Cities Transformed

Demographic Change and Its Implications in the Developing World

Edited by
Mark R. Montgomery, Richard Stren,
Barney Cohen, and Holly E. Reed

For the
Panel on Urban Population Dynamics,
National Research Council

EARTHSCAN

London

Pravin Visaria
(1937–2001)

This volume is dedicated to our colleague Pravin Visaria, who passed away during the completion of this project.

Pravin was director of the Institute of Economic Growth in Delhi and worked closely with the Indian government's Planning Commission, Department of Statistics, Office of the Registrar General, and Ministry of Health and Family Welfare. A distinguished scholar who held positions with the University of Bombay, the World Bank, and the Gujarat Institute of Development Research, Pravin was always involved in important policy-relevant economic and demographic research. He published numerous articles and books on mortality, fertility, migration, urbanization, labor force and employment, population projections, censuses and surveys, poverty, and population policy, especially in the Indian context. Pravin also held leadership positions with many important academic and policy organizations, including the Indian Association for the Study of Population, the National Sample Survey Organization of India, and the Gujarat Economic Association.

Pravin was an especially constructive and committed member of the Panel on Urban Population Dynamics. He not only provided much information about the rapid urbanization of one of the world's largest countries—India—but he also pushed the panel to evaluate its own thinking, insisting that we always consider our arguments from the viewpoint of policy makers in poor countries, who need to deal with very large rural, as well as urban populations. Pravin was a member of so many research networks and institutions over the years, and friends around the world mourned his sad and early death. We remember him as our friend who continually reminded us of the purpose of our research: to guide us towards better policy decisions.

PANEL ON URBAN POPULATION DYNAMICS

MARK R. MONTGOMERY (*Co-Chair*), Policy Research Division,
    Population Council, New York, NY, and Department of Economics,
    State University of New York at Stony Brook
RICHARD STREN (*Co-Chair*), Department of Political Science, University
    of Toronto, Canada
CHARLES M. BECKER, Department of Economics, University of
    Colorado, Denver, and Institute of Behavioral Science, University of
    Colorado, Boulder
ELLEN M. BRENNAN-GALVIN, School of Forestry and Environmental
    Studies, Yale University
MARTIN BROCKERHOFF,[1] Policy Research Division, Population
    Council, New York, NY
MICHAEL A. COHEN, International Affairs Program, The New School for
    Social Research, New York, NY
ALAIN DUBRESSON, Laboratoire Géographie des Tropiques, Université
    de Paris X-Nanterre, Paris, France
GUSTAVO GARZA, Center for Demographic and Urban Development
    Studies, El Colegio de México, Mexico City, Mexico
TRUDY HARPHAM, Division of Urban and Environmental Studies, South
    Bank University, London, United Kingdom
TERRENCE G. MCGEE, Institute of Asian Research, University of British
    Columbia, Vancouver, Canada
CAROLINE MOSER, Overseas Development Institute, London, United
    Kingdom
SASKIA SASSEN, Department of Sociology, University of Chicago
DAVID E. SATTERTHWAITE, Human Settlements Programme,
    International Institute for Environment and Development, London,
    United Kingdom
PRAVIN VISARIA,[2] Institute for Economic Growth, New Delhi, India
MICHAEL WHITE, Department of Sociology, Brown University,
    Providence, RI
YUE-MAN YEUNG, Shaw College, The Chinese University of Hong Kong,
    Hong Kong

National Research Council Staff

BARNEY COHEN, *Study Director*
HOLLY REED, *Program Officer*
BRIAN TOBACHNICK, *Senior Project Assistant* (until August 2001)
ANA-MARIA IGNAT, *Senior Project Assistant* (since October 2001)

---

[1]Resigned August 2000.
[2]Deceased February 2001.

CHRISTINE CHEN, *Senior Project Assistant* (August–October 2001)
ELIZABETH WALLACE, *Senior Project Assistant* (until October 2000)

**Liaison to the International Union for the Scientific Study of
Population (IUSSP) Working Group on Urbanization**

ANTHONY CHAMPION, Department of Geography, University of
Newcastle upon Tyne, United Kingdom

Acknowledgments

As co-chairs of the Panel on Urban Population Dynamics, we would like to say on behalf of the panel that we have been privileged and challenged by our task of examining the rapid urbanization of the developing world and its causes and consequences. *Cities Transformed: Demographic Change and Its Implications in the Developing World* is the product of a three-and-a-half-year effort in which we both reviewed the existing literature and conducted new analyses in the hope of encouraging demographers (and, by extension, other urban scholars) to take a fresh look at this topic. If others are moved to follow up, or to criticize some of the work we have presented in this volume, our time will not have been wasted.

This report would not have been possible without the help of numerous people and organizations. First, we wish to thank the reports' sponsors: the Andrew W. Mellon Foundation (whose program officer, Carolyn Makinson, was a fount of enthusiasm and intellectual energy), the Canadian International Development Agency, the United States Agency for International Development, and the William and Flora Hewlett Foundation. Their generous support for this project allowed us to draw creatively on a variety of resources that ultimately made for a stronger report.

This report is the collective product of panel members and staff. Its content reflects the deliberations of the full panel. The panel reviewed all contributions, and these have been revised and edited in light of panel reactions and the comments of outside reviewers. The purpose of the following list, therefore, is to give credit to individuals on the panel but not to assign final responsibility for the published text.

> Executive Summary: This is the collective product of the deliberations of the entire panel.
> Chapter 1: B. Cohen and M. Montgomery
> Chapter 2: M. Montgomery, H. Reed, D. Satterthwaite, M. White, M. Cohen, T. McGee, and Y. Yeung
> Chapter 3: B. Cohen, M. White, M. Montgomery, T. McGee, and Y. Yeung
> Chapter 4: M. White, M. Montgomery, E. Brennan-Galvin, and P. Visaria
> Chapter 5: D. Satterthwaite, M. Montgomery, and H. Reed
> Chapter 6: M. Montgomery, H. Reed, and M. White

Chapter 7: T. Harpham, H. Reed, M. Montgomery, D. Satterthwaite,
    C. Moser, and B. Cohen
Chapter 8: C. Becker, A. Dubresson, G. Garza, S. Sassen, M. Cohen,
    M. Montgomery, and B. Cohen
Chapter 9: R. Stren, T. McGee, C. Moser, and Y. Yeung
Chapter 10: R. Stren, B. Cohen, M. Montgomery, and H. Reed
Appendix A: E. Brennan-Galvin and M. Montgomery
Appendices B–F: M. Montgomery

It should be noted that although this list covers major sections of this volume, these sections frequently contain additional paragraphs or pages from other hands. Primary responsibility for the revision and editing of the volume was shared by Mark Montgomery, Richard Stren, Barney Cohen, and Holly Reed.

Anthony Champion, University of Newcastle upon Tyne, served as official liaison between the panel and the International Union for the Scientific Study of Population's Working Group on Urbanisation. Tony helped review the panel's report informally and offered important suggestions and advice. We are very grateful for his many contributions.

Numerous other individuals also made key contributions to the panel's efforts. We are especially indebted to Martin Brockerhoff, who was with the panel in its first year. His intellectual legacy to this volume is evident in Chapter 6, which evolved along the lines that Martin had anticipated in the panel's early deliberations. Paul C. Hewett of The Population Council devoted countless hours to the analysis of data from the Demographic and Health Surveys. Brian Pence, also of The Population Council, made a number of key contributions to analyses of mortality. Doreen Totaram of The Population Council skillfully prepared the massive reference list for the report.

Anne Kubisch of the Aspen Institute provided many leads to the neighborhood effects literature for the United States that is discussed in Chapter 2. Alice Clague of the United Nations generously made available a prepublication version of data from the *1998 Demographic Yearbook*, without which we could not have derived results for city size classes. Using these data, Edward Hui (at the time an undergraduate at Brown University) took on the difficult task of matching city-specific population data to the region and city size identifiers from the Demographic and Health Surveys datasets. Roberta Scheinman linked data on HIV-AIDS from the U.S. Census Bureau's database to the United Nations city population file. Ann Ilacque, librarian at the PSTC at Brown University, and Sara Colangelo, a Brown University undergraduate, contributed to the literature reviews for Chapter 4.

Sassy Molyneux (working from the Kenya Medical Research Institute, Wellcome Trust Centre for Geographic Medicine Research, Kilifi, Kenya) and Emma Grant (South Bank University, London) both contributed unequalled expertise to the early versions of Chapter 7. We also thank Gordon McGranahan, International Institute for Environment and Development, London, and John Seager, Medical Research Council, Cape Town, South Africa, for their comments on this chapter.

Several people participated in a planning meeting in December 1998 to help formulate a plan for the panel's contributions. We have been mindful of the advice we received from the following people at that meeting: Richard Bilsborrow, University of North Carolina at Chapel Hill; Sidney Goldstein, Brown University; Josef Gugler, University of Connecticut; and David Lam, University of Michigan at Ann Arbor.

The panel was fortunate to be able to hold several workshops on topics related to our undertaking. In this way, we were able to gain insights from a number of people outside of the panel. The first workshop we held, in October 1999, which addressed the topic of "world cities in poor countries," was organized with the help of Josef Gugler, University of Connecticut. We are grateful to Dr. Gugler for identifying an array of scholars from around the world who presented case studies: Janet Abu-Lughod, New School University; Maria Helena Moreira Alves, Instituto de Ciencias Aplicadas, Santiago, Chile; James H. Bater, University of Waterloo; Owen Crankshaw, University of Cape Town; Dean Forbes, University of South Australia; Susan Parnell, University of Cape Town; Sujata Patel, University of Pune; Janet W. Salaff, University of Toronto; Alvin Y. So, The Hong Kong University of Science and Technology; Peter M. Ward, University of Texas at Austin; Douglas Webster, National Economic and Social Development Board of Thailand; Weiping Wu, Virginia Commonwealth University; and Shahid Yusuf, The World Bank. The papers from this workshop will be published in the edited volume *World Cities in Poor Countries* by Cambridge University Press in 2003.

In February 2000, the panel was hosted by panel member Gustavo Garza and his colleagues for a meeting at El Colegio de México, where we had the opportunity to learn firsthand about urbanization processes in Mexico City. Gustavo organized a wonderful tour of the city for us, focusing on public services and housing. We thank him for his assistance and are grateful to our other hosts: Andrés Lira, President, El Colegio de México; Manuel Ordorica Mellado, Director, Center for Demographic and Urban Development Studies at El Colegio de México; and Gabriela Grajales, El Colegio de México. We benefited from the presentations of several guest speakers for this meeting as well: David Arellano, Center for Economic Research and Education; Andrés Lira, El Colegio de México; Orlandina de Oliveira, El Colegio de México; Rosa Maria Rubalcava, Mexican National Council on Population; Carlos Santos-Burgoa, Institute of Health, Environment, and Employment; and Willem VanVliet, University of Colorado, Boulder.

The panel's work on urban health was furthered and materially assisted by the participants in a workshop on social capital and urban health held in May 2000. Trudy Harpham and Mark Montgomery from the panel co-chaired this meeting. The participants shared their knowledge of the linkages between health and social capital in both richer and poorer countries. We thank the following people for their participation: Karen Hansen, Northwestern University; Ichiro Kawachi, Harvard University; Nan Lin, Duke University; Alberto Palloni, University of Wisconsin at Madison; Edith Parker, University of Michigan at Ann Arbor; Joseph Potter,

University of Texas at Austin; Vijayendra Rao, The World Bank; Carlos Rodriguéz, Fundación Para la Asesoria de Programas de Salud (FUNDAPS), Cali, Colombia; Amy Schulz, University of Michigan at Ann Arbor; John Townsend, The Population Council; Thomas W. Valente, University of Southern California; and Michael Woolcock, The World Bank. Emma Grant of South Bank University, London, was instrumental in organizing this workshop and wrote the workshop summary.

In September 2000, our panel was privileged to hold a meeting in Woods Hole, Massachusetts, where Seymour S. Cohen, a member of the National Academy of Sciences and father of panel member Michael A. Cohen, served as host. A workshop on urban governance held in conjunction with this meeting included the following participants: Koffi Attahi, Bureau National d'Etudes Techniques et de Developpement, Abidjan, Côte d'Ivoire; Jordi Borja, Urban Technology Consulting, Barcelona, Spain; Gu Chaolin, Nanjing University; Patricia McCarney, University of Toronto; AbdouMaliq Simone, New School University; and K. C. Sivaramakrishnan, Centre for Policy Research, New Delhi, India. The papers written by Dr. Attahi, Dr. Borja, Dr. Gu, Dr. Sivaramakrishnan, and Dr. Edgar Pieterse, Islanda Institute, South Africa, proved very helpful to the panel in our work on governance.

Many other colleagues supplied the panel with research in the form of background papers. These papers, which served as valuable resources for the report, were written by Kathryn H. Anderson, Vanderbilt University; Cris Beauchemin, Université de Paris VIII; Philippe Bocquier, Institut de Recherche Pour le Développement, Nairobi, Kenya; Pablo Ciccolella, Universidad Nacional de Buenos Aires; Simone Buechler, Columbia University; Christopher Dunn, University of Michigan; Valerie Durrant, National Research Council; Martha Galvez, Citizens Housing and Planning Council, New York; Emma Grant, South Bank University, London; Christopher D. Grewe, University of Colorado; Paul C. Hewett, Population Council; Åsa Jonsson, International Institute for Environment and Development, London; David Lam, University of Michigan; Sang-Hyop Lee, University of Hawaii; Zai Liang, City University of New York; Andrew Mason, University of Hawaii; Iliana Mignaqui, Universidad Nacional de Buenos Aires; Sassy Molyneux, Kenya Medical Research Institute, Wellcome Trust Centre for Geographic Medicine Research, Kilifi, Kenya; Erbolat Musabekov, Kazakhstan National Statistical Agency; Yiu Por Chen, Columbia University; Sueli Schiffer, Universidade de São Paulo; Ai-Gul Seitenova, Pragma Corporation, Kazakhstan; Sunil Kumar Sinha, Institute for Economic Growth, Mumbai, India; Cecilia Tacoli, International Institute for Environment and Development, London; and Dina Urzhumova, Pragma Corporation, Kazakhstan.

This report has been reviewed in draft form by individuals chosen for their diverse perspectives and technical expertise, in accordance with procedures approved by the National Research Council's Report Review Committee. The purpose of this independent review is to provide candid and critical comments that

ACKNOWLEDGMENTS

will assist the institution in making its published report as sound as possible and to ensure that the report meets institutional standards for objectivity, evidence, and responsiveness to the study charge. The review comments and draft manuscript remain confidential to protect the integrity of the deliberative process. We wish to thank the following individuals for their review of this report:

> Gordon Clark, Department of Geography, University of Oxford, Oxford, United Kingdom
> Susan Hanson, School of Geography, Clark University, Worcester, MA
> Kenneth H. Hill, Department of Population and Family Health Science, Johns Hopkins University, Baltimore, MD
> Akin L. Mabogunje, Development Policy Centre, Ibadan, Nigeria
> David R. Meyer, Department of Sociology, Brown University, Providence, RI
> Philip Rees, School of Geography, University of Leeds, Leeds, United Kingdom
> Barney L. Warf, Department of Geography, Florida State University, Tallahassee, FL
> John Weeks, International Population Center, San Diego State University, CA

Although the reviewers listed above have provided many constructive comments and suggestions, they were not asked to endorse the panel's conclusions or recommendations, nor did they see the final draft of the report before its release. The review of this report was overseen by Ronald Lee, Department of Demography, University of California, Berkeley, CA, and Brian J.L. Berry, School of Social Science, University of Texas, Richardson, TX. Appointed by the National Research Council, they were responsible for making certain that an independent examination of this report was carried out in accordance with institutional procedures and that all review comments were carefully considered. Responsibility for the final content of this report rests entirely with the authoring panel and the institution.

We especially wish to recognize the efforts of several staff of The National Academies, who provided critical support for the panel and our work. Jianjun Ji and Ito Toshima, interns with the Committee on Population, lent their energy and skills to background research for the report. Michelle McGuire assisted with proofreading and editing of the final manuscript. In the Reports Office of the Division of Behavioral and Social Sciences and Education, Kirsten Sampson Snyder helped guide the manuscript through review, editing, and finally publication. And Rona Briere applied her considerable editorial talent to this daunting text; we are deeply indebted to her.

Elizabeth Wallace organized our earliest panel meetings and skillfully assisted with other administrative tasks. We are also grateful for the help of Brian Tobachnick, who guided the panel through logistical arrangements for subsequent meetings and helped keep the finances and paperwork for the project under control. Christine Chen made arrangements for our crucial final meeting in Boulder,

Colorado, and helped transition the panel smoothly into the hands of Ana-Maria Ignat. Ana-Maria has been a steadfast help to the panel, not only by organizing logistical matters with ease and grace, but also by providing a great deal of research support and editorial expertise. Her assistance has made dealing with the final stages of editing and managing the manuscript a fluid and virtually worry-free process.

We are grateful to all the individuals who contributed to this immense undertaking. It would not have been possible without their continual, generous, and imaginative support.

Mark R. Montgomery and Richard Stren, *Co-Chairs*
Panel on Urban Population Dynamics

Contents

EXECUTIVE SUMMARY   1

1   INTRODUCTION   9
    The Demographic Transformation,   11
    The Transformation of Cities,   17
    The Panel's Charge,   25
    Study Scope and Approach,   27
    Organization of the Report,   28

2   WHY LOCATION MATTERS   29
    Places, Networks, Neighborhoods,   31
    Sustaining Diversity: Economic Interactions,   51
    City Systems and City-Regions,   58
    From Government to Governance,   64
    What Remains of the Urban/Rural Divide?,   67

3   URBAN POPULATION CHANGE: A SKETCH   75
    Cities Amid Global Forces,   76
    Key Demographic Features of the Urban Transition,   81
    Major Regional Differences,   95
    Conclusions, 106

4   URBAN POPULATION DYNAMICS: MODELS, MEASURES,
    AND FORECASTS   108
    The Simple Analytics, 110
    Fertility, Mortality, Migration, and Urban Age Structure, 120
    Core Issues in Definition and Measurement, 128
    Projecting Urban Populations, 141
    Statistical Systems for Disaggregated Data, 146
    Conclusions and Recommendations, 151

5   DIVERSITY AND INEQUALITY   155
    A Spatial Perspective, 157

Human Capital: Schooling, 160
Urban Well-Being: Concepts and Measures, 164
Access to Public Services, 167
Measuring Absolute Poverty in Cities, 180
Risk and Vulnerability, 184
Children's Lives, 188
Conclusions and Recommendations, 195

6   FERTILITY AND REPRODUCTIVE HEALTH   199
The Urban Dimension, 200
An Empirical Overview, 209
Fertility Transitions and Economic Crises, 226
The Urban Poor, 231
Migrants, 242
Urban Adolescents, 247
Urban Service Delivery, 251
Conclusions and Recommendations, 255

7   MORTALITY AND MORBIDITY: IS CITY LIFE GOOD FOR
YOUR HEALTH?   259
Distinctive Aspects of Urban Health, 262
The Disease Spectrum, 262
Recent Evidence on Children's Health and Survival, 272
A Penalty for the Urban Poor?, 284
Health Service Provision and Treatment Seeking, 289
Conclusions and Recommendations, 295

8   THE URBAN ECONOMY TRANSFORMED   300
Sector and Space, 302
Economic Returns to Schooling, 319
Migration and Economic Mobility, 322
The Informalization of Urban Labor Markets, 331
Earnings Inequality: Case Studies, 340
The Future of Urban Labor Markets: Global Links and Local
      Outcomes, 343
Conclusions and Recommendations, 352

9   THE CHALLENGE OF URBAN GOVERNANCE   355
The Concept of Urban Governance, 357
Major Challenges of Urban Governance in Developing Countries, 363
Is There a "Best" Model of Urban Governance?, 401
Conclusions and Recommendations, 407

10 LOOKING AHEAD 410
   Directions for Future Research, 412
   Improving the Research Infrastructure, 414

REFERENCES 419

APPENDICES

A Concepts and Definitions of Metropolitan Regions 481

B Mathematical Derivations 484

C Linking DHS Surveys to United Nations City Data 487

D United Nations Estimates and Projections 495

E Measuring Relative Poverty with DHS Data 499

F Recommendations for the Demographic and Health Surveys 503

Biographical Sketches of Panel Members and Staff 507

INDEX 515

Executive Summary

Over the next 30 years, most of the growth in the world's population is expected to occur in the cities and towns of poor countries. Cities are now home to nearly half of the world's total population and over three-quarters of the population of high-income countries. By 2020 the developing world as a whole is likely to have become more urban than rural. The changes under way are not only a matter of percentages, but also of scale. At the beginning of the twentieth century, just 16 cities in the world—the vast majority in advanced industrial economies—contained a million people or more. Today, almost 400 cities are of this size, and about three-quarters of them are in found in low- and middle-income countries.

In the very near future, then, it will no longer be possible to conceive of developing countries as being mainly rural. Both poverty and opportunity will take on an urban cast. This transformation will be a powerful force in shaping family, social, economic, and political life over the next century. And yet, in the research conducted to date on developing countries, demographers have devoted very little attention to the implications of urban contexts for marriage, fertility, health, schooling, and children's lives. As poor countries continue to urbanize, the distinctive features of urban life will have to be taken into consideration in demographic research and the policies it informs.

As the demographic trends unfold, the nature of urban life in low-income countries will itself be changing. The world is in the midst of a period of fundamental economic restructuring, driven by globalization and the revolution in information and communication technology. Many poor countries are industrializing rapidly, while advanced economies are shifting away from manufacturing toward finance, specialized services, and information processing. These changes are forcing countries—and, indeed, individual cities—to redefine their comparative advantages so as to be competitive in the global marketplace. As they link themselves to international markets, the cities that participate in global circuits are increasingly exposing their residents to the risks, as well as the benefits, that come from being more tightly integrated in world networks of finance, information, and production.

The speed and scale of these changes present many challenges. Of particular concern are the risks to the physical environment and natural resources, to health conditions, to social cohesion, and to individual rights. For many observers, however, the immediate concern is the massive increase expected in the numbers of the urban poor. In many countries in the developing world, at least one in four urban residents is estimated to be living in absolute poverty. The manifestations of poverty are clearly visible in all major cities: overcrowded neighborhoods; pollution; inadequate housing; and insufficient access to clean water, sanitation, and other social services. Compounding matters, each year cities attract considerable numbers of new migrants who, together with the increasing native population, can expand squatter settlements and shanty towns, exacerbate problems of congestion, and confound the ability of local authorities to provide infrastructure and basic amenities.

At the same time, the benefits derived from urbanization must not be overlooked. Cities are the locations where diverse social and economic resources are concentrated. This concentration can bring substantial benefits in the form of positive social and economic externalities, which are expressed in technological change and economic growth. Historically, urban growth has been most rapid where economic growth rates have been highest. This is clearly the case today in Pacific Asia, where urbanization is accelerating—and being accelerated by—a newly globalized economy that is changing the face of the planet.

As cities grow and evolve, the task of managing them becomes ever more complex, in part as a result of jurisdictional conflicts arising from the expansion of cities beyond existing administrative and political boundaries. The nature of management and governance is also undergoing fundamental change. The policy and program environment in urban areas is being transformed as national governments decentralize service delivery and revenue raising to lower tiers of government. In the areas of health, family planning, and poverty alleviation, many national governments are beginning to allow local governments to operate the levers of policy and programs. But at present, few local governments are equipped with the technical and managerial expertise they need to take on these new responsibilities.

THE RESEARCH GAP

Demographers are not now in a position to shed much light on the demographic aspects of the urban transformation, and they can provide little by way of guidance on urban-oriented programs and policies. Where urban/rural differences are recognized in demographic research, they still tend to be described in terms of simple urban/rural dichotomies. But urban growth is often accompanied by economic development, the restructuring and relocation of production, social and economic fragmentation, and spatial reorganization—and urban/rural dichotomies are increasingly inadequate even to describe these changes. In countries where the level of urbanization is already high, further measurement of change in the urban percentage adds little by way of insight. What is needed is a new emphasis on the inter- and intraurban differentials, and these are topics to which demographers have paid remarkably little attention. The neglect of intraurban research on developing countries is all the more surprising in view of the close attention given to neighborhood effects and other intraurban issues in research on cities in the United States.

THE PANEL'S CHARGE

Recognizing the need for a major new inquiry in this area, the National Research Council formed the Panel on Urban Population Dynamics. The panel's mandate was to develop a better understanding of the dynamics of urban population growth, as well as its causes and consequences, as a step toward helping governments better manage the environmental and social service problems that accompany the rapid growth of urban areas in poor countries. The panel focused on improving knowledge in six areas:

- Urban population dynamics and city growth

- Social and economic differentiation within and across cities

- Fertility and reproductive health in urban areas

- Mortality and morbidity in urban areas

- Labor force implications of a changing urban economy

- The challenge of urban governance

In addressing its task, the panel both reviewed the existing literature and conducted new data analyses. In particular, the panel relied heavily on a new database that it created by linking the Demographic and Health Surveys (DHS) with information on city sizes taken from United Nations (UN) sources.

URBAN POPULATION DYNAMICS AND CITY GROWTH

Almost all of the world's population growth for the foreseeable future will occur in the cities and towns of Africa, Asia, and Latin America. Although rates of urbanization in these poor regions today are similar in several respects to those in the Western historical experience, marked differences are also evident. Urban natural increase is as great a contributor to high rates of urban growth as is rural-to-urban migration, and because of lower mortality, natural rates of increase are higher in the modern era than in the historical record. Furthermore, many residents of poor countries will live their lives in very large cities whose sizes are historically unprecedented.

With increases in urban percentages and the growth of cities large and small comes a need for adequate population data that are comparable among and within cities, as well as between urban and rural areas. The demographic field is perhaps overly dependent on the United Nations Population Division for such city and urban population counts. The Population Division does an admirable job of producing urban population estimates and projections, but it lacks the resources—in terms of personnel, funds, and data contributed by member countries—to meet the demands placed upon it. The panel recommends that a critical review of the United Nations data and methodology be undertaken with the help of outside researchers to bring additional perspectives and intellectual resources to bear on this difficult work. In addition, the DHS data would be much more useful for urban research if spatial identifiers for all surveys were made available to researchers, and if measures of public services better reflected variations in service adequacy and reliability.

SOCIOECONOMIC DIFFERENTIATION

Diversity is a defining characteristic of urban life. Every city has relatively more affluent and relatively poorer neighborhoods, and large cities are often marked by the spatial segregation of rich and poor. Yet these important inter- and intraurban differences are lost from view in demographic analyses that concentrate on rural/urban dichotomies. In exploring cross-city differences, the panel found that large urban areas enjoy a marked advantage in the provision of piped water, waste disposal, electricity, and schools. Smaller urban areas—particularly those under 100,000 in population—are significantly underserved. In examining the effects of intraurban poverty, the panel found that the urban poor are in a distinctly inferior position relative to other urban residents in terms of access to basic amenities. The urban poor are also particularly vulnerable to economic, social, and political crises and environmental hazards and disasters.

Current systems of poverty measurement are inadequate for capturing all of the dimensions of urban poverty. The panel recommends improving data systems on access to services, income and assets, the multiple dimensions of poverty, and education, so that the data will be comparable among and within cities. Such data must also be disseminated widely to policy makers and program managers at the national and local levels.

FERTILITY AND REPRODUCTIVE HEALTH

The fertility levels of urban residents are shaped by urban constraints and opportunities. Typically, urban couples desire to have fewer children than their rural counterparts, so that the general level of demand for contraceptive services is higher in urban than in rural areas. This can be partially explained by higher levels of schooling among urban adults, and perhaps by the greater prevalence of women working outside the home.

But in considering theories of neighborhood effects, social learning, and diffusion, the panel found that urban socioeconomic diversity and the range of urban reference groups and role models are also likely to have an influence on fertility decisions. In particular, urban parents are apt to appreciate the advantages of having fewer but better-educated children. In some settings, urban environments are presenting women with novel behavioral options. The establishment of a garment manufacturing sector in Dhaka, for example, has created the opportunity for young unmarried adolescents to work outside the home in direct contact with men, a situation almost unimaginable a generation ago. This experience is likely to have significant implications for women's attitudes toward marriage, childbearing, and children's education.

The panel found considerable variation within urban settings in fertility; in factors relating to contraceptive use; and in other reproductive health indicators, such as place of delivery, birth attendance, and AIDS awareness. The urban poor and residents of smaller cities appear to be underserved in terms of access to reproductive health services as compared with their counterparts who are wealthier and living in larger cities. The panel's analysis revealed the need for policy prescription in four areas: improving services for the urban poor, enhancing services in smaller cities, creating appropriate services for adolescents, and augmenting HIV/AIDS prevention programs. Research is urgently needed to understand the implications of the decentralization of reproductive health services that is under way in many developing countries.

MORTALITY AND MORBIDITY

As is the case with fertility, many features of urban life have important implications for urban morbidity and mortality. Social infrastructural investments have historically been greater in cities than in rural areas, so that on average, urban dwellers (particularly, as noted above, those in large cities) enjoy better infrastructure and easier access to health services, as least as measured by the physical distance to services. Other factors influencing urban health include the greater prominence of the private sector in health care, weaker informal safety nets, lifestyle changes that affect diet and exercise patterns, and increased exposure to environmental contamination. In some developing countries, noncommunicable (i.e., chronic and degenerative) diseases, accidents, and injuries are becoming more important than infectious diseases as causes of death.

Since the mid-1980s, the long-assumed urban advantage in health has been called into question. The international debt crisis hit many poor countries hard, and the implementation of structural adjustment programs led to a retrenchment of government subsidies and social expenditures that probably affected urban residents disproportionately. In addition, high rates of overall population growth, together with significant rural-to-urban migration, have contributed to the rapid and unplanned expansion of low-income settlements on the outskirts of many large cities, which has occurred without a concomitant expansion of health services and facilities.

The panel's analysis of urban/rural differences in infant and child mortality reveals the existence of a substantial urban health advantage, at least on average. The dominant pattern in the DHS data is one of declines in both urban and rural mortality, with slightly greater declines taking place in urban areas. In the majority of the surveys analyzed, mortality risks facing the urban poor are found to be lower than those faced by rural children. In several surveys, however, the urban poor are found to face significantly higher risks than the general rural population, and in Latin America, the residents of smaller cities are disadvantaged in comparison with residents of cities with more than 5 million population. The spatially concentrated urban poor—such as those living in slums—may face additional health penalties that erase the urban health advantage. Scattered data for sub-Saharan Africa clearly indicate deteriorating conditions in a number of places. The panel recommends that governments focus attention on inter- and intraurban differences when designing health services for cities (recognizing that this will require better data and research), and adapt existing services and programs to address emerging health threats, including injuries, chronic diseases, mental health issues, and in some areas communicable threats such as HIV/AIDS.

THE URBAN ECONOMY AND LABOR FORCE

The urban economy generates many of the resources needed by governments to improve services in health, education, and other areas. The scale of the urban economy enables specialization to take place and allows for a broad range of productive activity to develop, leading, for example, to diverse urban private sectors in health services. Through urban labor markets, the economic returns to schooling are established, and for urban parents these returns may profoundly influence decisions about investments in children's schooling and family size. Urban labor and product markets also determine individual and family incomes and establish incentives for migration.

Rapid growth in the supply of urban labor might appear to threaten the economic returns to schooling. Yet analysis of several case studies shows that where macroeconomic growth has been moderate or strong, the urban returns to schooling have generally been maintained, and in some cases returns to university schooling have increased. Evidently, the accumulation of physical capital and technological progress can sustain educational returns even in the face of rapid shifts in supply. But where macroeconomic growth has been weak, as it has in much of sub-Saharan Africa, rapid increases in the supply of better-educated urban labor have resulted in marked declines in the returns to schooling.

Surprisingly little attention has been paid to individual income dynamics within urban areas. The few longitudinal studies available do not clearly reveal higher rates of upward or downward mobility in cities as compared with rural areas;

in both there is a great deal of flux. However, studies of migrants—based on cross-sectional surveys that may overrepresent the more successful migrants—generally show that rural migrants undergo a period of adjustment to city life during which their earnings are low, but subsequently achieve earnings levels that rival and sometimes exceed those of urban natives.

There has been much recent speculation about whether the globalization of economic relationships heightens urban inequalities. Case studies of Brazil, Taiwan, and China provide some evidence of rising inequality in urban incomes in the 1990s. Although the sources of the trends are not clearly identifiable, such empirical findings are consistent with the view that urban labor markets are increasingly heterogeneous and volatile, in part because of their exposure to world markets. An examination of the urban impact of international economic shocks and crises shows that city dwellers can be disproportionately affected—the evidence from Indonesia is especially clear on this point. The spatial effects are not always focused on cities, however, and urban residents also realize considerable benefit from their exposure to world markets. Further research on cities and their urban-regional economies, as well as the linkages between globalization and inequality, would help illuminate changing urban economic relationships and patterns.

THE CHALLENGE OF URBAN GOVERNANCE

The central challenge for the governments of poor countries—to improve the social and economic conditions of their citizens while preserving the natural environment for future generations—is becoming an urban challenge. The concept of urban governance has itself undergone a major transformation over the last decade and a half. Governance reforms have been affected by the movement toward democratization and political pluralism, an emphasis on decentralization, the rise of civil society, and the spread of powerful local social and environmental movements. Numerous legal and institutional reforms in many countries have given shape to institutional reform at the local and municipal levels.

Solutions to urban problems are increasingly being sought at the local level as central governments cede responsibilities in basic service delivery, giving local authorities more opportunity to take charge of services that affect the daily lives of their residents. New institutional forms of local governance are emerging in municipalities across the developing world. These new forms often involve larger roles for nongovernmental organizations and community groups, greater transparency and accountability, and the devolution of more legal and financial responsibility for urban affairs to the local, rather than the state or national level.

Although no consensus has emerged on the direction in which urban governance will develop, there is general agreement that as cities grow, some new form of governance response will be required. The panel identified five dimensions of the urban governance challenge facing all large urban areas: (1) capacity—the ability of local governments to provide adequate public services to their citizens; (2) financial—the ability of local governments to raise and manage sufficient revenue; (3) diversity—the ability of government to cope with the extraordinary internal variation within cities and to address the attendant issues of fragmentation and inequality; (4) security—the ability of government to deal with issues related to rising urban violence and crime; and (5) authority—which is related to the increasing complexity of managing the jurisdictional mosaic as large cities grow and spread out.

LOOKING AHEAD: NEW TECHNOLOGY, DATA, AND RESEARCH

If demographic research is to make a contribution, attention must be paid to the international infrastructure of research, as represented in the major international datasets. There is still considerable unexploited potential for urban research in existing databases and data collection mechanisms. At present, however, these data are often inaccessible or coded in such a way as to hinder cross-linkages to other datasets.

At the national and local levels, effective planning and governance require reliable and up-to-date information, which is a basic requirement for effective urban governance. Remotely sensed and geocoded data hold some promise for measuring the spatial extent of cities and certain aspects of urban change, but these are costly and difficult technologies. Many cities lack adequate intracity data, especially at the level of neighborhoods. There is a need to shift the focus of research from producing national datasets on social and economic differentiation to producing local datasets that are capable of reflecting local realities (including poverty lines adjusted to reflect local circumstances) and that can support local policy, planning, and investment decisions.

By 2030, more than 80 percent of the population of North America, Europe, Oceania, and Latin America and more than 50 percent of the population of Asia and Africa will be living in urban areas. In the long run, no doubt, this will be good news for global development. Over the next 30 years, however, the challenge will be to take full advantage of the potential benefits of urbanization in an inclusive way while reducing the risks of negative outcomes. Meeting this challenge will inevitably require better data and a deeper understanding of the changing demography of place—not just between rural and urban areas, but also across the urban spectrum and within large urban agglomerations. To date, these issues have been given inadequate attention. Until demographers develop an understanding of all facets of the urbanization process, their work will continue to be of marginal relevance to those charged with the design of better urban policies.

1

Introduction

Flying into São Paulo on a clear day, one can easily understand why this city has been called the locomotive that pulls the rest of Brazil. With a population in excess of 15 million, it is the largest city of the Southern Hemisphere. From its center thrust impressive clusters of modern buildings; beyond them the metropolitan complex stretches as far as the eye can see. This is the foremost industrial center of Latin America, and a dominant presence in finance and trade. São Paulo is home to Brazil's automobile industry, and accounts for much of its manufacturing in sectors as diverse as computers, electrical and mechanical appliances, chemicals and pharmaceuticals, textiles, furniture, and processed foods. With about one-tenth of Brazil's population, the city generates one-third of the country's net national product. In addition to being an economic powerhouse, São Paulo is a force in culture and intellectual debate, the site of four universities, a medical school, and many important museums. In economics, politics, and the arts, writes Alves (2003), "São Paulo has become an exporter of ideas."

This is a bird's-eye view of the city, but on closer inspection São Paulo takes on a more variegated appearance. It can be seen that poor neighborhoods and ramshackle housing surround some of the high-rise commercial clusters. Consider the situation of Marta, a young woman who lives in one of these *favelas*. Her husband once held a steady job in a manufacturing firm, but lost it in the economic downturns of the 1980s and now ekes out a living as a security guard for a rich family. Marta herself takes in work as a seamstress, but she keeps an eye out for any opportunity that might come her way. She is pleased that her daughters are about to complete primary school, unlike their cousins in the countryside who dropped out. Still, she worries incessantly about the children's safety, especially since their route to school wends through territory claimed by rival gangs. Marta's aunt, a formidable nurse in a clinic not far away, continually impresses upon her the need for the children to be well educated, but in looking ahead, Marta finds herself wondering whether the girls would really benefit from secondary school.

The pros and cons of schooling are much debated among her friends, some point-ing to success stories and others to children who wasted their education; they all complain, however, about the difficulties and costs of rearing children properly in São Paulo. Marta's friends are unanimous on one point: to have five or six children today, as was often done in their mothers' time, would be too exhausting even to contemplate.

In vignettes such as this, the positive and negative elements of urban life are thoroughly intermixed. Cities are the sites where diverse social and eco-nomic resources are concentrated, and that concentration can generate substantial economic benefits in the form of innovation and income growth (Jacobs, 1969; Glaeser, Kallal, Scheinkman, and Shleifer, 1992; Henderson, 2002). If cities could not offer such benefits, they would have little reason to exist, for the mass-ing of production and population also generates many costs—heavy congestion, high rents, and stress on the capacities of government. In the nineteenth century, this opposition of benefits and costs was well understood. The cities of that time were likened to "satanic mills" where one could seize economic opportunity only at some risk to life and health. In much of today's popular writing on cities, how-ever, the costs of city life tend to be vividly described, while the economic benefits are left unmentioned.

Cities are also the sites of diverse forms of social interaction, whether on the staging grounds of neighborhoods, through personal social networks, or within local community associations. The multiple social worlds inhabited by city res-idents must profoundly influence their outlooks and perceptions of life's possi-bilities. In city life, many family productive and reproductive strategies are on display, with the consequences being acted out by local role models and reference groups. The poor are often brought into contact with the near-poor and sometimes with the rich; these social collisions can either stir ambitions or fan frustrations. The social embeddedness and multiple contexts of urban life (Granovetter, 1985) would thus appear to present demographic researchers with a very rich field for analysis.

Over the past two decades, researchers interested in high-income countries have moved to take up this analytic challenge, with much of the intellectual energy being provided by the powerful writings of Wilson (1987) and Coleman (1988, 1990) on the roles of neighborhoods and local context in the cities of the United States. But the cities of poor countries have seen no comparable surge in demo-graphic research. Indeed, apart from the occasional study of migration, the main-stream literature has been all but silent on the demographic implications of urban life in developing countries. Not since Preston (1979) and the United Nations (1980) has there been a rigorous, comprehensive assessment of urban demogra-phy in these countries.

As we will discuss, the U.S. literature has emphasized many of the themes that are of central importance to the cities of low-income countries: children's schooling, reproductive behavior among adolescents and adults, health, spatial segregation, and employment. It has also advanced important theories and mechanisms—social learning, networks, collective socialization, and social capital among them—that have clear parallels in developing-country cities. Yet, at least to date, the theories and research strategies being vigorously pursued in the U.S. context have not been taken up elsewhere. On these grounds alone, a review of what is known about urban population dynamics would appear well overdue.

This chapter introduces some of the themes that will be explored in the chapters to follow, together with basic demographic information on the urban transformation. The chapter also describes the panel's charge, the main reasons for undertaking this study, and some of the major audiences for the report, with particular reference to the demographic research community.

THE DEMOGRAPHIC TRANSFORMATION

The neglect of urban research can only be reckoned astonishing when considered in light of the demographic transformations now under way. The world's population passed 6 billion in 1999, and 6 of every 7 people now reside in a low- or middle-income country.[1] The global rate of population growth has declined over the past 20 years; in absolute terms, however, the world remains in the midst of an era of historically dramatic population increase. According to the latest United Nations (2002a) projections, even as the rate of population growth continues to decline, the world's total population will rise substantially. The total is expected to reach 8.27 billion in 2030, this being a net addition of 2.2 billion persons to the 2000 population. Almost all of this growth will take place in the poor countries of the world, whose governments and economies are generally ill equipped to deal with it.

The Urban Future

As Figure 1-1 shows, over the next 30 years it is the world's cities that are expected to absorb these additional billions.[2] The total rural population is likely to undergo little net change over the period, declining by 30 percent in high-income countries and increasing by an expected 3 percent in low- and middle-income countries. Relatively small changes are also expected for the cities of high-income

---

[1] In this report we take as synonymous the phrases *low- and middle-income countries, poor countries,* and *developing countries,* although we recognize that they differ in emphasis and shades of meaning. We follow the World Bank (2002b) in classifying a country as high-income if its gross national income per capita in the year 2000 exceeded $9,266 in the World Bank's estimation. We also take the terms *urban areas, cities,* and *cities and towns* to be broadly synonymous, often employing the last of these to highlight the great size range of urban places.

[2] The great variety of definitions of "urban" used by national statistical agencies and deficiencies in the measures these agencies supply to the United Nations imply that the United Nations estimates and projections can be taken only as broadly indicative of levels and trends. Definitional and measurement issues are discussed at length in this report.

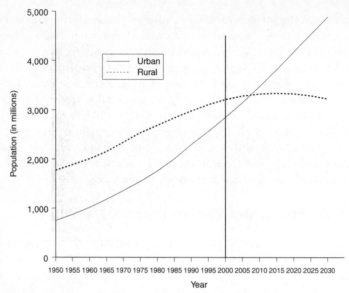

FIGURE 1-1 Estimated and projected urban and rural populations, world totals 1950–2030.
SOURCE: United Nations (2002a).

countries, whose populations will rise from 0.9 billion in 2000 to 1 billion in 2030. Hence, as can be seen in Figures 1-2 and 1-3, the net additions to the world's population will be found mainly in the cities and towns of poor countries. The prospects for the near future stand in stark contrast to what was seen during the period 1950 to 1975, when population growth was much more evenly divided between urban and rural areas.

The United Nations predicts that the total urban populations of Africa, Asia, and Latin America will double in size over the next 30 years, increasing from 1.9 billion in 2000 to 3.9 billion in 2030. These changes in totals will also be reflected in the urban percentages. In 1950 less than 20 percent of the population of poor countries lived in cities and towns. By 2030, that figure will have risen to nearly 60 percent. Rather soon, it appears, it will no longer be possible to speak of the developing world as being mainly rural. Both poverty and opportunity are assuming an urban character.

Each of the developing regions is expected to participate in this trend. As Figure 1-4 shows, a good deal of convergence is anticipated, but considerable differences will likely remain in levels of urbanization (the percentage of the population residing in urban areas) by geographic region. Latin America is now highly urbanized: 75 percent of its population resides in cities, a figure rivaling the percentages of Europe and North America. Africa and Asia are much less urbanized,

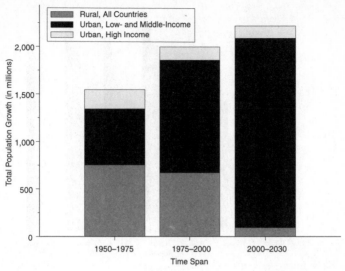

FIGURE 1-2 Distribution of world population growth by urban/rural and national income level. Estimates and projections for 1950–2030.
SOURCE: United Nations (2002a).

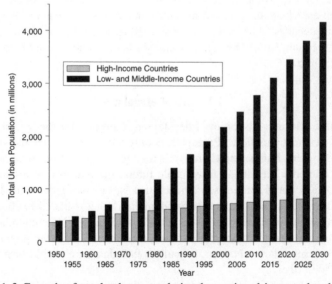

FIGURE 1-3 Growth of total urban population by national income level, 1950–2030.
SOURCES: United Nations (2002a); World Bank (2001).

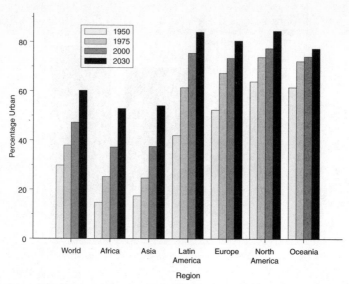

FIGURE 1-4 Estimated and projected percentage of population in urban areas, by region, 1950–2030.
SOURCE: United Nations (2002a).

however, with less than 40 percent of their populations being urban. However, Asia will contribute the greatest absolute number of new urban residents over the next three decades. Although both Africa and Asia will become more urban than rural in the near future, they are not thought likely to attain the 60 percent level before 2030.

A Future of Megacities?

In popular writing on the cities of developing countries, it is the largest cities that receive the most attention. Perhaps it is only natural that cities the size of São Paulo, Bangkok, Lagos, and Cairo come readily to mind when urban populations are considered. Yet for the foreseeable future, the majority of urban residents will reside in much smaller settlements, that is, in small cities with 100,000 to 250,000 residents and in towns with populations of less than 100,000. Data on these cities and towns are scarce and grossly inadequate. No comprehensive, reliable, and up-to-date database exists for cities under 100,000 in population, and as is discussed later, it is even difficult to find data in a usable form for cities under 750,000.

Despite these difficulties, some information on urban populations by size of city can be gleaned from the United Nations (2002a). Figure 1-5 presents the United Nations predictions, showing the number of urban residents who will be

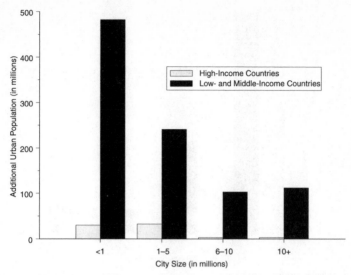

FIGURE 1-5 Net additions to urban population, by city size and national income level, 2000–2015.
SOURCES: United Nations (2002a); World Bank (2001).

added to cities of different sizes over the period 2000 to 2015. As can be seen, the lion's share of the increase will be taken by towns and cities with fewer than 1 million inhabitants. Figure 1-6 depicts the projected distribution (in 2015) of urban population by size of city. Towns and cities with a population of under 1 million will then account for about 60 percent of the developing-country urban total. Cities from 1 to 5 million in size will house another 26 percent.

As a rule, smaller cities tend to grow more rapidly than do larger ones. This tendency is evident in regression analyses with controls for confounding factors, and in the trajectories followed by individual cities over time. To be sure, there is considerable unexplained variation in the relationship between city size and growth. Nevertheless, as will be discussed later, the negative association between the two is sufficiently robust for the United Nations to have incorporated the relation in its forecasting methods.

We cannot recall a case in which a small city was the focus of an editorial lamenting rapid urban growth or the lack of public services. Nevertheless, the combined size of such cities makes them very significant presences in developing countries. As is shown throughout this report, smaller urban areas—especially those under 100,000 in population—are notably underserved by their governments, often lacking piped water, adequate waste disposal, and electricity. Indeed, they can exhibit levels of human capital, fertility, health, and child survival that are akin to those found in rural areas. The sheer scale of the challenges

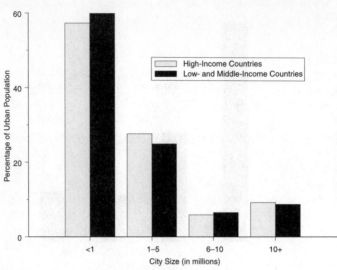

FIGURE 1-6 Projected distribution of urban residents in 2015 by city size for high-income countries, and for low- and middle-income countries.
SOURCES: United Nations (2002b); World Bank (2001).

presented by very large cities should not cause the difficulties of these small cities to be overlooked.

We are by no means suggesting that large cities be neglected in policy and research. The scale on which resources are concentrated in these cities presents governments with needs that are of a qualitatively different order than those of small cities and towns. At the beginning of the twentieth century, there were only 16 cities in the world with populations of 1 million or more, and the vast majority of these cities were found in advanced industrial economies. Today the world contains more than 400 cities of this size, and three-quarters of them are found in low- and middle-income countries. For the residents of these cities, scale is a defining feature of social, economic, and political life. It has many positive aspects: when urban activity is appropriately organized and governed, scale can enable specialization, reduce the per capita costs of service provision, and allow economic and social diversity to flourish. In poor countries, however, which lack all manner of the necessary administrative and technical resources, the challenges presented by large cities can be daunting indeed.

In these countries, the proportion of the population residing in large cities is approaching the levels seen in rich countries. In 2000, about one-third of the national populations of rich countries lived in cities of at least 1 million residents. Although poor countries have not yet reached the one-third mark, they are moving toward it. In 1975, only 9 percent of the national populations of poor countries lived in such cities. By 2000, the total had risen to 15 percent, and it is expected to rise further, to 17 percent, by 2015.

THE TRANSFORMATION OF CITIES

São Paulo, now Latin America's second-largest city and a megacity by any definition, had its origins as a minor commercial center. Although the story of São Paulo has unique elements, it can stand as an example of the changes under way in cities worldwide. In 1890, when Rio de Janeiro could boast a population of more than half a million, only 65,000 people lived in São Paulo. It was improvements in agriculture—widespread coffee cultivation in the region—that ushered in São Paulo's first era of prosperity. By the early 1900s, manufacturing had gained a foothold in the city, mainly in connection with the processing and marketing of coffee. Over the next half-century, industrialization began on a large scale, a development spurred by the collapse of world prices for coffee, which caused large landowners and major entrepreneurs to scramble for ways to diversify. By 1950 São Paulo had assumed its present position as the leading manufacturing center of Brazil. Industrialization then further accelerated, encouraged by the government's strategy of import substitution and the construction of a transportation system that made the city a central node. The city's rate of population growth in this era was truly spectacular—in the 1950s, São Paulo was one of the world's fastest-growing metropolitan areas. Although its growth rate subsequently declined, the population of the greater São Paulo metropolitan area is still increasing and is expected to exceed 20 million by 2015 (United Nations, 2001).

In this history are found several of the themes with which this report is concerned—the linkages of cities to their surrounding regions, the role of world markets, government development strategies and investments, and demographic transitions. In what follows we describe more systematically the principal themes that link the chapters of this volume.

Space and Measurement

As countries urbanize and proportionately more of their citizens find homes in cities, the need grows for spatially disaggregated data on the conditions of urban life. It is difficult to imagine how cities can be governed effectively without such data. But from what sources are spatially disaggregated data now available? National censuses can provide useful measures for small spatial units, but censuses are not often examined at such disaggregated levels. Few national surveys have samples sufficiently large to permit estimation at fine-grained spatial resolutions. To fill the gap, some countries have been making use of remotely sensed data and other measures organized in geographic information systems (GIS).

Such spatial detail could, in theory, provide a stronger basis for forecasts of city populations than now exists. We suspect, however, that the greatest value of

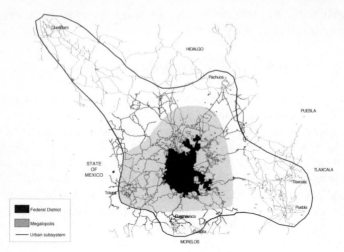

FIGURE 1-7 Mexico City urban subsystem, 1995.
SOURCE: Garza (2000), reprinted with permission.

spatially disaggregated data will lie in their potential to spark dialogue among urban units of government and groups of citizens. In Cape Town, South Africa, the metropolitan government is now displaying data drawn from a GIS on its Internet Web site, where residents can easily see how the provision of water and other services in their neighborhoods compares with that elsewhere in the city (for discussion, see Milne, 2001). This new technology has opened a channel through which poor groups might one day press government officials for greater equity in the provision of resources.

Spatial disaggregation may also enable progress to be made on a problem that has long bedeviled urban studies—how to define and measure the extent of a city. These measurement concerns are addressed later in the report, but to appreciate their implications, it may be useful to consider two examples here.

The extent of Mexico City is for some purposes defined to be the Federal District (*Distrito Federal*); for other purposes it takes in the Mexico City Metropolitan Area; and for still others it encompasses the large urban megalopolis centered on Mexico City but including the population of Toluca (see Figure 1-7). In the 2000 census, the population of the Federal District was estimated at 8.6 million, and that of the larger Mexico City Metropolitan Area at 17.9 million. The urban megalopolis was estimated to contain 19.1 million residents.[3] Evidently, one's choice of city definition can double or halve the reported city population and wholly reconfigure its socioeconomic profile.

---

[3] A still more expansive conception would acknowledge the system of cities in which Mexico City participates, including Toluca, Puebla, Cuernavaca, Querétaro, and Pachuca, among which the flows of people, goods, and services are considerable. This polynuclear metropolitan region (or megalopolis) had a population of 23.2 million inhabitants in 2000, representing 24 percent of Mexico's total national population and 35 percent of its total urban population (Garza, 2000).

TABLE 1-1 Comparison of Two Estimates of Population Size and Growth in Four
Extended Metropolitan Regions (EMRs)

	Bangkok		Jakarta		Manila		Taipei	
	1980	1990	1980	1990	1980	1990	1980	1990
Population								
Urban	4,723	5,901	5,985	7,650	5,955	7,968	2,217	2,711
Agglomeration								
Core	4,697	5,876	6,481	8,223	5,926	7,948	2,268	2,761
Inner Zone	1,947	2,706	5,413	7,676	2,820	4,107	3,070	4,035
Outer Zone	2,513	3,061	n.a.	n.a.	2,932	3,908	709	757
Whole EMR	9,157	11,643	11,894	15,899	11,678	15,963	6,047	7,553
1980–1990 Rate of Growth								
Urban		2.22		2.45		2.91		2.01
Agglomeration								
Core		2.23		2.38		2.93		1.96
Inner Zone		3.29		3.49		3.75		2.73
Outer Zone		1.97		n.a.		2.87		0.65
Whole EMR		2.40		2.90		3.12		2.22

NOTE: n.a. means not available.
SOURCES: Data on urban agglomeration from United Nations (2001); all other data
from Jones (2002).

The benefits of disaggregating data in spatial dimensions can also be seen by
considering four large metropolitan areas in Southeast Asia—Bangkok, Jakarta,
Manila, and Taipei. Just how large are these large cities? How rapidly are they
growing? Again the answers depend on how boundaries are drawn. Table 1-1
shows the urban agglomeration population estimates supplied by the United Nations (2001) and compares them with more spatially refined estimates that distinguish among a city core, an inner zone of settlement, and an outer zone (from
Jones, 2002). The core, inner, and outer zones together constitute an extended
metropolitan region. If the extended region is taken to be the appropriate measure, the United Nations estimates of city population size are understated by half
(Jones, 2002). In addition, rates of population growth differ a good deal among
the core, inner, and outer zones, with the inner zones growing much more rapidly
than the official urban agglomeration. If the city boundaries are drawn too tightly,
important developments may be missed in the periurban areas lying just outside
these boundaries (Jones, Tsay, and Bajracharya, 2000).

Socioeconomic Diversity Within Cities

Social, economic, and spatial diversity is a fact of life in cities, whether of the
size of São Paulo or smaller. Almost all cities contain elite neighborhoods that
are well served by schools, health facilities, and public utilities. Likewise, almost
all contain desperately poor neighborhoods whose residents live in dilapidated

housing and suffer from inadequate public services. In many countries in the developing world, at least one urban resident in four is thought to be living in absolute poverty (Hall and Pfeiffer, 2000). In the world's poorest countries, the conditions of life in slums and shantytowns can be extremely grim. Rural migrants to cities add another element of diversity; in many accounts they are said to be further swelling the slums.

A central theme of this report is the need to attend to the spatial aspects of diversity and inequality. As a country urbanizes, one naturally expects its cities to house a growing percentage of all poor citizens. To understand urban poverty, it is necessary to understand where within cities the poor live and to map the conditions of their neighborhoods. The analysis entails a study of spatial segregation, local social networks and social capital, and the localized features of government. Of course, not all urban inequality will be expressed spatially. As Caldeira (1999, 2000) reminds us for São Paulo, by establishing fortified enclaves the rich can quite effectively exclude the poor without putting them at any great distance. But the spatial aspects of segregation warrant close attention, not least because governments and nongovernmental organizations (NGOs) must often operate on a territorial basis.

Another aspect of urban diversity is more beneficial, or at least potentially so. Following the lead of Jacobs (1969), economists have been exploring the ways in which the diversity of economic activity in cities can stimulate innovation and productivity growth. At present, much of this literature is theoretical, but empirical studies are beginning to appear (e.g., Glaeser, Kallal, Scheinkman, and Shleifer, 1992; Moretti, 2000; Duranton and Puga, 2001; Henderson, Lee, and Lee, 2001; Henderson, 2002). These diversity effects are a form of what are termed "agglomeration economies," a phrase that refers to the productivity advantages stemming from the spatial concentration of production. The social theories mentioned earlier—concerning social learning and networks, reference groups, collective socialization, and the like—also emphasize the potential benefits of diversity, and in this respect closely parallel the economic theories. Space figures centrally in urban economic and social theory because proximity facilitates the gathering and exchange of information, lessens the costs of transport, and makes possible the exercise of some beneficial social controls.

Fertility and Reproductive Health

For developing countries there are surprisingly few careful studies of inter- and intraurban differentials in fertility and reproductive health. As is well known, urban residents face many constraints and opportunities that influence their childbearing. They typically want fewer children than their rural counterparts, making the general level of demand for contraceptive services higher in urban than in rural areas. Urban couples are probably more apt to appreciate the advantages of having fewer but better-educated children, choosing to make greater investments in their children's schooling and adopting childrearing strategies that place heavier demands on parental time. What is it about urban environments that encourages such reproductive strategies?

The fertility implications of urban contexts were once prominent in demographic transition theory, a collection of ideas about demographic change that Van de Kaa (1996), Kirk (1996), and Mason (1997) have recently reappraised. Indeed, Notestein (1953) went so far as to suggest that urbanization be considered as something of a precondition for fertility decline. The historical record shows that fertility was lower in urban than in rural areas in many historical populations, although debate persists on the relationship of urbanization to fertility decline. The Princeton European Fertility Project examined marital fertility in Europe during the nineteenth and twentieth centuries, and found urban fertility to be lower than rural in almost every region and time period. Fertility was also found to be lower in larger than in smaller cities (Sharlin, 1986). A detailed study by Galloway, Hammel, and Lee (1994) for Prussia makes a strong case that here, urbanization was linked to fertility decline, in the sense that measures closely associated with urbanization (percentages of the adult population employed in banking, insurance, and communication) were found to have exerted substantial influence on the pace of fertility decline.[4]

In what ways might fertility behavior be distinctively urban? Broadly speaking, the distinctive features have to do with the benefits of new family reproductive strategies, the costs of executing these strategies, and the features of urban social life that shape the perception of benefits and costs. In considering whether to have fewer children, urban parents may well be influenced by the consequences they can observe in their own social networks and neighborhoods. If these networks and neighborhoods are homogeneous, they may not provide a sample of experience with sufficient range to demonstrate the implications of innovative reproductive decisions. In cities, however, local networks and information are likely to be more diverse than in the countryside, and this diversity can enrich the information available to parents and give them the necessary confidence to take innovative actions. The mechanisms are those highlighted in multilevel theories of social learning and diffusion (National Research Council, 2001). By limiting the variety of social role models and reference groups on view, the spatial segregation of the urban poor may have the effect of increasing uncertainties about new strategies, thereby prolonging dependence on traditional strategies of high fertility.

The costs of obtaining family planning, health, and related services also have an urban aspect. Certainly the private health sector is far more prominent in cities.

---

[4]These authors examined Prussian *Kreise*—small administrative units—using fixed-effect regression methods. In addition to the banking, insurance, and communication measures, they included the urbanization level of each *Kreise*, but uncovered no additional effects of interest. Of course, there remains room for debate about the strength of the connection elsewhere in historical Europe. Other empirical studies of the European experience have not found a close connection between urbanization and fertility decline (Lesthaeghe, 1977; Coale and Watkins, 1986).

It is itself highly diverse and heterogenous. In large cities, one finds sophisticated clinics and teaching hospitals that cater to the elite operating alongside an assortment of pharmacists and traditional healers. The physical *distance* to services is no doubt less in many cities than in rural areas, but whether urban services are of any higher *quality* once reached is highly debatable. As will be seen, the few careful comparisons that have been made between urban and rural services show the supposed urban advantage to have been much overstated, especially where the urban poor are concerned.

Many other features of social life in the city can have important reproductive health implications. In some cases, urban settings present young unmarried women with completely new behavioral options. The establishment of a garment manufacturing sector in Dhaka, for example, has created the opportunity for unmarried women to work outside the home in direct contact with men, a situation almost unimaginable a generation ago (Amin, Diamond, Haved, and Newby, 1998). This experience is likely to transform the attitudes and social confidence of young women, influencing the terms upon which they enter marriage, engage in childbearing, and make decisions about their children's schooling. Men and women in urban areas tend to marry later than their rural counterparts, and therefore appear more likely to have transitory partnerships and (perhaps) to begin sexual activity prior to marriage. Early and unprotected adolescent sex is a familiar urban concern. Cities also contain disproportionately more young migrants, many of whom have postponed marriage or engage in extramarital sex. Urban areas usually have higher levels of prostitution than rural areas and have exhibited greater prevalence of HIV/AIDS and other sexually transmitted diseases.

Health

Urban inequalities are perhaps most vividly expressed in measures of health. Since the mid-1980s, the long-assumed superiority of urban areas with respect to health and child survival has been called into question (Brockerhoff and Brennan, 1998). Debt crises and structural adjustment have led to retrenchments of many government subsidies, which had disproportionately benefited urban residents. Yet even as these funds have been cut, high rates of urban population growth have generally continued. Population growth has often taken the form of rapid, unplanned expansion of low-income settlements on the peripheries of large cities, where health and other public services are lacking. Although the urban poor may be better equipped with some services than the rural poor, many of the urban poor also lack clean and affordable water, adequate sanitation, and electricity (Hardoy, Mitlin, and Satterthwaite, 2001; Jonsson and Satterthwaite, 2000b). In the absence of such services, the spatial concentration of urban poverty hastens the circulation of communicable diseases.

Researchers have recently raised the possibility of a reemergence of the urban health penalties seen in the nineteenth century. They have stressed repeatedly the need to pay close attention to the malign influences of spatially concentrated poverty (Harpham, Lusty, and Vaughan, 1988; Tabibzadeh, Rossi-Espagnet, and Maxwell, 1989; Stephens, 1996). Where data exist, studies of urban slums and shantytowns have often revealed rates of morbidity and mortality similar to those in rural areas, and in some cases far higher. Perhaps it is not surprising, then, that neo-Malthusians have portrayed large cities as centers of poverty and social collapse (see, for example, Kennedy, 1993, or Linden, 1996).

Although they have not entirely neglected the topic, demographers have devoted insufficient attention to the study of intraurban differentials in health. Only a few studies with a demographic focus, such as that of Timaeus and Lush (1995), have explored in detail how negative spillovers, or "externalities," influence health conditions in spatially concentrated urban populations. No longitudinal study of which we are aware has linked health or health-seeking behaviors to measures of neighborhood social interaction, networks, and social capital. Nor have interurban health differences received adequate attention. As the conventional wisdom has it, health conditions are better for residents of large cities than for those in smaller cities, towns, and rural villages. Can this be true if an urban penalty is emerging?

Cities, Their Regions, and the International Economy

Spatially disaggregated data are needed to understand the influence of local contexts on fertility and health, and are of particular interest in zones where urban and rural activities are interpenetrating. In some geographic regions—the phenomenon has been examined most closely in Southeast Asia—rural economies and lifestyles appear to be undergoing a qualitative change, increasingly assuming characteristics that were formerly considered urban. More rural residents work outside agriculture; rural economies are increasingly diverse, mixing agriculture with cottage industries, industrial estates, and suburban development; and many rural residents are, of course, linked to city life through spells of migration and even through commuting. In some developing regions, one sees the emergence of megaurban areas in which it is difficult to say where a particular city begins and ends. The reconfiguration of urban space is manifested in the outward spread of urban activities, such as industry, shopping centers, suburban homes, and recreational facilities, which are penetrating what was once rural territory.

In short, the functions and roles of cities that connect them to surrounding territory are changing in ways that threaten the relevance of administrative boundaries (McGee, 1991). By shading and obscuring boundaries, such changes are causing researchers to question the value of urban/rural dichotomies, which appear increasingly simplistic. The interpenetration of activity is also forcing a reassessment of the essential nature of rurality, attracting new attention to measures of the remoteness of rural sites from the cities of their regions (Coombes and Raybould, 2001; Hugo, Champion, and Lattes, 2001).

Much as the economy of São Paulo evolved over the course of the last century, with its evolution punctuated by crises in the international markets, we can expect modern cities to be reshaped by global economic forces over the course of the century ahead. Newly globalized circuits of finance, trade, and information exchange are linking rich countries with some poor countries, and connecting some urban residents of poor countries to their counterparts elsewhere. Many poor countries are industrializing rapidly, while advanced economies are taking steps away from manufacturing into the sectors of finance, specialized services, and information technology.

These changes are forcing countries—and individual cities—to rethink their comparative advantages. To be competitive in global markets, cities are finding that they need to establish themselves as strategic nodes in international networks of exchange. Cities increasingly compete against each other, striving to present the image and provide the infrastructure demanded by international firms so as to attract greater foreign investment and generate new jobs. As they link themselves to global markets, cities are increasingly exposing their residents to the risks, as well as the benefits, of being more tightly integrated into world networks of finance, information, and production. But cities vary greatly in their exposure to such risks and benefits, and the implications depend on national contexts and levels of development.

International orientations are emerging so quickly, especially in the Asia Pacific region, that it is difficult to discern the full implications for demographic behavior. It is obvious that the benefits of globalization are being distributed in a highly uneven fashion. Very few African cities have benefited from direct foreign investment in manufacturing, whereas foreign capital has gone to a number of cities in Asia and Latin America. To the extent that some cities succeed in attracting foreign capital and to the extent that this capital is spatially concentrated (Douglass, 1997), new loci of economic activity can be expected to emerge, with some areas experiencing rapid growth while others decline. Because foreign direct investment is usually distributed unevenly across national landscapes, patterns of migration are likely to be reshaped. Wage rates and the returns to schooling for some categories of workers may also be affected. Furthermore, as large cities enter the international competition for resources, they may lay claim to quantities of physical capital that might otherwise have gone to smaller cities. The result may be a further widening of the gap between resource-poor small cities and large cities that are already better endowed with private capital and infrastructure. But all this is speculation: although powerful forces are afoot, we cannot yet say where they will lead.

Cities are a nation's gateways to international markets, and city populations can be among the first beneficiaries of the waves of technological change that stream through these markets. City residents can also find themselves among the first victims of price spikes and exchange rate crises. Engagement with these markets may well come at the price of urban economic volatility. Still, it is not a given that international economic shocks will have greater impacts on urban than rural residents. As will be discussed later, the political economy of crises can be exceedingly complex, making the spatial distribution of their effects difficult to predict (Fallon and Lucas, 2002).

Governance

A remarkable transformation is under way in developing-country cities that may be of first-order importance to policies in the areas of health and reproductive health. We refer to the phenomenon of decentralization, a process in which national governments are devolving some of their powers and revenue-raising authority to regional, state, and local units of government. The rate of change is astonishing, as is the diversity of countries in which these reforms are being undertaken.

The pace and variety of decentralization initiatives have occasioned an outpouring of research in political science, public finance, and urban administration. In these literatures it is recognized that a new cast of policy makers is being assembled, and that many on the staffs of local and regional governments will be issuing policies and monitoring implementation in areas in which they have little previous experience or expertise. As municipal and regional governments take up new responsibilities for service delivery in health and education, among other things, on what basis will they make their decisions? In decentralized systems, where will the technical expertise be located in such areas as family planning? How will information be conveyed from national ministries of health to such lower-tier governments, and how will it be returned to the ministries to guide their allocation of resources? What role can be envisioned for private national medical associations? Who will attend to the question of equity in reproductive health service delivery when services are arranged and monitored by different units of government? These are large and difficult questions, and of course they extend beyond health to touch on many roles and aspects of government.

THE PANEL'S CHARGE

The transformations just reviewed suggest the need for a thorough reappraisal of what is new in the process of urbanization in developing countries, how demographic perspectives can enhance understanding of the process, and what policy revisions and initiatives are likely to be needed. At present, demographic researchers are ill positioned to shed light on these matters. Although vigorous programs of urban research are under way in other fields—including international health, political science, public finance, and, lately, economics—the lack of activity in demographic research circles has left these fields without the benefit of demographic insight. In economics, for instance, elegant theories have been fashioned to explain why large cities grow more slowly than small ones, evidently without taking lower fertility rates into account. And it can be argued that the low profile of urban demography has left important institutions without the resources they need to maintain the urban research infrastructure.

Reference was made earlier to Preston (1979) and the United Nations (1980), which are the landmarks in urban demographic research. The world of research has changed in many ways since these reports were issued. Sample surveys are utilized far more today than was the case in the 1970s, and demographic theories have come to emphasize individual-level motives and behavior, paying decidedly less attention to the behavior of population aggregates. Relatively few demographers now work with census data for developing countries, and fewer still are able to use data on the populations of the individual cities of these countries. The great demographic resources of the modern era—the Demographic and Health Surveys (DHS) and the city population data in the United Nations' *Demographic Yearbook* and *World Urbanization Prospects*—are not themselves directly linkable because until recently the necessary geographic identifiers were expunged from the DHS public-use datasets, and the United Nations datasets have not been publicly available in computerized form. It is disconcerting to realize that as we enter the twenty-first century, the world of demographic research lacks the basic infrastructure to address the urban challenge ahead.

Recognizing the need for a major fresh inquiry, the National Research Council formed the Panel on Urban Population Dynamics. The panel's mandate was to develop greater understanding of the dynamics of urban population growth, as well as its causes and consequences, as a step toward helping governments better manage the environmental and social service problems that accompany the rapid growth of urban areas in poor countries. The panel focused on improving knowledge in six areas:

- Urban population dynamics and city growth

- Social and economic differentiation within and across cities

- Fertility and reproductive health in urban areas

- Mortality and morbidity in urban areas

- Demographic implications of a changing global economy

- The challenge of urban governance

In each of these areas, the panel was charged with synthesizing results from existing and emerging research, as well as identifying new directions for research that are scientifically promising and have the potential to better integrate population and public policy.

STUDY SCOPE AND APPROACH

The panel's first concern was how to define the boundaries of its undertaking. Urbanization, itself the product of fundamental economic and technological change, arguably affects every aspect of social life (Davis, 1955). In reviewing developments from the onset of the industrial revolution to 1950, Bairoch (1988) maintains that there was really no aspect of the demography of cities that did not exhibit specifically urban traits. In sifting through priorities, the panel endeavored to isolate these distinctively urban features. We tried to determine the value added by an urban perspective on demographic behavior and policy. The dilemma throughout was to single out what is distinctive about urban environments without placing undue emphasis on urban/rural differences, which in some regions are beginning to fade.

To address its task, the panel reviewed the existing literature and conducted a substantial amount of new data analysis. We relied heavily on a database created by linking individual DHS surveys with information on city population sizes taken from the United Nations' *Demographic Yearbook*, a publication that includes data for cities as small as 100,000 in population and all national capitals. (Chapter 4 reviews the many difficulties encountered in linking the survey and city data.) The linked DHS–United Nations database contains comparable measures for a broad range of demographic outcomes from as many as 90 surveys in more than 50 countries.

For the reasons mentioned above, the DHS surveys have not been systematically analyzed from an urban perspective. The advantages of these surveys lie in their breadth, their consistency, and the comparability of questions and methods across surveys, as well as in good (if incomplete) regional coverage. These surveys also suffer from significant disadvantages—their samples are generally too small to permit reliable description at the level of individual cities, to say nothing of analysis of socioeconomic variation within individual cities. Only through the application of multivariate methods can one get a glimpse of this sort of variation.

In addressing its charge, the panel sought to confine its efforts to areas of the most pressing need. For example, we did not exhaustively review environmental problems in cities because recent and highly capable summaries of these issues are available elsewhere (see Hardoy, Mitlin, and Satterthwaite, 2001). Likewise, issues of housing are thoroughly examined by the United Nations Centre for Human Settlements (UNCHS) (1996, 2001) and Malpezzi (1999). To make best use of its limited resources, the panel focused on the critical need for more detailed demographic analysis of inter- and intraurban differentials in low- and middle-income countries. Although we could not conduct analyses at the level of neighborhoods, we developed a measure of relative urban poverty to explore the equity dimension of intracity variation. To determine the extent of intercity differentials, we analyzed the DHS–United Nations data by one measure of urban hierarchy—

city population size—recognizing the urgent need for measures of governance and other city-specific characteristics.

ORGANIZATION OF THE REPORT

The remainder of this volume reports the results of the panel's work. We first develop a theoretical rationale for studying urban contexts, giving an overview of recent thought on the importance of local social and spatial environments (Chapter 2). The report proceeds to sketch the regional context in which change occurs and reviews the basic demography of urbanization and city growth (Chapters 3 and 4, respectively). Chapter 5 examines the social and economic diversity in urban conditions of life. Despite the material advantages offered by urban life, it is evident that many city residents are unable to avail themselves of these advantages—they lack adequate food, water, and shelter. Chapter 5 documents several dimensions of urban poverty and presents new findings on the extent of poverty and inequality by city size and by region. Chapters 6 and 7 then consider fertility and health, respectively, raising the question of whether there exist distinctively urban demographic regimes with distinctive implications for service delivery.

The demographic changes examined in these chapters are rooted in the urban economy, which generates resources and establishes some of the constraints and costs that affect demographic behavior, and in urban governance, which influences how those resources are distributed and conflicting demands resolved. A defining characteristic of cities and towns at the beginning of the twenty-first century is their internal diversity; the management and mediation of difference is a central challenge in urban governance. Chapter 8 addresses the urban economy and its labor markets from a demographic perspective, and Chapter 9 examines the challenge of urban governance. Finally, Chapter 10 takes stock of what has been learned and offers some thoughts about the path forward.

2

Why Location Matters

This chapter explores the ways in which urban environments can influence demographic behavior. Although we refer to empirical findings, our main purpose is to provide a map of concepts, with emphasis on the features that give the urban socioeconomic landscape its distinctive character. The discussion begins at the micro level, examining how neighborhoods might affect individual and family demographic decisions. It then moves to successively higher levels of aggregation, surveying the linkages that cross neighborhoods, taking in the broader urban economy, exploring connections among cities, and finally examining the structures of government that are overlaid upon this varied terrain. The themes developed here have international extensions, but this chapter remains within national boundaries. In closing, the concepts that have entered the discussion are reviewed, and a few of the major features that distinguish urban from rural landscapes are identified.

Although the discussion in this chapter traverses a great range of contexts, it is guided by a mere handful of concepts: diversity, proximity, externality, network, and centrality. As they are assembled in different configurations, these concepts present a series of urban frameworks through which demographic behavior can be viewed. Urban frames do not always offer novel views of demographic phenomena, but they often provide a fresh perspective.

At the center of our argument is a proposition so unexceptionable as to be banal: individuals and families—demographic decision makers—are located or *embedded* in social contexts that determine what information is available to them and influence the decisions based upon that information. Health, fertility, and human capital investment decisions are influenced by multiple social contexts; so, too, are decisions about job search, migration, and labor force participation. The panel regards these demographic decisions as being inherently *multilevel* in nature, and in considering the individual-to-group links, emphasizes the roles of urban social interaction, feedback, and diffusion.

Had demographers but taken their cue from the Taichung experiment, we might now be in a position to summarize 30 years of intraurban multilevel research. That randomized intervention—its elements were described by Freedman and Takeshita (1969: 109–48)—began in 1963, when Taichung was a smallish Taiwanese city of some 325,000 inhabitants. The experimental design exploited the city's neighborhood structure, allocating 2,400 small neighborhoods, or *lin*, to treatment and control groups. The treatment took the form of provision of information about the intrauterine device (IUD), which was then a relatively new method of family planning. A key question in the analysis was whether such family planning information "spilled across" the boundaries of the treatment *lin* to benefit women in adjacent control *lin*.

Remarkably strong evidence of such informational spillovers emerged, and women's social networks were identified as the main mechanism by which news of the IUD was conveyed from the treatment women to those who had not heard of this method firsthand. A number of women outside Taichung proper were found to have learned of the IUD through their social network ties to city residents. These network contacts evidently had the effect of amplifying the program efforts undertaken in the treatment *lin*, acting as "social multipliers" through which information could be diffused across space and socioeconomic strata.

The Taichung case introduces several themes that figure prominently in this report. Informational externalities are one such theme. Neighborhood effects are another, as are the conceptual distinctions between neighborhood and social network. The Taichung experiment revealed urban/rural linkages that were stronger than expected, thus calling into question the sociological meaning of the city boundaries. It also showed how programs that must operate in specific neighborhoods—small *lin*, in this instance—can exert influence beyond those local spaces.

Had research only continued along these lines, a new "Chicago School" tradition of detailed spatial and social analyses of developing-country cities might well have developed, with demographic behavior as one focus. But as it happened, the urban themes of the Taichung experiment were left dangling, and the demographic literature took up entirely different lines of inquiry. By the late 1970s and 1980s, this literature had come to be dominated by individualistic models of behavior. Interest in contextual effects did not disappear, of course, and multilevel methods of analysis continue to be refined.[1] In developing countries, however, such methods have seldom been matched to data on urban neighborhoods and local contexts. A continuing difficulty—to which we return in Chapter 5—is that in these countries, census data are rarely processed at the level of local areal units. Lacking census data, researchers interested in multilevel approaches have often found themselves

---

[1] See, among others, Rosenzweig and Schultz (1982), Casterline (1985a,b), Tsui (1985), Entwisle, Casterline, and Sayed (1989), Entwisle, Rindfuss, Guilkey, Chamratrithirong, Curran, and Sawangdee (1996), Bilsborrow and Anker (1993), Pebley, Goldman, and Rodríguez (1996), Sastry (1996), Degraff, Bilsborrow, and Guilkey (1997), Axinn, Barber, and Ghimire (1997), Axinn and Yabiku (2001), and Mroz, Bollen, Speizer, and Mancini (1999).

restricted to rural sites, where sample surveys can be used to inventory the local environment.

For these reasons, the demographic literature on developing-country cities has never achieved the sophistication and keen appreciation of context that is seen in studies of Chicago (Sampson and Raudenbush, 1999), Oakland (Fischer, 1982), or Glasgow (Garner and Raudenbush, 1991). As we take up the issue of why location matters in Africa, Asia, and Latin America, we are therefore uncomfortably dependent on concepts and findings developed with other settings in mind. We shall, nevertheless, borrow wholesale from these developed-country studies, hoping to bring conceptual parallels and partial analogies to light.

PLACES, NETWORKS, NEIGHBORHOODS

Urban neighborhoods can be viewed as spatial units that might—or might not— have significant effects on demographic behavior. To clarify what form neighborhood effects could take, we must first separate the concept of place from that of community. As used here, place is a spatial concept, whereas community is a social concept, having to do with individual and group identities, senses of belonging, and the presumption of mutual interests and shared values.[2] A neighborhood might be defined as a type of community composed of spatially proximate individuals. When the discussion focuses on social capital, social learning, and other mechanisms through which neighborhood effects can be expressed, this community aspect of neighborhoods comes to the fore. But there may well be effects attributable to the local social–spatial environment that are due to the very lack of place-based community ties. In settings where local residents mistrust one another and recognize few shared interests and common values, they may see elements of social and physical risk in the local environment and behave accordingly. Hence, the concept of neighborhood effects encompasses two rather different influences on individual behavior—those stemming from local social ties and those due to their absence.

The identification of neighborhood with community has gone in and out of fashion in urban sociological research. In the early literature, it was argued that cities had once been home to coherent, functional "natural neighborhoods," or "urban villages," which were ethnic communities akin to rural villages. The forces of modernization were said to have swept away many of these local, place-based social relationships and dispersed their functions among a variety of urban institutions. Wirth (1938: 20–21) famously depicted the process as entailing a "substitution of secondary for primary contacts, the weakening of bonds of kinship, and the declining social significance of the family, the disappearance of the neighborhood,

---

[2]Different disciplines attach quite different meanings to the term "place." To geographers (e.g., Committee on Identifying Data Needs for Place-Based Decision Making, 2002: 55), place is an "ensemble concept" that encompasses both spatial and social elements and processes. See also Harvey (1973), Gregory and Urry (1985), Wolch and Dear (1989), and Golledge and Stimson (1997).

and the undermining of the traditional basis of social solidarity." In the urban way of life—or so it then appeared—place-based social ties were replaced by aspatial social relationships or by no relationships at all.

When empirical methods were brought to bear on such views, they were found to be simplistic and even misleading. As Chaskin (1994: 12) notes in reference to the bygone era of functional, natural urban neighborhoods, "There is no evidence that such a golden age ever existed." Sociologists began to examine broader conceptions of community and to conceive of individuals as participating in several sorts of communities at once, some of which are spatially grounded and others not. Social networks—including both personal social networks and those formed through formal and informal associations—began to be recognized as a key linking mechanism. Through such networks, any given person might have ties to spatially proximate and spatially distant partners. The idea of "communities without propinquity" (a phrase due to Webber, 1963) emerged, and sociologists began to think of individuals as being attached to each of their communities on a voluntary and contingent basis (Chaskin, 1994).

Empirical studies in the United States showed that urban residence is not necessarily associated with weakened personal ties and attenuated senses of community; rather, it affects the *types* of ties and communities in which people participate. Sampson and Morenoff (2000: 374) summarize the empirical record in this way:

> ... contrary to the popular belief that metropolitan life has led inexorably to the decline of personal ties, sociological research has shown that while urbanites may be exposed to more unconventionality and diversity, they retain a set of personal support networks just like their suburban and rural counterparts (see e.g., Fischer 1982).

Fischer (1982: 264) puts it succinctly: "Urbanism does not seem to weaken community, but it does seem to help sustain a plurality of communities."

If the social networks of urban residents contain sufficient links to other spatially proximate individuals, a basis exists for thinking of geographic neighborhoods as communities. Some social network researchers question whether modern urban networks are indeed this localized.[3] As Wellman and Leighton (1979: 365–67) argue in a memorable passage:

> To sociologists, unlike geographers, spatial distributions are not inherently important variables, but assume importance only as they affect such social structural questions as the formation of interpersonal networks and the flow of resources through such networks ... the

---

[3] Social network researchers maintain that their methods provide excellent tools for assessing the relative frequency and strength of place-based ties. For instance, Wellman and Leighton (1979: 365–67) write: "By leaving the matter of spatial distributions initially open, [the network perspective] makes it equally as possible to discover an 'urban village' (Gans, 1962) as it is to discover a 'community without propinquity' (Webber, 1963).... With this approach we are then better able to assess the position of neighborhood ties within the context of overall structures of social relationships."

identification of a neighborhood as a container for communal ties
assumes the a priori organizing power of space. This is spatial
determinism.

The empirical record confirms that U.S. urban residents are connected to a variety
of networks extending outside their neighborhoods. But it also shows that they
continue to value their neighborhood ties, making use of them for day-to-day so-
cializing and drawing upon them for social support. Evidently, some strong and
intimate ties—not all, to be sure—remain grounded in neighborhoods.[4]

If neighborhoods are subsets of networks, how are their spatial boundaries to
be delineated? Residents of poor U.S. communities often disagree as to the dimensions of the neighborhood—even residents of the same household can see things
differently (Furstenberg and Hughes, 1997: 34). The perspectives of adults and
youth can diverge, as can the views of younger and older children. For adolescents, "neighborhoods of sociability" may be at least as important as those defined according to residence (Burton, Price-Spratlen, and Spencer, 1997: 135). In
a study of Los Angeles, Sastry, Pebley, and Zonta (2002) find that better-educated
respondents conceive of their neighborhoods in broader spatial terms than do those
who are less educated. Recent immigrants to Los Angeles hold spatially con-
stricted views of their neighborhoods. Hence, even where local space is acknowledged to matter, the perceived perimeters of that space can be expected to vary
(Committee on Identifying Data Needs for Place-Based Decision Making, 2002).

This social construction of neighborhood is not a merely a subjective matter—
it may well have an influence on the use of public services and, through services, on demographic behavior. For instance, neighborhood residents may view
a nearby health or family planning clinic as being inaccessible if it happens to be
situated beyond a socially defined neighborhood boundary. Or, where privacy is
deemed essential—as it is often thought to be for adolescents—such services may
deliberately be sought outside the bounds of the neighborhood.

Is there any reason to question the social significance of neighborhood in
the cities of poor countries? To the extent that city residents face higher costs
of transport and information exchange than their counterparts in rich countries,
local social space would be expected to assume greater importance. For instance,
in a study of two poor neighborhoods in Santiago, Espinoza (1999) finds that
nearly three-quarters of residents' personal network partners live within walking

---

[4]Acknowledging this, Wellman and Leighton (1979: 385) nevertheless express skepticism about
the relative importance of the local ties: "Neighborhood relationships persist but only as specialized
components of the overall primary networks.... if we broaden our field of view to include other
primary relations, then the apparent neighborhood solidarities may now be seen as clusters in the
rather sparse, loosely bounded structures of urbanites' total networks." Geographers (see Committee
on Identifying Data Needs for Place-Based Decision Making, 2002) argue that people can inhabit
multiple "places" at the same time, some of these at local spatial scales, such as neighborhoods, and
others at larger scales. The spatially distant connections found in social networks serve to define
some of the larger-scale places.

distance. For these poor Chileans, distance is a constraining factor because of the high cost of transport in relation to their resources. For the United States, Fischer (1982: 251) shows that the social networks of the poorly educated are more spatially concentrated than the networks of the better educated. Also, the social networks of women are believed to be more localized than those of men, containing higher proportions of neighbors and kin (see Moore, 1990, and Stoloff, Glanville, and Bienenstock, 1999, as well as the extensive references cited therein). The panel is not aware of comparable social network research in the cities of low-income countries, but would expect that in these settings, too, the networks of women and the poor would tend to be disproportionately local. Because so much of family demographic behavior depends on the information and resources held by women, differences in the composition of their personal networks can have important demographic implications.

Many activities undertaken by governments and nongovernmental organizations (NGOs) are spatially organized and will surely remain so. These activities confer additional social meaning upon local space. Public services—water supply, electricity, sanitation—are of course spatially grounded. However hazy the boundaries of neighborhoods in the eyes of local residents, city planners are obliged to delineate them to arrange for the delivery of such services (White, 1987: 1–6). Politics and political access likewise have their territorial aspects.

For these reasons, neighborhoods are often taken to be the natural units for program interventions, whether on the part of NGOs, governments, or international agencies. The popularity of neighborhood-based programs testifies to a widespread belief in the organizing potential of spatial proximity. Chaskin (1994: 32–44) identifies four strands of thinking that have tended to orient program interventions to neighborhoods: the increasing value being placed on the concepts of local empowerment, control, and responsiveness; the need to operate pilot projects and experimental interventions on a manageable scale; the recognition that effective interventions must often have a comprehensive character, which is difficult to achieve without some spatial concentration of effort; and the expectation that important target populations are themselves spatially concentrated. The growing influence of these ideas is evident in many developing countries, and is being expressed in the decentralization of government functions and the devolution of governmental authority. The twin processes of decentralization and devolution—discussed later in this chapter and in full detail in Chapter 9—are causing governments to be rescaled into spatial units that can approximate clusters of neighborhoods. All this suggests that urban neighborhoods are likely to retain a good deal of social meaning in low-income countries.

Neighborhoods and Demographic Behavior: Theory

This section explores the implications of neighborhood contexts for two types of demographic behavior: first, investments in "child quality," which have to do with children's schooling and the adoption of time-intensive modes of child care on the part of parents; and second, household knowledge of health care and the nature of health outcomes.

For well over a century, specialists in public health have understood that the spatial proximity and intermixing of diverse city populations must amplify the risks of contagious disease. The resources shared within neighborhoods—a neighborhood well in the famous health puzzle solved by John Snow (1855)—present opportunities for social interaction that can have profound epidemiological consequences. An appreciation for the neighborhood aspects of child quality investments, however, is comparatively recent. Some of the theories reviewed below stress the acquisition of information about the labor market and the economic returns to children's schooling; others address the time and opportunity costs of child rearing; and still others consider the location of services and institutions. To the panel's knowledge, none of these theories has been properly tested in low-income countries, but we comment on the features that would appear most salient.[5]

Social learning via social networks

Theories of social learning draw attention to the information that is exchanged through peer groups and personal social networks. Such individual-to-group linkages are a prominent feature of models in many social science disciplines, including anthropology, sociology, economics, cognitive psychology, and the communication sciences. The common thread is this: In situations of flux and uncertainty, when new choices and strategies are being debated, people naturally look to their reference groups and role models to understand the benefits, costs, and uncertainties of these new choices. In the demographic realm, social learning can prompt a rethinking of broad family strategies, or it can be narrowly focused on new tools and behavioral options.[6]

Social learning about education provides one example of the transformation of family strategies. If left to their own perceptual devices, adolescents and their parents would probably have only the haziest sense of the economic returns to schooling. In diverse urban settings, however, they can gain a keener appreciation of these returns by observing local adult role models and reference groups (Wilson, 1987; Borjas, 1995). Professional and middle-class adults exemplify distinctive life-course strategies; in so doing, they help others understand the implications of educational investments and decision points. If social learning enhances

---

[5]This review closely follows the presentation of Gephart (1997: 6–7), who draws in turn from Jencks and Mayer (1990).

[6]A large literature in sociology, geography, and economics focuses on diffusion and social learning processes—see Montgomery and Casterline (1993, 1996) and National Research Council (2001) for extensive reviews with attention to demographic implications. Although the behavioral mechanisms suggested are often plausible, this literature presents few rigorous empirical tests of their significance. We revisit this point later in the chapter.

the perceived returns to schooling (it can also raise concerns about educational costs and risks), urban families can be led to make deeper investments in their children's schooling and to forego traditional strategies of high fertility.

Social learning about the tools of fertility control—modern contraceptives— was central to the success of the Taichung family planning experiment discussed above (Palmore and Freedman, 1969). The learning mechanisms uncovered in that early experiment are being revisited in models of social networks and the diffusion of modern contraceptive use in sub-Saharan Africa. Montgomery and Casterline (1993, 1996) develop the theory with reference to contraceptive use, and strong confirmation is found in empirical estimates made by Behrman, Kohler, and Watkins (2001) for Kenya and Casterline, Montgomery, Agyeman, Aglobitse, and Kiros (2001) for Ghana. These findings—based on longitudinal designs with repeated measures of networks—show how contraceptive use (and knowledge of AIDS) can be spread within localized social networks, diffusing as if by force of example.

Although these empirical studies have focused on diffusion in either rural (Behrman, Kohler, and Watkins, 2001) or rural and periurban (Casterline, Montgomery, Agyeman, Aglobitse, and Kiros, 2001) networks, there is no reason to expect the effects to be limited to these contexts. Indeed, as the Taichung experiment strongly suggests, the socioeconomic diversity of cities and the heterogeneity of the information that circulates within them probably enhance the prospects for informational spillovers. But surprisingly little is known about urban/rural differences in the composition and function of social networks. Beggs, Haines, and Hurlbert (1996) find that in the United States, rural social network ties are "stronger" in the sense of involving greater intimacy, more frequent contact, and longer duration; that rural networks are more homogeneous (especially in terms of religion) and smaller than urban networks; and that they are more dominated by kin. We know of no comparisons of this sort for developing countries.[7]

Clustering, common resources, and contagion

In describing social learning, some researchers refer to the "contagiousness" of ideas and social examples, and make use of mathematical models drawn from epidemiology to trace out the implications (e.g., Rosero-Bixby and Casterline, 1993). If models of social contagion are still relatively new and untested, models of biological contagion are by now well established. In epidemiology it is understood that, with other things being equal, the risks of disease transmission among spatially proximate urban populations must be higher than the risks facing dispersed rural populations. Clustering obviously affects the likelihood of person-to-person

---

[7]Mitchell (1969) offers many clues as to the nature of urban social networks in southern Africa in the 1950s, but the studies collected here are on such a small scale that they might almost be regarded as anecdotal. More recent evidence on urban social networks in Africa can be found in Tostensen, Tvedten, and Vaa (2001).

contagion, whether due to airborne or sexually transmitted disease. Also, because concentrated urban populations share certain resources (notably water), the sanitary practices of one group can generate externalities that affect the health of another.

As a result, urban populations start from a position of health disadvantage relative to rural populations. Where this disadvantage is erased or reversed, one looks for the cause in several areas: in the investments and regulation undertaken by governments to improve water supply and sanitation, in the provision of both public- and private-sector health services, and in the economic factors that supply urban residents with the means to purchase better health care in private markets (see, among others, Preston and van de Walle, 1978; Ewbank and Preston, 1990; Preston and Haines, 1991; van Poppel and van der Heijden, 1997). As discussed below and in Chapter 7, neighborhood health externalities are not wholly a local affair—they also reflect actions taken by the public and private institutions that transcend neighborhoods.

Collective and institutional socialization

Theories of *collective socialization* also highlight the linkages from individuals to groups, but these theories emphasize a form of group influence that is distinct from social learning and contagion. The mechanisms of collective socialization are powerfully described by Wilson (1987) and Coleman (1988), whose work generated a resurgence of interest in neighborhood effects in the cities of the United States. Their research focuses attention on the role of adults residing in the neighborhood, who can supplement the child-rearing efforts of parents by acting as extraparental sources of authority and social control. Directly and by example, these neighborhood adults can teach the young the boundaries of acceptable behavior.

What if city neighborhoods lack such trusted adults? As will be seen in Chapter 6, parents in developing-country cities often complain of the need for extra vigilance in child rearing, describing this as one of the costs of family life that is decidedly higher in cities. This is, perhaps, the other side of the notion that "it takes a village to raise a child": in city neighborhoods where neighbors are distrusted, the burden of child rearing can fall heavily on parents' own shoulders. Furstenberg (1993) describes how in poor U.S. neighborhoods, apprehensive parents take pains to isolate their children from the surrounding population and thereby shield them from social risk. Girls in such high-risk settings may be especially closely supervised (Furstenberg and Hughes, 1997: 28). If similar views prevail in the cities of poor countries—we strongly suspect that they do—the costs entailed in close parental supervision could strongly discourage high fertility.

Institutional socialization refers to the nonresident adults who are figures of influence in a neighborhood because they hold positions in local schools, clinics, police departments, or other institutions. In these roles, adults can affect the young both directly and indirectly. If schools in poor neighborhoods are staffed by inferior teachers, the direct effects may be seen in delayed child development and discouraged human capital investment. Indirect influence can be exerted when teachers or health clinicians require the young to adhere to strict standards of comportment. In such ways, nonresident adults can wield influence much like that of the resident adults envisioned in collective socialization theory.

Although institutional socialization theory has generally focused on micro-level outcomes for children and adolescents, it is closely linked to the allocation of societal resources to neighborhoods (White, 2001). Political and economic processes that deliver good schools and high-quality health clinics to some neighborhoods while leaving others ill served can affect the young by altering the depth and form of institutional socialization.

Social comparisons and subculture conflict

The focus of *social comparison* theory is on the perception of relative deprivation and the possibility that when young people judge their own situation to be relatively unfavorable, the reaction may be either to redouble efforts to improve or to abandon these efforts and drop out of the competition. The theory is described by van den Eeden and Hüttner (1982: 42–6) as one of comparative reference groups. The specifically urban aspect is the relative ease with which diverse reference groups can be observed in cities as a result of the spatial proximity and socioeconomic heterogeneity of urban residents.

When frustrated by blocked opportunities, the young may respond by forming subcultures of resistance. Their individual motivations may be the product of social comparisons, as sketched just above, but the emphasis in *cultural conflict* theory is on how such motivations are voiced and reinforced by groups (Jencks and Mayer, 1990: 116). Chapter 9 examines urban gangs and violence from this perspective; see Durlauf (1999) on how disaffected urban groups may constitute a "perverse" form of local social capital.

The types of social comparison addressed in these theories have not been explored in much demographic research. A rather different form of social comparison, however, has attracted a modest amount of attention. We refer to the consumption possibilities exhibited in the behavior of upper-income groups and displayed in advertisements and television soap operas. In rural areas, the social chasm between high-income families and the bulk of the population may be wide enough to render the consumption habits of the rich irrelevant to most residents. In economically diverse cities, however, a greater range of social groups may find some modern consumer durables affordable, and as these items are taken up by middle-class households, they may come to be seen as potentially within the reach of the upwardly striving poor. In this form of social comparison, individuals are influenced by the consumption patterns exhibited in their reference groups.[8] As Freedman (1979) argues, aspirations for modern consumer goods can exert a powerful influence on fertility decisions, particularly when the costs of consumption are understood to compete with the costs of childrearing.

Services and the physical environment

A prominent theme in demographic research is that the services available in local neighborhoods can either complement or act as substitutes for individual and family resources.[9] In the area of health, for instance, it is thought that mothers who are educated are equipped with information of direct relevance to health care, and that education also helps mothers process the information provided by the media and government, and supplies them with the social confidence needed to seek care for themselves and their children (Caldwell, 1979). Local health services might therefore complement and enhance the positive effects of maternal education, and in this way could increase the health differentials associated with education. But it is also possible that well-functioning services could supply information to women of low education that they might not have been able to acquire by other means. If so, local services could act as substitutes for maternal education, and the presence of services in the community might then reduce the health differentials associated with education.

Examining child mortality rates in Brazil, Sastry (1996) conducts an unusually thorough examination of substitution and complementarity between community measures, on the one hand, and mothers' education, on the other. He finds evidence of substitution between mothers' education and community sanitation and water supply in Northeast Brazil. In this region, community infrastructure appears to be more beneficial for the survival of children of less-educated mothers than for that of children of the better educated. But as Sastry notes, even for Brazil the literature offers mixed results, and there is reason to think that the substitution and complementarity effects must be highly context-specific, depending on policies, prices, and levels of development.

The theories outlined above are concerned with social interactions and ordering, but the ways in which local space is physically ordered may also have demographic implications. Highways, waterways, and other physical features of neighborhoods can establish barriers, corridors, and niches that shape social interactions and distribute risks across space. As Sampson and Morenoff (2000: 379) observe for the United States,

> ... the ecological placement of bars, liquor stores, strip-mall shopping outlets, subway stops, and unsupervised play spaces play a

---

[8]For economic explorations of consumption reference groups, see Alessie and Kapteyn (1991) and Kapteyn, van de Geer, van de Stadt, and Wansbeek (1997).

[9]Sastry (1996) provides an excellent review of the salient concepts and literature, touching on earlier studies by Rosenzweig and Schultz (1982), Thomas, Strauss, and Henriques (1991), and others.

direct role in the distribution of high-risk situations ... not only do mixed-use neighborhoods offer greater opportunities for expropriative crime, they offer increased opportunity for children to congregate outside the home in places conducive to peer-group influence.

Sampson and Raudenbush (1999: 622) point out that such physical barriers limit the scope of beneficial adult surveillance and can inhibit children's social interactions, blocking possibilities for collective socialization and weakening the capacity of residents to organize for common goals.

In the literature on neighborhood effects and crime, the so-called *broken windows* theory stresses the dynamic implications of disordered physical environments. According to this theory, the physical state of a neighborhood testifies to its social cohesion and likely vulnerability. Visual evidence of disorder can suggest that residents are indifferent to their neighborhood or incapable of defending it, all but inviting the attention of potential criminals. Such visual cues can also discourage outsiders from investing economic resources in a neighborhood and can cause residents to disengage from community affairs (Sampson and Raudenbush, 1999: 604).

Social Capital

The preceding discussion has emphasized the role of social networks in neighborhood effects, but certain features of these effects are perhaps more readily seen from a social capital perspective. The distinctions between social networks and social capital are imprecise (Lin, 1999) but may be understood as follows. The term "network" is often employed when the focus is on mechanisms of information exchange and diffusion dynamics, or when specific linkages to resources are being highlighted. The phrase "social capital" is used when networks and local associations are being described as *structures* that might support collective action, enforce norms, generate expectations of reciprocity, or foster feelings of mutual trust (Kawachi, Kennedy, and Glass, 1999; Putnam, 2000; Sampson and Morenoff, 2000). Because it places emphasis on the more durable features of networks and assigns prominent roles to associations and institutions, social capital is often invoked in discussions of civil society and governance.

Health and social capital

In the field of health, social capital effects have drawn considerable attention, especially in relation to mental health. Networks and groups are thought to play two roles: they can offer general economic and emotional support on a sustained basis, and can make specific resources available in times of severe health stress (Kawachi and Berkman, 2001; Lin, Ye, and Ensel, 1999). As James, Schulz, and van Olphen (2001) note, the spatial proximity of network members may be something of a requirement if they are to provide one another with day-to-day

---

BOX 2.1 Social Capital and Mortality Crisis in Russia

Social capital is often defined in terms of features of social organization—the density of civic associations, levels of interpersonal trust, and norms of reciprocity—that act as resources for individuals and facilitate collective action. Using household survey data from 40 regions of Russia, Kennedy, Kawachi, and Brainerd (1998) find empirical links between life expectancy at birth and several indicators of social capital—mistrust of government, crime, quality of work relations, and civic engagement in politics. In the impoverished Russian institutional environment, people may be forced to rely on family, friends, and other informal sources of support to meet their health needs. Until formal institutions can be rebuilt, those who lack informal means of support may be especially vulnerable.

---

assistance. The point would appear to apply with special force to the cities of low-income countries, where the costs of transport and communication are relatively high.

In the empirical analyses of Kawachi, Kennedy, and Glass (1999), two measures of local social capital—civic trust and participation in voluntary associations—are shown to enhance individuals' assessments of their health. In addition to material resources, these associations can bring order, coherence, and meaning to the daily lives of their members (James, Schulz, and van Olphen, 2001). Box 2.1 describes empirical findings on the supportive functions of local social capital in Russia. The Russian context is one of difficult transition to a market economy—a transition that has been accompanied by a breakdown of formal health care institutions, a widespread decline in life expectancy, and an increased dependence on informal mechanisms of support.

Social capital and community dynamics

From the viewpoint of social network theorists, social capital is formed by an accretion of individual investments. When individuals establish a new social network tie or choose to strengthen an existing one, they contribute to a mass of social capital. If social capital is constructed when individuals thus invest, it likewise depreciates when they choose to disinvest: as individuals neglect their neighborhood ties and withdraw from local associations, they weaken the foundations of local capital (Astone, Nathanson, Schoen, and Kim, 1999). In describing these processes, social capital theorists tend to stress investments that take the form of participation in local voluntary associations and formal institutions (Narayan and Pritchett, 1999). They sometimes reconceptualize properties of social networks so as to highlight the links to associations.

The differences in emphasis can be seen by reconsidering the theory of collective socialization. Social capital is thought to be strengthened by the "intergenerational closure" of individual social networks (Coleman, 1988; Gephart, 1997; Sampson, 2002). Network closure occurs when parents come to know the parents of their children's friends; this personal link encourages adult monitoring and supervision. But closure of personal networks is greatly facilitated by the presence of formal associations and institutions (Aber, Gephart, Brooks-Gunn, and Connell, 1997: 53–54):

> ... living in socially organized or "functional" communities should increase parents' contact with their children's friends and with the families of their children's friends.... A weak community organizational base impedes participation in local organizations and development of informal social networks, such as friendship ties among community adults. These, in turn, reduce the collective supervision of youth in the community and diminish the resources available for child care.

Such individual-to-group linkages can generate complex feedbacks and path dependencies in the life of local communities. Individual behavior can either reinforce local social capital and buttress local institutions, or set diffusion processes into motion that ultimately erode the associational base of the neighborhood.

Child-rearing strategies provide one case in point. As noted above, families in risky neighborhoods may choose to restrict their neighborhood ties in favor of cultivating outside ties. Once such strategies become widespread, they effectively disconnect local personal networks and undermine the sense of local community, and this in turn further reduces incentives to invest in local ties. As Furstenberg (1993) writes:

> The social world of transitional communities contracts as neighbors become strangers. Low participation at school meetings and neighborhood improvement associations reduces the networks.... We see in transitional neighborhoods a shift from collective to individualistic strategies of family management. Fewer parents are willing to delegate authority to formal institutions which have lost their credibility and command of external resources. Informal networks become attenuated as kin and close friends move out and are replaced by new residents who are regarded as outsiders. The perception of normative consensus in the community diminishes accordingly.

Sampson (2002) writes in a similar vein on the dynamic feedbacks between crime rates and social capital, whereby crime erodes the bonds of community, and weakening community institutions allow for the further penetration of crime. Some demographic processes—such as residential mobility—can undermine attachments to the local community and make it more difficult to preserve local social capital (Chaskin, 1994; Sampson and Morenoff, 1997; Sampson, 2002).

Spatial Segregation

In his presidential address to the Population Association of America, Massey (1996) argued that the urban poor and the urban affluent increasingly inhabit separate spaces. Massey warned of increasing segregation in high- and low-income countries alike. One spatial expression of segregation can be seen in Figure 2-1, which shows how levels of income (measured here by an index of proxy variables) vary across the metropolitan area of Mexico City. As can be seen, the poorest areas (those with the darkest shading) are concentrated in the city's periphery. Does this spatial patterning of poverty have implications for demographic behavior?

Spatial segregation can have the effect of enforcing homogeneity in local social network ties and resources, suppressing some of the diversity in social relations that can benefit the poor. To appreciate this point, imagine an alternative organization of Mexico City, one in which poor families are distributed uniformly across the urban space. If spatial proximity promotes social network ties and heightens the visibility of beneficial role models and reference groups, the redistributed poor would be expected to have more connections to higher-income network partners. The life-course possibilities exemplified by the nonpoor might then be more easily appreciated by the poor and factored into their own family strategies. But when the poor are spatially segregated, such local socioeconomic diversity is diminished, and, as Sampson and Morenoff (1997: 19) write,

> ... the social isolation fostered by the ecological concentration of urban poverty deprives residents not only of resources and conventional role models but also of cultural learning from mainstream social networks that facilitate social and economic advancement in modern industrial society....

In this way, spatial segregation blocks avenues for social learning and severs some of the weak ties that could provide information and pathways to resources.[10]

Labor market ties are of particular importance. The social networks of adults shape their job-search strategies and, through search, the nature of employment that can be secured. Montgomery (1992) formalizes the role of social network connections in the job-search theory used by economists, developing the idea that weak network ties may supply information about job openings more frequently than do strong ties.[11] By affecting wages and incomes, restrictions on labor

---

[10]Granovetter (1973) is usually credited with the distinction between weak and strong ties in social networks. A tie between two network members is said to be strong if they have a long and durable association, if they meet frequently, and if their relationship is multistranded in the sense of joining different types of social relations (e.g., neighbor and kin). Weak ties are generally of shorter duration, can involve infrequent contact, and can be more specialized (say, if two people know each other only as coworkers). Granovetter's contribution was to suggest that weak ties are often those along which novel information is conveyed: they can provide "bridges" leading from dense, strongly tied, and homogenous networks to diverse outside information and resources. Hence, weak ties are thought to be important to innovation, and strong ties to the maintenance of norms and collective identities.

[11]If weak ties increase the frequency with which job offers are made known, job searchers with more weak ties in their networks would be expected to have higher reservation wage thresholds, and (other things being equal) higher expected wages as well.

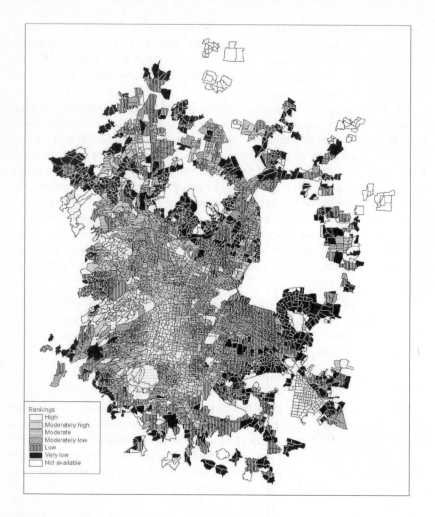

FIGURE 2-1 Mexico City metropolitan area: socioeconomic levels by geostatis-
tical areas, 1990.
SOURCE: Rubalcava and Schteingart (2000: Map 4.7.2). Reprinted with permission.

market information can powerfully (albeit indirectly) constrain demographic decisions.

In a study of Los Angeles, Stoloff, Glanville, and Bienenstock (1999) explore the links between social network diversity (or *range*) and women's employment outcomes, focusing on the influence of network ties that reach outside the neighborhood and those that cross lines of race, gender, and education. Stoloff and colleagues find that women are more likely to be employed when they have more outside-neighborhood ties and more ties to other women with university schooling. As Chapple (2002) notes for San Francisco, many poor women face transport costs that restrict the geographic reach of their employment contacts and find themselves locked into local low-paying jobs. Poor women may look locally for work because long commutes are incompatible with the child-care options they can afford; with spatially restricted social networks, they are unlikely to hear of better jobs that might be available elsewhere.[12]

In addition to constraining employment information, the spatial concentration of the poor may heighten their exposure to external, macroeconomic shocks. Consider a shock that initially reduces each poor family's income by a given percentage. If the poor are spatially concentrated, this initial effect will be magnified by local economic multipliers. As the shock is propagated locally, businesses that serve the poor will be placed under stress, and when local businesses give way, some neighborhoods may spiral downward (Massey, 1990). If the poor were not so spatially concentrated, the effects of such shocks would be dispersed and thereby muted.

Not all aspects of spatial segregation need be negative. The isolation of the poor can sometimes enhance their sense of mutual dependence (Lee and Campbell, 1999). The resulting "compression" of social relationships can increase the importance of neighborhoods and other localized ties, creating a possibly beleaguered sense of neighborhood as community.[13] In situations in which groups are segregated mainly along racial or ethnic lines, it is even possible for social compression to increase local diversity in the dimensions of income and class, bringing disadvantaged poor households into closer proximity to their better-off ethnic or

---

[12]See Hanson and Pratt (1991, 1995) and McDowell (1993a,b). But note that in some cases, poor women seek employment far from home, as discussed in Hondagneu-Sotelo (1994) for Mexican immigrant women working in the United States. The trade-offs between job search time and the spatial extent of search are well recognized in the human geography literature (e.g., Committee on Identifying Data Needs for Place-Based Decision Making, 2002) as leading examples of what geographers term the space–time prism (Hägerstrand, 1975).

[13]Comparing white with black households in Nashville, Lee and Campbell (1999) find that black households have more intimate ties to their neighbors and activate these ties more frequently. Among all network partners from whom support might be sought—the authors analyze several dimensions of support, including job search, financial assistance, care during illness, and help with important decisions—blacks are more likely than whites to list partners who live in their neighborhoods (support in arranging transportation is an exception). To be sure, in the dimensions of social support examined here, neighbors make up only a minority of all network partners. Even for Nashville blacks, most supportive network ties reach outside the neighborhood.

racial counterparts (Massey, 1990; White, 2001). In this way, the compression mechanism could set the stage for the development of social capital in some poor neighborhoods.

The spatial element in social interaction and resource distribution should not be overemphasized. Many urban residents participate in multiple social networks and communities, and these can operate at multiple spatial scales. As we have discussed, spatially dispersed social and economic ties could be as important to information flow, access to services, and social comparisons as spatially localized ties. Proximity may well facilitate the formation of social network ties and lessen the costs of maintaining such ties, but proximity certainly does not guarantee that social linkages will be formed.[14] Nor does spatial proximity necessarily imply socioeconomic homogeneity. But it is reasonable to think that even where localized factors are not dominant, they may still exert appreciable influence. The demographic implications of spatial segregation therefore deserve careful consideration.

Neighborhoods and Larger Structures

As the foregoing discussion makes clear, neighborhood effects are not wholly attributable to neighborhoods. They reflect the situation of neighborhoods within larger social and economic structures and the roles assumed by institutions that operate across the urban space. The crucial interactions among neighborhood and more widely dispersed actors can be illustrated by a demographic example from a century ago, concerning the diffusion of new ideas in the sphere of urban public health.

As early as the 1880s in the United States, proponents of what was then known as "sanitary science" adopted the elements of the germ theory of disease and worked in multiple forums, using multiple media, in an effort to spread new health messages and transform personal hygienic behavior (Tomes, 1998). There was an outpouring of popular advice on how to keep the home free of germs—advice conveyed through manuals on domestic hygiene, pamphlets, newspaper columns, public lectures, exhibits, and posters. Plumbing and toilet manufacturers aided the cause, together with entrepreneurs specializing in disinfectants and ventilating devices. City and town governments assisted by enacting detailed plumbing codes and regulations. Among the affluent and those striving to join their ranks, the fear of germs was fanned by apprehensions about the infective power of newly arrived immigrant populations and was intermixed with social attitudes equating cleanliness with gentility (Tomes, 1998: 62, 111).

---

[14]Mere residence in a neighborhood with superior institutional and social resources does not ensure access to them. See Jarrett (1997) on the experience of black families in affluent U.S. communities, who can be excluded from participation in important community networks and social circles. See also Chapters 5 and 9, where the "proximity but high walls" modes of segregation are discussed.

Even by the late 1890s, it was still mainly the literate who were in a position to hear the new sanitary advice, and few but the affluent could afford to safeguard their homes. Beginning in the 1890s, however, local and national associations began to be organized with the aim of preventing contagious disease (especially tuberculosis), adopting commercial advertising techniques to deliver their messages to the poor and illiterate in a vivid and memorable form (Tomes, 1998: 114–21). Of course, these efforts to improve personal hygiene and home sanitation would have produced little improvement in health were it not for the massive complementary investments made by governments in extending sewerage, cleaning water supplies, and enforcing regulations to keep milk and food free from contamination (Preston and van de Walle, 1978; Ewbank and Preston, 1990; Preston and Haines, 1991; van Poppel and van der Heijden, 1997).

This tale illustrates several of the distinctive features of urban social interactions. Externalities were at the core of the urban public health problem—the communicable diseases to which urban populations were vulnerable because of their proximity and dependence on common resources. Technological change and the emergence of new theories of disease transmission provided the opportunity for such biological externalities to be fought by way of beneficial social externalities, which took the form of diffusion of information about personal hygiene. In the resulting diffusion processes, novel forms of information were propagated through social networks (as in the Taichung experiment), as well as through multiple media. Because urban settings were socially heterogeneous, juxtaposing the literate and the illiterate, the urban poor were exposed to greater heterogeneity in health information than might otherwise have been the case. The process was further aided by two types of social comparison—one that linked cleanliness to gentility, and another that linked anxieties about infection to the presence of diverse urban immigrant populations. The economic diversity of urban settings was also evident in the roles assumed by private markets and businessmen. Finally, decisive actions were taken by city governments and by the kinds of associations we would now call NGOs, illustrating the institutional diversity seen even then in the urban arena.

As these examples show, macro-level economic, social, and political structures can determine what resources are made available to local communities and rendered accessible through the personal social networks of community residents. In the case of the public health revolution, these larger structures brought enormous benefits to individuals and neighborhoods. But as James, Schulz, and van Olphen (2001: 178) note, structural forces can sometimes have the effect of "circumscribing the range of resources that may be mobilized within social networks and decreasing their flexibility in responding to the social environment." The point is that resources cannot simply be expected to materialize, as if by spontaneous generation, in the personal social networks and local associations of poor city residents. Links are needed to the powerful actors and institutions that generate resources and influence how they are distributed.

BOX 2.2 A Federation of Low-Income Groups in Mumbai

Appadurai (2001) recounts how three local associations in Mumbai, India—SPARC (the Society for the Promotion of Area Resource Centres), NSDF (the National Slum Dwellers Federation), and Mahila Milan (an organization of poor women) have formed an alliance to raise the political visibility of issues affecting the poor and to promote creative solutions. These three organizations share concerns about the security of land tenure; adequate housing; and access to electricity, transport, sanitation, and related services. They have extensive links to other poor groups across India, and are forming international partnerships with similarly composed associations in South Africa, Thailand, Cambodia, and the Philippines. (These and other groups are described in the October 2001 issue of the journal *Environment & Urbanization*.) Their international reach is evident in the founding of Shack/Slum Dwellers International (SDI), an alliance of poor peoples' federations that spans 14 countries across four continents.

The Mumbai federation is built upon several principles: (1) a reliance upon local informal savings and microcredit groups, which not only give the poor a means of amassing modest amounts of capital, but also instill patience and discipline, thus reinforcing a sense of community; (2) recognition that the conditions of the poor must be documented if they are to be made visible to outsiders, this insight being reflected in a commitment to periodic socioeconomic surveys of the slums in which federation members live; (3) use of "precedent-setting" pilot projects and public exhibitions, which draw attention to feasible, low-cost designs for affordable housing and sanitation (the latter dramatized in "toilet festivals" that showcase functioning public toilets designed by the poor with careful attention to systems of collective payment and maintenance); and (4) adherence to a political stance of resolute nonalignment with any local or national political party, and a commitment to negotiation rather than confrontation in political tactics.

Of the three groups involved, SPARC (formed in 1984 by social work professionals) is the best connected to the state and corporate elites of Mumbai and elsewhere. It provides many of the bridges that reach to local and national Indian governments and to the international funders. By presenting a professional face to these outsiders, SPARC gives the funders a means of funneling their resources to its affiliates. SPARC also provides its local allies with a buffer that prevents the agendas of the funders from dominating the concerns of the poor.

The question of how resources can be drawn into poor communities can be addressed in terms of the "bridging" role of social networks and local social capital in developing countries. Box 2.2 recounts one of the most successful cases involving groups of the poor. Beginning in the mid-1980s, local groups in Mumbai, India, gradually acquired sufficient visibility, reach, and political mass to attract resources from various levels of the Indian government and international agencies. As Appadurai (2001) and others have observed, some of the most sophisticated alliances of poor groups are making contacts in international networks of like-minded groups and funders, engaging in what some have termed "advocacy without borders." Box 2.3, by contrast, shows how difficult it can be to establish durable institutional mechanisms for delivering resources to poor communities.

BOX 2.3 Participatory Urban Poverty Programs in Bangalore: Lessons Learned

The experience of the Bangalore Urban Poverty Alleviation Programme (BUPP), a Dutch-funded pilot project implemented in 1993–99, illustrates many of the difficulties that face participatory urban initiatives (de Wit, 2002). This ambitious program drew together Bangalore government departments, local NGOs working in the city slums, and the community-based organizations (CBOs) of these slums. On-the-ground activities were to be carried out by newly formed Slum Development Teams, local groups whose members were to be elected by local inhabitants, with women assuming a full share of the leadership positions. Although the project did record some successes (notably in establishing savings and credit schemes for slum women), the partnerships it fostered among government, NGOs, and CBOs could not be sustained once external funding had ceased. After 1999, these organizations largely reverted to their preprogram, independent modes of operation.

According to de Wit (2002), part of the problem had to do with the question of "ownership" of the project. BUPP was conceived as a separate organizational entity, connected to but standing apart from government departments, NGOs, and preexisting CBOs. This autonomy was meant to encourage experimentation and learning-by-doing, but it had unintended side effects. Government departments proved reluctant to channel scarce resources to a program not housed within any unit of government; local NGOs found themselves being asked to play generalist, supervisory roles for which they had neither the experience, the expertise, nor the resources; and the CBOs that had already been in existence in the Bangalore slums often viewed the new program and its slum development teams as competitors for local influence, and even as threats to the interests of their own leaders. (The local community groups tended to be both male-dominated and inegalitarian; they were in some instances the product of local systems of patronage.) As a result, none of the slum development teams could survive after the end of Dutch funding in 1999. As de Wit (2002: 3941) remarks, in retrospect "it might have been better to start from, foster and link to proven well-functioning traditional, endogenous or pragmatic groups (informal credit groups, women's networks, user groups)" and to encourage these groups to gradually adopt more open and participatory approaches.

In Bangalore a well-conceived participatory program that enlisted units of government, local NGOs, and slum community organizations fell victim to sharply conflicting interests.

Summary

This section has described features of local social and spatial environments that could influence demographic behavior. In each of the areas mentioned, neighborhoods provide the staging grounds upon which social interactions take place; personal networks provide the circuits along which externalities and information flow; and, together with networks, associations and institutions provide the base of local social capital. There is good reason to think that neighborhoods, networks, and social capital can exert a great deal of influence on demographic behavior in developing-country cities. It is certainly possible that their effects are powerful and pervasive. To date, however, almost all of the literature on these issues is concerned with the cities of developed countries. Chicago has been well documented, but Cairo has not. In its present form, the research literature can offer little more to those interested in poor countries than intriguing analogies and potentially fruitful lines of inquiry. Even the field of urban health still lacks the multilevel, longitudinal research programs that could identify the effects of neighborhoods, social networks, and social capital in developing-country cities.

In the literature on the United States, where theoretical propositions about networks, neighborhoods, and social capital have been in circulation for well over a decade, convincing empirical tests also remain scarce. This chapter is not the place for a thorough critique of research strategies, but several aspects deserve mention.[15] The dominant research strategy used in U.S. studies matches individual data, often drawn from sample surveys, to areal data drawn from censuses. In view of the many difficulties involved in defining neighborhoods, the approach is acknowledged to be imperfect and defensible only as a first pass at the issues. But in most developing countries, no data are available on units akin to census tracts, rendering even this crude approach infeasible.

Mixed results have emerged from the pairing of cross-sectional individual and areal data in the first generation of U.S. research.[16] Strong neighborhood composition effects have been found in some studies of adolescent fertility and contraceptive use (see the review in Jencks and Mayer, 1990). However, the estimated effects of neighborhood on measures of child development have generally been small (see Gephart, 1997; Brooks-Gunn, Duncan, Leventhal, and Aber, 1997). In part this is because in highly segregated cities, it is empirically difficult to separate the effects of individual and family characteristics (e.g., family income) from those of the neighborhood (e.g., the percentage of low-income families in the neighborhood).

It is only recently that research studies have been designed explicitly to test neighborhood effect theories (Sampson and Raudenbush, 1999; Sastry, Pebley, and Zonta, 2002) and that randomized experiments have been mined for evidence on neighborhood effects. Large-scale housing voucher experiments—notably the "Moving to Opportunity" experiment conducted in Boston, Baltimore, Los Angeles, and a few other U.S. cities—are proving to be a rich source of neighborhood effect studies (Del Conte and Kling, 2001; Sampson, Morenoff, and Gannon-Rowley, 2002). Nonexperimental longitudinal designs are only now going into the field. Furstenberg and Hughes (1997) suggest that studies of this sort should

---

[15]Sampson, Morenoff, and Gannon-Rowley (2002) provide a recent insightful review. Duncan, Connell, and Klebanov (1997) and Durlauf (1999) give a concise account of the statistical difficulties that confront tests of neighborhood effects and diffusion/social interaction theories—difficulties that are formidable if only cross-sectional data are available. Manski (1993) develops a special case that nicely exposes these difficulties.

[16]See Hogan and Kitagawa (1985) for an early effort focused on teen childbearing and the recent study of Upchurch, Aneshensel, Sucoff, and Levy-Storms (1999), which addresses the timing of teenage sexual activity.

begin by mapping local perceptions and definitions of neighborhood, that questionnaires should employ several such concepts to enable comparison, and that neighborhood residents should be asked about social ties extending outside their residential communities. This would appear to be sound advice for new studies in developing-country cities.

SUSTAINING DIVERSITY: ECONOMIC INTERACTIONS

Much demographic behavior is rooted in individual and family perceptions of economic costs, benefits, and uncertainties. The lines running from economy to demography are readily seen in the case of migration, which is a behavioral response to spatial differences in income and consumption opportunities. Urban economic structure can also be expected to affect women's wage rates and, through wages, the opportunity costs of time spent in child care. These opportunity costs have long been identified as important factors in fertility decisions.

Earlier we drew attention to the economic returns to schooling. Models of the "quantity–quality trade-off" suggest that as returns to schooling increase, parents may be persuaded to forego high fertility to have fewer but better-educated children. By implication, then, the returns to schooling evident in urban areas could induce lower fertility and greater investment in human capital. Incomes obviously affect the full range of urban demographic decisions—including decisions about health as well as children's schooling. There are also macro-level effects to be considered. When urban income growth raises government revenues, it provides governments with the means to extend investments in public services (such as water supply and sanitation) and education. Rising incomes support the development of specialized private markets, such as in the delivery of health services. For all these reasons, economic factors are fundamental to an understanding of urban demography.

The preceding discussion has been concerned mainly with what might be termed *social and biological externalities*, which arise from social interactions in differentiated populations. Proximity matters to the social side of the argument because it reduces the costs of information acquisition and exchange. To economists, these are familiar ideas; indeed, if the theories were to be relabeled as theories of information exchange among firms and workers, involving both production and search networks, they would be recognizable as the basis for much of urban economics.

The fundamental building blocks of urban economic theory are the costs of communication and transport, spatial heterogeneity, returns to scale, and the set of *pecuniary and technological externalities* known as agglomeration economies. Recently, the special role of economic diversity has attracted attention—whether the diversity displayed in a city's portfolio of economic activities (Jacobs, 1969, 1984; Glaeser, Kallal, Scheinkman, and Shleifer, 1992) or that embedded in the preferences of consumers for a range of goods (Fujita, Krugman, and Venables,

1999; Neary, 2001). Taken as a group, the economic theories seek to explain both the existence and the growth of cities; that is, they have static and dynamic implications. Here we present a sketch of the main arguments, drawing from reviews by Anas, Arnott, and Small (1998), Glaeser (1998), Henderson, Shalizi, and Venables (2000), and Quigley (1998), while reserving a fuller treatment for Chapter 8.

Spatial Theories

Costs of transport and communication lie at the heart of urban economic theory. When these costs are very high, they have the effect of fixing people, goods, and ideas to specific locations; production and consumption then occur as in autarky. When transport and communication costs approach zero, by contrast, space ceases to matter, and geography might then be said to disappear. It is in the middle range, where costs are appreciable but not prohibitive, that the economics of spatial clustering are of interest (Henderson, Shalizi, and Venables, 2000).

Today, with declines in the costs of information exchange due to the telephone, the Internet, and other innovations, spatial proximity might be thought to have lost some of its former economic significance. Technological progress presumably removes much of the need for face-to-face exchanges of services and information, and it would appear only logical that exchange mediated by technology must substitute for personal exchange. Although plausible, this substitution hypothesis needs further scrutiny. Technological and personal exchanges may often be complementary; when freed to conduct their routine interactions by e-mail or telephone, for example, economic actors may increasingly prize and seek to exploit the special advantages of face-to-face exchange (Glaeser, 1998). Perhaps in personal contacts there are ways of communicating trustworthiness, ensuring confidentiality, and displaying interest and commitment that simply cannot be equaled by technological devices, at least in their present form. We return to this point below in the context of "economies of diversity." A very different approach to questions of agglomeration comes from an emphasis on the increased uncertainty of global markets, coupled with the increased speed of electronic markets (see Sassen, 2001a).

In a world in which transportation and communication costs remain significant, the heterogeneities of space present one fundamental rationale for the clustering of economic activity. The physical features of land—the presence of natural harbors, the confluence of rivers, the sites of mineral deposits—confer comparative advantages and disadvantages upon locations. Firms move to exploit the advantages of specific sites; trade then links locations much as it does in the standard models of international trade among countries. Spatial clustering and differentiation can thus be explained, up to a point, by Ricardian comparative advantage.

It is when the productivity benefits of scale and proximity are brought into the picture that urban economic theories take on their distinctive character. Two forms of productivity benefits are of interest: those that are internal to the firm or production unit or that involve links through markets, and those that are external, which can take the form of technological externalities and informational spillovers. We consider these in turn.

Internal economies of scale and proximity

When production is characterized by increasing returns to scale—a doubling of inputs yielding more than a doubling of output—firms have additional motivation to concentrate their production spatially. And as long as there are significant transport costs involved in moving people, the concentration of production will imply a concentration of the labor force.

Many factors determine whether firms choose to locate near supplies of other inputs or near the final markets for their goods. Historically, cities have grown around transshipment points so as to exploit scale economies in the loading and unloading of goods (Anas, Arnott, and Small, 1998). In an earlier era, the weight of final goods and inputs and the weight lost in the processing of inputs into final goods were regarded as the dominant factors in models of locational choice. But as transport costs for goods have declined, this rationale has lost something of its historical force. Speed and market uncertainty have today replaced weight (Sassen, 2001a).

When the firms of a given industry cluster spatially, this permits the suppliers of inputs tailored to that industry to save on transport costs, and may allow for further specialization in the production of inputs. For instance, heavy government investment in urban health facilities can foster specialization among private-sector suppliers of health services. From this base, a broader private health sector can develop, offering services that parallel those in the public sector. As will be seen in Chapters 6 and 7, such private markets in health services are far more prominent in cities than in rural areas, and are a more significant presence in larger than in smaller cities.

Similar arguments apply to the cross-industry clustering of firms and the suppliers of inputs used across a variety of industries.[17] When firms are spatially clustered, workers can search among them more efficiently, expending less time and fewer resources in locating jobs that are well matched to their human capital. Consumers, too, can benefit from the spatial concentration of differentiated goods (Quigley, 1998).

An important role in the theory pertains to the services that are provided by the public sector—water supply, sanitation, electricity—which are thought to exhibit significant economies of scale and proximity. The issue is not simply how cost varies with the number of units produced, but also how it varies with distance to consumers of services, whether individuals or private firms (Montgomery, 1987, 1988). Where these economies of proximity are significant, there are decided cost advantages to spatial clustering. The cost reductions derived from proximity can

---

[17]In some accounts of the theory, the within-industry and cross-industry effects are termed, respectively, localization and urbanization effects. We reserve the phrase "localization effects" for true externalities associated with spatial proximity, as contrasted with effects mediated through markets.

bring further savings; for example, private firms may not be able to secure lower production costs from their own internal scale economies until they are assured of access to reliable public services.

The benefits of proximity can also be seen in the desires of workers to protect themselves against firm-specific random shocks. A worker with industry-specific human capital may agree to take a lower-wage position with one firm if there are many similar firms in its immediate vicinity. Likewise, a firm anticipating idiosyncratic shocks in its markets may choose to locate near other firms in the industry if by so doing it can reduce buffer stocks of inventories. Presumably such motives would be evident in industry wage levels and in the nature of in-traindustry, firm-to-firm contracts. If the economic shocks are anticipated to be industry-wide rather than firm-specific, however, equivalent protections may be secured through interindustry clustering. For instance, the "thick labor markets" of cities, involving many firms and workers mutually engaged in search, may confer some protection against long layoffs, prolonged unproductive searches, and persistent difficulties in filling selected skilled positions (Glaeser, 1998).

In summary, the internal scale and proximity arguments are concerned mainly with the cost savings firms can achieve through spatial concentration of production. These savings may depend, in turn, on the economies of specialization, scale, and proximity realized by suppliers of inputs, including workers and the providers of public services. These issues are well illustrated in the case of producer services, described in Box 2.4.

External economies of proximity

External productivity benefits of proximity are true externalities in that they involve spillovers not directly mediated by markets. Such external effects are generated by economic interactions partly as a response to the complexity of corporate services today (Sassen, 2001a), search, and the exchange of ideas (Anas, Arnott, and Small, 1998). *Localization effects* arise from the spatial concentration of firms in a given industry. They may be produced when one firm is able to observe the innovations, experiments, production processes, or competitive strategies of another. Workers carry such innovative ideas with them as they circulate among firms (Glaeser, 1998). Striking evidence of such spillovers is seen in the spatial clustering of patent applications in the United States (Jaffe, Trajtenberg, and Henderson, 1993), which suggests that innovations undertaken by one firm can indirectly benefit another (see also Audretsch and Feldman, 1996).

Within this literature, *diversity effects* refer to the positive externalities generated by information exchange in heterogeneous environments; here the emphasis is on the variety of urban economic activity and the stimuli that are provided by diversity. The concept owes much to Jacobs (1969, 1984) and is expressed by Glaeser, Kallal, Scheinkman, and Shleifer (1992) in terms of cross-industry economic diversity.[18] The argument is that creative, innovative energies

---

[18]Quigley (1998) gives a good account of the issues.

BOX 2.4 Producer Services and High-Skill Labor Markets

Although much of any city's daily economic activity must be given over to the routine needs of its residents, there can be analytic returns to a focus on a specialized sector. A narrow focus can shed light on urban dynamics and suggest the course of future developments. When examined from this vantage point, the specialized, high-end business service sector amply repays study (Sassen, 1991, 2001a).

In regions that are already well endowed with telecommunications infrastructure, advanced producer services might be expected to locate outside the major cities so as to escape high rents and congestion. Contrary to expectation, however, it appears that producer services are often concentrated in large cities. The reasons for this may have to do with urbanization economies and the economic rewards to cross-industry, intraurban diversification (Jacobs, 1969, 1984; Glaeser, Kallal, Scheinkman, and Shleifer, 1992).

Producer service firms are not necessarily dependent on being close to the businesses they serve. There are cost savings and efficiencies to be found in locating near suppliers and professional collaborators, especially when the service involves a form of joint production. Assembling a financial instrument, for example, can require inputs from firms in fields as diverse as accounting, advertising, law, economic consulting, public relations, design, and printing. An accounting firm may serve its clients at a distance, but the quality of its service depends on proximity to specialists, lawyers, and programmers. Additional motives for concentration arise from the needs of the professionals who are employed in such high-skill jobs; they are often attracted to the amenities and lifestyles that large urban centers can offer, and can be reluctant to live elsewhere (Sassen, 1991, 2001a).

The political economy of all this warrants attention. Growing numbers of high-level professionals and specialized service firms can increase urban spatial and socioeconomic inequality. Markets and politicians may prefer to develop housing for high-income professionals; commercial space may be dominated by firms selling high-priced goods and services; and these tendencies can be reinforced by the growing share of the city's total payroll and tax revenues due to the specialized services core.

---

are stimulated most effectively by the collision of disparate ideas. Just how disparate these ideas may be is difficult to formalize, but the theory envisions a creative ferment in which entrepreneurs, scientists, artists, and firms find themselves struck by analogies and by the observation of activity in spheres that overlap but do not wholly coincide with their own.

The benefits stemming from urban diversity are often linked to the product development cycle, that is, to the stages in the life of a good or service as it moves from experimentation and design to routine production. The benefits of urban diversity are believed to be greatest in the initial stages of product development. Once a production process becomes standardized, some of its elements can be relocated to suburban or rural sites where wages and rents are lower (Duranton and Puga, 2001). Services and production in high-technology sectors are thought to derive special benefits from economies of diversity (for Korea, see Henderson, Lee, and Lee, 2001, and Henderson, 2002). As noted in Box 2.4, there are some services that must be assembled with speed and that require the collaboration of many professionals from diverse fields; services such as these may never become sufficiently standardized to be relocated.

Network effects are implicated in these theories in that information exchange and creative partnerships will sometimes form along social network lines and can be facilitated by spatial proximity. The social capital aspect of networks can matter when economic decisions must be made swiftly. To seize opportunities when they arise, economic actors may need assurance that their partners are trustworthy and can keep strategic information confidential. Network effects may be especially important in fast-moving sectors such as finance. According to Meyer (1998), in this sector the face-to-face exchanges made possible by spatial concentration foster trust and allow for the growth of social networks that permit the sharing of private information.

Given the importance of education to demographic behavior, it is interesting to consider how it might figure in such theories. It is often said that while ideas depreciate, education has enduring value: in the process of acquiring it, the educated also acquire conceptual flexibility, an openness to innovation, and a capacity to identify and exploit the possibilities that present themselves in disequilibrium. It may be that in urban areas, which are continually roiled by economic shocks and waves of technological change, the economic returns to schooling lie precisely in these abilities. Black and Henderson (1999b) develop this theme in terms of the social returns to schooling in urban areas, arguing that spillovers cause the social returns to exceed private returns. Supportive empirical results are presented by Rauch (1993) and Moretti (2000). They find that individual returns to schooling increase with the average level of schooling in the local labor market, a result that hints at the benefits to be derived from urban diversity.

The diseconomies of proximity

As cities grow, the economies derived from spatial proximity are eventually offset by diseconomies. The economic value of space rises with concentration, but this increased value drives up rents. Commuting times grow longer as cities become larger and transport grids seize up with congestion (Glaeser, 1998; Henderson, Shalizi, and Venables, 2000). Crime rates may also be linked to city size.[19] Levels of pollution can increase with city size as well, although it may be that size is less a root cause than an exacerbating factor.

In many dimensions, then, congestion costs and diseconomies would be expected to rise as producers, workers, and consumers become more spatially concentrated. At some point, the benefits of further growth and concentration are overtaken by the marginal costs. The city size at which marginal benefits just equal marginal costs can be regarded as an optimal city size.[20]

---

[19]As Glaeser (1998) explains, crime may be associated with city size because the diversity of big-city life lets criminals function with anonymity. He speculates that there may be economies of scale in the distribution of stolen goods and an easier flow of information among diverse networks of criminals.

[20]At one time it was thought that optimal city sizes might be identified empirically, and a number of heroic efforts to do so made appearances in the literature. This quest has largely been abandoned.

Summary

The theories discussed above provide a framework for thinking about the urban economy—its size, diversity, and trajectory of growth—in terms closely analogous to those used to describe social interaction and neighborhood effects. Indeed, the economic arguments can be applied at spatial resolutions below the level of the city. Operating at micro scales, they can shed light on the organization of neighborhoods and other small clusters of economic activity (Anas, Arnott, and Small, 1998). As discussed further in Chapter 8, dynamic theories, in which an urban concentration of resources spurs innovation, are now attracting a great deal of research interest.

Still, as with neighborhood effects and social interaction, the economic theories discussed here have run well ahead of empirical tests. The statistical difficulties that confront dynamic theories of agglomeration are precisely those that confront theories of neighborhood effects. In both cases, unmeasured factors operating at an aggregate level (a neighborhood or city) exert influences at lower levels (families or firms) that can easily be mistaken for spillover effects at that lower level. For instance, an unmeasured natural advantage can attract firms in an industry to a particular site and raise the productivity of the firms that cluster about it. The unwary analyst might well take this productivity benefit to be evidence of a cross-firm localization effect. The risks of such mistaken inference are much reduced when repeated observations are available on the actors and their contexts, whether these are families in the context of neighborhoods or firms in the context of local industries and markets. Because credible tests of dynamic theories require multilevel, longitudinal research designs, it should be no surprise that progress on the empirical front has been slow. Even in the United States, where the effects of urbanization, localization, diversity, and innovation have been most closely examined, the literature cannot yet offer a consensus as to the size of these effects.

Theories inevitably overlook many features of urban economic life. Although we have stressed theories of innovation and dynamics, it can be argued that *inertia* is of equal importance to the arrangement of urban economic space. Public infrastructure and private capital are durable, and even networks and patterns of social interaction can be long-lasting.[21] These features of the urban scene can continue to attract and concentrate resources even as other elements of the economic rationale begin to weaken. Durability and sunk costs provide yet another reason to think that the dynamics of cities must be highly path-dependent and difficult to predict.

---

[21] The cities of South Africa illustrate the enduring imprint of inertia. On this point, Pieterse (2000: 10) quotes Lindsay Bremner, a South African planner: "The marks apartheid left on human lives will fade in the course of time. But its spatial logic will continue to affect people's daily lives for generations to come. Because of apartheid, people live great distances from where they work; standards of urban infrastructure vary enormously; parts of the city are devoid of shops, businesses, entertainment venues and schools, while others are saturated with them; chasms separate one citizen from another, so much so that people feel like tourists in each other's worlds."

CITY SYSTEMS AND CITY-REGIONS

This chapter began with a focus on families interacting within neighborhoods and through their social networks. In considering the urban economy, it then shifted to a higher level of aggregation at which interactions among firms and workers can be conceived of as taking place city-wide. But we cannot be content to leave off here, with individual cities as the units of analysis. Cities exist within wide-ranging social and economic systems that connect them to other cities and to the rural populations of their regions. Because such a large proportion of the urban population resides in small cities—those under 500,000 in population—it is especially important to consider the roles of these cities in the wider system. In the chapters that follow, we repeatedly draw attention to the demographic conditions that prevail in small cities and show that, at least on average, their residents generally fare worse on the various demographic indicators than do residents of large cities. To understand such findings, one must consider what theory has to say about systems of cities.

It should be acknowledged at once that city and regional systems are entities far too complex to be understood through theory alone.[22] As noted above, even the evolution of a single city presents issues of path dependence, historical lock-in, and agglomeration dynamics that render theoretical conclusions indeterminate. The difficulties involved in explaining a single city's growth trajectory are magnified many times when city systems and regions are considered.

A further complication is that the networks in which cities participate are increasingly international in character, and therefore involve economic and social forces that operate at supranational scales. Although this chapter is confined to the national scene, international networks in information, trade, and finance are considered in Chapter 3.

City Size Distributions and Primacy

Henderson (1988) summarizes the implications of localization economies for the size distribution of cities. Consider an industry for which such economies are significant, giving its firms an incentive to cluster. If the benefits of clustering were exhausted at relatively small cluster sizes or rose so slowly with size that they were soon overtaken by diseconomies, this industry would tend to be located in relatively small cities. There would be little payoff to larger-city locations because there the industry's firms (and its workers) would expose themselves to additional penalties from diseconomies without any offsetting productivity gain. Large cities are thus composed of the industries for which clustering confers net benefits even in large concentrations. Acting in this way, localization effects can frame the

---

[22]Economists are being guided by models of interaction in complex systems, developed in physics and other disciplines, in their efforts to understand urban change; see Anas, Arnott, and Small (1998) for a recent review.

architecture of a national system of cities. Firms that benefit from cross-industry, urbanization economies (including economies of diversity) then sort themselves among cities of differing size and composition, seeking sites where the marginal benefits from urbanization economies exceed the marginal costs from congestion and other diseconomies.

Are industries with close links to agriculture likely to be found in smaller cities? If so, then by the theory sketched above, these industries should show only mild benefits from spatial clustering. An empirical analysis for Korea by Henderson, Lee, and Lee (2001) confirms that localization effects for food, wood and paper products, furniture, textiles, and apparel are significantly smaller than the effects for heavy industries, transport, machinery, and the high-tech sectors. These findings may well apply more generally. Of course, many other factors—such as the savings on transport costs achieved by processing raw agricultural outputs and natural site-specific advantages—may be just as important as localization effects to the economic life of small cities. Although in poor countries these cities account for a large share of the urban population, researchers have yet to understand just how their economic health is sustained (but see Hardoy and Satterthwaite, 1986a,b).

Much more attention has been paid to the other end of the city size distribution. A country's largest city may have attracted much of its core employment by way of localization and urbanization effects, but its character is also likely to have been shaped by the political economy of national development. Discussions of primacy—the share of urban population taken by a country's largest city—often begin with an argument due to Williamson (1965) that emphasizes sequential development strategies. Enormous public and private resources are required to organize cities efficiently, and these resources—capital and managerial capacities among them—are likely to be very scarce in a country's early stages of development. To conserve resources, policy makers may at first restrict their attention to one region, and turn to others only when the potential of that region appears to have been well exploited. High levels of primacy are thus to be expected in countries in the early stages of development. Eventually, however, deconcentration and lower levels of primacy should accompany, and will themselves stimulate, sustained economic growth (Henderson, 2002).

Decentralized city systems cannot be expected to evolve until substantial investments are made in interregional and intercity transport. In the case of Korea, a massive program of investment in intercity infrastructure in the 1970s led to significant industrial deconcentration in the 1980s. Here, political factors—especially access to Seoul bureaucrats—proved to be important in delaying deconcentration, as were the time lags involved in extending good-quality education and other public services to areas outside the capital (Henderson, Shalizi, and Venables, 2000; Henderson, 2002). As discussed in Chapter 8, persistent urban biases in government pricing and social investments can also prolong the life of overconcentrated and inefficient city systems.

In highly urbanized regions such as Latin America, an appreciation of urban change requires a reconceptualization of the linkages among cities. The most interesting aspect of Mexico's urban transformation between 1980 and 2000 is not that its urban population share rose from 55 to 67 percent, but that its city system evolved from a monocentric structure dominated by Mexico City to a complex polycentric structure linking the country's nine largest cities (Garza, 2002). In some densely populated regions of the developing world, large cities are overlapping as they expand, merging to form extended metropolitan areas. To appreciate the rapidity of such developments, consider that it was just 40 years ago when the first "megalopolis" was identified along the northeastern seaboard of the United States (Gottman, 1961). Today such city systems are much in evidence in poor countries (Ginsburg, Koppell, and McGee, 1991; Hugo, Champion, and Lattes, 2001).

Spaces and Networks at the Urban/Rural Interface

Increases in rents, prices, and congestion in the central areas of large cities, together with the operation of product development cycles, would be expected to encourage the spatial deconcentration of manufacturing. Many researchers have noted that city centers tend to cede new manufacturing jobs to the urban periphery. Having done so, the central areas are freed to host a new generation of specialized services in telecommunications, banking, law, financial management, management consulting, and information technologies (recall Box 2.4). As reliable transport and communication systems reach into the urban periphery, large-scale projects requiring land and extensive capital—whether for new airports, manufacturing plants, or office space—can be relocated in that periphery. Residential housing obeys a similar spatial logic.

Something of this dynamic can be seen in the recent history of São Paulo, as depicted in Figure 2-2. In the 1970s, rates of (residential) population growth were relatively high across the *municipio*—on the order of 3.7 percent on average. By the 1980s, however, net population declines were already being seen in the central and interior areas, and by the 1990s, population growth rates had collapsed in these areas, falling well below -2.0 percent. Although population growth rates also declined somewhat outside the core areas of São Paulo, growth rates in the outskirts remained well above those in the city core. Yet even while residential growth was declining in the core areas of the city, these areas were accounting for a large share of new employment growth, especially in producer services (not shown in the figure).

If the general nature of these developments is predictable, their spatial expressions are surprisingly varied and complex. Many large cities are extending outward in an irregular and seemingly haphazard fashion. Development is not evenly spread, but spatially concentrated at transport nodes (railway stations, river ports, and highway intersections), at scattered industrial sites (such as quarries and

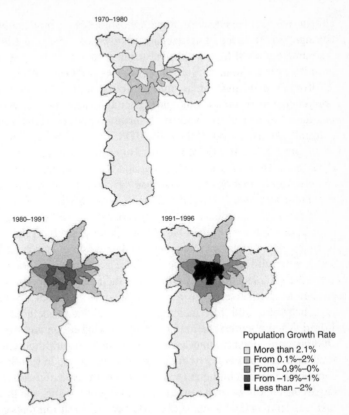

FIGURE 2-2 Population growth rates within metropolitan São Paulo, 1970–1980, 1980–1991, and 1991–1996.
SOURCE: Taschner and Bógus (2001).

landfill sites), and in residential "bedroom" communities. The villages, towns, and small cities in the vicinity of a large city often develop their own diverse workforces, whose fortunes are tightly bound to the major city. It has been estimated that almost half of urban development in poor countries occurs outside established city boundaries, where local governments are often fragmented and poorly equipped to handle the demands of city building (Webster, 2000a).

Urban and rural activities can be interwoven in ways that thoroughly refashion the social and spatial fabric. In Southeast Asia, for instance, zones have emerged in the intersections between cities and their rural areas that are neither urban nor rural in any conventional sense (Ginsburg, Koppell, and McGee, 1991). McGee (1991) refers to these as *desakota* zones, a word derived from the Indonesian words for village (*desa*) and town or city (*kota*). The casual visitor to a *desakota* zone sees a landscape that appears to be rural, with almost all land under

cultivation. But despite appearances, most income is now derived from nonagricultural sources, many of these being urban based. The nature of agricultural production has also shifted, with subsistence production giving way to higher-value
products targeted to urban and world markets (McGee, 1991).

Data on such rural areas underscore the importance to rural well-being of
nonfarm employment and other nonagricultural activities. Diversification of rural
income sources gives the rural poor a means of protecting themselves against agricultural risks (Bryceson, 1999; Ellis, 1998; Lerise, Kibadu, Mbutolwe, and Mushi,
2001; Schejtman, 1999). Risks are also reduced through spells of migration to
urban areas (Blitzer, Davila, Hardoy, and Satterthwaite, 1988). As discussed in
Chapter 8, information about the urban jobs open to migrants often filters through
to rural areas by way of social and family networks.[23]

If the rural dependence on the city economy is well recognized, it is less often
appreciated that many urban-based households depend on rural-based assets and
incomes. Urban migrants frequently make investments in rural housing, land, or
cattle, with rural relatives overseeing these assets in the migrant's absence (Afsar,
1999; Krüger, 1998; Smit, 1998). Like their rural counterparts, the urban poor
have little alternative but to rely upon income and asset diversification; better-
off urban households also maintain a mix of assets to accumulate capital (Baker,
1995). The networks of economic flows linking urban and rural households include not only the remittances sent from urban to rural households, but also the
foodstuffs that are conveyed in the opposite direction. In sub-Saharan Africa, it is
common for urban children to be fostered into the care of their rural relatives when
city living conditions make urban child care problematic. On their part, the urban
relatives lend critical support to newly arrived rural migrants. As all this suggests, it is more than a little artificial to describe households as being wholly rural
or urban—many of them are deliberately multispatial in their economic strategies,
especially in the zones surrounding large cities.

As cities extend themselves and bid for rural land, this process inevitably dis-
rupts rural economic relationships and redistributes income. Urban expansion can
increase rural productivity by giving landed farmers better access to roads, ports,
airports, credit, and information about market opportunities. But tenant farmers,
sharecroppers and others without land may find their livelihoods curtailed by the
city incursions; only some of them will be able to secure more lucrative nonagricultural employment. The rural residents most at risk would appear to be those
with little or no land, who are dependent on wage or casual agricultural labor and
lack the skills, contacts, capital, or freedom of movement to take advantage of new
opportunities (Rakodi, 1998).

The terms on which rural and urban populations engage are determined in part
by national development strategies. A study of Hebei province in China shows

---

[23]Other types of information also flow across the urban/rural boundary, as was the case with contraceptive information in the Taichung experiment discussed earlier.

how national economic restructuring can impinge upon the rural populations living near cities (Benziger, 1996). In the prereform era in China, when the prevailing ideology of "self-reliance" directed state industries and national investments to relatively small Chinese cities, it was the rural counties near such cities that captured the productivity benefits. But in the 1980s, as economic reforms began in earnest, the role of the Chinese state in resource allocation came to be supplanted by that of the markets. Larger and more dynamic Chinese cities began to take the lead in attracting foreign investments and engaging with world markets, and, as Benziger (1996) shows, it was their rural counties to which the greatest productivity benefits then accrued.

Rural and urban households are knit together in numerous mutually beneficial economic and social networks; as groups, however, rural and urban populations have distinct and at times sharply conflicting interests (Douglass, 1989; Kelly, 1998). The urban/rural interface is contested terrain, especially where urban and rural populations both make demands on common natural resources, such as water (UNCHS, 1996: 150–151). Cities and their industries consume great quantities of water; in many countries they also depend on rural rivers and dams to generate electricity. Urban wastewater is deposited in the rural areas near cities and can flow into coastal fishing grounds, which are often overwhelmed by its content and volume. As Showers (2002) documents for sub-Saharan Africa, when such urban demands are imposed upon fragile rural and coastal ecologies, the environmental stress can leave some areas unfit for agriculture.

In principle, at least, pricing schedules for water and electricity could be devised to take these social costs into account. To ensure that the rural costs are fully appreciated, such pricing policies would probably have to be administered by the governments that oversee the rural and urban populations involved. But the zones around cities would present these governments with vexing problems of equity and efficiency. If water were indeed to be priced according to its social marginal costs, this practice would likely restrain urban growth and increase the costs of living for the urban poor. But slower urban growth would also damage the prospects of some of the rural poor. Regional governments would have to balance the interests not only of urban and rural populations, but also of the poor in each of these populations.

The multiple linkages between rural and urban populations imply that rural and urban poverty cannot be viewed as presenting wholly separate and distinct sets of problems. An increase in urban poverty usually leaves fewer city jobs for rural dwellers, reduces flows of remittances from urban to rural households, lessens urban demand for rural products, and may even spur urban-to-rural migration. Likewise, falling crop prices or declining rural productivity may have initial impacts on rural poverty, but urban incomes may suffer as demand declines for the goods and services provided by urban firms to rural areas. Curiously, however, most governments and international agencies operate as if rural and urban poverty were wholly separable.

To sum up, with cities having grown and projected their influence across space, the "city-region" now deserves consideration as a unit of analysis for governance and policy. Although difficult to define with precision, a city-region is identifiable by the extent and nature of economic activity in an economic zone surrounding a large city. Many such regions have grown enormously over recent decades. The Extended Bangkok Region, for example, now contains more than 17 million people; by 2010 it is expected to extend some 200 kilometers from its current center (Kaothien and Webster, 2001). Such new regional forms, with their highly diverse populations, will require innovative approaches to planning and administration.

FROM GOVERNMENT TO GOVERNANCE

Governments provide the legal and regulatory structures within which social and economic interactions take place; they arrange for the delivery of public services; and they attempt to manage the externalities and conflicts that inevitably accompany social interaction. For these reasons, governments are inescapable presences in local urban spaces. As we have just seen, however, cities are assuming complex spatial forms, often extending into terrain where the lines of governmental authority are muddled and casting influence across regions that include substantial rural populations. These developments are presenting governments with new needs to mediate among diverse demands (Simmonds and Hack, 2000; Scott, 2001).

The forms in which governments project themselves into these spaces have also been rapidly changing. In many developing countries, local and regional governments are taking on greater prominence, while national governments are stepping back into indirect and seemingly less intrusive roles. As described in Chapter 9, a process of decentralization is under way, whereby national governments are devolving to lower-level governments many political, fiscal, and administrative powers. Across the developing world, new local governmental forms and units are proliferating at a rate that is little short of astonishing. This phenomenon is in part the result of growing agreement that effective urban management requires new formal structures of government (Sivaramakrishanan, 1996). It also owes a great deal to the introduction of democratic principles in many countries, and to the increased importance being accorded to citizen and community voice (UNCHS, 1996). These are welcome developments in many quarters; yet they imply that for some time to come, the levers of local policy will be manipulated by new and inexperienced governmental actors.

As governments are rescaled into smaller spatial units, they are engaging more directly with private-sector actors and NGOs. The term *governance* describes this engagement. It refers to a set of relationships: between the state and civil society, between rulers and the ruled, and between governments proper and those who are governed. Good governance is, in part, the outcome of government processes that are transparent, as executed by bureaucracies instilled with a professional ethos and accountable for their actions. In a healthy system of governance, these structures of government are engaged with a civil society that for its part takes an active role in public affairs; in such a system, all parties adhere to the rule of law (Sivaramakrishanan, 1996). The reciprocity and mutual engagement entailed in good governance should build trust and lend support to the development of local and national social capital (World Bank, 2000a).

As Stren (2002) observes, there is a certain romantic quality to some discussions of governance, which imply that moving governments closer to the people (the "grass roots") must heighten sensitivity to local needs and bring more democracy and transparency to the processes by which these needs are addressed. The current wave of decentralization is far more widespread than its historical predecessors—Stren notes two comparable "moments" of decentralization in Africa and Asia, the first in the period surrounding independence and the second in the 1970s—but many of the warnings sounded earlier about limits and risks still warrant attention.

It is exceedingly difficult to measure the efficiency and responsiveness of local governments, and empirical evidence on their performance is thus far mixed (World Bank, 2000a). Theories of public finance point to several potential advantages of small, localized governmental units. In decentralized systems, local governments acquire a stake in local economic prosperity. They can arrange the menu of local public goods to suit local preferences, although the quantities supplied will still be constrained by local revenue-raising capacities and transfers from other levels of government. In such systems, local consumers can express their preferences for bundles of public goods by voting or by moving to other jurisdictions (Tiebout, 1956). Under ideal conditions, local politics can then achieve something of the efficiency of markets. The increasingly globalized nature of economic relations is another factor to be considered. Local firms working with nimble, entrepreneurial local governments can collaborate to attract foreign direct investment, sometimes by sidestepping central government authorities or involving them only minimally (UNCHS, 2001).

At the same time, however, small governmental units can suffer from significant disadvantages. Some aspects of governance and regulation may lie well beyond their technical and revenue-raising capacities. Unless transfers from higher-level governments are well designed (see Box 2.5), local governments in have-not regions will rarely be able to marshal the resources available to those in wealthier regions, and if such tendencies are left unchecked, the result can be pronounced regional inequities.[24] In decentralized systems, higher-level governments need to devise ways of managing the externalities that spill across local governmental boundaries.[25] In addition, when the national government cedes power

---

[24] Discussing how systems of intergovernmental transfers can be designed to promote efficiency and equity, Bird and Smart (2002) note that adverse selection and related behavior on the part of local governments can defeat the good intentions of the system designers.

[25] Some observers blame weak national states and porous national safety nets for the growth of megacities and the expansion of slums in developing countries, whose cities simply lack the tools to manage national-level demographic and economic flows (Tulchin, 1998).

BOX 2.5 Intergovernmental Transfers and Targeted Social Assistance

Alderman (2001) describes the case of intergovernmental transfers from the national to the local (*commune*) level of government in Albania, where a social assistance program is in place to help the poor. The Albanian national government lacks all but the most rudimentary data on poverty at the local level. To allocate its transfers among local governments, the national government employs ad hoc criteria that appear to be very weakly related to local poverty rates. Although funds are evidently well distributed once they reach the local level, the system as a whole fails to make the best use of resources. Alderman (2001: 50) concludes that "to take advantage of local governments' assumed access to local information, there must be a corresponding flow of information to the center as well as an incentive to use this information." For instance, census data can be used to generate poverty rankings at the level of local governments, and such spatially disaggregated data can provide the national government with tools to improve its resource allocation.

---

to local governments, representation is not guaranteed to all local interest groups. In some cases, the devolution appears to do little more than transfer power from national to local elites. Partnerships of local firms and local governments can invite corruption and render local political processes opaque where transparency is the ideal. Finally, decentralization can threaten macroeconomic stability if central governments lose control over total public outlays.

The phenomenon of decentralization—with all its attendant risks and benefits, often heatedly debated in the countries involved—does not yet appear to have engaged the attention of the international demographic research community. Perhaps in many countries, health and family planning services are still being delivered through vertically organized ministries of health, much as they have been for decades. But in many other countries, the decentralization of these services is being actively contemplated, and in some it is already well under way. A recent analysis by Schwartz, Guilkey, and Racelis (2002) in the Philippines employed rare before-and-after data on local governmental units to determine whether decentralization has affected rates of child immunization and the use of family planning. In this case, it appears that the transfer of resources from national to local authorities has increased local resources overall. The additional resources have evidently encouraged the use of family planning, although they do not appear to have had the same impact on immunization.

Until researchers can assemble more case studies such as this, the implications of decentralization for reproductive health will remain highly uncertain. When decentralization confers greater authority over health and family planning services on municipal governments, which have long lacked professional staff and managerial expertise, on what basis will these governments make their decisions about resources and policies? Will they possess the requisite technical abilities, and the revenue-rasing capacities, to wield their newly assumed powers effectively? What role should national-level professional associations play, along with the national ministries, in seeing that technical expertise is made available to small governments? Perhaps the only certain element in all of this is that the international policy dialogue in reproductive health, which has in the past been a matter of discussion with national ministries and NGOs, will soon have to engage on a broader front with the many new units of government and local NGOs that populate decentralized settings.

WHAT REMAINS OF THE URBAN/RURAL DIVIDE?

In concluding, we survey the broad concepts that have entered this discussion and ask whether they point to specific features that distinguish urban from rural landscapes. The urban/rural distinction is one that has been contemplated by generations of thoughtful scholars, few of whom have failed to note its many intricacies. The urban concept is an abstraction that involves multiple distinct but interrelated social, economic, political, and ecological factors (McGee and Griffiths, 1998; Frey and Zimmer, 2001). Furthermore, when carefully considered, the differences between urban and rural populations are almost always seen to be differences in degree rather than in kind. In almost any aspect that might be considered, urban and rural populations have something in common, and they often overlap substantially. The conceptual challenge, then, is to identify the central tendencies without denying the commonalities.

At the outset we referred to five concepts that tap distinctive aspects of urban social and economic relations—proximity, diversity, externality, network, and centrality. While giving attention to the first four of these, we have not commented much on the fifth. Centrality is a summarizing concept: in our usage it refers to the multiple strands of economic and social interchange that are knit together in cities (Sassen, 2002). These strands also reach to rural areas, and they have links that extend to the international arena. But they intertwine in cities, and from the many knots and nodes there emanates a quality that might be described as urbanness. In employing this sort of language—abstract and rather tentative—we are of course signaling the many difficulties that would be involved in moving from summary concepts to their empirical measures.

This report takes the position that urbanness is best conceived in terms of a continuum, or gradient, along which individual populations are arrayed. The discussion earlier in this chapter referred to city-regions and *desakota* zones, phrases that are suggestive of a blurring between urban and rural populations. Are urban and rural areas now so thoroughly intermixed that the urban/rural distinction has lost its analytic value? We think not. As will be seen repeatedly in the chapters to come, even very crude indicators of position on the urban/rural continuum—the definitions of urban and rural that are adopted by national statistical agencies—are empirically powerful in explaining demographic behavior. Whatever these conventional measures may mean, they somehow succeed in capturing important locational differences. But the empirical performance of crude indicators notwithstanding, the concept of an urban/rural divide appears to be losing whatever intellectual appeal it may once have had. The difficulty is how to devise satisfactory measures of the alternative concept—of an urban/rural continuum—with attention to the many ways in which rural residents are now partaking of urban life.

To appreciate the empirical challenge, consider the case of Real Montecasino, a settlement of about a thousand residents located just south of Mexico City, wedged between the Federal District and the Metropolitan Zone of Cuernavaca. The 2000 Mexican census classified Real Montecasino as rural. Yet only 1.8 percent of the its labor force is engaged in the primary sector; 83 percent of its houses have electricity, piped water, and waste disposal; 70 percent of its households own telephones; 66 percent own cars; and 92 percent have televisions (Garza, 2002). Despite its small population size, Real Montecasino is arguably an outpost of Mexico City.

To distinguish such fine gradations in the urban/rural continuum, criteria such as the degree to which cities are accessible from rural areas (or remote from them) will need to be explored in some detail, making use of all available census and survey data on commuting times and spells of short-term city residence (Coombes and Raybould, 2001; Hugo, Champion, and Lattes, 2001). Appendix A gives an account of recent efforts in the United States to rethink urban measurement, and very similar issues face the national statistical services of many developing countries. Advances in geocoding may enable researchers to link many different sorts of data, thus permitting more sophisticated measurement (Hugo, Champion, and Lattes, 2001). A glimpse of the possibilities is given in Box 2.6 for Cairo, where a combination of remotely sensed and census data permits a gradient of urbanness to be distinguished within the Greater Cairo metropolitan area. But to measure the micro-level aspects of social and economic interaction will surely require entirely new forms of data collection; it is doubtful that data gathered routinely by censuses or satellites will suffice. Although the concept of an urban/rural divide should perhaps be readied for the scrap heap, much more research will be required for the concept of a continuum to be put into a useful and operational form.

Table 2-1 summarizes the main urban/rural differences as seen from a demographic perspective. This chapter has emphasized the *social embeddedness* of information and behavior (Granovetter, 1985), drawing attention to the ways in which individuals and families are linked to their social networks, neighborhoods, and local associations; how they are connected to the larger structures of government; and how they may be engaged as groups in relations of governance. Although a multilevel perspective can be highly informative about rural societies, we would maintain that such that a perspective is essential to an understanding of urban demography. As our review of the U.S. sociological literature shows, this is hardly a novel or controversial perspective, but its insights have yet to be developed in the contexts of developing-country cities.

BOX 2.6 Using Multiple Data Sources to Define Urbanness: The Case of Cairo

This figure, adapted from ongoing research by Weeks (2002), depicts a composite index of urbanness derived from an unusual blend of remotely sensed data on land cover (indicators of vegetation, impervious surfaces, bare soil, and the shade cast by buildings) and census data on population density and the proportion of the labor force in nonagricultural occupations. The spatial units represented are *shiakhas*, of which there are some 300 in Greater Cairo.

The map shows a gradient with the highest values of urbanness (portrayed in dark shading) in the center of the city straddling the banks of the Nile. Urbanness declines as one moves toward the newer urban areas to the west of the Nile (in Giza governorate). Weeks has found that the composite urbanness index is correlated with several demographic measures at the *shiakhas* level: the areas classified as more urban have lower fertility, later ages at marriage, and greater education.

TABLE 2-1 Dimensions in Which Urban Environments Differ from Rural

Social: (1) The spatial proximity of social and economic diversity; (2) the range and weak ties of social networks; (3) a social delineation of neighborhoods, with neighborhood ties being subsets of wider network ties; (4) informational spillovers and other externalities; (5) spatial segregation; and (6) distinct forms taken by urban social capital (including gangs and "perverse" forms), and the possibility of "bridges" to government and funding resources.

Economic: (1) Scale, spillover, and diversity effects; (2) far greater specialization and diversity in private markets, such as in health services; and (3) greater utilization of physical capital and infrastructure.

Human Capital: (1) Easier access to middle and secondary schooling; (2) greater visibility of educated reference groups and role models; and (3) greater social risks attending child rearing, implying higher costs in parental time.

Prices and Consumption: (1) Costs of living and incomes more monetized; (2) greater exposure to variation in wages and prices, hence greater subjective sensitivity to their levels; (3) a greater range of goods and services available; and (4) greater visibility of diverse consumption reference groups.

Livelihoods: (1) Nonagricultural occupations far more prevalent; (2) fewer possibilities for own production and consumption of food; (3) possibly greater returns to human capital; (4) for urban households, nothing quite comparable to Green Revolution agricultural technology in raising productivity; (5) greater economic value of urban housing; and

(6) higher urban incomes on average, possibly with greater income disparities.

Health: (1) Greater inherent risks of communicable disease, including those that are sexually transmitted; (2) possibly lower unit costs for provision of clean water; (3) a different range of occupational health and safety risks; (4) greater numbers of urban poor at risk from some natural disasters because of population concentration; (5) possible economies of proximity in health media campaigns, and informational spillovers from the educated to the less-educated and through social networks; (6) greater access to health services through private markets and mixed public–private provision; (7) quicker access to emergency services, of great importance to maternal mortality; and (8) composition of disease within the population altered by higher incomes and better public provision of services.

Basic Services: (1) Greater percentage of households with water supply, waste disposal, and electricity; (2) different dimensions of access, with quality, reliability, and adequacy of service taking on greater importance, and time costs often of lesser importance; and (3) a greater reliance on illegal forms of access to basic services and housing.

Government: (1) Greater dependence on government implied by urban population concentration and diversity; (2) greater exposure to a multiplicity of laws and regulations; (3) possibly greater vulnerability to "bad" government; (4) especially in large cities, multiple layers and units of government; and (5) possibly (in some cities) greater ability of local governments to raise their own revenues.

Many of the points mentioned in Table 2-1 have already been described at length or are taken up in more detail in later chapters. Our comments here can be brief. A number of the distinctively urban social features stem from one source: *spatial proximity brings socioeconomic diversity into focus.* Proximity allows information to flow more easily among social network members; it highlights social reference groups and role models; and it puts diverse consumption possibilities on view. As mentioned earlier, spatial segregation is likely to have profound demographic implications because it suppresses diversity in the local environs. In the economic realm, proximity enables firms and entrepreneurs to learn from the experiments, successes, and failures of their competitors. The spatial dispersion of rural populations and the greater homogeneity of much agricultural production generally raise the costs of such social and economic exchange.

In advancing such broad and general claims, we are mindful of important counterexamples. It was in the context of agriculture, after all, that the early theories of information diffusion and adoption of new technology were formulated (Griliches, 1957; Hägerstrand, 1952), and recent data drawn mainly from rural sites provide the most convincing demographic demonstration of diffusion operating through social networks (Behrman, Kohler, and Watkins, 2001; Casterline, Montgomery, Agyeman, Aglobitse, and Kiros, 2001). Moreover, some may object to giving urban diversity greater emphasis than city size. Large cities do tend to exhibit greater diversity than small ones (Henderson, 2002), and in the economic arena, scale is something of a precondition for specialization and diversity. Nevertheless, scale and diversity are conceptually and empirically separable features of urban environments. As Henderson has shown for high-technology industries in the United States and Korea, it is diversity rather than city size as such that generates productivity advantages for these industries.

Where *social capital* is concerned, there are likely to be many differences between its urban and rural expressions; to our knowledge there has been no systematic study of those differences. Residential mobility and migration are thought to weaken the basis for cooperation in city neighborhoods. Yet it is difficult to know whether urban areas are, in general, sites of high residential mobility. In the panel's own research experience, many city neighborhoods have proven to be residentially stable (see UNCHS, 1996: 206 for confirmation).

Certainly urban environments do not prevent the mobilization of social capital. The literature offers numerous examples of strong, effective, and inclusive urban community organizations; recall Box 2.2 on the alliance of SPARC, Mahila Milan, and the National Slum Dwellers Federation in Mumbai. Indeed, urban settings would often appear to provide more opportunities for community organizations to negotiate with government agencies (Appadurai, 2001; Boonyabancha, 2001; Baumann, Bolnick, and Mitlin, 2001; Tostensen, Tvedten, and Vaa, 2001). The urban engagement between government and civil society is especially apparent in countries with democratic systems, where there are political and legal restraints on the power of government to suppress community mobilization.

The differences in *human capital* are explored further in Chapters 5 and 8. As is shown there, urban residents are more educated on average than rural residents, and would appear to enjoy easier access to middle and secondary levels of education for their children. Less often appreciated, however, is the diversity of educational opportunities for urban adults and children. What matters in cities, we would argue, is not only the higher average levels of educational attainment, but also the greater diversity of educational experiences. As discussed in Chapters 5 and 6, in addition to the demands on parental time associated with children's schooling, time costs arise from the distinctive social risks of urban child rearing.

Of course, these urban/rural differences should not be exaggerated. Urban returns to schooling vary across economic sector and by city size and diversity; education is known to help rural farmers exploit new agricultural technologies. As is shown in Chapter 5, school enrollment rates among the children of the urban poor often are hardly greater than those among rural children. In both rural and urban settings, the need for child labor can keep children from attending school regularly or at all.

It is a commonplace that urban populations rely more heavily than rural populations on *cash income for access to necessities*—including food, fuel, fresh water, housing (which is more commercialized in cities), transport, and waste disposal. Monetization reduces transactions costs and raises real standards of living, but with these benefits comes a greater vulnerability to changes in money wages and prices. The fact that most urban goods and services are monetized may also induce in urban populations a keener appreciation of relative costs in general, and may draw special attention to the relative costs of child rearing. To be sure, monetization is probably more characteristic of larger than smaller cities. In many countries, a significant proportion of rural dwellers are also dependent on cash income, and they, too, can face variable prices for some goods and services.

As discussed in Chapter 5, it is difficult to know just how much the prices of essentials differ between urban and rural populations. The costs no doubt vary enormously among rural areas themselves, among cities, and among different neighborhoods within cities. In rich countries, advances in transport and communications, together with sophisticated systems of wholesale and retail trade, have suppressed much spatial variation in prices. These factors operate with far less force in most poor countries. In many of their cities, the urban poor face particularly high costs for such essentials as water and health care because public services are not reliably provided to poor neighborhoods, and the private markets offering substitutes can be highly imperfect or exploitative.

Still, rural populations may face high money costs for some goods as well. As recent economic studies have shown at the national level (Limão and Venables, 2001), the costs of transporting goods to rural areas are reflected in two sorts of penalties: higher prices and severe limits on the range of goods available. Much like landlocked countries, rural populations often suffer both of these penalties.

For many rural dwellers, access is limited by the inconvenience and relatively high cost of transport, which for a given physical distance renders less accessible schools, health centers, emergency services, courts, banks, politicians, and the institutions meant to enforce the rule of law. For the urban poor, it is not so much distance to services and institutions that matters, but rather exclusion from them for economic, social, or political reasons. A squatter household living 200 yards from a hospital, secondary school, or bank can be as effectively excluded as a rural dweller living 20 miles away. Proximity may ease access, but does not guarantee it.

Discussions of urbanness often begin by noting the prevalence of *nonagricultural occupations*, and it is certainly true that urban livelihoods are less directly dependent than rural on access to land, water, and other natural resources. Urban residents cannot easily turn to subsistence production to cope with rising prices or declining incomes. However, urban agriculture is more important to low-income residents than is commonly realized. Also, as discussed earlier, many urban dwellers maintain some claims on rural assets. In the same way, rural households can depend on nonfarm income, whether from wages, nonagricultural production, or urban remittances.

Housing is a key economic resource for low-income urban residents: it can supply income (from the renting out of rooms or as space for household-based enterprises); it has value as collateral; and it reflects trade-offs made in access to employment, as when the poor accept low-quality or dangerous locations to save on transport costs. Rural housing can also play an economic role (as with food processing and crafts), but generally this role is of lesser importance to household economic strategies.

Earlier in this chapter, we described the greater risks of *communicable disease* faced by city populations in the absence of adequate infrastructure and good governance. Higher levels of health risk are very much to be expected in urban areas lacking provisions for infrastructure, services, and waste management. Dispersed rural populations enjoy a measure of natural protection from much communicable disease. (Some large rural villages can also suffer from urban-like concentrations of population and pollution due, for instance, to livestock and agroprocessing.) Massive public-sector investments are required to convert an inherent urban health disadvantage to the urban advantage that is often taken as a given in modern populations.

Cities exhibit a different range of *occupational health and safety risks* than is seen in rural areas as a result of differences in the kinds of work undertaken (involving industrial chemicals and wastes, dust, heat, or dangerous machinery). Particular groups (such as waste pickers) face especially high occupational risks. But rural occupational health and safety risks should not be understated. There are high levels of health risk in many rural areas due to poorly managed irrigation (schistosomiasis, malaria), agricultural chemicals, dangerous machinery, and excessive physical demands. Finally, the spatially concentrated urban poor are vulnerable to *natural disasters* because they live on land at high risk from floods, landslides, or earthquakes. Rural populations are also vulnerable to natural disasters in many countries.

A central theme in this discussion is the pervasive influence of *governments*. Cities are marked by a multiplicity of laws, official norms, rules, and regulations that can be applied to land use, construction, economic enterprises, and production. To many observers, it appears that a regrettably common use of these regulations is to render illegal many of the means by which the urban poor gain access to their housing and livelihoods (Hardoy and Satterthwaite, 1989). Because access to services is less a matter of distance than of ability to pay and political clout, one finds in cities a greater reliance on illegal solutions for access to services—such as illegal taps of piped water and electricity—and this carries over to illegally occupied or subdivided land. Illegal or informal settlements are often concentrated on land sites subject to flooding or at risk from landslides or other natural hazards, especially where these sites offer low-income settlers the best chance of establishing a home or avoiding eviction. Often these sites also prove to be difficult to equip with basic infrastructure (Hardoy, Mitlin, and Satterthwaite, 2001).

The spatial concentration and visibility of urban populations may well leave them at the mercy of bureaucracies and powerful vested interests. On occasion, however, spatial concentration can also confer on the poor a certain political mass and even a measure of power. Stren (2002) notes that in Latin America, a common strategy among poor groups was to stage mass "land invasions" in an effort to secure access to urban land. Although not always immediately successful, this strategy enabled some poor groups to voice effectively their claim to a share of public resources.

In summary, Table 2-1 shows the main elements the panel believes lend urban landscapes their distinctive character. In considering each of these elements and in highlighting exceptions and counterexamples, we have endeavored to show how along each dimension, the urban/rural distinction is mainly a question of degree. The quality of urbanness—which eludes definition, but is somehow easy to sense—emanates less from any single dimension listed than from their combination.

3

Urban Population Change: A Sketch

The first section of this chapter reviews the international extensions of the themes explored in the previous chapter, examining how cities occupy positions in the larger contexts of regional and global networks of trade, finance, and information. The term "globalization" is often invoked to describe the remarkable changes under way in communications and economic relations worldwide. The processes of globalization are surely as old as human history, but recent years have seen unprecedented developments in the speed, scale, scope, and complexity of change. In its modern forms, globalization is characterized by a rapid evolution of the international division of labor, increased trade and foreign direct investment (FDI), a quickening pace of transnational communication, and a dramatic expansion of cross-border business alliances (Cohen, 1981; Berry, Conkling, and Ray, 1997). In the eyes of critics, the modern forms of globalization are also associated with rising inequality and social polarization.

Historically and today, globalization has taken effect mainly through networks of trade. These networks link geographically distant consumers and producers, establishing relationships of identification and interdependence, and provide a vehicle for cultural exchange. In the modern era, flows of goods between countries offer parallel opportunities to expand trade in services. Trade is intertwined with other elements of globalization, such as movements of financial capital and highly skilled labor. Today, transnational corporations—firms that operate in more than one country, whether directly or through affiliates and subsidiaries—form much of the basis for the international system of trade (Sassen, 1994a).

Cities have historically functioned as the nodes of such global trade networks. Indeed, it is sometimes useful to envision large cities as junctions for flows of goods, information, and people, rather than as fixed locations at which goods and services are produced. This view helps bring city networks—whether transportation and communication networks or networks involving finance and culture—into focus (Batten, 1990).

These are large topics, but our treatment of them must be brief. As mentioned in Chapter 1, the demographic implications of globalization are, at present, quite difficult to discern. The changes under way in trade, finance, and communication are still too recent, and their effects too seldom traced to the level of individuals and families, for a demographic accounting to be possible. In closing this first section of the chapter, we offer some speculations about the areas in which demographic effects might be seen most clearly.

In the following sections of the chapter, we take up the task of linking demographic data to the concepts that have dominated the discussion thus far. Globalization may set cities in new contexts, but, as will be seen, the demographic features of their urban transitions are a mix of novel and familiar elements. We give a brief summary, describing in broad strokes the scale of recent urban change, with particular attention to the emergence of large cities in the developing world, the pace of change, and the main differences in urban experience by demographic regime and level of national income. Having sketched this background, we then return to the regional context and explore the similarities and differences among the transitions of African, Asian, and Latin American countries. These regional comparisons leave little doubt about the unevenness of globalization and the great variety of socioeconomic contexts in which urbanization is taking place.

CITIES AMID GLOBAL FORCES

Over the past 20 years, cities have become decidedly more international in their orientation. In a world of easier cross-border flows of information, capital, goods, and people, the firm control once exercised by nation states appears to have been loosened by deregulation, privatization, and the growth of foreign investment. As national governments adopt new forms of governance and allow markets and smaller governmental units to assume more prominent roles, cities find themselves having to redefine their positions in the international arena.

As nation states step back somewhat from center stage, it becomes possible to discern an emerging transnational system in which cities and corporations are key players, operating within complex networks of relations (Taylor, 2000; Gipoulou, 1998). Increasingly, we believe, it will be membership in such networks that serves to define "global cities." Investments in infrastructure and human capital will give some cities access to strategic international circuits of exchange, allowing them to present themselves as viable sites for foreign direct investment. Other cities will lack the necessary capital and will be restricted to regional or domestic roles.

A paradox of globalization is that, while creating more linkages and interdependencies, it also underscores the importance of comparative advantage at the subnational and local levels. Transnational corporations become increasingly aware of the niches where cheap and reliable labor can be found, and learn in detail of the constraints of local transport and infrastructure. Hence, when seen from a global corporate perspective, the cities of low-income countries are likely to appear increasingly diverse (Sassen, 2002).

To appreciate the scale of the changes that are under way, consider the breathtaking physical and structural transformations occurring in some cities of Pacific Asia.[1] Shenzhen, the border city just north of Hong Kong, is perhaps the most remarkable example. In 1979, when it was designated a Special Economic Zone, Shenzhen was an obscure fringe settlement of some 35,000 inhabitants. Over the course of the next two decades, it rose to become a metropolis of 4 million inhabitants, boasting the highest wage levels in China, and having one of China's two stock markets and its heaviest concentration of foreign investment. The city of Pudong—the part of Shanghai lying to the east of the Huangpu River—has since 1990 been transformed from a constellation of villages into an urban agglomeration premised upon technology and innovation. Kuala Lumpur has also reinvented itself, acquiring a modern image with the construction of the 88-story Petronas Twin Towers, the starting point of a new development corridor that extends 70 kilometers to the Kuala Lumpur International Airport.

In these cases, countries and cities have proven themselves capable of mobilizing great quantities of human and physical capital in remarkably brief spans of time. Such concentrations of resources must eventually reshape patterns of migration and other demographic behavior, although the forms these demographic responses will take are not yet fully apparent. In what follows, we touch briefly on several of the important developments in the globalization of cities.

Financial Services and Foreign Direct Investment

In the realm of finance, it appears probable that today's powerful centers—New York, London, and Tokyo—will continue to dominate the world markets. Although financial transactions can now be executed over great distances, the firms that mediate the risk of these transactions are themselves located in only a few major cities. At the regional level, the scale of investment required makes it unlikely that very many cities can soon expect to attract a critical mass of international financial firms. The regional centers of finance will probably be located in those few cities whose political and economic systems are relatively secure, and where the legal system provides effective regulation, mediating disputes, prosecuting offenders, and providing compensation for wrongdoing. The situation of Hong Kong bears watching, because its recent change in political status has raised fears about the continuity of legal protections under Chinese rule.

---

[1] These changes are both the cause and the consequence of spectacular economic growth. In the period 1970–1990, some cities in the region registered increases in gross domestic product (GDP) in excess of 1,000 percent. These included Seoul and Tokyo, which recorded increases of 2,127 and 2,994 percent, respectively. During the same period, Hong Kong's GDP rose 15-fold, and its exports rocketed upward 27-fold (Savitch, 1996).

The role of FDI, described more fully in Chapter 8, has become exceedingly important in certain regions of the developing world. Such investments, which involve south-to-south flows as well as flows from northern economies, are significant in several respects. They are notable for being highly concentrated in just a few developing countries, with Brazil, China, and Mexico taking about half of the current flows, and are equally notable for their absence from much of sub-Saharan Africa and South Asia (World Bank, 2002a). Foreign investments are also spatially concentrated within countries, although the favored locations have tended to change with time. In an earlier era, FDI was often concentrated in extractive industries and natural resources, but more recently these investments have gone into manufacturing and urban locations (for the case of Indonesia, see Douglass, 1997).

The increasing prominence of FDI reflects the extent to which international firms headquartered in high-income countries now prefer to operate with multiple international affiliates, partners, and subcontractors. In some accounts, as will be discussed, these collaborative efforts are said to facilitate the transfer and local adaptation of new technologies. International networks of emigrants are also believed to provide important conduits for foreign investment and technology transfer (Rauch, 2001). For instance, a study of Fujian province shows that its Chinese emigrants have been a major source not only of capital, but also of commercial information and technical know-how (Yeung and Chu, 2000). Age-old Chinese business networks are being refitted to the needs of a globalizing era, tapping resources that flow through formal financial systems (Olds and Yeung, 1999).

Emerging Regional Networks

In Pacific Asia, the emergence of several "growth triangles" testifies to the increasing importance of regional linkages. Figure 3-1 depicts these economic systems, which can present unique cross-border challenges to governance. Singapore, for example, has sought to establish a regional growth network with links to the Riau Islands in Indonesia and Malaysia's province of Johor (Macleod and McGee, 1996; Yeung, 2000). Another growth triangle is developing in Southern China. It incorporates Fujian and Guangdong provinces on the mainland with Hong Kong and Taiwan, establishing a web of relations in which emigrant networks are much involved. Figure 3-1 depicts several other regional networks, which differ in maturity and depth of integration (Yeung, 2000). The Pacific Asia region is also witnessing the formation of "urban corridors" that connect cities across the region. Perhaps the best example of this is the Beijing–Seoul–Tokyo (BESETO) "ecumenopolis," which stretches for 1500 kilometers and connects 77 cities of more than 200,000 inhabitants each (Choe, 1996).

Markets and Volatility

Regional and international markets are the conduits through which new technologies and demands are conveyed to city populations. Open borders also put local

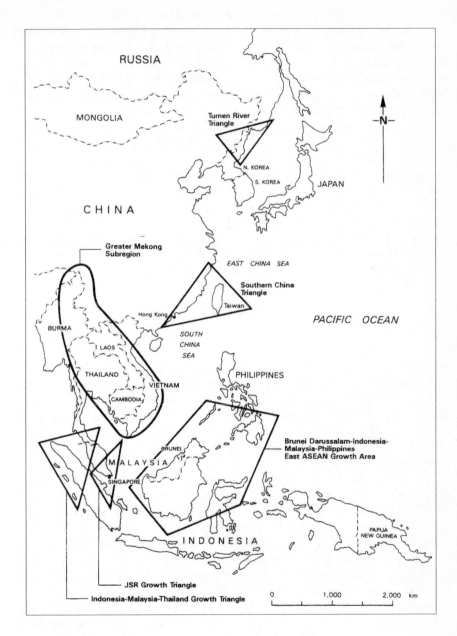

FIGURE 3-1 Regional urban linkages: The Asian "triangles."
SOURCE: Yeung (2000).

firms at risk of losing their markets to imports. As discussed in Chapter 8, in poor countries the dismantling of barriers to trade presents efficient firms with new opportunities, but can subject inefficient firms to withering international competition. Because cities are the gateways between national and international markets and because they are often the sites of inefficient firms dating to the import-substitution era, city populations can be exposed more openly than rural populations to the risks of market engagement.

Perhaps the greatest volatility and potential for contagion is seen in world markets in stocks, bonds, and currencies (World Bank, 2002a). The computerized, round-the-clock operation of these markets means that when a problem surfaces in one major market, it can very quickly affect others. The global stock market collapse of 1987 provided an early warning of the contagiousness of financial shocks, as did the Mexican financial crises of 1982 and 1994. The most serious episode of recent years, however, took place in the latter part of 1997, when in the span of a few months most countries along the western Pacific Rim found themselves in the grip of financial and political crisis. Chapters 6 and 8 explore the demographic and economic implications of such crises.

World Cities

With the unfolding of new forms of global economic relations, urban scholars have been exploring new ways to categorize cities. Over the past two decades, there has been an outpouring of research on the roles played by cities and systems of cities in the global economy (e.g., Knox and Taylor, 1995; Yeung, 2000; Sassen, 2000, 2001b; Taylor and Walker, 2001). In the formative stages of the debate, Hall (1966) and Friedmann and Wolff (1982) drew attention to a class of cities—termed "world cities"—that assume pivotal roles in the global economy. New York, London, and Tokyo occupy the uppermost tier because of their dominance of finance and specialized services, their importance as sites of production and innovation, and their role as markets for new products and services (Sassen, 2001b). Friedmann (1986) identifies 30 cities with claims to world city status, although arranging them in well-ordered hierarchies has proven to be difficult (Friedmann, 1995). The common thread in this research is the idea that a few cities form the dominant loci in today's global economy, contributing disproportionately to the internationalization of capital, production, services, and even culture (Yeung, 1995).

As cities are becoming more interdependent, they are also becoming more self-consciously competitive. This competition is conducted partly through economic investment strategies, but it also has something of a marketing and promotional aspect. Some city competitions, such as those for the World Cup, the Olympics, and the Asian Games, are meant to capture the headlines. These events are opportunities to project positive city images. As cities aspire to compete in regional and global arenas, they also invest in building human capital, modernizing conference facilities, upgrading physical infrastructure, beautifying the built environment, and protecting the natural environment. In globalized settings, a city's comparative advantage lies not only in the tangible resources it can offer, but also in its sets of networks and contacts (Gipoulou, 1998). As cities prepare themselves for competition, their municipal governments can help create environments in which business firms can explore new networking opportunities.[2]

Demographic Implications?

The full demographic implications of these developments are, at this point, still difficult to discern. As cities undertake ambitious investment plans, human capital and social infrastructure figure prominently among their strategic themes. Decisions to invest in schools, transportation, and faster communication undoubtedly raise urban productivity and can serve to better integrate rural areas. These investments also generate new types of inequality, benefiting some groups while displacing others. It is reasonable to think that patterns of migration will be reshaped in response. If capital accumulation and new technology raise the returns to schooling, this may encourage families to shift to reproductive strategies of lower fertility and higher education per child.

The implications of globalization for smaller cities are potentially disturbing. If capital is diverted from smaller cities to prepare larger cities for their global debuts, significant costs for many of the developing world's urban dwellers could result. When judged in relation to present resources, the challenges faced by small cities in a globalizing era may well be proportionately greater than those faced by megacities (Hall and Pfeiffer, 2000).

KEY DEMOGRAPHIC FEATURES OF THE URBAN TRANSITION

By the above account, the economic and social environments facing today's cities have many novel and unprecedented features. Is the urban transition equally novel in its demography? The transitions now under way differ in many respects from the experiences of Europe and the United States in the first half of the twentieth century. They also have much in common with these earlier transitions (Brockerhoff, 2000; Hall and Pfeiffer, 2000; Sassen, 2001a; Yeung, 2000). The scale of change—the absolute numbers of people involved—is clearly unprecedented, as are the typical rates of growth of total urban populations. It is less certain that the demographic components of growth differ much from historical experience. Not enough evidence remains in the record to separate the share of

---

[2]Hong Kong's recent economic success has owed much to its enterprising and resourceful businessmen, who have been extending the city-state's economic reach. For instance, Huchison Whampoa, one of the most successful listed corporations in the territory, has made port and technology investments in 24 countries, from which the bulk of its earnings is derived (Yeung, 1999). Some 35 percent of Hong Kong's gross national product has been derived from revenues from trade support activities situated outside its borders (Hong Kong Trade Development Council, 1998).

natural increase in historical urban growth (the balance of urban births against deaths) from that of net migration and territorial reclassification. The changes in the urban percentages of today's developing countries, rapid as they may appear to be, are not at all unlike the historical precedents. Urbanization does appear to be taking place at generally lower levels of per capita income than in the historical experience, and in the case of Africa, may have become decoupled from indus-trialization. Some of these empirical regularities are traceable to national-level demographic regimes, which can differ a great deal from the regimes that were in place in the histories of developed countries.

Before we describe the demographic features of today's urban transition, a word of explanation is needed on the ways in which demographers measure urban levels and trends. We have already mentioned the share of urban growth due to natural increase and migration, a measure to which demographers give consider-able attention. Four additional measures are also employed, and although they are quite distinct in meaning, their labels are sufficiently similar to invite confusion. The four measures are (1) the absolute annual increase in urban (or city) popula-tion size, (2) the urban (or city) population growth rate, (3) the level of urbaniza-tion, and (4) the rate of urbanization. The first of these is commonly described as a measure of scale, an indicator of the numbers of people involved in urban growth. Of course, the annual increase is affected by the urban growth rate, but growth rates are measures of proportional rather than absolute change. The level of ur-banization is the percentage of a country's population that lives in its cities and towns. This is to be distinguished from the rate of urbanization, which is defined in two ways: either as the growth rate of the urban percentage (we prefer this def-inition) or as the absolute annual change in the urban percentage. It is also impor-tant to maintain a distinction between the growth of the total urban population and that of individual city populations. Total urban growth can be distributed across individual cities, and thus across a range of city sizes, in many different ways.

In describing the main demographic features of the urban experience, we draw extensively on the estimates and projections of the United Nations Population Division. In so doing, we are mindful of the problems in concepts and measures that plague the study of urban change. As will be seen in Chapter 4, the data series available to the United Nations suffer from many limitations and inconsistencies, and the Population Division cannot resolve all of these. For instance, the United Nations cannot impose on its member countries a uniform definition of urban areas, and this fact of life renders problematic all cross-country comparisons of urban levels and trends. Nevertheless, for present purposes—to identify the broad features—these data will suffice.

The Scale of Change

The sheer number of new urban residents gives perhaps the clearest indication of the challenge facing governments and urban planners in poor countries. As

TABLE 3-1 Population Size and Growth, Urban and Rural, by Region

Region	Midyear Population (millions)				Growth Rate (percent)		
	1950	1975	2000	2030	1950– 1975	1975– 2000	2000– 2030
Urban							
World total	751	1,543	2,862	4,981	2.9	2.4	1.8
High-income countries	359	562	697	825	1.8	0.9	0.6
Middle- and low-income countries	392	981	2,165	4,156	3.7	3.2	2.2
Asia	244	592	1,376	2,679	3.5	3.4	2.2
Africa	32	102	295	787	4.6	4.2	3.3
Europe	287	455	534	540	1.8	0.6	0.04
Latin America and Caribbean	70	198	391	608	4.2	2.7	1.5
North America	110	180	243	335	2.0	1.2	1.0
Oceania	8	15	231	32	2.5	1.7	1.1
Rural							
World total	1,769	2,523	3,195	3,289	1.4	0.9	0.1
High-income countries	219	187	184	139	−0.6	−0.07	−0.9
Middle- and low-income countries	1,550	2,336	3,011	3,151	1.6	1.0	0.2
Asia	1,155	1,805	2,297	2,271	1.8	1.0	−0.04
Africa	188	304	498	702	1.9	2.0	1.1
Europe	261	221	193	131	−0.7	−0.5	−1.3
Latin America and Caribbean	97	124	127	116	1.0	0.1	−0.3
North America	62	64	71	61	0.1	0.4	−0.5
Oceania	5	6	8	10	0.7	1.2	0.7

NOTE: High-income countries have gross national income per capita of $9,266 or more based on World Bank estimates.

SOURCES: United Nations (2002a); World Bank (2002b).

discussed in Chapter 1, the urban population of the world is projected to increase from 2.86 billion in 2000 to 4.98 billion by 2030, with the total for all developing countries reaching 4.16 billion (see Table 3-1). In these countries, urban growth rates have ranged over time from spectacular to merely alarming levels. The period from 1950 to 1975 saw rates of urban growth of 3.7 percent across the developing world; had these rates persisted to 2000, the total urban population would have grown to six times what it was in 1950, with consequences that can only be imagined. Fortunately, the growth rates did decline, falling to 3.2 percent from 1975 to 2000, and further declines, to 2.2 percent, are anticipated for the next 30 years. As can be seen in the table, although they have faded away in Latin America, high rates of urban population growth are still characteristic of Africa, and African growth rates are expected to remain high for the foreseeable future.

Large Cities

Increases in total urban populations can have different spatial manifestations; in theory, a rapid increase in the total might be accommodated by the very rapid replication of small cities. But perhaps it is not surprising that urban growth has generally been expressed in the number and average size of large cities. At the beginning of the nineteenth century, Beijing (then Peking) was the only city in the world with a million or more residents (Chandler, 1987), and at the advent of the twentieth century, there were only 16 cities of this size. By 1950, however, the number of such cities had risen to 86, and, as can be seen in Figure 3-2, there are about 400 such cities today. For the next 15 years, the United Nations anticipates the addition of a further 150 cities to the list of those with at least a million residents. The average size of the world's largest cities is also growing. In 1800 the world's largest hundred cities averaged only 165,000 in population; today that average exceeds 6 million (Chandler, 1987; United Nations, 2002a).

The very upper end of the city size distribution is occupied by the megacities, which are conventionally defined as agglomerations with populations of 10 million or more. These cities have also become more numerous and considerably

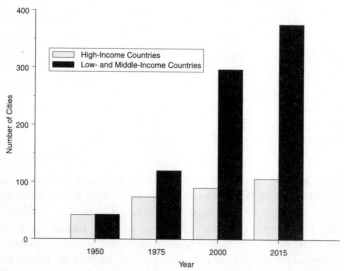

FIGURE 3-2 Number of cities with a million residents or more, 1950–2015.
SOURCES: United Nations (2002a); World Bank (2001).

TABLE 3-2 Number of Urban Areas and Total Urban Population by Size, 1950–2015

City Size	Number of Cities				Urban Population (in thousands)			
	1950	1975	2000	2015	1950	1975	2000	2015
World total								
10 million or more	1	5	16	21	12,339	68,118	224,988	340,497
5 to 10 million	7	16	23	37	42,121	122,107	169,164	263,870
1 to 5 million	75	174	348	496	144,335	331,576	674,571	960,329
500,000 to 1 million	106	248	417	507	75,134	176,414	290,113	354,448
Fewer than 500,000	n.a.	n.a.	n.a.	n.a.	481,455	844,296	1,502,920	1,950,323
High-income countries								
10 million or more	1	2	4	4	12,339	35,651	67,403	70,641
5 to 10 million	4	7	5	6	26,389	54,550	37,650	45,359
1 to 5 million	38	64	81	95	76,504	n.a.	183,635	211,578
500,000 to 1 million	32	28	n.a.	n.a.	24,138	n.a.	n.a.	n.a.
Fewer than 500,000	n.a.	n.a.	n.a.	n.a.	n.a.	n.a.	n.a.	n.a.
Middle- and low-income countries								
10 million or more	0	3	12	17	0	32,467	157,585	269,856
5 to 10 million	3	9	18	31	15,732	67,557	131,514	218,511
1 to 5 million	40	110	267	401	67,831	n.a.	490,936	748,751
500,000 to 1 million	74	220	n.a.	n.a.	50,996	n.a.	n.a.	n.a.
Fewer than 500,000	n.a.	n.a.	n.a.	n.a.	n.a.	n.a.	n.a.	n.a.

NOTE: n.a. means not available.
SOURCE: United Nations (2002a).

larger in average size. Tables 3-2 and 3-3 show how the number, size, and geographic distribution of the world's largest cities have changed over time. To better portray the trends, Table 3-3 lists all cities with populations in excess of 5 million.

In 1950, there were only 8 cities in the world with populations of 5 million or more. At that time, New York, London, and Tokyo were the world's largest agglomerations, containing 12.3 million, 8.7 million, and 6.9 million residents, respectively. Cities such as Mumbai (formerly Bombay), Mexico City, and Rio de Janeiro were still relatively small, each having about 2.9 million residents.

TABLE 3-3 Urban Agglomerations with 5 Million People or More, 1950–2015

Region	1950	1970	2000	2015
High-income countries				
Europe	Paris	Paris	Paris	Paris
	Rhein-Ruhr	Rhein-Ruhr	Rhein-Ruhr	Rhein-Ruhr
	London	London	London	London
		Milan		
North America	New York	New York	New York	New York
		Los Angeles	Los Angeles	Los Angeles
		Chicago	Chicago	Chicago
				Toronto
Asia	Tokyo	Tokyo	Tokyo	Tokyo
		Osaka	Osaka	Osaka
			Hong Kong	Hong Kong
Middle- and low-income countries				
Asia	Shanghai	Shanghai	Shanghai	Shanghai
		Beijing	Beijing	Beijing
		Tianjin	Tianjin	Tianjin
		Seoul	Seoul	Seoul
		Bombay	Bombay	Bombay
		Calcutta	Calcutta	Calcutta
			Bangalore	Bangalore
			Delhi	Delhi
			Hyderabad	Hyderabad
			Madras	Madras
			Wuhan	Wuhan
			Jakarta	Jakarta
			Teheran	Teheran
			Istanbul	Istanbul
			Bangkok	Bangkok
			Metro Manila	Metro Manila
			Karachi	Karachi
			Lahore	Lahore
			Dhaka	Dhaka
				Kabul
				Chongqing
				Shenyang
				Pune
				Chittagong
				Riyadh
				Baghdad
				Jidda
				Hanoi
				Ho Chi Minh
				Ahmedabad
				Surat
				Yangon
				Bandung
Africa		Cairo	Cairo	Cairo
			Lagos	Lagos
			Kinshasa	Kinshasa
				Addis Ababa
				Luanda
				Abidjan
Latin America	Buenos Aires	Buenos Aires	Buenos Aires	Buenos Aires
and the Caribbean		Rio de Janeiro	Rio de Janeiro	Rio de Janeiro
		São Paulo	São Paulo	São Paulo
		Mexico City	Mexico City	Mexico City
			Lima	Lima
			Santiago	Santiago
			Bogota	Bogota
				Guatemala City
				Belo Horizonte
Europe	Moscow	Moscow	Moscow	Moscow

SOURCE: United Nations (2002a).

By 1975, there were 21 cities with more than 5 million people and 5 massive urban agglomerations with more than 10 million: Tokyo, New York, Shanghai, Mexico City, and São Paulo. Today there are 39 cities with populations estimated at 5 million or more, and 16 have surpassed the 10 million mark. Its 12.3 million residents made the New York City of 1950 the largest city in the world; a city of that size would not rank among the world's 10 largest today.

Although additional large agglomerations have emerged in the high-income countries, the balance has clearly tipped to the developing world.[3] United Nations projections indicate that between 2000 and 2015, some 19 cities will be added to the total of those with at least 5 million residents; only 1 of these will be located in a high-income country (United Nations, 2002a). Among the world's 30 largest urban agglomerations in 2015, 18 are expected to be found in Asia, 6 in Latin America, 3 in Africa, and the remaining 3 elsewhere. It is anticipated that each of them will house more than 8 million residents, with the biggest 3 (Tokyo, Dhaka, and Mumbai) projected to contain more than 22 million residents apiece.

The percentage of the national population living in large cities is especially high in Latin America, where some 32 percent of the population resides in cities with a least a million residents. By 2015, almost 38 percent of the population of this region will live in such cities (United Nations, 2002a). This is a much higher percentage than is found in either Africa or Asia; by 2015, the latter regions are expected to have only 15 and 19 percent of their populations, respectively, living in million-plus cities (United Nations, 2002a).

In many developing countries, a high percentage of the national population lives in the country's largest city, which is usually its capital. This is not generally the case in high-income countries, whose urban populations tend to be more spatially dispersed. Some 17 Latin American countries have 15 percent or more of their national populations in their largest city, and in 8 of these, that city houses more than one-quarter of the national population. In Africa, there are 9 countries with more than 15 percent of their populations in the largest city (in Libya and Congo, the figure is more than 30 percent). And in Asia, 15 countries have at least 15 percent of their total populations in the largest city, although 1 of these countries is Singapore, a city state.

Chapter 1 drew attention to a feature of large cities that is often overlooked: they generally grow more slowly than small cities. It is not at all uncommon to find small cities and towns growing at double-digit rates, but rarely do cities of several million inhabitants grow by more than 5 per cent per annum, and their

---

[3] A list of the 10 largest cities in the world in 1950 contained 7 cities from the developed world, including all of the world's 5 largest: New York, London, Tokyo, Paris, and Moscow. Today, the largest urban agglomerations in the world are mainly in the south. According to the latest United Nations data, for 2000, 7 of the world's 10 largest cities are in middle- or low-income countries, and 3 of the world's 5 largest cities—perhaps more accurately called urban agglomerations—are in the south: Mexico City, São Paulo, and Mumbai (the other 2 are Tokyo and New York). Cities in Europe such as London and Paris are now dwarfed in demographic terms by cities such as Calcutta, Dhaka, Delhi, Karachi, Mumbai, Shanghai, São Paulo, and Mexico City.

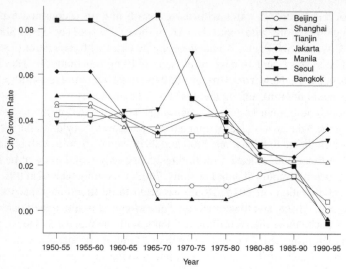

FIGURE 3-3 Selected city growth rates in East and Southeast Asia, 1950–1995.
SOURCE: United Nations (2001).

growth is typically much slower than this (Hardoy, Mitlin, and Satterthwaite,
2001). The link between city size and growth can be seen in Figure 3-3, which
shows how the growth rates of some of Asia's large cities have declined over time
as their total populations have increased. (The trends also reflect the declines under way in national population growth rates, as will be discussed shortly, and of
course city growth rates may decline when new growth occurs just beyond the
official boundaries.) Most of today's largest cities grew far more rapidly several
decades ago. Indeed, for cities such as São Paulo and Buenos Aires, one has to go
back to the late nineteenth or early twentieth century to find the most rapid epochs
of growth (Hardoy, Mitlin, and Satterthwaite, 2001).

The point that large cities tend to grow more slowly is often lost in accounts
that stress the growth of the total urban population in the largest of the city size
classes. As the United Nations (1980) warns, the growth rate of the largest city
size class is a misleading indicator of typical rates of growth of large cities
themselves. Consider the number of people living in agglomerations of 10 million
or more, which rose from 68 million in 1975 to 225 million in 2000 (Table 3-2).
This growth was partly the result of a piling up of population in the largest size
class, as cities having populations under the 10 million threshold in 1975 passed
over that threshold between 1975 and 2000. City size classes can be useful indicators for some purposes, but it is individual city growth rates that more directly
confront urban planners and others who must arrange for service delivery.

Rapidly growing megacities are not limited to Asia, Africa, and Latin
America. That cities such as Shanghai, Buenos Aires, and Calcutta grew from

between 4 and 5 million in 1950 to around 13 million today does not greatly distinguish their experience from that of Los Angeles over the same period of time. The rates of growth of these cities are considerably slower than the rates seen in such U.S. cities as Atlanta, Dallas, Miami, and Phoenix (Satterthwaite, 1996a). To be sure, some of today's megacities have experienced high rates of population growth over the last quarter century. Dhaka and Lagos, for example, may well have grown at rates of 7 and 6 percent, respectively, from the 1980s to the early 1990s, although the record is too incomplete for this to be verified. But these are the exceptions. Among the 16 megacities of today, only 3—Dhaka, Delhi, and Karachi—grew at rates consistently above 3 percent per annum during the 1980s and 1990s. The others experienced moderate or low growth, with rates under 2 percent. The United Nations projects that over the next 15 years, only 4 megacities— Dhaka, Delhi, Jakarta, and Karachi—will experience growth rates of more than 3 percent per year, while 9 will see annual growth rates under 1 percent.

Components of Growth: Natural Increase and Migration

Observers of rapid city growth are often tempted to think of migration as the dominant demographic factor. Demographers, however, have long emphasized the contribution of natural increase to urban growth. Reclassification, whereby urban status is conferred on formerly rural residents and territory, also deserves consideration. One type of reclassification occurs when a settlement passes beyond a minimum size or density threshold, thereby qualifying to be termed an urban place. A second type occurs when a government changes its definition of "urban," as did the United States in 1950 and China in the 1980s. Cities can also annex neighboring territory.

Where natural increase is concerned, urban growth in developing countries is being driven by birth and death rates that hardly resemble those of 100 to 150 years ago, when Europe and North America were urbanizing. Today's fertility and mortality rates generate (stable) rates of national population growth that often exceed 1 percent annually. Western historical populations seldom saw growth that rapid—their rates were usually on the order of 1 percent and below (Livi Bacci, 1997). High rates of national population growth are transmitted to urban growth, with the connection being direct in the case of urban natural increase and indirect, through migration, for rural increase.

The contribution of migration to urban growth

The most recent effort to separate natural increase from other components of urban growth is that of Chen, Valente, and Zlotnik (1998). This research, which draws on censuses from Africa, Latin America, and Asia, covers 35 pairs of censuses in the 1960s, some 39 pairs in the 1970s, and 26 in the 1980s. Table 3-4 summarizes

TABLE 3-4 United Nations Estimates of the Contributions of Migration and Reclassification to Urban Growth in Developing Countries

Source	Census Pairs	Decade	Migration and Reclassification Percentage (Median)	Range
United Nations (1980)	39	1950s	37.2	7.3–61.9
Chen, Valente, and Zlotnik (1998)	35	1960s	40.7	8.8–77.4
	39	1970s	43.2	13.2–65.6
	26	1980s	40.1[a]	6.6–71.9

[a] These data include estimates for China, whose migrant share is 71.9 percent.

the findings.[4] A first point to note is that the Chen et al. analysis reconfirms earlier estimates of the share of urban growth due to migration and reclassification (United Nations, 1980), which put their combined contribution at about 40 percent in the median country. The remaining part of urban growth—roughly 60 percent—is due to urban natural increase. The Chen et al. findings underscore a point made repeatedly by demographers: both migration and natural increase make substantial contributions to urban growth. The case of China, for which the migrant share is estimated at 71.9 percent, is something of an outlier.

The estimates assembled by Chen, Valente, and Zlotnik (1998) permit an examination of trends in migration shares for some countries. In Latin America, the region in this sample best covered by censuses, there has been a slight shift downward in the share of urban growth due to migration. This has occurred despite the decline in natural increase in the region, perhaps because of a contemporaneous decline in the rural out-migration rate.

Rural-to-urban migration rates

Are modern rates of rural-to-urban migration unusual by historical standards? Relying on indirect evidence, Preston (1979) conjectures that migration rates in Western countries must have been somewhat higher a century ago than they are in developing countries today. However, the United Nations (1980: Figure III) examines estimates for 11 developing countries that suggest increases in rural-to-urban migration rates with time. Probing further into its small sample, the United Nations finds that migration rates tend to be higher in developing countries with

---

[4]The method used to generate these estimates is described in Chapter 4. Note that estimates for Puerto Rico and Israel are excluded from Table 3-4.

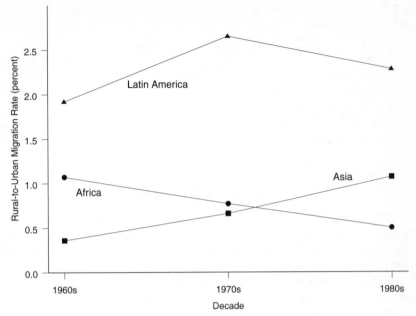

FIGURE 3-4 Estimates of rural-to-urban migration rates, 1960s–1980s.

higher levels of income per capita, suggesting that with economic development may come a greater spatial dispersion of economic opportunities.

Chen, Valente, and Zlotnik (1998: Table 2-7) provide updated estimates of rural-to-urban migration rates for a selection of countries in Africa, Asia, and Latin America. These estimates are shown in Figure 3-4. As can be seen, the African trend is distinct: on this continent, rates of rural-to-urban migration have declined over the three decades shown in the figure. This trend would be surprising given Africa's relatively low level of urbanization, but for the 1980s, at least, it may have been the result of the decade's economic crises and retrenchments that reduced the attractions of cities.[5] The Asian trend is in the opposite direction: here the migration rate is low but increasing. (The Asian estimate for the 1980s includes China; if China were excluded, the estimate for that period would rise to 1.37 percent.) In Latin America, the region exhibiting the highest migration rates, the data series indicate that a decline in migration began in the 1980s, this being, perhaps, yet another reflection of the economic crises of that decade.

---

[5]Bocquier and Traoré (1998) find evidence of substantial urban-to-rural migration flows in West Africa, but the cross-sectional data available to them shed no light on trends. A study of 14 sub-Saharan African cities during 1960–1985 finds that the proportion of city growth due to migration fell over the period, and city growth rates also declined (Makannah, 1990).

TABLE 3-5 Estimates of the Rate of Urbanization in More-Developed and
Less-Developed Countries

Geographic Area	Predicted Annual Change in Urban Percentage	
	Unweighted	Population-Weighted
MDCs, 1875–1925	0.390	0.431
LDCs, 1950–2000	0.457	0.416
United States, 1790–2000	0.402	—

NOTE: The figures shown are coefficients on time (measured annually) in a simple
regression of the country's urban percentage on time.

The Rate of Urbanization

Does the current rate of urbanization differ from historical experience? To pursue
this question, we assembled data on urbanization levels by decade for 7 of today's
high-income countries in the period 1875 to 1925, and compared their rates of
urbanization with those of 17 low- and middle-income countries in the 1950–
2000 period.[6] Different starting points and urban definitions render comparisons
of urbanization levels problematic, but we believe useful comparisons of the rate
of urbanization are nonetheless possible.

Table 3-5 shows that, on average, the high-income populations increased their
urbanization levels by about 0.39 percentage points annually from 1875 to 1925.
In the modern era, the low- and middle-income countries exhibit only a slightly
higher pace of urbanization of 0.457 points per annum. When we repeat this
analysis weighting the data by country population size—see the second column
of Table 3-5—the present-day rates of urbanization move even closer to the 1875–
1925 historical experience.

For the United States, a longer time series on urbanization is available, extending from the first census in 1790 to the present.[7] Across the full span of these data,
the average annual rate of urbanization is again about 0.4 percentage points. On
closer scrutiny these data reveal eras of more rapid urbanization (the mid- to late
nineteenth century) and eras when the pace of urbanization slowed (the 1970s and
1980s). Yet when viewed over the nation's 200-year history, U.S. urbanization
rates are seen to fall well within the historical bounds.

These analyses strongly reconfirm the findings of Preston (1979) and the
United Nations (1980): the *rate of urbanization* experienced by today's developing

---

[6]The high-income countries include Canada, France, Germany (entered separately for East and
West during partition), Italy, Japan, Russian Federation (including Soviet Union), Sweden, United
Kingdom, and United States. Data for Germany and Russia (former Soviet Union) were merged.
Data are from World Bank and United Nations sources. We include from 40 to 50 annual observations
per country. The low- and middle-income set includes Argentina, Brazil, Colombia, Congo, Egypt.
Ethiopia, India, Indonesia, Mexico, Pakistan, Peru, Russian Federation, and South Africa.

[7]Urban definitions have changed in the United States, most notably in 1950, and territory has been
reclassified, but this should not seriously compromise inferences about the long-term trend.

countries is much like that experienced by developed countries a century ago. Between 1975 and 2000, the percentage of the population living in urban areas in developing countries grew from 29 to 41 percent, a change remarkably similar to the experience recorded by the more-developed world during the first quarter of the twentieth century (Brockerhoff, 2000). But if the rate of urbanization is similar, the typical *rate of urban growth* is much more rapid than what was seen in the Western experience.

Urbanization Without Development?

Urban growth is not in itself a cause for alarm. The pace of urbanization is usually closely associated with that of industrialization and economic growth. As countries develop, their economies undergo predictable changes, the relative importance of agriculture declining while that of manufacturing and services rises. Industrialization and economic growth are almost always accompanied by urbanization (World Bank, 2000a), and urbanization can be viewed as a measure of progress toward industry and services (Davis, 1965). Furthermore, as we have argued, there is good reason to think that urbanization itself stimulates economic growth. Viewed in this way, moderate rates of urban population growth might be taken as emblems of success.

In some parts of the world, however, and particularly in sub-Saharan Africa, cities have been growing without a concomitant expansion of economic activity. In Africa, high rates of city growth owe more to high rates of national population growth than to economic development. On this point a comparison of Africa with Southeast Asia may be instructive. At first glance their urbanization experiences appear to have been remarkably similar over the past 35 years. In 1950, some 14.7 percent of Africa's population lived in urban areas, as did 14.8 percent of the population of Southeast Asia. The level of urbanization then rose in Africa, reaching 20.8 percent in 1965 and 37.2 percent in 2000. Meanwhile Southeast Asia recorded nearly identical changes, with its level of urbanization reaching 19.0 percent in 1965 and 37.5 percent in 2000 (United Nations, 2002a). But if the urban percentages rose in parallel, the economic experiences of these regions could hardly have been more different. Incomes per capita in Southeast Asia have shot up, while in Africa they have stagnated or declined (World Bank, 2000c). As the World Bank (2000a: 130) observes, "...cities in Africa are not serving as engines of growth and structural transformation. Instead they are part of the cause and a major symptom of the economic and social crises that have enveloped the continent."

National Demographic Regimes

Since the middle of the twentieth century, the demographic regimes prevailing in most developing countries have been thoroughly reconfigured. Soon after the end of World War II, rapid declines in mortality occurred throughout much of the developing world, due largely to the use of Western drugs and medical practices. Gains in life expectancy that took 50 or 100 years to achieve in the developed world required little more than a decade or two in the developing world (National Research Council, 2000). The beginnings of a dramatic change in fertility in developing countries can be traced back to the 1960s, albeit with considerable regional variation (National Research Council, 2000; Caldwell and Caldwell, 2001). In 1950, women in the developing world gave birth to about 6 children, on average, over the course of a reproductive lifetime. By 1990–1995, this figure had fallen to 3.3 children per woman in all developing countries combined, a decline of nearly half from the level at midcentury. Commenting on the modern transitions, Bongaarts and Watkins (1996: 653) note, "The pace of fertility decline in the developing world as a whole has been substantially more rapid than observed in Europe around the turn of this [twentieth] century...."

Speedy declines in mortality and fertility can bring substantial economic benefits. Declining fertility has been credited with a major contribution to the high growth rates of income per capita experienced by South Korea, Taiwan, Thailand, Singapore, Indonesia, Malaysia, and the former Hong Kong territory. With lower fertility comes an increase in the share of working-age persons in the population. Even if income per worker remains constant, this increase in the working percentage will be expressed in more rapid growth in income per capita.[8] Lower fertility may also ease the task of accumulating human and physical capital. It results in slower growth in the number of school-age children, which in turn permits an increase in educational investments per child. Moreover, reduced age dependency ratios can encourage higher national savings rates and reduce the need for certain types of public expenditure (see Mason, Merrick, and Shaw, 1999).

Cities are full participants in these national demographic transitions, and in some cases are thought to take leading roles (Shapiro and Tambashe, 2001). Because urban fertility rates are lower than rural rates, and cityward migration occurs disproportionately among the young, urban age structures are even more concentrated in the productive (and reproductive) ages than are those of national populations. Examples of this distinctive age structure are provided in Chapter 4. It may be that the economic "bonus" delivered by changes in age structure is largely an urban phenomenon, due to earlier and steeper declines in mortality and fertility in urban areas. Unfortunately, time-series data on the evolution of urban and rural vital rates and age structures were not available to the panel—the time spans covered by the Demographic and Health Surveys (DHS) are too short for such changes to be clearly discerned—and we are left to speculate about the urban role in national demographic transitions.

---

[8]An examination of national data shows substantial variation in the age dependency ratios among countries that are moving through the fertility transition at different rates (Casterline, 1999). The swings in age structure are wider when an abrupt fertility decline follows an abrupt decline in mortality, as occurred in much of East and Southeast Asia.

As demographic transitions mature, further declines in fertility, coupled with declines in adult mortality, have the effect of aging the population, increasing both the average age of the general population and the proportion of the population that is elderly. Progress against adult mortality is always desirable; when it is achieved rapidly, however, governments are given little time to adjust to the ensuing economic, social, and political disruptions. In some European countries, population aging has been a gradual process. In 1865 some 7 percent of the French population was age 65 or older. Some 115 years later, in 1980, the 65-plus percentage had crept up to 14 percent. Today, about 7 percent of China's population is aged 65 or older, and according to the U.S. Bureau of the Census (2001), it will take only 25 years for this proportion to reach 14 percent. The Chinese transition will thus occur in about one-fifth of the time that was required for the transition in France.

Some cities in developing countries are already beginning to face the challenges associated with population aging. In Argentina, for example, population aging began sooner and occurred more rapidly than in neighboring countries, so that by the 1990s, the country contained a disproportionately high number of elderly (Lloyd-Sherlock, 1997). In Greater Buenos Aires, several neighborhoods have large proportions of elderly residents, who have particular demands for specialized health and other public services (Lloyd-Sherlock, 1997). As in so much of urban demography, however, very little is known of the specifically urban features of aging. At the intersection of two major trends in the developing world—urbanization and population aging—lies very little research.

MAJOR REGIONAL DIFFERENCES

The simple description of events presented above masks enormous regional differences. There is substantial variation in the pattern of urbanization among regions and even greater variation in the growth of individual countries and cities. As noted earlier, Latin America is far more urbanized than Africa or Asia. The level of urbanization in Latin America—75 percent—already matches that of Europe and North America. Consequently, the region's rate of urbanization is now relatively slow. (Using simple mathematical methods, Chapter 4 shows why this should be so.) At the other end of the spectrum, Asia and Africa remain predominantly rural, with less than 38 percent of their populations in urban areas. Being less urbanized today, these two regions are expected to experience the most rapid rates of urbanization over the next 30 years. By 2030, some 55 percent of Africa's population and 53 percent of Asia's population are expected to be found in urban areas. The continents are also quite different in terms of total population size—Asia is much the largest—so that there are almost twice as many urban residents in Asia as in Latin America and Africa combined.

All of these regions are in the midst of major political, social, and economic transitions driven by the forces of globalization, democratization, and decentralization. The remainder of this chapter highlights some of the major differences among and within the regions. Because much of the demographic analysis in the following chapters relies on the DHS, maps are provided for each region that show the locations of the major cities and indicate which countries have been covered by a DHS survey.

Latin America

The national populations of Latin America and the Caribbean grew very rapidly during the twentieth century, with the period from 1950 to 1970 being one of exceptionally rapid growth. Population growth rates peaked in the early 1960s at 2.75 percent per annum. Latin America's population increased from 167 million in 1950 to 519 million in 2000. Three-quarters of the region's population now resides in just six countries: Argentina, Brazil, Columbia, Mexico, Peru, and Venezuela. The two largest of these, Brazil and Mexico, account for more than half of the total population of the region. Figure 3-5 shows the large cities of the region.

As noted above, Latin America has become predominantly urban, with the urban proportion having risen from 42 percent in 1950 to 75 percent in 2000. In terms of totals, the region's urban population grew from 70 million in 1950 to 391 million in 2000. With urban growth has come an increase in the number of large cities in the region. The number of million-plus cities increased from 6 in 1950 to more than 50 in 2000. (As we remarked earlier, the spatial distribution of Latin America's population is unusual in that high fractions reside in these large cities.) Latin America's four largest cities—Buenos Aires, Mexico City, Rio de Janeiro, and São Paulo—have reached sizes that could hardly have been imagined a century ago. In 1950 the largest city of the region was Buenos Aires, which at that time had a population of around 5 million; Mexico City and Rio de Janeiro each had populations of 2.9 million; and São Paulo's population was 2.4 million. By 2000, these cities had grown enormously—to 18.1 million in the case of Mexico City, 18.0 million in São Paulo, 12.0 million in Buenos Aires, and 10.7 million in Rio de Janeiro. Today Mexico City and São Paulo are two of the world's three largest urban agglomerations.

The United Nations projects that Latin America's total population will grow to 723 million by 2030. All of this growth is expected to be absorbed by its cities; indeed, the total rural population of Latin America is expected to decline slightly as the total urban population rises by more than 200 million. The year 2030 will likely see four of every five Latin Americans living in cities, in many cases substantially increasing the demand for already overburdened public services. Nevertheless, there has been a dramatic and somewhat unanticipated slowdown in the growth of some of the most important megacities in Latin America, as congestion costs and government incentives have diverted new investment beyond metropolitan boundaries. In some cases, such as in the São Paulo region of Brazil, new plants have located as far as 200 kilometers from the central core (Gilbert, 1994). In addition, many large Latin American cities were profoundly

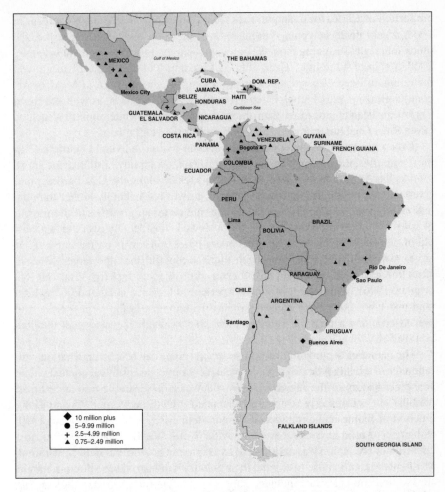

FIGURE 3-5 Cities of more than 750,000 population in Latin America and the Caribbean.

NOTE: Shading indicates that a DHS survey fielded in the country was included in the panel's dataset (see Table C-1).

SOURCES: Adapted from United Nations Centre for Human Settlements (UNCHS) (1996); United Nations (2002a).

affected in the 1980s and 1990s by severe economic recession and programs of structural adjustment.

The countries of the region differ greatly in the extent of urbanization and the pace of urban growth. At one end of the spectrum, countries such as Argentina, Chile, and Uruguay were already highly urbanized by 1950, and their rates of urbanization over the ensuing 50 years were relatively moderate. The urban proportion of Chile, for example, rose from 58 percent in 1950 to 86 percent in 2000, a gain of 28 percentage points. Over the same period, Brazil urbanized much more rapidly, going from 37 percent urban in 1950 to 81 percent urban by 2000, a gain of 44 points. Even after half a century of sustained urban growth, there remain large disparities across the region. Countries such as Mexico, Argentina, Brazil, Chile, French Guiana, Uruguay, and Venezuela, as well as several Caribbean Islands, are more than three-quarters urban, while countries such as Costa Rica, Guatemala, and Guyana remain less than half urban.

Urban growth has also been highly uneven within individual countries. In most countries, the national capitals have grown most rapidly. But in some areas, such as the Amazonia region of Brazil or in Mexico along the U.S. border, rapid economic expansion has generated rates of growth considerably higher than the national average. Generally speaking, the rate of urban growth and the growth of some of the region's largest cities have slowed considerably over the last couple of decades. In many places, secondary cities and towns on the outskirts of large metropolitan regions have been more successful than the larger cities in attracting new investment and have begun to grow more rapidly (Villa and Rodriguez, 1996). Thus the region has experienced "reverse polarization," as high land and labor costs have created urban diseconomies in the largest cities and persuaded manufacturers to relocate their plants outside the main metropolitan boundaries.

The nature of the growth of Latin American cities can best be understood with reference to the larger demographic, social, economic, and political contexts. The economic history of the region since World War II is separable into three broad periods: an era of fairly strong and sustained growth between 1945 and 1980; a period of major economic recessions and debt crises between 1980 and 1990; and an era of mild recovery thereafter. After World War II, urban growth in most countries of the region was accelerated by economic growth and industrialization. Most governments chose to expand their country's industrial base through import substitution strategies that included support for infant industries and the erecting of protective trade barriers. The majority of new industry was concentrated in a few major cities, most of them national capitals.

Urban growth slowed in Latin America in the early 1980s as the region entered a period of major social and economic upheaval and fell into a prolonged economic recession. Many Latin American countries were forced to implement stabilization and adjustment policies designed to restore their economies by reducing the size of the public sector and improving efficiency in their labor markets. As part of these reforms, governments were obliged to rethink state-driven initiatives for industrialization based on import substitution, and most governments came to place greater emphasis on the role of market forces in determining the location and nature of new economic growth. Many industries that had been developed on the basis of import substitution were forced to contract or close as local consumer markets shrank and protective barriers were removed (UNCHS, 1996).

Although there was a measure of economic recovery in the 1990s, living standards in many of the region's major cities remain lower than they were in the 1970s (Gilbert, 1996). Evidence of both absolute and relative poverty is clearly visible in all Latin American cities: large shanty towns; large numbers of poor people; high levels of underemployment and (in some cases) unemployment; insufficient urban infrastructure; poor public services; crime; and high levels of air, water, and noise pollution. Latin America remains the region with the greatest income inequality in the world, and in many Latin American cities, slum and shanty dwellers still make up a large fraction of the population of the city (see, for example, Garza, 2000; Cohen, 2002).

Africa

Africa has long been one of the least urbanized regions of the world. Most African economies are still heavily dependent on agriculture, principally at the subsistence level. In 1950, only 15 percent of the Africa population was living in cities, as compared with 17 percent in Asia and 42 percent in Latin America. Nevertheless, over the past 50 years the region has undergone relatively high rates of urban growth, a function, in part, of having relatively fewer urban residents to begin with. By 2000, some 37 percent of the region's population lived in urban areas, compared with 38 percent of Asia's population and 75 percent of Latin America's. In absolute terms, Africa's urban population grew from 32 million in 1950 to 102 million in 1975 and 295 million in 2000 (United Nations, 2002a).

Most cities in Africa are small by international standards: Cairo and Lagos, with estimated populations of 9.5 and 8.7 million, respectively, in 2000, are the only two African urban agglomerations to make the United Nations' list of the 30 largest urban agglomerations in the world (see Figure 3-6). According to the United Nations, Kinshasa, with 5.1 million residents in 2000, is the only other African city with more than 5 million residents. The United Nations estimates that there are 40 cities with 1–5 million residents. This list includes Johannesburg, which the United Nations treats as a city with an estimated population of 2.3 million in 2000, whereas other estimates put the population of the Greater Johannesburg Metropolitan Region at around 7.3 million in 1996 (Crankshaw and Parnell, 2003). The United Nations estimates that there are 39 cities with populations of 500,000 to 1 million and an unknown number with fewer than 500,000 residents. Africa's large cities play important economic and political roles, but it should be remembered that just 8 percent of Africa's urban population lives in cities of 5 million or more. The majority of urban Africans (61 percent) resides in towns or cities with fewer than 500,000 residents.

African fertility is expected to fall substantially in the coming decades, but the total population of the region is expected to continue to increase, from 794 million in 2000 to 1.5 billion in 2030, with the annual growth rate being about 2.1 percent. According to the latest United Nations projections, the urban population

FIGURE 3-6 Cities of more than 750,000 population in Africa.
NOTE: Shading indicates that a DHS survey fielded in the country was included in the panel's dataset (see Table C-1).
SOURCES: Adapted from United Nations Centre for Human Settlements (UNCHS) (1996); United Nations (2002a).

is expected to increase from 295 million in 2000 to 787 million in 2030, and its annual growth rate will be 3.3 percent. According to these projections, African society will cross the 50 percent urban threshold sometime before 2025, reaching 53 percent urban by 2030. It is expected that a large fraction of the Africa urban population will continue to reside in small towns and cities, and urban development planning for such communities should probably be given high priority.

As is the case elsewhere, understanding urban change in Africa requires consideration of the social, economic, and political history of the region. In Africa's case, the role of the colonial experience merits special consideration (Stren and

Halfani, 2001). Colonialism, which in much of Africa lasted from the late nineteenth century until at least the early 1960s, influenced the structure and pattern of African urban growth in a number of ways. Several of today's more prominent African cities—Abidjan, Johannesburg, and Nairobi—simply did not exist before colonial rule. They were founded and developed during colonial times as centers of commerce and administrative activity. More generally, however, colonialism led to the formation of an urban system that displaced the traditional networks of trade and influence that had developed over many centuries. The new urban system reflected colonial economic priorities, which emphasized the exploitation of Africa's mineral resources, primary agricultural production (including plantations), and transportation and communication activities (Stren and Halfani, 2001). These new patterns of commerce and trade, in turn, led to higher levels and new patterns of migration as Africans sought work in mines, plantations, and newly developing urban areas.

Colonial urbanization also affected the physical structure and layout of many cities. Perhaps the most obvious characteristic of colonial urban planning was the partitioning of urban space into two highly distinct zones: a "European" space that enjoyed a high level of urban infrastructure and services, and an "indigenous" space that was marginally serviced (Poisnot et al., 1989, cited in Stren and Halfani 2001). The relative indifference to the needs of the African majority is said by Stren and Halfani (2001: 468) to be "a characteristic of urban planning that was rooted in the very fabric of the colonial state."

Following independence, the population of many African cities grew rapidly, even in the absence of significant industrialization. City growth was fueled by high levels of both national population growth and spatial mobility. The availability of large numbers of jobs in a newly formed public sector and better access to health and education services, together with an urban bias in the terms of trade between primary products and manufactured goods, combined to make urban life attractive.

Since the 1970s, urban growth in Africa has been greatly affected by the region's economic crisis. A current list of ailments includes declining productivity in agriculture and industry, persistent shortfalls of foreign exchange, increasing indebtedness, worsening balance-of-payments positions, and declining real wages. In addition, in several countries the legacy of long civil wars, together with years of economic mismanagement, has generated massive and rapid population flows into cities and left economies teetering on the verge of collapse. As a consequence of these and other prolonged economic problems, many sub-Saharan African countries have been forced to implement stabilization and adjustment policies, often under the auspices of the International Monetary Fund. These policies appear to have caused considerable social and economic distress, particularly among urban residents.

The essential feature of current Africa urbanization, however, is that, unlike cities in much of Asia and Latin America, African cities are economically marginalized in the new global economy. African cities are growing despite poor macroeconomic performance and without the benefit of significant FDI in their economies. Several large cities are growing at an average rate of 4 to 5 percent, making it next to impossible to provide low-income housing, high-quality urban services, or sufficient employment.

Asia

Asia is too vast and heterogeneous a region to yield easily to generalization. Altogether the region contains 3.7 billion people, about three-fifths of the world's population, rising from around 1.4 billion in 1950 and 2.4 billion in 1975. Although population growth rates for Asia as a whole have been declining since the late 1960s, the enormous base populations to which these rates have been applied have resulted in very large increases in the population totals over the past 50 years.

Despite its relatively low level of urbanization (37.5 percent in 2000), Asia contains 1.38 billion urban residents, nearly half of the world's urban population (United Nations, 2002a). Since 1950 the region's urban population has increased by more than a factor of five, rising from 244 million in 1950 to 1.38 billion in 2000. By 2030, 53 percent of Asia's population is expected to be living in urban areas, a substantial increase from the current figure of just over 37 percent. Dominated statistically by China and India, the region contains almost 200 cities with 1 million or more residents and 22 cities with 5 million or more (see Figure 3-7). The most recent United Nations projections indicate that more than 1.25 billion people will be added to Asia's population by 2030, all of whom will be absorbed in the region's cities and towns. By 2015, 18 of the world's 30 largest megacities will be found in Asia.

Few generalizations can be meaningful for a continent that combines some of the richest countries in the world with some of the poorest and some of the largest countries and economies with some of the smallest (Hardoy, Mitlin, and Satterthwaite, 2001). Given the diversity of experience across Asia, it is useful to classify the various countries in the region according to their level of urbanization and economic development. Perhaps the most important distinction is that between Pacific Asian and non–Pacific Asian countries, but further distinctions need to be made within both of these categories.

Many cities in Pacific Asia have experienced dramatic economic growth as the region has become integrated into the global economy. Cities on the forefront of global restructuring, such as Hong Kong, Singapore, Seoul, and Taipei, enjoyed unprecedented growth rates of more than 10 percent per annum throughout the 1970s and early 1980s. All of these cities rank among the top trading cities in the world; the level of gross national product (GNP) per capita in Hong Kong and Singapore exceeds that of many European countries. Similarly rapid urban transformation is now being seen in the "new" newly industrializing economies (NIEs) of Malaysia, Thailand, and Indonesia.

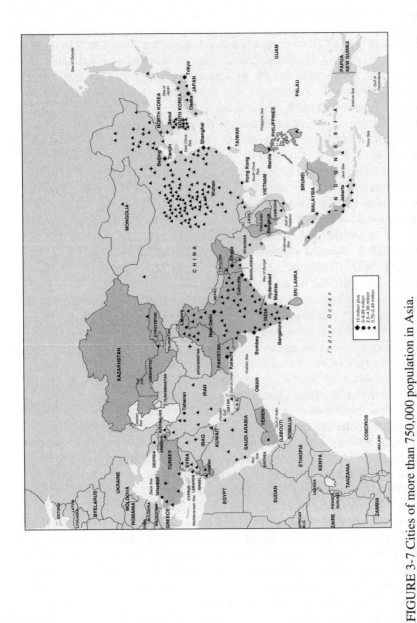

FIGURE 3-7 Cities of more than 750,000 population in Asia.

NOTE: Shading indicates that a DHS survey fielded in the country was included in the panel's dataset (see Table C-1).

SOURCES: Adapted from United Nations Centre for Human Settlements (UNCHS) (1996); United Nations (2002a).

At the national level, China remains a predominantly rural country with a level of GNP per capita that places it in the lower–middle-income range. But parts of China resemble the rapidly developing Pacific Asian economies. Its coastal region has witnessed very rapid urban and industrial development since 1978, when the government departed from its earlier policy of self-reliance and initiated a new "open policy" designed to attract foreign investment and technology. In the early years of this policy, foreign investment was limited to the four Special Economic Zones (SEZs)—Shenzhen, Zhuhai, Xiamen, and Shantou—which were to serve as testing grounds for a country-wide export-oriented development strategy. Gradually, other special zones have been established. The result has been phenomenal economic growth for these zones and a massive increase in export-led foreign exchange earnings for China as a whole (Yeung and Hu, 1992).

In Shenzhen, for example, which was chosen as one of the four initial SEZs because of its close proximity to Hong Kong, the value of industrial output in 1987 was almost 70 times its 1980 value, implying an annual rate of growth of 60 percent per annum (Wong, Cai, and Chen, 1992; Yeung and Chu, 1998). Similarly, Xiamen, located directly opposite the island of Taiwan, has enjoyed extraordinarily rapid export-led growth and industrialization over the last 20 years, thanks in large part to strong ties with overseas Chinese that brought an influx of FDI (Yeung and Chu, 2000). Xiamen's gross domestic product (GDP) increased by a factor of 57 between 1980 and 1997, implying an average rate of growth of 23 percent per annum (Howell, 2000). Similarly, coastal cities such as Dalian, Guangzhou, Qingdao, and Tianjin have all undergone remarkable transformations over the last 20 years since the government's open policy began (Yeung and Hu, 1992).

In Shanghai, the transformation is more recent but perhaps even more striking. Long the largest industrial city and the economic powerhouse of socialist China, Shanghai was one of the 14 cities designated open in 1984. The city initially experienced relatively modest growth, lagging well behind Guangdong, Fujian, and other parts of Southern China (Yeung and Sung, 1996; Yeung, 2000). The pace of urban development in Shanghai picked up after 1990, when the central government announced the development of Pudong New Area, a large area of agricultural and marginal land east of the central city. Since 1991, the growth of FDI in the city has been nothing short of astonishing. In 1985, Shanghai attracted US$759 million in FDI. By 1996, this figure had increased to $15.14 billion (Wu, 2000). The city is now being dramatically restructured (Wu, 2000; Wu and Yusuf, 2003).

Even after taking these various success stories out of the mix, it remains difficult to characterize the remainder of Asia, particularly when one considers that this part of the world contains tens of thousands of urban centers. In India alone, according to its 2001 census, there are more than 300 cities of over 100,000 population and 35 with more than a million residents (Government of India, 2001). For the most part, the non–Pacific Asian countries have significantly lower levels of GNP per capita than the Pacific Asian countries, but there is considerable diversity within and among countries in their economic and urban characteristics. Relative to some cities in Pacific Asia, urban growth in such cities as Bombay, Calcutta, Delhi, Karachi, and Dhaka, for example, has probably been fueled less by economic dynamism and more by rural poverty and continued high fertility.

Cities in the former Soviet republics—Kazakhstan, Kyrgyzstan, Tajikistan, Turkmenistan, and Uzbekistan in central Asia; Armenia, Azerbaijan, and Georgia in western Asia—have followed a somewhat different pattern. Until the collapse of the former Soviet Union, these countries operated under systems of centralized planning in which government decisions rather than market forces determined the nature, scale, and spatial distribution of economic activity (Kostinskiy, 2001). Oddly distinctive patterns of urban development resulted. For example, the lack of a market for land in Soviet cities led them to grow in concentric rings with vast amounts of unused land dispersed throughout (Becker and Morrison, 1999). The limited role permitted to private housing markets and private enterprise and the emphasis on large-scale housing estates imposed a very different logic on the form and spatial distribution of cities than that seen in the West (Harloe, 1996; UNCHS, 1996). In addition, there was a general tendency among Soviet policy makers to favor large-scale industrial production over the service and retail sectors, and industries were often located in a manner that a market economy would not have tolerated. There was also a tendency to keep plants in production long after they would have been deemed unprofitable or too expensive in the West.

The end of the Cold War and the collapse of the Soviet Union have had enormous social, economic, and demographic consequences. Political destabilization and exposure to world market forces have resulted in an unprecedented decline in economic output and widespread poverty, which in turn have forced a reassessment of the location, functioning, and organization of productive activity and engendered great uncertainty about the future. These developments are most apparent in cities, and in some countries they appear to have sent large and small cities in very different directions.

Between 1987 and 1994, marriage rates in the newly independent states fell by 25–50 percent, divorce rates in some newly independent states rose by 25 percent, birth rates declined by 20–40 percent, and male life expectancy fell by about 6 years (Cornia and Paniccià, 1999; Becker and Hemley, 1998). Death rates among middle-aged male adults rose dramatically as the result of a large increase in cardiovascular disease and other preventable diseases, such as tuberculosis, bronchitis, pneumonia, and dysentery, as well as accidents, injuries, and violence (Becker and Bloom, 1998). In addition, the republics on the periphery of the former Soviet Union witnessed significant ethnic-based migration, partly as a response to deteriorating urban living conditions and economic and social stress and partly as a response to growing regional nationalism. In Kazakhstan, for example, 11 percent of the population emigrated between 1990 and 1999, leading to deurbanization in the aggregate (Musabek, Becker, Seitenova, and Urzhumova, 2001). A similar pattern of outmigration of Russians and other non-Kyrgyz ethnic groups was also recorded in neighboring Kyrgyzstan in the years immediately following the breakup of the Soviet Union (Anderson and Becker, 2001).

CONCLUSIONS

The United Nations predicts that almost all of the world's population growth for the foreseeable future will occur in the cities and towns of developing countries. In Africa, Asia, and Latin America alike, population growth is becoming largely an urban phenomenon. By 2030, almost 60 percent of the population of poor countries will live in urban areas, and this spatial transformation can be expected to reshape social, economic, and political realms. For many if not most of the urban residents of poor countries, city life will take place in the context of very large cities whose scale will present residents and their governments with distinctive challenges. Without doubt, the challenges of city scale that will be faced in poor countries are unprecedented, and will call for flexible and novel responses.

As this chapter has shown, the regional and international settings in which cities find themselves are roiling with change, presenting cities and governments with many unsettling developments. Globalization is bestowing its benefits and bestrewing its costs in a highly uneven fashion, with the benefits being most apparent in Pacific Asia and parts of Latin America. Most African economies stand apart from the global circuits, and they seldom partake of the FDI and technological changes that are being experienced elsewhere.

The novelty, pace, and distribution of globalization suggest that the phenomenon may well transform the demographic aspects of urban transitions. It is possible to conceive of profound effects, but empirical linkages between demographic behavior and measures of globalization have not yet been established. Insightful demographic studies might be focused on the cities and surrounding rural regions of Pacific Asia, with attention to fertility and marriage, as well as migration. We can imagine research designs for Pudong or Shenzhen that might be highly illuminating about the local demographic expressions of global economic forces. For instance, as capital flows to the large cities of these regions, are their small cities likely to be starved of the capital they need, or will large-city growth be accompanied by beneficial economic spillovers? Studies of such issues have yet to be undertaken.

Conventional demographic approaches reveal that when compared with the historical precedents, recent urban transitions differ sharply in some aspects but differ rather little in others. As the analysis in this chapter has shown, rates of urban population growth are high relative to the historical standard, although it appears that rates of urbanization are not. High rates of urban growth in today's developing countries are at least as much the product of high rates of urban natural increase as of rural-to-urban migration. Recent estimates by the United

Nations strongly confirm earlier estimates, which attributed some 60 percent of urban growth to urban natural increase, with the balance left to migration and reclassification. Policy makers do not appear to have fully understood the contribution of urban natural increase. If it is typically the greater part of urban growth, a correct assessment of the situation should bring a renewed appreciation of the role that might be played by urban family planning programs in restraining urban growth.

4

Urban Population Dynamics: Models, Measures, and Forecasts

This chapter brings analytic tools to bear on the urban levels and trends described in the previous chapter. Our treatment of the issues is narrowly demographic, particularly at the outset, focusing on what might be termed the proximate causes of urban growth. Rural-to-urban migration is one of these proximate causes; of equal importance are the rates of urban and rural natural increase and the relative sizes of the urban and rural populations. Territorial reclassification must also be considered. In placing emphasis on this small set of demographic variables, we are mindful of their uncertain causal status. Rates of migration and natural increase are at once the cause and the consequence of larger social and economic forces. Even reclassification touches on economic, fiscal, and political concerns. In the chapters to follow, the socioeconomic content of the demographic variables will be explored in depth.

This chapter begins by describing the features of urban population dynamics that can be seen even with the simplest of analytic mechanisms. A model of urban and rural population growth is developed to show how an initial urban and rural population distribution, when subjected to fixed demographic rates, can produce a variety of demographic outcomes: annual increases in the total urban population, the share of those increases due to migration, rates of urban growth, levels of urbanization, and their rates of change. Using projections, we highlight several regularities that can help in understanding the empirical record.

The chapter then draws upon the Demographic and Health Surveys (DHS) for evidence on the main contributors to urban population growth—fertility, mortality, and migration—which act together to determine urban age composition. As will be seen, urban populations are much more concentrated in the productive and reproductive ages than are rural populations. Where age is concerned, urban populations are configured for higher potential economic productivity. With respect to the reproductive ages, however, these populations are also configured in a way that enhances the potential for high fertility—although later marriage and greater contraceptive use generally keep this potential from being realized—and that raises the profile of reproductive health concerns and other diseases affecting young adults.

To shed light on the contribution of migration, we analyze the DHS data on recent moves, linking these data to measures of city size. This analysis exposes several weaknesses in the basic infrastructure of urban population research. First, because the DHS surveys are generally restricted to women of reproductive age, they reveal little about the situations of men and other migrants. Second, the geographic identifiers supplied with DHS datasets are so coarse that it is difficult to determine even the name of the city in which a survey respondent lives, unless that city happens to be the nation's capital. Third, the population of the city in question is available from United Nations sources if the city is a capital, but otherwise can be determined only for cities above 100,000 in population. Moreover, only "raw" estimates of city size, taken from the United Nations *Demographic Yearbooks*, are available for cities in the range of 100,000 to 750,000 population. The expertise of the United Nations Population Division, as expressed in its influential series *World Urbanization Prospects*, is focused only upon cities larger than this. In short, a rather mundane analysis task brings alarming research gaps into view.

The next section turns a critical eye on the two United Nations databases used in urban population research—the annual *Demographic Yearbooks* and the biennial *World Urbanization Prospects*. In this field, *World Urbanization Prospects* has assumed the role of a standard reference work; it is the authoritative, comprehensive source of urban population estimates and projections upon which most researchers and institutions rely. Because it assembles data over time, *World Urbanization Prospects* provides an especially rich set of materials on urban growth, with detailed time series for all of the world's large cities. But the occasional user of these data is apt to be misled by their attractive packaging, and may need to be reminded of the weaknesses and heterogeneities of the population series that are available to the United Nations and the difficulties it faces in adequately estimating and projecting urban populations.

The chapter then examines the record of urban population projections, an issue of fundamental importance that has attracted curiously little attention apart from the efforts of the United Nations and Brockerhoff (1999). As will be seen, the history of city size projections does not inspire confidence. The urban record of success is so thin that a recent authoritative assessment of national-level demographic projections (National Research Council, 2000) does not even consider the possibility of projecting the national populations of developing countries by conducting separate rural and urban projections. Evidently we are still some distance from being able to apply modern statistical techniques to urban population time series.

Having reviewed the aggregate databases, we turn to new developments in the area of spatially disaggregated geographic information systems (GIS). As a locus of several new technologies, GIS holds promise for restoring a spatial dimension to the (typically) aspatial data gathered through demographic surveys and related sources. There is at least the possibility that data collected according to GIS principles might strengthen the foundation for urban population projection. GIS technology is perhaps even more promising as a political device, that is, as a mechanism for fostering dialogue among the units of government that collect data, those that supply services, and the urban residents who wish to make use of such services. We document several of the encouraging efforts now under way. The chapter ends by emphasizing the infrastructure that will be needed to support urban population research.

THE SIMPLE ANALYTICS

Five demographic indicators are required to sketch the main developments in an urban transition: the absolute annual increase in the urban population, the share of that increase attributable to migration, the urban growth rate, the level of urbanization, and the rate of urbanization. In the model presented below, all five indicators result from the repeated application of constant demographic rates to an initial population distribution.[1]

Key Concepts and Notation

To highlight the essentials, we abstract from the problem of reclassification and focus on a hypothetical country divided into rural and urban sectors that are fixed in geographical terms. Age dependence in fertility, mortality, and migration rates is initially ignored. The results thus obtained would generally continue to hold in an age-differentiated simulation (Rogers, 1995).

In this stylized representation, national population size in year t is denoted by P_t, the size of the urban population by U_t, and that of the rural population by R_t. Given the sizes of the rural and urban populations in a base year—R_0 and U_0, respectively—the totals U_t and R_t evolve in a manner determined by four demographic rates, each of which is expressed on a per annum basis:

n_u the rate of natural increase in the urban population, that is, the difference between urban birth and death rates

n_r the rate of natural increase in the rural population

$m_{r,u}$ the migration rate from rural to urban areas, expressed per rural resident

$m_{u,r}$ the migration rate from urban to rural areas, expressed per urban resident

---

[1] For more detail on the equations and their derivation, see Appendix B and United Nations (1974, 1998b).

As discussed in Appendix B, which presents more of the mathematical detail, from these simple ingredients the model can generate time paths for the five urban outcome measures mentioned above.

To proceed, we must define some terms. The *urban population increment* is the net addition to the urban population from year $t - 1$ to year t, or

$$\Delta U_t = U_t - U_{t-1}.$$

We make use of an equivalent representation,

$$\Delta U_t = U_{t-1} \cdot (n_u - m_{u,r}) + R_{t-1} \cdot m_{r,u}, \tag{4.1}$$

in which the roles of the demographic rates and the population distribution are more clearly evident.[2] The *urban growth rate* is another measure of change in the total urban population over a single year; it is expressed not in absolute terms, but as a fraction of the initial urban population:

$$UGR_t = \frac{U_t - U_{t-1}}{U_{t-1}} = \frac{\Delta U_t}{U_{t-1}}.$$

This, too, can be given a useful alternative form:

$$UGR_t = n_u - m_{u,r} + \frac{R_{t-1}}{U_{t-1}} \cdot m_{r,u}. \tag{4.2}$$

The *migrant share* of urban growth, denoted MS_t, is the proportion of net urban growth that is due to migration from rural areas. The share can be written as

$$MS_t = \left(1 + \frac{U_{t-1}}{R_{t-1}} \cdot \frac{n_u - m_{u,r}}{m_{r,u}}\right)^{-1}. \tag{4.3}$$

As is evident in equations (4.2) and (4.3), the urban growth rate and the share of growth due to migration are determined by several constants—the rate of urban natural increase and rates of migration to and from urban areas—as well as a time-varying factor, U_{t-1}/R_{t-1}, the urban/rural population balance.

Because urban population increments, growth rates, and migrant shares are closely related, they are often discussed as a group. So, too, are the following measures, which concisely summarize levels and trends. The *level of urbanization* is simply the urban proportion (or percentage),

$$P_{u,t} = \frac{U_t}{P_t},$$

---

[2] A counterpart expression for the rural increment would include the term $n_r - m_{r,u}$. This term is generally positive. See, for instance, Oucho and Gould (1993) on net rural increase in sub-Saharan Africa.

and the *rate of urbanization* is the rate of growth in this proportion over time. It can be written as

$$\frac{\Delta P_{u,t}}{P_{u,t-1}} = \frac{U_t - U_{t-1}}{U_{t-1}} - \frac{P_t - P_{t-1}}{P_{t-1}},$$

which is the difference between the urban and national population growth rates.

Even a model as simple as this can help clarify otherwise puzzling and counterintuitive aspects of urban transitions. We use it to address several questions. First, if urban growth results from both migration and natural increase, which of these accounts for the greater share of growth? Should the migration share be regarded as a constant or as a time trend? How are urban growth rates linked to the rate of urbanization? Do national population growth rates translate directly into rates of urban growth (according to Preston [1979], a 1-point decline in national growth reduces urban growth by the same amount), or can we anticipate a systematic change in the relationship between the rates as urbanization proceeds?

City Growth: Migration or Natural Increase?

Much of the concern surrounding urban growth has to do with the annual additions to their populations that cities must somehow absorb, and with the contribution to growth that is made by rural-to-urban migrants. As discussed earlier, demographers often find themselves emphasizing the role of urban natural increase (see United Nations, 1980; Chen, Valente, and Zlotnik, 1998), if only to counter the impression that migration must be the dominant factor. To disentangle migration from natural increase is more difficult than might be supposed; an analytic model is helpful in showing just where the problems lie.

As Rogers (1982) explains, to understand whether migration or natural increase is the dominant source of growth, one must first decide on terms. Much depends on whether one conceives of the problem in terms of *flows* or *stocks*. Flows are, by definition, short-term measures. Their empirical counterparts are found in the decompositions of intercensal urban growth that separate urban natural increase on the one hand from the sum of net migration and reclassification on the other. According to such flow estimates—as discussed in Chapter 3—the share of migration in urban growth is in the neighborhood of 40 percent in most developing countries. Stocks, by contrast, are cumulative measures. If the migrant contribution is to be assessed in terms of stocks, the estimate should take into account not only the migrants themselves, but also their descendants. To understand the cumulative contribution of migration to urban growth, one would compare the size of an urban population with what it would have been in the absence of rural-to-urban migration (i.e., with $m_{r,u} = 0$) or with lower rates of migration than occurred. Of course, if migration is permitted cities will grow larger than they would otherwise, but the size of the difference is of interest.[3]

Because flows depend on stocks—for example, the flow of rural-to-urban migrants is $m_{r,u} \cdot R_{t-1}$, with R_{t-1} being the stock of rural population—one cannot cleanly separate them. For analytic purposes, it is preferable to distinguish *direct effects* from *feedback effects* and to focus attention on the implications of changes in the fundamental rates. Consider, then, the consequences of a change in n_u, the urban rate of natural increase. Returning to the migration share equation (4.3), we see that at time t, the direct effect of an increase in n_u is to reduce the share of migration in urban growth, as would be expected. Likewise, the direct effect of an increase in the rural-to-urban migration rate, $m_{r,u}$, is to increase the migration share, again as would be expected. In either case, the amount of change produced in the migration share depends on several factors, one of which is the urban/rural balance, U_{t-1}/R_{t-1}.

Once rates have changed, feedback effects come into play, and these effects exert further influence on the migrant share. Higher rates of urban natural increase, n_u, tip the population balance toward urban areas, causing U_{t-1}/R_{t-1} to rise with time. The more rapid population shift toward cities diminishes the relative size of the rural sector, and this in turn diminishes the relative contribution of rural migrants to city growth. The direct and feedback effects of n_u work in the same direction; through both routes, a higher rate of urban natural increase reduces the migrant share of urban growth.

Applying the same kind of analysis to the rural-to-urban migration rate, we find that an increase in $m_{r,u}$ generates feedbacks that work against the direct effect. As explained above, the direct effect is to increase the share of urban growth due to migrants; but with faster rural outmigration, the population balance begins to shift toward urban areas. Over time, this feedback acts to reduce the migrant share.

The opposition of forces can be seen in Figure 4-1, which shows the share of urban growth due to migration for values of $m_{r,u}$ ranging from 0.5 percent per annum to 3.0 percent.[4] Higher migration rates are associated initially, and through most of the projection period, with larger migrant shares. As feedback

---

[3]The flows–stocks perspective has often proven helpful; for instance, it was used by the National Research Council (1997) to analyze the full contribution of international migration to the population of the United States.

[4]All projections begin with an urban proportion of $P_{u,0} = 0.15$. For the other parameters of the projections, we have been guided by Livi Bacci (1997) for natural increase and by the United Nations (1980) and Chen, Valente, and Zlotnik (1998) for migration. Chen, Valente, and Zlotnik (1998) present regional estimates of $m_{r,u}$ that range from 0.5 percent (Africa in the 1980s) to 2.65 percent (Latin America in the 1970s). Earlier, the United Nations (1980) provided estimates ranging from 0.05 percent for Nepal in the 1960s to 3.7 percent for Venezuela in the 1950s. We restrict $m_{r,u}$ to lie between 0.5 and 3 percent. The reverse urban-to-rural migration rate, $m_{u,r}$, is set to 0.25 percent throughout.

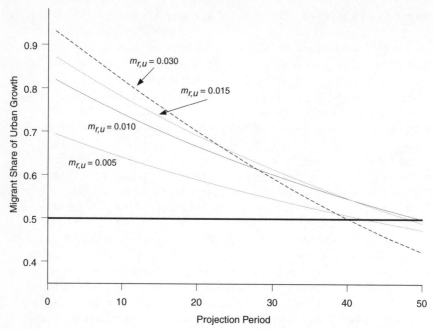

FIGURE 4-1 Declining migrant shares of urban growth.

effects exert their influence, however, all these curves decline and show a tendency to converge.

The point at which the migrant share of growth reaches one-half has been termed the *cross-over point* by Keyfitz and Ledent (Rogers, 1982, citing their papers). As can be seen in the curve with $m_{r,u} = 0.03$, depicted by a dashed line in Figure 4-1, very high rates of rural-to-urban migration can hasten the arrival of the cross-over point and produce lower migrant shares thereafter than would be seen in a regime of lower migration rates. The apparent paradox is an expression of a feedback effect.

Urban Growth and the Rate of Urbanization

The rate of urban growth obeys a similar logic. Urban natural increase, n_u, has a positive direct effect on the rate of urban growth (see equation (4.2)). The direct effect of the rural-to-urban migration rate, $m_{r,u}$, is also positive, but its strength varies with the urban/rural population balance. When $m_{r,u}$ rises, the rural sector begins to decline in relative importance, and the urban growth rate then falls. Over the long term, the urban growth rate will approach

$$\overline{UGR} = n_u - m_{u,r} + \frac{m_{r,u}}{b},$$

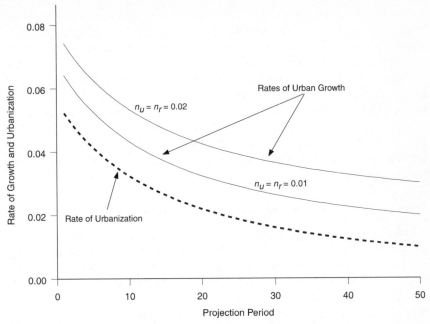

FIGURE 4-2 Rates of urban growth and urbanization.

where b is the long-term urban/rural balance, that is, the value taken by U_t/R_t in the limit.[5]

As was shown earlier, high rates of natural increase have been a defining feature of the demographic regimes of many developing countries and distinguish their urban transitions from the Western historical experience. As just noted, a higher n_u produces more rapid urban growth; working indirectly through migration, a higher rural n_r also produces more rapid urban growth. Although they have powerful effects on the urban growth rate, n_u and n_r need not have any particular implications for the rate of urbanization. As can be seen in Appendix B, equation (B.6), if n_u and n_r happen to be equal, they can be scaled up or down with no direct effect on the rate of urbanization. The projections depicted in Figure 4-2 illustrate the point. In this figure, the rates of natural increase are set to 2 percent (the upper curve) and 1 percent (the middle curve). These two curves exhibit high initial urban growth rates that are followed by growth rate declines. Meanwhile, the rate of urbanization—shown with the dashed line—remains wholly unaffected, adhering to the same trajectory whether the natural rates of increase are high or low.

If equality in urban and rural rates of natural increase appears to be a special case, consider data from the United Nations (1980: Tables 10–12). These

---

[5]Of course, the rates must be such that the limit exists; see Appendix B.

data show that in the 1950s and 1960s, a number of developing countries had values of n_u and n_r that were roughly equal. In the 27 developing countries examined by the United Nations, fertility and mortality rates were lower in urban than in rural areas, but the differences between fertility and mortality were about the same.[6] When n_u is approximately equal to n_r, as in these cases, the rate of urbanization is all but entirely attributable to migration. If $n_u \neq n_r$ or if these rates change by different amounts, their effects will be expressed in the rate of urbanization, producing a different path of urbanization than that which appears in Figure 4-2. For example, countries with slower rates of urban than rural natural increase ($n_u < n_r$) will tend to have slower rates of urbanization, other things being equal.

Urban and National Population Growth

As noted in Appendix B, equation (B.5), national population growth rates can be written as a weighted average of the urban and rural rates of natural increase, with the weights being the proportions of urban and rural residents in the national total. In the fixed-rate analytic model—compare equations (B.2) and (B.5) in Appendix B—it is clear that national and urban growth rates depend on n_u and n_r in much the same way, and this implies that national and urban growth will tend to be positively correlated.[7]

Figure 4-3 charts the relationship between the two rates of growth over the course of one projection.[8] The two rates are positively associated, as expected, although they are linked in a nonlinear fashion. At the outset of the projection (see the upper right portion of the figure), both the urban and national growth rates are high; as the country urbanizes, both rates fall. With increasing urbanization, the slope of the relationship between urban and national growth rates flattens.

One might well expect to see the main features of Figure 4-3 reproduced in empirical urban growth regressions. Indeed, demographers have uncovered strong regularities in the association between urban and national rates of growth. In one analysis using a sample of cities in both developing and developed countries (Preston, 1979; United Nations, 1980), a regression of urban growth rates on national growth rates yielded a coefficient for national growth that was very close to unity. The relationship was revisited by Brockerhoff (1999) with a sample limited to

---

[6]The United Nations tables show that even in this era, rural rates of natural increase were often slightly higher than urban rates. It is not clear whether the generalization $n_u \approx n_r$ still stands. An inspection of recent data (United Nations, 2000: Tables 9 and 18) shows that in the 10 countries with data available for the 1990s (most of these 10 being in West Asia), the urban rate of natural increase falls well short of the rural rate. However, according to Visaria (1997), rates of natural increase in India are about the same in urban and rural areas.

[7]Of course, if $n_u = n_r$, the national growth rate would be invariant to the distribution of population between urban and rural areas.

[8]In this projection, $n_u = 0.01$, $n_r = 0.02$, and $m_{r,u} = 0.01$. Recall that $m_{u,r} = 0.0025$ in this and all other projections.

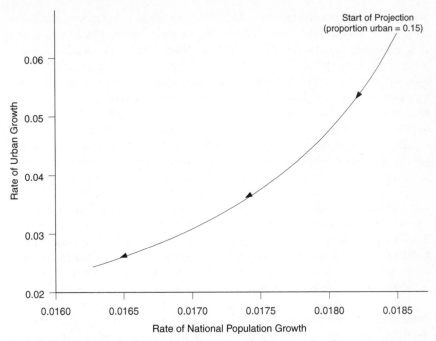

FIGURE 4-3 Rates of urban and national population growth, given $n_u < n_r$.

developing countries; his regression yielded a coefficient estimate of about 0.8. Such differences in regression coefficients are to be expected when the analysis samples differ in the average level of urbanization.[9] In this case, however, the countries in the Brockerhoff sample are less urbanized on average, leaving it doubtful that the lower coefficient estimate found by Brockerhoff is due to the changing curvature of Figure 4-3.

Note that when $n_u < n_r$, a higher rural-to-urban migration rate $m_{r,u}$ reduces the national population growth rate because it speeds the transfer of population to the urban sector where the natural rate of growth is lower. At the same time, a higher $m_{r,u}$ increases the rate of urban growth. Hence, changes in the migration rate would cause urban and national population growth rates to be negatively correlated, other things being held equal.

Migration and Urban Age Structure

As is well known, rural-to-urban migration rates are strongly influenced by age, and this age dependence is reflected in urban and rural age distributions. As

---

[9] In reaching these conclusions, both Preston (1979) and Brockerhoff (1999) use multivariate regression and include covariates other than national growth rates in their specifications. The initial level of urbanization, used in both analyses, proves to have a negative, strongly significant influence on the rate of urban growth. The link to the level of urbanization is implicit in Figure 4-3.

will be documented shortly using DHS data, in urban populations proportionately more residents are found in the prime working and reproductive ages, and proportionately fewer residents are children. Such differences are attributable to lower urban fertility and the age selectivity of rural-to-urban migration. But the relationship between migration and urban age composition is more complex than it might at first appear. In supplying cities with more young adults, rural-to-urban migration also tends to increase the urban crude birth rate, and higher birth rates, in turn, partly offsets the direct effects of migration on age structure.

To further clarify the role of migration, we constructed an age-differentiated demographic simulation that makes use of model schedules of fertility, mortality, marriage, and migration. The approach is inspired by Rogers (1986) and draws on demographic schedules developed by Rogers (1995), Coale and Trussell (1974), and Ewbank, de León, and Stoto (1983). Consider two hypothetical populations, one rural and the other urban, between which there is no migration. Both populations share the same (high) mortality rate ($e_0 = 45$) and total fertility rate ($TFR = 6.0$), and we assume that they have each attained stable age distributions. We then open the border between the two populations and allow for migration in both directions. We assume, however, that the rural-to-urban migration rates are higher.[10]

Figure 4-4 depicts the consequences. The first wave of rural-to-urban migrants increases the proportion of urban residents of reproductive age (shown on the right scale of the figure). As these new urban residents marry and bear children, the urban crude birth rate increases from its initial stable population value. Meanwhile the rural crude birth rate declines from its stable value; although there is migration in both directions, the schedules we have adopted ensure a net transfer of young adults to urban areas. Once the urban crude birth rates have been driven higher, the share of those aged 15–49 in the urban population begins to fall as the proportion of children rises (the latter proportion is not shown).

The inflation of urban crude birth rates is temporary; it subsides as the first cohorts of rural migrants work their way through the urban age distribution, and the urban and rural birth rates then approach each other. The urban crude birth rate remains higher than the rural rate, however, as a result of the continuing influence of rural-to-urban migration. All this occurs even though the rural and urban rates of fertility, marriage, and mortality are assumed to be equal at each age. The effects displayed in the figure are purely compositional. Even so, they serve as a reminder of one important role of rural-to-urban migration: it increases the share of the urban population in the reproductive ages.

The analytic models we have been using are based on assumptions of fixed demographic rates—whether these are aggregate rates of natural increase and migration in the simpler projection model, or fixed underlying schedules in the model with age structure. If such models are to help in sorting out the empirical record,

---

[10]Initially, the urban share of the combined population is 15 percent; by the end of the projection, this share has risen to about 56 percent.

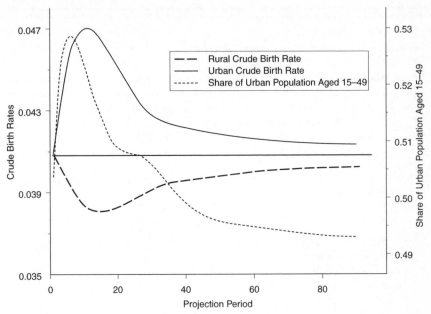

FIGURE 4-4 Changes in rural and urban crude birth rates and age structure with migration. Results from projections using model schedules.

care must be taken to separate the dynamic implications of fixed rates from the implications of changing rates. To appreciate this point, consider again the urban growth rate and the migrant share of that growth. In a fixed-rate regime, we would expect to see a decline in the urban growth rate with time as rural-to-urban migration diminishes in relative importance (equation (4.2)). The migrant share of growth would also be expected to decline with time (equation (4.3)). But when the demographic rates are changing, the forces that propel the trends may need to be reinterpreted. For example, the urban rate of natural increase, n_u, may fall as a result of reductions in urban fertility. If n_u falls, urban growth rates will also tend to fall, but the share of urban growth due to migration will tend to rise—an outcome not predicted by a fixed-rate model.

On balance, then, it is sensible to view empirical trends as resulting from a combination of fixed-rate dynamics and the dynamics stemming from demographic transitions. Without additional evidence, empirical time series provide ambiguous testimony as to the relative importance of these dynamic forces. The ambiguity is evident in the empirical record of urban Brazil, described in Box 4.1. Here, over the course of three decades, one can see clear evidence of decline in the growth rates of the country's six largest cities. However, that decline can be variously interpreted: as the workings of a fixed-rate model, as the result of declines over time in urban fertility and rates of natural increase, or as a combination of the two.

BOX 4.1 Declining Growth Rates Experienced by Brazil's Six Largest Cities, 1970–1996

São Paulo's average annual growth rate (UGR) fell from 4.36 percent in the 1970s to 1.42 percent during 1991–1996. Annual growth in Rio de Janeiro also fell, from 2.41 to 0.75 percent (Lam and Dunn, 2001). Likewise, growth slowed in the next four of Brazil's largest cities. For all these cities combined—they contained nearly 40 million persons in 1996—the growth rate fell from 3.59 percent in the 1970s to to 1.29 percent by 1991–1996, leaving the UGR at slightly more than one-third of its 1970s level. Reductions in fertility rates are believed to have played an important part in the UGR decline. Meanwhile, the city populations continued to grow in absolute terms even as their rates of growth waned. The annual population increments (ΔU_t) to these six large cities were on the order of 1 million persons in the 1970s, fell to about 600,000 persons in the 1980s, and fell further to some 500,000 persons in the 1990s.

City	Total Population (in thousands)				Average Annual Growth Rate		
	1970	1980	1991	1996	1970–80	1980–91	1991–96
São Paulo	8,137	12,589	15,445	16,582	4.36	1.86	1.42
Rio de Janeiro	7,082	9,014	9,815	10,192	2.41	0.77	0.75
Belo Horizonte	1,606	2,540	3,436	3,803	4.59	2.75	2.03
Porto Alegre	1,531	2,231	3,028	3,245	3.77	2.78	1.39
Recife	1,793	2,347	2,920	3,088	2.69	1.99	1.12
Salvador	1,149	1,767	2,497	2,709	4.30	3.14	1.63
TOTAL	21,298	30,488	37,140	39,619	3.59	1.79	1.29

SOURCE: Lam and Dunn (2001).

FERTILITY, MORTALITY, MIGRATION, AND URBAN AGE STRUCTURE

This section brings data from the DHS to bear on the demographic concepts outlined in the previous section. We preface the discussion with a note on how migrant shares of growth are usually calculated from aggregate census data. This aggregate procedure, which offers estimates of a component of urban growth that cannot be reliably obtained from sample surveys of the size usually fielded, has both weaknesses and strengths. We then present estimates from the DHS for recent migration, examine the place of urban-origin migrants among all migrants, and conduct an analysis of migration by the size of the destination city. Finally, estimates of urban and rural fertility and mortality are presented, and urban age structures are illustrated.

Migrant Shares as Calculated from Censuses

Methodological problems bedevil all attempts to determine the relative contributions of migration, natural increase, and reclassification to urban growth. When data are lacking on migration as such, the contribution of migrants to urban growth can be estimated only imprecisely. The usual "residual" method, which generated the findings of Chen, Valente, and Zlotnik (1998) described in the previous chapter, begins with a comparison of population counts in two censuses. The urban population of the second census is projected from that of the first, making an allowance for intercensal mortality.[11] When the projected urban population is subtracted from the total counted in the second census, what remains is an estimate of the sum of net migration and territorial reclassification. Errors in the census data and in the assumptions are also embedded in this residual. Although errors are always a concern, the residual method gives at least a rough estimate of the relative contributions of natural increase on the one hand and migration coupled with reclassification on the other.[12] Migration data can be gathered by other means, such as through sample surveys, but it is difficult to imagine how survey interviewers could collect any meaningful information about reclassification from their respondents. In this limited sense, the aggregate census-based method delivers information that surveys cannot.

---

[11] Suppose that the two censuses are exactly a decade apart. Let $N_u^1(a)$ be the number of persons of age a recorded in the first census. Let $\mu_u(a)$ be the urban mortality hazard function. If all urban residents found in the first census remain urban, a decade later one would expect to find

$$P_u^2(a+10) = N_u^1(a) \exp\left(-\int_a^{a+10} \mu_u(x)dx\right)$$

survivors in urban areas. Let $N_u^2(a+10)$ represent the number of urbanites aged $a+10$ who were actually recorded in the second census. The difference $D_u(a+10) = N_u^2(a+10) - P_u^2(a+10)$ is then an estimate of the sum of net migration and reclassification for this age group. Net migration is the difference between the number of rural migrants, $M_{r,u}(a+10)$, who arrived between the censuses (and survived to the date of the second census) and the number of formerly urban residents, $M_{u,r}(a+10)$, who left. Any remainder in $D_u(a+10)$ is attributable to net reclassification. Summing $D_u(a+10)$ over all $a > 0$ yields a total for net migration and reclassification in the population above 10 years of age at the time of the second census.

There remains a need to calculate something akin to $D_u(a)$ for the population aged 10 and under, and assumptions about urban fertility must be invoked to do so. The United Nations (1980) explains the method, which relies on urban child–woman ratios. The key assumption is that the same fertility schedule applies to all women in urban areas, whether they are intercensal migrants or not. As will be seen in Chapter 6, there is some empirical justification for the assumption that, relatively soon upon arrival, rural-to-urban migrants exhibit about the same age-specific fertility rates as urban natives. But counterexamples doubtless exist, and the literature has not yet settled into consensus.

Another complication is that it is rather rare to have estimates of $\mu_u(a)$ that are actually derived from urban data. Generally the urban mortality curve must be calculated from national data that include the rural population, and assumptions about relative risks are required to extract an urban estimate. As explained by Chen, Valente, and Zlotnik (1998), the United Nations assumes that the rural mortality hazard function $\mu_r(a) = 1.25 \cdot \mu_u(a)$, that is, the rural hazard rate is assumed to be 25 percent higher than the urban at each age a. Taken together with estimates of urbanization, this proportionality assumption yields estimates of the urban mortality hazard. The United Nations (1980) describes some experiments in which rural mortality was assumed to be as much as 50 percent higher than urban. These experiments revealed that the decomposition of urban growth into natural increase and net migration is robust to variations in assumptions about the relative risks of mortality.

[12] Scattered, order-of-magnitude estimates suggest that of the migration and reclassification total, about one-quarter is attributable to reclassification; see United Nations (1980: 25) and Visaria (1997: Table 13.5).

Migrants as Recorded in the Demographic and Health Surveys

Another way to gauge the contribution of migrants is to examine their numbers in relation to the urban population total, rather than in relation to urban growth.[13] Data from the DHS provide a measure akin to this, although it is restricted to an urban subpopulation. Using these surveys, one can examine the migration status of urban women of reproductive age. That men and other women are excluded is unfortunate, but the DHS surveys do not usually gather migration data for these groups.[14] Some DHS surveys collect month-by-month retrospective migration histories that cover the 5 years before the survey and occasionally go back further in time. Other surveys simply ask the woman how long she has resided in her current community and record the responses in terms of years of residence.[15] In what follows, we define recent migrants to be those women who moved to their current (urban) residence in the 5 years before the DHS survey.

Among urban women of reproductive age, recent migrants are a numerically important group. As Table 4-1 shows, nearly one urban woman in four in the age range 15–49 is a recent migrant.[16] The figure ranges from a low of 15.6 percent in the Latin American surveys to a high of 29.4 percent in the surveys from sub-Saharan Africa.[17] As would be expected given the age pattern of migration, younger women are much more likely to be recent migrants. Some 36 percent of urban women under age 25 are recent migrants, as compared with only 9–12 percent of women in their 40s. Even this lower percentage might be judged high by providers of reproductive health and related services if migrants have special

---

[13]In the analytic model developed above, this measure could be expressed as $(R_{t-1}/U_{t-1}) \cdot m_{r,u}$.

[14]Census data from Mexico in 1990 show that, compared with male migrants, female migrants were more heavily concentrated in the age groups 15–19 and 20–24. Migrants were slightly more likely to be married or in a consensual union than nonmigrants (De la Paz López, Izazola, and de León, 1993). The concentration of female migrants in the 15–24 age range is generally greater than is the case for males and is greatest for migrants moving to metropolitan areas rather than to urban areas in general (Hugo, 1993). See Recchini de Lattes and Mychaszula (1993), Findley and Diallo (1993), and Alvi and Wong (1993) for studies of the age and marital status of female migrants compared with nonmigrants.

[15]According to the Demographic and Health Surveys (2001), the term "community" refers to the village, town, or city of residence.

[16]Here and throughout the volume, we report summaries of estimates derived from analyses of individual DHS surveys. The statistical models were estimated with an allowance for unmeasured effects specific to sampling clusters, so that all discussions of statistical significance refer to robust standard errors. Sampling weights were not used at the estimation stage, but were applied to convert the estimates to representative summary values for each survey. In assembling the tables, we then averaged such survey-specific values. Survey results from countries that fielded more than one DHS survey were downweighted in proportion to the number of surveys fielded. Hence, the unit described in the tables is the country.

[17]Note that the "total" row of the table is dominated by estimates from sub-Saharan Africa and Latin America, where the greatest number of DHS surveys have been fielded. In no region of the developing world have all countries participated in the DHS program, and within regions some countries have fielded more surveys than others. Hence, the "total" row cannot be interpreted in terms of averages across the whole of the developing world.

TABLE 4-1 Percentages of Urban Women of Reproductive Age Who Are Recent Migrants, by Age and Region

DHS Surveys in Region	N^a	All Women	Women of Ages						
			15–19	20–24	25–29	30–34	35–39	40–44	45–49
North Africa	3	20.7	44.6	39.6	28.5	20.4	13.7	10.1	7.9
Sub-Saharan Africa	25	29.4	35.3	38.7	31.9	24.7	18.5	14.1	10.9
Southeast Asia	3	24.2	45.5	42.2	32.8	22.6	16.3	12.5	10.7
South, Central, West Asia	10	23.2	47.5	41.8	27.3	17.8	13.5	9.9	6.9
Latin America	11	15.6	21.2	21.3	16.8	13.2	9.5	8.4	8.0
TOTAL	52	24.5	35.8	35.9	27.7	20.6	15.2	11.8	9.3

NOTE: The age-specific entries are summaries of predicted values from a probit model. The table gives the average value of proportions estimated separately from each DHS survey with migration information. Estimates from countries with more than one such survey were downweighted in proportion to the number of surveys fielded in the country.

[a] Number of countries with DHS survey information on migration.

TABLE 4-2 Percentages of Urban Women of Reproductive Age Who Are Recent
Migrants, by City Population Size and Region

DHS Surveys in Region	City Population Size				
	Under 100,000	100,000 to 500,000	500,000 to 1 million	1 to 5 million	Over 5 million
North Africa	22.1	27.4	20.9	16.7	10.0
Sub-Saharan Africa	31.5	29.0	29.6	22.9	22.5
Southeast Asia	21.3	26.8	22.9	26.0	26.5
South, Central, West Asia	21.9	23.5	26.7	20.3	28.0
Latin America	17.9	16.6	16.8	14.1	9.0
TOTAL	25.5	24.8	23.8	19.6	22.0

NOTE: The entries in this table are summaries of age-standardized predictions from a
probit model; they represent the migrant status of women aged 25–29. See also notes
to Table 4-1.

health needs or deficits in knowledge compared with urban natives. In any case, it
is plain that migrants account for a substantial percentage of urban women at both
ends of the reproductive age span.

Table 4-2 presents data on migrant status according to the population size of
the city in which the woman resides.[18] A methodological note is in order here.
Appendix C describes how the panel linked DHS survey records to United Nations
data on city size. The linkage is very difficult to effect, involving approximations
and a good measure of guesswork, because the DHS datasets that were available
to the panel did not include adequate spatial identifiers. In concluding this chapter
we will revisit this point, which has a bearing on how spatially coded urban data
can be used in survey-based studies of individuals and families.

Returning to the question of migration, the results for the average DHS country, shown in the "total" row of Table 4-2, indicate that cities with 1 million or
more residents have proportionately fewer migrants than smaller cities, although
these differences are on the order of a few percentage points. In Latin America
and sub-Saharan Africa, clearer evidence of a negative relationship emerges.[19]
A negative relationship is also apparent in North Africa if one sets aside the
smallest cities. There is little here to suggest that migrants are systematically
overrepresented in the larger cities, and yet that would appear to be a common
belief.

---

[18]See Table C-3 in Appendix C for a list of cities in the population size range from 1 to 5 million
whose countries have fielded a DHS survey. The cities of over 5 million are, by region; *North Africa*,
Cairo; *sub-Saharan Africa*, Lagos; *Southeast Asia*, Bangkok, Jakarta, and Manila; *South, Central, and
West Asia*, Dhaka, Madras, Delhi, Calcutta, Mumbai, Karachi, and Istanbul; and *Latin America*, Rio
de Janeiro, São Paulo, Mexico City, and Lima.

[19]For similar findings in Mexico using a special migration survey, see Brambila Paz (1998).

TABLE 4-3 Type of Origin Area for Recent Urban Migrants, by
Region

DHS Surveys in Region	N^a	Type of Origin Area		
		City	Town	Rural
North Africa	3	40.4	28.9	30.7
Sub-Saharan Africa	23	33.3	28.0	38.8
Southeast Asia	3	31.2	23.6	45.2
South, Central, West Asia	7	34.5	28.0	37.5
Latin America	9	38.7	31.8	29.6
TOTAL	45	34.9	28.5	36.6

NOTE: Towns are defined by the DHS as urban areas with fewer
than 50,000 residents; cities are all urban areas larger than this.
See also notes to Table 4-1.

[a] Number of countries with DHS survey data on migrant origin.

Most of the DHS surveys with data on migration also gather data on migrants'
areas of origin, classified as city, town, or rural.[20] Table 4-3 shows that roughly
equal percentages of urban migrants come from cities and rural areas, with smaller
but still substantial percentages coming from towns. As can be seen, only about
one in three urban migrants is of rural origin; the table shows that, taken together,
cities and towns are far more important sources of urban migrants. When city
size differences are examined (see Table 4-4), a somewhat mixed picture emerges.
The percentage of migrants with city origins is generally higher in the larger cities
of destination, but there are exceptions and irregularities in the evidence. In Latin
America, the larger the destination city, the greater is the share of city-origin migrants among all migrants. This pattern is also evident in North Africa, although
it is less apparent in other regions.

All of these findings cast doubt on the common view of migrants as predominantly rural folk. The DHS data also call into question the value of simplistic
analytic models, such as ours, which treat the urban population as an undifferentiated mass. As these data show, considerable migration takes place *within* the
urban sector, and the implications of circulation among towns and cities may be
quite different from the implications of rural-to-urban migration.

Urban and Rural Levels of Fertility and Mortality

Unlike data on migration, which are available only for a subset of the DHS surveys, all of the surveys provide information on levels of fertility, infant mortality

---

[20] See Appendix C. In this context, "origin" refers to the nature of the area from which a migrant
has most recently come, rather than to place of birth. Bilsborrow (1998) warns that survey respondents
may describe their origin areas in terms that bias the urban percentages upward. The panel is not aware
of any empirical assessments of such a bias.

TABLE 4-4 Type of Origin Area for Recent Urban Migrants, by Region and Population Size of Current Residence

DHS Surveys in Region	Origin	City Size				
		Under 100,000	100,000 to 500,000	500,000 to 1 million	1 to 5 million	Over 5 million
North Africa	City	22.0	42.9	46.8	59.9	42.5
	Town	41.6	26.3	24.5	16.2	23.9
	Rural	36.4	30.8	28.7	23.9	33.6
Sub-Saharan	City	28.0	36.3	40.1	30.0	35.6
Africa	Town	31.1	27.5	30.1	32.7	47.2
	Rural	41.0	36.2	29.8	37.2	17.2
Southeast Asia	City	21.3	22.2	26.2	15.9	42.0
	Town	17.9	24.4	40.4	29.6	20.4
	Rural	60.7	53.4	33.4	54.5	37.6
South, Central,	City	24.7	38.7	39.1	23.7	12.0
West Asia	Town	30.4	28.1	25.5	30.9	57.6
	Rural	44.9	33.2	35.4	45.4	30.3
Latin America	City	36.6	46.5	40.3	38.2	60.7
	Town	26.5	27.9	38.9	33.2	26.8
	Rural	37.0	25.6	20.8	28.6	12.5
TOTAL	City	28.5	38.1	39.4	35.1	42.2
	Town	30.1	27.3	32.2	29.8	30.4
	Rural	41.4	34.6	28.4	35.1	27.4

NOTE: See notes to Tables 4-1 and 4-3.

(deaths under age 1), and child mortality (deaths under age 5). Both fertility and mortality are examined later in this report (see Chapters 6 and 7, respectively), and the treatment of these data here is brief and introductory in nature.

Table 4-5 provides estimates of total fertility rates (TFRs) for urban and rural women. This table confirms that urban and rural areas have quite different fertility rates. The widest gaps in fertility are seen in Latin America, where the difference is on the order of 2.1 children, and in sub-Saharan Africa, where urban women are estimated to have 1.4 fewer children than rural women over a reproductive lifetime. The urban/rural differences are smaller in the other regions, although still appreciable. Of course, much of this is due to urban/rural differences in socioeconomic composition, as will be seen in Chapter 6. But lower urban fertility is hardly a modern development—it is a well-documented feature of the European historical record (Sharlin, 1986). Lower fertility is, and long has been, an indicator of urban-specific productive and reproductive family strategies.

Table 4-6 gives an overview of urban/rural differences in infant ($_1q_0$) and child ($_5q_0$) mortality levels. Here again we see sizable differences between urban and rural areas. That urban mortality falls below rural is unsurprising, perhaps, but it

TABLE 4-5 Total Fertility Rates, Rural and Urban Areas, by Region

DHS Surveys in Region	N^a	Rural Fertility	Urban Fertility
North Africa	3	4.82	3.59
Sub-Saharan Africa	27	6.50	5.07
Southeast Asia	3	3.37	2.81
South, Central, West Asia	10	3.93	3.29
Latin America	13	5.49	3.36
TOTAL	56	5.55	4.16

NOTE: Calculated from 90 DHS surveys, with survey-specific results downweighted for countries with multiple surveys. The fertility estimates are derived from a Poisson model with a set of age dummies. The Poisson coefficients are then converted to estimated rates, using additional correction factors supplied by the DHS for the surveys restricted to ever-married women.

[a] Number of countries with survey information on fertility.

is worth remembering how recently this advantage has emerged and how tenuous it may be. Communicable diseases are a predominant cause of deaths in infancy and childhood, and if other things were equal, urban residents would be placed at greater risk by their spatial proximity and dependence on common resources, such as water. After all, it was not until the late nineteenth and early twentieth centuries in the West that urban mortality levels fell below rural levels (Preston and van de Walle, 1978; Preston and Haines, 1991). The marked urban mortality advantage seen in Table 4-6 is thus a departure from the historical norm; it reflects advances in public health and scientific knowledge, and testifies to the ability of

TABLE 4-6 Infant and Child Mortality, Rural and Urban Areas, by Region

DHS Surveys in Region	N^c	Infant Mortality[a]		Child Mortality[b]	
		Rural	Urban	Rural	Urban
North Africa	3	73.8	45.8	88.5	50.3
Sub-Saharan Africa	27	101.7	81.0	153.6	122.0
Southeast Asia	3	49.7	30.4	60.6	36.8
South, Central, West Asia	10	69.7	54.2	84.6	62.2
Latin America	13	63.3	46.9	80.7	57.0
TOTAL	56	82.8	63.7	115.9	87.8

[a] Table entries are means of Kaplan-Meier estimates of $_1q_0$ derived from 90 DHS surveys, with survey-specific estimates downweighted for countries with multiple surveys.

[b] Kaplan-Meier estimates of $_5q_0$, from the same set of surveys.

[c] Number of countries with information on infant and child mortality.

higher-income urbanites to purchase protection against disease. In Chapter 7 we return to the issue, asking whether poor urban residents can avail themselves of any similar protections.

Urban Age Structure

The fact that urban fertility rates are generally lower than rural, when combined with the influence of rural-to-urban migration, yields urban age profiles with a distinctive shape. The age composition of urban populations is illustrated in Figures 4-5 and 4-6 for Brazil (based on its 1996 DHS survey) and in Figures 4-7 and 4-8 for Ghana (based on its 1998–99 survey). For each country, the urban population pyramid is shown first; below that pyramid, the figures depict the urban proportion at a given age in relation to the rural proportion at that age. Figures 4-6 and 4-8 reveal a relative deficit of children in the urban areas of Brazil and Ghana and a relative surplus of men and women in the working and reproductive ages.

As these illustrations suggest, urban populations are older than rural populations on average. Table 4-7 shows that, as in Brazil and Ghana, cities generally have lower percentages of children (those aged 0–14) in their populations, higher percentages of working-age and reproductive-age adults (aged 15–64), and slightly lower proportions of older adults (aged 65 and above).

Table 4-8 provides a further analysis of age structure in urban areas of different population size, focusing on the proportion of the household population in the working ages. As can be seen, there is a noticeable increase with city size in the working-age proportion, with the occasional exception of the largest city size category. These differences may well stem from the lower fertility rates characteristic of larger cities.

CORE ISSUES IN DEFINITION AND MEASUREMENT

The preceding section presented results by city size, which required that a linkage be made from DHS survey data on individuals to aggregate data from United Nations sources on the population sizes of cities. We have already mentioned the difficulties involved in establishing such a linkage; at this point we must assess the quality of the city population data themselves. They are derived from reports made by national statistical agencies to the United Nations, and therefore reflect the criteria applied by these agencies to define urban areas and delimit the boundaries of individual cities. The reports are usually (if not always) taken from national censuses, and thus depend on the regularity with which censuses are conducted and the completeness of population counts. What is known of the quality of such urban and city size data?

It was not until the nineteenth century that formal urban and rural classifications were introduced into the compilations of European population statistics. The systematic compilation of such data is still more recent. In 1948, shortly

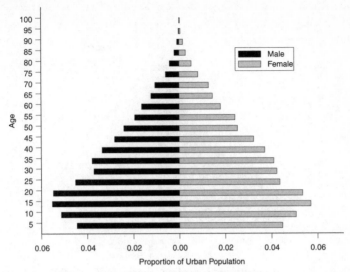

FIGURE 4-5 Population pyramid for urban Brazil, 1996.

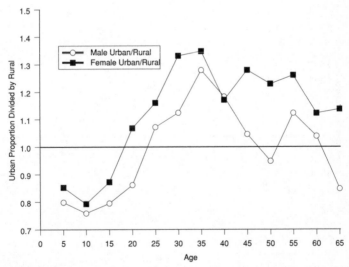

FIGURE 4-6 Urban relative to rural age composition, men and women by age, Brazil, 1996.

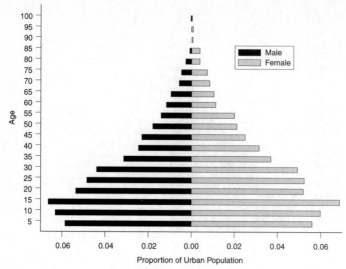

FIGURE 4-7 Population pyramid for urban Ghana, 1998–1999.

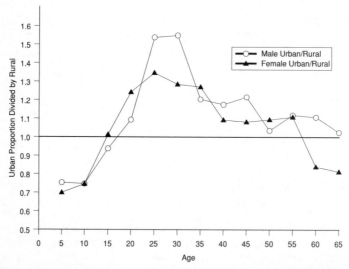

FIGURE 4-8 Urban relative to rural age composition, men and women by age, Ghana, 1998–1999.

TABLE 4-7 Household Age Composition, Rural and Urban Areas by Region

DHS Surveys in Region	N^a	Percentages of Population					
		Aged 0–14		Aged 15–64		Aged 65+	
		Rural	Urban	Rural	Urban	Rural	Urban
North Africa	3	43.2	35.5	52.4	60.5	4.5	4.1
Sub-Saharan Africa	27	48.3	42.8	47.5	54.8	4.3	2.4
Southeast Asia	3	37.2	31.0	58.3	65.2	4.6	3.8
South, Central, West Asia	10	40.6	34.9	54.3	60.1	5.1	4.9
Latin America	12	43.4	35.9	51.8	59.6	4.8	4.5
TOTAL	55	44.9	38.8	50.5	57.7	4.5	3.5

NOTE: Calculated from the household rosters of DHS surveys, with survey-specific results downweighted for countries with multiple surveys.
[a] Number of countries with age data in the DHS household roster.

after its founding, the United Nations assembled information on the rural and urban populations of 58 countries with recent censuses (United Nations, 1949). By 1952, the United Nations *Demographic Yearbook* already contained rural and urban population counts for 160 countries and could offer an introductory chapter on urban/rural differentials (United Nations, 1953).

These early efforts paved the way for systematic international research on urbanization, and problems in standardizing urban definitions and measures were among the first issues to be studied (Davis, 1958, 1969; Gibbs and Davis, 1958). From the outset, researchers at the United Nations and elsewhere wrote frankly about the deficiencies of urban data. As they discovered, the difficulties involved

TABLE 4-8 Percentages of Urban Population in the Working Ages (15–64), by Region and City Population Size

DHS Surveys in Region	City Population Size				
	Under 100,000	100,000 to 500,000	500,000 to 1 million	1 to 5 million	Over 5 million
North Africa	58.2	59.6	61.3	63.6	61.8
Sub-Saharan Africa	52.1	55.4	56.3	60.1	55.2
Southeast Asia	59.6	64.3	62.7	64.3	68.7
South, Central, West Asia	56.9	59.7	61.8	62.5	62.3
Latin America	56.1	59.4	61.0	61.9	64.7
TOTAL	54.5	58.1	59.6	61.7	63.9

in establishing concepts and improving measures could not be speedily overcome. Even by 1969, the United Nations (1969: 22) was forced to concede that "... at least a rough overview of world urbanization trends is now so much needed that tolerably usable results had to be preferred over more refined estimates obtainable only with much additional labor." This 1969 report presents estimates and projections of urban population according to national urban definitions, but contrasts them with results from a proposed alternative standard whereby urban areas are defined as agglomerations with populations of 20,000 or more. Noting the many interdependencies of rural and urban areas and the ambiguous status of much territory surrounding urban areas, the report also expresses concern over simplistic urban/rural classifications.

As compilations of urban data were being expanded to cover more nations and longer spans of time, methods for estimating and projecting urban populations were being devised and then revised. By 1974 the United Nations had developed the urban/rural growth difference (URGD) method, now usually termed "the United Nations method," which continues to feature centrally in its estimates and projections (United Nations, 1974). The method (see Appendix D for more detailed discussion) is based on an extrapolation of differences between urban and rural growth rates, with the results expressed in terms of levels of urbanization. A method similar in spirit (if different in details) has been devised to project the populations of individual cities. In the late 1970s, the URGD method was modified so as to force a decline in projected urban/rural growth differences as the level of urbanization rises (United Nations, 1980), and the city projections were similarly revised.

Over the past three decades, while making such minor adjustments to its methods, the United Nations Population Division has continued to prepare estimates and projections of total urban and rural populations and of urban agglomerations, issuing reports and major updates on a biennial basis. The results are widely cited by researchers and journalists alike. At present, the United Nations provides the only comprehensive, international source of urban population data—all the more reason, then, to understand the data limitations.

Inconsistent Urban Definitions

No definition of urban places has been universally adopted by national governments, and it must be said that the prospects for consensus are dim. A great variety of national definitions is now in use. To briefly summarize current practice, in just over half of the 228 countries for which the United Nations Statistical Office compiles data, urban definitions are based on administrative considerations equating urban areas with the capitals of provinces or with areas under the jurisdiction of certain types of local authority. In less than a quarter of countries (22 percent) are urban areas distinguished mainly on the basis of population size and density, and in these countries, the lower limit at which a settlement is considered urban varies from 200 to 50,000 inhabitants. In 39 countries, including all of the successor states of the former Soviet Union and many Eastern European countries, explicit mention is made of socioeconomic criteria, such as the proportion of the labor force employed in nonagricultural activities and the availability of urban-type facilities (e.g., streets, water supply, sewerage systems, electric lighting). Some two dozen countries provide the United Nations with no explanation at all of their defining criteria.

A few examples will illustrate the variety of urban definitions in use. Some countries define urban residents as those people living within well-specified administrative boundaries—in *municipios* (as in El Salvador); municipality councils (as in Iraq); or places having a municipality or municipal corporation, a town committee, or a cantonment board (as in Bangladesh and Pakistan). In Angola, Argentina, and Ethiopia, urban areas are those localities with 2,000 inhabitants or more; in Benin, the threshold is set at 10,000 inhabitants. Botswana sets the threshold at 5,000 people but requires that 75 percent of economic activity be nonagricultural. In Cuba, places with as few as 2,000 inhabitants are considered urban, but even smaller places than this can qualify if they have paved streets, street lighting, piped water, sewerage, a medical center, and educational facilities (United Nations, 2001). As Hardoy, Mitlin, and Satterthwaite (2001) note, the percentage of the world's population living in urban areas could be increased or decreased by several percentage points if China, India, or a few other large countries were simply to adopt new urban definitions. It is not implausible to think that such changes might occur; as Box 4.2 shows, China made major revisions to its urban criteria in the 1980s.

What, then, are the prospects for a uniform international standard in urban definitions? Some researchers have defended current practice on the grounds that "national statistical offices are in the best position to distinguish between urban and rural-type areas in their own countries" (United Nations, 1980). But in keeping with its earlier scientific reviews, as late as 1980 the United Nations (1980: 5) was urging consideration of a four-fold classification distinguishing urban and rural places both inside and outside metropolitan regions—to no apparent effect. As one United Nations report drily observes (United Nations, 1969: 9), "greater homogeneity of definition could be achieved in the unlikely event that forms of local government became more standardized throughout the world." If the probability of such an event appeared remote in 1969, it has now reached the vanishing point as developing countries decentralize their governments and establish wholly new municipal and regional entities.

The lack of an official consensus greatly constrains the efforts of the United Nations, but it need not deter all researchers. If nationally determined urban criteria were to be made fully and publicly available in the major urban datasets, published alongside population size and density data, researchers would be free to study the implications of applying alternative urban criteria. Many recent censuses contain detailed information on the percentages of population living in

---

BOX 4.2 Changing Urban Definitions in China

China's current urban definition reflects both settlement patterns and administrative regulations for persons and places. China's urban concept has taken several forms over the last two decades (Zhang and Zhao, 1998). At present, four factors determine the size of the urban population and the urbanization level: the criteria for designating a settlement as urban, the physical and administrative boundaries of places so designated, the household registration (*hukou*) system, and the urban status of the unregistered or "floating" population.

The criteria for urban designation have changed over time, reflecting the prevailing urbanization policy, economic development, and political ideologies. The criteria focus on the administrative status of a settlement, the minimum absolute size of its resident population, and its occupational structure. The 1984 revisions in urban classification reduced the requirements for minimum population size and nonagricultural workforce share (Goldstein, 1990). These revisions increased both the number of cities and their populations. In further revisions since 1993, additional characteristics of settlements have been taken into account.

The Chinese urban system now consists of two main components: cities (*shi* or *chengshi*) and towns (*zhen*). The urban hierarchy is divided into three levels, roughly analogous to provinces, prefectures, and counties. Provincial status has been granted to four urban regions: Shanghai, Beijing, Tianjin, and Wuhan. Towns fall under the authority of counties. Territorial reorganization and annexation leave the number of counties in the municipal jurisdiction of each city far from standardized.

The Chinese government has long exerted influence over the growth of urban population; since 1954 it has sought to maintain control through the *hukou* system. This system divides the population into agricultural (*nongye renkou*) and nonagricultural (*fei nonye renkou*) categories, which among other things determine rights of access to public-sector subsidies (e.g., grain distributions). In the *hukou* system, there are two official indicators of urban population: the total population of cities and towns (TPCT) and their nonagricultural population (NPCT). TPCT counts as urban those who are living in a designated urban area under the administration of residents' committees for at least a year and absent from their former *hukou* registration place for over a year. NPCT, by contrast, counts as urban those living in a designated urban area who are engaged in nonagricultural work. A person's *hukou* status, defined administratively as "agricultural" or "nonagricultural," need not reflect his or her actual occupation.

---

settlements in specified size ranges. Although these census data could be employed to develop a uniform standard for research, they have not yet been put to this use (Satterthwaite, 1996a). A number of regional databases could also support the development of a consensus standard. For instance, the GEOPOLIS database for sub-Saharan Africa has adopted a homogeneous definition of urban areas, counting as urban only those settlements with populations of more than 10,000 (Moriconi-Ebrard, 1994). Although such alternatives are promising, researchers will doubtless continue to rely on the United Nations data, with their heterogeneous urban criteria, for the forseeable future.

Differences in urban definitions affect mainly the status of smaller towns and cities, those settlements that might be classified as either rural or urban. In cross-national comparisons, one can skirt much of the problem by focusing not on a country's total urban population, but on the urban population that resides in settlements above a given size. In following this line of reasoning, we are led away from the national estimates and toward the United Nations' city-level estimates and projections.

City-Level Population Data

At present, the United Nations offers two sources of data on city population size— one gathered by its Statistical Office and the other prepared by the Population Division. The more extensive data, processed by the Statistical Office, are found in the annual *Demographic Yearbook*. Every year since 1955, this publication has recorded the population sizes of capital cities and all cities of 100,000 or more population according to the most recent official counts. The population counts are themselves taken from national or municipal censuses.[21] The *Demographic Yearbook* presents only the most recently reported census results and estimates. For countries that do not regularly conduct censuses, do not tabulate population at the level of cities, or do not report their data to the United Nations, the figures may refer to counts taken years or even decades earlier. For such countries, city population data are available only at isolated or irregularly spaced points in time.

The second major source of data, the biennial *World Urbanization Prospects* volumes (the most recent edition being United Nations, 2002a), presents population estimates and projections at regular 5-year intervals for urban agglomerations with populations of 750,000 and above; it includes all capital cities, irrespective of size. In preparing *World Urbanization Prospects*, the United Nations Population Division evidently draws its raw materials from the same population counts that are published in the *Demographic Yearbook*, which it then extrapolates to cover years for which census counts are unavailable.[22] Curve-fitting techniques akin to the URGD method are used to form city estimates and projections, involving city population growth rates (where they are available) and growth rates of the total population; further adjustments are made (it appears) on the basis of country-specific factors. Appendix D describes these procedures in more detail.

---

[21] In addition to census counts, estimates of city population based on sample surveys and other sources are presented in the *Demographic Yearbook*. According to the United Nations (2000: 44), data drawn from sources other than a census or complete survey are potentially unreliable.

[22] The data files and empirical methods used by the Population Division are not publicly accessible, so we can only speculate about the details of its procedures. The panel's understanding is that the Population Division gives considerable attention to the possibility of errors and cross-country differences in reporting.

It is not clear just why the estimates and projections in *World Urbanization Prospects* are limited to cities of 750,000 and above, with exceptions for capitals.[23] Perhaps the URGD approach has proven unreliable when applied to smaller cities. The exclusion of smaller cities is unfortunate given the United Nations' projection that over the next few decades, roughly half of the urban population of developing countries will be found in cities with populations of 500,000 and below (recall Chapter 1, and see United Nations, 1998b: 27).

City boundaries

As noted in Chapter 1, the delineation of city boundaries affects both population counts and growth rates. Indeed, cities such as Buenos Aires, Mexico City, London, and Tokyo can correctly be said to be declining or expanding in population, depending on how their boundaries are defined. In the United Nations publications, urban population counts are reported for several types of boundaries or city concepts:

- **City proper:** the inhabitants residing within the formal administrative boundaries of the city.

- **Urban agglomeration:** the population found within the contours of a contiguous territory inhabited at urban levels of residential density, without regard to administrative boundaries.

- **Metropolitan area:** the most expansive of the measures. It includes the territory covered by the urban agglomeration, but also incorporates lower-density settlements, including areas that might otherwise be designated as rural when under the direct influence of the city through networks of transport and communication. That, at any rate, is the principle; in practice, metropolitan regions can be defined as large administrative entities that include rural areas even if these areas have no particular city linkages.

The United Nations (2000: 43–45) provides further discussion of these urban concepts.

In *World Urbanization Prospects*, the urban agglomeration is the preferred unit for which urban estimates and projections should be prepared. Unfortunately, as

---

[23] According to the United Nations (1998b: 34), it is the responsibility of the Population Division to "monitor the size of all of the world's cities once they reach 100,000 as recorded by a population census or other reliable observational procedure." As recently as 1985, the populations of all cities with populations of 100,000 and above were estimated, although they were not listed city by city in the annexes of the report. (The 1985 report includes a size category of under 100,000, but the estimates for this smallest size class may have been derived by subtracting the total of the other size classes from the estimated all-urban total.) The United Nations (2001) provides estimates by city size class that include all urban areas with populations under 500,000, but gives city-specific estimates only for urban agglomerations with populations of 750,000 and above.

noted by the United Nations (1998b: 34–35, 37, 55–80), when countries do not report their city populations in terms of agglomerations or when their reporting criteria vary over time, the United Nations' estimates and projections cannot be interpreted in terms of urban agglomerations as such. In these cases, the *World Urbanization Prospects* estimates often represent the size of the city proper; occasionally, they represent metropolitan areas rather than urban agglomerations.

Examples

The figures that follow illustrate some of the difficulties of interpretation that surround the United Nations' city population estimates. Because the estimates that attract most attention are those published in *World Urbanization Prospects*, these are emphasized in the discussion.

Figures 4-9 and 4-10 present the full data series available to the panel for the Egyptian cities of Cairo and Shubra-El-Khema. The line of connected points is taken from the *World Urbanization Prospects* dataset (United Nations, 2001). The points marked by boxes are estimates of the population size of the city proper, as presented in various years of the *Demographic Yearbook*. (Egypt does not publish estimates for the agglomeration of Cairo.) Figure 4-9 thus conforms to expectations: it shows that the *World Urbanization Prospects* estimates, which refer to the urban agglomeration of Cairo, lie well above the various *Demographic Yearbook* estimates for the city proper.

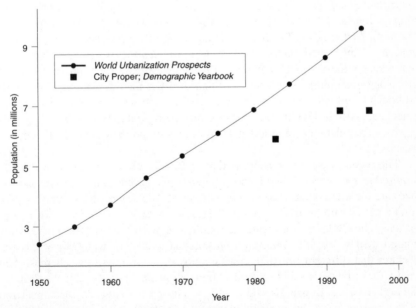

FIGURE 4-9 Cairo: United Nations population estimates.

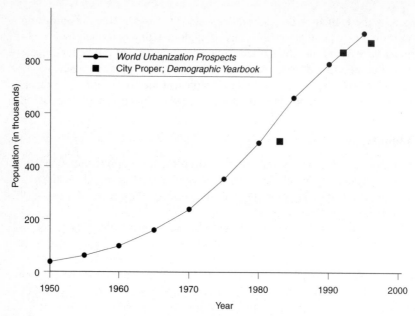

FIGURE 4-10 Shubra-El-Khema: United Nations population estimates.

It is then disconcerting to discover that for Shubra-El-Khema, the *World Ur-banization Prospects* estimates are very close to those published in the *Demographic Yearbook* for the city proper; a larger gap would have been expected if the *World Urbanization Prospects* estimates faithfully represented urban agglomerations. The United Nations (1998b: 62) provides the explanation, indicating that whereas the *World Urbanization Prospects* estimate for Cairo refers to the urban agglomeration, its estimate for Shubra-El-Khema refers to the city proper. Although listed in the tables as if it were a physically separate entity, Shubra-El-Khema actually lies within the greater Cairo metropolitan area, and perhaps this is why its population is reported in terms of the city proper (no rationale is stated explicitly).

The second case we consider is that of Brazil. Here, according to the *Demographic Yearbook* (United Nations, 1998a: 301, footnote 13), city population sizes are recorded in terms of the populations of "*municipios* which may contain rural areas as well as urban centre[s]." This description is ambiguous—it is suggestive of both administrative and metropolitan area definitions. The units issue is complicated by *World Urbanization Prospects* (United Nations 1998b: 58), which declares that different Brazilian cities employ different reporting schemes. São Paulo, for instance, is said to record its population data in terms of the metropolitan area, whereas Brasília is said to use the city proper concept. A comparison of the *Yearbook* and *Prospects* estimates for São Paulo injects further confusion.

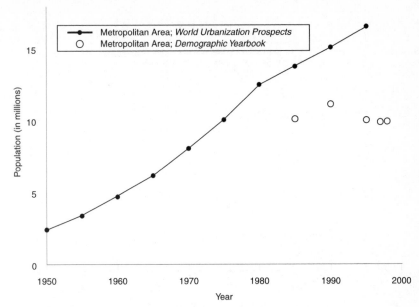

FIGURE 4-11 São Paulo: United Nations population estimates.

Figure 4-11 shows a marked difference between these estimates, with the *Prospects* figure exceeding that of the *Yearbook* by more than a million persons. It is not obvious how discrepancies of this size can be resolved. If both estimates refer to the population of the metropolitan area, the metropolitan measure used by *Prospects* must be considerably more expansive. For Brasília (Figure 4-12), the *Yearbook* counts are higher than the extrapolated values of *Prospects* in the mid-1980s and 1990, as expected given the difference in urban concepts, but this gap unexpectedly closes in the mid-1990s.

Finally (see Figures 4-13 and 4-14), a city such as Niamey, the capital of Niger, has had too small a population to be included in the main series of estimates and projections in *World Urbanization Prospects*. Nevertheless, because Niamey is a capital city, its population is estimated using techniques similar to those applied to larger cities. In Kitwe, Zambia—a small city in Zambia's Copper Belt, but not a national capital—only the *Demographic Yearbook* population counts are available.

Evidently, there is a great deal of heterogeneity in the nature of the United Nations' city population estimates. The fundamental problem is the variety of units used to report city populations to the United Nations; as noted, the city proper, the urban agglomeration, and the metropolitan area are all used, and some countries employ two of these measures. The units problem is explicitly acknowledged in the footnotes and technical appendices of the United Nations publications, but is not much appreciated, we suspect, by the casual user.

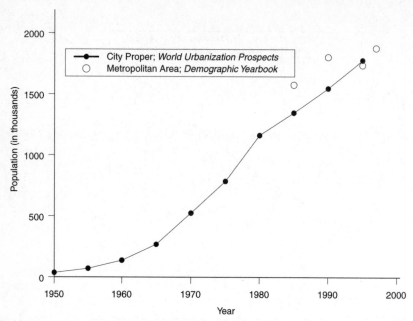

FIGURE 4-12 Brasília: United Nations population estimates.

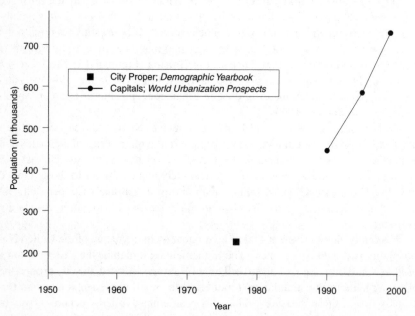

FIGURE 4-13 Niamey, Niger: United Nations population estimates.

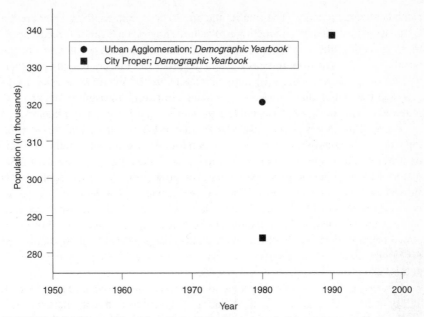

FIGURE 4-14 Kitwe, Zambia: United Nations population estimates.

Further interpretive difficulties may arise from applying the URGD method—involving simple extrapolation and projection assumptions—to these heterogeneous data series. Although the broad outlines of the URGD method are known from the United Nations publications, the details of its application to city populations have not been placed in the public domain. Hence, little is known about the gains that might result from more sophisticated statistical modeling. In the panel's view, it is doubtful that more sophisticated methods could surmount the many measurement errors and other problems, stemming mainly from differing units, that plague the raw data series. Nevertheless, rigorous research on alternative projection methods is in order.

PROJECTING URBAN POPULATIONS

A first issue with regard to urban projections is to identify the populations of interest: projections can be applied to national urban poulations, to the populations of individual cities, and to metropolitan subregions and even neighborhoods. Such diversity calls for the use of diverse techniques and data sources, and there are interrelationships that need to be considered. As national populations grow, especially in conjunction with economic growth, the number, spatial location, and size distribution of cities can be expected to evolve. As individual cities grow, they often become more diverse internally, and their neighborhoods and subareas can take divergent paths. The smaller the unit to be examined, the greater are the demands placed on data and methods to achieve any given level of forecast accuracy. Indeed, at the submetropolitan level, it may be that the greater part of the benefit to be derived from forecasts lies in the processes that are bound up in their generation—the gathering, collating, and reconciling of diverse sources of disaggregated population and socioeconomic data. But some measure of accuracy is required to sustain the exercise and to give sensible guidance to city planners.

Even for the largest units—consider the total urban population of the developing world—demographic forecasts have been found to exhibit substantial error after the fact. The United Nations' 1999 projection of the urban population for 2000 is fully 12.4 percent below the level of its 1980 projection. As Brockerhoff (1999) shows, the United Nations projections of total urban populations have tended to be overestimates. Although the United Nations has also had to revise downward its projections of national populations, these reductions have been small by comparison with the urban reductions. For instance, the projected total populations of developing countries were reduced by just 2 percent in the 1996 projection relative to the 1980 projection (Brockerhoff, 1999).

It is easy to find examples of projections at the city level that have proven to be wildly in error. For instance, United Nations projections of the population of Lagos for 2000 have fluctuated with each successive update of *World Urbanization Prospects*. The *1994 Revision* indicated that the 2000 population of Lagos would be 13.46 million; the *1996 Revision* slashed about 3 million from that total, reducing the forecast to 10.47 million; and the *1999 Revision* added these people back, raising the projected total to 13.43 million in 2000. After finally being granted access to more recent Nigerian data, the United Nations (2002a) again cut the 2000 population of Lagos, which it found in retrospect to have been only 8.67 million. Although Lagos can hardly be considered a fair test case—most demographers would be skeptical of the accuracy of any data available for this city—gyrations of this magnitude are worrisome.

Error is to be expected in any forecast, no matter how sophisticated and well grounded in the data. The question is whether the level of error is tolerable given the purposes for which a forecast is required. Unfortunately, population forecasts are often understood differently by demographers and nondemographers. To demographers, forecasts and projections are devices for extrapolating the logical implications of *current* demographic forces by simple mathematical or (less often) statistical means. Economic, social, and environmental considerations are not generally factored into the forecasting equations. The process of urbanization is exceedingly complex, involving feedbacks and counterpressures on many social, political, spatial, and economic fronts—and these are too varied to be incorporated in formal projection models. However, nondemographers often assume that population forecasts are based on professional judgments about the full range of socioeconomic and environmental influences. This interpretation may be encouraged by the presentation of high, low, and medium projection variants, a demographic practice that might suggest that medium projections represent consensus views.

Clearly mindful of the difficulties involved, the United Nations has generally advanced only the most modest of claims for its city size projections. The United Nations (1980: 45) warns:

> Projection of city populations is fraught with hazards.... There are more than 1,600 cities in the data set, and it is obviously impossible to predict precisely the demographic future of most of them.... In most cases, national and local planners will have access to more detailed information about a particular place and could supply more reliable information about its prospects.

With reference to Mexico City, whose population was to rise to 31 million by the turn of the century according to the 1980 projection, the United Nations (1980: 57) observes:

> Whether such size can actually be attained is, of course, questionable. It has been noted, for example, that population growth at Mexico City theatens to destroy tree cover that is necessary to prevent erosion and flooding. Water-supply also appears to be a potentially constraining factor in this case. Natural or social limits to growth could be encountered well before a size of 31 million is reached, or of 26 million for São Paulo, and so on down the line.

In the event, neither São Paulo nor Mexico City reached the sizes predicted for them in the 1980 United Nations projections. The 2000 Mexican census recorded a population of 18.1 million for Mexico City, and São Paulo's population is reckoned at 17.9 million for the same year.[24]

Are these isolated cases that illustrate the inevitable errors of any projection, or are the United Nations projections assembled in a way that somehow tends to impart an upward bias to the projections for large cities? Because the United Nations does not place its city projection materials and methods fully in the public domain, we cannot say whether particular assumptions or data errors might produce systematic biases. But the United Nations cannot be accused of neglecting the possibility of error. As discussed in Appendix D, the Population Division has imposed a number of restrictions in an effort to rein in its projected city growth rates.

Nevertheless, the record of projections gives considerable cause for concern. Table 4-9 reports mean percentage errors (MPEs) and mean absolute percentage errors (MAPEs) for 169 countries and territories whose boundaries have not changed substantially over the past 20 years (i.e., it excludes countries in the former Soviet Union). The MPE is positive if projections are too high on average,

---

[24]Of course, it is possible that the projected massive population increases spurred government action to deter growth in these cities in favor of growth in smaller cities.

TABLE 4-9 Mean Percentage Error (MPE) and Mean Absolute Percentage Error (MAPE) in Urban Population Projections for the Year 2000, by Length of Forecast, Region, Level of Development, and Size of Country

Category	MPE[a]			MAPE[b]		
	20 years[c]	10 years[d]	5 years[e]	20 years	10 years	5 years
Region						
East Asia and Pacific (EAP)	0.039	0.267	−0.028	0.113	0.289	0.043
EAP excluding China	0.184	0.098	−0.004	0.295	0.166	0.053
Europe	0.140	0.130	0.088	0.140	0.130	0.088
Latin America and Caribbean	0.198	0.054	−0.009	0.226	0.075	0.021
Middle East and North Africa	0.133	0.068	0.085	0.245	0.123	0.105
South Asia	0.272	0.197	0.027	0.291	0.197	0.070
Sub-Saharan Africa	0.218	0.234	0.055	0.382	0.274	0.097
Organisation for Economic Cooperation and Development	0.068	−0.024	−0.018	0.110	0.048	0.020
Other High-Income	−0.183	−0.102	−0.056	0.334	0.199	0.072
Level of Development						
Low	0.231	0.183	0.032	0.312	0.199	0.080
Lower Middle	0.069	0.261	−0.013	0.115	0.283	0.049
Lower Middle excluding China	0.256	0.099	0.037	0.279	0.161	0.066
Upper Middle	0.128	0.089	0.008	0.199	0.115	0.026
High	0.060	−0.027	−0.019	0.117	0.053	0.022
Size of Country						
0–2 million	0.074	0.063	0.030	0.528	0.268	0.169
2–10 million	0.120	0.098	0.019	0.282	0.199	0.082
10–50 million	0.216	0.108	0.027	0.329	0.163	0.070
50+ million	0.124	0.192	0.001	0.168	0.208	0.049
50+ million excluding China	0.189	0.126	0.018	0.227	0.149	0.054
World	0.141	0.171	0.007	0.206	0.199	0.055
Excluding China	0.190	0.120	0.020	0.257	0.156	0.060

NOTE: Based on 169 countries and territories whose boundaries have not changed substantially over the last 20 years. Excludes former Soviet Union. All figures are weighted by population size.

[a] MPE = mean percentage error. Positive error associated with projections being too high and negative error with projections being too low.

[b] MAPE = mean absolute percentage error.

[c] 20-year comparison based on comparing 1980 projections for the year 2000 in United Nations (1980) with actual data in United Nations (2002a,b).

[d] 10-year comparison based on comparing 1990 projections for the year 2000 in United Nations (1991) with actual data in United Nations (2002a,b).

[e] 5-year comparison based on comparing 1996 projections for the year 2000 in United Nations (1998b) with actual data in United Nations (2002a,b).

and negative if they are too low; as such, the MPE is a measure of bias. By contrast, the MAPE is always positive and is usually taken to be a measure of imprecision.

As is evident from the positive values for MPEs in the first three columns of Table 4-9, urban projections have been too high more often than too low. This is attributable in part to the fact that fertility has declined in many places more rapidly than was expected. At the global level, the forecasts of the urban population in 2000 that were made 20 years ago were approximately 14 percent too high; forecasts made 10 years ago were approximately 17 percent too high; and forecasts made 5 years ago were nearly perfect as a result of the fortuitous canceling out of roughly equal numbers of high and low errors. The general pattern is much as expected, in that projections typically are more accurate over shorter projection periods.

The inclusion of China in the calculations makes a considerable difference to the results. Urbanization trends in China, which is home to 30 percent of the urban population of Asia, have fluctuated greatly over the years. These fluctuations stem both from historical events, such as the Cultural Revolution and its aftermath, that retarded or even reversed urbanization in China, and from several revisions (since 1983) in the official criteria defining cities and towns (recall Box 4.2). If the Chinese data are set aside, a more consistent pattern is revealed in which projections over shorter periods are more accurate.

Table 4-9 also shows that there has been considerable diversity in the quality of urban projections by geographic region, level of economic development, and size of country. The United Nations urban projections have been most reliable for Organisation for Economic Cooperation and Development (OECD) countries, on average, and least reliable for countries in sub-Saharan Africa and other high-income countries, many of which are quite small. United Nations projections also tend to be better for larger than for smaller countries, perhaps because larger countries tend to receive more attention.

Similarly, focusing on the largest countries in each developing region and the largest city in each, Brockerhoff (1999) compares two projections for 2000—one taken from the 1980 United Nations projections (United Nations, 1980) and the other from the 1996 projections (United Nations, 1998b). He finds the 1996 projections of city size to be far lower, implying that they had to be revised substantially downward. Among all cities of 750,000 or more residents whose populations were projected in 1980, the median reduction in projected city size was 15.1 percentage points. Upward revisions in the projections were far less common than downward revisions.

Such forecast errors stem from several sources. The baseline data can be absent or unreliable. Censuses may well undercount urban populations: crowded cities with their mobile populations present a challenge to census takers in every part of the world. Recent censuses in Indonesia and Pakistan are believed to have seriously undercounted the populations of Jakarta and Karachi (Jones, 2002). As demographers incorporate the results of recent census rounds, they often find that their estimates of urban populations at earlier points in time need to be revised. Also, as noted above, total population growth in developing countries has been slower than projected, apparently as a result of fertility declines that were more rapid than anticipated. Many economic and social changes have taken place that simply could not have been foreseen 20 years ago.

We conclude that urban and city size projections must be treated with a good deal of caution. It appears that projections at higher levels of aggregation (such as total urban populations) have been slightly more reliable. Regionally aggregated data may benefit to a certain extent from the cross-cancellation of country-level errors. Nevertheless, the urban future is highly uncertain even for some regions. The United Nations projection for Africa, for example, is that by 2025, the continent will have become predominantly urban. This is a reasonable extrapolation of current trends, but of course one wonders whether the decoupling of urbanization from economic growth in Africa and the economic crises plaguing the continent's cities will again cause the level of urbanization to fall short of the prediction.

STATISTICAL SYSTEMS FOR DISAGGREGATED DATA

Evidently, the aggregate databases on city size and growth are in need of substantial repair. But the United Nations demographers cannot be charged with this task: although they have great expertise and a store of critical knowledge, they must depend on the figures contributed by national statistical agencies. What factors are likely to motivate these agencies to rethink and reform their procedures and give them the means to do so?

One thinks first of the role of national censuses. Censuses are large and often politically charged undertakings, and although they are regularly fielded in some developing countries, in others they are held irregularly, while in still others the census taking enterprise appears to have ground to a halt. In any case, not all statistical agencies will process census data into the small spatial units that are needed for accurate counts of city populations and informative assessments of socioeconomic conditions within cities. At the local level, planning is further hindered by limited information about local land markets. Most large cities lack sufficient, accurate, and current data on patterns of land conversion and infrastructure deployment. Urban maps are not infrequently 20 to 30 years out of date, lacking any information on newly emerging periurban areas.

We cannot hope to understand the motivations and constraints of national and local statistical agencies, but we can point to two developments that may be encouraging. The first is the move toward governmental decentralization that is occurring in many countries of the developing world, which places new responsibilities in the hands of municipal and regional government units. In the national debates that accompany decentralization, the appropriate role for information in the processes of governance is often discussed. For instance, as noted in

Chapter 2, national budget allocations to regions can be based on regional population sizes and indicators of poverty, and similar criteria can be applied to the transfers from regional to municipal levels of government. The need for information exchange and feedback among units of government is often recognized in the national debates, although what is likely to come of the insight is generally less than clear.

The second development, not unrelated to the first, is the rise of civil society and the recognition that when they can be assembled, proper socioeconomic maps can be powerful political tools. A city map of differences in service delivery or health conditions can give residents a means of assessing their relative standing and staking claims to resources. For example, maps of Accra and São Paulo showing differentials in health status, mortality rates, and environmental conditions among city districts produced considerable local debate—and some policy change—in both of these cities (Stephens, Akerman, Avle, Maia, Campanareio, Doe, and Tetteh, 1997). Maps highlighting the city neighborhoods with far-above-average mortality rates or unusual concentrations of environmental health problems both inform and help mobilize the inhabitants of these areas and the politicians who represent them.

Assembling such maps is a daunting task, however. In most large cities, each municipal agency or department maintains its own database, often organizing the data in an idiosyncratic manner and rarely sharing them with other agencies. Computerization of data is still relatively uncommon. Many city agencies continue to rely on paper files and paper maps, which may be stored in formats and at scales that all but prohibit comparison, collation, and revision (Bernhardsen, 1999). There are almost no examples of fully integrated databases for the constituent parts of large metropolitan regions. At best one finds data of reasonable quality for the central areas of the city, with little comparable information for the outlying areas.

Looking to the skies for help, some countries have seen remotely sensed and geocoded data as an alternative to data gathered on the ground. Here there are encouraging technical developments. Sutton (2000), for example, has made estimates of intraurban population density based on measures of light intensity; total city populations were estimated by measuring the areal extent of the city in the imagery. These remotely sensed data alone were found to be strongly correlated with census population counts, and the use of ancilliary socioeconomic information further strengthened the correlation. Methods such as these have good potential to improve estimates of the spatial extent of city populations. They can be used to inform "smart interpolation" programs that can improve on existing maps and other population data in areas where good census data are unavailable. The possibilities are attracting considerable research interest—Weeks (2002) provides a guide to some of the very recent technical developments.

The essential principle of GIS is that when information is systematically geocoded, it becomes possible to integrate data from highly diverse sources. Many recent GIS applications draw information from maps, satellite images, videos taken from low-flying aircraft, statistical data from tables, photographs, and other sources. When such data are overlaid, they permit cities to to be described and their socioeconomic conditions monitored more quickly and accurately than was previously possible. Geocoded data can assist governance in many ways, such as planning for infrastructure and transportation, tracking crime and improving law enforcement planning, allowing comparisons of program effectiveness across jurisdictions, strengthening taxation bases and record keeping, facilitating site selection for services, and promoting better evacuation plans in the event of emergencies (O'Looney, 2000). Under ideal circumstances, common databases can help instill habits of cooperation among the units of local, regional and even national governments, or at least among their technical departments.

GIS technology is still in its early stages of development in most poor countries, and even where the enterprise is under way, it tends to be a single-office operation, usually located in a planning or engineering department. And of course, the usefulness of GIS technology is dependent on the availability of appropriate GIS-coded data. But encouraging initiatives can be seen in a number of developing countries, as described below.

Qatar

At the forefront of geographic information technology in the developing world stands Qatar, whose GIS activities began in 1988. The country is now completely covered by a high-resolution, digital topographic database, which draws together images; estimates of land elevation; and information on streets, buildings, zoning, land use, soils, and urban utilities (Tosta, 1997). These data are meant to be available to all government agencies that need them. In one successful application, the availability of digital parcel and building records for the entire country allowed the Central Statistical Organization to conduct an extremely comprehensive housing and population census in a single day.

To be sure, Qatar's situation must be very nearly unique. Factors favoring the country's advanced use of GIS technology include its small geographic size, high-level political support for GIS initiatives (including the authority to mandate and enforce uniform standards), outstanding technical leadership, and adequate funding (Tosta, 1997).

African Initiatives

Many African governments record substantial amounts of data in the form of maps. The major sources of spatial data are the national mapping agencies; many municipal authorities also gather spatial data, with particular attention to cadastral records. Efforts are under way in a number of African countries to create digital databases through the conversion of such maps. In Botswana, for example, the Department of Town and Regional Planning has developed a digital database to monitor land use compliance in Gaborone. Lesotho's Mapping Agency is engaged in a large-scale digital mapping exercise for its urban areas. In most countries, however, metadata—the sets of organized spatial data and information about those data (e.g., where the data are located, how and by whom they were collected and maintained, how they can be accessed, and what their major characteristics are)—remain in a rudimentary form.

In Lagos, GIS technology has been employed effectively to resolve conflicts over land use. The goverment owns large portions of land in certain sections of the city, and residents are supposed to pay "ground rents." But owing to the multiple claims on many parcels and a history of poor record keeping, the government has been collecting only 5 to 10 percent of the rents it is due. To improve collection rates, a land information system is being developed that will provide access to all documents for each parcel of government-owned land. The geographic boundaries of each parcel have been derived from digital orthophotos in conjunction with various legal plot maps that have been digitized.

India

Although circumstances in India appear to strongly favor GIS advances, the country's spatial data infrastructure remains curiously limited. The great Survey of India, which dates to the mid-eighteenth century, covered the entire country with rigorous cartographic surveys. India is also the birthplace of the IRS (Indian Remote Sensing) series of satellites, which provide high-resolution remote sensing data to global markets. And India is home to a remarkable software industry. Why, then, has its use of GIS technology not progressed further?

Most Indian government agencies simply do not understand the value of their data for government functions or for the private sector. Much as in African countries, enormous quantities of valuable material are stored in paper form and seldom computerized. Security concerns have led to restrictions on access to maps, as well as to aerial photographs. Despite these obstacles, a number of diverse GIS initiatives are under way in some of India's largest cities; examples are described in Box 4.3.

Malaysia

Since the mid-1980s, several federal and state land agencies have explored GIS technology and developed stand-alone systems with valuable information. But these systems have not been integrated across agencies. In an effort to draw the information together, the Malaysian government is developing a national land information system, which will provide access to spatial data for all levels of government, the commercial sector, the nonprofit sector, academia, and the general

---

BOX 4.3 GIS Initiatives Across India

Greater Mumbai Remote sensing and GIS are much involved in land use planning, with indicators ranging from soil type to air pollution. Maps have been produced on decadal population growth, population distribution, employment, the distribution of socioeconomic facilities, agriculture and forest land uses, and traffic patterns. These maps have illuminated spatial and temporal trends in each settlement within the Mumbai Metropolitan Region. GIS technology has also been used to assess alternative locations for a proposed second international airport and for a solid waste disposal site, and is assisting in the preparation of a rehabilitation and resettlement program for encroachments at Bandra-Kurla Complex, site of a planned international finance and business center. The government is using GIS technology to map features related to fire hazards and risk assessment, as well as service delivery.

Perhaps the most interesting development in Mumbai is that a proposed land use plan for the metropolitan region has been transferred to village maps. Citizens and other concerned groups are thereby able to understand the implications of the proposed plan and to file objections and suggestions.

Hyderabad The Center for Resource Education undertook a project on spatial mapping of industrial estates and environmental hazardous sites in or near residential areas. The maps depict the contribution of each industry to pollution, show the likely environmental impact, and indicate monitoring points. Hyderabad has also been developing a GIS-based integrated emergency response management system for Hyderabad City. The project incorporates maps depicting land use, road networks (including travel time estimates), and the locations and numbers of fire and police stations and water-filling points.

Chennai City (Madras) A GIS database has been developed for road networks. With this database, priorities can be assigned to road improvements in the context of an integrated transportation information system.

Bangalore The Bangalore Development Authority has used GIS applications for route planning and tracking of 200 (and eventually 2,000) private buses. The Global Positioning System (GPS) is used to monitor the locations of the buses and to generate appropriate bills based on distance traveled.

---

public. The private sector is being encouraged to contribute products and services (Mahid Bin Mohamed, 1998).

Other Applications

Elsewhere around the world, GIS technology is being applied in innovative ways to improve urban management. The Kuwaiti Ministry of Public Works has launched a large-scale computerized management system to assist in the maintenance of roadways, bridges, sanitary and storm sewers, and street rights-of-way. The Water Authority of Jordan has employed GIS technology to restructure the water supply network in Amman. This project has involved a complete redesign of the water supply system in the city's congested, densely populated core. In Dhaka, GIS technology has been applied to the problem of drainage in Dhaka City. A digital elevation model was established for the catchment area; inundation maps were then produced, and various flooding scenarios of the past were simulated. Use of this technology, found to be cost-effective, has enabled the government to develop sustainable flood alleviation schemes.

The Future of GIS

Although the above are all promising developments, each involves substantial costs, ranging from those of personnel and training to those of purchasing and converting maps. GIS entails much more than technology, and because it requires cooperation among units and levels of government that have little experience in this regard, it may be perceived as threatening. Effective use of the technology requires both new organizational structures and experienced staff. The few case studies available do not demonstrate that the novel techniques and ways of thinking about information and interrelated services made possible by GIS will necessarily make successful transitions from the technical staffs of engineering and planning departments to the broader (and more powerful) realms of government. But clearly this is a development that bears watching, and one that may well bring new energies to bear on the collection of spatially disaggregated data.

CONCLUSIONS AND RECOMMENDATIONS

This chapter has addressed a wide range of issues, touching on both methods and substance. In concluding, we pass rather lightly over the empirical findings presented earlier in the chapter and emphasize implications for the infrastructure needed to support urban population research.

Conclusions

The analytic models examined in this chapter highlight a point that is often overlooked: urban growth rates and the migrant shares of growth will both tend to be high when a country is in its initial stages of urbanization; both will then tend to decline as the level of urbanization rises. The linkages of urban natural increase to the rate of urbanization can also be misperceived. If urban natural increase happens to equal rural natural increase, rural-to-urban migration will be the dominant factor in urbanization. This is the argument of the United Nations (1980). Although there was evidence of equal rates of natural increase in the 1950s and 1960s, it is unclear whether equality in the rates persists. If it does not, differences in the rates of natural increase will also exert an important influence on the rate of urbanization. Migration has a distinctive role to play in affecting urban age structures—together with lower urban fertility, it confers upon city age distributions a distinctive shape in which greater proportions of the population are found in the productive and reproductive ages. Hence, other things being held equal, rural-to-urban migration will tend to inflate urban fertility rates. Moving back one link in the chain, we find that rural natural increase, working through migration, exerts an influence on urban fertility. The interlinkages of urban and rural populations are as clearly evident in analytic models as in empirical studies.

Using data from the DHS, we have found that among urban women of reproductive age, nearly one woman in four is a recent migrant, having moved to her current city or town less than half a decade earlier. In studies of urban change, the term "migrant" calls up the image of a rural-to-urban migrant. The DHS data show, however, that most urban migrants come from other towns and cities; only about one migrant in three arrives directly from a rural area. It appears that the common view of migrants needs to be tempered by empirical realities. Researchers need to consider more carefully the implications of migration within the urban sector. There is little evidence to support another common perception—that migrants are more prevalent in the populations of large than small cities. For women, at least, the DHS data do not confirm this supposition.

Turning to the aggregate data sources on urban and city populations, we underscored a familiar point, one that is mentioned in many scientific reviews of urbanization: countries define urban areas in a great variety of ways. This definitional heterogeneity is of concern mainly with respect to small settlements, but because these are so numerous, differences in definition can have a large impact on the urban totals reported at national levels. In an ideal world, it might be thought desirable for countries to adopt a common definition, but this is unlikely to occur.

How damaging is the absence of consensus? As discussed in Chapter 2, the theories that animate contemporary urban research are increasingly dismissive of simple urban/rural dichotomies, and point toward richer conceptualizations involving centrality, communication, and relational networks. These theoretical developments would appear to be leading away from simple prescriptions and definitions of urban areas. As discussed earlier, however, the measurement of such concepts is still in the early stages, and much remains to be learned about their value for empirical research, planning, and policy making. Furthermore, as can be seen throughout this report, simple urban and rural classifications retain considerable explanatory power. It is probably unwise to set such useful measures aside while better ones are being developed. In any case, because much of the international heterogeneity in definition applies to smaller settlements, analyses based on cities above a certain size (e.g., 100,000 population) can escape many of the difficulties.

Unfortunately, the United Nations estimates of city size, as presented in *World Urbanization Prospects*, are more heterogeneous and subject to measurement error than is commonly realized. We reviewed several cases and found that only the most attentive and dogged researcher would be likely to understand the idiosyncracies of the city population data. As discussed below, if the United Nations were to make its data and methods publicly available, a wider community of researchers could assist in improving measures and methods. Much the same can be said of the United Nations projections, which have often proven to be so far off the mark that consideration of alternative projection methods is now badly needed.

Recommendations for Urban Research Infrastructure

As countries urbanize, the proliferation of cities and increases in average city sizes heighten the need for adequate urban population data. There is, first, a need for acceptable estimates of city population size. Second, and especially for the larger cities, there is a greater need for intracity data, which are required both for understanding social and economic diversity and for extending services. Spatial information is essential in both of these areas, for not even city sizes can be determined without good information on city boundaries. The potential for use of spatially collected data is perhaps even greater within cities.

The difficulty lies in determining where among the many local, national, and international statistical systems there exists a combination of motivation and resources sufficient to generate such spatially disaggregated data. Of course, the major burden of responsibility must rest with the national statistical agencies themselves, but international researchers and agencies can make a contribution through focused research and coordination. The panel is hopeful that GIS and related technology advances will bring new energy and ideas to the problem, but sustained efforts and international technical assistance will clearly be required.

The panel's impression is that where city and urban population data for developing countries are concerned, most demographers believe the United Nations Population Division will somehow take care of things. Yet the Population Division is but one small group of expert professionals with many responsibilities extending beyond the maintenance of urban databases. If the panel understands correctly, the Population Division manages to assemble its urban estimates and projections with very few resources, evidently dedicating less than the equivalent of a single full-time staffer to the task. The United Nations Statistical Office likewise has many responsibilities. It would be unrealistic to suppose that these units are about to receive major new infusions of funds and personnel.

Yet the status quo is a precarious arrangement. It places responsibility for urban databases essential to the demographic field on the shoulders of a very few individuals. If city and urban population data series are to be adequately and critically reviewed on an ongoing basis and if alternative forecasting methods are to be explored in any depth, a way must be found to bring greater resources to bear. More researchers, especially from the countries that contribute the data series, need to be involved, and more methodological perspectives taken into account. In the panel's view, on which we elaborate in this volume's concluding chapter, the best way to attract more resources to the problem is to place the United Nations data and methods in the public domain, giving the Population Division the task of coordinating full-scale critical reviews.

There is an urgent need for review of the empirical basis for city and urban population projections. United Nations projections of the populations of large cities have displayed a tendency toward upward bias. Total urban populations have also been projected to grow at rates that, in retrospect, were much too rapid. Although the United Nations has taken special care to restrain projections of city and urban population growth, it appears that these efforts have been insufficient. If the United Nations were to place its sources and methods fully in the public domain, the problems that produce such projection errors might be diagnosed more effectively.

Where the DHS program is concerned, the problem on which this chapter has shed light is the lack—until quite recently—of adequate spatial identifiers in the datasets released for public use. The problem, as we understand it, is that disclosure of the spatial locations of sampling clusters might compromise the privacy of respondents and threaten the exposure of confidential information. These are important concerns. As the research for this volume drew to a close, the DHS moved to address such concerns with a permissions policy that gives researchers access to GIS spatial identifiers for its recently fielded surveys. This is a welcome change in procedures; over time it will much enhance the value of DHS data for urban demography. We hope that the DHS will now do what it can to provide spatial identifiers for the surveys it fielded before 1999. There are potential benefits for rural analyses as well as urban. It may be that indicators of distance to nearby cities would suffice to measure concepts of rural "remoteness." In a world that is increasingly urban and in which rural areas are coming under the influence of city economies and societies, it is difficult to imagine a next generation of demographic research that does not attend more closely to the implications of space.

5

Diversity and Inequality

Diversity is among the defining features of city life. Seen from one perspective, diversity is a manifestation of the concept of the city as lottery, a social arena where risks and rewards are on display. It is evidence of mobility and possibility. But from another perspective, diversity is experienced as inequity, a reminder of immobility and possibilities frustrated. This chapter explores several of the dimensions of urban socioeconomic diversity and inequality. Particular attention is paid to the circumstances of the urban poor.

On close inspection, the housing and living conditions of the urban poor prove to be more varied than might have been thought, and it is not easy to reduce indicators of urban housing quality to estimates of the population living in slums. Even the term "slum" tends to be avoided in careful research on urban housing, although it can be employed as a convenient shorthand. The tone adopted in scientific studies resembles that of the United Nations Centre for Human Settlements (UNCHS) (1996:205): "How simplistic and often inaccurate it is to assume that most low-income groups [live] in 'slums' or 'slums and squatter settlements'." On the question of changes in the percentages of urban dwellers in slums, UNCHS (1996) does not find sufficient evidence to draw conclusions, although it does concede that the total numbers living in such settlements are large and probably have been rising. Not until 1990, when UNCHS began its Housing Indicators Programme, was a sustained effort made on a large scale to bring order and coherence to empirical measures of urban housing, enabling cross-country comparisons in a few key dimensions. This study (described in UNCHS [1996:196]; see also Malpezzi [1999]) laid the groundwork for a more nuanced understanding of urban living conditions and drew attention to the variety of housing markets in which the urban poor participate.

We approach urban poverty with the understanding that it has many facets that need to be considered. Housing is of interest, as are levels of income and consumption. Other aspects also warrant attention. When poverty is conceptualized as having multiple dimensions, the focus of analyses extends from individuals and households to groups, encompassing measures of the economic and political power held by groups and the qualities and capacities of local and national governments. As will be seen, a recognition of poverty's multiple dimensions suggests broader roles for programs and policies than could be deduced from a consideration of income and consumption alone.

As we seek to understand how diversity and inequality manifest themselves spatially, we initially examine city maps of socioeconomic indicators. It is disappointing that the analysis cannot then proceed systematically to the level of city neighborhoods and districts. As mentioned in Chapter 2, the conceptual and empirical tools that have been applied to the cities of rich countries await further application to the cities of poor countries. We are confident that the neighborhood data exist, though at present they are inaccessible.

To be sure, the literature on poor countries presents many fine-grained portraits of selected city neighborhoods. The micro studies give vivid and compelling accounts of the absolute poverty and serious deprivation that can be found in some city neighborhoods, but such studies provide an uncertain basis for wider generalization. Household surveys fielded at the national level can offer such a generalized overview—in what follows, we rely heavily on the Demographic and Health Surveys (DHS)—but they usually lack the sample sizes needed to detect socioeconomic differentiation at the neighborhood level or even at the level of cities. However, household surveys will generally support *aspatial* analyses of urban populations taken as a whole, and will often allow the urban population to be subdivided by city size class or separated into other broad categories.

In the first section of the chapter, then, we can only briefly examine the spatial aspects of inequality and diversity within cities. The remainder of the chapter is necessarily less spatial in orientation. Conditions among urban populations are compared with those among rural populations; within the urban populations, we explore how socioeconomic conditions vary across cities of differing population size and by measures of relative poverty.

Applying this aspatial approach, the chapter's second section examines schooling. For adults, schooling is an important determinant of socioeconomic wellbeing and demographic behavior. We show the distributions of adult education in urban and rural areas and pay special attention to the educational diversity that marks urban areas. The section following considers the distinctive features of urban poverty, describing recent research that leads to a multidimensional perspective on disadvantage. We then explore one of these dimensions in detail, examining how access to basic public services differs between rural and urban populations, and differs within urban populations along the lines of city size and relative poverty. Next, we critically assess current estimates of urban poverty in developing countries, arguing that national and international statistics are likely to have understated its prevalence. This assessment is followed by a brief discussion of the risk and vulnerability faced by the urban poor.

The chapter ends with a consideration of children's lives. How well do children fare in the cities of poor countries? If adult schooling represents the socioeconomic diversity of the current generation, children's schooling represents the potential for differences to emerge in the next generation. Schooling is the result of social investments of several kinds—those made by parents, communities, and the state. As will be seen, these investments give urban children a decided advantage in terms of school enrollment, on average, as compared with their rural counterparts. However, the urban averages conceal substantial variation. When other aspects of children's lives in the city are examined—we review what is known about street children—a fuller picture emerges of diversity and inequality in urban children's lives.

A SPATIAL PERSPECTIVE

In the cities of Africa, Asia, and Latin America, the spatial expressions of poverty and affluence are often as vivid as they are in Chicago, Los Angeles, and New York. Figure 5-1 shows the concentration of the affluent in Santiago, Chile, an urban area with some 4.7 million residents within the bounds of the city proper. Here the elites are clustered in the northeastern sections of the city. (Wealthier areas are depicted in darker shading.) The ways in which rich and poor are spatially arrayed vary greatly across cities (compare Figure 5-1 with the complex pattern seen in Mexico City in Figure 2-1 in Chapter 2), but in one form or another, many cities exhibit spatial evidence of exclusion and segregation. As we have mentioned, however, not all aspects of exclusion express themselves spatially, and researchers are beginning to explore the nonspatial forms.

The complexities can be appreciated in a recent study of Buenos Aires (Torres, 2001) that examines the increase in this city's "gated" communities—the protected enclaves of upper-income groups. Figure 5-2 depicts the changes seen in Buenos Aires during the 1990s, when many such enclaves sprang up. (The white squares represent the locations of gated communities in 1990–1991, and the black dots represent the new communities of this type that emerged by 2001.) As can be seen in Figure 5-3, a number of these enclaves lie adjacent to the neighborhoods of the poor. (In this figure, the gated communities are shown as white dots, and the darker areas indicate where the poor live.) In locating near the poor, the rich gain easy access to a pool of cheap labor, persons who can be hired as security guards, gardeners, and maids. The rich separate themselves from the poor not so much by putting them at a distance (though there is some of that), but by fortifying the borders of their enclaves and restricting the terms on which the poor are allowed to come into contact with them. This is a strategy of "proximity and high walls" (a phrase taken from Caldeira, 1996). If transport costs allow some of the poor to make longer journeys to work, the rich are permitted the additional luxury of distance. As can be seen in Figure 5-3, most of the gated communities

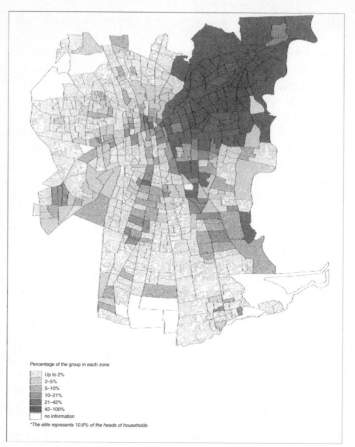

Percentage of the group in each zone

- Up to 2%
- 2–5%
- 5–10%
- 10–21%
- 21–42%
- 42–100%
- no information

*The elite represents 10.6% of the heads of households

FIGURE 5-1 Spatial concentration of the elites of Santiago, Chile. Wealthier neighborhoods are depicted in darker shading.
SOURCE: Sabatini and Arenas (2000).

of Buenos Aires are situated far from poor neighborhoods but close to the main transport routes.

A recent analysis of poverty and inequality in Argentina demonstrates that there are great differences in the quality of basic infrastructure among the neighborhoods of greater Buenos Aires. Inequality as measured by differences in provision of basic services (water, sanitation, and housing) is three times greater than inequality measured in terms of education and health status. These striking intraurban differentials illustrate the insights that can be derived from a focus on neighborhoods (Cohen, 2002).

Another spatial dimension to be considered is the situation of small relative to large cities. As noted earlier, there are a number of reasons to believe that economic conditions in small cities are often worse than those in large cities,

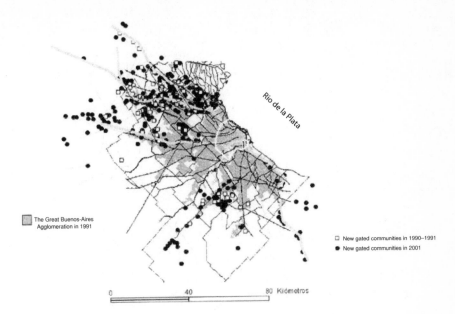

FIGURE 5-2 Increase in the number of gated communities in Buenos Aires in the 1990s.
SOURCE: Torres (2001).

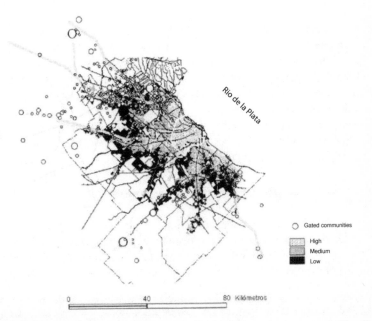

FIGURE 5-3 A number of gated communities lie adjacent to poor neighborhoods in Buenos Aires.
SOURCE: Torres (2001).

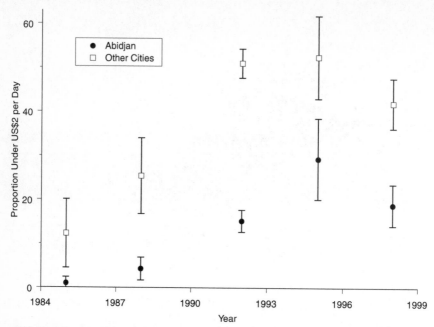

FIGURE 5-4 Poverty in Abidjan compared with that in the secondary cities of Côte d'Ivoire, 1985–1995.
SOURCE: Grimm, Guénard, and Mespleé-Somps (2002).

at least on average. Some evidence to this effect is available for Côte d'Ivoire. For the period 1985–1998, Figure 5-4 shows the levels and trends in poverty in Abidjan relative to those in the country's secondary cities. (Point estimates are given with their confidence bands.) As can be seen, the proportion of residents estimated to be living on less than US$2 per day has consistently been lower in Abidjan than in the smaller cities. Through the mid-1990s, macroeconomic deterioration drove up the poverty rates of Abidjan along with those of secondary cities, but never erased Abidjan's advantage. We report evidence of such smaller-city disadvantages throughout this chapter.

HUMAN CAPITAL: SCHOOLING

As a principal measure of human capital, adult educational attainment is of fundamental importance to incomes and socioeconomic standing. Figure 5-5 depicts the distributions of schooling in urban and rural areas, and Table 5-1 provides further region-specific detail.[1] It is not surprising to see that the average level of schooling

---

[1]The figure and table present summaries of estimates from 61 surveys fielded by the DHS program in 44 developing countries between 1985 and 1999 (see Table C-1 in Appendix C for a list of

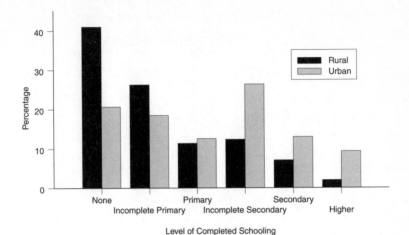

FIGURE 5-5 Completed schooling for adults, rural and urban areas. See footnote 1.

is higher in urban than in rural areas, with higher percentages of urban adults having secondary schooling or more, and lower percentages having no schooling. But to focus on the extremes of these educational distributions is to overlook another important feature: the urban distribution is less concentrated than the rural, with appreciable percentages of urban adults appearing in each of the educational categories. Here is evidence of an urban advantage—higher levels of schooling on average—coupled with evidence of greater urban diversity.

Urban/rural differences in education stem from many causes. Among these, we would single out migration because it is known to be selective of those with higher levels of schooling. A portion of the urban/rural difference might well be due to the outmigration of better-educated, formerly rural residents.[2] As will be seen later in this chapter, however, urban children have strikingly higher levels of school enrollment than their rural counterparts. Hence, the urban/rural differences shown above must also reflect long-standing differences in educational investments between the countryside and the city.

countries). The estimates refer to both women and men. The numbers shown are based on survey-specific estimates, which are weighted so that an estimate from a country with two surveys receives a weight that is one-half that of a country with only one survey. Estimates from countries with three or four surveys are similarly downweighted. This is our practice throughout the report. Note, however, that the number of surveys and countries varies depending on what is being analyzed. Educational attainment is measured in the DHS household modules, but before the recent rounds of the DHS program, not all surveys included education questions for all household members. Although fertility data are available for 90 surveys, adult educational data are available for far fewer surveys.

[2]Unfortunately, we cannot isolate the migration component. DHS surveys generally do not identify the former residences of adults in the household, other than the woman selected for the main interview.

TABLE 5-1 Adult Educational Attainment, Rural and Urban Areas

DHS Surveys in Region[a]		Percentage of Adults with					
		None	Some Primary	Complete Primary	Some Secondary	Complete Secondary	Higher
North	Rural	59.5	14.0	4.9	11.5	7.7	2.4
Africa	Urban	28.0	13.6	9.9	22.9	15.0	10.7
Sub-	Rural	51.5	27.6	9.7	9.5	1.2	0.5
Saharan Africa	Urban	27.7	22.5	13.3	27.2	5.9	3.8
Southeast	Rural	11.0	26.7	25.6	20.5	12.0	5.7
Asia	Urban	3.9	11.9	17.2	27.0	26.6	17.8
South,	Rural	33.2	8.4	9.9	17.2	26.3	5.0
Central, West Asia	Urban	17.3	6.6	8.5	22.8	27.0	17.8
Latin	Rural	23.8	41.3	15.4	13.8	4.0	1.7
America	Urban	7.9	21.2	13.9	28.5	15.1	13.3
TOTAL	Rural	41.0	26.3	11.4	12.4	7.1	2.0
	Urban	20.7	18.5	12.6	26.4	13.0	9.4

[a] Number of countries surveyed: North Africa, 2; sub-Saharan Africa, 23; Southeast Asia, 2; South, Central, and West Asia, 8; Latin America, 9; all regions, 44.

Why does educational diversity matter? In Chapter 2 we referred to the economic and social theories that draw out its implications. The collective socialization theory of Coleman (1988) and Wilson (1987) posits that educated adults may wield beneficial influence in poor neighborhoods; the economic theories of Jacobs (1969), Rauch (1993), and Moretti (2000) suggest that economic interactions between the better and less educated may generate positive externalities in city labor markets and firms. What is central to these theories, but missing from Figure 5-5, is the aspect of *interaction*. It is one thing to note that cities contain a diversity of educational levels, but quite another to say that adults with different levels of education commonly interact, whether in their social or economic relations. Spatial segregation and exclusion no doubt inhibit interaction, but individuals may interact in their workplaces and other settings across a metropolitan region. (Measuring such interactions is admittedly difficult.) Still, the mere presence of educational diversity in cities raises the possibility of beneficial spillovers in city neighborhoods and labor markets.

Comparing educational attainment across city size classes (see Figure 5-6), we find that adults living in large cities (especially in those of 1 million or more population) tend to have acquired more schooling than those in small cities and towns. This is easily seen in the percentages having secondary and higher schooling.

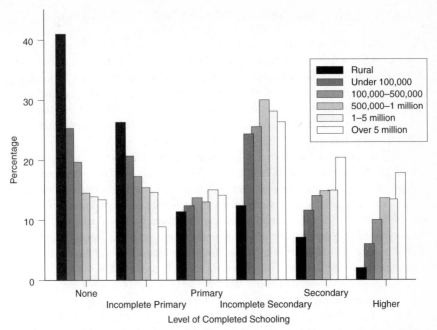

FIGURE 5-6 Completed schooling for adults, rural and urban areas by city size.

Again, however, there is evidence of substantial diversity in schooling levels, even in the larger cities.

For the 16 countries having two or more DHS surveys, we are able to examine changes over time in the educational attainment of adults.[3] Over the period between surveys—about 5 years on average—there was a decline in the percentage of adults having no schooling or at most incomplete primary schooling. In 11 of the 16 countries, the percentage of adults with no schooling fell in both rural and urban areas, with the rural decline generally being larger than the urban. In 7 countries, the percentage of adults with incomplete primary education also declined in both rural and urban areas, but here the decline tended to be larger in urban areas. Examining the other end of the educational distribution, we find that the percentage of adults with higher schooling increased in 9 countries, with the urban increase again being greater than the rural on average, and much the same was true at the level of completed secondary schooling. In summary, where the trends in adult schooling can be examined, the data show that the relative situation of rural and urban populations remains much as it is portrayed in Figure 5-5: an urban advantage on average, together with greater urban diversity.

---

[3]The countries are Bangladesh, Bolivia, Cameroon, Colombia, the Dominican Republic, Egypt, Ghana, Guatemala, Indonesia (where three time points can be compared), Kenya, Madagascar, Niger, Peru, the Philippines, Tanzania, and Zambia.

URBAN WELL-BEING: CONCEPTS AND MEASURES

The path from educational attainment to living standards and well-being is complex and indirect, involving, among other things, many mediating institutions and policies. Although education data are helpful in understanding socioeconomic diversity, they inevitably tell something less than the full story. This section takes up the problem of how to define urban living standards, treating the issues in broad, conceptual terms, but commenting in passing on measurement concerns to be discussed at length later.

A glance at the literature shows that the conceptualization of urban poverty by researchers is increasingly diverging from the methods used by governments to measure it. Recent research has taken to describing poverty in multidimensional terms, even as the official poverty measures continue to be expressed in highly simplified, unidimensional terms. Poverty measures typically take the form of income-based or consumption-based poverty lines, with the thresholds defined mainly in terms of food consumption. Such restricted definitions testify to the difficulties involved in measuring poverty's multiple dimensions, but they can also distort understanding of its causes and may unnecessarily narrow the scope for intervention on the part of local and international agencies.

Box 5.1 lists some of the key dimensions of urban poverty identified in the literature.[4] Although we emphasize its implications for urban poverty, this research owes a great deal to studies of rural poverty (see especially Chambers, 1983, 1995; Beck, 1994). The roles of income and assets are central and well recognized in the new research, but other dimensions of poverty are also singled out for consideration. A leading example is a lack of voice within political systems that keeps the concerns of the poor from being heard; another example is the poor's inadequate security and lack of protection from violence, theft, and fraud.

It is the multiplicity of deprivations and the connections among them that characterize the circumstances of many urban poor. As Navarro (2001) notes, a low-income family with only one income earner living in an illegal settlement on a flood plain cannot really be said to have three distinct problems (low income,

---

[4]This box draws on a typology developed by Baulch (1996) to describe rural poverty, modified to reflect the dimensions of poverty that are common in urban areas. It is meant only to illustrate different aspects of urban poverty; others could certainly be added. The multiple aspects of poverty are described by Moser (1993, 1996, 1998), Moser, Herbert, and Makonnen (1993), Amis (1995), Wratten (1995), Rakodi (1995), Satterthwaite (1996b), and Anzorena, Bolnick, Boonyabancha, Cabannes, Hardoy, Hasan, Levy, Mitlin, et al. (1998), among others.

Perhaps the best-known of the multidimensional indices is the Human Poverty Index (HPI), developed by the United Nations Development Programme and introduced in the 1997 Human Development Report (United Nations Development Program, 1997b). This index, generally applied to national populations but sometimes to population subgroups, takes three factors of poverty into account: vulnerability to death before age 40; the illiteracy rate, and the standard of living, this last being measured on the basis of access to health services and safe water and the percentage of children under age 5 who are malnourished.

BOX 5.1 The Multiple Dimensions of Urban Poverty

Income and consumption Poverty is conventionally defined ~~~~~
inadequate to permit the purchase of necessities, incl'
sufficient quantity. Because incomes can be transitor
levels of consumption are often used as indicators of the ~~
income.

Assets The nature of household assets also bears on the longer-term aspects of poverty
and the degree to which households are shielded from risk. A household's assets
may be inadequate, unstable, difficult to convert to monetized form, or subject to
economic, weather-related, or political risks; access to credit may be restricted or
loans available only at high rates of interest. For many of the urban poor, significant
proportions of income go to repay debts (see, e.g., Amis and Kumar, 2000).

Time costs Conventional poverty lines do not directly incorporate the time needed for
low-income households to travel to work or undertake other essential tasks. Such
households often try to reduce their monetary expenditures on travel by walking or
enduring long commutes (Moser, 1996). Time costs also affect the net value of
some goods and services.

Shelter Shelter may be of poor quality, overcrowded, or insecure.

Public infrastructure Inadequate provision of public infrastructure (piped water, sanitation, drainage, roads, and the like) can increase health burdens, as well as the time
and money costs of employment.

Other basic services There can be inadequate provision of such basic services as health
care, emergency services, law enforcement, schools, day care, vocational training,
and communication.

Safety nets There may be no social safety net to secure consumption, access to shelter,
and health care when incomes fall.

Protection of rights The rights of poor groups may be inadequately protected, there being
a lack of effective laws and regulations regarding civil and political rights, occupational health and safety, pollution control, environmental health, violence and crime,
discrimination, and exploitation.

Political voice The poor's lack of voice and their powerlessness within political and
bureaucratic systems may leave them with little likelihood of receiving entitlements
and little prospect that organizing and making demands on the public sector will
produce a fair response. The lack of voice also refers to an absence of means to
ensure accountability from public, private, and nongovernmental agencies.

---

insecure tenure, and exposure to environmental risk)—its difficulties are manifestations of a fundamental deprivation. Of course, if the multiple dimensions of
poverty were always so closely related, a single poverty measure might suffice to
identify poor households. Why, then, is it necessary to elaborate on each of the
multiple dimensions?

itlin and Satterthwaite (2001) develop the rationale. First, a number of case dies show how the deprivations associated with low income can be eased without increasing income as such. Several routes have been explored: increasing asset bases, improving basic infrastructure and services, and fostering political changes that give low-income groups a means of negotiating for greater governmental support or less harassment (see Patel and Mitlin, 2001; Baumann, Bolnick, and Mitlin, 2001).

Second, governments and nongovernmental organizations (NGOs) may have few direct means of increasing the incomes of the poor, but may be better equipped to address other dimensions of poverty. Recent experience with micro finance in cities (and with funds that support public works and employment) suggests a greater scope for raising urban incomes than many had supposed. In most cities, however, the prospects for effective direct intervention will doubtless remain limited (see Benjamin, 2000; Amis and Kumar, 2000; Etemadi, 2000).

Third, an effective intervention in the nonincome dimensions of poverty sometimes has the potential to increase real incomes. Better-quality housing and improved public services can enhance income-earning opportunities for home enterprises, allowing rooms to be rented out and small enterprises to be maintained. The provision of piped water can reduce a household's water bill, which in turn may permit consumption of more food; see Cairncross (1990) on the mechanisms. Improved infrastructure and services protect health and reduce fatigue (as when water piped into the home replaces a long trek to a standpipe) and in this way may increase net income (as when reduced illness and injury mean less time taken from work and lower medical costs).

Fourth, even increased incomes may not enable households to escape poverty. In many cities, the provision of infrastructure and services is so limited and the capacity to expand them so weak, that families with incomes above the poverty line can find it difficult to locate housing with adequate services and protections against risk (Hardoy, Mitlin, and Satterthwaite, 2001). These families may suffer from most of the deprivations of poverty without being officially classified as poor by the standard income criteria.[5] The deprivations identified in Box 5.1 are not problems of the income-poor alone; those with adequate income can also lack political voice and suffer from inadequate protection.

Fifth, a nuanced understanding of urban poverty helps policy makers expand the set of agencies charged with roles in poverty reduction. Most municipal agencies do not see their principal responsibilities as lying in the area of poverty alleviation when poverty is defined in terms of income alone. But if the definition is expanded, as in Box 5.1, then public transport authorities, hospitals, occupational health and safety agencies, and water companies may come to understand that the

---

[5] See McDade and Adair (2001) for an empirical assessment of the overlap in three dimensions of poverty in Cebu, Philippines—levels of consumption, access to infrastructure, and access to health services.

services for which they are responsible can affect poverty. When poverty is described in expanded terms, the poor are given a new vocabulary with which they can assert claims to state resources.

Links to the state and to external private groups can be critical in bringing resources to poor communities (Anzorena, Bolnick, Boonyabancha, Cabannes, Hardoy, Hasan, Levy, Mitlin, et al., 1998; Mitlin and Satterthwaite, 2001). In Chapter 2, this point is discussed in connection with the bridging role of local social capital, and illustrated by the experience of the Mumbai-based alliance of SPARC, the National Slum Dwellers Federation, and Mahila Milan (recall Box 2.2). As that case shows, the quality of the relationship between the poor and external organizations depends on organizational transparency and the degree to which outside organizations are accountable to the poor. A number of case studies demonstrate how much the urban poor can achieve when they have good relationships with local and external organizations (Baumann, Bolnick, and Mitlin, 2001; Patel and Mitlin, 2001).

A broad conception of poverty also draws out its implications for women. Because women take responsibility for care of children and the sick, in addition to routine household management, they often bear much of the burden of the time costs described above. Poor women can be exposed to greater health or social risks than poor men (Moser, 1996, 1987, 1993; Beall and Levy, 1994; Lee-Smith and Trujillo, 1992; Crewe, 1995; Sapir, 1990; Songsore and McGranahan, 1998). For instance, women are often responsible for the disposal of their households' human wastes when provision for sanitation is inadequate, and this can elevate the risks to their own health.

ACCESS TO PUBLIC SERVICES

Most countries gather data on the provision of infrastructure and public services, although few include access to services in their official definitions of poverty. The official reports on service provision make their way into the international databases, where they are duly recorded as national, urban, and rural percentages. It is unclear, however, whether these reports are reliable. What counts as "adequate provision" is often left vague in the official accounts. For example, are households that take water from a standpipe that works for 2 hours a day as adequately served as households whose water is piped to the home (Hardoy, Mitlin, and Satterthwaite, 2001)? Even in countries with sophisticated data collection abilities, such as Argentina, local authorities often know surprisingly little about the quality of service provision in their jurisdictions (Navarro, 2001). In an effort to improve the situation, some international agencies are beginning their own programs of data gathering and monitoring. Box 5.2 describes the *Cities Data Book* project under way at the Asian Development Bank.

In what follows, we rely on the data on access to services gathered by the DHS in the course of its household interviews. Although these data are not all

---

BOX 5.2 The Asian Development Bank's *Cities Data Book*

The *Cities Data Book* project for the Asian and Pacific Region was organized by the Asian Development Bank in 1998. The objectives of the project are:

- To build the capacity of local governments to collect and use urban indicators to improve coverage and operational performance.

- To develop criteria and methods for the measurement and evaluation of urban service delivery.

- To enhance interaction and information exchange among local governments.

The project, which involves some 17 local governments from 15 countries, lends assistance to local governments in developing methods for collecting and analyzing data. The core questionnaire covers such social indicators as population, land use, income and employment, poverty, health, and education, as well as sectoral areas of service provision such as shelter, transport, communication, energy, water supply, and sanitation. Data on local governments cover the structure of revenues and expenditures, measures of satisfaction with services, and indicators of the roles of public corporations and privatized urban services companies. Over the course of the project, quantitative and qualitative analyses will address city organizations, relationships with higher levels of government, major issues in service provision, and the effectiveness of service delivery.

The *Cities Data Book* also includes theme papers that explore the implications of the local government data for urban development strategies, capacity building for efficient data collection and analysis, best practices in urban monitoring and data collection, and the role of local data in promoting efficient and sustainable urban management.

---

that could be desired, they have the important advantage of being recorded at the household level. There is some variation from survey to survey in how access to services is measured, but the DHS has imposed a coding scheme that keeps this variation within reasonable bounds. By choosing to define broad categories of access—see Box 5.3 for the scheme adopted by the panel—we have organized the data in a way that should permit valid comparisons across countries and over time, at the cost of omitting some of the country-specific detail.

Urban and Rural Access to Services

Table 5-2 summarizes the data on services for the rural and urban sectors as a whole. The urban advantage can be seen at a glance. There is an enormous gap between urban and rural areas in the provision of piped drinking water: the percentages in urban areas range from nearly 5 times those of rural areas in the case of sub-Saharan Africa to a ratio of about 2 to 1 in the case of North Africa.[6] Access to drinking water through standpipes and other neighborhood sources is less unevenly distributed, with the rural and urban percentages being roughly equal in sub-Saharan Africa and Southeast Asia, but higher in rural areas in the

---

[6]The only countries surveyed in North Africa are Egypt and Morocco.

TABLE 5-2 Percentages of Households with Access to Public Services, Rural and Urban Areas

DHS Surveys in Region	Area	Piped or Well Water on Premises	Water in Neighborhood	Water from Other Sources	Time to Water[a]	Flush Toilet	Pit Toilet	Other Toilet	Electricity	Lacks 3 Services
North Africa	Rural	41.6	37.3	21.0	30.8	41.3	17.5	41.2	52.7	35.9
	Urban	85.0	13.1	1.9	22.6	93.2	4.0	2.8	91.7	3.4
	(N)[b]	(2)	(2)	(2)	(2)	(3)	(3)	(3)	(3)	(3)
Sub-Saharan Africa	Rural	7.8	55.7	36.5	29.4	1.1	51.0	47.9	4.3	88.5
	Urban	40.8	50.1	9.2	17.7	21.7	66.8	11.6	41.5	43.9
	(N)	(22)	(22)	(22)	(20)	(20)	(20)	(20)	(20)	(20)
Southeast Asia	Rural	18.6	53.7	27.7	13.1	55.5	24.3	20.1	50.8	29.4
	Urban	46.6	47.6	5.8	9.4	81.8	12.7	5.5	89.9	5.0
	(N)	(2)	(2)	(2)	(2)	(1)	(1)	(1)	(2)	(1)
South, Central, West Asia	Rural	28.1	53.6	18.3	25.6	4.3	55.4	40.3	55.2	39.5
	Urban	73.7	23.2	3.0	19.8	56.9	26.3	16.7	90.7	6.7
	(N)	(9)	(9)	(9)	(8)	(9)	(9)	(9)	(9)	(9)
Latin America	Rural	31.4	36.4	32.2	19.9	12.6	44.0	43.4	40.5	46.4
	Urban	68.4	28.1	3.5	18.8	56.5	35.0	8.5	92.1	4.9
	(N)	(8)	(8)	(8)	(6)	(6)	(6)	(6)	(6)	(6)
TOTAL	Rural	18.5	50.7	30.8	26.3	7.5	48.2	44.3	25.2	65.9
	Urban	55.1	38.5	6.3	18.1	41.7	46.8	11.5	64.9	25.4
	(N)	(43)	(43)	(43)	(38)	(39)	(39)	(39)	(40)	(38)

[a] In minutes, calculated for households lacking in-home access to water.

[b] The numbers in parentheses are the numbers of countries in the region whose surveys included the item.

BOX 5.3 Measures of Access to Basic Public Services in the Demographic and Health Surveys

---

Drinking water For the panel's analyses, access to drinking water is coded in three categories: (1) water delivered through in-residence pipes or an in-residence well, the latter accounting for a small proportion of cases; (2) water available not in the home but in the neighborhood, usually via standpipes or neighborhood wells, but including cases in which water is purchased from vendors and tanker trucks; and (3) water drawn from other sources, such as from open streams and rainwater. These access measures are meant to represent the household's main water source, and only one response per household is recorded in a DHS interview. No data are available from DHS surveys on water costs, the variability of water supply, or perceived levels of contamination.

In addition, many countries have fielded a question on the time required to fetch water and return. This indicator is presumably sensitive to congestion (waiting) costs, as well as to the distance of the household from its main water source.

Waste disposal The household's access to a method of waste disposal is measured by whether the household (1) has access to a flush toilet; (2) uses a pit toilet or latrine; or (3) uses some other method of disposal, such as "throw-aways" or deposits in the bush. As with access to water, each surveyed household responds in terms of its principal method of waste disposal, and multiple methods are not recorded.

Some DHS surveys include additional questions on the privacy of access to flush toilets, pit toilets, and latrines, which could show how many households must share such facilities. Unfortunately, not enough surveys include these questions to justify exploring them in the panel's analyses. No information is gathered on the frequency with which facilities other than flush toilets are cleaned, or on the time costs of access in the case of shared facilities.

Electricity Access to electricity is measured crudely through a "yes–no" question that omits the dimensions of cost, reliability, and adequacy of power.

---

other regions. The drawing of water from other sources is seen mainly in the countryside.

These urban/rural differences in types of access to water are reflected in the time costs of access as well, as shown in the "time to water" column of Table 5-2. Even when attention is limited to households lacking in-home access to water, as is the case here, rural households need substantially more time than urban to fetch water and return, with Latin America being the exception.

Where waste disposal is concerned, a marked urban advantage is seen in access to flush toilets, an advantage that is due mainly, no doubt, to differences in the provision of piped water. The use of pit toilets and latrines is quite common in the cities of sub-Saharan Africa, where about two-thirds of urban households dispose of their wastes in this manner. A significant fraction of households also use pit toilets and latrines in South, Central, and West Asia and in Latin America.

What does it matter that a pit toilet is used rather than a flush toilet? In rural areas, a well-constructed and -maintained pit latrine can provide the same health advantages as a flush toilet if water is available for washing after defecation. The use of other methods of waste disposal also merits comment. In small, uncrowded rural villages, defecation in the bush or in the open can pose little risk of contact with feces or contamination of water sources. In crowded urban areas, however, poorly maintained pit toilets, open defecation, and "wrap and throw" may present substantial health risks. Table 5-2 shows that significant percentages of urban households use such methods of waste disposal in sub-Saharan Africa; in South, West, and Central Asia; and even in Latin America.

According to the estimates in Table 5-2, some 90 percent or more of urban households have access to electricity except in the case of sub-Saharan Africa, where only 42 percent of households are electrified. Rural households in sub-Saharan Africa are rarely supplied with electricity, although 41 to 55 percent of rural households have access to it in other regions.

The last column of Table 5-2 presents a composite indicator of disadvantage that summarizes lack of access to public services. This measure identifies households that lack three such services: in-home access to drinking water, a flush toilet, and electricity. The households that are least well served are the rural households of sub-Saharan Africa, almost 89 percent of which lack all three services. The best-served households are those in urban North Africa, only 2 percent of which lack these services.

Can such composite measures of disadvantage be used to define residence in an urban slum? The measure just described makes no reference to housing as such; neither does it address the spatial concentration of disadvantage. But with these limitations noted, how might it perform? In sub-Saharan Africa, the composite measure would place some 44 percent of the urban population in slums. In North Africa, Southeast Asia, and Latin America, however, it would suggest that only 5 percent of the urban population resides in slums. Many researchers, we suspect, would reject 5 percent as being far too low a number. But if a services-based definition is rejected, what properly defines a slum? Is crowded and dilapidated housing sufficient to capture the essence of the concept?

In considering trends in service delivery, which can be examined for only 17 pairs of DHS surveys, we find some evidence of improvement outside sub-Saharan Africa. For provision of electricity, the average increase recorded between DHS surveys (over a span averaging 5 years) is 5.9 percentage points in rural and 6.3 points in urban areas. The gains recorded in piped water and access to flush toilets are smaller, on the order of 2 percentage points in rural areas and less than 1 percentage point in urban areas. Little progress is seen for sub-Saharan Africa, as might be expected given its chronic economic malaise. Outside this region, however, the urban/rural gap is maintained as the levels of provision rise.

These analyses reveal striking urban advantages in almost all of the service indicators. In most of the countries surveyed, the average urban resident enjoys much better access to services than the average rural resident. This is hardly surprising. The presence of middle- and upper-income groups in cities undoubtedly drives up the urban averages, insofar as access to services improves with ability to pay. Another urban advantage lies in the significant economies of scale, scope, and proximity that (at least in principle) reduce the costs per user of some public services. Of course, government investment priorities have often favored cities, whether as a result of political bias or because of the lower unit costs of service provision.

Differences by City Size

Within the urban population, are large and small cities equally well served? As discussed in Chapters 1 and 3, much of the urban population of developing countries is found in smaller cities, which are also likely to accommodate much of the developing world's future population growth. If current levels of service delivery in small cities and towns are any indication, large programs of capital investment are likely to be needed.

Table 5-3 shows why. Smaller towns and cities—particularly those under 100,000 in population—are significantly underserved by comparison with larger cities.[7] The association between city size and the proportion served is not entirely uniform—irregularities are apparent in the region-specific estimates—but the general picture is one of poorer services in smaller cities.

Differentials such as these do raise a question about the substantive meaning of city size. Population size is but a crude proxy for more fundamental city characteristics on which data are lacking. It is probable that city size and the quality of public-sector management are correlated only loosely, if at all. Larger cities have bigger municipal staffs and greater total resources to deploy than small cities, but their staff and resources can be defeated by the greater scale of the management tasks they face. Across the range of cities examined by the United Nations Population Division, it is the smaller cities that tend to have higher population growth rates (see Chapters 1 and 3), and this may subject their generally thinner management teams to greater stress. Many other factors are doubtless involved in the relationship between city size and public-sector performance.

Note, however, that even the smallest cities—those with fewer than 100,000 residents—exhibit levels of service provision that are well above those seen in rural areas (compare Tables 5-2 and 5-3). Settlements of this size may not be thought to have a strong claim to "urbanness," and of course it is in this size range that countries differ greatly in how they distinguish urban from rural places (see Chapter 4). Referring back to Figure 5-6, we find that a gap of this sort also characterizes adult educational attainment, with small towns and cities having higher levels of schooling than rural areas. Such gaps reappear in many contexts

---

[7]The contrasts in the table are statistically significant less often in sub-Saharan Africa than in other regions.

TABLE 5-3 Percentages of Urban Households with Access to Public Services, by City Population Size

DHS Surveys in Region	City Size				
	Under 100,000	100,000 to 500,000	500,000 to 1 million	1 to 5 million	Over 5 million
Piped or Well Water on Premises					
North Africa	79.6	89.0	91.2	82.6	94.8
Sub-Saharan Africa[a]	35.4	45.1	42.3	55.1	
Southeast Asia	36.1	50.2	39.2	56.1	53.2
South, Central, West Asia	64.0	72.4	67.0	74.1	61.0
Latin America	66.0	73.8	79.8	64.9	90.1
TOTAL	49.2	60.3	60.6	65.5	69.5
Minutes Needed to Fetch Water Outside the Home					
North Africa	23.2	20.2	20.9	22.8	22.6
Sub-Saharan Africa	19.1	14.1	19.7	13.5	
Southeast Asia	8.6	9.1	8.4	7.2	11.4
South, Central, West Asia	26.1	15.0	13.1	14.2	20.3
Latin America	17.9	19.4	18.0	19.4	20.8
TOTAL	20.0	15.3	17.0	15.9	18.2
Access to Flush Toilet					
North Africa	88.3	95.4	95.4	93.1	98.5
Sub-Saharan Africa	18.0	20.6	25.4	30.5	
Southeast Asia	78.1	82.5	89.1		84.8
South, Central, West Asia	36.8	56.0	71.5	75.9	82.1
Latin America	42.6	57.7	61.6	65.3	82.3
TOTAL	32.2	44.1	55.0	59.4	84.5
Access to Pit Toilet or Latrine					
North Africa	6.9	3.5	1.7	4.2	1.0
Sub-Saharan Africa	65.7	70.6	72.6	63.5	
Southeast Asia	14.4	10.3	9.2		13.9
South, Central, West Asia	44.4	25.9	17.2	19.2	13.5
Latin America	44.1	29.9	30.1	28.6	14.5
TOTAL	52.3	44.3	39.1	35.2	12.2
Availability of Electricity					
North Africa	90.9	94.4	93.8	88.7	99.1
Sub-Saharan Africa	33.8	46.7	52.0	65.5	
Southeast Asia	83.7	90.4	85.6	97.2	98.8
South, Central, West Asia	81.0	89.1	93.3	94.3	91.6
Latin America	84.0	89.9	97.4	98.0	99.1
TOTAL	57.1	70.4	77.1	85.0	96.2

(continued)

TABLE 5-3 (*continued*)

DHS Surveys in Region	City Size				
	Under 100,000	100,000 to 500,000	500,000 to 1 million	1 to 5 million	Over 5 million
	Household Lacks Piped Water, Flush Toilet, and Electricity				
North Africa	3.7	1.2	2.9	5.6	0.2
Sub-Saharan Africa	50.1	41.1	34.5	21.7	
Southeast Asia	8.1	5.7	5.7		0.2
South, Central, West Asia	14.1	8.5	4.6	4.2	5.1
Latin America	10.1	5.7	1.6	1.5	0.4
TOTAL	31.4	22.1	15.4	9.8	2.3

[a] The DHS survey for Nigeria (1990) did not include questions on access to services in the household section of the questionnaire; hence, Lagos does not appear in this table.

throughout this report. Evidently, for reasons that are difficult to pin down, small urban places are somehow quite distinct from rural villages. Although we cannot assign any precise meaning to small or large city sizes, we draw attention throughout the report to the differences associated with size and urge that the factors behind these differences be investigated.

Services and the Poor

To probe further into intraurban inequalities in service access, we make use of a *relative urban poverty* measure based on the data available in the DHS. These surveys do not collect information on income or consumption expenditures, but they do collect data on a number of proxies for living standards. The proxies—which concern ownership of consumer durables and housing quality—can be distilled into an index of relative urban poverty. Appendix E explains the essence of the method, and Hewett and Montgomery (2001) give a full account. The approach yields a single relative poverty measure that defines the lowest quartile of urban households to be poor by comparison with other urban households. By "poor," we mean that these households own fewer consumer durables and have a lower quality of housing than do the other urban households in the same DHS survey. In the terms used by McDade and Adair (2001), ours is a "relative affluence" indicator.

Table 5-4 compares levels of access to services among three groups: rural households, urban households that are relatively poor by our definition, and urban nonpoor households.[8] The remarkable aspect of this table is the near uniformity of the results. For several of the key service access measures—piped water, access

---

[8]The table summarizes the results of a multivariate analysis, using probits, in which the explanatory variables for the urban subsample include measures of city population size and urban relative poverty. The results were converted to predicted values and then summarized with the aid of the sampling weights so they can be compared with the rural weighted means.

TABLE 5-4 Percentages of Poor Urban Households with Access to Services, Compared with Rural Households and the Urban Nonpoor

DHS Countries in Region	Category	Piped Water on Premises	Water in Neighborhood	Time to Water[a]	Flush Toilet	Pit Toilet	Electricity	Lacks 3 Services
North Africa	Rural	41.6	37.3	33.4	41.3	17.5	52.7	35.9
	Urban poor	67.3	27.8	23.1	83.7	8.5	78.7	13.5
	Urban nonpoor	90.8	7.8	22.8	96.3	2.6	96.4	3.7
	Poverty significant[b]	3 of 3	3 of 3	0 of 3	3 of 3	3 of 3	3 of 3	1 of 3
Sub-Saharan Africa	Rural	7.8	55.7	29.4	1.1	47.6	4.3	88.5
	Urban poor	26.9	61.6	17.5	13.0	65.9	19.7	62.9
	Urban nonpoor	47.6	45.8	16.9	27.4	67.2	52.2	34.2
	Poverty significant	29 of 30	25 of 30	3 of 30	27 of 30	20 of 30	30 of 30	28 of 30
Southeast Asia	Rural	18.6	53.7	13.1	55.5	24.3	50.8	29.4
	Urban poor	34.0	53.7	9.8	61.8	22.9	68.9	17.5
	Urban nonpoor	55.8	40.1	10.1	89.0	9.4	97.4	0.6
	Poverty significant	5 of 5	5 of 5	0 of 5	2 of 5	2 of 5	5 of 5	2 of 5
South, Central, West Asia	Rural	28.1	53.6	26.4	4.3	55.4	55.2	39.5
	Urban poor	58.0	36.3	20.4	39.8	34.1	61.3	28.9
	Urban nonpoor	80.2	17.7	19.9	64.0	23.2	94.9	3.1
	Poverty significant	9 of 10	9 of 10	2 of 10	10 of 10	9 of 10	6 of 10	6 of 10
Latin America	Rural	31.4	36.4	19.9	12.6	44.0	40.5	46.4
	Urban poor	58.7	35.2	18.8	33.6	47.0	79.4	14.4
	Urban nonpoor	72.7	24.9	18.4	63.7	31.6	96.4	2.8
	Poverty significant	12 of 13	10 of 13	1 of 13	13 of 13	13 of 13	10 of 13	10 of 13
TOTAL	Rural	18.5	50.7	26.5	7.5	46.6	25.2	65.9
	Urban poor	41.5	49.4	18.1	28.3	51.7	41.8	46.1
	Urban nonpoor	61.5	34.0	17.6	48.4	46.5	70.6	21.8
	Poverty significant	58 of 61	52 of 61	6 of 61	55 of 61	47 of 61	54 of 61	47 of 61

[a] In minutes, calculated for households lacking in-home access to water.

[b] These are the results of significance tests comparing the urban poor with the urban nonpoor, the tests being assessed at the 0.05 level. The figures show the number of DHS surveys, out of the number of surveys in which the test could be performed, in which the contrast is significant.

to a flush toilet, and electricity—we find that the urban poor are in a distinctly inferior position compared with other urban residents, but in a decidedly better position than the average rural household. The situation is more complex when we consider access to drinking water in the neighborhood, a case in which poor urban households can be on a par with rural households (as in Latin America) or in which higher proportions of rural households can have access (as in South, Central, and West Asia). The countries surveyed in sub-Saharan Africa show higher levels of access to water in the neighborhood among the urban poor than in rural areas, and taking the two water sources together gives the urban poor a decided advantage. (Note that the time costs of access to water for those households lacking in-home connections are similar for the urban poor and nonpoor.) A similar regional pattern is evident in the use of pit toilets and latrines.

The differences in the access of relatively poor urban households and rural households are almost always statistically significant.[9] In the case of piped and in-home water, all of the estimates shown in Table 5-4 indicate that the urban poor are significantly more likely to have access than rural households. Much the same is true for the likelihood of having a flush toilet and electricity.[10] In the cases of water in the neighborhood and access to either pit toilets or latrines, however, the urban poor are not always significantly advantaged relative to rural households.[11]

Are Migrants Poor and Underserved?

We now ask whether city households containing recent migrants—more precisely, recent migrants who are women of reproductive age—differ from other households in their access to services. Surprisingly, an empirical analysis uncovers few important differences. The details can be found in Appendix E, Tables E-1 and E-2.

Households with a migrant woman in residence are only slightly more likely than other households to be defined as "poor" by our relative definition, with the differences ranging from 1 to 5 percentage points depending on the region.[12] Likewise, in comparing access to services between migrant and nonmigrant households, we uncover only the slightest of differences. The migrant–nonmigrant gap in the likelihood of access typically amounts to no more than 2 to 3 percentage

---

[9]We compute standard errors for this test using the delta method. The frequency of significant results is due in part to the relatively large sample sizes for rural areas and the usually generous sample size of the urban sector, one-quarter of which is "poor" according to our relative definition of poverty.

[10]In each of these cases, only one DHS survey gave an insignificant result.

[11]In some 28 of the 59 DHS surveys, the urban poor were significantly less likely to have access to water in the neighborhood than were rural households, whereas in 31 surveys, the urban poor were significantly more likely to have such access. A similar split emerged in access to pit toilets and latrines, with poor urban households being significantly less likely to have access than rural households in 20 of the 56 surveys, but significantly more likely in 34 surveys.

[12]Recall that by definition, one-quarter of urban households are relatively poor. The relationship is statistically significant in 19 surveys out of the total of 78. A significant relationship emerges in 25 surveys, but 6 of these suggest that migrant households are *less* likely to be poor.

points, and it rarely attains statistical significance. Even when the rural-origin mi-grants are separated out—they are about one-third of all recent migrants—the differences in service access are estimated to be small. This is not at all what we had expected to find.

Is the conventional view of migrants so wrong? Can it really be that recent migrants are hardly distinguishable from urban natives and longer-term residents in these socioeconomic dimensions? Is the notion that migrants are found mainly in ill-served urban slums simply incorrect? Or is the problem one of inadequate measurement and an overly restricted sample? After all, the DHS data on migrants pertain only to women of reproductive age, and these women cannot represent the situation of all migrants.

We suspect that an analysis of China's unregistered migrants, known as the "floating population," would uncover very large migrant disadvantages (see Chapter 8), and doubtless such disadvantages can be found elsewhere as well. Data from the DHS, from which male migrants are generally excluded, simply do not speak to these situations. For the case of women of reproductive age, however, the DHS data cannot be so easily dismissed. Although they are far from being definitive, these data suggest that the conventional views of migrant disadvantage may need to be reconfirmed.

Discussion

The DHS household-level data on service provision are broadly consistent with the findings of city-level reviews of water and sanitation in African, Asian, and Latin American cities (e.g., Hardoy, Mitlin, and Satterthwaite, 2001). Studies of individual cities confirm what was seen in the DHS data—that members of many poor urban households must defecate outside or resort to unsanitary "wrap and throw" methods. The DHS results for sub-Saharan Africa are also consistent with other evidence. Whereas case studies of large cities in Latin America usually show considerable improvements over time in the provision of water and sanitation, this trend is less evident or absent in sub-Saharan Africa (Hardoy, Mitlin, and Satterthwaite, 2001). For example, a review of how access to water changed in 10 urban sites in East Africa between 1967 and 1997 found that for those lack-ing in-house connections, the average queueing time for water rose from 28 min-utes per day in 1967 to 92 minutes in 1997 (Thompson, Porras, Wood, Tumwine, Mujwahuzi, Katui-Katua, and Johnstone, 2000). Such increases in waiting time appear to be due to the increased congestion and competition for scarce public resources that often accompany city population growth. Even households with piped supplies experienced deterioration in the quantity and reliability of their water.

Micro studies of individual neighborhoods—see Boxes 5.4 and 5.5 and Table 5-5 for examples—can penetrate more deeply than the DHS surveys into some aspects of services. Perhaps the most important finding to emerge from

---

BOX 5.4 Examples of Intracity Differentials in Water Supply

Accra (Ghana) In high-income residential areas with water piped to the home and water closets for sanitation, daily water consumption is likely to be well in excess of the recommended figure of 200 liters per person. By contrast, in slum neighborhoods such as Nima-Maamobi and Ashiaman where buying water from vendors is common, daily consumption is only about 60 liters per person (Songsore, 1992).

Dar es Salaam (Tanzania) A 1997 study of domestic water use in four sites, all with piped supplies, found large differences in water use and reliability. The average per capita water use for households interviewed in Oyster Bay (a high-income area) was 164 liters a day. Water use was much less in two lower-income areas: in Changombe, it was 44 liters a day and in Temeke, 64 liters. Some 70 percent of the households interviewed in Oyster Bay received a 24-hour supply, as compared with just 10 percent of households in Temeke and 11 percent in Changombe. The unreliability of the piped water supplies in Changombe and Temeke meant that more than 60 percent of the interviewed households with piped supplies used vendors as their primary source, despite the higher costs (Thompson, Porras, Wood, Tumwine, Mujwahuzi, Katui-Katua, and Johnstone, 2000).

Guayaquil (Ecuador) In 1990, average daily consumption ranged from 307 liters per person in the well-to-do parts of the city to less than 25 liters for the poor supplied by private water sellers (Swyngedouw, 1995).

Monterrey (Mexico) The proportion of houses with running water varied from 49 to 93 percent among the eight municipalities that made up the metropolitan area in 1990; the proportion with adequate drainage varied from 35 to 96 percent (Garza, 1996).

---

neighborhood studies is the high money cost of water. Evidently it is not uncommon for low-income households to spend 10–20 percent of their cash income on water; some case studies show even higher percentages (Cairncross, 1990). The regularity of water supply also deserves attention: many studies have documented intermittent flows and long outages of supply. One study of water provision in 50 cities in Asia and the Pacific during the mid-1990s (Asian Development Bank, 1997) showed that the utilities often supply water for only a few hours each day.[13] Very few neighborhoods of Mombasa enjoy a continuous supply of water (the average is only 3 hours a day), and some have seen no water in their pipes for several years (Rakodi, Gatabaki-Kamau, and Devas, 2000). This dimension of water supply could be examined much more thoroughly in standard demographic surveys.[14] Survey questions could also be fashioned to elicit information about the adequacy and regularity of electricity supply.

---

[13]This study reports an average for Karachi of 4 hours per day, and similarly for Madras/Chennai (4 hours), Mumbai (5 hours), Bandung (6 hours), Kathmandu (6 hours), and Faisalabad (7 hours).

[14]Understandably, the DHS surveys do not make inquiries about water quality and contamination, which probably could not be recorded reliably through survey questions.

BOX 5.5 Citywide Study of Environment and Health Among Households in Port Elizabeth, South Africa

A 1996–1997 study of a representative sample of 1,000 households in Port Elizabeth (population 800,000) explores environmental and health conditions at the household level across the city. As in the case of the DHS analyses, consumer durables were used as proxies for living standards. Stark contrasts between the rich and poor emerged in both environmental conditions and access to services, as can be seen in the following table for the case of water supply:

	Socioeconomic Status					
Water Source	Low	Lower-middle	Middle	Upper-middle	High	Total
Piped inside house	11	27	57	82	98	56
Piped to yard	36	37	35	14	2	24
Communal tap	51	36	9	4	1	20
Other[a]	2	0	0	0	0	0
Number of Households	186	210	207	227	193	1023

SOURCES: Potgieter, Venter, Thomas, Seager, McGranahan, and Kjellén (1999); Thomas, Seager, Viljoen, Potgieter, Rossouw, Tokota, McGranahan, and Kjellén (1999).
[a] Includes water from, e.g., a neighbor or river.

Although the wealthier areas of Port Elizabeth are highly homogeneous in measures of income and services, the poorer areas exhibit a surprising amount of internal variation. Here the poor often have relatively rich neighbors despite the high average level of poverty in the neighborhood. The variation evident in these poor neighborhoods suggests that services might be funded in part through cross-subsidization.

Little information has been collected by the DHS surveys on the number of people who share toilets, the quality of toilet maintenance, and the monetary or time costs of access.[15] In some cities, pay-as-you-go public latrines consume a not-insignificant percentage of the cash incomes of poor households (for Kumasi, Ghana, see Devas and Korboe, 2000; for Bhilwara, India, see Ghosh, Ahmad, and Maitra, 1994). With all the aspects of reliability and adequacy taken into consideration, it is likely that the simple indicators used by the DHS tend to overstate the advantages of urban residence with regard to securing access to public services. The degree of overstatement is not known, but the issue clearly warrants further study.

---

[15]The DHS has formulated standardized questions on the privacy of access, but few countries have made use of these questions as yet.

TABLE 5-5 Household Environment Indicators in Accra, by Affluence of Neighborhood

Indicator	Percentage of Sample		
	Poor	Middle	Affluent
No water at source of residence	55	14	4
Share toilets with more than 10 households	60	17	2
No home garbage collection	94	77	55
Main cooking fuel wood or charcoal	85	44	30
Flies infesting kitchen	91	56	18
Number of households	790	160	50

SOURCE: Benneh, Songsore, Nabila, Amuzu, Tutu, Yangyuoru, and McGranahan (1993).

MEASURING ABSOLUTE POVERTY IN CITIES

There is broad agreement on the principles underlying official poverty lines: the lines should be determined by the monetary income required for an individual or household to meet basic consumption needs in a specified neighborhood.[16] In practice, however, few developing-country governments adjust income-based poverty lines to take full account of locational differences in the prices of food and nonfood essentials. The amount of adjustment needed is a matter of debate in high-income and low-income countries alike. In the United States, for instance, there is considerable uncertainty about whether and how to implement location-specific adjustments for differences in the costs of living (see Box 5.6). Adjusting for housing costs alone would significantly shift the U.S. poverty profile, with the likely effect of raising estimates of poverty in metropolitan areas. Much the same could be expected from locational cost-of-living adjustments in poor countries.

Locational Price Differences and Nonfood Needs

There is reason to believe that the official poverty lines adopted by developing countries can be seriously deficient in two aspects—the treatment of locational price differences and allowances for nonfood essentials. Income-based poverty lines are usually determined according to estimates of the cost of an adequate

---

[16]Most governments use the household as the unit of analysis and do not examine intrahousehold differentials in access to income. Although undoubtedly important (Levin, Maxwell, Ammar-Klemesu, et al., 1999), intrahousehold differences in consumption and control over resources are very difficult to measure. Many governments also ignore differences in household size and number of dependents, although there is some evidence suggesting that adjustments for size can make a significant difference to poverty estimates (Grewe and Becker, 2001).

BOX 5.6 Adjusting Poverty Rates for Geographic Differences in Prices: The U.S. Experience

At present, the official poverty measure used in the United States makes no adjustment for geographic differences in the cost of living. Although strong recommendations have been made to adjust for locational differences (Citro and Michael, 1995), there is disagreement about how best to implement the recommendations given the data available. According to Short (2001), the least contentious issue is that of housing costs, which are thought to be the factor accounting for the greatest portion of locational differences in the costs of living.

Building on the methods outlined in Citro and Michael (1995) and Short, Garner, Johnson, and Doyle (1999) and linking these to hedonic methods to adjust for variation in housing quality, Short (2001) shows that locational adjustments bring little change to national-level estimates of poverty, but have important effects at the state level. Poverty rates tend to fall in states with relatively low housing costs (e.g., Alabama and Arkansas) and rise in states where housing costs are higher (e.g., New York and California). The change in poverty by metropolitan and nonmetropolitan area is difficult to summarize (laws regarding confidentiality and disclosure of census data prevent detailed inspection of the data at these levels), but the analysis suggests that estimated poverty rates would tend to rise in large metropolitan areas if housing cost adjustments were made.

---

diet, with a further allowance, typically on the order of 15 to 30 percent, for all nonfood expenditures. If the prices of food and other necessities range widely and systematically across locations, there is a potential for systematic misestimation of poverty. The size of the nonfood allowance and the means by which this allowance is calculated also need attention.

It has not escaped notice that poverty lines ought to be adjusted for locational differences in prices, and a number of governments have established different poverty lines for urban and rural areas (e.g., the Philippines). For several reasons, however, adequate adjustments for locational differences are difficult to put in practice. First, prices can vary widely within locations. Second, households make decisions about where to live and what to consume that cause difficulties in formulating criteria appropriate to any given location. In making such decisions, households may accept high prices for some goods (or deficient services) in return for lower prices on others (or better services). Without knowledge of the full range of circumstances in each neighborhood or district, it is difficult to specify the level of income required to reach a "nonpoor" threshold of subjective well-being. Local and national authorities have very limited knowledge of the particulars and must do what they can to establish simple, administratively feasible poverty lines. Inevitably some families will be misclassified; the question is whether the errors are tolerable.

There is evidence of considerable variation within cities in the prices of water and food. In some accounts, the cost per liter of good-quality water is said to vary by as much as a factor of 10 depending on location (Hardoy, Mitlin, and Satterthwaite, 2001). As shown earlier in this chapter, middle- and upper-income households generally enjoy better access to piped water, and neighborhood studies show they can pay much less per liter than lower-income groups that rely on water vendors. Poorer households also tend to pay more for food than higher-income groups (Ruel, Haddad, and Garrett, 1999). The poor depend to a greater extent on food bought in the street because they lack a means of preparing it in bulk at home and face time constraints in their travels to work. To calculate the costs of food in a manner consistent with the eating habits of the poor would require detailed household-level quantity and expenditure data, which are seldom available (Hentschel and Lanjouw, 1996).

The unit costs of nonfood essentials may also be higher for the poor. Rents and quality of housing vary both within and across cities (UNCHS, 1996; Malpezzi, 1999). In many cities, the poor keep their expenses down by building their own homes on the urban periphery, but doing so may entail high transport costs in both time and monetary terms (Barter, 1999). Other households choose to live in rental housing on more centrally located sites, accepting the high rents because of easier access to jobs and lower transport costs.

In poor countries the adjustments made to account for nonfood needs tend to be ad hoc and are seldom grounded in careful assessments of the prices faced by the poor (Jonsson and Satterthwaite, 2000a). Housing is the most important nonfood item.[17] A 1989 survey of poor households in six South Korean cities found that 64 percent of their incomes were spent on nonfood items; this proportion had increased over the previous 25 years, mainly because of increases in the real costs of housing (United Nations Development Program, 1998). Other studies confirm that significant shares of income are spent on housing (see Barbosa, Cabannes, and Moraes, 1997; Richmond, 1997; UNCHS, 1993; United Nations Development Program, 1998; Rakodi, 1995). In addition, many poor households face high costs for transport (Urban Resource Centre—Karachi, 2001; Malawi, National Statistics Office, 1994; Barter, 1999); school fees and related expenses (Kanji, 1995; Bigsten and Mugerwa, 1992); health and child care; energy (Islam, Huda, Narayan, and Rana, 1997; Ghosh, Ahmad, and Maitra, 1994); and other expenses, such as payments to community-based organizations, bribes to the police, and payment of fines. Is an allowance equivalent to 15–30 percent of minimum food expenditures really sufficient to account for all such needs?

When official income-based poverty lines were calculated in the United States in the 1960s, it was thought reasonable to set the poverty threshold at three times the cost of a minimum food basket, rather than at 1.15 to 1.3 times that cost as is current practice in many developing countries. The U.S. approach recognized the many nonfood expenditures that households need to make to avoid poverty

---

[17]There are difficulties in defining the income needed for the acquisition of any durable good, which requires the computation of service flows, imputation of rental values for owner-occupied housing, and the like (e.g., Mozambique Ministry of Planning and Finance, Eduardo Mondlane University, and International Food Policy Research Institute, 1998).

(Citro and Michael, 1995). Some researchers have suggested that the appropriate adjustments may be even greater in the cities of poor countries (see Beck, 1994).

Comparisons of Urban and Rural Poverty

It is an encouraging sign that an increasing number of governments and international agencies have adopted separate urban and rural poverty lines—this is evidence of a growing recognition of the importance of location in the costs of living (Tabatabai and Fouad, 1993; Jonsson and Satterthwaite, 2000a). In the views of many researchers, the urban adjustments give insufficient attention to the prices faced by the urban poor. But not all considerations indicate that urban poverty is understated relative to rural poverty. Some nonfood essentials (e.g., clothes and medicines) can be much more expensive in rural areas, and much of the deprivation faced by the rural poor is measured less by prices than by the unavailability of goods and services. If levels of urban poverty are understated for the reasons outlined above, this certainly does not imply that they are understated relative to rural.

There is by no means a consensus on the adjustments needed to put urban and rural poverty on a comparable basis. In examining urban and rural price levels in India, Deaton and Tarozzi (2000) find evidence that prices are about 15 percent higher in urban areas, but this is far short of the 41 percent estimate adopted for India's official poverty lines on the recommendation of its Expert Group Report of 1993 (Government of India, 1993). The lower estimate derived by Deaton and Tarozzi—which, incidentally, is roughly equal to the official adjustments made before that Expert Group report—excludes housing and transportation, which account for at least a third, and possibly more, of urban household budgets. Even with allowance for the omitted items, Deaton and Tarozzi maintain that the official poverty lines overstate urban costs of living and thus the extent of urban poverty relative to rural. Evidently there is ample room for controversy and dispute, even in countries with sophisticated statistical systems.

What, then, can be said about comparisons of urban and rural poverty? The World Bank has developed country-specific estimates of the number of poor people in cities and rural areas for all of the developing regions. These estimates are based on an international poverty line that is set at (approximately) US$1 per person per day. The World Bank's estimates have been highly influential in public debates on development and development assistance; they are in many respects beneficial in bringing attention to the poverty levels of developing countries.

Whether the methods used to derive these estimates give a correct assessment of urban poverty levels is another matter. The World Bank (2000a: Figure 11) presents an estimate that some 495 million urban poor lived in developing countries in 2000. This figure implies that of every 4 urban residents, 3 are not poor. In some countries, according to these estimates, the percentage of city residents who are poor is very low. For instance, by the US$1 per day standard, fewer than

2 percent of China's city residents are judged to be poor (World Bank, 2000a: 236). Is proper account being taken of urban price differences and the costs of housing and other nonfood essentials? We stress this point because estimates such as these have considerable influence in public debates about development and international aid. As China and other poor countries become more urban, the limitations of urban poverty estimates cannot be left to delicately worded footnotes and rueful caveats. Urbanization underscores the need for rigorous justification of the basis for urban poverty estimates and clear statements of the limits and uncertainties that surround such estimates.

RISK AND VULNERABILITY

Because they must live in the narrow margin above subsistence, the urban poor face many difficulties in managing risks—in coping with rising prices, falling incomes, and other personal and societal shocks. Low incomes constrain savings and limit the accumulation of assets on which the poor can draw. The limited asset bases of the poor leave them vulnerable to sudden economic shocks, as well as to longer-term crises such as serious illness or injury (Moser, 1996). It is usually the poorer groups in urban areas that lose their homes and assets to floods, landslides, and earthquakes (Hardoy, Mitlin, and Satterthwaite, 1992; International Federation of Red Cross and Red Crescent Societies, 1998; Sanderson, 2000).

Social networks can provide some important resources for the poor in times of stress (Cox and Jimenez, 1998). Such networks can facilitate transfers of income or services when a network member is in distress, whether from a shortfall in income, illness, or some other shock. Social networks functioning in this way can be likened to informal insurance systems.

Although a substantial literature now exists on risk-sharing networks in rural villages (e.g., Townsend, 1994), there has been comparatively little investigation of risk-sharing arrangements in urban communities. Cox and Jimenez note that rural and urban settings differ in two aspects that affect informal insurance mechanisms. In cities it can be more difficult for network members to monitor the causes of income shortfalls, allowing a negligent or lazy member to make claims for assistance. In rural areas, by contrast, the major causes of income shocks (such as droughts) can be readily verified. Such moral hazard problems could make it difficult to maintain the mutual trust needed to sustain urban informal networks of insurance. Effective monitoring in urban areas might require that the network members reside in the same neighborhood or be linked in other ways (such as through family ties) that maintain trust. But urban areas also present some advantages for insurance networks. The greater diversity of city economies and occupations in comparison with those of rural areas could allow urban social networks to include more members whose incomes are negatively correlated. In rural areas, by contrast, common price and weather shocks could depress the incomes of all network members simultaneously, leaving little possibility for beneficial transfers.

In their study, set in a low-income section of Cartagena, Colombia, Cox and Jimenez (1998) find substantial evidence of transfers in urban social networks.[18] Members who had experienced recent spells of unemployment were more likely to have been given assistance by their networks; those with higher incomes were less likely to have been assisted.[19]   The diversity of network composition also made a difference: a household whose networks contained other households better off than itself was more likely to have received assistance. Most of the network members—some 60 percent—lived in Cartagena, and the poorer households tended to have larger networks, perhaps because they needed to spread their social safety nets wider.

In addition to relying on social networks, low-income households make use of many other day-to-day coping strategies to survive such stresses without irreversible damage to their productive capacities. Methods of coping with shocks and stresses include supplying more labor (taking second jobs, working longer hours, entering children and other household members into the labor market); reducing consumption; changing diets; selling household assets; and, in the extreme, resorting to prostitution or theft (Dinye, 1995; Moser, 1996). Box 5.7 describes some of the coping strategies adopted by low-income households in Dar es Salaam (CARE/Tanzania, 1998).

The Dar es Salaam study notes that before seeking outside assistance, urban households "self-adjust" to the extent that they can. It appears that households will restrict food consumption before they borrow money or take food on credit. Those with higher incomes take their children out of school less often and do not cut back on medical expenses to the same extent as lower-income groups. The study also notes that about half of city households regularly send remittances to family members, thereby maintaining extended family relationships that can be drawn upon in times of crisis; some 10 percent report receiving regular remittances from other households.

By using means such as these, poor households can protect themselves against some external shocks, but not all households can adjust to the same extent, and the assets on which the poor rely can be rapidly depleted. In addition, many short-term survival strategies have negative longer-term consequences—as when all available assets are sold, children are withdrawn from school, and women take up dead-end jobs offering low pay for long hours (Moser, 1996). Other risky and potentially damaging strategies include compromising the quality of medical care and reducing food consumption.

---

[18] According to the World Bank (2000b), about half of these Cartagena households received a transfer in cash or in kind in the month before the survey. For the poorest quintile of households, transfers accounted for 40 percent of household income for male-headed households and 52 percent for female-headed households.

[19] A related study of the urban and rural Philippines, that of Cox, Hansen, and Jimenez (1999), shows that informal transfers are responsive to the income levels of the poorest households. For urban Filipino households, total transfers received decline with household income among households in the lowest income quartile, but are constant with respect to income for higher-income households.

BOX 5.7 Shocks and Coping Strategies: Dar es Salaam

A study of shocks and coping strategies in Dar es Salaam, drawn from interviews with 298 households in six wards, gives insight into the coping strategies used by low-income households. In the year leading up to the interview, many households had suffered a severe shock, whether from having a member lose a main income-generating activity, from a major expense such as medical bills, or from necessary festival or ceremony contributions. More than 1 in 10 households had been evicted during the year. The table below (adapted from CARE/Tanzania, 1998: Table 13) shows the coping strategies used.

Coping Strategy Used	Percent Using
Seek more sources of income	24
Pull children out of school	24
Reduce quality of medical care	52
Return to home village	25
Obtain food from rural areas	37
Consume less-preferred or less-expensive foods	78
Borrow money	39
Purchase on credit	36
Reduce the number of meals per day	52
Reduce food portions	56
Limit adult food to give more to children	41
Borrow food	21
Send children to neighbors to eat	8
Skip eating for complete days	16

In cities, environmental hazards represent another dimension of the risk faced by poor households. Vulnerability to environmental risk depends on many factors: income and assets, which determine access to good-quality housing and reduce exposure to some locational hazards; the availability of health care and emergency response capabilities in the community, which can mitigate the health consequences of injury and acute disease; occupational roles that increase exposure to risk, such as picking through garbage or disposing of excreta; and other coping mechanisms in a household's repertoire that come into play when a hazard has caused illness or injury—knowing what to do, whom to visit, and how to reconfigure survival strategies (Chambers, 1989; Corbett, 1989; Pryer, 1989).

The greater exposure of the poor to environmental hazards may threaten in particular infants, young children, and the elderly, as well as pregnant women.[20] Susceptibility to environmental hazards is determined by various factors: (1) for many

---

[20] According to the World Health Organization (1992: 121), "Every stage of the multi-step process of reproduction can be disrupted by external environmental agents and this may lead to increased risk of abortion, birth defects, fetal growth retardation and perinatal death."

biological pathogens, weak body defenses (some related to age and nutritional status, others to acquired immunity, such as through vaccines); (2) for physical hazards, limited mobility, strength, and balance, as in the cases of young children, the elderly, and the physically disabled; and (3) for exposure to chemicals, age and the state of health at the time of exposure. Micronutrient deficiencies are likely to exacerbate the effects of air pollutants (Romieu and Hernandez, 1999). Asthmatics and the elderly with chronic respiratory disease appear to be particularly susceptible to certain air pollutants.

There are few data available on individual exposure to environmental hazards in developing-country urban environments. Most of the data are aggregate in nature, taking the form of areal averages. But some micro-level implications can be pieced together from the aggregate clues. According to the World Health Organization (1992), low-income families in many cities use lower-cost fuels and cook on less-efficient portable stoves or open fires. These practices put poorer families at risk from indoor and localized air pollution. Air pollution levels in low-income neighborhoods may also be elevated because of spillover effects within the neighborhood, as when many neighborhood households use polluting fuels. The correlations of poverty with other forms of outdoor air pollution, however, may not be especially strong. Exposure may be heightened when the poor live adjacent to quarries, cement factories, and other air-polluting industries. (There is also a tendency for polluting industries, waste dumps, and waste management facilities to concentrate in low-income neighborhoods, a tendency that is evident in high-income nations as well, as the literature on environmental racism has helped document [Wing, Grant, Green, and Stewart, 1996].) The burning of garbage can be a significant source of air pollution in neighborhoods lacking regular garbage collection (Surjadi, 1993). But the correlations are less clear when an entire city suffers from air pollution or when winds help disperse pollution.

Floods and landslides are risks that affect the poor disproportionately because housing and land markets price low-income groups out of safe, well-located, and well-serviced sites. High percentages of the urban poor live in housing that is vulnerable to fire, made of inflammable materials such as wood and cardboard. The risk of accidental fires is much increased when these households cook on open fires or use portable stoves and when kerosene lamps or candles are used for light.

As do other urban residents, poor city families also face risks stemming from macroeconomic forces and political restructuring. These issues are discussed in Chapter 8, but it may be useful here to note the spatial distribution of their effects. Macro shocks and political disruptions can have very different impacts in large than in smaller secondary cities. Box 5.8 gives an account of the turbulence surrounding the breakup of the former Soviet Union, the repercussions of which were felt differently in Bishkek, the capital of Kyrgyzstan, and the secondary cities of that new country. In the capital, the disruption appears to have been sharp but short; the secondary cities, however, appear to be in a sustained funk.

BOX 5.8 The Economic Transition in Kyrgyzstan: Bishkek and the Secondary Cities Compared

A number of the countries once part of the Soviet Union have experienced large declines in living standards. In Kyrgyzstan a series of surveys allows the determinants of earnings to be studied over the periods of chaos, stagnation, and nascent recovery (Anderson and Becker, 2001). The study shows that Bishkek, the national capital, is apparently more resilient than the secondary cities.

Kyrgyzstan weathered a loss in gross domestic product of 50–60 percent following the collapse of the Soviet Union, and per capita income today is only about US $300 at official exchange rates. For the nation as a whole, poverty rates peaked in 1996. Since then Bishkek has experienced declining levels of poverty. The situation in the secondary cities, however, is mixed: they have a lower incidence of poverty than rural areas (in particular, lower levels of extreme poverty), but there is no clear time trend and apparently little prospect for long-term improvement. Bishkek's resilience is evidently due to its skilled workforce, the favorable composition of its industries, and the fact that it is Kyrgyzstan's entry point for international trade and foreign aid.

CHILDREN'S LIVES

Children's lives reflect many of the aspects of inequality and diversity discussed in this chapter. This section begins by focusing on children's schooling, which is a measure of the human capital that governments and families invest in children. (Child health and survival are examined in Chapter 7.) Earlier in this chapter, we presented evidence of a decided urban advantage in adult schooling. Here we ask whether urban residence is also associated with higher levels of investment in children's education. We investigate whether children in relatively poor urban families are at a disadvantage by comparison with other urban children and examine their position relative to rural children. We then explore what is known about a subpopulation of urban children who suffer from serious deprivation—street children. We show that urban children as a group are advantaged and that poor urban children retain some of that advantage by comparison with rural children. However, street children are burdened not only by poverty, but also by the special social and health risks to which urban life exposes them.

School Enrollments in Urban Areas

The tables and figures that follow show enrollment proportions for two age groups of children: those aged 9–10, who are of an age to be enrolled in primary school, and those aged 15–16, whose enrollment rates are likely to reflect a mix of the late primary, middle, and early secondary school levels.[21]

For both age groups, Table 5-6 shows strikingly large differences in enrollment between urban and rural children. On average, the difference is on the order of

---

[21]These analyses are based on 62 DHS surveys from 45 countries; see Table C-1 in Appendix C.

TABLE 5-6 Percentages of Children Enrolled at Ages 9–10 and 15–16, Rural and Urban Areas

DHS Surveys in Region	Number of Countries	Proportions of Children Enrolled			
		Aged 9–10		Aged 15–16	
		Rural	Urban	Rural	Urban
North Africa	2	61.7	91.7	33.8	66.6
Sub-Saharan Africa	23	57.1	78.6	39.3	57.3
Southeast Asia	2	93.1	97.0	57.2	75.0
South, Central, West Asia[a]	8	79.4	90.2	51.6	67.0
Latin America	9	84.8	93.4	48.6	76.7
TOTAL	44	68.9	85.3	44.0	64.3

[a] India (1992) collected enrollment data only for children aged 6–14.

16 percentage points for the 9–10 age group and reaches nearly 20 percentage points for those aged 15–16. In Latin America, only 49 percent of rural children are enrolled at the latter ages, whereas almost 77 percent of urban children are still in school at those ages.

Focusing on variation in enrollment rates by city population size, we find smaller differences than those seen in the urban/rural comparisons. Table 5-7 presents the city size findings. As one might expect, enrollment rates in the smallest cities are somewhat lower than in the larger cities, but the differences are on

TABLE 5-7 Enrollment Percentages for Urban Children, by City Population Size

DHS Surveys in Region	City Population Size				
	Under 100,000	100,000 to 500,000	500,000 to 1 million	1 to 5 million	Over 5 million
	Enrollment at Ages 9–10				
North Africa	90.5	93.2	93.4	91.7	93.8
Sub-Saharan Africa	75.3	79.6	85.9	83.7	95.7
Southeast Asia	97.4	96.1	96.3	98.7	97.5
South, Central, West Asia	86.1	90.5	90.7	91.6	87.5
Latin America	92.5	92.8	95.0	95.1	97.2
TOTAL	82.6	86.6	90.6	90.4	92.9
	Enrollment at Ages 15–16				
North Africa	64.5	69.3	67.2	63.2	77.9
Sub-Saharan Africa	56.4	57.9	60.6	55.2	70.7
Southeast Asia	70.4	78.2	74.1	73.9	79.2
South, Central, West Asia	61.2	68.6	68.2	66.4	52.7
Latin America	74.0	76.9	79.0	80.3	85.6
TOTAL	61.9	66.0	68.6	66.7	70.7

NOTE: See note to Table 5-6.

TABLE 5-8 Predicted Enrollment for Children Aged
15–16 by Residence and, for Urban Areas, by Relative Poverty

DHS Surveys in Region	All Rural	Urban Poor	Urban Nonpoor
North Africa	33.4	47.4	72.4
Sub-Saharan Africa	39.0	42.9	61.5
Southeast Asia	58.8	63.0	80.3
South, Central, West Asia	43.2	44.2	67.0
Latin America	50.7	66.2	82.1
TOTAL	42.7	49.0	67.9

NOTE: See note to Table 5-6. Estimates based on probit models
with controls for child's age and sex in rural areas and for age,
sex, and city size in urban areas. Some surveys employed in
Table 5-6 could not be used in analyses of poverty, causing the
rural estimates shown above to differ slightly from those of the
earlier table.

the order of 9 percentage points for younger children and 6 percentage points for
older children. In sub-Saharan Africa, however, the enrollment differences are
much larger—nearly 20 and 13 points for the younger and older groups of children, respectively.[22]

Table 5-8 explores the implications of urban poverty for levels of school
enrollment, presenting a comparison of urban poor children, their urban peers
from nonpoor households, and rural children. We find that poor urban children
are more likely to be enrolled than rural children, but less likely to be enrolled
than nonpoor urban children.[23] As was the case with public service provision,
the urban poor generally occupy the middle position. Note, however, that in sub-
Saharan Africa and both regions of Asia, the margin of difference between the
urban poor and rural children is very thin. To judge by enrollment rates, poor urban children are not receiving much more in the way of human capital investment
than children in the countryside. This finding is dismaying in view of its implications for urban inequality in the future. Table 5-9 provides further evidence on
the situation of poor children, with attention to differences by sex. Although there
are important differences in enrollment between girls and boys, these differences
are not as large as those associated with poverty, which apply with nearly equal
force to both sexes.[24]

---

[22]These differences by city size are usually statistically significant—they are significant in 46 of 58
surveys for enrollment at ages 9–10 and in 50 of 58 surveys for those aged 15–16.

[23]The contrast between urban poor children and urban nonpoor children is almost always statistically significant, being so in 53 of the 57 DHS surveys in which the test could be performed.

[24]Statistical significance tests were applied to the poverty and sex variables in an effort to discrimi-
nate among the four categories shown in the table. The results indicate a strong main effect for poverty
in all regions, with poor children less likely to enroll. Enrollment rates for poor boys are significantly
different from those for nonpoor boys in 52 of 63 surveys; rates for poor girls are statistically different

TABLE 5-9 Predicted Enrollment for Urban Children Aged 15–16 by Relative Poverty and Child's Sex

DHS Surveys in Region	Poor Urban Girls	Poor Urban Boys	Nonpoor Urban Girls	Nonpoor Urban Boys
North Africa	43.3	51.2	69.7	75.1
Sub-Saharan Africa	37.7	48.2	55.1	68.4
Southeast Asia	64.2	62.1	78.1	82.8
South, Central, West Asia	38.4	49.2	62.2	71.8
Latin America	65.8	66.7	81.2	83.2
TOTAL	45.0	52.9	63.3	72.9

NOTE: See note to Table 5-6. Estimates based on probit models with controls for city size, the child's age, household poverty status, and their interaction in urban areas.

In summary, there can be little doubt of an urban advantage in children's school enrollment. The source of this advantage is less clear. Family background must have a strong influence; we saw earlier that the average level of adult schooling is higher in urban areas, and this is surely associated with higher levels of children's schooling. In addition, urban residence can be associated with higher enrollment because urban areas are better equipped with schools than rural areas. At the primary school level, the urban/rural differences in the availability of schools are far less important than they once were, although substantial differences remain in many countries. However, at the middle and secondary school levels, and certainly where tertiary schooling is concerned, access to schools is decidedly greater in the urban areas of many, and perhaps most countries. As discussed in Chapter 2, the presence of more-educated adults in cities may present urban parents with more role models exemplifying the implications of human capital investments, as well as more opportunities for social learning. These urban social interactions could well enhance the perceived returns to children's schooling. Better-educated adults are not distributed uniformly across the urban space, however; they are less likely to be encountered in city neighborhoods of concentrated disadvantage.

Street Children

Street children must represent an extreme in terms of urban disadvantage. Although they are a highly visible presence in many developing-country cities, little is known of the total numbers of such children, their characteristics and origins, and the long-term consequences of their life on the street. Researchers agree that

from those for nonpoor boys in 54 of 63 surveys. The enrollment difference by sex is more prominent among the nonpoor than among the poor. Among nonpoor boys and girls, the male–female enrollment difference is significant in 43 of 63 surveys. Among the poor, however, it is more difficult to distinguish enrollment rates for poor girls from those for poor boys; the contrast is significant in 26 of 63 surveys.

two characteristics of street children must be taken into account—where they sleep and the amount of family contact they have—but have not yet reached a consensus on matters of sampling and measurement. This lack of agreement on methods hinders generalization and leaves room for substantial imprecision in determining who is and who is not a street child.

UNICEF distinguishes among three types of children: *children of the street*, who live and sleep on the street; *children on the street*, who spend most of their time on the street with little adult supervision but sleep at home; and a broader category of which these two are subsets, denoted *children at high risk*, consisting of those who live in absolute poverty with little adult supervision (Lusk, 1989). This three-part classification has been widely adopted by researchers and policy makers and helps clarify important differences among children. Unfortunately, the implementation of these concepts in research protocols has been inconsistent. Further methodological difficulties arise from the transient and elusive nature of street children's lives—their circulation among shelters, homes, and the streets—which makes them very difficult to study. The result is that researchers often adopt different definitions of street children and employ different sampling strategies.

Research on street children remains largely descriptive, based on small, localized studies of doubtful generalizability. Few studies make use of sampling techniques that permit statistical tests or introduce controls for confounding factors. Likewise, few studies make use of comparison groups, either comparing street children from different neighborhoods or comparing them with non–street children. The lack of well-specified comparison groups makes it difficult to situate street children in a larger context and to separate the risks and consequences of life on the street from the more general disadvantages of poverty (for exceptions, see Gross, Landried, and Herman, 1996; Panter-Brick, Todd, and Baker, 1996).

Researchers agree that the number of street children is all but impossible to assess with rigor. Obstacles are presented by definitional problems, the mobility of the population, the lack of reliable data, widespread use of purposive sampling techniques, and the fact that many street children elude detection or give inaccurate information when interviewed (Aptekar, 1994). Nevertheless, the available evidence suggests that the number of street children is large and may well be growing. An often-cited 1989 estimate by UNICEF gives a global total of 100 million street children (Barker and Knaul, 1991). This total includes children of the street, as well as those who work on the street. An estimated 40 million of these children live in Latin America, some 25 to 30 million in Asia, and 10 million in Africa (Barker and Knaul, 1991). For children living and sleeping on the street, the estimated total is about 10 million.

Demographic profile

Over half of the street children in most studies report sleeping at home, which in the UNICEF classification defines them to be children "on" the street. Among those who sleep away from home, most give the street as their residence, though others report staying in shelters or with friends. Even among children who do not sleep at home, many report that they maintain some contact with their families, often remitting a portion of their earnings to parents or other family members. The spells of time children spend on the street vary greatly in length, but it appears that most street children, particularly those "of" the street, spend several years in this situation.

The majority of street children are boys. Girls also work and live on the street, but when children of the street are considered, the great majority are boys. This imbalance is probably due to gender differences in the socialization of children, different opportunities for work, the greater vulnerability of girls to physical and sexual assault, and the better protection they sometimes receive (Aptekar and Ciano-Federoff, 1999; Martins and Ebrahim, 1995).

Most street children are in their early adolescence, with the modal age being about 13 years. Children of the street have a mean age of 15–16; they are slightly older on average than children who are on the street. Studies often define the upper age limit of street children to be 18 years; when they pass this threshold, street children are redefined as working or homeless adults.

Just over half of street children either live with or come from intact birth families; the next most common family background includes single-mother families and families containing partners of the child's parents (i.e., stepparents or the equivalent). Contrary to what might be supposed, relatively few street children are orphans, with the percentage of orphans being higher among children of the street than among those on the street.

Most street children have attended school at some point, although few have gone so far as to complete primary school, and of course very few remain in school. It is difficult to assess their literacy. Despite a lack of schooling, many street children are numerate, and many are sufficiently entrepreneurial to have acquired critical economic and survival skills.

Life on the street and its consequences

There can be no doubt that life is harsh and brutalizing for children who live and work on the street. They are exposed to pollution, disease, harassment, abuse, and violence. They generally earn meager wages and are often forced into exploitative or dangerous occupations. They face a constant challenge in finding food, toilet and bathing facilities, and a protected place to sleep. Because of their poverty and exposed living conditions, street children also tend to have many health afflictions. Infectious diseases, particularly respiratory illnesses and skin conditions, are pervasive in this population (Mejia-Soto, 1998; Senanayake, Ranasinghe, and Balasuriya, 1998; Wright, Kaminsky, and Wittig, 1993). Moreover, street children lack access to health care; some are suspicious of the health care system and actively resist treatment (Reddy, 1992).

Street children also engage in activities that put them at risk for other health problems. Alcohol and drug use is widespread in this population; many of the

children use inhalants (mostly glue) and tobacco (Campos, Raffaelli, and Ude, 1994; Forster, Tannhauser, and Barros, 1996; Wittig, Wright, and Kaminsky, 1997). Street children also have sexual intercourse at younger ages (whether willingly or as the consequence of coercion), and they tend to engage in riskier sexual behaviors (e.g., prostitution, multiple partners, infrequent condom use) than those of non–street children of similar ages (Eisenstein and de Aquino, 1992; Swart-Kruger and Richter, 1997). These behaviors are much more prevalent in children who are of the street.

Only a handful of studies have compared street children with other poor and nonpoor children of similar ages. Although the nutritional status of street children can be a problem, they are often found to be healthier than poor children who are not on the street (Gross, Landried, and Herman, 1996; Panter-Brick, Todd, and Baker, 1996). When they can, street children make use of their varied repertoire of survival and entrepreneurial skills, and their own social networks, to meet basic needs. Although many street children are at great risk for a variety of health problems, at least one study finds that street children in Chandigarh, a medium-sized city in India, learn a variety of useful life skills and coping mechanisms from their work and play in the streets. Their developmental maturity in terms of survival skills is high, but other measures of physical and mental health give cause for concern, and of course the future opportunities for street children are likely to be severely limited (Verma, 1999).

Origins and causes

Life on the street is the outcome of many factors, some of these being society-wide and others the result of family and personal circumstances. Given the thin research base, researchers can do no more at present than to speculate about the most important causes. There is agreement that many societal factors—increasing urbanization and migration, economic recession, civil unrest, conflict, famine, high levels of HIV/AIDS—contribute, intensifying poverty and disrupting household structure (Aptekar, 1994; Barker and Knaul, 1991; Martins and Ebrahim, 1995; Rizzini, 1998). Likewise, researchers agree that there are many factors involved at the family level—poverty, family conflict and dissolution, and both physical and sexual abuse. Street children themselves most often cite poverty or the need to find work as their motivation for leaving home, although family disruptions and conflicts, abandonment by or death of parents, and a desire for "street life" also come into play. Many researchers describe street life as the product of combinations of factors (Aptekar and Ciano-Federoff, 1999; Matchinda, 1999), but little is known of the critical stress points and thresholds.

Interventions

Policy makers, human rights activists, and NGOs are paying growing attention to street children. In governmental policies and programs for children and families, street children are increasingly identified as a group with special needs (Lusk, 1989; Agrawal, 1999). At one time, institutionalization and rehabilitation efforts were proposed as the main interventions, but emphasis is now being given to programs focused on basic needs, skill development and training, counseling, and related services. Many current programs engage volunteers or "street educators" who enter the communities of street children to provide them with assistance and services.

The change in intervention strategies reflects a shift in the conceptualization of street children. If formerly they were viewed as a "deviant population," they are now being seen as an "at-risk" population. Multisector and multilevel interventions, particularly at the community level, are being promoted, and the emphasis is moving, albeit gradually, to prevention efforts aimed at combating poverty and strengthening families. Programs are beginning to target the aspects of street life that are particularly risky, including HIV/AIDS prevention, drug and alcohol intervention, and prevention of violence (Crane and Carswell, 1992; World Health Organization, 1997).

Some researchers argue that, when considered in relation to their numbers, street children may now be receiving disproportionate attention compared with other disadvantaged children (MacArthur, 1993). The fact that the health of street children is often no worse than that of other poor children is compelling testimony to the many disadvantages of poverty from which all poor children suffer. Yet street children are undoubtedly seriously disadvantaged, and their elusiveness means that many of them are neither offered nor receive the services they are due.

CONCLUSIONS AND RECOMMENDATIONS

If within the compass of urban life one finds both street children and the gated communities of the rich, inequality and diversity must be among its defining features. This chapter has explored intraurban and interurban differences in social and economic characteristics. By training an urban lens on human capital investment, poverty and well-being, access to basic services, risk and vulnerability, and the lives of children, we have sought a better understanding of urban/rural differences and intraurban diversity. Our main findings can be summarized in broad strokes: in the dimensions analyzed here, urban residents are better off on average than rural residents; residents of smaller cities are generally disadvantaged by comparison with those of larger cities, although advantaged by comparison with rural villagers; and the urban poor suffer from deprivations that can sometimes leave them no better off than rural residents, but generally situate them between rural residents and the urban nonpoor.

In contemplating the rich array of concepts and methods being applied to the study of socioeconomic diversity in the cities of rich countries (Chapter 2), we are struck by the promise they hold for understanding the cities of poor countries. The concepts of neighborhood and social capital are well recognized in the literature on poor countries and are illustrated by many vivid urban examples. Less has been seen of social network analysis, and yet this perspective might fruitfully be applied to the study of job search in cities, to health-seeking behavior, and even to the survival strategies of street children. Although to date the analysis of neighborhoods and social capital has been conducted mainly through powerful and evocative case studies, we see no reason why statistical tools could not also be brought to bear once neighborhood data become available.

Conclusions

Access to public services

The provision of basic services is much better in cities than in rural areas, but smaller cities are less well served than larger ones. The urban poor have significantly less access to basic services than other urban residents. Analyses of the DHS surveys reveal that in almost every country surveyed, the average urban resident enjoys better access to basic public services—piped drinking water, flush toilets, and electricity—than the average rural resident. This finding is not surprising given differences in abilities to pay for services, government investment priorities, and (possibly) lower urban unit costs of service provision.

Within and between urban areas, however, there are substantial differences in levels of basic service provision. Smaller urban areas—especially those under 100,000 population—are underserved by comparison with larger cities in all regions. With regard to intraurban differences, the urban poor are significantly ill served relative to other urban residents. The effects of urban poverty are strongly corroborated by microstudies of city slums and city-level reviews of service provision. In the DHS survey data, which generally record migrant status only for women of reproductive age, there is surprisingly little evidence that households with recent migrants are disadvantaged in terms of service access.

Human capital

Urban educational levels are higher on average than rural levels, but the urban educational spectrum is also more diverse. Educational levels are higher on average in larger than in smaller cities, but there is substantial diversity in cities of all sizes. It is to be expected that cities will have higher average levels of educational attainment than rural areas. But cities also exhibit greater educational diversity. Residents of larger cities (particularly cities of 1 million or more population) have higher average levels of schooling compared with their counterparts in smaller urban centers. Important theories suggest that educational diversity can have beneficial social and economic effects, although these theories have not yet been tested in the cities of developing countries.

Higher percentages of urban than rural children are enrolled in school, and enrollments are somewhat higher in larger than in smaller cities. In addition, urban poor children are much less likely than other urban children to be enrolled.

There is a decided urban advantage in children's school enrollment, which is likely attributable to differences in family background and access to schools. Although smaller cities have lower enrollment rates than the largest cities, these differences are not especially great except in sub-Saharan Africa. Poor urban children are also much less likely to be enrolled in school than other urban children, and in some regions (notably in sub-Saharan Africa), they are hardly more likely to be enrolled than children in the countryside.

Poverty and well-being

Urban poverty is being conceptualized in terms of multiple dimensions, many of which are not summarized by income and assets. Considering the income dimension alone, the poverty lines currently being used in many developing countries appear to need substantial upward revision. The research literature increasingly points to a variety of dimensions of urban poverty, and yet the official methods used to measure poverty continue to be simplistic and one-dimensional. Other dimensions should be considered, including shelter, access to public infrastructure and other basic services, safety nets, protection of rights, time costs, and political voice. Failure to recognize the multiple dimensions of poverty can skew understanding of its causes and needlessly narrow the scope of poverty alleviation efforts.

In addition, the official methods used to establish income-based poverty lines often fail to account adequately for locational differences in prices and the high proportion of income that many of the urban poor must spend on nonfood essentials, especially housing. Urban poverty may well be underestimated in many countries because of these methodological deficiencies. We cannot say, however, that urban poverty is underestimated relative to rural poverty, because formidable methodological and empirical problems prevent direct comparisons.

Because they lack significant financial assets and are dependent on cash incomes, the urban poor are left vulnerable to risks associated with economic shocks, political and social crises, and environmental hazards and disasters. Although low-income households are resilient and employ many coping mechanisms to adjust, some are harder hit than others and less able to adapt. The loss of assets, homes, and primary income earners that comes in the wake of disasters and shocks can cause poor families to supply more labor, reduce or change consumption patterns, borrow, sell household assets, or even resort to prostitution or theft. Poor households are likely to send children to work, cut back on medical care, or restrict food consumption before turning to others for credit or charity. The consequences can be dire; many street children cite poverty and the need to earn money for their families as their main reason for living on the street.

Recommendations

The analysis presented in this chapter indicates several directions for policy and research in the areas of service delivery, data collection, and a research agenda on intraurban and interurban differences in social and economic well-being in low-income countries.

Service delivery In the area of service delivery, we single out several elements of an agenda for basic public services, including water supply, sanitation, electricity, and education:

- Reach the urban poor
- Improve services in smaller cities
- Increase the school enrollment rates of urban poor children;
- Create or strengthen social safety nets

Data collection Where data collection is concerned, there is an urgent need for collating of available data on socioeconomic conditions within cities, with a particular focus on city neighborhoods and subdistricts. New data collection efforts should also be encouraged, particularly data on access to services, income and assets, the multiple dimensions of poverty, and education that are comparable among and within cities. Surveys such as the DHS can make an important contribution, especially if measures of the reliability and adequacy of basic services (water supply, electricity, sanitation) can be enriched and made sensitive to urban circumstances. Community-level surveys also have a useful role to play. It is critical that these data be collected, and also that they be disseminated widely to policy makers and program managers at the national and local levels.

It is disappointing that national statistical offices, which appear to be in the best position to supply spatially disaggregated data on their populations, have seldom done so in the past. The published data from national sources are notably weak in spatial terms. The importance of urban areas must be brought to the attention of the national statistical agencies, and they must bring their resources to bear by supplying adequate local data. Countries need to increase the availability of disaggregated social and economic data by social class, gender, age, and local area to inform policy makers and planners at the local level. These intraurban data-gathering mechanisms are needed to better understand the socioeconomic aspects of spatially concentrated disadvantage, as well as the extent and nature of urban "slums," for which there is no current agreement on a generally accepted definition.

Research Research is also needed on how to define and measure the multiple dimensions of poverty, how to identify vulnerable groups (with attention to migrants), and how to create linkages from poor urban communities to their governments and external sources of funds.

6

Fertility and Reproductive Health

Many aspects of urban life have the potential to affect fertility and reproductive health, but not all of these can be said to be distinctively urban. The broad features of the urban economy—its dominance by industry and services, its workplaces situated outside the home—were noted so long ago in discussions of the demographic transition (Notestein, 1953) that they have almost ceased to be regarded as urban. Indeed, as discussed earlier in this report, many rural areas have been assuming similar characteristics, especially in the regions surrounding large cities. Lower infant and child mortality is also broadly characteristic of cities, and lower mortality reduces some of the risks parents face in adopting strategies of low fertility. But the mechanisms are not obviously urban in character; surely lower mortality would exert much the same sort of influence in rural villages. Migrants are a distinctive presence in urban environments, and the fact that they have recently made transitions from other contexts raises issues of disruption, adjustment, and selectivity. Apart from migration, however, there remains the question of what is gained by situating fertility and reproductive health decisions within specifically urban contexts. What does this "embedding" achieve? Does it bring to light any implications for services and programs?

To begin, we should offer a word of explanation on the meaning of the phrase "reproductive health." It refers to "a state of complete physical, mental, and social well-being and not merely the absence of disease or infirmity, in all matters relating to the reproductive system and its processes" (United Nations, 1994: 202). The concept provides a framework for thinking about sex and reproduction, highlighting not only family planning, conception, and birth, but also the imbalances in decision-making autonomy between men and women, the possibilities of coercion and even violence in their relations, and the different health risks to which they may be knowingly or unknowingly exposed. A broad perspective is especially helpful where adolescents are concerned, because young men and women are often woefully ignorant about matters of conception and health risk, are still testing the limits of their autonomy in decision making vis-à-vis their elders and the other sex, and yet must often make choices that can foreclose options for adult life and compromise their later decision-making powers. Programs in the area of reproductive health include those dealing with contraception, but also encompass initiatives aimed at sexual violence; reproductive tract infections; and sexually transmitted diseases (STDs), including HIV/AIDS. They extend as well to services intended to ensure healthy pregnancies and deliveries and safe abortion.

With this set of issues in mind, we turn in the first section of the chapter to the distinctive features of urban environments. Two features warrant special attention. First, the socioeconomic diversity and the forms of social interaction found in cities may encourage urban parents to make deeper investments in their children's schooling, a strategy that typically entails lower fertility. Social interaction may also focus attention on the means by which lower fertility can be achieved, that is, on modern contraception. It is possible that urban environments influence the ways in which adolescents make their transitions to adulthood and the terms upon which marriage search is conducted. Second, the urban services and program environment differs in many ways from that of rural areas. It is much more diverse, especially in the roles taken by the private sector and in the multiplicity of governmental units that have a say in the management and delivery of health services.

It is remarkable how little research attention has been paid to the specifically urban aspects of reproductive health programs. The problem is not that these programs are mainly rural; especially in the areas of STDs and HIV/AIDS, many programs are situated in cities and address health issues that are of special concern to urban populations. Rather, the problem is that the conceptual frameworks that inform program design and evaluation do not appear to have been thoroughly appraised from an urban perspective. The service providers who work in cities may well be attentive to urban possibilities and constraints, but the research literature has conspicuously failed to provide them with concepts and guidelines tailored to their environments.

Having set forth the main concepts in the first section of the chapter, we give in the second section an empirical overview of urban fertility, contraceptive use, and selected measures of reproductive health, drawing from the survey data supplied by the Demographic and Health Surveys (DHS). We next explore the fertility transitions that are under way in cities, seeking to differentiate the transitions that accompany economic development from those produced by economic crises. The succeeding sections of the chapter consider three urban groups of particular importance: the urban poor, migrants, and adolescents. We then offer reflections on the distinctive features of urban service delivery. The final section presents conclusions and recommendations.

THE URBAN DIMENSION

Urban residents face a variety of constraints and opportunities that influence decisions about marriage search, the number of children to bear, and the manner

in which children are raised. Like rural parents, those in urban areas strive to protect their children's health and their own. Rural and urban parents no doubt hold
similar fundamental values, but they face different economic and social environments and may find that they must adopt productive and reproductive strategies
specific to these environments. In what follows, we first discuss the features of
urban settings that can influence family building and the pursuit of reproductive
health. We then examine the programs and services that can determine whether
urban families have access to the means to reach their goals.

Social and Economic Contexts

There can be little doubt that a great number of family reproductive strategies are
on display in cities. Consider the case of Natal, a Brazilian city of some 680,000
residents within the urban agglomeration. By no current standard would Natal be
considered a megacity, and yet across its neighborhoods one sees an astonishing
range of fertility levels. Franca (2001) illustrates this diversity, showing that the
total fertility rates (TFRs) of Natal's neighborhoods can be as different as those of
Switzerland and Nigeria (see Figure 6-1). This spatial expression of reproductive
diversity suggests, although it does not prove, that urban neighborhoods must exert
an important influence on fertility decisions. As argued in previous chapters, the
fact that cities exhibit a diversity of reproductive strategies is not sufficient to make

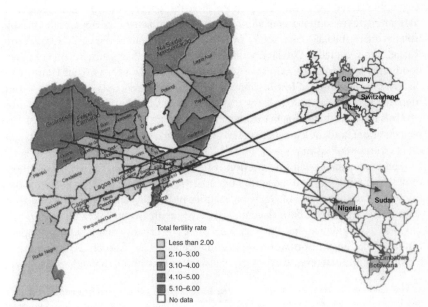

FIGURE 6-1 Total fertility rates in the neighborhoods of Natal, Brazil, as compared with rates in Europe and sub-Saharan Africa.
SOURCE: Franca (2001).

the case for neighborhood effects. The spatial diversity must persist when controls are introduced for individual socioeconomic characteristics, and it must be shown that forms of interaction take place within neighborhoods that shape individual knowledge and behavior. Of course, interactions limited to defined spaces, such as neighborhoods, do not exhaust the possibilities. As Chapter 2 makes clear, city residents can participate in multiple networks and associations, only some of which may intersect in their neighborhoods of residence. For example, the separation of workplace from place of residence that is characteristic of cities allows for the development of spatially separated reference groups.

In our view, the theories set forth in Chapter 2 make a persuasive case for the proposition that neighborhoods, networks, and reference groups influence fertility and reproductive health decisions in the cities of poor countries. But this case rests mainly on analogies with the experience of rich countries. For the poor countries with which we are concerned, the empirical evidence on urban social interaction and fertility is meager indeed. In a few aspects of urban reproductive health—sexual networks and STDs in particular—the social interactions are better documented. In the broader realm of health, the empirical record is quite rich, offering many examples that illustrate the operation of neighborhood effects and the influence of spatially concentrated disadvantage (see Chapter 7). But with respect to fertility and much of reproductive health, research is still in a documentation and data-gathering phase.

A first step in assembling the documentation is to show that spatial units such as neighborhoods are something more than the aggregation of their residents' characteristics. To merit consideration, they must have some separable, durable traits with an urban character.[1] In very recent research, Weeks, Getis, Yang, Rashed, and Gadalla (2002) assemble evidence that is suggestive of neighborhood effects in Cairo. Examining geocoded census data for Greater Cairo, they discover a wide range of fertility rates across the city's *shiakhas* (see Box 6.1) and, more to the point, are able to show that substantial spatial differences remain after controls are introduced for the usual socioeconomic predictors of fertility. It appears that in Cairo, at least, the spatial component is durable enough to withstand this first round of testing.

But evidence of social interaction, whether in the confines of neighborhoods or in social networks arrayed across the urban space, is required to isolate the distinctively urban features of decision making in fertility and reproductive health. As we have argued, the early Taichung study (Freedman and Takeshita, 1969) provided strong evidence that the social networks of urban women supply conduits for the exchange of information about contraception (see Chapter 2). Recent multilevel, longitudinal research on social networks in the periurban and rural areas of

---

[1] In multilevel models with individuals clustered within areas, statisticians often introduce unmeasured areal traits—termed "random" or "fixed" effects, depending on their relation to the measured traits—and commonly find these effects to be statistically important even with controls in place for individual characteristics.

BOX 6.1 Spatial Differences in Fertility Rates: Greater Cairo

In ongoing research using geographic information systems (GIS) in Greater Cairo, Weeks, Getis, Yang, Rashed, and Gadalla (2002) have uncovered substantial differences in fertility rates across this city's neighborhoods. Census data were used to map fertility rates by *shiakhas*—small districts within the Cairo metropolitan area that are akin to U.S. census tracts. As can be seen in the map below, the lowest fertility rates were found near the center of Cairo (near Talaat Harb Square) and the highest at the suburban edges, where men and women tend to be less educated, higher percentages of women are married, and fewer women work outside the home. Many of the high-fertility *shiakhas* have fertility levels similar to those of rural Egyptian villages.

Multivariate analyses revealed that neighborhood context has a substantial impact on fertility even net of controls for conventional predictors of fertility. Weeks and colleagues also discovered substantial variation by *shiakha* in the coefficients of these predictors.

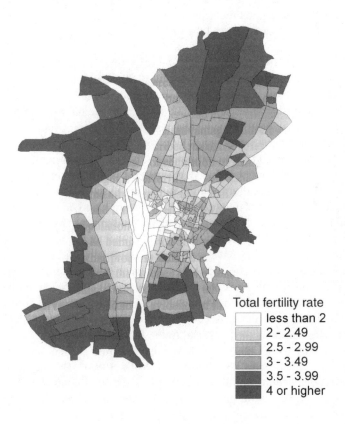

Total fertility rate
less than 2
2 - 2.49
2.5 - 2.99
3 - 3.49
3.5 - 3.99
4 or higher

Ghana, Kenya, and Malawi has reconfirmed the importance of these networks to contraceptive use (Behrman, Kohler, and Watkins, 2001; Casterline, Montgomery, Agyeman, Aglobitse, and Kiros, 2001). We are not aware of any other studies of this sort that are set in the cities of developing countries. For the moment, therefore, the urban case must rest almost entirely on a persuasive theory.

The key theoretical concepts are those of *diversity* and *spatial proximity*. Because they are highly diverse in social and economic terms but relatively compact in spatial terms, urban populations present a greater range of accessible models of behavior than is seen in rural areas and offer greater possibilities for social comparison. In cities, for instance, an uneducated young mother may find a few better-educated friends and peers in her social networks. Whether through conversation or by example, these women can give her a keener sense of the time that is involved in properly preparing a child for success in school. When the urban poor live near others with somewhat higher incomes, they may be able to recognize in their neighbors' behavior new strategies for upward economic mobility. Urban settings also present a parade of new consumption possibilities (as seen in consumer durables, for example), and the prospects for securing them may motivate desires for smaller families.

As Granovetter (1973) argues, individuals are often connected to novel information and social examples by the "weak ties" of their social networks. For the urban poor, social exclusion and spatial segregation can inhibit the formation of such weak ties, or disconnect them. The poor then lose out on opportunities to evaluate novel behavioral strategies and lack the full range of local models who could illustrate their implications.

As urban parents and would-be parents survey their environments, they are likely to come upon some examples illustrating how important education is to upward mobility and others illustrating either its relative unimportance or the risks of squandering educational investments. The examples provided in networks and neighborhoods may also demonstrate that substantial infusions of parental time and resources are needed to protect and support human capital investments in children. Recognizing that they have limited time and money, parents may conclude that only a few children can be afforded if such an innovative reproductive strategy is to be pursued. By this route, they may be prompted to consider modern contraception, another relatively new dimension of choice, with each contraceptive method presenting uncertain benefits, costs, and (perceived) risks to health.

These considerations are packaged in the literature under the heading of the "quantity–quality trade-off" (see, among others, Willis, 1973; Knodel, Chamratrithirong, and Debavalya, 1987; Parish and Willis, 1993). The theory describes how in certain situations, families will find it in their best interest to bear fewer children but to invest more in developing the human capital of each child. In Chapters 4 and 5, we present empirical evidence showing that children's school enrollment rates are decidedly higher in the cities of developing countries than in rural villages, and that fertility rates are decidedly lower. These are not isolated empirical regularities, but alternative positions along the two axes of a quantity–quality transition. The costs and benefits perceived by rural households tend to produce family strategies involving higher fertility and lower human capital investments in children.[2] Urban configurations of benefits and costs, however, lead to lower-fertility, higher-investment strategies (Caldwell, 1976; Stecklov, 1997; Lee, 2000).

Two motivating factors are involved in the quantity–quality transition: the perceptions that net economic returns to schooling are high and that the full costs of child-rearing strategies supportive of schooling are also high (Montgomery, Arends-Kuenning, and Mete, 2000). Some parents can see at first hand how schooling is required for advancement in the workplace. Others must acquire a sense of schooling's economic returns from social observations and comparisons and from the media. Parents may also need to acquire information about appropriate child-rearing strategies. As some research has shown (notably LeVine, Dexter, Velasco, LeVine, Joshi, Stuebing, and Tapia-Uribe, 1994; Stuebing, 1997), mothers who have had some schooling themselves tend to employ more verbal, time-intensive styles of interaction with their children. Such attentiveness has the effect of raising the costs of child rearing for parents while increasing the present and future benefits for their children. Other opportunity costs of schooling also need to be weighed: time in school is time subtracted from family or wage work, and this may be an important consideration for the poor. Even if poor parents agree that schooling promises their children substantial returns, they may not be able to invest in it to the extent that richer parents can.

The negative and threatening aspects of urban diversity can also affect parental views of the time and supervisory effort required in child rearing. As Randall and LeGrand (2001: 31) note for Senegal:

> The city (especially Dakar) is viewed as an environment in which bringing up children well is particularly difficult, where parents must face the effects of the economic crisis (poverty, unemployment, crowding), the presence of bad elements, and the ease for children to escape from parental authority and bring themselves up in the streets.

---

[2]In traditional rural societies, children provide status, resources, and old-age support to their parents, and these are incentives for higher fertility. But rural populations are not excluded from the quantity–quality transition. The rural fertility transitions of Kenya (Brass and Jolly, 1993) and Thailand (Knodel, Chamratrithirong, and Debavalya, 1987) can be viewed as examples in which rural parents invested in their children so as to better prepare them for urban livelihoods. In a sense, urban populations provide distant reference groups for rural populations, and in some cases, connections through migration and relatives can provide rural villagers with specific urban examples. In Vietnam, as noted by White, Djamba, and Dang (2001: 3), "Parents must now cope with rising costs of education and other expenses, if they want to guarantee the social mobility of their children. This strategy of grooming children for good jobs started among the rich and urban residents, but it expanded to other groups across the society."

Compared to life in villages, in cities more parental time and investment is required to produce a well-brought up child, and this, along
with the costs of supporting a family, motivates family size limitation.

As these authors describe the situation, in Dakar the temptations and proximity of
social risks for children have the effect of raising the full costs of child rearing.
Parental anxieties are no doubt heightened by the ubiquitous presence of street
children, who serve as vivid reminders of what can happen if parents do not remain
vigilant.

For urban adolescents and young unmarried adults, the surrounding social and
economic environment also presents a great diversity of novel and untested behavioral options. Indeed, in some countries the very notion of adolescence—a
period interposed between childhood and full adulthood—is a recent development, and adolescents may lack guidance on how to negotiate this new terrain.
Amin, Diamond, Haved, and Newby (1998) describe the case of young female
garment workers in Dhaka, Bangladesh, who must reconcile the strictures of *purdah* (the strict isolation of women inside the home) with their own factory wage
work, which takes them outside the home and into direct contact with men in the
roles of coworkers, bosses, and potential social partners. As most of these young
women are recent migrants from rural villages, their own parents can provide little
by way of guidance about city environments and risks. In conversation, the garment workers exhibit a mix of pride and anxiety about their new situations. They
take up distinctive habits of dress to signal their special status while allowing their
parents to conduct marriage search in the traditional manner. These women will
enter marriage with cash dowries that they have amassed through their own work,
and will also be equipped with some knowledge of how to negotiate with men as
partners—resources unknown to the Bangladeshi brides of generations past. The
terrain such young women are traversing is new for them; in Hong Kong and Singapore, by contrast, women began to face similar choices a quarter-century ago
(Salaff, 1981).

The Program and Services Environment

The services and reproductive health programs found in cities offer some resources that can be of use in spacing and limiting births, other resources meant
to ensure safe conditions at delivery and swift assistance should complications
arise, and still others that provide protection against sexually transmitted and
related diseases. Rural areas also have services and programs of this general
kind. What, then, are the important urban/rural differences in the program
environment?

Many of the studies that touch on these issues are found in what might be
called a "gray literature," that is, in project reports and memoranda. These materials must reflect a great deal of specific expertise and experience in reproductive
health that could be drawn upon in a comprehensive review. To date, however,

researchers have not collated and organized this knowledge in a way that distills its lessons for program design, service delivery, and evaluation. The panel's own efforts to survey the literature identified seven distinctive features of urban service environments that deserve further consideration.

First, the diverse composition of cities and the absence of certain social controls on behavior that are exercised in rural villages may raise the profile of some reproductive health problems. Urban sexual networks, the role of prostitution, subpopulations of drug users, and communities of migrants separated from their families all can increase the risks of STDs and HIV/AIDS. In city life, adolescents can elude the watchful eyes and discipline of family elders and neighbors and find themselves at risk of violence, pregnancy, and disease. Urban socioeconomic composition is also expressed in the levels of demand for preventive services, such as contraception, and at least on average, city residents have greater abilities to pay for preventive and curative care.

Second, many countries are undertaking ambitious programs of governmental decentralization, and these political reforms are introducing new municipal, state, and regional units of government (see Chapter 9 for a full account). In the era before these reforms were initiated, responsibility for the delivery of family planning and reproductive health services generally rested with national ministries, which held the requisite funds and technical expertise. Decentralization has introduced many uncertainties. As vertically organized delivery systems give way to more complex forms involving multiple units of government, what becomes of the expertise and funds previously concentrated in the national ministries? Are national staff relocated and reassigned, or are municipal and regional units of government asked to acquire their own staff to oversee service delivery (Aitken, 1999)? What sorts of transfers from upper to lower tiers of government will sustain the reproductive health care system? How is information about health to be returned from the local to the national level to guide resource allocation?

These appear to be highly complex matters, and it is surprising that they have attracted relatively little research attention to date. Scattered case studies are available—Chapter 2 describes interesting recent results for the Philippines (Schwartz, Racelis, and Guilkey, 2000; Schwartz, Guilkey, and Racelis, 2002)—but nothing akin to a comprehensive review has been published. Of course, decentralization is still new, and it is often difficult to distinguish between the reforms being proposed and those actually being implemented. In principle, at least, the developments at the municipal and local levels might generate opportunities for local governments to engage indirectly in service delivery through monitoring and contractual relationships with the local private sector and nongovernmental organizations.

Third, the private sector is a distinctive and prominent presence in urban reproductive health, and indeed, in urban health care more generally (see Chapter 7). The urban private sector is highly heterogeneous, offering an array of expertise that ranges from traditional healers to chemist shops to highly trained surgeons.

Fee-for-service arrangements take on greater importance in the private sector, and service pricing raises questions of equity and ability to pay.[3] In some countries, private providers interact with their clients through health insurance mechanisms, especially when patients are in the employ of the public-sector or "formal-sector" private firms. Rural areas generally lack the scale, diversified economies, and concentrations of resources needed to support much private-sector activity in health. Some drugs and supplies can be purchased in rural markets, and traditional forms of health care are much in evidence, but on the whole it is the public sector that must provide rural villages with modern forms of care.

Fourth, the question of access to services takes on a different cast in urban areas. In urban settings, it is inadequate—and potentially misleading—to conceive of access as being measured by the physical distance to services. The greater density and variety of urban transport can greatly reduce the time it takes to reach services by comparison with access time in rural areas. Much less time is likely required to locate emergency care, such as that needed in cases of hemorrhage and other complications of childbirth, than is the case in most villages. However, time costs can still loom large in discouraging preventive and nonemergency forms of care. These costs should not be underestimated, particularly when services are located far from main transport routes and the clusters of residence and employment for the urban poor. Moreover, delays in obtaining care are not just a matter of time and transport. In poor city neighborhoods, there can be as little knowledge of reproductive health as in remote rural villages. In both settings, delays in seeking health care can arise from the need to consult with men and family elders and obtain from them the funds needed to purchase care.

Fifth, the quality aspect of service delivery merits comment. It is a common assumption that urban reproductive health services are of higher quality than rural services. As will be seen, careful comparisons have not always supported this view. Some aspects of quality have been found to differ—for instance, urban clinics are more likely than their rural counterparts to have electricity—but in terms of the interactions between staff and clients, the information exchanged, and the availability of essential supplies, the situations of urban and rural clinics can be much the same.

Sixth, the roles that may be played in service delivery by communities and community organizations no doubt differ a great deal between cities and rural villages. Urban neighborhoods can be defined according to social criteria, involving notions of belonging, inclusion, and exclusion that may be difficult for outsiders to discern. The social capital of urban communities—the matrix of formal and informal associations that can provide support, information, and a means of linking individuals to services—also appear to have a distinctive character. Some service delivery systems that were developed for rural populations, such as

---

[3] Public-sector services, even if ostensibly free, often require patients to pay for drugs and supplies or to make side payments.

community-based distribution networks, may need to be substantially adapted to serve urban populations (Tsui, Wasserheit, and Haaga, 1997).

Strategies for communicating about reproductive health that work well in rural villages may also need to be adjusted to the circumstances of urban life. Cities are characterized by a diversity and multiplicity of information. In large cities, information emanates from so many sources that a potential user of contraception may well find herself overwhelmed and unable to discern the quality of any single source. Individuals may have to rely on their social networks and local associations for guidance to services. The localized networks of the urban poor may not offer them many leads, and the poor may not learn of new reproductive health services and initiatives unless special efforts are made to reach them.

Seventh, urban/rural differences in the costs of service provision need to be considered (Tsui, Wasserheit, and Haaga, 1997). It is difficult to persuade highly skilled health personnel to locate in remote rural villages absent a substantial wage premium. Professionals with school-age children are generally reluctant to sacrifice their urban educational opportunities and often can do no more than take a tour of duty in the countryside. Rural health services requiring this sort of labor must pay higher real wages and cope with higher rates of turnover. Health services that depend on electricity and piped water may well be costlier to organize in rural areas. On the other hand, there may be offsetting savings stemming from the lower costs of rural housing, and some health professionals may prefer the slower pace of rural life.

AN EMPIRICAL OVERVIEW

This section provides a sketch of fertility, marriage, contraceptive use, conditions at childbirth, and HIV/AIDS that draws comparisons between urban and rural areas and, where possible, highlights differences among cities by population size.[4] It is the common view that, with regard to reproductive health, cities are far better served than rural areas. Expert assessments often suggest that urban services are more plentiful and generally of higher quality. Table 6-1 can be taken as representative of this consensus. The figures shown are summaries of the responses of in-country evaluators of maternal care to a questionnaire that was standardized across countries (Bulatao and Ross, 2000). In each of the dimensions shown in the table, the experts are more likely to classify urban than rural services as being adequate.

One does expect cities to exhibit advantages in many aspects of reproductive health. But as will be seen, the advantages that are suggested by averages taken over urban populations as a whole often conceal a great deal of intraurban heterogeneity. In fertility and contraceptive use, the urban averages appear to indicate an urban socioeconomic advantage. On closer inspection, however, cities are found to be more varied than might have been thought. As we consider more

---

[4]See Table C-3 in Appendix C for a list of cities in the 1–5 million range and those over 5 million.

TABLE 6-1 Percentages of Experts Rating Access to Urban and Rural Maternal Health Services as "Adequate" for Pregnant Women

Maternal Service	Urban	Rural
District hospitals open 24 hours	81	58
Antenatal care	89	56
Delivery care by trained professional attendant	75	44
Postpartum family planning services	61	36
Treatment for postpartum hemorrhage	69	35
Management of obstructed labor	69	33
Treatment of abortion complications	68	32
Provision of safe abortion services	45	21

SOURCE: Bulatao and Ross (2000: Table 4).

refined measures of fertility control and reproductive health and probe the circumstances of urban subgroups and smaller cities, the urban advantage becomes less and less obvious. In particular, the urban poor can be shown to suffer from disadvantages that often resemble those of rural populations.

Figure 6-2 presents a regional comparison of TFRs in the urban/rural and city size dimensions. On average, the urban TFR falls short of the rural TFR by about one child per woman, a difference that is evident in all regions except Southeast Asia. Fertility levels tend to fall with city size. This tendency is especially marked in Latin America; it is apparent to a degree in sub-Saharan Africa, with the excep-

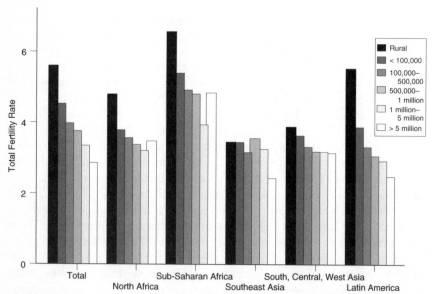

FIGURE 6-2 Total fertility rates in rural and urban areas, by region and city population size.

tion of Lagos (the only city of 5 million population or more in this region), but is less evident in the other regions. Southeast Asia exhibits little fertility difference by city size until one considers Bangkok, Manila, and Jakarta (the cities of over 5 million), where fertility rates are decidedly lower. Outside Southeast Asia (a region in which rural populations have often been given high priority in government family planning programs), the fertility rates of the smallest towns and cities (those of under 100,000 population) appear to fall well below those of rural areas. This gap between rural areas and small cities again raises the question of what qualities of "urbanness" such small urban areas can possess to render them so distinctive in relation to rural villages.

The intraurban diversity in the TFRs of Natal and Cairo (see Figure 6-1 and Box 6.1) is well hidden in the fertility averages presented in Figure 6-2. Natal falls in the middle rank of Latin American cities, but by Franca's (2001) account, its fertility levels cover the full range shown in the figure. Likewise, Cairo's fertility average does not begin to suggest the extent of its intracity range. Chapter 8 presents evidence from Lam and Dunn (2001) on the variation in urban earnings, showing that most of the total variation is intraurban in nature, the cross-city variation making a relatively small contribution. It is tempting to speculate that were fertility rates similarly decomposed, the greater portion of their variation would also be found within cities.

The fertility patterns seen in the DHS data are not unlike what was seen in the 1970s and early 1980s in the World Fertility Surveys (WFS).[5] As with the DHS analyses, an inspection of fertility levels by place of residence revealed important urban/rural differences, although these were seldom as large as the differences in fertility by level of woman's education. The differences emerged most clearly in the regions of the developing world that were already urbanized, such as Latin America and a few countries in the Middle East. In many countries surveyed by the WFS, the differences between the smaller cities and rural areas (1.5–2.5 children per woman) were found to be larger than the differences between large and small urban areas, which were on the order of 1.0 child or less (Cleland, 1985; World Fertility Survey, 1984). It is curious, in retrospect, that this aspect of the urban/rural fertility difference failed to attract much attention.

If the WFS analyses yielded clear results as to fertility levels, they left unresolved the question of the urban connection to fertility transitions. Some researchers (Cleland, 1985; Cleland and Hobcraft, 1985; Cleland and Wilson, 1987) saw little in these surveys to suggest any strong relationship between urbanization and fertility decline. Indeed, some WFS surveys suggested that urbanization could increase marital fertility by discouraging breastfeeding and other traditional

---

[5]The WFS was an international comparative survey program carried out in 42 developing countries and 20 developed countries between 1972 and 1984 (World Fertility Survey, 1984). In these surveys, place of residence was classified in terms of major urban areas, other urban areas, and rural areas.

birth-spacing practices.[6] We return to the subject of fertility transitions in the next section of the chapter.

All social and economic forces influencing fertility, including those operating in urban environments, must exert their influence indirectly through a set of what are termed "proximate determinants" (Bongaarts and Potter, 1983). These determinants fall into three categories: the formation and maintenance of sexual unions; the deliberate control of fertility (exercised mainly through contraception and induced abortion); and residual factors affecting fertility in the absence of deliberate control, such as fecundability, sterility, postpartum infecundability, and intrauterine mortality. Little can be said about the urban aspects of this third set of proximate determinants, but the DHS surveys allow an inspection of the first two.[7]

Sexual Unions and First Marriage

Cities are often portrayed as social arenas in which a variety of sexual pressures are brought to bear on unmarried adolescent girls. Some of the adult social controls applied in rural settings are probably ineffective in cities, and parental supervision has its limits. One therefore expects to find evidence of earlier sexual experimentation and intercourse in cities; with marriage typically occurring at a later age, this would leave urban adolescents facing longer periods of exposure to pregnancy and the risk of STDs.

There must be a great deal of truth to these views, but it is difficult to find them confirmed in the standard demographic surveys. To judge from the DHS surveys, urban women have their first experience of intercourse, on average, when they are 1.0–1.5 years older than the average rural woman.[8] In examining data

---

[6]This possibility has been examined in other research. A study in Cebu (Philippines) found urban women to be significantly less likely to breastfeed than rural women, and among those who breastfed, the urban durations of feeding were shorter. The differences may be attributable to work outside the home, interventions by hospital staff, and the availability of free infant formula (Adair, Popkin, and Guilkey, 1993). Analyses by Muhuri and Rutstein (1994) of DHS survey data for Africa revealed that average breastfeeding duration was 3 months shorter in urban than in rural areas. Brockerhoff (1994) examined the breastfeeding practices of rural-to-urban migrants, and found that their breastfeeding lengths were closer to those of urban natives than those of rural nonmigrants, although a tendency was evident for migrants to lengthen their breastfeeding with longer durations of city residence (Brockerhoff, 1995b). The shorter breastfeeding lengths of recent migrants may be evidence of the "disruptive effects" of migration described later in this chapter.

[7]Sterility may be more common in urban areas because of STDs. Evidence on this point is weak. One study of male temporary migrants in Burkina Faso suggested that sterility (probably from STDs acquired in Abidjan, where many Burkinabe go for work) may have been among the causes of their lower fertility levels (Hampshire and Randall, 2000).

[8]Our results were derived from the reports of ever-married women aged 25 and over. We expect that their reports of first intercourse, although retrospective, would tend to be more reliable than the reports of young unmarried women. The basis for this expectation is admittedly thin. See Mensch, Hewett, and Erulkar (2001) for a review of what little is known regarding the reliability of survey responses on adolescent sexual activity in developing countries. This study compares several interviewing techniques and, rather surprisingly, finds little in the comparison to suggest that conventional survey methods (such as those employed by the DHS teams) are clearly biased.

TABLE 6-2 Average Age at First Marriage for Women, Rural and Urban Areas

DHS Surveys in Region	Number of Surveys	Rural Women	Urban Women
North Africa	6	17.98	19.86
Sub-Saharan Africa	42	17.51	18.48
Southeast Asia	7	18.48	20.10
South, Central, West Asia	11	17.61	18.59
Latin America	24	19.09	20.15
TOTAL	90	18.05	19.16

NOTE: Restricted to ever-married women aged 25 and older.

on premarital intercourse, the panel found that, although urban women are more likely than their rural counterparts to report having had premarital intercourse, the differences are rather small, amounting to a few percentage points.[9] The reliability of survey data on first intercourse is simply unknown; one can neither dismiss these data nor vouch for their trustworthiness. It is worth emphasizing that the DHS data are for women, and data for men might well show evidence of earlier urban sexual activity.

Other studies have found that urban adolescents become sexually active at young ages, although comparisons with rural adolescents are not always made. Agyei, Birirwum, Ashitey, and Hill (2000) examined age at first intercourse in a sample of unmarried Ghanaians aged 15–24, and found little difference among those living in Accra, in periurban areas, and in rural villages.[10] For urban Botswana, Meekers and Ahmed (2000) found that the great majority of adolescents were sexually experienced by the age of 17 to 18; many of them had had multiple sexual partners. Interestingly, girls who were enrolled in school were less likely to be sexually active, but the enrolled boys were more likely to be active. Meekers and colleagues interpreted this finding as a reflection of the better economic prospects facing boys with secondary schooling, which enhances their attractiveness as potential marriage partners.

If data on sexual intercourse are of unknown reliability, survey data on age at first marriage are believed to be relatively trustworthy, although in some regions (e.g., sub-Saharan Africa), there are stages in the process of becoming married that do not allow the event to be confined to a single age or date. Table 6-2 summarizes DHS data on mean age at first marriage for urban and rural women, the

---

[9]The DHS question on first intercourse allows a response of "at marriage." Premarital intercourse is identified in DHS surveys by a gap of a year or more between age at first intercourse and age at first marriage; women with a shorter gap than this cannot be identified as having had premarital intercourse.

[10]In this sample, 67 percent of the boys had had intercourse and 78 percent of the girls; the authors do not present urban/rural breakdowns. The mean age at first intercourse was calculated for the adolescents who had ever had intercourse; the lack of an urban/rural difference may be partly an artifact of selection bias.

estimates being based on the reports of all ever-married women aged 25 and older at the time of the survey interview.[11] Urban women marry about a year later than rural women on average. In some regions, such as North Africa and Southeast Asia, the difference in marriage age is closer to 1.5 years. Table 6-3 provides reassurance that these differences in age at marriage are not attributable to the use of ever-married samples. This table summarizes data from the DHS surveys that include never-married women. Only a few surveys in Asia and North Africa are represented in the set, but all sub-Saharan and Latin American surveys are included. In all regions and for all age groups, the proportion of women married by a given age is consistently lower in cities than in rural areas. The urban/rural differences are especially pronounced for women in the 15–19 age group.

Several factors could account for the urban/rural difference in age at marriage. Young urbanites of both sexes are likely to postpone marriage while they are enrolled in secondary school. City economies may provide more productive niches for women than are found in rural villages, thereby giving women a measure of economic independence not easily obtainable in the countryside. Young men may find it necessary to experiment with different types of city jobs before they locate one with sufficient stability and earnings to support family building. Migration can produce an imbalance in the number of unmarried men and women, thus creating a mismatch among potential mates. And if young migrants come to the city alone, they may not live near family members who could engage in marriage search on their behalf.

Contraception

For many of the reasons mentioned, urban women are generally thought to be more likely than their rural counterparts to use contraception, and an analysis of the DHS data confirms this supposition. As can be seen in Figure 6-3, the level of modern contraceptive use is markedly higher in urban than in rural areas, and it increases with city size when the full sample is considered. Within regions, the strongest association between city size and contraceptive use appears in Latin America and North Africa, with high levels of use appearing in Cairo (the only city of 5 million and above in North Africa) and the largest cities of Latin America. As is the case with TFRs, Southeast Asia shows little urban/rural or city size difference in contraceptive use. In sub-Saharan Africa, current use is progressively higher as one moves along the continuum from rural areas to cities in the 1–5 million population range, although it then falls somewhat in Lagos. A similar pattern—a slightly lower level of use in the largest cities—is evident in the rather eclectic region of South, Central, and West Asia, whose largest cities are Dhaka, Madras, Delhi, Calcutta, Mumbai, Karachi, and Istanbul.

---

[11]The restriction to ever-married women allows surveys from North Africa, South Asia, and parts of Southeast Asia to be included, these being regions where never-married women were ineligible for interviews in a number of countries.

TABLE 6-3 Proportions Ever-Married by Age, All Women, Rural and Urban Areas

DHS Surveys in Region	Number of Surveys	Rural				Urban			
		Under 15	15–19	20–24	25–29	Under 15	15–19	20–24	25–29
North Africa[a]	1	0.08	0.56	0.85	0.94	0.06	0.39	0.68	0.85
Sub-Saharan Africa	38	0.16	0.70	0.91	0.95	0.11	0.57	0.83	0.92
Southeast Asia[b]	2	0.03	0.42	0.77	0.88	0.02	0.28	0.63	0.81
South, Central, West Asia[c]	3	0.00	0.49	0.90	0.96	0.00	0.38	0.86	0.94
Latin America	24	0.09	0.57	0.84	0.91	0.05	0.44	0.75	0.87
TOTAL	68	0.13	0.64	0.88	0.94	0.08	0.50	0.80	0.90

NOTE: Based on DHS surveys that included women irrespective of marital status, from all three rounds of the DHS program. The estimates for ages under 15 are based on the reports of women who were aged 15 or older at the time of the survey; likewise, the estimates for those aged 15–19 are based on women who were at least 20 years old, and so on for the other age categories.

[a] Morocco (1992) is the only survey in this region.
[b] Surveys of the Philippines (1993 and 1998).
[c] Surveys of Kazakhstan (1995), the Kyrgyz Republic (1997), and Uzbekistan (1996).

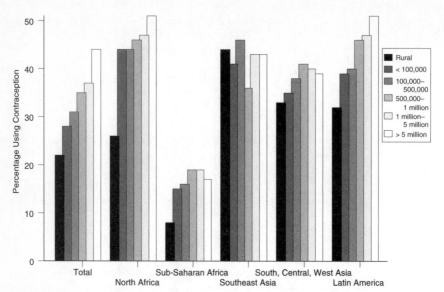

FIGURE 6-3 Current use of modern contraceptives, rural and urban areas, by city size.

The larger role of the private sector in urban than in rural contraception is evident in Table 6-4 and Figure 6-4. Table 6-4 summarizes the sources employed by current users of contraception. Both rural and urban women depend on public sources for their contraceptive supplies—the urban percentage ranges from 39 to 67 percent—but the percentage among rural women is much higher, and urban women are far more likely to use private medical sources. This is to be expected, for rural areas generally lack the diversity of pharmacies, chemist shops, private clinics, and hospitals that is found in cities. As shown in Figure 6-4, the use of private sources generally increases with city size, although these sources are used somewhat less commonly in the largest cities.

Unmet Needs and Unintended Fertility

An unmet need for contraception exists when a woman who says she wants no more children (or none soon), and who is in a sexual union and believes herself capable of conceiving, nevertheless uses no modern contraception. Her situation, as she herself depicts it, appears to indicate a demand for contraception, but something intervenes to prevent its use. Unmet need is often interpreted as a measure of the extent to which demand is satisfied through existing public and private sources of contraceptive supplies. There is some controversy about whether this emphasis on the supply side is really warranted. Unmet need is inferred from the reports of women, who may have to contend with husbands and family elders who

TABLE 6-4 Proportions of Current Users of Contraceptive by Source of Method, Rural and Urban Areas

DHS Surveys in Region	N^a	Rural			Urban		
		Public	Private Medical[b]	Other Private	Public	Private Medical[b]	Other Private
North Africa	3	0.51	0.48	0.01	0.39	0.60	0.01
Sub-Saharan Africa	31	0.68	0.24	0.08	0.62	0.31	0.07
Southeast Asia	5	0.75	0.22	0.03	0.55	0.44	0.02
South, Central, West Asia	10	0.81	0.14	0.05	0.67	0.25	0.07
Latin America	14	0.50	0.48	0.03	0.39	0.59	0.03
TOTAL	63	0.66	0.29	0.05	0.56	0.39	0.06

[a] Number of surveys. Analyses restricted to ever-married women.

[b] This category includes private hospitals, doctors, and clinics; it also includes pharmacies and (in some countries) chemist shops and other providers who can claim some professional expertise.

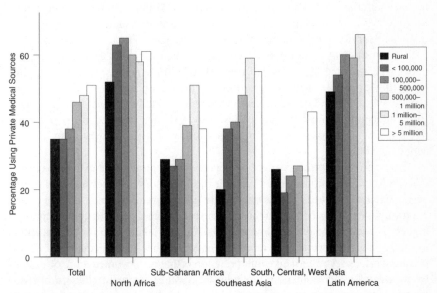

FIGURE 6-4 Percentage using private medical sources among current users, rural and urban areas, by city size.

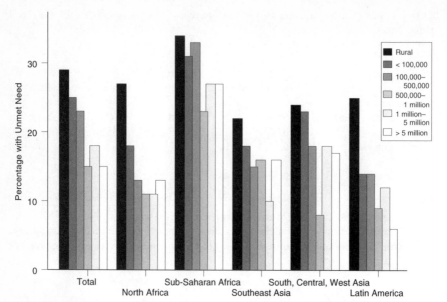

FIGURE 6-5 Unmet need for contraception, rural and urban areas, by city size.

do not share the woman's views about whether additional children are desirable. Moreover, it may not be the availability of contraceptive supplies as much as the quality of service provision that hinders method use. The unmet need measure focuses on modern contraception, whereas women may find their contraceptive needs well satisfied by traditional methods of birth spacing. With these points noted, however, it is useful to approach the analysis of unmet need by thinking broadly of supply and demand. Urban women are likely to have greater demand for contraception, and cities are believed to be better supplied with contraceptive services—but this leaves open the possibility of a greater urban gap between supply and demand.

Figure 6-5 depicts the extent of unmet need for contraception in the urban/rural and city size dimensions. It is plain that rural areas have higher levels of unmet need. Even in Southeast Asia, where little urban/rural difference in fertility and contraceptive use has been seen thus far, the rural unmet need for contraception is higher. Evidently, despite the lower levels of potential demand for contraception in rural areas, rural women are relatively undersupplied with adequate public and private services. An alternative interpretation is that rural women more often confront husbands and mothers-in-law whose pressures for more children override the woman's own preferences.

The city size differences seen in Figure 6-5 are intriguing. Viewed on the average (the set of bars labeled "Total"), they suggest generally lower levels of unmet need in larger cities. But inspection of the regional detail reveals a richer pattern. In several regions, it appears that levels of unmet need are higher in the largest cities or in the largest two city size categories than in cities in the middle range. The smallest cities and towns generally have the highest levels of unmet need among all urban areas. In view of the role that will be played by small cities in accommodating future population growth, it is clear that attention must be given to their need for services.

Unmet need provides one measure of exposure to the risk of unintended pregnancy and childbearing. But even women who use modern contraception—those whose needs are "met" by the standard criteria—do not necessarily use their methods consistently and effectively. To understand the degree of fertility control that is actually exercised in cities and rural areas, it is necessary to examine the incidence of unwanted and mistimed pregnancy.

To take this step is to enter an area riven by methodological controversies and plagued by fundamental gaps in the data (Bongaarts, 1990). Surveys are not thought to provide reliable estimates of induced abortion, and survey-based estimates of unintended pregnancy are therefore limited to the pregnancies that are taken to term. Survey questions have been devised to assess whether these births were unintended at the time of conception, but there is considerable dispute about the meaning of such retrospective assessments.

The DHS surveys provide women's reports of the intendedness of their recent births, and the panel examined reports on unwanted and mistimed births occurring during the 3 years preceding the interview. To a first approximation (detailed results not shown), the rural and urban rates of unwanted childbearing are found to be about equal, as are the rural and urban rates of mistimed childbearing. The differences by city size are also quite small.[12] The contrast with the patterns of unmet need for contraception is interesting. It appears that although urban women are more likely than their rural counterparts to use modern contraception when they wish to avert births, they may not use their contraceptive methods effectively and may then experience unintended births at about the same rate as do rural women. The urban/rural differences in this aspect of reproductive health are surprisingly small.[13]

Indeed, if rates of abortion could only be taken into account, it might be found that urban women experience even higher rates of unintended pregnancy than are suggested by their levels of unintended births. In a sample of unmarried

---

[12]These findings are based on the application of Poisson models to births in the 3 years preceding the DHS survey. Some 62 surveys contained data on unwanted and mistimed fertility. A woman with a birth in this period was asked whether, at the time of conception, she had not wanted any more children or had not wanted a child soon. The former are the unwanted births and the latter the mistimed births. An age-specific fertility rate is the sum of the rate of unwanted births at that age, the rate of mistimed births, and the rate of intended births.

[13]An analysis of urban/rural differences in eight of the Indian states covered in that country's 1992 DHS survey (Kulkarni and Choe, 1998) revealed higher unwanted fertility in the urban areas of four states (those with higher fertility overall) and higher rural unwanted fertility, or little urban/rural difference, in the remaining four states.

Ghanaians (Agyei, Birirwum, Ashitey, and Hill, 2000), some 37 percent of young women (aged 15–24) had been pregnant, and among those residing in Accra, about half had had an abortion. This study included a (small) sample of rural women, who were somewhat less likely to have been pregnant and also less likely to have had an induced abortion. We know of no other direct comparisons of abortion between urban and rural women, but there are several revealing analyses of urban subgroups.[14] One recent study found abortion to be widespread in Abidjan (Desgrées du Loû, Msellati, Viho, and Welffens-Ekra, 2000). Abortion is illegal in Côte d'Ivoire, yet nearly one-third of the women surveyed who had ever been pregnant had had one. Studies set in Shanghai, Havana, Santo Domingo, and Ile-Ife and Jos in Nigeria revealed that city natives had higher rates of abortion than city residents of rural origin (Shi-xun, 1999; Vasquez, Garcia, Catasus, Benitez, and Martinez, 1999; Paiewonsky, 1999; Okonofua, Odimegwu, Aina, Daru, and Johnson, 1996). In a low-income neighborhood in Santiago, Chile, women living in poor housing were more likely to have had an abortion than those with good-quality housing (Molina, Pereda, Cumsille, Oliva, Miranda, and Molina, 1999). Women in three squatter settlements in Karachi, Pakistan, were estimated to have a lifetime rate of 3.6 abortions per woman (Jamil and Fikree, 2002a). And rural migrants were found to be likely to seek clandestine, illegal abortions in cities where illicit providers were more plentiful (Tamang, Shrestha, and Sharma, 1999; Tai-whan, Hee, and Sung-nam, 1999; Jamil and Fikree, 2002a,b).

In Santiago, researchers found that focusing family planning interventions on women at high risk for abortion could help lower the abortion rate in a low-income neighborhood (Molina, Pereda, Cumsille, Oliva, Miranda, and Molina, 1999). Women who have just had an abortion are often more than willing to consider the use of family planning; however, family planning counseling is not always made a part of postabortion care. In a study of incomplete abortion in hospitals in Karachi, 49 percent of women said they had wanted to use contraceptives after aborting, but only 27 percent had been given any family planning counseling (Jamil and Fikree, 2002b).

It appears, then, that the lower levels of fertility found in cities relative to rural villages and the higher levels of contraceptive use may not be reliable indicators of the urban state of reproductive health, even in the family planning dimension. Differences between small and large cities need to be considered, as do more refined measures of fertility control. The panel's examination of unmet need for

---

[14] At the national and urban–regional level, there appears to be a strong inverse relationship between rates of contraceptive use and abortion rates. Evidence to this effect is found in Bogota, Colombia, and Mexico City during the 1970s and 1980s: here, as abortion rates dropped, contraceptive prevalence increased (Singh and Sedgh, 1997). Reducing abortion rates by providing adequate access to contraceptives is especially important in light of the dangerous complications that can result from unsafe, clandestine abortions performed by unskilled providers. The World Health Organization (1998) estimates that 20 million unsafe abortions are performed annually worldwide and that almost all of these are in Africa, Asia, and Latin America. Approximately 80,000 women die every year from complications of unsafe abortions.

contraception indicated more diversity across city sizes and regions than is often recognized, and an analysis of unwanted and mistimed fertility gave little hint of an urban advantage. To be sure, these are simple descriptive analyses, and a much more thorough investigation is in order than this panel was able to undertake. We return to these issues below in examining the situation of the urban poor.

Maternal Care

Although we cannot examine each facet of urban maternal health, we can consider two of the most important from the programmatic standpoint. We focus here on the attendance of trained personnel at the time of childbirth and the place of delivery, which are indicators of the resources at hand in situations of high risk for mother and child. As can be seen in Figure 6-6, the percentage of women whose deliveries are attended by trained physicians or nurse/midwives is very low in rural areas and generally increases with city size. On average, only 20 percent of rural births are attended, a level far below the range of 40–60 percent seen in urban areas. It is also noteworthy that the smallest towns and cities have lower proportions of attended births than do the larger cities. No doubt this difference is due to the lack of skilled health personnel in such small places.

A private–public split in maternal care is evident in the kinds of institutions in which childbirth takes place. Figure 6-7 summarizes results on the percentage of women delivering their recent births at home, in a public-sector institution, and

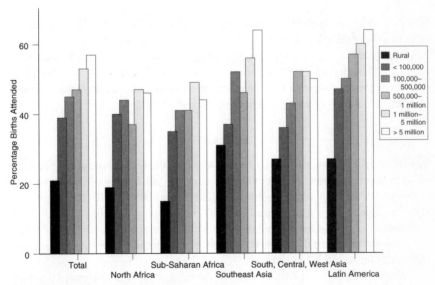

FIGURE 6-6 Percentage of women with all recent births attended by physicians or nurse/midwives, rural and urban areas, by city size.

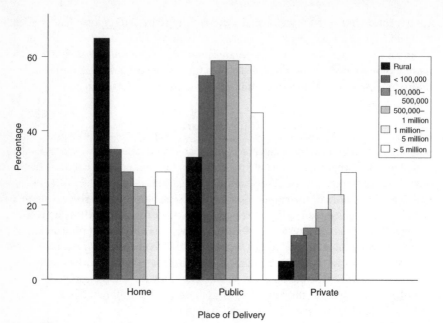

FIGURE 6-7 Percentages of women delivering recent births at home, in a public-sector institution, or in a private-sector institution, rural and urban areas, by city size.

in a private-sector institution. In general, as one moves up the city size scale, relatively fewer women deliver at home, and more deliver in private institutions. Regional analyses (not shown) reveal that this relationship generally holds within regions, although the largest cities can be exceptions. The most striking finding is that the majority of rural women deliver their children at home, while the majority of urban women give birth in public institutions.

HIV/AIDS

The anonymity of city life, more permissive social and sexual norms, the presence of sex workers, migrants with new sexual networks, and many other factors may contribute to the high urban prevalence of STDs and HIV/AIDS. Although rural HIV prevalence rates are approaching and even surpassing urban rates in some countries, it is still generally true that prevalence is higher in urban areas. There is substantial evidence that large cities have higher prevalence than smaller cities (Boerma, Nunn, and Whitworth, 1999).

In urban sub-Saharan Africa, HIV seroprevalence rates are estimated to be not only high but still on the increase in many populations (see Table 6-5). To judge from studies of pregnant women, over 31 percent of women in urban Botswana,

TABLE 6-5 Estimated Levels and Trends in Seroprevalence for Pregnant Urban Women, Selected Countries[a]

Country	Initial Date	Sero-positive (%)	Later Date	Sero-positive (%)	Percentage Point Change
Angola	1995	1.20	1999	3.40	2.2
Benin	1994	1.10	1998	2.50	1.4
Botswana	1994	27.80	1997	34.00	6.72
Burkina Faso	1991	7.80	1996	10.00	2.2
Burundi	1986	14.70	1998	19.10	4.4
Cameroon	1992	3.95	1994	5.70	1.75
Chad	1995	2.40	1999	6.20	3.8
C.A.R.	1986	4.70	1996	11.70	7
Congo (Brazzaville)	1987	3.10	1993	7.20	4.10
Congo (Kinshasa)	1985	6.90	1991	9.20	2.3
Djibouti	1993	4.00	1995	6.10	2.1
Cote d'Ivoire	1989	6.00	1997	15.90	9.9
Ethiopia	1991	10.70	1996	17.90	7.2
Gabon	1998	0.50	1994	1.70	1.2
Ghana	1992	1.20	1996	2.20	1
Guinea	1990	1.10	1996	2.10	1
Guinea-Bissau	1990	0.90	1997	2.50	1.6
Kenya	1992	14.40	1995	18.50	4.1
Lesotho	1991	5.50	1996	20.60	15.1
Liberia	1992	3.70	1993	4.00	0.30
Malawi	1991	22.00	1995	27.60	5.60
Mali	1988	1.30	1994	4.40	3.10
Mozambique	1994	10.70	1998	17.00	6.30
Namibia	1991	4.20	1996	16.00	11.80
Niger	1988	0.50	1993	1.30	0.80
Nigeria	1992	2.90	1994	5.40	2.50
Rwanda	1989	26.80	1992	28.90	2.10
South Africa	1994	6.40	1997	16.10	9.70
Swaziland	1993	21.90	1998	31.60	9.70
Tanzania	1986	3.70	1996	13.70	10
Togo	1995	6.00	1997	6.80	0.80
Uganda	1996	15.30	1997	14.70	−0.6
Zambia	1990	24.50	1994	27.50	3
Zimbabwe	1990	23.80	1995	30.00	6.20
Bahamas, The	1990	3.00	1993	3.60	0.60
Barbados	1991	1.30	1996	1.10	−0.2
Belize	1993	0.20	1995	2.30	2.10
Dominican Republic	1995	1.20	1999	1.70	0.50
Guatemala	1991	0.00	1998	0.90	0.90
Guyana	1990	1.50	1991	1.87	0.37

(continued)

TABLE 6-5 *(continued)*

Country	Initial Date	Sero-positive (%)	Later Date	Sero-positive (%)	Percentage Point Change
Haiti	1989	7.10	1993	8.40	1.30
Honduras	1992	2.00	1995	4.10	2.10
Panama	1993	0.80	1995	0.90	0.10
Trinidad & Tobaggo	1991	0.20	1999	3.40	3.20
Burma[b]	1992	0.50	1997	1.42	0.92
Cambodia	1995	3.00	1998	4.90	1.90

SOURCE: Urban and rural data are from the HIV/AIDS Surveillance Data Base, International Programs Center, U.S. Census Bureau, January 2000. Estimated total country HIV percentage is from UNAIDS (2000).

[a] Estimated Total Country is for Jan. 1, 2000, except for Djibouti which is from 1995.

[b] Military recruit data.

32 percent in urban Rwanda, and 27 percent in urban Malawi and Zambia are HIV-positive. Even in West Africa, where HIV prevalence has been estimated to be low, it is on the increase in urban Nigeria and Cameroon (United States Government, 1999). Seroprevalence rates for 1997 in capital or major cities indicate that on average, almost one-quarter of the adult population of Eastern and Southern Africa has contracted the disease, a level much higher than that in rural areas (Caldwell, 1997). According to the U.S. Census Bureau's HIV/AIDS Surveillance Data Base, estimates of HIV prevalence are significantly higher in most urban areas as compared with rural areas, particularly among high-risk subgroups (United States Government, 1999).

Many researchers believe the colonization and subsequent urbanization of sub-Saharan Africa brought about shifts in family formation patterns and gender relations that have contributed to the spread of the AIDS epidemic. Dislocation and migration caused by economic, political, and environmental crises and war have created an atmosphere permissive of multipartner relationships in societies where polygyny had always been somewhat common (Cohen and Trussell, 1996; Caldwell and Caldwell, 1993; Quinn, 1996; Caldwell, 1995, 2000).

In Asia, HIV levels have fallen slightly in Bangkok (a major center for the epidemic) after rising throughout the early 1990s. In urban Cambodia and Burma (Myanmar), however, HIV rates continue to increase. Between 1992 and 1996, for example, HIV prevalence among sex workers in Phnom Penh increased from 10 to 42 percent. In India, the epidemic appears to be taking hold in Mumbai but remaining steady in Calcutta (United States Government, 1999).

HIV transmission in Latin America and the Caribbean is increasing in many cities, mainly as a result of heterosexual transmission and needle sharing among injection drug users. For example, in Tegucigalpa, HIV rates among sex workers increased from 6 percent in 1989 to 14 percent in 1997. In Rio de Janeiro only 3 percent of sex workers were estimated to be infected in 1987, but by 1993, 11 percent were HIV-positive (United States Government, 2001).

Migration has been a major factor in the spread of HIV, especially in Africa, where it has introduced the disease into many smaller cities and rural areas. International migration—often by refugees displaced by civil war, famine, and political crisis—also moves HIV across borders and into cities and countries where it has not previously been prominent. Commercial sex work is a viable source of income for many migrants, but a risk factor for AIDS. Truck drivers, military personnel, traders, and other transient populations also spread the disease. In the regions surrounding large cities such as Bangkok, circular migration appears to play a role, combined with a globalized sex tourism industry and widespread use of injected heroin (Quinn, 1995). Poor migrants are likely to be at high risk for AIDS. In Abidjan, for instance, it is believed that more than one-half of all prostitutes are Ghanaian migrants (Decosas, Kane, Anarfi, Sodji, and Wagner, 1995), and over 80 percent of these prostitutes are thought to be HIV-positive. Because they are of foreign origin and low status, these Ghanaian prostitutes are highly unlikely to seek treatment or services from reliable sources, and it is difficult for intervention programs to reach them (Decosas, Kane, Anarfi, Sodji, and Wagner, 1995).

Using data from the DHS, the panel examined the proportion of ever-married women who are aware of AIDS and, among those who are aware, the proportion knowing that condom use or limiting sex partners reduces risk. Figure 6-8

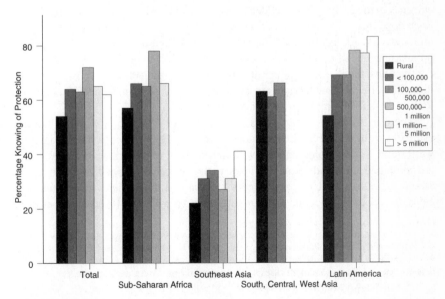

FIGURE 6-8 Among women aware of AIDS, percentage knowing that using condoms or limiting sexual partners reduces risk, rural and urban areas, by city size.

summarizes this information.[15] Relatively few DHS surveys collect data on AIDS awareness, and these data do not suggest a clear relationship between knowledge and city size. Although they are not well informed about risks, urban women appear to be somewhat better informed than rural women.

FERTILITY TRANSITIONS AND ECONOMIC CRISES

A comparison of trends in urban and rural fertility is desirable on several counts. To project populations, it is important to know how national fertility rates are likely to be affected by urban/rural differences in fertility. As noted earlier, urban TFRs are generally lower than rural rates. If the difference between these rates is expected to remain roughly constant over time, national fertility rates will approach the urban rates as greater proportions of the national population become urban. Matters are more complicated when urban and rural fertility rates follow different trajectories over time.

A comparison of trends also sheds some light on the socioeconomic mechanisms producing national fertility decline. Urban areas are often said to be the "leaders" in fertility decline and rural areas the "laggards," with lower-fertility attitudes and behavior diffusing from the cities to the countryside (for a critical view, see Montgomery and Casterline, 1993). Especially in recent decades, fertility declines appear to be linked to the economic crises that have gripped many low-income countries. The notion of a "crisis-led" fertility transition first achieved currency in the early 1990s, the idea being that changes in behavior initially forced upon populations by economic crises can persist even as economic recoveries get under way (Working Group on Factors Affecting Contraceptive Use, 1993). City populations are often believed to be among the first to suffer from real income contractions, the ill effects of privatization, and the removal of government subsidies. The effects of such crises are explored in more detail in Chapter 8; an initial look at the fertility implications is taken here.

The time trends in urban TFRs are depicted in Figure 6-9, which combines estimates from the WFS with estimates from the DHS.[16] In each region, a downward trend is detectable, together with a good deal of variation. If all estimates are combined and an adjustment is made to net out country-specific time-invariant factors (i.e., the country "fixed effects"), a regression coefficient for trend indicates that the annual decline in urban total fertility is about 0.08 children per year,

---

[15]We combine the answers to survey questions on the awareness of AIDS with questions on whether condom use and partner limitation can reduce risk. Women who are not aware of AIDS are scored as 0; women aware of the disease but with no knowledge of these preventive measures are also scored 0; and women who are aware of the disease *and* know of the preventive measures are scored 1. The estimates shown in the figure are age-adjusted to reflect the knowledge of ever-married women aged 25–29.

[16]The WFS data on urban TFRs are taken from Ashurst, Balkaran, and Casterline (1984). To derive a figure for all urban areas, we averaged the WFS estimates for major cities and other urban areas.

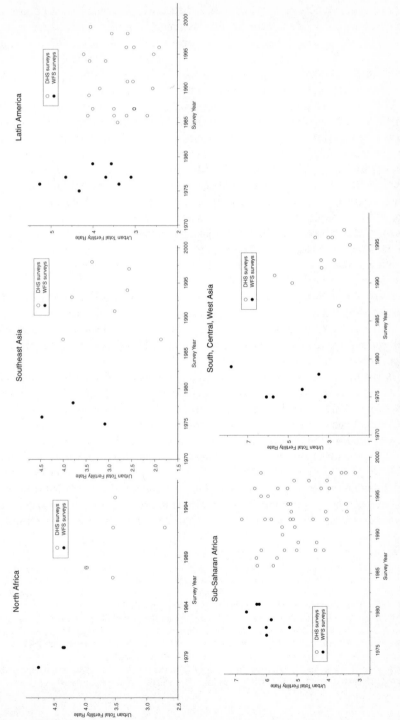

FIGURE 6-9 Urban total fertility rates by region and survey year, estimates from WFS and DHS surveys.

this being statistically significant.[17] It is difficult to determine what portion of this trend is attributable to economic development. In a fixed-effects regression applied to the full sample, using the log of gross national product (GNP) per capita as an explanatory variable, the GNP measure did not attain statistical significance. Region-specific estimates were more variable, however, and it appears that the role of GNP cannot be effectively isolated by these regressions.

The rural/urban differences in fertility can be seen in Figure 6-10, where the vertical axis of each figure represents the rural TFR for a given survey less the urban rate for that survey. (Similar patterns emerge from relative measures, i.e., rural fertility rates divided by urban.) No trend is obvious to the eye. The application of fixed-effects regression methods to the full sample produces a trend coefficient of about -0.01, which is both substantively and statistically insignificant. Region-specific estimates suggest an increasing urban/rural gap in sub-Saharan Africa (at about 0.04 children per year) and a decreasing gap in Latin America (-0.03 children per year), but neither of these is large enough to be of real interest. In the full sample, there is evidence of offsetting effects of GNP per capita and time, with the regression yielding positive coefficients for trend and negative for GNP, but within regions the evidence is mixed.

Confining attention to the DHS surveys, one can examine 34 pairs of surveys covering some 23 countries.[18] For these countries, urban TFRs declined in 31 of the 34 pairs of surveys; they also declined in rural areas in 24 survey pairs. Where fertility declined in both rural and urban settings (22 surveys), the urban decline slightly exceeded the rural on average.[19]

In summary, insofar as broad patterns and trends can be revealing, it appears that urban/rural fertility gaps are surprisingly durable. Fertility declines are under way in both rural villages and cities, but there is no clear indication as yet of steeper declines in the villages. It is reasonable to think that the urban/rural gap must eventually close, but for the moment it appears persistent.

The question of whether fertility rates have been driven down by economic crisis has often been raised with respect to sub-Saharan Africa, a region where the beginnings of fertility decline in the late 1980s and 1990s coincided with economic crises and slow economic growth. There is a surface plausibility to the suggestion that crisis has provoked fertility decline, but the mechanisms need careful inspection.

---

[17]The region-specific trend estimates from fixed-effects models are -0.085 for North Africa; -0.108 for sub-Saharan Africa; -0.068 for Southeast Asia; -0.090 for South, Central, and West Asia; and -0.053 for Latin America. All these estimates are significant at the 0.001 level.

[18]The countries where fertility change can be examined are Bangladesh, Bolivia, Brazil, Cameroon, Colombia, the Dominican Republic, Egypt, Ghana, Guatemala, Indonesia, Kenya, Madagascar, Mali, Morocco, Niger, Peru, the Philippines, Senegal, Tanzania, Togo, Uganda, Zambia, and Zimbabwe. The gap between DHS surveys ranges from 3 to 10 years, but on average is 5.3 years.

[19]If the surveys are weighted, the weight being the inverse of the number of surveys fielded in the country, the mean declines are 0.68 and 0.53 children in urban and rural areas, respectively.

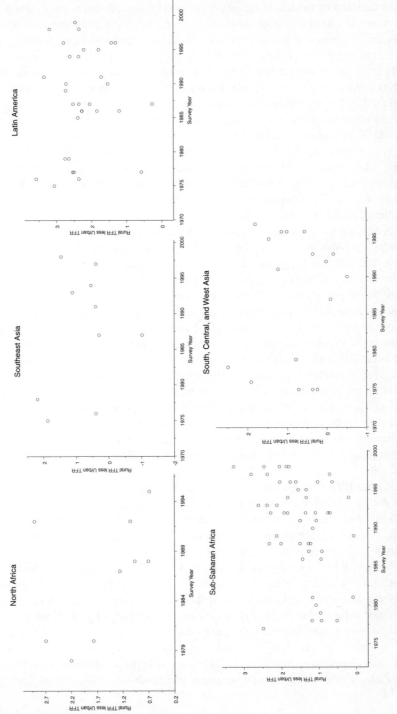

FIGURE 6-10 Rural total fertility rates less urban rates by region and survey year, estimates from WFS and DHS surveys.

In the standard models of fertility developed by economists, roles are reserved for the current level of household income and for expected future income. Wage rates and the prices of goods enter the budget constraints of these models, also in current and future periods. Theories of the quantity–quality transition make a place for the economic returns to investments in schooling, and sophisticated versions of the theory (e.g., Parish and Willis, 1993) recognize the liquidity constraints that, by preventing poor families from borrowing against future income, require them to adjust their behavior to fit within current income. Economic models of marriage draw attention to the differences in current and future wages between women and men, which are hypothesized to influence the returns to marriage. The theories that focus on economic crises do not introduce any new concepts to this list. Rather, they draw attention to the net effects of *combinations* of forces. Boserup (1985) gives the essence of the crisis argument, which is further developed by Lesthaeghe (1989).

A crisis-led fertility transition is brought on by several simultaneous or nearly simultaneous shocks: contractions in real incomes, associated with programs of privatization and exchange rate devaluation in some countries; price increases due to the removal of subsidies and the imposition of fees and user charges for services that previously had none; and reductions in the quality of public services in health and education. According to the Working Group on Factors Affecting Contraceptive Use (1993), which examined the implications for sub-Saharan Africa in the early 1990s, such shocks appeared to have the potential to unsettle what had been high-fertility demographic regimes, removing much of the economic logic that supported high fertility. Whether economic recovery would restore the old logic was unclear in the view of these authors. While economic crises offered opportunities for governments to seize upon temporary motivations for lower fertility by extending services, the crises also reduced the funds available for governments to do so. Hence, in the view of this group, whether crises could lead to sustained fertility transitions was much in doubt. The empirical basis for the argument was closely scrutinized in a companion study (Working Group on Demographic Effects of Economic and Social Reversals, 1993), which concluded that the demographic effects of crisis varied from country to country in Africa, with no clear empirical connection to macroeconomic performance. As of the early 1990s, then, fertility decline could not be linked definitively to economic crisis or stagnation in sub-Saharan Africa.

Many of the socioeconomic elements shaken by the African crises of the 1980s have now settled into place, leaving the economies of the region with drastically reconfigured prices and public sectors, and leaving in tatters much of the logic that supported high fertility in earlier eras. Recent research in Dakar, Bamako, Yaoundé, and Antananarivo shows that residents of these cities are adjusting their marriage and fertility behavior in response to high unemployment rates and reduced access to formal-sector salaried employment (Antoine, Ouédraogo, and Piché, 1999; Antoine, Razafindrakoto, and Roubaud, 2001). Agyei-Mensah

(2002) sees signs across a wide range of settings that urban fertility is declining precipitously, with the declines being especially notable in capital cities. TFRs have fallen below 3.0 children per woman in Accra (2.66 in 1998), Nairobi (2.61 in 1998), Lomé (2.91 in 1998), and Harare (2.98 in 1999), and the TFR is rapidly approaching that level in Yaoundé (3.1 in 1998, down from 4.4 in 1991).

In a careful study of Addis Ababa, Yitna (2002) documents a decline in TFRs from 5.26 children per woman in 1974–79 to 3.17 a decade later, further to 2.2 children in 1989–1994, and further still to 1.76 children in 1998. The largest declines took place in teenage fertility, and these are attributable to a postponement of marriage. In 1978 only 6.5 percent of women aged 25–29 in Addis Ababa had never married; by 1995, that figure had risen to 41.8 percent. Yitna also suggests that an urban housing shortage and strict housing controls contribute to delayed marriage, as does a high level of unemployment among young adults. (See Box 6.2 for a similar analysis of economic crises in Mongolia.) By comparison with marriage, rising levels of contraceptive use appear to have had only a modest impact on fertility, and even that appears to be confined to the 1990s.

Shapiro and Tambashe (2001) argue that a general fertility transition is well under way across sub-Saharan Africa, typically unfolding in three phases: an initial urban decline; then rapid urban fertility decline and the beginnings of rural decline; and, eventually, more rapid rural than urban decline.[20] As did the earlier Working Group on Demographic Effects of Economic and Social Reversals (1993), these authors attempted to assess the role of economic crises, using change in gross domestic product (GDP) per capita as an explanatory variable, but they could find almost no evidence of direct linkage. The effects of economic decline are most likely to be indirect, operating through postponement of marriage, as in the case of Addis Ababa. Although the effects cannot be traced confidently from national macroeconomic indicators to the level of individuals and families, there is every reason to think that the macro factors must operate with a concentrated force on the lives of the urban poor.

THE URBAN POOR

In this and the next two sections of the chapter, we consider several subgroups of the urban population that are of particular interest: the urban poor, migrants, and adolescents. This section documents some of the demographic disadvantages

---

[20] As noted above, evidence for more rapid rural decline is slim. According to a previous analysis of data on sub-Saharan Africa from the DHS (Cohen, 1998a), fertility in the urban areas of all countries surveyed by 1996 was lower than fertility in the rural areas. However, in the countries that experienced relatively large fertility declines, these declines occurred in both rural and urban areas. In countries that had only small national fertility declines, fertility dropped only in urban areas, and therefore, urban/rural gaps in fertility rates increased. In the late 1970s and early 1980s, many African countries had urban fertility rates of more than 6.0 children per woman. By the mid-1990s, urban fertility rates in several African countries had fallen to under 4.0 children (Cohen, 1998a).

BOX 6.2 Demography During Crises: The Mongolia Case

Fertility declines associated with social and economic crisis often take a distinctive form, expressed in a collapse in rates of marriage (sometimes accompanied by a rise in out-of-wedlock births) and postponement of fertility among married couples. The effects of economic crisis can be seen in a number of countries of West Asia, and the case of Mongolia has been examined by Becker and Hemley (1998).

In the decade between 1989 and 1999, Mongolia's total fertility rate declined by half, from 4.6 to 2.3 children per woman. The decline was especially great for women over age 30. Only crude birth rate data are available for *aimag* (provinces), but these data (shown in the figure below) suggest that fertility has declined more rapidly in Mongolia's three large cities than in the country as a whole, with an especially rapid decline in the secondary cities of Erdenet and Darhan. The fertility collapse has been accompanied by a large decline in registered marriages, which fell by some 35 percent over the decade.

The demographic indicators reflect the economic trends. Per capita gross domestic product in constant prices declined by 22 percent between 1989 and 1995 but recovered thereafter, rising slowly from 1995 to 1999. Most of the response appears to have been completed by 1996, when the Mongolian economy stabilized.

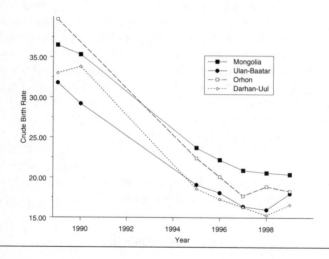

that are associated with urban poverty. It begins by contrasting the circumstances of poor urban women with those of urban nonpoor and rural women, relying on data from the DHS. It then examines the implications of *spatially concentrated* poverty, drawing on a set of case studies of urban slums and squatter communities.

Poverty: An Aspatial Analysis

Recall that for the DHS analyses, poverty is defined in relative terms, with the lowest quartile of urban households in each survey being classified as poor (see Appendix E). The poverty measure refers to individual households and does

TABLE 6-6 Fertility Rates Among Poor and Nonpoor Urban Women in Relation to Rural Fertility, by Region

DHS Surveys in Region	Urban Poor	Urban Nonpoor	Urban Poverty Statistically Significant[a]
North Africa	0.89	0.78	5 of 6
Sub-Saharan Africa	0.92	0.85	13 of 41[b]
Southeast Asia	1.11	0.93	7 of 7
South, Central, West Asia	0.97	0.82	6 of 11
Latin America	0.90	0.67	21 of 22
TOTAL	0.93	0.80	52 of 87

[a] Statistical significance is assessed at the 0.05 level for each survey that permits a hypothesis test. The test controls for age, marital status, and city size. The estimates shown in the two columns are based on predicted values for ever-married women aged 25–29.

[b] In two cases, urban poverty was statistically significant but negatively related to fertility.

not encompass the spatially concentrated aspects of poverty. Although more refined measures of poverty are badly needed, the measure we use allows at least a glimpse into the circumstances of the poor. In the next section we consider evidence drawn from selected micro studies of low-income urban communities to get a sense of how spatially concentrated poverty may be expressed in reproductive health.

The fertility rates of poor urban women are not very different from those of rural women, but are well above those of other urban women. In Table 6-6, which displays these differences, rural fertility rates serve as the reference category, and levels of urban fertility are expressed relative to those rates. As can be seen, the fertility of poor urban women generally falls below that of rural women—on average their ratio is 0.93, a 7 percent shortfall. (Note that in Southeast Asia, the urban poor exhibit higher fertility than rural women.) Poor urban women have significantly higher levels of fertility than urban women who are not poor.

Modern contraceptive use varies in much the same way. Among all urban women, those who are poor are significantly less likely to use contraception (see Table 6-7). They are generally more likely to use contraception than rural women, but in some regions there is little to separate the two groups, and in Southeast Asia, rural women are more likely to use contraceptive methods than the urban poor (see the notes to the table). In short, there is a large subgroup of urban women whose fertility and contraceptive use closely resemble those of rural women.

As noted earlier, the urban private sector is quite important as a source of contraception, but for the poor, the prices charged for contraceptives can put the private sources out of reach. As shown in Table 6-8, poor urban women using

TABLE 6-7 Predicted Contraceptive Use for Women Aged 25–29 by Residence and, for Urban Areas, Poverty Status

				Statistical Significance	
DHS Surveys in Region	All Rural	Urban Poor	Urban Nonpoor	Urban Poor vs. Urban Nonpoor[a]	Urban Poor vs. Rural[b]
North Africa	0.26	0.37	0.48	5 of 6	6 of 6
Sub-Saharan Africa	0.08	0.13	0.22	31 of 41	37 of 40
Southeast Asia	0.44	0.40	0.47	6 of 7	7 of 7
South, Central, West Asia	0.33	0.35	0.44	11 of 11	11 of 11
Latin America	0.32	0.37	0.47	18 of 22	22 of 22
TOTAL	0.22	0.26	0.35	71 of 87	83 of 86

NOTE: See notes to Table 6-6.

[a] Significance assessed at the 0.05 level. The figures listed are the numbers of surveys in which a test could be applied.

[b] Significant difference (at the 0.05 level) in predicted values, as assessed using the delta method for estimating variances. The differences between the urban poor and rural women are positive and significant in 66 cases (North Africa, 6; Sub-Saharan Africa, 34; East and Southeast Asia, 1; South, Central, West Asia, 9; and Latin America, 16). Of the 17 surveys showing a negative and significant difference, the cases of Indonesia (all 4 surveys), and the Dominican Republic (all 3 surveys) are noteworthy. Colombia (1990) and Uzbekistan (1996) have significant negative differences of more than 8 percentage points, the largest in this set of surveys.

TABLE 6-8 Proportion of Contracepting Women Using Private Medical Sources of Contraception, by Residence and Poverty Status

DHS Surveys in Region	All Rural	Urban Poor	Urban Nonpoor
North Africa	0.52	0.49	0.62
Sub-Saharan Africa	0.29	0.33	0.37
Southeast Asia	0.20	0.29	0.46
South, Central, West Asia	0.26	0.23	0.36
Latin America	0.49	0.49	0.64
TOTAL	0.35	0.36	0.46

NOTE: See notes to Table 6-4. The figures shown are predicted values for ever-married women who currently use a modern method of contraception, based on estimates from a probit model adjusted for age in rural areas and for age and city size in urban areas. The predicted values are for women aged 25–29. Surveys from several countries were excluded because they had too few users of contraception from private sources to allow multivariate estimation.

contraception are much less likely than other urban women to obtain their methods from private sources.[21] Indeed, the urban poor are only slightly more likely than rural women to use such sources, which is surprising in view of the prominence of the urban private sector. That the urban poor rely less on private sources may well reflect their inability to pay. It is also possible, however, that public-sector family planning programs have targeted the communities of the urban poor as sites for clinics and outreach programs, in this way making the public sources of methods more convenient.[22]

Higher fertility and lower contraceptive use are not necessarily indicative of disadvantage: the urban poor may find it rational and in their interest to adopt strategies of higher fertility. To conclude that there is a disadvantage in fertility, one must have measures suggesting that the poor are less able to exercise control over the number and spacing of their births. Estimates of unmet need for contraception provide one such indicator. Examining these estimates by poverty status (Table 6-9), we find that the urban poor suffer from a clear disadvantage relative to other urban women, having higher levels of unmet need. As we have come to expect, in Southeast Asia they have slightly higher levels of unmet need than rural women.

Poor urban women can also be exposed to higher levels of other reproductive health risks than urban nonpoor. When poor women give birth, they are much less likely than other urban women to have their deliveries attended by a physician or nurse/midwife (see Table 6-10). The gap between poor and nonpoor urban women is statistically significant and is as large as 20 percentage points in the case of Southeast Asia.[23] The urban poor are, however, relatively fortunate by comparison with rural women, whose deliveries are attended even less often. The absence of trained personnel at childbirth may result in unnecessary delays in diagnosing the need for medical intervention, and by leaving it to family and neighbors to decide where emergency care should be sought, may create further delays in reaching modern care. In times of crisis, trained nurses and midwives are voices of authority whose recommendations can override the concerns of husbands and family elders about the monetary costs of care.

Poor urban women are also less likely to know how to protect themselves against the risks of STDs, including HIV/AIDS. As can be seen in Table 6-11, poverty status makes a significant difference in the level of AIDS

---

[21] In sub-Saharan Africa, urban poverty is rarely a statistically significant influence on the use of private sources, attaining significance only in 3 of 25 surveys. In other regions, however, urban poverty is almost always significant (24 of 29 surveys).

[22] Findings from a study in Jakarta, Indonesia, revealed that poor mothers were significantly more likely to use *posyandus* (local health posts established by the Indonesian government) than were wealthier mothers (Kaye and Novell, 1994).

[23] Again the relative poverty measure fails to distinguish clearly among urban women in sub-Saharan Africa, where it is statistically significant in only 13 of 40 surveys. In the other regions, however, the poverty measure is significant in 38 of 44 surveys.

TABLE 6-9 Predicted Unmet Need for Ever-Married Women Aged 25–29 by Residence and, for Urban Areas, Poverty Status

DHS Surveys in Region	All Rural	Urban Poor	Urban Nonpoor	Statistical Significance	
				Urban Poor vs. Urban Nonpoor	Urban Poor vs. Rural[a]
North Africa	0.27	0.16	0.12	2 of 3	3 of 3
Sub-Saharan Africa	0.34	0.31	0.24	12 of 30	26 of 30
Southeast Asia	0.22	0.23	0.16	5 of 5	5 of 5
South, Central, West Asia	0.24	0.22	0.15	4 of 9	7 of 9
Latin America	0.25	0.16	0.10	10 of 13	13 of 13
TOTAL	0.29	0.25	0.19	33 of 60	54 of 60

NOTE: See notes to Table 6-6.

[a] Significant difference (at the 0.05 level) in the predicted values of unmet need for the urban poor and rural residents. Of the 54 surveys with significant differences between the urban poor and rural residents, 39 showed lower levels of unmet need among the urban poor (the difference is 7.5 percentage points in the average survey), and some 15 showed that the urban poor have significantly higher levels of unmet need (an average difference of 5.3 percentage points). The level of unmet need for the urban poor exceeded that for rural women in no surveys in North Africa; 9 surveys in Sub-Saharan Africa; 3 in East and Southeast Asia; 2 in South, Central, and West Asia; and 1 in Latin America. The difference exceeded 3 percentage points in the surveys for Burkina Faso (1993), Côte d'Ivoire (1994), Ghana (1993), Mozambique (1997), Rwanda (1992), Senegal (1992 and 1997), and Zambia (1992).

TABLE 6-10 Proportion of Women with All Recent Births Attended by Physicians or Nurse/Midwives, by Residence and, for Urban Areas, Poverty Status

DHS Surveys in Region	All Rural	Urban Poor	Urban Nonpoor
North Africa	0.19	0.39	0.57
Sub-Saharan Africa	0.15	0.32	0.41
Southeast Asia	0.31	0.47	0.67
South, Central, West Asia	0.27	0.34	0.49
Latin America	0.27	0.44	0.59
TOTAL	0.21	0.37	0.50

NOTE: The estimates shown in the table are age-adjusted to reflect the experience of ever-married women aged 25–29.

TABLE 6-11 Among Those Aware of AIDS, Knowledge
That Using Condoms and Limiting Sexual Partners Can
Reduce the Risk of AIDS, by Residence and, for Urban
Areas, Poverty Status

DHS Surveys in Region	All Rural	Urban Poor	Urban Nonpoor
Sub-Saharan Africa	0.57	0.64	0.73
Southeast Asia	0.22	0.25	0.39
South, Central, West Asia	0.63	0.69	0.71
Latin America	0.54	0.66	0.81
TOTAL	0.54	0.62	0.72

awareness and prevention,[24] although the level of knowledge is even lower in rural areas.[25]

Urban health services in several African cities are quite weak in terms of prevention programs for HIV/AIDS and other STDs (Rossi, 2000), but even here there is evidence that targeted interventions can make a difference. One such program—in Kinshasa, Zaire, for female sex workers—was highly successful in reducing STD and HIV incidence and prevalence (Laga, Alary, Nzila, Manoka, Tuliza, Behets, Goeman, St. Louis, and Piot, 1994). Social marketing programs appear to have had some success in urban settings in Mozambique, Zambia, and Zimbabwe (Agha, Karlyn, and Meekers, 2001; Agha, 1998; Meekers, 2001). These programs promote the use of condoms by advertising and distributing them at bars, nightclubs, hotels, and other areas where individuals who are at high risk of exposure to HIV congregate. However, those who use condoms are less likely to use them with their spouse than with other partners and may not use them in each sexual encounter. A study of men in urban Zimbabwe, for example, found that 91 percent used condoms with casual partners and 77 percent used them with nonmarital regular partners, but only 11 percent used them with their spouses (Meekers, 2001).

To sum up, poor urban women appear to be more exposed to the risks of unintended pregnancy than are nonpoor urban women; at the time of delivery, they are not as likely to be protected by trained medical personnel; and they lack the knowledge to protect themselves effectively against the risks of HIV/AIDS and other STDs. In most of the surveys we examined, these poor women retain an advantage over rural women, but the margin of difference can be very slim, and in

---

[24]In sub-Saharan Africa, the poverty measure is statistically significant in 12 of 21 surveys; in the other regions, it is significant in 2 of 2 surveys in Southeast Asia; not significant in the single survey for South, Central, and West Asia; and significant in 7 of 7 surveys in Latin America.

[25]Evidence from other studies also suggests that poor women lack information about AIDS. In South Africa, for example, researchers found that better-educated women were more aware of AIDS (Pick and Cooper, 1997).

some instances, rural women appear to be less disadvantaged than the urban poor. If there is an urban advantage in reproductive health in general, it is obviously distributed most unevenly.

Spatially Concentrated Poverty

The DHS analyses are helpful in describing the situation of the poor, but they do not allow the spatially concentrated aspects of urban poverty to be seen clearly. To understand the implications of concentrated poverty, one must leave the generalized terrain of the DHS and examine studies of specific city neighborhoods and low-income communities. The selective nature of these micro studies is a cause for concern. Researchers might be drawn to study the poorest of urban neighborhoods because these are the places most likely to supply vivid illustrations of the deprivations of poverty. It is possible that micro studies tend to exaggerate the deprivations experienced by the urban poor. We do not know whether any serious bias arises from the selection of research sites, but it is a point to bear in mind.

Sample selection issues were carefully considered for the recent Nairobi Cross-Sectional Slums Survey (African Population and Health Research Center, 2002), which was designed so as to represent statistically those Nairobi settlements that have been designated as "informal settlements" by the national statistical office. Box 6.3 describes a number of findings from this study. The design permits comparison of low-income communities with other settlements in Nairobi, as well as with cities elsewhere in Kenya and with the Kenyan rural population. This assessment reveals a number of dimensions in which poor urban women are disadvantaged or at risk, including earlier ages at first intercourse, involvement with multiple sexual partners, lack of knowledge of contraceptive sources, and absence of trained personnel at the time of childbirth.

As the conditions of the urban poor are scrutinized, it often appears that the time and money costs of access to services are understood by women less as economic than as social barriers. When services require payment in cash, women must often negotiate for the money with their husbands and other family members. A lack of independence and autonomy in decision making emerges in many accounts. For instance, a study set in Lahore, Pakistan, found that poor urban women lacked control over their fertility because they were unaware of the contraceptive methods available and had to defer to husbands in decisions about their use (see Box 6.4). Likewise, Pasha, Fikree, and Vermund (2001) studied the unmet need for contraception in a Karachi squatter settlement, finding that it stemmed from several sources: a divergence between the woman's own fertility goals and those of her mother-in-law, a perceived lack of autonomy and economic self-sufficiency, and a lack of communication about sexual matters with the woman's spouse. In a study of urban Mumbai, poor women complained that they had neither the time nor the money to seek out reproductive health care. A number of the Mumbai

---

BOX 6.3 Fertility and Reproductive Health in Nairobi's Slums

A study was recently undertaken to document the demographic and health characteristics of slum residents by comparison with other residents of Nairobi, other Kenyan cities, and rural areas (African Population and Health Research Center, 2002). The table below shows some of the results on fertility and reproductive health.

Measure	Nairobi Slums	Nairobi	Other Cities	Rural	Kenya
Total Fertility Rate	4.0	2.6	3.5	5.2	4.7
Ideal Family Size	3.2	2.9	3.3	4.0	3.8
Use Modern Contraceptives[a]	39.1	46.8	37.0	29.0	31.5
Obtain Contraceptives from Private Sources[b]	41.7	46.9	45.5	29.3	33.2
Births at a Health Facility	52.3	75.6	64.4	36.2	42.1
Births Attended by Doctor, Nurse, Trained Midwife	54.3	76.4	67.9	38.4	44.3
Median Age at First Intercourse, Women 15–24	16.9	17.9	17.3	17.2	17.3
Had Multiple Sexual Partners in Past 12 Months	13.5	7.4	n.a.	n.a.	6.8
Know a Source for Condoms	56.0	65.0	n.a.	n.a.	60.0

NOTE: n.a. means not available.

[a] Currently married women.

[b] Current users.

The Nairobi slums have a significantly higher total fertility rate (at 4.0 births per woman) than the rest of Nairobi (2.6) and other Kenyan cities (3.5), although fertility is lower in these slums than in the countryside (5.2). Yet residents of the slums say they think 3.2 children would be the ideal, a number only slightly above that found elsewhere in Nairobi and in other Kenyan cities. Contraceptive use is lower in the slums, and there are indications of an unmet need for family planning services.

Only half (52.3 percent) of births to the women living in these low-income communities were delivered in a health facility, and only about half (54.3 percent) of the deliveries were attended by a doctor, nurse, or trained midwife. To be sure, these are higher than the national proportion, but much lower than for the remainder of Nairobi and other cities.

The median age at first intercourse for women aged 15–24 is 17, about a year younger than elsewhere in Nairobi, but not much different from the ages seen in other cities and rural areas. Other analyses indicate that age at first intercourse may have been declining in recent years (African Population and Health Research Center, 2002). When compared with women living elsewhere in Nairobi, slum women are nearly twice as likely to have had multiple sexual partners in the past year. A significant proportion of unmarried women with low educational attainment living in the slums did not know how to avoid HIV infection. Even though the majority of the women were aware of condoms, almost half did not know where they could be obtained.

BOX 6.4 Intraurban Differences in Women's Autonomy and Fertility Control in Lahore, Pakistan

---

Some 650 women from low, middle, and high socioeconomic communities in Lahore were interviewed to assess the degree of control they could exercise over their fertility (Hamid, 2001). Women were said to have control of their fertility if they were aware of at least two modern methods of contraception; had access to such methods; and were able to decide whether to use them, independently or jointly with their husbands. By this definition, 75 percent of women in the low socioeconomic area lacked control over their fertility, as did 65 percent in the middle socioeconomic area. By contrast, only 36 percent of women in the high socioeconomic communities lacked control.

---

women expressed fears that their husbands or mothers-in-law might prevent them from going to the clinic (Mulgaonkar, Parikh, Taskar, Dharap, and Pradhan, 1994). It appears that intrahousehold conflicts and a lack of decision-making autonomy for women are urban as well as rural concerns.

Although they would be exceptionally revealing as summary measures of reproductive health, comparisons of maternal mortality rates in rural and poor urban communities are rare, doubtless because large samples are required for reliable estimates of these rates. Box 6.5 describes one of the few studies available, in which comparisons were made among several low-income settlements in Karachi and a variety of rural Pakistani communities. Although the estimated maternal mortality ratio for Karachi was the lowest in the group, it does not differ significantly from the estimates for some of the rural sites. Yet Karachi has a number of modern hospitals and clinics, and the options for transport would appear to be plentiful. Why is there no greater urban advantage? In Karachi's poor neighborhoods, it has not been customary for husbands and other male decision makers to be present at the time of childbirth, and delays arise from the need to consult them when complications arise. In addition, poor families tend to seek local care first, going from place to place in the neighborhood before making an effort to reach the modern facilities outside the neighborhood (Fariyal Fikree, personal communication, 2002).

The reproductive morbidities affecting poor urban women were examined by Mayank, Bahl, Rattan, and Bhandari (2001), who studied some 1700 pregnant women in Dakshinpuri, a New Delhi slum. The maternal mortality rate in this urban sample was estimated at 645 deaths per 100,000, a level not much different from that of rural India. The Dakshinpuri study was prospective in design, recording evidence of reproductive morbidities during each woman's pregnancy and following the women through to childbirth. Pregnant women in this low-income community were found to have little understanding of the health risks associated with their pregnancies. A number of them suffered from potentially serious ailments—over two-thirds were clinically diagnosed as anemic, and 12 percent were found to be seriously anemic. Lower reproductive tract infections were

BOX 6.5 Urban/Rural Differences in Maternal Mortality: Pakistan

Fikree, Midhet, Sadruddin, and Berendes (1997) fielded a large sample survey in 1989–1992 that included low-income settlements in Karachi, together with four rural comparison districts in the province of Balochistan (Pishin, Loralai, Lasbela, and Khuzdar) and two rural districts (Abbottabad and Mansehra) in the North-West Frontier. Among the rural sites, Pishin and Lasbela lie within 20 miles of Karachi, whereas Loralai and Khuzdar are far from modern sources of maternal care. Both of the sites in the North-West Frontier are remote, but one (Abbottabad) has a university hospital.

Estimates of maternal mortality ratios (MMRs), together with their confidence bands, are shown in the figure below. As can be seen, the MMR estimate for Karachi is the lowest among all sites, but the rural estimates are significantly different only for the remote districts of Loralai and Khuzdar. The rural district of Pishin has an estimated MMR very similar to that of low-income Karachi. The rural North-West Frontier district of Abbottabad, no doubt benefiting from its university hospital, also has an MMR that differs insignificantly from that of low-income Karachi. It appears that the urban poor can suffer from health disadvantages not unlike those that afflict rural residents.

In the poor communities of Karachi, some 68 percent of births are delivered at home, and 59 percent are attended by traditional birth attendants (TBAs). Yet rural women are even more likely to deliver at home and have family members or TBAs in attendance. Why, then, is the urban health advantage not greater? An earlier study of Karachi slums (Fikree, Gray, Berendes, and Karim, 1994) suggests that when acute pregnancy and delivery complications arise, local care is sought before women are brought to the hospital, and there can be delays in locating male decision makers and obtaining their consent to hospital care.

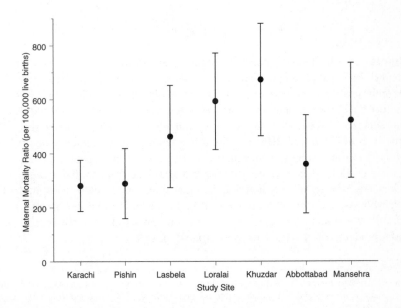

discovered in 35 percent of pregnant women.[26] Yet relatively few women understood that high fevers and swelling of the face, hands, or feet might be symptoms of conditions that could endanger their pregnancy. (The symptoms of anemia, recognizable by a characteristic pallor or shortness of breath, antenatal bleeding, and convulsions, were better appreciated as indicators of serious risk.) In this community, antenatal care is provided free of charge in the local health clinic, and the vast majority of women make use of this care. However, the quality of the care the women receive is grossly inadequate; for example, fewer than 10 percent of women attending the clinic were given any advice about the danger signs of pregnancy.

Better-educated women in Dakshinpuri tend to be more attentive to indications of ill-health and report more episodes of serious morbidity. In the low-income areas of Karachi as well, literate women and those of somewhat higher economic status are more likely to make use of contraception (Fikree, Khan, Kadir, Sajan, and Rahbar, 2001). It may be that the potential benefits stemming from socioeconomic diversity *within* low-income neighborhoods have not been fully appreciated. In communities such as Dakshinpuri, for example, do illiterate families learn about pregnancy risks and danger signs from the experiences of their literate neighbors? Or are there social barriers and forms of exclusion operating even within these low-income settlements that limit beneficial social interaction? A study of Bulawayo, Zimbabwe, draws attention to a lack of communication within the community about new reproductive health services, which appears to have suppressed demand (Rossi, 2000).

MIGRANTS

Migrants are distinctive among all urban groups in that they have recently exchanged one spatial–social context for another. What might be the implications for their fertility and reproductive health? It is difficult to give a definitive answer because the literature on migrants has been dominated by studies of rural-to-urban migrants, even though this may not be the largest group in numerical terms. The panel's examination of DHS data for urban women of reproductive age (Chapter 4) found that among the women who had moved to their current residence in the preceding 5 years, about two-thirds had arrived from another town or city. Urban-origin migrants may find that their new environment closely resembles the old, whereas rural-origin migrants would be expected to find the contrast much starker. We summarize below what is known about fertility, contraceptive use, and reproductive risk among rural-to-urban migrants.

---

[26]The clinical tests found higher percentages of women with anemia and reproductive tract infections (RTIs) than women's self-reports would have indicated. This may be because RTIs are often asymptomatic, or because the vaginal discharge associated with RTIs is considered to be a normal part of a woman's life.

Three propositions have been advanced about the urban demographic behavior exhibited by such migrants. The *selectivity* hypothesis holds that as a group, rural-to-urban migrants are socioeconomically distinct from the populations of their rural origins in terms of education, work experience, age, marital status, and family-size preferences (Ribe and Schultz, 1980; Goldstein and Goldstein, 1981, 1983; White, Moreno, and Guo, 1995). In some respects, then, rural-to-urban migrants might have more in common with their new urban neighbors than with their counterparts in the village. Migrants are also likely to have distinctive personal traits, such as tolerance of risk, an openness to innovation, and uncommon energy and drive, these being qualities that might manifest themselves in any context.

The *disruption* hypothesis focuses on the period surrounding the move. Childbearing can be interrupted by the stress that accompanies migration and by the physical separation of spouses. According to this theory, fertility is displaced in time by migration—the short-term fertility deficit emerging at the time of a move is later erased (Ribe and Schultz, 1980; Potter and Kobrin, 1982; Hervitz, 1985; Goldstein and Goldstein, 1981, 1983, 1984; White, Moreno, and Guo, 1995).

Finally, without denying that migration can be disruptive, the *adaptation* hypothesis emphasizes the urban environments in which migrants find themselves after their move, arguing that migrants refashion their fertility behavior to fit the realities of their new environments. As Bond, Valente, and Kendall (1999) find in a study of Chiang Mai, Thailand, migrants begin to construct new social networks upon moving to the city, taking up with new friends, mixing with city workmates, and engaging with romantic and sexual partners. These urban networks supply new contexts for decisions affecting fertility and reproductive health. According to the adaptation hypothesis, rural-to-urban migrants take up many of the outlooks and reproductive strategies of urban natives (Goldstein and Goldstein, 1983). This hypothesis has attracted a good deal of empirical support (e.g., Farber and Lee, 1984; Lee and Farber, 1984).

The well-documented age pattern of migration, in which rates peak in the late teens and early twenties (Rogers and Castro, 1981; Rogers, 1995), implies that many migrant women will begin their reproductive careers in the city. Drawing on DHS surveys in Africa, Brockerhoff (1995b) found that unmarried rural women were more than twice as likely as married women to migrate to urban areas.[27] The married women who migrated were found to be less likely than urban natives to live with their husbands during their first few months in the city, as predicted by the disruption hypothesis.

Evidence from the DHS generally conforms to the hypothesis of adaptation. A study of DHS data from 13 surveys in Africa between 1986 and 1992 found that rates of pregnancy among migrant women were lower than those among urban

---

[27]The unmarried women were found no more likely to marry subsequently than their rural counterparts, making it doubtful that their moves could have been driven by near-term prospects for marriage.

natives during their first 3 years in the city, rose slightly higher by the fifth year, and then declined to levels like those of natives (Brockerhoff, 1995b). The panel examined all DHS surveys with information on migration and subsequent urban fertility and came to a similar conclusion (detailed results not shown). There is some evidence (not always strong) of disruption effects immediately following a move, but when fertility rates are estimated for migrants with 5 years' duration in the city, the rates are not generally distinguishable from those of urban natives (and longer-term migrants) of the same age. In short, the literature appears to have settled on a consensus: within a few years of moving, rural-to-urban migrants exhibit urban birth rates that are about the same as those of natives when age, education, and other factors are taken into account (White, 2000).

There are cases in which migrants are found to have lower lifetime fertility than urban natives. White, Djamba, and Dang (2001) examined the case of Vietnam, where fertility at the national level fell from an average of 5.6 children per woman in 1979 to 2.3 children in 1997. Using data on individual birth histories, which permit comparisons of fertility before and after migration, White and colleagues found that migration is strongly implicated in the Vietnamese fertility decline. A relaxation of governmental controls over migration accompanied the introduction of the *Doi Moi* program of economic reforms, and the combination of policies appears to have spurred rural-to-urban migration, especially of the temporary variety. There is evidence of a disruption effect from migration in individual birth histories, but Vietnamese migrants generally tend to marry later than nonmigrants and to delay their first births. Other things being held constant, the migrants' delay of marriage and first birth yields somewhat fewer children over a reproductive lifetime than is the case for urban natives. The effects found by White and colleagues are surprisingly strong for temporary migrants, who may postpone childbearing because they expect they may need to undertake yet further moves.

The case of China, where controls over migration were also relaxed at roughly the same time that economic reforms were introduced, exhibits features similar to those of Vietnam. It was thought in the 1980s that "temporary" rural-to-urban migrants (those lacking an urban registration) might be moving to cities to evade the one-child policy, raising fears of an increase in urban birth rates.[28] These fears proved to be groundless. A study of Hubei Province showed that migrant fertility was no higher there than the fertility of urban natives, and might well be lower because of spousal separation (Goldstein, White, and Goldstein, 1997). A study in Anhui province came to a similar conclusion, suggesting that temporary migrants in China may actually have lower fertility than long-term urban residents (Liu and Goldstein, 1996). This is similar to what White, Djamba, and Dang (2001) found for Vietnam.

---

[28]By moving out of their *hukou*, families could avoid having to register and pay fines for second- and higher-order births.

The achievement of rough equality in levels of fertility says little about the other reproductive health needs of migrants, however, especially since their fertility is often suppressed by spousal separation rather than by modern contraceptive use. The family planning needs of China's temporary migrants are likely to go unaddressed because they lack the easy access to government family planning agencies that is enjoyed by registered city residents (Goldstein, White, and Goldstein, 1997). Brockerhoff (1995b) argues that in Africa, many rural-to-urban migrants are unfamiliar with modern contraceptives, and upon arrival in the city may continue with the familiar traditional methods or use no method at all.[29]

Although they may come to agree with urban small-family norms, migrants may lack the information that would enable their desires to be acted upon—they may be unaware of the available services, have poor access to them, or be unable to pay. Rural-to-urban African migrants were found to have lower levels of contraceptive use during their first 2 years of city residence than urban married women (Brockerhoff, 1995b). In this study, levels of contraceptive use among migrants begin to approximate those of natives in the second and third years of residence, but the temporary deficits in contraceptive use could put some migrants at risk of unintended pregnancy.

To address such concerns, the panel analyzed the DHS data on unmet need for contraception with attention to the woman's migration status (whether she had moved to her current residence in the preceding 5 years) and found surprisingly little difference between migrants and nonmigrants. Likewise, analyses of unwanted and mistimed fertility revealed little by way of a migrant–nonmigrant difference. Even when separate effects were estimated for rural-origin migrants, few significant findings emerged. Simple descriptive analyses such as these are far from being definitive, however, and it may be that migrants who live in poor neighborhoods have distinctive needs that could be uncovered by a more detailed investigation.

Several studies of access to urban maternal health services have found that the poor, and rural migrants in particular, are less likely to seek prenatal care. In Cochabamba, Bolivia, young rural migrants living in periurban areas are significantly less likely to use prenatal care and to have a trained birth attendant at delivery (Bender, Rivera, and Madonna, 1993). Similar findings from Cape Town, South Africa, indicate that in large squatter settlements with many rural migrants, women tend to postpone prenatal care and have fewer prenatal visits, and are likelier to have preterm and low-birthweight babies than other women in the city (Rip, Keen, Woods, and Van Coeverden De Groot, 1988). Studies such as these provide evidence of the joint effects of poverty and migration, but do not separate out the migrant component.

---

[29] It is sometimes suggested, however, that migrant women may be more likely to try different contraceptive methods and may share information about their experiences with families and friends in their rural home villages (Lim, 1993).

It is well known that male migrants who are single or living apart from their spouses often frequent prostitutes and take other sexual partners. In order to understand the implications of this for the transmission of HIV/AIDS, VanLandingham, Suprasert, Sittitrai, Vaddhanaphuti, and Grandjean (1993) conducted an extensive survey of single men in Chiang Mai, Thailand, where some 62 percent of men are migrants from villages in the north of the country. Among the men who had ever had sexual intercourse, some 90 percent had visited a prostitute at some time, and 38 percent had done so in the 6 months preceding the survey.[30] With reference to these recent visits, only about half (53 percent) of the Thai men said that they always used a condom; some 6 percent never did, and another 19 percent used them intermittently.[31] In this part of Thailand, where the prevalence of HIV/AIDS is high, such behavior courts fatal risks. Furthermore, because men who visit sex workers also tend to engage in intercourse with their girlfriends, the potential is high for infection to spread beyond the circles of sex workers and their clients.[32]

As VanLandingham, Suprasert, Sittitrai, Vaddhanaphuti, and Grandjean (1993) note, the circumstances of Chiang Mai are not unlike those found in many cities of Southeast Asia, where migrants can dominate employment in the personal service industries. Prostitution is not an uncommon profession among women who move from the countryside (Jones, 1984; Rodenburg, 1993). Prostitutes are in need of reproductive health services to protect themselves, including contraceptives and both information and services related to STDs and HIV/AIDS, but there is also a powerful public health rationale based on externalities. The direct connections of prostitutes to male migrants and the broader sexual networks of migrants, encompassing girlfriends and wives, make prostitutes critical targets for health interventions.[33]

Although the expanded urban social networks of migrants may increase the likelihood of exposure to HIV/AIDS and other STDs, these networks can also provide opportunities for education and intervention. Bond, Valente, and Kendall (1999) describe several promising approaches based on peer group meetings moderated by health educators, as well as initiatives set in dormitories and other sites where migrants live and work.

---

[30]The study focused on several groups of men: university students, soldiers, clerks, and a group of construction workers and municipal employees. The students were much less likely to have had intercourse (34 percent had done so, against 80 percent or more for the other groups of men).

[31]In this study, men who had migrated from rural areas were found to have had their first intercourse at a slightly younger age than nonmigrants, and were somewhat more likely to have visited a sex worker recently.

[32]Bond, Valente, and Kendall (1999) document the overlaps among several types of high-risk behavior in Chiang Mai, including drug use, smoking, heavy consumption of alcohol, and unprotected sex.

[33]For an introduction to health interventions that emphasizes the roles of social networks, sexual networks, and networks of high-risk behavior, see Friedman and Aral (2001).

URBAN ADOLESCENTS

An enormous population of young people is coming of age in Africa, Asia, and Latin America. In sub-Saharan Africa, about one person in every four is between 10 and 19 years old (Population Reference Bureau, 2001). As countries continue to urbanize, more and more of these adolescents will be growing up in cities. Yet the nature of urban adolescent life is not well understood, and much remains to be learned about its distinctive features. Vulnerable groups of adolescents—orphans, street children, and sex workers—have not been given sufficient research attention (Rossi, 2000). Although no comprehensive treatment of the issues is available, the literature can offer revealing portraits of adolescence in selected countries.

Mensch, Ibrahim, Lee, and El-Gibaly (2000) explore the gender differences in the experiences of unmarried Egyptian boys and girls aged 16–19 using both urban and rural samples. Egyptian boys generally gain autonomy and mobility as they proceed through adolescence. Upon reaching puberty, by contrast, girls see an end to the relative freedom they enjoyed as children, and are expected to withdraw from public spaces and exhibit modesty in all their behavior. Secondary schooling extends somewhat the ages at which adolescent girls are able to circulate in public spaces, but domestic work and other constraints tend to keep Egyptian girls at home. They spend less time than boys visiting friends, relatives, and peers. These divergent gender trajectories may well be expressed in the social confidence and decision-making authority that young men and women bring to marriage.

By comparison with rural adolescents in Egypt, urban boys and girls express beliefs in somewhat later marriage—by about a year in this study's urban sample (net of own and parental education and household economic status). In other respects, however, it is not obvious that urban boys and girls hold any more progressive views than their rural counterparts. With regard to decision making within households, urban girls place some emphasis on the need for shared decision making between spouses and greater gender equality. However, these attitudes are not commonly shared by urban boys. Schooling is associated positively with an emphasis on equality and joint decision making, but the link is decidedly stronger for girls than for boys. In summary, urban environments in Egypt are linked to later desired ages at marriage, but at least for boys, these environments do not appear to exert much influence on beliefs about gender equality within marriage.

The fertility behavior of urban adolescents is also poorly documented in general. Part of the difficulty is that in some regions, surveys cannot ask fertility-related questions of unmarried adolescents. Hence, if information about adolescents is scanty in general, it is especially so for those living in cities, who are less likely to be married. To judge from the scattered studies available, it appears that out-of-wedlock teen births have been common in urban sub-Saharan Africa and Latin America, and may be increasingly so (Alan Guttmacher Institute, 1998).

In South Africa, however, there is little evidence of any long-term upward trend in the percentage of women giving birth in their teens, which has consistently ranged between 30 and 40 percent (Kaufman, de Wet, and Stadler, 2000). The determinants of teen sexual activity were examined in a large survey of adolescents in urban and rural areas of South Africa's province of KwaZulu–Natal (Kaufman, Clark, Manzini, and May, 2002). This study examined the likelihood of sexual intercourse in the 12 months preceding the survey, and among those adolescents with recent sexual partners, the likelihood of consistent use of condoms. The study is especially noteworthy in the context of this report—it gives careful attention to the neighborhood and other multilevel effects that figure prominently in the discussion of Chapter 2.

In KwaZulu–Natal province, some 49 percent of the boys and 46 percent of the girls reported having had intercourse in the preceding year; among those who had had intercourse, condoms were reported to have been used at the time of last intercourse by 49 percent of the boys and 46 percent of girls. Recent intercourse was much more likely among the black South African adolescents than among the whites or Indians in the sample, but for blacks no urban/rural difference could be detected, other things held constant.[34]

For adolescent girls—but not for boys—several measures of neighborhood context appeared to reduce the likelihood of recent sex. These context measures included the proportion of other neighborhood adolescents enrolled in primary or secondary school, and, among those aged 20 and above, the proportion who had graduated from secondary school. These indicators were strongly associated with lower likelihood of recent intercourse, other things being held constant. Such contextual effects are consistent with theories of social learning and peer or role model effects, as described in Chapter 2, in which local reference groups draw attention to the returns to schooling and underscore the dangers of activities, such as early sex, that might threaten school completion.[35] In the South African neighborhoods in which wage rates for adolescents were relatively high, the likelihood of recent intercourse was found to be relatively low for girls, although no effect on the likelihood of intercourse could be detected for boys.

Among those adolescents who were sexually active, measures of household poverty were associated with a lesser likelihood of condom usage (for girls), and having an adult in the household with secondary schooling sharply increased the

---

[34]The factors held constant included the adolescent's age, quality of housing, and whether the household contained an adult with 12 or more years of schooling, the last of these having a pronounced negative effect on the likelihood of girls having had recent sex, although no apparent effect for boys.

[35]Note, however, that teen mothers in South Africa have schooling options open to them that would not have been available in other developing countries (Kaufman, de Wet, and Stadler, 2000). They are permitted to return to school after giving birth, and many teen mothers evidently take advantage of this opportunity (a practice that gives rise to unusually long intervals between first and second births). The keen desire to continue schooling is due partly to its connection with brideprice: schooling is regarded as much enhancing the woman's economic potential in marriage.

likelihood of condom use for both girls and boys.[36]   The educational context measures, however, displayed inconsistent effects, and other contextual measures (neighborhood levels of involvement in community groups, sports associations, and religious groups) exhibited little interpretable influence on either intercourse or condom use. The effects of local labor market conditions were similar for boys and girls, with higher wages being associated with a greater likelihood of condom use. As Kaufman et al. (2002: 25) conclude, "if young people perceive that it is possible to work for reasonable wages, they are more likely to engage in safer sex practices."

A complementary study of teen childbearing in urban South Africa provides a glimpse of the complexities of adolescence in this environment. Kaufman, de Wet, and Stadler (2000) examined the consequences of teen pregnancy and childbearing through interviews with teen mothers and young men in their early twenties, many of whom were already fathers. (The urban interviews were conducted in Soweto, the collection of townships to the southwest of Johannesburg.) Although accounts of rape and coercion often appear in studies of adolescent pregnancy elsewhere, the participants in this South African study infrequently mentioned coercion and forced sex in discussions of why girls get pregnant; these were acknowledged as possibilities, but not represented to the interviewers as common occurrences. (It may be that in South Africa, a certain amount of coercion in sexual relationships is taken to be "normal.") In both Soweto and the study's rural sites, young women readily admitted that they had considered abortion upon discovering their pregnancies, and they tried to give the interviewers a realistic sense of the pros and cons involved in the decision to take their own pregnancies to term. As in the KwaZulu–Natal study described above, Kaufman and colleagues found no sharp urban/rural differences here.

The recent Nairobi Cross-Sectional Slums Survey, mentioned above, found that adolescents in the slums initiate sex earlier than those in the rest of Kenya (almost 1 year earlier for girls and 6 months earlier for boys). Moreover, in contrast to what was found in the South African study, one-quarter of Nairobi girls reported that coercive pressures were applied in these first encounters (Magadi and Zulu, 2002). In some cities, many young women are believed to be involved with much older men—"sugar daddies," as they are known—who supply them with money and gifts in exchange for sex. Poor adolescents are believed to be especially vulnerable to such relationships. In cities such as Nairobi and Yaoundé, sugar daddies appear to be much in evidence (Luke, 2002; Meekers and Calves, 1997). They are especially risky sex partners because sugar daddies have more nonmarital sex in general than other urban men, and more relationships with prostitutes in particular.

---

[36]The effects of poverty on teen pregnancy have been highlighted in other studies of South Africa, one example being that of Pick and Cooper (1997) for a periurban area of Cape Town, in which teenage pregnancy was found to be very common among less-educated women.

Adolescent girls present special difficulties for reproductive health programs because their need for protection comes into conflict with traditional values emphasizing that for girls, sex is to occur only within marriage. Even clinic staff and outreach workers can be uncomfortable in dealing with adolescents (Magnani, Gaffikin, Leão de Aquino, Seiber, de Conceição Chagas Almeida, and Lipovsek, 2001). For their part, adolescents may fear being recognized in clinics or scolded by clinic staff (for South Africa, see the discussion in Kaufman, de Wet, and Stadler, 2000). Several studies have shown that urban youth are unlikely to approach their parents for advice about reproductive health but willingly seek such information from their peers, which is unlikely to be reliable (Senderowitz, 1995; Center for Population Options, 1992; Dietz, 1990; Meekers, Ahmed, and Molatlhegi, 2001; Magnani, Seiber, Zielinkski Gutierrez, and Vereau, 2001; Speizer, Mullen, and Amegee, 2001).

Not surprisingly, studies of the services that succeed in attracting teens find that services need to be perceived as being conveniently located and of high quality (Magnani, Gaffikin, Leão de Aquino, Seiber, de Conceição Chagas Almeida, and Lipovsek, 2001). It is interesting that adolescents appear to be much concerned about whether their communities accept and endorse the provision of services for youth. Studies of Salvador, Brazil, and Lusaka, Zambia, revealed that community acceptance was more important to adolescents than the "youth-friendliness" of the services that were provided (Magnani, Gaffikin, Leão de Aquino, Seiber, de Conceição Chagas Almeida, and Lipovsek, 2001; Nelson, Magnani, and Bond, 2000). Effective programs also take account of the diversity of sexual experiences among youth; they strive to build on existing skills and knowledge; and they make use of a greater variety of providers, including those in the private sector (Hughes and McCauley, 1998).

The private sector may be especially important in supplying teens with protection against HIV/AIDS and other STDs. Condoms and birth control pills are readily available at many urban pharmacies, and adolescents often feel that such settings offer them greater anonymity and convenience than is the case for public-sector clinics (Meekers, Ahmed, and Molatlhegi, 2001). As will be discussed later, the quality of care available at pharmacies can be poor; they can fail to provide teens (and others) with correct and adequate information about contraceptives and STDs (Magnani, Gaffikin, Leão de Aquino, Seiber, de Conceição Chagas Almeida, and Lipovsek, 2001; Meekers, 2001). Social marketing programs (including Social Marketing for Adolescent Sexual Health [SMASH], which has run projects in Botswana, Cameroon, Guinea, and South Africa) are beginning to focus on how to make best use of the private sector in marketing contraceptives to youth.

In many countries, both adolescents and adults regard condom use as unnecessary and even insulting within steady sexual relationships (Van Rossem and Meekers, 2000; Population Services International and Population Reference Bureau, 2000). It has proven difficult for reproductive health programs to counter this view. For instance, a program among city youth in Cameroon drew upon peer education, promotions in night clubs, mass media campaigns, and other strategies and evidently succeeded in increasing the use of condoms for birth control. However, its efforts did not increase condom use for prevention of STDs (Van Rossem and Meekers, 2000; Population Services International and Population Reference Bureau, 2000).

In addition to clinics, schools and workplaces are potentially important intervention sites for adolescents. In contrast with the situation in high-income countries, where most adolescents attend secondary schools, in poor countries many adolescents remain in middle or even primary school, and many never proceed to secondary schooling. The age heterogeneity of primary and middle school students probably discourages frank talk by health educators about the specifics of reproductive health. Successful programs have been implemented outside schools, such as through employers of young people (e.g., garment factories, hotels), through advertising targeted to youth, and through private health providers. These programs are just as important as school-based efforts, especially in regions where school enrollment among adolescents is low (Senderowitz and Stevens, 2001).

A focus on school and work may miss urban girls, however. Girls are much less likely than boys to take part in school-based or community youth activities; they may be expected to work at home and, as in Egypt, may be required to refrain from public interactions. Reaching girls in such environments requires creative effort. In one example, a program in Maqattam, a community on the outskirts of Cairo, offers cash to girls who delay marriage until age 18. The monetary reward gives girls some leverage with their parents, as well as a sense of empowerment (Mensch, Bruce, and Greene, 1998).

URBAN SERVICE DELIVERY

As we noted at the beginning of this chapter, to date there has been no comprehensive appraisal of reproductive health services in urban areas. In discussing the urban poor, migrants, and adolescents, we referred to literature specific to these subgroups. Below we discuss aspects of service delivery that can affect urban populations as a whole. The panel's review of the reproductive health literature indicated several areas in which research is much needed.

Decentralization of Reproductive Health Services

In many countries, the political economy of reproductive health care is undergoing a fundamental transformation. With decentralization and health-sector reform, local authorities are becoming responsible for implementing what were once centralized, vertically organized programs of service delivery. The full implications of these developments are not yet known, but there are likely to be both positive and negative aspects. The allocation of responsibilities to local government units should increase the flexibility of service delivery and heighten sensitivities to local needs and resources. Yet the division of responsibilities also raises questions about how effort will be coordinated across governmental lines, which tiers of government will monitor equity in access to services, and how health externalities that spill over local governmental boundaries will be managed. Free-rider problems can arise in decisions about the siting of hospitals and clinics, as when one local government is reluctant to finance services for fear that they will be used by residents of a neighboring locality. Governmental responsibilities can be disputed, as in the case of periurban areas where lines of governmental authority are unclear, and small cities may be placed within large regional frameworks in which their needs are given insufficient attention.

In theory, decentralization puts management in the hands of those "closer to the ground," who are thought to better understand local conditions and needs. It allows flexible allocation and use of resources, promotes capacity building through local investment in personnel and systems, and gives communities the opportunity to participate in decision making about health. But decentralization also requires greater management capabilities and knowledge of reproductive health at all levels of government, and such systems can work effectively only if there are strong linkages and two-way communication across levels of government. The increase in the number of contending groups and interests in a decentralized system can hinder service delivery, as noted by Aitken (1999: 117):

> In the Philippines, a newly appointed provincial governor stopped the implementation of a ... health project in his province because he opposed the family planning component. In Colombia, a National Women's Health Policy was passed in 1992 under a sympathetic minister, but three years later there was still no action because no funds had been budgeted at the state level. More recently, as part of the Colombian health-sector reform, new agencies called Empresas Promotoras de Salud (EPSs) have been made responsible for the purchase of health services for individuals. Because the law did not specify which family planning services were to be covered by the new health plan, the EPSs decided that contraceptives were not preventive health measures and have been unwilling to cover them.

In addition, local participation need not imply any openness to the local poor, who can be effectively excluded unless mechanisms for monitoring their participation are put in place (Policy Project, 2000; Langer, Nigenda, and Catino, 2000; Hardee, Agarwal, Luke, Wilson, Pendzich, Farrell, and Cross, 1998).

In view of the difficulties involved, it would not be surprising to find gross inefficiencies arising in the early stages of decentralization reforms. In India and Nepal, for example, lack of experience with reproductive health at the local level appears to have led to poor planning and implementation of reproductive health programs (Hardee, Agarwal, Luke, Wilson, Pendzich, Farrell, and Cross, 1998).

In the Philippines, where a devolution of responsibilities for primary health care took place in the early 1990s, cities and municipalities began to spend more per capita on health, sometimes by reducing expenditures on other local services. Although the share of local expenditures going to family planning remained low, the increase in total expenditures appears to have had a positive influence on the use of family planning (Schwartz, Guilkey, and Racelis, 2002). In Uganda, decentralization led local governments to invest heavily in the construction of new clinics, perhaps with an eye to their local political constituencies, but they gave less emphasis to programs in family planning and maternal and child health, which could be used by nonresidents. Cross-district effects were also seen in this case. Where their neighbors were investing in public health care, some health districts responded by shifting their own spending to private health care (Akin, Hitchinson, and Strumpf, 2001). It is not obvious that decentralization will improve social welfare unless higher-level tiers of government can establish systems of transfers and incentives that constrain and, when necessary, redirect the actions of local governments.

Improving the Quality and Accessibility of Care

Is the quality of reproductive health services higher in urban than in rural areas? That is the common belief (recall Table 6-1), and it receives support from some studies, but not from all. To assess the evidence on family planning services, the Family Planning Service Expansion and Technical Support (SEATS) project conducted a comprehensive examination of family planning service delivery in the urban and rural areas of several countries in Africa (Rossi, 2000). This study found surprisingly little evidence of an urban advantage in the quality of service delivery (Pearlman, Jones, Gorosh, Vogel, and Ojermark, 1998). However, evidence in support of an urban advantage in service quality has appeared in a comparison of clinics in Lima with those in the rural areas of Peru (Mensch, Arends-Kuenning, Jain, and Garate, 1997). Direct urban/rural comparisons of the kind made in these studies are unusual, and the lack of research makes it impossible to draw strong conclusions. Clearly, however, it should not be assumed that urban services are superior in the quality of care provided.

Somewhat more research is available on the time costs borne by urban residents to reach and receive reproductive health services, which have not been fully appreciated. Time costs are increased when clinics are open for only a few hours each day, when services are located far from the workplaces and homes of clients, and when crowding produces long waits at the clinic. Because many city residents work full-time, some of them juggling two or more jobs, they can find it difficult to attend health clinics during working hours and would benefit from longer hours of operation.

According to a study of a family planning program in Jakarta, short hours at the government-sponsored clinic were a contributing factor in discouraging adoption of contraception (Lubis, 1986). In Kingston, Jamaica, facilities were found to be highly concentrated near hospitals, major roads, and suburban commercial zones, sites that are inconvenient for many residents and particularly so for the urban poor (Bailey, Wynter, Lee, Jackson, Oliver, Munroe, Lyew-Ayee, Smith, and Clyde, 1996). Similarly, in Cape Town, South Africa, access to many facilities was found to require private transportation (Hoffman, Pick, Cooper, and Myers, 1997). Rip, Keen, Woods, and Van Coeverden De Groot (1988) examined prenatal care in a periurban area of Cape Town, trying to discover why many women did not use antenatal health services until the second trimester of their pregnancies. It became clear that use of the clinic was being discouraged by its inconvenient location, and that a clinic sited in the neighborhood would be likely to encourage prenatal care. (Women were also discouraged by long waiting times.) Similar research in the *barrios* of Caracas, Venezuela, and other sites (Rakowski and Kastner, 1985; Wawer, Lassner, and Hanff, 1986) revealed the importance of service location to access. Even if the time costs of access are lower than those in rural areas, these costs can play an important role in the reproductive health of poor urban residents.

The Private Sector in Family Planning

Services funded and delivered by the public sector have been a mainstay of reproductive health in rural and urban areas alike. As we have seen, the urban poor can be as dependent on the public sector as rural residents. Even though they are generally more expensive, private services are often preferred by urban women—even by poor women—because they are more accessible and appear to be of higher quality (Bailey, Wynter, Lee, Jackson, Oliver, Munroe, Lyew-Ayee, Smith, and Clyde, 1996; Lubis, 1986). The *favelas* of Rio de Janeiro, for example, have many public health clinics and more than a few public hospitals, but most women obtain their contraceptives through private physicians and pharmacies. Women may prefer these sources for their convenience, greater privacy, and shorter waiting times and longer hours of operation, as well as the greater range of contraceptive choices available by comparison with public clinics (Wawer, Lassner, and Hanff, 1986). However, the poorest women have little choice but to rely on free or low-cost public clinics.

In some countries, the private sector consists mainly of pharmacies because nonprofit and other for-profit services are not well developed. In countries such as Bangladesh, the public sector appears to have all but abandoned cities to the private sector (Tantchou and Wilson, 2000; Ross, Stover, and Willard, 1999; Hardee, Agarwal, Luke, Wilson, Pendzich, Farrell, and Cross, 1998). Recent research in Dhaka found that 80 percent of contraceptive users pay for their family planning services (Routh, Thwin, Kane, and Baqui, 2000). A study of Faisalabad and

Larkana, Pakistan, also found that both current family planning users and those who intend to use family planning in the future are willing and able to pay for hormonal methods of contraception. This was found to be true even for the very poor, probably because the monetary cost of family planning is so low (Kress and Winfrey, 1997; Afolabi Bambgoye and Ladipo, 1992).

Many residents rely on pharmacies and commercial vendors to provide them with quick, convenient, and relatively inexpensive access to a variety of family planning methods, including condoms and even treatment for some reproductive health problems, such as STDs. In urban Nepal, it was found that social marketing of contraceptives through shops was successful because the shops were located close to workplaces and homes; they were also well stocked with supplies and appeared to offer some measure of privacy (Shrestha, Kane, and Hamal, 1990).

The quality of private care at such outlets is not necessarily better, and sometimes appears to be worse, than the care supplied by government health services (Kaye and Novell, 1994). Private services may specialize in meeting narrowly medical or surgical needs and fail to offer basic services where these are unprofitable. Among the private-sector health facilities in several African cities, only 35 percent offer family planning services (Rossi, 2000). In urban Nepal, for example, contraceptive retailers proved to be relatively well informed about some aspects of the oral pill, but in need of training about its side effects and the contraindications for use, as well what to do should a pill be missed (Shrestha, Kane, and Hamal, 1990). A study of private pharmacists in Hanoi, Vietnam, also found that many of them were treating patients for STDs without referral to a physician. The pharmacists were often providing incorrect treatment and giving either wrong or grossly inadequate advice for follow-up care, partner notification, and condom use (Chalker, Chuc, Falkenberg, Do, and Tomson, 2000).

Nongovernmental organizations (NGOs) can be quite successful in establishing private, nonprofit reproductive health programs, particularly when government programs are limited and the poor need greater access to services. In Santiago, Chile, an integrated maternal and child health program was set up by an NGO in a very poor neighborhood. This NGO clinic offered a greater number of family planning choices—all free of charge—than did the public clinic. The program appeared to have positive results with regard to contraceptive use, breastfeeding, and child health. Patients judged the quality of the program to be high, and the providers themselves believed they had learned new skills and gained acceptance in the community (Alvarado, Zepeda, Rivero, Rico, López, and Díaz, 1999). Sometimes NGO programs can fill a need that is not already being addressed by either government or private for-profit clinics.

CONCLUSIONS AND RECOMMENDATIONS

It has long been known that urban levels of fertility are lower than rural levels (this was the case even in historical Europe, as noted in Chapter 1) and, in the modern era, that urban women are more likely to use contraception. Lower fertility is an element of family reproductive strategies that emphasize investments in the human capital of children and modes of child rearing that are time-intensive. The combination of lower fertility and greater educational investments in children distinguishes urban populations from rural. On theoretical grounds, as we have noted, there is reason to think that patterns of social interaction in cities may serve to focus attention on the benefits of children's schooling. But rural families are beginning to adopt similar strategies, perhaps to prepare their children for urban or urbanized livelihoods, and fertility rates are also falling in rural areas.

In studies of historical populations, delayed marriage is accorded a large role in lower urban fertility, and it still plays a major part. Demographers and demographic surveys have tended to focus exclusively on age at marriage as the indicator of interest, but another and possibly more interesting aspect has to do with the nature of marriage search and the terms upon which marriage is entered. Urban economies in some settings can now offer young unmarried women a modest measure of economic resources and enable them to enter marriage with a greater degree of autonomy and social confidence than might previously have been possible. Studies of adolescence are beginning to focus on how attitudes toward gender equality in marriage take shape; it appears that schooling has an influence, but it is possible that girls may be more influenced than boys. The urban element in gender beliefs has not been much studied, but we suspect that the diversity of urban life and the variety of urban reference groups and role models may well affect how adolescent girls come to understand the limits and possibilities of adult life.

Our major conclusions relate to differences and similarities in reproductive behavior and outcomes across space and class, and are based on reviews of the literature and analyses of the DHS–United Nations urban database. These conclusions provide the foundation for a set of recommendations for programs and research.

Conclusions

Fertility behavior and trends

The urban/rural gap in fertility levels has remained roughly constant since the late 1970s in each of the developing regions of Africa, Asia, and Latin America. The panel's analysis of urban and rural fertility trends since the late 1970s uncovered no clear tendency for rural fertility rates to fall more rapidly than urban rates. As far as could be determined, the urban/rural gap in fertility levels has not changed much in these regions. Eventually, however, some measure of convergence is to be expected, as rural fertility rates continue to decline and urban fertility rates level off.

Reproductive health and access to services

The urban advantage in terms of reproductive health and access to family planning and health care services is smaller than anticipated. The question of whether an urban advantage exists in reproductive health might not have been thought especially interesting. Cities are obviously better endowed with health services of all kinds than rural areas and have both a larger and a more diverse private sector. This would appear to imply easier access to reproductive health services, greater effective control over the number and spacing of births, and a lower incidence of unintended pregnancy. Yet as the panel explored the issues with the data available, we found evidence of a smaller urban advantage than would have been anticipated. Urban women do have lower levels of unmet need for contraception than rural women, and in general, the levels of unmet need tend to be lower in large cities than in small. But the incidence of mistimed and unwanted births does not appear to be any lower in cities, and it appears to vary little by city size. The urban advantages for maternal health are more clearly evident. Urban women are much more likely than rural women to have a physician or nurse/midwife present at childbirth, and we found this to be the case even among the urban poor.

The urban poor are little better off than rural residents in several dimensions of reproductive health and access to services, and in some cases, they appear to be worse off. When attention is focused on poor urban residents, especially those who live in settlements of concentrated poverty, the urban advantage in terms of unmet need for contraception and mistimed and unwanted births almost disappears, and can even be reversed to become a disadvantage. In other areas of reproductive health, too, the situation of the urban poor resembles closely that of rural populations. In a comparison of a Karachi slum with rural areas of Pakistan, the maternal mortality rates suffered by the urban poor were found to be similar to those of some rural areas. Likewise, in one of the few studies in which the quality of urban reproductive services could be compared with that of rural services, little quality difference could be detected (Rossi, 2000). In summary, as we pass from broad generalizations about urban populations as a whole to a narrower focus on the urban poor, the contrasts with rural populations become much less marked.

The urban poor operate with very little of the information they need to make good decisions about reproductive health. Time costs and transport pose difficulties for the poor that should not be underestimated. Pregnancy risks are not well understood by poor women or men, nor are other reproductive morbidities. There is some evidence to suggest that social interaction within low-income communities may be beneficial, helping to circulate information about new services, and the mechanisms by which the poor come to be aware of health services deserve further study.

Smaller cities are significantly underserved in terms of reproductive health services compared with larger cities. The disadvantages of smaller cities are evident in several (if not all) of the health dimensions considered in this chapter.

Levels of unmet need are higher in these cities, and levels of contraceptive use are lower. Women in small cities are also less likely to know how to protect themselves against HIV/AIDS. As this infection spreads from the large cities to rural areas and smaller cities, both the urban poor and the residents of small cities need to be carefully considered in health policies and programs.

Recommendations

Decentralization of reproductive health The decentralization initiatives being undertaken by many national governments are introducing a new cast of policy makers and program implementors at the regional and local levels of government. The implications of decentralization for reproductive health are not well understood, and an analytic comparative review of country experience is now badly needed.

Service delivery The panel's analysis revealed four priority areas for service delivery:

- Reach the urban poor.
- Improve services in smaller cities.
- Create appropriate services for adolescents.
- Augment HIV/AIDS prevention programs.

Data collection Although national-level demographic measures are available in the DHS and other national-level surveys, the samples are not generally of a size that permits cities to be characterized reliably, to say nothing of neighborhoods within cities. As countries urbanize, however, data at finer spatial resolutions will increasingly be needed. High priority should be given to collecting demographic data that will allow comparisons among the situations of rural areas, smaller cities, poor neighborhoods in large cities, and nonpoor neighborhoods in these cities. National-level surveys will continue to play an important role in comparative analyses of urban and rural populations. We make specific recommendations for the DHS in Chapter 10 and Appendix F.

Research We have advocated multilevel perspectives on fertility and reproductive health research, with a focus on the implications of intraurban diversity, neighborhood effects, social networks, and social capital. In view of the deficiencies in reproductive health information that characterize poor urban populations, research is much needed on how the poor acquire information about reproductive health and how they are linked to health services.

7

Mortality and Morbidity:
Is City Life Good for Your Health?

What is it that is distinctive about urban health? Health is both an outcome and a determinant of economic development and in this way must be associated with urbanization. But when considering health in cities and rural villages, can one identify a distinctive urban health profile, or are the urban/rural differences less a matter of kind than of degree? In what ways are the concepts of urban diversity and social–spatial proximity reflected in health?

The concept of an epidemiological or health transition provides a starting point for discussion of these questions. This transition is expressed in a shift from a situation in which communicable diseases are the primary causes of morbidity and mortality to one in which noncommunicable diseases predominate. As will be shown, the health transition is well under way in some cities, especially in the developing countries that have relatively high levels of income per capita. As the transition proceeds, urban populations will experience relatively more chronic disease, including cancers and heart disease; mental health will also be of growing concern. In many and perhaps most cities, however, the health transition is still in its early stages, and these cities will continue to grapple with communicable diseases for the foreseeable future. In addition to such long-standing challenges to health, some cities will face grave threats from new diseases (e.g., HIV/AIDS) and diseases that are reemerging with heightened virulence or resistance (e.g., tuberculosis).

The spatial proximity of urban residents and their reliance on common public resources leave them more vulnerable to communicable health threats than are rural residents, who enjoy a measure of protection owing to their spatial dispersion. This "urban penalty" was first observed in the Victorian era when city dwellers died at higher rates than their rural counterparts despite their greater average incomes, but it has been in force throughout most of human history. It was only

259

when urban populations had begun to be protected by public health investments and when advances in the understanding of disease had progressed to the point that higher incomes could purchase effective treatments that urban populations could achieve higher levels of health on average (Preston and van de Walle, 1978; Ewbank and Preston, 1990; van Poppel and van der Heijden, 1997).

In a sense, then, the urban advantage that we now take for granted is a recent and possibly fragile development. Nothing locks this advantage into place. Deteriorating economic conditions, disinvestment by governments in urban public health infrastructure, and newly virulent communicable diseases could conceivably cause the penalties last seen in the nineteenth century to reemerge. Of course, some urban groups may never have enjoyed much of an urban advantage; the poor and the politically overlooked may have been at least as exposed to disease as their rural cousins, and perhaps more so. In this chapter, we look carefully for evidence of a reemergent urban penalty. As will be seen, the evidence is mixed and contradictory, but that in itself may present a challenge to complacency.

The uneven distribution of health is clearly apparent within cities; it can be seen, for example, in the spatial variation of crude death rates in Accra, depicted in Figure 7-1. Although age-adjusted mortality measures would be preferred, the variation in crude death rates is suggestive of stark intraurban inequities that are unlikely to be due to age composition alone. The spatial concentration of poor health has long been recognized by epidemiologists, and its economic and social aspects are increasingly being emphasized in the public health journals. One now

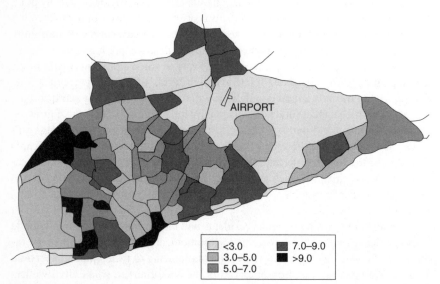

FIGURE 7-1 Crude death rates by neighborhood in Accra, 1991.
SOURCE: Stephens, Timaeus, Akerman, Avlve, Maia, Campanario, Doe, Lush, Tetteh, and Harpham (1994b).

sees much discussion of the roles of local social capital and social networks in urban health, and efforts are under way to bring empirical content to these concepts. Although few longitudinal studies of urban sites are fully functioning as of this writing (see Kahn and Tollman, 2002, for a list of new urban research sites), there is some prospect for linking sophisticated prospective social science research to the sophisticated programs of epidemiological research already under way.

The socioeconomic diversity of urban populations makes possible the development of many specialized markets and functions. Some of these can directly affect the communicability of disease; consider, for example, the markets in which sex workers participate. Rural prostitution exists, of course, but its epidemiological role in the spread of sexually transmitted diseases (STDs) and HIV/AIDS is quite different from that of urban prostitution, which probably involves denser and more highly interconnected sexual networks (Yirrell, Pickering, Palmarini, Hamilton, Rutemberwa, Biryahwaho, Whitworth, and Brown, 1998; Pickering, Okongo, Ojwiya, Yirrell, and Whitworth, 1997). At the same time, urban diversity supports the development of markets that are beneficial to health. As was seen in the previous chapter in connection with reproductive health, the role of the private sector is far more prominent in urban than in rural areas. Urban health providers in the public sector operate alongside a great variety of private-sector providers, who range from traditional healers to highly specialized surgeons. Various fee-for-service arrangements are found in this variegated private sector, and fees are seen increasingly in the public sector as well. These arrangements raise issues of ability and willingness to pay on the part of urban residents. The urban poor who are unable to pay fees may remain as dependent on subsidized public-sector services as their rural counterparts.

This chapter begins by considering the distinctive aspects of urban health in more detail. Then, guided by the concept of the health transition, it reviews the spectrum of diseases that afflict urban residents and compares this spectrum with the rural burden of disease. Much of the discussion concerns adult health; special emphasis is placed on risks—for injuries and mental ill-health—that have interesting urban features and have too readily been overlooked.

The chapter next turns to children's health, presenting results from analyses of the Demographic and Health Surveys (DHS) on children's nutrition (as measured by height for age and weight for height) and child survival. (The panel could not explore trends over time going back to the DHS predecessor surveys—the World Fertility Surveys (WFS)—but this would be a useful exercise for future research.) Although the DHS data are limited in their spatial resolution and usually do not allow neighborhood effects to be discerned, they do enable a general assessment of whether urban children suffer from a newly emergent urban penalty. To this end, results from the DHS surveys are compared with findings from spatially focused studies of urban slums and squatter settlements. The chapter then turns to a discussion of treatment-seeking behavior in urban populations and the new configurations of urban health systems. The final section presents conclusions and recommendations.

DISTINCTIVE ASPECTS OF URBAN HEALTH

To understand whether and how urban health is distinct from rural, two questions need to be addressed: (1) whether the determinants of urban health are the same as those of rural health, and if so, (2) whether the levels of these determinants differ. Among the subdisciplines of health research, one finds such questions addressed most directly in the field of urban nutrition. Ruel, Haddad, and Garrett (1999: 1887) argue that there are important, urban-specific aspects of food security and nutrition, which include the following:

> (a) the greater dependence of urban dwellers on cash income and less reliance on surrounding natural resources, which means that having a secure source of income is critical; (b) the likelihood that, even if formal safety net programs are more prevalent, informal social networks are weaker, possibly reducing the ability of the poor to deal with economic shocks; (c) the higher levels of women who participate in the formal labor force and work away from home, with potentially negative consequences for their ability to care for other household members and their children; (d) the changes in diet and exercise patterns that may increase risk of chronic disease and obesity even among low-income groups; (e) the significant obstacles that the poorest segments of the population may still face to gain access to public services, such as water, sanitation, and garbage disposal, even when these services are more available than in rural areas; (f) the increased exposure of urban-dwellers to environmental contamination, which increases risk of illness and, especially, infectious disease; and (g) the legal obstacles that urban-dwellers face in attempting to improve their livelihoods in such areas as employment, land, and water use.

Box 7.1, which draws on Harpham, Lusty, and Vaughan (1988) and Ruel and Garrett (1999), shows how the characteristics of urban life may be expressed in health outcomes and the distribution of illness. Poverty, environment, and psychosocial problems may lead to specific diseases or health conditions that are more common in urban areas, including STDs, accidents, and depression. However, some conditions, including malnutrition and malaria, are prevalent in both urban and rural areas.

THE DISEASE SPECTRUM

In Latin America, the health transition has generally appeared first in urban locations (Pan American Health Organization , PAHO; Tanner and Harpham, 1995) and has tended to proceed more rapidly in countries with higher levels of

---

BOX 7.1 Urban Problems and Their Health Implications

Poverty-Related Problems	Environmental Problems	Psychosocial Problems
Cash income and markets	Hazardous informal sector	Stress
High intake of fats and refined sugars ("junk food")	Inadequate water and sanitation	Alienation
		Instability
		Insecurity
Out-of-home female labor force participation	Within-house and community overcrowding	Smoking
Prostitution	Lack of land to grow food	Drug abuse (including alcohol)
Street children	Lack of rubbish disposal	Limited social support
	Traffic	Insecurity of tenure
	Industrial pollution	Violence
	Air, water, and food contamination	

	Implications	
Lack of breastfeeding	Accidents	Depression
Malnutrition	Parasitic disease	Anxiety
Sexually transmitted diseases, including HIV/AIDS	Malaria	Suicide
	Dengue	Cancer
	Respiratory infections	Heart disease
	Tuberculosis	Injuries
	Cancer	
	Other infectious diseases (especially diarrheal)	

---

urbanization. A link to urbanization is seen in studies of other developing regions as well. These studies document higher urban rates of cardiovascular disease, cancers, coronary heart disease, and accidents, and higher rural rates of malaria, malnutrition, maternal mortality, and respiratory disease.[1] Evidently, urban and rural health profiles do differ.

---

[1] On the rural disease pattern, see Mbizvo, Fawcus, Lindmark, and Nystrom (1993), Mock, Sellers, Abdoh, and Franklin (1993), McCombie (1995), Fawcus, Mbizvo, Lindmark, and Nystrom (1995, 1996), and Root (1997). On the urban pattern, see reviews by Beevers and Prince (1991), Muna (1993), Walker (1995), Walker and Sareli (1997), and Walker and Segal (1997), and studies by McPake et al. (1999), Steyn, Fourie, Lombard, Katzenellenbogen, Bourne, and Jooste (1996), Ceesay, Morgan, Kamanda, Willoughby, and Lisk (1996), and Delpeuch and Marie (1997). Some of these studies present data on risk factors associated with disease, rather than rates of disease as such.

The reasons why they differ are of course complex, stemming from the many environmental, socioeconomic, and cultural changes that are associated with urbanization. Lower rates of communicable disease and urban advantages in child survival can be linked to lower urban fertility, better immunization coverage, and easier access to and greater use of health services.[2] As communicable diseases begin to decline in urban areas, noncommunicable diseases (including the so-called "diseases of affluence") and diseases associated with social instability can be expected to rise in relative importance, particularly among adults (Feachem, Kjellstrom, and Murray, 1990). The growing impact of mental ill-health, violence, accidents, and chronic disease is evident in disability-adjusted life year (DALY) predictions.[3] It has been predicted that by 2030, depression, traffic accidents, and heart disease will be the leading burdens of disease in developing countries overall, replacing the 1990 leaders, which were respiratory disease, diarrhea, and perinatal conditions (World Health Organization, 1996).

Health transitions generally progress unevenly, producing more rapid change in some population groups than in others. This unevenness can be seen in comparisons of adult and child mortality. In some cities, data registers allow the main causes of death to be identified and permit comparisons of adult and child causes. A 1996 analysis by Ministerio de Salud de Perú (1996) showed the main causes of adult death in Managua, Nicaragua, to be acute respiratory infection (which accounted for 11 percent of adult deaths), hypertension (8 percent), road traffic accidents (7 percent), stroke (6 percent), and pneumonia (5 percent). Adults in Managua die from a mix of communicable and noncommunicable diseases. The children of this city, however, still die mainly of communicable diseases, which account for the five leading causes of death. Acute respiratory infections and diarrhea alone are responsible for 39 percent of infant and child deaths.[4] Other cities in Latin America have reached a more advanced stage of the health transition. In San Pedro Sula, a rapidly growing city in Honduras with about half a million residents, the Honduras Ministry of Health (1999) found the main causes of adult death in 1999 to be violence (43 percent), cardiovascular disease (19 percent), cirrhosis (15 percent), cancer (13 percent), and AIDS (8 percent). Even child deaths are dominated by noncommunicable causes (by rank, violence, cancer, cranial trauma, and anemia).

---

[2]See Bah (1993), Bahr and Wehrhahn (1993), Taylor (1993), Fawcus, Mbizvo, Lindmark, and Nystrom (1995), Brockerhoff (1994, 1995a), Brockerhoff and Brennan (1998), and Gould (1998).

[3]The DALY measure combines the years of life lost as a result of premature death with years spent in an unhealthy state. A death is premature if it occurs before age 82.5 for a woman and age 80 for a man, these being the life expectancies achieved in Japan, which is the world's current leader in longevity. To be included in the DALY measure, disabilities must be classified by severity and duration such that one DALY is equivalent to a year of fully healthy life. These concepts and measures are explained in the executive summary of The Global Burden of Disease and Injury Series, available at http://www.hsph.harvard.edu/organizations/bdu/summary.html.

[4]These figures should be interpreted cautiously; the quality of cause-of-death reporting is not known.

TABLE 7-1 Disability-Adjusted Years of Life Lost in Mexico, by Cause and Residence

Cause	Rural	Rural Rank	Urban	Urban Rank	Rural/Urban
Diarrhea	12.0	1	2.8	9	4.28
Pneumonia	9.3	2	3.9	7	2.39
Homicide and violence	9.2	3	7.4	2	1.23
Motor vehicle–related deaths	7.9	4	8.3	1	0.95
Cirrhosis	7.5	5	6.3	4	1.19
Anemia and malnutrition	6.8	6	2.4	11	2.86
Road traffic accidents	5.5	7	6.8	3	0.81
Ischemic heart disease	5.1	8	5.3	6	0.96
Diseases of the digestive system	4.7	9	1.7	15	2.74
Diabetes mellitus	4.1	10	5.7	5	0.72
Brain vascular disease	3.0	11	3.0	8	1.02
Alcoholic dependence	3.0	11	1.9	13	1.56
Accidents (falls)	2.8	13	2.6	10	1.09
Chronic lung disease	2.6	14	1.9	13	1.39
Nephritis	2.2	15	2.2	12	1.01

NOTE: 1991 estimates, expressed per 1000 population.
SOURCE: Lozano, Murray, and Frenk (1999: 130).

Not only do cities differ as to their stage in the health transition, but some countries challenge the generalization that urban areas take the lead in the transition. As Table 7-1 shows for Mexico, the 15 leading causes of DALYs lost in rural and urban areas are the same, although they appear in different rank order. Of the top five causes in urban areas, three (deaths related to motor vehicles, homicide and violence, and cirrhosis) are also in the top five in rural areas.

The implications of the health transition are far-reaching, encompassing factors as various as the range of drugs needed in urban primary health centers and the emphases required for effective health promotion programs. The discussion that follows focuses mainly on adults and addresses three types of disease—injuries, mental health, and "lifestyle" diseases—whose impact has not been sufficiently appreciated.

Injuries

Drawing on a DALYs analysis, Zwi, Forjuoh, Murugusampillay, Odero, and Watts (1996: 593) call attention to the effects of injuries on health and well-being:

> ... world-wide, intentional injuries (suicide, homicide and war) account for almost the same number of DALYs lost as either sexually transmitted diseases and human immunodeficiency virus (HIV) infection combined, or tuberculosis. Unintentional injuries cause as many

DALYs lost as diarrhea, and more than those lost from cardiovascular disease, malignant neoplasm, or vaccine-preventable childhood infections. In developing regions of the world, in 1990, injuries in males aged 15–44 years led to 55 million DALYs lost, over one-third of those lost from all causes in this sex and age group.

As this quotation makes clear, violence is one of the major causes of injuries. Much of the empirical work on violence has been carried out in Latin America and the Caribbean. This is for good reason: Latin America has the world's highest burden of homicides, which occur at a rate of 7.7 per 1,000 population, more than twice the world average of 3.5 per 1,000. Approximately 30 percent of all homicide victims in Latin America are adolescents, and young men are the most affected group (Frenk, Londoño, Knaul, and Lozano, 1998; Pan American Health Organization , PAHO, cited in Grant, 1999).

Violent crime is particularly prevalent in Latin America's large cities, and in these cities, it disproportionately affects men living in low-income neighborhoods (Barata, Ribeiro, Guedes, and Moraes, 1998; Grant, 1999). Data collected between 1991 and 1993 in São Paulo suggested that men aged 15–24 in low-income areas were more than 5 times likelier to fall victim to homicide than were men of the same age in higher-income areas (Soares et al., cited in Grant, 1999).

Gender roles and relations put men and women at risk of different types of violence. Higher rates of homicide are reported for men, but rape and domestic violence rates are higher for women. Heise, Raikes, Watts, and Zwi (1994) reviewed community-based data for eight urban areas from different regions of the developing world and found that mental and physical abuse of women by their partners was common, with damaging consequences for women's physical and psychological well-being.

Traffic accidents are another major but often overlooked cause of urban death and injury (Mock, Abantanga, Cummings, and Koepsell, 1999; Kayombo, 1995; Byarugaba and Kielkowski, 1994). Urban residents are often thought to be at greater risk of being involved in an accident than rural residents (Odero, Garner, and Zwi, 1997). This supposition enjoys some empirical support (Mock, Abantanga, Cummings, and Koepsell, 1999), but higher rural accident rates—at least for accidents causing injuries—have been recorded (Odero, 1995). Poor countries invest less in their roads than do rich countries; they have fewer laws related to traffic and enforce them unevenly; and they probably have rates of alcohol consumption that are at least as high as those of rich countries. The combination puts men, adolescents, and young adults at particularly high risk of involvement in an accident. Traffic accidents account for 30 to 86 percent of all trauma-related hospital admissions, with a mean length of stay of 20 days (Odero, Garner, and Zwi, 1997, citing 15 and 11 studies, respectively). Since the majority of trauma facilities are located in cities, accidents not only are responsible for significant mortality and morbidity among urban residents, but also place a heavy burden on urban health systems.

Little is known about the urban incidence of other types of accidents, such as accidental falls, drownings, poisonings, and injuries from fire. Some unintentional injuries are likely to be more common in urban areas because of overcrowding and related factors (Bartlett, Hart, Satterthwaite, Barra, and Missair, 1999; Mock, Abantanga, Cummings, and Koepsell, 1999; Knobel, Yang, and Ho, 1994). Urban communities are vulnerable to some forms of natural disaster, such as landslides, earthquakes, and floods. The urban poor in Rio de Janeiro, for example, are forced to live where landslides kill or leave homeless thousands every year.[5]

Mental Health

According to the World Health Organization (1996), by 2020 unipolar depression is expected to account for the greatest burden of disease in developing countries. Indeed, community-based studies of mental health in developing countries already show that 12 to 51 percent of urban adults suffer from some form of depression (see 16 studies reviewed by Blue, 1999). Although these studies employ a range of samples, definitions, and instruments, their conclusions underscore the importance of mental ill-health in the urban spectrum of disease. A diverse set of risk factors is implicated, including lack of control over resources, changing marriage patterns and increased divorce rates, cultural ideology, long-term chronic stress, exposure to stressful life events, and lack of social support (Harpham, 1994). There are differences across urban neighborhoods and even from person to person in abilities to devise successful coping strategies. Anxiety and depression are typically more prevalent among urban women than men and more prevalent in poor than in nonpoor urban neighborhoods.

Those suffering from stress may be able to call upon various forms of emotional support, as well as material support in the form of goods, services, and information. These resources can help in coping with stress and mitigating its damage (Thoits, 1995). Nonetheless, urban environments in general, and poor urban environments in particular, have a number of harsh physical and social aspects, including poor housing and services and limited prospects for good jobs and incomes (Ekblad, 1993; Fuller, Edwards, Sermsri, and Vorakitphokatorn, 1993; Satterthwaite, 1993, 1995). Day-to-day life in poor communities can subject individuals to sustained, chronic stress. As discussed in Chapter 5, poor urban residents often show great resilience and creativity in meeting such challenges. Nevertheless, they can be beaten down by the chronic stresses of poverty, jolted by other stressful life events, and wearied by the constant need to improvise new coping strategies.

---

[5] Of the 568 major natural disasters that occurred in the world between 1990 and 1998, 94 percent took place in developing countries, and 97 percent of all natural disaster–related deaths occurred in those countries as well (World Bank, 2001).

In empirical analyses, differences in social support—the degree to which basic social needs are gratified through interaction with others—have been estimated to account for 5 to 10 percent of the variance in levels of mental ill-health (of all types) in different areas (Harpham, 1994; Committee to Study Female Morbidity and Mortality in Sub-Saharan Africa, 1996; Aidoo and Harpham, 2001; Harpham and Blue, 1995). Urbanization can be associated with reductions in social support resulting from the breakdown or reorganization of family life, a potential increase in single-parent households and decrease in the support networks of extended families, reduced fertility (and thus fewer children to care for parents in old age), and the need to work outside the home (Harpham, 1994; Parry, 1995; Harpham and Blue, 1995). Although some of these aspects of stress appear to be worse in large developing-country cities than in small cities, researchers have not yet compared levels of social support and stress in large and small cities.

Another knowledge gap has to do with the interrelationships between mental illness and social support. Most of the available research is cross-sectional, leaving open the possibility that mental illness itself reduces social support and that the positive relationship between social support and mental health may be overstated. Also, the literature has yet to explore the contribution of community-level factors, such as levels of violence and social cohesion (Blue and Harpham, 1998). Regarding the latter, an ecological variable that may play a role is social capital, or the density and nature of the network of contacts and connections among individuals in a given community. Strong social capital has been linked to reduced mortality at the state level in the United States (National Research Council, 2000). In low-income urban communities, social capital has been found to weaken as households' ability to cope decreases and community trust breaks down, and to be severely eroded by various forms of violence (Moser and McIlwaine, 1999).

Chronic "Lifestyle" Diseases

As noted above, urban areas have higher risk factors for and rates of diabetes, obesity, cardiovascular disease, cancers, and coronary heart disease. These are sometimes termed chronic "lifestyle" diseases, the idea being that they are at least partly attributable to behavior. Risk factors associated with this group of diseases include smoking; alcohol consumption; increased intake of fat and reduced intake of fiber; lack of exercise; and inhalation of potentially toxic pollutants, such as carbon monoxide, sulfur dioxide, nitrogen oxides, and suspended particulate matter.

In many developing countries, substantial proportions of the population are either underweight or overweight, with the increase in the overweight percentage being a recent development. One review (Delpeuch and Marie, 1997) suggests that over 30 percent of the national population is overweight in Latin America, the Caribbean, the Middle East, and Northern Africa. (The highest prevalence of obesity is found in Pacific and Indian Ocean island populations.) In Asia and sub-Saharan Africa, the prevalence of obesity is low on average but is evidently higher in urban than in rural areas. Obesity tends to appear first among the affluent and then among low-income groups, including young children and teenagers. Its main causes include the adoption of lipid-rich diets and (more important) the reduction in physical activity that often accompanies city life. Malnutrition during fetal development and early childhood is a predisposing factor for later obesity.

Undernutrition, food insecurity, dietary excess, and obesity often coexist in urban populations. Popkin (1999: 1908) shows that more urbanized developing countries have a higher consumption of sweeteners and fats, noting that "a shift from 25 percent to 75 percent urban population in very low income countries is associated with an increase of approximately four percentage points of total energy from fat and an additional 12 percentage points of energy from sweeteners." Although this pattern is often attributed to the urban rich, Monteiro, Benicio, Conde, and Popkin (2000) show that in urban Brazil, it is the city residents with more education who are less likely to be overweight. Much the same pattern has been observed in South Africa (South African Department of Health, 1998).

In Latin America, there is an upward trend in cancer mortality, which is especially marked for cancers of the lung, gallbladder, and breast (Timaeus and Lopez, 1996). In Accra and São Paulo, circulatory disease has been found to be the second most important cause of death among those aged 15–44 and the most important cause for those aged 45–64 (Stephens, Timaeus, Akerman, Avlve, Maia, Campanario, Doe, Lush, Tetteh, and Harpham, 1994a). Community-based urban studies among the elderly likewise have documented high rates of mortality and morbidity due to chronic and lifestyle diseases (Bella, Baiyewu, Bamigboye, Adeyemi, Ikuesan, and Jegede, 1993; Allain, Wilson, Gomo, Mushangi, Senzanje, Adamchak, and Matenga, 1997). The prevalence and increase of risk factors for these diseases among urban populations, coupled with gradual population aging, imply that they will become increasingly important causes of death. Yet they remain poorly described, particularly in African and Asian cities.

Unfortunately, the DALYs data available from the Global Burden of Disease studies have not been systematically disaggregated by rural and urban place of residence. Diagnoses of chronic diseases may be better in urban than rural areas, and the studies cited above suggest that urban populations will continue to be at the forefront of health transitions. It remains uncertain just how urban disease patterns will be influenced by urban population growth, poverty, and emerging and reemerging communicable diseases.

New and Reemergent Communicable Diseases

Communicable diseases continue to be important causes of adult mortality in many urban areas. In Dar es Salaam, HIV/AIDS is the main cause of death among urban men and, along with maternal mortality, is the primary killer of urban women (Kitange, Machibya, Black, Mtasiwa, Masuki, Whiting, Unwin,

Moshiro, Klima, Lewanga, Alberti, and McLarty, 1996). This study also found that when desperately ill, city residents sometimes return to their rural homes to die: 11 and 19 percent of the adult deaths recorded in two rural study sites occurred to formerly urban residents who had become ill. Where this pattern is common, it may result in underestimates of adult mortality in urban-based community surveys.

The importance of STDs is suggested by a study of Harare, where these diseases are the most common presenting complaint among adults at primary care clinics, accounting for one-quarter of the total case load (Wellington, Ndowa, and Mbengeranwa, 1997). As discussed in Chapter 6, many factors are involved: numbers and types of sexual contacts, gender roles and relations, and poor knowledge about or access to contraceptives (Mamdani, Garner, et al., 1993; Agyei, Mukiza-Gapere, and Epema, 1994; Pick and Obermeyer, 1996; Wellington, Ndowa, and Mbengeranwa, 1997). The role of STDs in facilitating HIV transmission further underscores their importance.

Tuberculosis is among the leading causes of death to adults in developing countries, killing an estimated 3 million people in 1995 (Dolin et al., 1994; cited in Boerma, Nunn, and Whitworth, 1999). The interactions between HIV and tuberculosis and the spread of multi-drug-resistant strains of tuberculosis have increased concerns about a global resurgence of the disease. Urban crowding increases the risk of contracting tuberculosis (van Rie, Beyers, Gie, Kunneke, Zietsman, and Donald, 1999), and this fact, together with the higher prevalence of HIV in cities, implies that tuberculosis will probably become increasingly prevalent. High-density low-income urban communities may be particularly at risk. The socioenvironmental conditions of urban areas are also implicated in vector-borne diseases, such as malaria, filariasis, dengue, chagas disease, plague, and typhus (Knudsen and Slooff, 1992). Studies highlighting the potential inadequacies of health systems in preventing and treating these conditions (Molbak, Aaby, Ingholt, Hojlyng, Gottschau, Anderson, Brink, Gansted, Permin, and Vollmer, 1992; Atkinson and Cheyne, 1994; Byass, Adedeji, Mongdem, Zwandor, Brew-Graves, and Clements, 1995; Sodermann, Jakobsen, Molbak, and Aaby, 1997) also point to the role of local and national governments in the provision of environmental sanitation and health services.

The Urban Penalty

The prospect of communicable diseases proliferating in countries with weak governmental and public health capacities has raised concerns about new forms of urban penalties. The phrase "urban penalty" arose from analyses of English mortality data from the industrial revolution of the nineteenth century, which revealed that urban mortality rates (particularly from tuberculosis) were much higher than rural rates (Kearns, 1988, 1993). Similar urban disadvantages were evident elsewhere in Europe. In 1875, for example, the urban infant mortality rate was

240 per 1,000 in Prussia, as against 190 per 1,000 in rural Prussia (Vögele, 2000). To the extent that such differences were due to communicable disease, the spatial concentration of urban populations rendered them more vulnerable to infection. Special risks faced the inhabitants of port cities, who were repeatedly exposed to new or newly mutated pathogens carried by sailors, passengers, and vermin. The urban disadvantage persisted until urban public health measures, such as investments in the provision of clean water and sanitation, were introduced on a wide scale. These investments, when accompanied by increases in literacy and supporting socioeconomic change, began to drive down urban infant mortality rates in Prussia, with clear evidence of decline emerging as of 1893. By 1905, the urban infant mortality rate had reached parity with the rural rate at a level of 170 per 1,000.

The eradication of urban penalties was seen throughout much of Europe at the turn of the century. The reduction in urban mortality rates owed as much to social and political forces as to technical and scientific factors. In Great Britain, for example, constitutional arrangements and political organizations that recognized the importance of the sanitary movement are thought to have been critical (Szreter, 1997). As discussed in Chapter 2, a similar configuration of public health, political, and social dynamics proved to be influential in the United States (Preston and Haines, 1991). Likewise, in Japan an early appreciation of the public health benefits achievable through concerted public information campaigns stressing hygiene and sanitation yielded infant mortality rates rivaling those of England at the turn of the century. This was a notable achievement given average levels of income in Japan, which at the time were far below those of England. But from 1908 until after World War II, an urbanizing Japan failed to marshal the infrastructure investments needed to consolidate and sustain its early gains, and began to fall well behind England in progress against infant mortality (Johansson and Mosk, 1987).

As this brief review of the historical experience makes clear, the emergence of an urban advantage in mortality is the product of several complementary developments: sufficient public-sector resources to undertake infrastructure investments, the engaged attention of nongovernmental groups, concentrated political will, and both scientific and public health expertise. Higher levels of national and household income are also important. Higher national incomes supply governments with the means to extend public health investments and training, and lay the foundation for the development of private health care markets. Higher household incomes enable effective health care to be purchased. Household incomes are also associated with literacy and education, which can heighten attention to health, foster a sense of personal agency, and encourage beneficial social and political interaction (Montgomery, 2000).

In view of the many factors involved in reducing mortality and the natural disadvantages faced by spatially concentrated urban populations, it would not be surprising to find evidence of slippage in the urban health advantage, nor would it be surprising to see instances in which rural populations have regained their earlier advantage. Given the importance of income levels noted above, such reversals might well occur in regions that are enduring severe economic distress.

RECENT EVIDENCE ON CHILDREN'S HEALTH AND SURVIVAL

What empirical evidence is there of an emerging urban penalty for children in developing countries? For an overview, we turn first to data from the DHS on children's height and weight, and then consider child survival.

Children's Height and Weight

The DHS collects information on the height and weight of young children and provides age- and sex-standardized measures of height for age and weight for height. These measures are expressed in terms of standard deviations from the medians of international reference populations. The units are such that a value of −100 represents 1 standard deviation below the reference median. Most of the values seen in these data for the developing world are negative, reflecting the many health disadvantages that face developing-country children.

A child whose height for age falls 2 or more standard deviations below the reference median is often described as "stunted," and one who is of similarly low weight for height is said to be "wasted." Low height for age is often taken to represent the cumulative effects of long-term deprivation, whereas low weight for height is interpreted as reflecting more recent, shorter-term deprivation. Although conventional, these interpretations are understood to be a bit simplistic. In any case, cross-sectional data do not allow the long- and short-term influences on health to be easily distinguished.

The children whose height and weight are measured by the DHS range in age from newborns to 5-year-olds, depending on the survey. To reduce errors that may arise from measuring the youngest children and to maintain a degree of comparability across surveys, we have included in the present analysis only children in the age range of 3–36 months. In poor countries—that is, in most of the countries surveyed—there are often substantial age differences in the extent to which children fall short of the reference medians, and to see clearly how children's health varies in other dimensions, a method of further standardizing the data by age is needed. We do this by estimating ordinary least-squares regressions in which the dependent variable is either the child's height for age or weight for height, and the explanatory variable is the child's age. The results of these regressions are summarized in predicted values for children at 24 months of age.

Table 7-2 summarizes estimates of children's height and weight for the rural and urban sectors as a whole.[6] As can be seen, only one country in Southeast Asia

---

[6]As elsewhere in this report, the table entries are mean values of survey-specific estimates, and countries with more than one DHS survey are downweighted in proportion to the number of surveys. The "total" row of each table provides averages across all countries, but these averages are dominated

TABLE 7-2 Children's Height for Age and Weight for Height at 24 Months, Rural and Urban Areas

DHS Surveys in Region	N^a	Rural Height for Age	Urban Height for Age	Rural Weight for Height	Urban Weight for Height
North Africa[b]	2	−155.0	−94.9	10.8	32.2
Sub−Saharan Africa	24	−184.9	−135.9	−62.5	−43.3
East, Southeast Asia[c]	1	−139.0	−64.5	−78.4	−51.6
South, Central, West Asia	10	−176.8	−131.6	−52.5	−42.8
Latin America	10	−144.7	−92.4	−10.6	2.9
TOTAL	47	−172.4	−122.5	−46.6	−30.3

[a] Number of countries with DHS data on children's height and weight.
[b] Egypt and Morocco only.
[c] Thailand only.

(Thailand) gathered height and weight data, and only two did so in North Africa (Egypt and Morocco). The table documents clearly what might well have been expected: in each geographic region, children in urban areas are significantly more healthy, judging by their height for age, than children in rural areas. The height differences are on the order of half a standard deviation in the usual case (in the units shown here, this is about 50 points in the average survey; see the "total" row of the table). A country-by-country inspection of urban/rural differences shows that in all but one case (Uzbekistan), children's height for age is greater in urban than in rural areas, and this difference is statistically significant in all countries.

The urban/rural differences in weight for height are smaller, being somewhat less than 17 points in the average survey, although slightly larger differences appear in North Africa, Southeast Asia, and sub-Saharan Africa. In only six surveys (those of Comoros Islands in 1996, Mali in 1995, Kazakhstan in 1995, the Kyrgyz Republic in 1997, Turkey in 1993, and Yemen in 1991) is rural weight for height greater than urban; in all but one survey (that of Kazakhstan in 1995), the urban/rural difference is statistically significant.

Among urban children, do these measures of health vary according to city population size? Table 7-3 shows that differences in children's height by city size range from substantial (on the order of 0.9 standard deviation for surveys in Latin America) to trivial. There is a suggestion in these estimates that in some regions (notably in South, Central, and West Asia), children in the largest cities (those of over 5 million population) are disadvantaged relative to those living in intermediate-sized urban areas (with populations over 100,000 but less than 5 million). This is not a pattern common to all regions, however, as is evident in

by the estimates from sub-Saharan Africa and Latin America, the regions that have fielded the greatest number of DHS surveys. When we discuss statistical significance, we refer to standard errors that are calculated with an allowance for unmeasured effects at the level of sampling clusters.

TABLE 7-3 Height for Age and Weight for Height in Urban Areas, by City Size

DHS Surveys in Region	Population Size					City Size Statistically Significant
	Under 100,000	100,000 to 500,000	500,000 to 1 million	1 to 5 million	Over 5 million	
			Height for Age			
North Africa	−103.0	−82.2	−93.4	−102.9	−99.5	2 of 4
Sub-Saharan Africa	−141.4	−127.9	−129.4	−99.1	−125.4	18 of 33
Southeast Asia		−73.1			−57.5	0 of 1
South, Central, West Asia	−166.5	−127.4	−105.3	−104.6	−144.2	7 of 10
Latin America	−104.4	−108.2	−68.7	−89.0	−29.3	12 of 18
TOTAL	−137.2	−120.1	−103.7	−98.3	−106.2	39 of 66
			Weight for Height			
North Africa	31.4	33.2	30.2	33.7	21.6	2 of 4
Sub-Saharan Africa	−46.1	−40.9	−42.2	−21.0	−46.9	9 of 33
Southeast Asia		−43.5			−58.1	1 of 1
South, Central, West Asia	−56.5	−39.8	−63.2	−18.5	−54.9	4 of 10
Latin America	−1.1	8.0	22.1	1.0	45.8	10 of 18
TOTAL	−35.2	−27.4	−23.4	−8.9	−27.6	26 of 66

NOTE: Statistical significance is assessed at the 0.05 level for each survey that permits a hypothesis test.

the case of Latin America, where height for age is greater in the largest cities than elsewhere. Indeed, each region exhibits some irregularities in the relationship between city size and children's height. Much the same story emerges when one considers children's weight for height, as shown in the second panel of Table 7-3. The differences by city size are small and irregular, although again it appears that children in the largest cities of Latin America enjoy better health than children in smaller urban areas. Differences by city size in weight for height do not appear to be closely associated, in general, with differences in height for age.

The rightmost column of Table 7-3 presents the results of statistical significance tests applied to the survey-specific data. Shown in this column are the numbers of surveys in which the city size variables make a statistically significant contribution to explaining health in relation to the total number of surveys in which such a test could be applied. The figures shown provide a sense of the strength of the association across surveys in each region. Of 66 surveys in which the test could be applied, statistically significant differences emerged in 39 surveys for children's height but in only 26 surveys in the case of weight for height.

Poverty and children's health

Using the relative poverty measure described in previous chapters, one can assess whether children's height and weight vary significantly with poverty status in urban areas. Table 7-4 summarizes the results of a multivariate analysis in which the explanatory variables for the urban subsample include the child's age, the city population size, and the household's poverty status. The remarkable aspect of the table is the near uniformity of the results. The children of poor urban households are shorter and weigh less than the children of nonpoor urban households, but poor urban children are taller and heavier than their rural counterparts. The intraurban differences are usually statistically significant with regard to height for age (being so in 46 of 67 surveys), but are less often significant where weight for height is concerned (meeting the criterion in only 23 of 67 surveys).

When we compare the height of poor urban children with that of rural children, we find that in almost all surveys (60 of 67), the former are significantly taller for their age than the latter. In only five surveys—those for the Comoros (1996), Madagascar (1997), Bangladesh (1996), India (1992), and Guatemala (1987)—is there evidence of poor urban children being significantly shorter. Apart from the Comoros estimate, which puts poor urban children about 0.3 standard deviations further below the median than rural children, the differences in these surveys are quite small in absolute terms, being less than 0.1 standard deviation. With regard to height for age, almost all surveys suggest that poor urban children fare at least as well as rural children, and generally fare better.

Comparisons of weight for height are less definitive. In 44 of 67 surveys, urban poor children are estimated to be significantly heavier given their height than rural children, but in 16 surveys, urban poor children weigh significantly less.

TABLE 7-4 Children's Height and Weight by Residence and, for Urban Areas, Poverty Status

DHS Countries in Region	All Rural	Urban Poor	Urban Nonpoor	Statistical Significance[a]		Number of Surveys
				Urban Poor vs. Urban Nonpoor	Urban Poor vs. Rural	
		Height for Age				
North Africa	−155.00	−122.35	−86.53	3	4	4
Sub-Saharan Africa	−184.60	−153.64	−125.86	18	32	34
Southeast Asia	−139.01	−106.46	−48.18	1	1	1
South, Central, West Asia	−176.78	−157.95	−120.31	8	6	10
Latin America	−157.09	−130.28	−80.61	17	17	18
TOTAL	−173.51	−145.43	−109.37	46	60	67
		Weight for Height				
North Africa	10.83	21.47	35.48	3	3	4
Sub-Saharan Africa	−63.28	−53.12	−40.01	7	24	34
Southeast Asia	−78.43	−66.13	−48.23	1	1	1
South, Central, West Asia	−52.50	−61.99	−36.39	4	3	10
Latin America	−7.51	−1.64	10.36	8	13	18
TOTAL	−42.28	−36.35	−21.55	23	44	67

[a] The column "Urban Poor vs. Urban Nonpoor" shows the number of DHS surveys in which the urban poor variable was negative and statistically significant (at the 5 percent level) in a regression that included city size and the child's age. The column "Urban Poor vs. Rural" shows the number of surveys in which the predicted value of height or weight for urban poor children significantly exceeded the predicted value for rural children.

Differences favoring rural children emerge in surveys of the Comoros (1996), Kazakhstan (1995), the Republic of Kyrgyzstan (1997), Mali (1995), and Yemen (1991), each of these being on the order of 0.2–0.4 standard deviations. Where this measure of children's health is concerned, there is substantial variation in the health advantage of poor urban children in relation to their rural counterparts. One finds an urban advantage more often than not, but in a substantial minority of surveys, rural children fare no worse than poor urban children.

Changes over time in children's health

In a subsample of 18 countries, one can examine changes over time in children's health from one survey to the next.[7] Trends in children's height differ markedly across the regions. In North Africa (only Egypt and Morocco) and Latin America, the time trends in height are positive in both rural and urban settings, whereas in sub-Saharan Africa, either no change or a decline in children's height for age is typical.

Contrary to some hypotheses, our analysis suggests that the urban advantage in health has persisted over the period covered by the DHS surveys, at least with regard to children's height for age. The changes over time in rural areas are of roughly the same magnitude and in the same direction as the urban changes. The rural change in height for age is about 70 percent of the urban change, on average.

Summary

Our comparisons of children's height and weight between urban and rural areas show that on average, urban children are indeed advantaged. The differences in these measures of health are both statistically significant and substantively important. Examining countries with two or more DHS surveys, we could find no evidence of erosion in the urban advantage in these measures of child health. That an urban advantage is found is not especially surprising, although it would have been thought an anomaly a century ago.

The more revealing comparisons involve urban children in poor households, those in nonpoor households, and rural children. There is strong evidence that the children of the urban poor are disadvantaged relative to other urban children. The evidence is equally strong in showing that, by the measure of height for age, the urban poor enjoy better health than do rural children, at least on average. Only a handful of surveys suggests that poor urban children fare worse than rural children in height for age, but a greater number of surveys indicate that in terms of weight for height, poor urban children may be less healthy than rural children.

---

[7]The countries are Bolivia, Brazil, Cameroon, Colombia, the Dominican Republic, Egypt, Ghana, Guatemala, Kenya, Madagascar, Mali, Morocco, Niger, Peru, Senegal, Tanzania, Zambia, and Zimbabwe.

Chapter 5 documents sharp differences between urban poor and nonpoor households in access to public services (water supply, sanitation, electricity) that fall into a similar pattern, with the access of the urban poor to services being worse than that of the urban nonpoor but better than that of rural households. It is likely that poverty-related differences in children's health are due, at least in part, to such differences in access to services.[8] If poor households have worse access to sanitation and clean water, for example, children in those households may be at greater risk of exposure to communicable diseases, in particular diarrheal diseases.

Infant and Child Survival

In their interviews with mothers, DHS fieldworkers collect information on the dates of birth of all children who were born alive and ascertain the child's length of life in cases in which a child died. The panel estimated the probabilities of infant and child death using Weibull and Kaplan-Meier models of mortality risks, allowing the correlation in risk across children in the same survey cluster to influence the standard errors of the estimates. For univariate, descriptive analyses, we used the Kaplan-Meier estimator; when covariates were included, we restricted the analyses to infant mortality and used a Weibull estimator.

Some comment is in order about the way in which we handled migration and exposure to risk. In rural areas, all children born in the 5 years preceding the survey date were considered in the analysis. In urban areas, however, the question arose of how to deal with families that migrated to their current residence during the 5-year period. A child of a migrant family (1) could have been born in the family's previous location and died there, or (2) could have survived through the move and then faced the risk environment of the family's current residence, or (3) could have been born in the family's current place of residence and faced those risks from the beginning of its life. For migrant families, one clearly must differentiate these segments of a child's history so as not to confuse the risks of the current with those of the previous residence. A first difficulty is that there is very little information on the nature of the previous residence; generally, no more is known than that the residence was rural or urban. A second difficulty is that the date of the move is imprecisely defined. In the great majority of surveys, this date is known only in terms of years of duration in the current residence. For 18 countries, however, there is a monthly migration calendar in which the most recent move can be pinpointed to the month, and we used these calendars when possible.

Faced with such complications, we decided to focus only on the migrant child's exposure to risk in the current urban location. Unless a monthly migration calendar happened to be available, the children of families who moved in the year leading

---

[8]Haddad, Ruel, and Garrett (1999) used DHS data from 11 countries (5 Latin American, 4 African, and 2 Asian) to demonstrate that the ratio of stunting prevalence between poorer and wealthier quintiles was greater within urban than within rural areas, and that intraurban differences (among socioeconomic groups) were greater than the urban/rural differentials.

up to the survey could not be included in our analysis since there was no way of knowing when in that year the move took place, and thus no way of determining precisely when the child was first exposed to the risks of the current urban environment. The conservative decision appeared to be to drop the case entirely. The results of the survival regressions are summarized in predicted values for infant mortality (denoted by $_1q_0$) and, where possible, for child mortality ($_5q_0$) as well.

Chapter 4 summarizes infant and child mortality in urban and rural areas (see Table 4-6). The results given there provide evidence of a substantial urban advantage, at least on the average. Here we explore the differentials by subgroup, focusing first on differences in urban children's mortality according to city population size. Table 7-5 shows the extent to which infant and child mortality rates vary by city size. At the aggregate level, there are sizable differences in both infant and child mortality by city size. Within particular regions, however, the results are not especially robust, and they are often not statistically significant, attaining significance in only 16 of 86 surveys in the case of infant mortality.

The effects of poverty are more substantial. The estimates for infant mortality shown in Table 7-6 suggest that the urban poor often, but not invariably, face mortality risks that are significantly greater than those faced by the urban nonpoor. The point estimates (converted to predicted values) shown in this table place urban poor children at a point midway on the risk spectrum, falling between the urban nonpoor and rural children. In comparing urban poor and rural children, we find that in some 57 of 87 surveys, the mortality risks facing the urban children are significantly lower. In 25 surveys, however, the urban poor face significantly higher risks.[9]

Changes in child mortality can be examined for 34 pairs of DHS surveys.[10] On average, child mortality fell by roughly the same amount in both urban and rural areas. The average change in the estimated $_5q_0$ between surveys is -9.3 points per 1,000 in rural areas and -8.1 points per 1,000 in urban areas. (The gap between surveys averages 5.2 years.) In 20 of the 34 cases examined, mortality fell in both rural and urban areas, with the declines being about equal in size. In 6 countries—all in sub-Saharan Africa—child mortality rose between the surveys, and in these cases the increases in mortality were slightly larger for urban than for rural children. But the sub-Saharan story is complicated: in the remaining 6 cases from this region, mortality fell in both rural and urban areas, with the urban declines being slightly larger on average.

In summary, although the details of the situation need further clarification and there are a number of counterexamples to consider, especially in sub-Saharan Africa, the dominant pattern evident in the DHS data is that of decline in both urban and rural mortality, with the urban decline being greater in relative terms. Overall, this evidence does not support the hypothesis of an eroding urban

---

[9]These findings are derived from an application of the delta method to predicted values from the mortality models.

[10]See Chapter 6, footnote 18, for the list of countries.

TABLE 7-5 Infant and Child Mortality in Urban Areas, by Population Size

DHS Surveys in Region	City Population Size				
	Under 100,000	100,000 to 500,000	500,000 to 1 million	1 to 5 million	Over 5 million
	Infant Mortality $_1q_0$				
North Africa	0.057	0.039	0.052	0.038	0.047
Sub-Saharan Africa	0.081	0.076	0.079	0.064	0.064
Southeast Asia	0.045	0.041	0.035	0.039	0.031
South, Central, West Asia	0.065	0.054	0.063	0.048	0.050
Latin America	0.052	0.056	0.043	0.048	0.028
TOTAL	0.067	0.061	0.058	0.051	0.038
	Child Mortality $_5q_0$				
North Africa	0.065	0.042	0.053	0.042	0.051
Sub-Saharan Africa	0.125	0.123	0.121	0.092	0.092
Southeast Asia	0.052	0.054	0.050	0.046	0.038
South, Central, West Asia	0.072	0.064	0.067	0.060	0.057
Latin America	0.061	0.068	0.048	0.056	0.037
TOTAL	0.092	0.087	0.076	0.066	0.046

TABLE 7-6 Infant Mortality Estimates for Urban Poor, Urban Nonpoor, and Rural Populations, by Region

DHS Surveys in Region	Rural	Urban Poor	Urban Nonpoor	Urban Poverty Statistically Significant	Urban Poor Better off Than Rural	Urban Poor Worse off Than Rural
North Africa	0.081	0.060	0.043	3 of 6	6 of 6	0 of 6
Sub-Saharan Africa	0.103	0.089	0.074	9 of 41	28 of 41	10 of 41
Southeast Asia	0.059	0.053	0.027	4 of 7	4 of 7	3 of 7
South, Central, West Asia	0.074	0.069	0.049	3 of 11	5 of 11	4 of 11
Latin America	0.069	0.062	0.039	13 of 22	14 of 22	8 of 22
TOTAL	0.086	0.075	0.056	32 of 87	57 of 87	25 of 87

NOTE: Estimates from Weibull models; urban estimates adjusted for city size.

advantage. But there may well be urban subpopulations—such as the urban poor—whose advantage *is* eroding. Moreover, the DHS program has continued to field surveys in Eastern and Southern Africa, where the effects of the HIV/AIDS epidemic are being seen in infant and child mortality. As the epidemic proceeds, our conclusions about trends will need to be reassessed.

In analyzing data from a number of DHS surveys, Brockerhoff and Brennan (1998) did find evidence of erosion in the urban advantage for large cities (those of over 1 million population). Relying on retrospective reports by mothers on the survival of their children, Brockerhoff and Brennan determined that mortality rates in the large cities were not declining as rapidly as those in smaller cities (of 50,000 to 1 million population) or rural areas.[11]

In light of these contradictory findings, as well as other case studies suggesting deteriorating health conditions among slum dwellers, we cannot draw strong conclusions about trends in the urban health advantage. It may be possible to incorporate data from the late 1970s gathered in the WFS to bring the trends by city size into clearer focus. The city size categories used in the WFS resemble those employed in the DHS, but considerable effort would be required to put the two in a strictly comparable form. Although the panel lacked the resources to pursue this issue further, it should be given high priority in future research.

Epidemics and Economic Crises

As we have seen, data for sub-Saharan Africa clearly indicate deteriorating health conditions in a number of cases. As noted in Chapter 6 and earlier in this chapter, there is substantial evidence of higher HIV prevalence in large cities than in small cities and rural areas in Africa, although the epidemic is spreading outside the large cities (Boerma, Nunn, and Whitworth, 1999). The implications for child mortality are spelled out by Timaeus (1998: S25):

> The main determinant of the impact of HIV on child mortality is the scale of the epidemic on adults ... child mortality could be expected to rise substantially in urban areas; towns with seroprevalence of 30 percent or more would experience a rise of one-third (in eastern and central Africa) and three-quarters (in Southern Africa).

In these regions of Africa, where the epidemic is currently at its worst, it is difficult to imagine that an urban survival advantage can be maintained.

Hanmer and White (1999) found a substantial rise in under-5 mortality in Zambia, one of the countries hardest hit by HIV/AIDS. The rise in mortality has been greater in cities than in rural areas and has led to a narrowing of the urban/rural differential. Child-rearing practices, immunization, and the use of oral rehydration therapy have all been improving, and if other things were held equal,

---

[11]To derive estimates specific to cities from the DHS retrospective birth histories, Brockerhoff and Brennan were forced to make strong assumptions about women's migration histories, which are not generally available in the same retrospective form. It is unclear whether the results thus derived are sensitive to assumptions about migration.

mortality should have declined. The HIV/AIDS epidemic may have produced a rise in infant mortality of about 5 points per 1,000 in rural areas and 13 per 1,000 in urban areas (it accounted for a quarter of urban under-5 mortality in 1996). But precise estimates are difficult to make because, in addition to the HIV/AIDS epidemic, Zambia has experienced a marked economic decline, reduced health spending, some deterioration in the quality of health services, and an increase in child malnutrition.

Changes in health associated with macroeconomic crises have been closely studied in the case of Indonesia, which suffered a sharp economic contraction in 1997–1998. Frankenberg, Beegle, Thomas, and Suriastini (1999) were able to trace the health impacts of this crisis. (Other aspects of the Indonesian crisis are examined in Chapter 8.) Use of health services declined overall during the crisis, and the composition of use shifted from public to private and traditional practitioners. There was a significant reduction in the proportion of children receiving vitamin A, which protects against various illnesses. There was also a decline in the quality of public health services relative to private providers, but both raised their fees. Interestingly, little change took place in contraceptive use; according to Frankenberg, Thomas, and Beegle (1999a: 1), this was because "contraception is a more appealing option than the risk of having an additional child in the current economic environment." The nutritional status of adults substantially worsened, but as far as short-term health measures are concerned, children appear to have been largely shielded from the worst effects of the crisis.

Perhaps the most dramatic effects of economic crisis have been seen in the former republics of the Soviet Union, which have experienced sharp increases in adult mortality. Box 7.2 describes the effects of the crisis in Kazakhstan and the subsequent recovery in the country's major cities.

BOX 7.2 Rising and Recovering Mortality During Transition in Cities of Kazakhstan

The collapse of the socialist world generated a demographic as well as an economic crisis, the most prominent feature of which was sharply rising adult mortality. High-quality data clearly document these disruptions in Kazakhstan (Becker and Urzhumova, 2001).

From the late Soviet period through the initial postindependence crisis, life expectancy in Kazakhstan as a whole declined by 6.5 years among men and 5.6 years among women. As in most of the other former Soviet republics, rising mortality in Kazakhstan can be attributed to diseases of the circulatory system and to a pronounced increase in accidents, injuries, and traumas. As elsewhere, rising mortality was accompanied by sharply declining incidence of fertility and marriage (Urzhumova and Becker, 1999).

Life expectancy began to recover in 1996. The recovery has been strongest among women and in Almaty (the commercial capital) and Astana (the political capital), where women have regained the survival rates characteristic of the late Soviet era. Indeed, for Almaty women under 40 and above 65 years of age, 1999 mortality rates were already below those recorded in 1991. In much of the country, however, recovery has not yet been firmly established, and whether it is imminent is unclear.

A PENALTY FOR THE URBAN POOR?

Although we did not find compelling evidence of a declining urban advantage overall, there remains the possibility that a health penalty is in force for some urban subgroups. Do the spatially concentrated urban poor face such a penalty? The last major urban health review for developing countries (Bradley, Stephens, Harpham, and Cairncross, 1992) consolidated studies highlighting intraurban inequities in morbidity and mortality. Taken as a group, these studies raise the possibility that the urban poor may suffer a double burden of both communicable and noncommunicable disease. Bradley, Stephens, Harpham, and Cairncross (1992: viii) advance the view that "urban poor households sometimes have worse nutritional status than rural households, contributing to ill-health related to nutrition." The panel's review of DHS data uncovered no systematic tendency for poor urban children to fare worse than rural children, but identified a number of exceptions to the general rule. The urban poor may face a double burden not because of poverty alone, but rather due to its depth and spatial concentration. These possibilities cannot be pursued in detail with DHS data, but they can be explored through case studies of selected cities and low-income neighborhoods within these cities.

Stephens, Timaeus, Akerman, Avlve, Maia, Campanario, Doe, Lush, Tetteh, and Harpham (1994a) and Stephens (1996) analyze data on socioeconomic status, indicators of environmental quality, and mortality from Accra and São Paulo, uncovering evidence of enormous disparities in the health status of urban populations living in the most and least deprived areas of these cities.[12] This was the first empirical study to demonstrate that the most deprived neighborhoods suffer relatively high mortality rates due not only to diseases of the respiratory system and infectious and parasitic diseases, but also to diseases of the circulatory system. In São Paulo, deaths from external causes (homicides and traffic accidents) are three times higher in the most deprived area of the city. The figures for homicide are particularly striking: there is an 11-fold difference between the least and most disadvantaged subdistricts. The authors estimate that in Accra, up to two-thirds of adult deaths in the poorest three zones of the city could have been avoided had these areas faced the lower mortality risks of the most advantaged areas. Similarly, if São Paulo had had a uniform socioeconomic and environmental profile rather than a profile of substantially unequal risks, more than half of the deaths in its most disadvantaged neighborhoods might have been avoided.

As earlier writers on urban health have noted (Harpham, Lusty, and Vaughan, 1988; Harpham and Stephens, 1991), the effects of the clustering of residential poverty on health can be devastating. The negative externalities that accompany life in slum and squatter settlements can magnify the effects of individual poverty and inadequate public health services, such as a lack of clean water and sanitation. High mortality rates in urban slums have long been documented. For example,

---

[12]The most deprived areas in both of these cities account for a significant proportion of the population (44 percent in São Paulo and 67 percent in Accra).

TABLE 7-7 Intraurban Differences in Infant Mortality Rates, Bangladesh, 1991

Gender	National	Rural	Urban	Urban Slum
Total	90	93	68	134
Male	98	97	70	123
Female	91	89	65	146

NOTE: National rates are from Bangladesh Demographic Statistics, Bangladesh Bureau of Statistics, Government of Bangladesh; rural and urban rates are extrapolated from 1990 data in the *Statistical Yearbook of Bangladesh*. Urban slum rates are from the Urban Surveillance System, Urban Health Extension Project, International Centre for Diarrhoeal Disease Research, Bangladesh.
SOURCES: Harpham and Tanner (1995: 36).

infant mortality rates in the slums of Dhaka, Bangladesh, were found in 1991 to be significantly worse compared not only with the rates among other urban residents, but also with rural rates (see Table 7-7). Several recent empirical studies have highlighted urban neighborhood and contextual effects on health outcomes and mortality, indicating that the urban poor, especially those living in majority-poor communities, suffer from urban penalties based on their geographic location and its interrelationship with poverty, segregation, and other forms of deprivation.

Infant mortality rates in the municipalities that make up Greater São Paulo varied in 1992 from 18 per 1,000 (in São Caetano do Sol) to 60 per 1,000 in Biritiba-Mirim. In 1980, the best-performing municipality had a rate of 29.3, while the worst had a rate of 152 (Indústria de Embalagens Plásticas Ltda, 1994). All of these municipalities have seen substantial declines in their infant mortality rates since 1980. At that time, the average infant mortality rate for Greater São Paulo was 51.8 per 1,000, but by 1992 the rate had fallen by half, to 25.5 per 1,000. Moreover, the differences across municipalities have narrowed. Even so, if the subdistricts of São Paulo municipality are classified into four categories according to social, economic, and environmental criteria, the mortality rates from infectious diseases for children under age 4 living in the worst of the four categories were more than four times higher than those for children living in the best of the four categories; there was also a nearly fourfold difference in deaths from respiratory diseases (Stephens, Timaeus, Akerman, Avlve, Maia, Campanario, Doe, Lush, Tetteh, and Harpham, 1994b). Similarly, in Buenos Aires in 1990, infant mortality rates within local government areas (municipalities and the central federal district) varied from a low of 15 in the federal district to a high of 30 in San Fernando and Tigre (Arrossi, 1996).

Findings of a recent study in Rio de Janeiro indicate that intraurban variations in the postneonatal mortality rate are associated with the geographic pattern of poverty—that is, neighborhood poverty clustering—even after adjusting for the neighborhood poverty rate. These poverty clusters are associated not only with economic poverty, but also with poor access to services, a poor environment, and deprivation and segregation, which affect health and mortality through cultural and social factors (Szwarcwald, de Andrade, and Bastos, 2002).

Finally, results of a recent comprehensive survey of the slums of Nairobi reveal that slum residents who lack basic services, adequate housing, and health services and who live amid others similarly disadvantaged, are worse off in almost every health dimension than those who reside elsewhere in Nairobi, rural Kenyans, and Kenyans overall (African Population and Health Research Center, 2002). In terms of infant and child morbidity and mortality, children living in the slums have lower survival odds, significantly lower immunization levels (with the exception of tetanus), and a higher incidence of infectious disease. During the 1990s, infant mortality rates declined in urban Kenya and in Nairobi overall, increased in rural areas, but appear to have increased even more sharply in the Nairobi slums. Figure 7-2 compares the infant mortality rate (0–1 year) and the under-5 mortality rate for rural Kenya, urban Kenya, Nairobi, and the Nairobi slums. The mortality rates are highest in the slums, where they are more than twice the rate for Nairobi as a whole (African Population and Health Research Center, 2002).

The extent of poverty can be gauged by the risk factors that are present for different diseases. Table 7-8 lists some of the risk factors for child diarrhea in Accra. Among Accra households facing fewer than three of these risk factors, only 2 percent reported diarrhea; among those facing three or four risk factors,

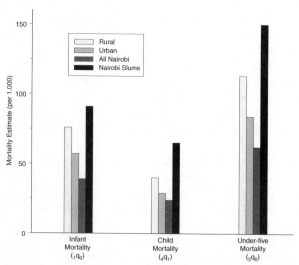

FIGURE 7-2 Levels of infant and child mortality in Nairobi slums as compared with other parts of Kenya.

SOURCE: African Population and Health Research Center (2002).

TABLE 7-8 Approximate Relative Risk of Diarrhea Among Children Under Age 6 in Accra

Factor	Odds Ratio	95% Confidence Interval
Use pot for storing water	4.3	1.7–11.1
Water interruptions are common	3.1	1.4–6.6
Share toilet with more than 5 households	2.7	1.2–5.8
Purchase vendor-prepared food	2.6	1.1–6.2
Open water storage container	2.2	1.1–4.3
Outdoor defecation in locality	2.1	1.1–3.9
Many flies in food area	2.1	1.1–3.8
Do not always wash hands before preparing food	2.0	1.1–3.8

NOTE: Number of observations is 500.

SOURCES: McGranahan, Songsore, and Kjellén (1999), Songsore and Mc-Granahan (1998).

the percentage rose to 14; and among those facing more than four risk factors, the percentage rose to 39. The deeper it is in poverty, the more risk factors an Accra household is likely to face. Children's health (in terms of diarrhea and acute respiratory infections) is associated with environmental correlates of poverty.

With regard to migrant health, Brockerhoff (1994, 1995a) analyzed DHS data from 15 and 17 countries, respectively, to explore inter- and intraurban health differentials. Regional variations in patterns of mortality, health, and social indicators rendered generalization difficult. Nevertheless, socioeconomic status, short birth intervals, young maternal age, parental education, and (after controlling for these variables) in-migration of mothers from rural areas were found to be powerful predictors of infant survival in cities with populations of over 1 million. (Recall that most recent migrants to urban areas come not from rural areas but from other towns and cities; see Chapter 4.) The factors that might explain excess mortality among the children of migrants could not be assessed with the available data, but may include the threat of new infectious disease agents, temporary residence on arrival in particularly poor housing environments, changes in care-giving practices, termination of breastfeeding, a decrease in income, and incomplete immunization due to a lack of familiarity with services.

In summary, the research on intraurban inequalities highlights the diverse experience of different countries and communities, but in general provides evidence that the double burden of disease is not equally shared by all groups within cities. Rather, the urban poor die disproportionately of both infectious and chronic, degenerative diseases.

Finally, it is understandable that much research on urban health is focused on absolute poverty rather than on measures of relative poverty. There are enormous intraurban differences in housing, income, sanitation, drainage, piped water, environment risk, and access to services, whether expressed in absolute or relative terms (Mitlin, Satterthwaite, and Stephens, 1996; Mutatkar, 1995; Wang'ombe, 1995; Atkinson, Songsore, and Werna, 1996; Todd, 1996; Harpham, 1997). How might an emphasis on the relative aspects of poverty bring a fresh perspective to the issues?

Because city residents are spatially proximate, the poor constantly confront visible reminders of their relative deprivation. Social comparisons are all but forced upon them. At times, presumably, the higher living standards enjoyed by other urban groups may exemplify the rewards to upward mobility. But for the discouraged and frustrated poor who have lost confidence in their prospects, these visible symbols of inequity are no doubt highly stressful. The very diversity of urban life may then increase anxiety and even threaten psychosocial well-being. Box 7.3 describes the work of Wilkinson (1996), who identifies the implications of urban inequalities for health and social cohesion.

BOX 7.3 Wilkinson on Inequality

In Wilkinson's view, social comparisons—knowledge of "how the other half lives"—can have a powerful effect on individual psychosocial well-being. With economic growth and the beginnings of the epidemiological transition, some groups secure access to higher living standards, while others continue to face severe deprivation. As inequities become more visible, the relative aspects of poverty affect subjective experience, and the consequent tensions and anxieties can have further damaging effects on health. The impact of relative poverty is powerfully described (Wilkinson, 1996: 215, cited in Blue, 1999:21):

> From the point of view of the experience of people involved, if health is being damaged as a result of psychosocial processes, this matters much more than it would if the damage resulted from the immediate physical effects of damp housing and poor quality diets.... To feel depressed, cheated, bitter, desperate, vulnerable, frightened, angry, worried about debts or job and housing insecurity; to feel devalued, useless, helpless, uncared for, hopeless, isolated, anxious and a failure: these feelings can dominate people's whole experience of life, coloring their experience of everything else. It is the chronic stress arising from feelings like these which does the damage. It is the social feelings which matter, not exposure to a supposedly toxic material environment. The material environment is merely the indelible mark and constant reminder of the oppressive fact of one's failure, of the atrophy of any sense of having a place in a community, and of one's social exclusion and devaluation as a human being.

As Wilkinson sees it, relative inequalities in income can lead to a breakdown in social cohesion, creating chronic psychosocial stress that adversely affects physical and mental health. The deterioration of community life and subsequent rise in violence and crime have a detrimental impact on all members of society, not only the poor. It is the proximity of the urban poor to what are frequently some of the richest people in the world that has been linked to urban tensions and social unrest (Massey, 1996).

The terms in which poverty is described have political implications. As Mitlin, Satterthwaite, and Stephens (1996) note, when poverty is described in absolute rather than relative terms, this can suggest that the responsibility for alleviating poverty rests with poor individuals and households themselves. Somehow the societal mechanisms that bring about and maintain deprivation tend to be over-looked. A focus on relative poverty and inequality, by contrast, may force a recognition of inequities and thereby encourage governments and the poor to grapple with the institutional and societal factors that perpetuate poverty.

HEALTH SERVICE PROVISION AND TREATMENT SEEKING

A defining feature of urban health systems is the diversity of providers who offer a multiplicity of services. These providers include government services run by district councils, municipal councils, or state or central ministries; private (for-profit) hospitals, laboratories, and practitioners (offering modern or traditional services); and a variety of nongovernmental providers, including missions and charities (Lorenz and Garner, 1995). Medications are also available in shops, pharmacies, markets, and various clandestine outlets. This diversity of providers in urban settings is an expression of the demand for private (for-profit) services; the very different ideas, needs, and purchasing power of diverse urban popula-tions; the availability of social or private health insurance coverage for some formal-sector employees; and a continuing urban bias in the provision of gov-ernment health services (Hanson and Berman, 1998). Official statistics often fail to convey this diversity; as Hanson and Berman (1998) note, there are almost no data on pharmacies, nurses, traditional healers, and kiosks.

The conceptual distinctions we have mentioned between the public and private sectors, for-profit and not-for-profit providers, the formal and informal sectors, and modern and traditional providers can be difficult to detect (see Giusti, Criel, and Bethune, 1997; Londoño and Frenk, 1997; Ferrinho, van Lerberghe, and Gomes, 1999). The urban health sector presents many arrangements that defy easy categorization—dual public and private practices by government-employed physicians, the introduction of private wards in public hospitals, the self-referral of patients between healers and Western doctors and between public and private facilities, and the introduction of user fees into government services. The urban system is less a system than a patchwork: there is often little formal interaction or cooperation among the different types of providers (Ogunbekun, Ogunbekun, and Orobaton, 1999).

Urban Treatment Seeking

The pluralism of urban health care provision is both an outcome and a determinant of treatment-seeking patterns. In urban as in rural areas, household responses to illness are highly complex, influenced by perceptions of illness severity, views of causation and appropriate therapy, and access to sources of treatment. Recognition of symptoms, their definition in terms of recognized illnesses, and decisions about treatment are all influenced by a plethora of macro-, meso-, and micro-level factors (Igun, 1979; Kleinman, 1980; Phillips, 1990; Berman, Kendall, and Bhattacharya, 1994; Andersen, 1995). Responses can therefore vary for different illnesses or syndromes, and in many cases more than one therapy source is contacted over the course of an illness. Against this general background of diversity, empirical studies have identified a number of key features of urban treatment-seeking patterns.

Self-medication

When they fall ill, many urban residents turn to the drugs available in private for-profit shops and pharmacies (see also Chapter 6). For example, community studies show that at least 40 percent of those seeking treatment for fever purchase drugs from these sources, and for most this is their first response to illness (Glik, Ward, Gordon, and Haba, 1989; Carme, Koulengana, Nzambe, and Bodan, 1992; Mwenesi, 1993; Kilian, 1995; Chiguzo, 1999; Molyneux, Mung'Ala-Odera, Harpham, and Snow, 1999). From the viewpoint of many urban residents, such self-treatment is a sensible first step because formal clinics and hospitals are less convenient and more expensive in time and money terms. Small shops can offer drugs on credit or sell them in small, affordable doses (Molyneux, Mung'Ala-Odera, Harpham, and Snow, 1999).

Traditional healers

Herbalists, diviners, midwives, fertility specialists, and spiritualists are an important source of health care in Africa and in much of Asia and Latin America. These traditional healers are thought to be the main source of health care for up to 80 percent of rural residents in developing countries, and Good (1987) argues that they are retaining and even expanding their influence in many cities. Healers have their specialties: empirical studies suggest that urban healers are more likely to be consulted for convulsions, nonspecific pains, and psychological problems than for other illnesses and symptoms (Winston and Patel, 1995; Carpentier, Prazuck, Vincent-Ballereau, Ouedraogo, and Lafaix, 1995). Many urban residents are eclectic, using healers even while they are attending modern health facilities, and healers often assume an important role when modern services fail to effect a cure or are perceived to fail (Molyneux, Mung'Ala-Odera, Harpham, and Snow, 1999).

Private providers

Private facilities are an important urban treatment source for STDs, malaria, tuberculosis, and diarrhea (Brugha, Chandramohan, and Zwi, 1999; Brugha and Zwi,

1999; Hotchkiss and Gordillo, 1999; Molyneux, Mung'Ala-Odera, Harpham, and Snow, 1999; Ngalande-Banda and Walt, 1995). The relatively high costs of private for-profit services might appear to put them out of the reach of the poor, but a growing body of research shows that many low-income urban residents are heavily dependent on such services (Ogunbekun, Ogunbekun, and Orobaton, 1999; Ngalande-Banda and Walt, 1995; Yesudian, 1994; Molyneux, Mung'Ala-Odera, Harpham, and Snow, 1999; Thaver, Harpham, McPake, and Garner, 1998; Develay, Sauerborn, and Diesfeld, 1996; Hotchkiss, 1998; Hanson and Berman, 1998). The preference for private services despite their higher costs as compared with public services is attributable to the availability of staff and drugs, easier physical access, shorter waiting times, extended or more flexible working hours, better interpersonal communication between staff and patients, and the promise of greater confidentiality.

Nevertheless, government health services remain an important source of health care. Wyss, Whiting, Kilima, McLarty, Mtasiwa, Tanner, and Lorenz (1996), for example, interviewed residents of Dar es Salaam about their use of services in the previous 2 weeks. They found that although poor and rich alike use private facilities, the poor rely more often on government health services. In some settings, richer households are as likely as poorer households to depend on public facilities (Hotchkiss, 1998; Makinen, Waters, Rauch, Almagambetova, Bitran, Gilson, McIntyre, Pannarunothai, Prieto, Ubilla, and Ram, 2000).

Selected Issues in Health Service Provision and Use

Aspects of urban health service use that have attracted research attention include the (mal)functioning of the referral system, the impact of user fees on rates and patterns of use, quality of care as a key influence on treatment seeking, and urban/rural linkages. These are addressed in turn below.

The referral system

In many cities, those seeking treatment often bypass clinics and other facilities at the lower tiers of the public health system and present themselves directly to the outpatient clinics of city hospitals (World Health Organization, 1993; Holdsworth, Garner, and Harpham, 1993; Sanders, Kravitz, Lewin, and McKee, 1998; Akin and Hutchinson, 1999). This behavior may be sensible from the viewpoint of those seeking treatment, given their perceptions of the low quality of services available at the lower tiers. From the perspective of the health system overall, however, such behavior contributes to overcrowding and to poor quality of care in hospitals, which arguably should be specializing in the severe health problems that require more sophisticated treatments.

Basic primary care and first-contact services have been introduced in many cities, although they often cannot keep pace with urban growth. Secondary and tertiary services (offering major inpatient and specialist care) are also generally located only in cities. The principal weakness identified in urban health systems is at the second tier of services, these being the units that should manage referrals, supervise primary care and first-contact services, and provide basic care for patients with obstetric difficulties and trauma (Lorenz and Garner, 1995). A World Health Organization strategy to strengthen this tier is to promote the development of urban intermediate-level health services or "reference centers," either by upgrading health centers or by giving referral hospitals authorization to provide different levels of care in the same institution (Sanders, Kravitz, Lewin, and McKee, 1998).

As shown by a study of patient flow in a national referral hospital in Lesotho (Holdsworth, Garner, and Harpham, 1993), however, clinicians may not be quite as overburdened by patients as they appear to be. Patient load as such may be less of a factor than poor management of the patient flow resulting in the overcrowding and long delays experienced in outpatient waiting rooms. Nor is it clear that establishing reference centers would necessarily ease such crowding. In Zambia, Atkinson, Ngwengwe, Macwan'gi, Ngulube, Harpham, and O'Connell (1999) found that accessible, inexpensive reference centers could well attract even more patients to the public health system, including many who would otherwise have used self-medication.

User fees

Proponents of health-sector reforms have often given top priority to financing, proposing that user fees be introduced or raised and urging consideration of prepayment and insurance schemes. The impact of such policies on the poor has been a subject of intense debate, with empirical studies yielding conflicting findings (see, for example, McPake, 1993; Gilson and Mills, 1995; Gilson, Russell, and Buse, 1995; Gilson, 1997; Stierle, Kaddar, Tchicaya, and Schmidt-Ehry, 1999). In some urban areas, the poor spend a higher proportion of total household funds on health than do the nonpoor. In 1992, for example, the poorest tenth of Mexican urban families spent 5.2 percent of their income on health care, as compared with 2.8 percent for the richest tenth of families (Londoño and Frenk, 1997). Although many studies have found that user fees reduce utilization of care, particularly for low-income households, some studies suggest that fees have little effect on demand and can even increase demand if higher fees are thought to be linked to better-quality care.[13] Quality of care and the perception of services may be as

---

[13]Even where utilization has not decreased, it is important to distinguish between willingness to pay and ability to pay. Where willingness to pay among low-income groups exceeds ability to pay, the strategies adopted by the poor to pay for health services (such as claims on kin, loans, sales of assets, and shifting of resources from other critical needs) can have broader consequences for livelihoods and health (Russell, 1996).

important as price and income in the use of health services (McPake, 1993; Russell, 1996; Okello, Lubanga, Guwatudde, and Sebina-Zziwa, 1998).

The introduction of user fees can price some low-income groups out of the market unless more effective exemption or third-party payment mechanisms are devised (Stierle, Kaddar, Tchicaya, and Schmidt-Ehry, 1999). It is not yet clear, however, how such mechanisms can be developed. Some researchers stress the need for better ways to identify the poor families that need exemptions; others stress the need to better monitor exemptions so as to prevent use of the subsidies by groups who can afford care; and still others stress the need to focus on the fundamental causes of poverty and inequity.

Quality of care

Sanders, Kravitz, Lewin, and McKee (1998: 366) conclude that "the inappropriate utilization of referral facilities will remain a problem until quality accessible (and affordable) primary and secondary level care is available." Quality of care is now mentioned frequently, and, as just noted, its importance is underscored by studies exploring how user fees affect utilization. The aspects of quality found to be associated with use include drug availability, prescribing and dispensing practices, the physical condition of health facilities, service availability, number of personnel, crowding and length of waiting time, attitudes displayed by health workers toward clients, and the degree of confidentiality (Hotchkiss, 1998; Brugha and Zwi, 1999; Bassett, Bijlmakers, and Sanders, 1997).

A study of rural and urban Zimbabwe highlights the interactions between nurses and women from the community (Bassett, Bijlmakers, and Sanders, 1997: 185):

> All groups were agreed in much of their assessment of the state of health services. Clinic fees, drug shortages and long waiting times were all identified as sources of dissatisfaction and declining quality of care.... To community women, the expectation of abrupt or rude treatment was the main complaint about the health services. Community complaints were voiced most strongly in the urban areas, where accusations of patient neglect and even abuse suggested a heightened hostility between the clinic and community in the urban setting. Several explanations for nurse behavior were put forward, chief among them was elitism.... it is in urban areas that class differentiation is most advanced. [The perspective of nurses differed. For them] overwork and low pay promote the adoption of the attitude of an industrial worker—to do what is required and no more. Most nurses work more than one job, not to get rich but to survive. As elsewhere, efforts to professionalize nursing have benefited only a few.

As noted above, the main reason for use of private facilities, despite what are often high costs relative to government services, has to do with quality of care. Private practitioners appear to be more responsive to patient needs, both in inter-personal relations and in the establishment of opening and closing times that suit community needs (Bennett, 1992; Thaver, Harpham, McPake, and Garner, 1998). Nevertheless, the relatively few studies that have explored the quality of care in private facilities from the technical point of view (Nichter, 1996; Brugha and Zwi, 1999) have produced disturbing findings, such as inappropriate prescription of antibiotics as a prophylaxis for STDs.

Urban/rural linkages

At a time when thinking on urban health is broadening to include social aspects of the environment and recognizing the multiple factors that operate at different levels, attention must also be paid to the sociodemographic linkages between rural and urban areas. The importance of urban/rural links in health is most frequently illustrated in the transmission patterns of HIV (and other infectious diseases). As noted in Chapter 6, a number of studies in sub-Saharan Africa have reported large differences in HIV prevalence among urban areas, roadside settlements, and ru-ral areas (Boerma, Nunn, and Whitworth, 1999), with prevalence generally being higher in urban areas. In Africa, however, many urban/rural links spread HIV to rural areas. The spread of disease from rural to urban populations can also result when migrants lack immunity to an endemic urban disease and spread it upon their return to rural areas or when urban residents lack immunity to diseases prevalent in rural areas.

In some contexts, then, the interaction between urban and rural populations contributes to a sharing of disease patterns and risk factors. Poor urban and ru-ral populations may also exhibit similar responses to ill-health. One study on the Kenyan coast demonstrated similar treatment-seeking patterns on the part of low-income urban and rural mothers in response to childhood fevers and convul-sions (Molyneux, Mung'Ala-Odera, Harpham, and Snow, 1999). The similarity in responses was unexpected given the significant differences between the two groups in socioeconomic status and distance to health services. It may be that urban and rural households exchange information and ideas about illnesses and appropriate therapies through migration and mobility, as well as through com-munication among spatially dispersed family members. Molyneux et al. (1999) found urban/rural ties to be strong:

- One of every three lifelong rural-resident mothers had a husband who lived elsewhere, most of them (80 percent) in urban areas.

- One of three urban-resident mothers had spent at least 10 percent of her nights elsewhere during the previous year (or since migration into the current household of residence), mainly in rural areas.

- Some 10 percent of lifelong rural-resident mothers had spent at least one-fifth of their nights during the previous year with urban residents (either in visiting cities or in hosting city visitors in their households), and 14 percent of urban residents had spent at least one-fifth of their nights with rural residents.

- Over 60 percent of urban-resident mothers reported regularly assisting one or more persons living elsewhere, and most of those who were assisted (90 percent) resided in rural areas.

- Fully 74 percent of urban-resident mothers stated that they wished to "retire" in a rural area.

The importance of moving beyond the urban/rural divide in urban health thinking is also highlighted by studies exploring referral systems within districts and countries (see, for example Akin and Hutchinson, 1999; Okello, Lubanga, Guwatudde, and Sebina-Zziwa, 1998) and by studies documenting the return migration to rural areas of ill urban family members (Kitange, Machibya, Black, Mtasiwa, Masuki, Whiting, Unwin, Moshiro, Klima, Lewanga, Alberti, and McLarty, 1996).

CONCLUSIONS AND RECOMMENDATIONS

This chapter has reviewed the extant knowledge about urban health, including health services. It has explored urban/rural, interurban, and intraurban differences in health and examined access to and quality of health care services, emerging health threats, and treatment-seeking behaviors. The major findings presented relate to urban and rural differences in health and health services; the relatively disadvantaged health status of the urban poor; and the shift from communicable diseases to chronic diseases, injuries, and mental health problems in low-income cities. These findings, based on a comprehensive literature review and analysis of the DHS–United Nations urban database, serve as the basis for the conclusions and recommendations presented below.

Conclusions

Child survival and child health

Infant and child mortality rates are higher on average in rural than in urban areas. Rural infant and child mortality is higher on average for a variety of reasons, including better urban public infrastructure, higher levels of maternal education, and better access to health care. Infant and child mortality risks also differ by region, with mortality being predictably and significantly higher in sub-Saharan

Africa than in other regions. However, rural areas still have relatively high mortality rates in all regions. Within the urban hierarchy, mortality varies little by city size.

There is no clear evidence of systematic erosion over time in the urban advantage in infant and child survival, except in some areas of sub-Saharan Africa. However, urban poor children face mortality risks that are significantly greater than those faced by the urban nonpoor. On average, infant and child mortality has declined over time by about the same amount in both urban and rural areas in most countries for which data are available. In six sub-Saharan African countries, however, mortality has increased in both urban and rural areas, slightly more so in the former. In the other half of the African cases examined, however, infant and child mortality has declined somewhat, with slightly larger declines evident in urban areas. The rapid urban spread of HIV/AIDS in some African countries may help explain their urban mortality increases, although it is difficult to disentangle the effects of the epidemic from other contributing factors. Although urban poor children have lower mortality risks than rural children in a majority of countries examined by the panel, rural children exhibit lower mortality risks in 25 of 87 surveys reviewed.

If health is assessed in terms of height for age, children in urban areas are significantly healthier than those in rural areas. Considering variation by city size, the panel found children living in the largest cities to be better off than those in the smallest cities in Latin America, but other regions showed no clear pattern. In terms of height for age, urban children are on average 0.5 standard deviation taller than rural children. Although urban and rural differences in weight for height are smaller than those in height for age, they display the same general pattern. In North Africa, Southeast Asia, and sub-Saharan Africa, urban children are significantly heavier for their height than rural children, although the reverse is true in six countries. City size differences in weight for height show no interpretable pattern except in Latin America, where children in the largest (5 million plus) cities are better off than those in the smaller cities.

With health measured by children's height and weight, we find no clear evidence of systematic erosion in the urban health advantage for children during the past two decades. However, poor urban children are much less healthy than nonpoor urban children, and they are sometimes not as healthy as their rural counterparts. Although there are few countries for which changes over time can be examined, it appears that the urban health advantage for children has not changed during the past two decades. In North Africa and Latin America, children's height for age has increased in both urban and rural areas over time. In both urban and rural areas of sub-Saharan Africa, however, there has been either no change or a decline in children's height over time, perhaps because of severe famine, war and civil conflict, and economic crisis.

Urban children overall may be healthier on average than rural children, but some urban children—those in poor families—are worse off in some countries. In nearly all countries, poor urban children are shorter and weigh less than nonpoor urban children. And although urban poor children are usually taller for their age than rural children in most countries examined by the panel, they are shorter in a few countries. Considering weight for height, poor urban children are generally heavier than rural children, but in 16 countries the reverse obtains.

The urban health penalty

In summary, there is no clear and compelling evidence of an emerging urban health penalty that puts urban children at greater risk than rural children. However, the urban poor are generally worse off than the urban nonpoor and in several cases may fare worse than rural children. The panel's review of the literature and analysis of the data yielded a somewhat conflicting picture of urban health. Micro studies of selected urban neighborhoods often suggest an erosion of the urban advantage in health, yet the DHS data show little evidence of this erosion. Of course, DHS surveys do not allow the effects of spatially concentrated poverty to be examined in any depth, and it may well be the spatially concentrated disadvantage that produces the urban penalties seen in the micro studies. This is a high-priority area for future research.

The disease spectrum

Urban populations face growing health threats in terms of injuries, mental health problems, and chronic lifestyle diseases. Although environmental risks and communicable diseases continue to be important, urban populations are increasingly at risk of injuries due to violence and accidents, mental health problems, and chronic diseases (e.g., heart disease, diabetes). This transformation, commonly known as the epidemiological or health transition, means that communicable diseases such as malaria and cholera become less of a threat in urban areas as these areas continue to grow. Some communicable diseases, however, including HIV/AIDS and tuberculosis, are still important factors in cities.

Recommendations

Although health policy makers clearly must not abandon rural areas, those working within urban areas should focus on reaching the urban poor. The panel's analysis clearly indicates priority areas for policy analysis and action in urban health, and strongly suggests the need for more comparative inter- and intraurban data and research on health and health service delivery. The following recommendations generally dovetail with those given in Chapter 5 regarding social and economic differentiation and access to public services, and with those in Chapter 6 regarding reproductive health service delivery, fertility, and reproductive health research. It may be that integrating services and synthesizing research in all of these areas would help identify problems and solutions in the three interrelated domains. Policy, data, and research needs are addressed below.

Service delivery The deficient health status of poor urban children in comparison with their nonpoor urban counterparts and sometimes in comparison with rural children leaves no doubt as to the importance of a focus on urban poverty in nutrition and health programs. Urban policy makers in Africa in particular should focus on improving environmental conditions and access to health services, as well as curbing the spread of AIDS, to reduce infant and child mortality among the urban poor. Dealing with emerging health problems will require a shift in health services, including different drugs and medical equipment and training, as well as different types of health promotion campaigns. The panel has identified four substantive areas of focus for policy makers. The following recommendations are made in the hope that they will be clarified and augmented by future research:

- Governments should consider both inter- and intraurban differences when designing health services and public health infrastructure in cities.

- Both governments and international agencies should place high priority on the urban poor in increasing access to health services and improving public health infrastructure.

- Closer attention should be paid to health conditions in smaller cities, especially in sub-Saharan Africa.

- The urban health sector should adapt its programs and communication strategies to address emerging health threats such as injuries, mental health issues, and chronic disease.

Data collection Apart from a few small-scale individual city and neighborhood studies, inter- and intraurban data on mortality and health are generally unavailable. Data on mortality, morbidity, health service delivery, and public health infrastructure should be collected for cities of different sizes and for various socioeconomic groups and neighborhoods within cities. National surveys will remain very important—the panel's specific recommendations for the DHS are provided in Appendix F—but we encourage the collection of data in small-scale studies that could complement and enrich the findings from such national surveys. Studies that permit comparisons among the urban poor and rural populations are of particular interest. In addition, much could be learned about mortality through the judicious use of data from national censuses, especially when a census contains information on the areas of origin of recent migrants.

Research A lack of data has led to gaps in research in the areas of urban mortality, health, and health services and infrastructure. There is an urgent need for comparative research on inter- and intraurban differentials in he[...] treatment seeking, the quality of urban health services, and percept[...] quality. Although the urban advantage would appear to have persisted [...] time, research on urban penalties is urgently needed in sub-Saharan Afric[...] where there are credible accounts of stagnation and even declines in child health in some countries. We were unable to fully explore health and mortality trends over time using data from the WFS in addition to those from the DHS, but this could be a fruitful avenue for future research.

8

onomy Transformed

Much of development economics is concerned with fostering economic growth, alleviating poverty, and improving the general standard of living of people in low- and middle-income countries. Employment and earnings from labor are central concerns because for most households, labor earnings represent the largest portion of total income, and poverty is often the result of insufficient access to adequate employment. As urban population projections make clear, the urban economies of many developing countries are facing an unprecedented challenge—to generate a sufficient number of new jobs at reasonable wages to absorb a growing and better-educated labor force. The purpose of this chapter is to examine several of the critical elements in the nature of urban labor supply and employment. Of course, no single chapter can do justice to the complexities of urban economic relations, and the attempt made here is far from comprehensive. From the great variety of issues associated with urban economies, we focus on a selected few that have the greatest demographic resonance.

In many ways, the urban economy shapes urban demography. Urban economies generate the resources upon which governments draw to extend public services, whether in family planning, education, or health, and to undertake investments in the public health infrastructure. The scale of the urban economy can enable specialization in economic activities and foster the growth of private markets, with the markets in health services being of particular significance. At the level of families, income from labor and economic enterprises provides a means of purchasing health, education, and other services. The incomes of women, when considered in relation to those of men, have much to do with the returns to marriage. The economic returns to schooling have been a central theme in this report, and we have repeatedly emphasized their importance to family strategies involving lower fertility but greater schooling per child. Urban incomes and educational returns also affect migration, whether from rural areas or from other urban areas. For these reasons, no study of urban demography can neglect its economic underpinnings.

To set the discussion in context, we begin with an introductory section that sketches the main sectoral and spatial features affecting labor markets and urban economies. This section highlights the analogies between the social externalities that arise from urban diversity and proximity and the economic externalities that arise from the same general sources. As will be seen, there is an economic role for social networks, one of the mechanisms highlighted in previous chapters. Our treatment of sectoral and spatial factors must be brief, but several superb literature reviews can be consulted for more detail (see, for example, Williamson, 1988; Eberts and McMillen, 1999; Becker and Morrison, 1999). Unemployment and poverty in urban labor markets in developing countries are often attributed to labor market failure, but our review highlights how the differences between labor markets in high- and low-income countries have probably been overemphasized. Economists are now reexamining the structure of wages and earnings within urban labor markets in low-income countries to assess more carefully the role of human capital and institutional factors in determining earnings. Many of the issues now being raised have long been themes in research on industrially more-developed economies.

In the following section, attention turns to urban growth and the economic returns to schooling. The potential contribution of education to improving economic productivity, lowering income inequality, and promoting growth and development is well known, and almost all governments allocate a considerable share of their budgets to public expenditures on education. For many capital- and natural-resource-starved countries, human resources may represent the only route to successful development. As noted above, the economic returns to schooling are also important determinants of demographic behavior. They influence parental assessments of the payoffs for investment in children's education and fertility decline. Also, to the extent that schooling returns are higher in urban than in rural areas or differ across cities, they exert influence on both the rate and direction of migration. Yet when the urban supply of educated labor is increasing rapidly, as it appears to be in most developing countries, one wonders how high returns to schooling can be maintained. This section explores the issues by way of case studies.

Migration, another central element in the size and nature of the urban labor force, is discussed in the next section, where we reassess the conceptual frameworks that so dominated thinking in the 1970s and 1980s—the Todaro (1969) and Harris and Todaro (1970) migration models. Given the changing nature of urban systems, to what extent are the assumptions made by Todaro and Harris—about the attractions of urban "formal-sector" jobs and dualistic conceptions of the urban economy—still valid and useful? In considering the issues, we examine migration as it is influenced by urban economic structure, review what is known of urban economic mobility and income dynamics, and then explore (in the next section) dualistic assumptions about segmented urban labor markets. Here we look critically at the proposition that sectoral barriers and rigidities are a root cause of urban economic inequalities, and examine the evidence for increasing hetero-geneity in the urban informal sector. We next review several case studies showing how labor demand and supply factors have come together to generate inequality in urban Brazil, Taiwan, and China, countries that can offer rich longitudinal data on urban earnings.

The penultimate section of the chapter examines international facets of urban economies, factors that doubtless will increasingly condition urban labor markets in developing countries in the future and affect their labor absorption capacity. We present evidence on the urban implications of foreign direct investment, discuss the role of globalized networks of high-end business services, and examine how heightened exposure to world markets—with their attendant benefits, costs, and uncertainties—can affect the lives of urban residents disproportionately. The final section of the chapter presents conclusions and recommendations.

SECTOR AND SPACE

At the outset, we must distinguish *sectoral* from *spatial* influences. To see why, consider Engel's law—that the income elasticity of demand for manufactured goods and services is greater than that for primary products. When demand conforms to Engel's law, an increase in a country's income per capita shifts the composition of its demand toward manufacturing and services and away from agriculture, mining, and related sectors. Shifts in the demand for labor (and other inputs) in each sector accompany these changes in final demand.

Although it is tempting to think of manufacturing and services as urban activi-ties and to conclude that national income growth leads inexorably to urbanization, nothing in Engel's law actually implies this. Engel effects are *aspatial*. Addi-tional argument is needed to show why manufacturing and services tend to be located in cities, that is, in spatially concentrated clusters of labor and production. Spatial concentration offers some cost and productivity advantages, but because these come bundled together with disadvantages (e.g., congestion, negative exter-nalities), the spatial side of the story has its own logic. Engel effects that steadily shift the composition of demand can at first be expressed in spatial concentration and higher levels of urbanization, but later be expressed in the spatial deconcen-tration of the urban population, if not in lower levels of urbanization as such.

In this section, we first examine sectoral effects, aiming mainly to show how urbanization can be a natural consequence of national economic growth or, more precisely, a consequence of the factors that produce national growth. We then take up spatial effects by considering both the benefits and costs of urban spatial con-centration. A review of the productivity advantages associated with spatial clus-tering suggests that urbanization may well be a cause of national economic growth in addition to being a consequence. The mechanisms involved are the spatial counterparts to the forces highlighted by the "new growth theory" in economics (e.g., Lucas, 1988).

In sorting through the many linkages between national and urban growth, we really cannot hope to disentangle cause from consequence. Even so, it may be useful to review the strong associations that have been documented repeatedly in the literature. We note four points. First, where national statistical systems permit such a decomposition, studies have shown that the urban share of the national economy can be far greater than its population share alone would suggest. In the case of Mexico, a careful analysis of 1998 economic census data at the municipality level by Sobrino (2002) shows that the five largest metropolitan areas accounted for 53 percent of national value added in industry, commerce, and services while housing only 28 percent of Mexico's population (United Nations, 2001). Mexico's 10 largest cities, with only one-third of the country's population, generate 62 percent of national value added. Figures such as these underscore the importance of city economies to national levels of income. Even from an accountant's perspective, it is difficult to conceive of national economic activity and urban activity as somehow occurring in separate spheres.

Second, because the size of the urban informal sector tends to be poorly measured in national income accounts—we discuss the informal sector later in this chapter—there is reason to think that the urban share of the national economy may often be underestimated. One study of West Africa reconstitutes the production and trade flows of 1960 by applying social accounting matrix techniques (Cour, 1994). These revisions suggest that national gross domestic product (GDP) was understated by as much as 30 to 50 percent in the national income accounts. The revised methods reveal that West African cities provided two-thirds of real GDP, rather than the mere 38 percent indicated in the conventional accounts.

Third, to get a sense of the urban contribution to national growth, one can look at cross-country data on growth in value added (World Bank, 2000a). Of the total growth in national value added among low-income countries from 1980 to 1998, fully 86 percent is attributable to growth in industry and services.[1] The urban contribution must be somewhat less than this because some services and industries are located in rural areas. Nevertheless, the figure suggests the extent to which national economic growth derives from urban growth, and it conveys something of the force of Engel's law.

Fourth, a number of statistical studies have found that higher levels of national income and faster national growth spur urbanization. Among the many studies that have examined such correlations, we single out the following few. Moomaw and Shatter (1996), using data from 90 countries for 1960, 1970, and 1980, show that the urban share of the population increases with national income per capita; the share is also increased by industrialization, trade orientation, and

---

[1] Excluding India and China, calculations by the panel put the industry and services share of growth at 83 percent.

foreign capital inflows. Brockerhoff (1999) examines the population growth rates of a large number of developing-country cities. He finds that growth in gross national product (GNP) per capita encourages city growth. In earlier work, Becker and Morrison (1988) reach a similar conclusion for the countries of sub-Saharan Africa. Gaviria and Stein (2000) also find a strong positive effect of growth in GDP per capita on the population growth rates of large cities.[2] Although studies such as these do not firmly establish the direction of causation, they do show that the association between urban and national economic growth is robust and worthy of attention.

Sectoral Effects

Kelley and Williamson (1984) give a highly instructive account of the sectoral factors involved in urban growth. They formulate what is termed a "computable general equilibrium" model and use simulations to illustrate their main analytic points.[3] These authors consider the case of a hypothetical country that is a price taker in international markets, which is to say that the prices of its agricultural and manufactured goods are taken to be externally determined. Changes in the relative price of manufactured goods affect the relative demand for labor in manufacturing. If manufacturing is indeed an urban activity, then an increase in the relative price of its products leads to faster urban growth and, in time, to a higher urban population share. In this way, changes in the international terms of trade between manufactured and agricultural goods can have an impact on the national level and pace of urbanization.

Two types of technological progress are considered in the Kelley–Williamson framework. Neutral or "balanced" technical change—which enhances the productivity of both agricultural and manufacturing activities to the same extent—acts much like an increase in average national income and exerts an influence on relative demands for labor through Engel effects. Unbalanced technical change, in which faster progress is made in manufacturing than in agriculture, is expressed in labor markets by faster growth in the demand for manufacturing jobs. This focused impact on manufacturing is augmented by the Engel effects that generally accompany technological progress. In the Kelley–Williamson simulations, unbalanced technological change is shown to exert a powerful influence on the pace of urban growth.

Technological change is less potent, however, when prices are determined in domestic rather than world markets, especially when those domestic markets are

---

[2]The Gaviria and Stein estimate retains its strength in the presence of country fixed effects. Although urban population growth and national income growth are correlated because both depend on country-specific fixed factors, there is clearly more to the story than this.

[3]The model contains a number of sectors, but for convenience we refer here only to manufacturing and agriculture. Other sectors play key mediating roles. In particular, the prices of nontradeable goods and services, such as urban housing, are bid up as the model's population shifts to urban areas. These changes in the urban cost of living keep the extent and pace of urbanization in check.

competitive. In such cases, technological progress favoring manufacturing will reduce marginal costs in that sector; under competitive pressures, the result will be lower prices for manufactured goods. Price declines, in turn, slow growth in the derived demand for manufacturing jobs. The differences in the effects of technological progress can be seen by comparing the price-taking, open-economy model of Kelley and Williamson with a similar model developed for India (Becker, Williamson, and Mills, 1992) in which prices are determined largely in domestic markets. In the latter case, technological progress continues to exert some influence on urban population growth, but this influence is mild by comparison with the price-taking open-economy case.

Just how technological change takes place in poor countries has been much debated. A number of studies suggest that when these countries are able to export manufactured goods, supplier–customer linkages are established that facilitate the adoption of new technologies and spread commercial know-how (Pack and Page, 1994; Tybout, 2000). The recent literature is ably summarized by Rauch (2001), who describes how exports can give firms and entrepreneurs an entreé to international business networks. Technological progress is generally thought to be skill-biased, in the sense that adoption of new technology raises the relative demand for educated, skilled labor (Johnson, 1997). This may explain in part why cities possess (and attract) better-educated workers. But as Rodrik (1997) points out, it is very difficult to separate the effects of technological change from those of physical capital accumulation, which is also thought to be strongly complementary to skills (Fallon and Layard, 1975).

The process of capital accumulation is acknowledged to be central to economic growth—some authors (e.g., Young, 1995) assign it the leading role—and of course a large portion of any country's investment in plant, equipment, and infrastructure will be found in its cities. But the size of a country's capital stock is one matter and its spatial concentration another. The agglomeration economies that urban sites offer to private firms (discussed in the next section) provide a partial explanation for the urban concentration of capital. However, these private advantages depend crucially on governments' complementary capital investments in urban public services and infrastructure (Eberts and McMillen, 1999). Productive cities must be highly capital-intensive. An urban bias in government expenditures may further concentrate capital in cities, as discussed below.

But does urbanization itself help mobilize the savings from which such investments are made? It is certainly reasonable to think so.[4] As documented in Chapter 4, city populations are more concentrated in the working and saving ages than are rural populations, and they contain relatively fewer young dependents.

---

[4]Two gaps between domestic savings and investment are worth mentioning here. First, urban savings are not necessarily invested domestically; capital flight is evident in sub-Saharan Africa, where, as Collier and Gunning (1999b) show, about 39 percent of all domestic savings is invested outside the region. Second, as discussed later in this chapter, foreign direct investment is an increasingly important source of capital in the cities of some developing countries.

BOX 8.1 Industrialization and Social Capital in Indonesia

There is much interest in the linkage between social capital and industrialization, but as yet very little by way of data with which to explore this linkage. Cross-sectional studies have suggested that the two are positively associated, but such studies leave it unclear whether social capital supports economic development, economic development gives rise to social capital, or the two are linked in a system of mutual causation.

Exploiting unusual panel data on Indonesian districts in the period 1985 to 1997, Miguel, Gertler, and Levine (2001) find that growth in a district's manufacturing employment appears to spur the development of local social capital, as measured by participation in arts and recreational groups and some types of credit cooperatives. However, the spatial impact is uneven. Because some districts become sites of flourishing manufacturing growth while others do not, social capital also grows unevenly. Outmigration occurs as migrants seek manufacturing jobs in nearby districts, and migration, in turn, erodes individual incentives to invest further in social capital in the origin districts. The loss of social capital is particularly evident for informal credit and mutual assistance groups, which depend for their survival on an assumption of stable and reciprocal exchange.

Upon examining the other direction of causation, the authors find no compelling evidence that social capital either attracts or fosters manufacturing growth. (As they acknowledge, establishing causation is difficult even with longitudinal data.) A complicating factor is that the local groups studied in this research are often chapters or affiliates of national groups, and are overseen by their national boards and by government. Hence, local groups probably cannot be viewed as groups that fade or flourish according to purely local circumstances.

In national populations, at least, lower dependency ratios have been shown to foster higher average savings rates (Higgins, 1997; Deaton and Paxson, 2000; Lee, Mason, and Miller, 2000). Urban incomes are higher than rural on average, and this must also encourage savings (Loayza, Schmidt-Hebbel, and Servén, 2000b). In addition, cities house the financial institutions that should allow savings to be monetized rather than held in the form of illiquid physical assets. In formulating their general equilibrium model, Kelley and Williamson (1984: 59–60, 218–20) thought it safe to assume that urban households have higher savings rates than rural households.

All this notwithstanding, however, one finds surprisingly little research in which urban savings rates are compared directly with rural rates.[5] Indeed, the recent evidence suggests that the savings rates of rural households may well be higher than urban rates. In analyses based on cross-national datasets, Loayza, Schmidt-Hebbel, and Servén (2000a,b), show that with other things held constant, the level of urbanization is negatively associated with average savings rates.

---

[5] Severe conceptual and measurement difficulties—the valuation of flows from consumer durables such as urban housing (Gersovitz, 1988), the measurement of business savings (retained profits), and the absence of spatially disaggregated data on government savings—render such comparisons uncommon.

Loayza and Shankar (2000) explore the case of India in detail, using time-series data for 1960–1995. They find private savings rates to be positively associated with the share of agriculture in GDP. From such aggregate data, it would appear that rural Indians, who lack other means to diversify the risks they confront, engage in more precautionary savings than do urban residents. Weather and related sources of risk introduce a substantial element of uncertainty in rural areas, and rural economies often lack the protective institutions found in cities.

In China, replacement of the commune system with a system of household responsibility—reforms that spurred income growth but also removed some institutional protections against risk—evidently led to sharp increases in rural savings rates (Kraay, 2000). By contrast, the protections extended in urban areas through work units and state subsidies left these populations without the same incentives to save, at least until recently. According to Kraay, urban household savings rates remained well below rural rates into the mid-1990s. Unfortunately, the data available to Kraay did not include savings among urban temporary migrants, who undoubtedly save higher fractions of their income than do permanent residents.

If a household's educational expenditures were considered alongside its monetized savings, might this broader view show that urban savings rates rival rural rates? Tsai, Chu, and Chung (2000) explore the possibility for Taiwan, and discover that metropolitan households engage in less monetized saving but make greater investments in their children's schooling. Schooling investments can substitute in several ways for savings, especially given the obligation for educated Taiwanese to repay their parents by providing them with support in old age. Still, the result is surprising because Taipei and the country's other large cities contain many financial institutions that should facilitate savings.[6]

Spatial Effects: Agglomeration Economies

To examine how the sectoral effects sketched above are expressed in spatial terms, we turn to the theory of agglomeration economies, which addresses the productivity and cost advantages derived from the spatial concentration of production and labor. The main elements of this theory date to the pioneering work of Marshall (1890), Weber (1909), Christaller (1933), and Lösch (1954) in economic geography. The outlines of the theory were set forth in Chapter 2, and here we need only mention the extensions and specific features that appear to be of particular salience for developing countries.

In a world with transportation and communication costs, agglomerating tendencies arise from several sources. Scale economies in production can lead firms to concentrate their activities instead of spreading production across spatially dispersed small plants. If production is broadly conceived to include the recruitment and training of labor, the maintenance of inventories, and the formulation of

---

[6]See Gersovitz (1988) for a review of other attempts to include educational expenditures with monetized savings.

contractual relations with other firms, and if transport and communication costs affect each of these elements, firms can derive many productive advantages from locating in large, diverse economic clusters. As discussed in Chapter 2, the advantages of spatial concentration can be grouped into two categories: *localization economies*, which pertain to the benefits of clustering with other firms in a given industry, and *urbanization economies*, which have to do with the benefits obtained from the size and diversity of the cluster. Localization economies arise when spatial concentration gives firms easier access to industry-specific inputs, such as specialized labor or services. Urbanization economies stem from the need for inputs used across industries and sectors, such as generalized legal and financial services and well-educated labor. Some of these productivity benefits are market-mediated, termed *pecuniary* externalities, whereas others are *pure* externalities, which often take the form of informational spillovers.

Agglomerating forces can be either strengthened or weakened by the natural heterogeneities of space. For instance, rivers and natural harbors often form the kernel of urban economies. Yet when valuable mineral deposits are geographically isolated, firms engaged in their extraction may find it necessary to establish operations in locations remote from cities. Although the spatial outcomes differ, in each case firms choose their locations by balancing scale economies against transport costs. Because sites with natural advantages tend to attract more firms and people, it can be very difficult to separate natural advantages from localization and urbanization effects. Even where longitudinal data are available, they seldom provide sufficient over-time variation in urbanization and localization measures for their effects to be clearly distinguished. One study attempting to isolate the role of natural advantage, that of Ellison and Glaeser (1999) for the United States, finds that as much as one-fifth of the geographic concentration of production, and quite possibly more, can be explained by such natural, location-specific features. Still, even this estimate leaves a large portion of concentration to be explained by localization and urbanization economies, as well as by other factors.

A point much stressed in reviews of the literature (notably that of Eberts and McMillen, 1999) is that the advantages of clustering may or may not materialize, depending on the availability and quality of public services. Public provision and regulation of transport is one example of critical infrastructure; another is the reliable delivery of such inputs as electricity and water (World Bank, 1994: 30–31). As discussed in Chapter 5, the provision of basic public services is far from being complete in the cities of most poor countries, especially when account is taken of the reliability and adequacy of supply, and it is likely that there are significant clustering advantages still to be realized in most cities. Other publicly provided services—such as health and education services—may have significant complementary effects on the costs of production. For instance, highly educated workers may much prefer to live where their children can be assured of good-quality schools. To live elsewhere, they might insist on a wage premium that would raise costs for firms. In short, when public services are unavailable or unreliable, the advantages of spatial concentration are likely to remain largely theoretical and to be threatened by congestion and the other diseconomies of agglomeration.

Evidence for developing countries

What is the special relevance to poor countries of the general points made above? In high-income countries, transportation costs have greatly declined as a share of total costs, and this has weakened one rationale for spatial concentration (Quigley, 1998). In most poor countries, however, transportation and communication costs surely remain high. Are economies of scale in production then sufficiently great to induce spatial concentration? On this point the empirical evidence suggests caution. In reviewing a number of empirical estimates for developing-country manufacturing, Tybout (2000) finds evidence that scale economies are either slight or altogether absent.[7] Without stronger evidence of scale effects, a theory built on transport costs and conventional scale economies alone appears inadequate.

At least for the moment, the more promising findings are contained in the literature on cross-firm and cross-industry spillovers. Several empirical studies of localization and urbanization effects have been conducted in Brazil and India, although studies are regrettably scarce in the remainder of the developing world (Henderson, 1982, 1988; Shukla, 1996; Mitra, 1999). In his analysis of Brazilian cities, Henderson (1982, 1988) detects little evidence of urbanization economies, but finds substantial evidence of within-industry localization economies. For the industries he studies, the elasticity of a firm's output with respect to local employ-ment in its industry (his preferred measure of localization) generally exceeds one-tenth. With reference to India, Shukla (1996) examines the elasticity of a firm's output with the size of the surrounding urban population, this being a measure of urbanization economies. She also finds significant positive elasticities averaging about one-tenth and ranging as high as one-fifth in the case of the basic metals and alloys industries. These are effects of considerable substantive importance, as can be appreciated by comparing the productivity of a firm located in a town with that of an otherwise identical firm located in a large city.

In tests comparing urbanization with localization measures, Shukla finds that the urbanization effects are larger in 11 of the 13 industries she examines. Mi-tra (1999) also examines the case of India, estimating production functions for electrical machinery and cotton and cotton textiles. His estimates suggest that economies of urbanization are greater in cities of intermediate size than in either smaller or larger cities. For instance, electrical machinery firms derive the great-est productivity benefits from locating in cities of 1.5–2.5 million; for firms in the cotton-related industries, the maximum benefit is obtained from cities of 2.5–5.0 million. Although Mitra and Shukla stress urbanization economies in their

---

[7]Likewise, in high-income settings, scale economies in manufacturing are perhaps less important than they once were, owing to declining fixed costs in computing and the use of techniques permitting smaller, more specialized production runs.

work, Henderson is not alone in emphasizing localization economies. A study of Mexican manufacturing by Grether (1999) shows that within-industry spatial concentration generates substantial productivity benefits.

Eberts and McMillen (1999) call attention to a curious gap in research on developed countries: agglomeration effects are examined in some studies and the effects of public infrastructure in others, while very few studies test for public–private complementarities. The situation is hardly different in poor countries. Using an array of measures of provision of infrastructure and social services, Shukla (1996) examines the implications for industry productivity in Maharashtra. In this Indian state, public-sector capital inputs are shown to enhance the productivity of private firms. Water supply, roads, electricity, and health and educational facilities are evidently gross complements in their direct impact on private output; they appear to be substitutes for private industries and public enterprises. Jimenez (1995) and the World Bank (1994: 15) review similar findings from a range of developing and developed countries. What is lacking, however, is direct evidence on whether public capital itself enhances the returns to spatial clustering.

Spatial concentration and growth: Dynamic elements

Over the past decade, the dynamic effects arising from agglomeration have attracted an increasing amount of research attention. The surge of interest is often dated to the emphasis on scale and externalities in new theories of economic growth (Lucas, 1988), but economists have long been intrigued by the idea that proximity and diversity can combine in forms of social learning that generate innovation. Alfred Marshall (1890) anticipated the current interest by more than a century, writing on both the static and dynamic aspects:

> ... great are the advantages which people following the same skilled trade get from near neighborhood to one another. The mysteries of the trade become no mysteries: but are as it were in the air.... Good work is rightly appreciated, inventions and improvements in machinery, in processes and the general organization of the business have their merits promptly discussed: if one man starts a new idea, it is taken up by others and combined with suggestions of their own; and thus it becomes the source of further new ideas.

Modern theoretical treatments have drawn out the implications of such social interaction for innovation (e.g., Jovanovic and Robb, 1989). As noted in Chapter 2, one important theme is that spatial proximity and urban diversity are especially important in the design and testing phases of product development and become less important once the production process has been standardized (Duranton and Puga, 2001). Empirical tests of these ideas are not yet common, in part because convincing tests require longitudinal data on the social and economic interactions highlighted in the theory.[8]

One important strand in this literature addresses the question of whether social interactions can affect the economic returns to schooling. As was seen in Chapter 5, developing-country cities differ from rural areas not only in the average level of adult schooling, which is of course higher in cities, but also in the diversity of educational attainment. Cities are locations where well- and poorly educated workers are more likely to come into contact. Might this proximity improve the prospects for informational spillovers and other beneficial externalities?

Some evidence to this effect has emerged for the United States. Rauch (1993) examines the earnings of individual workers in U.S. metropolitan areas. He finds that with individual education and experience held constant, individual earnings in these areas tend to increase with average level of education. The effect is robust to the inclusion of a variety of individual and metropolitan covariates. This is intriguing but hardly conclusive proof of beneficial spillovers: the marginal productivity of any one input (say, unskilled labor) is apt to increase with the levels of other productive inputs (say, skilled labor) in the local economy, even in the absence of spillovers.[9] Stronger evidence of spillovers is provided by Moretti (2000), who finds that the earnings of individual well-educated workers increase with the proportion of similarly well-educated workers in a metropolitan area, again holding individual characteristics constant. This positive effect is inconsistent with conventional theories of marginal productivity, and may therefore represent a true beneficial spillover. Moretti's estimate is strong enough to withstand a battery of tests for selection effects and other statistical biases. If well-educated labor does indeed generate positive spillovers, an increase in the proportion of well-educated labor in the local economy will raise the earnings of the less educated, as is seen in the earlier work by Rauch (1993). These are U.S. examples, to be sure, and we are not aware of comparable research in the cities of poor countries. However, there is no compelling reason to rule out similar effects in these cities.

If social interaction has the effect of increasing productivity and spawning innovation, what is the mechanism by which this occurs? Nothing appears to be known about this for workers, but where investment and innovation in manufacturing are concerned, some researchers see a key role for the social networks of owners and entrepreneurs. Collier and Gunning (1999b) give a general account

---

[8]In developing countries, of course, even conventional longitudinal studies of firms and industries remain rare. In a follow-on to the Indian research described above, Mitra (2000) examines productivity growth using panel data on a number of industries from the late 1970s to the early 1990s. Only a third of the industries studied show significant urbanization effects (as measured by the urban population of the state). These are weaker results than those obtained by Mitra (1999).

[9]Consider a Cobb–Douglas production function $Y = U^\alpha S^{1-\alpha}$, with U being unskilled labor and S skilled labor. The marginal product of unskilled labor is $\alpha U^{\alpha-1} S^{1-\alpha}$, which increases with the level of S. Without spillover effects, the marginal product of unskilled labor U will fall as the level of U increases. Hence, tests for spillovers focus on the empirical evidence *against* diminishing marginal productivity.

of the role of social networks in sub-Saharan Africa, and Murphy (2002) explores their specific role in Mwanza, a small Tanzanian town.

In keeping with the long tradition of network analysis in sociology, these authors stress two roles for social networks. First, networks are viewed as important mechanisms for the transmission of new information, especially when they contain individuals who can serve as "bridges" between otherwise unconnected groups. Networks can thus present their members with new economic options and offer examples of the consequences of innovative decisions. (This idea is well expressed in the above quotation from Marshall.) Second, from the viewpoint of a given network member, his or her contacts constitute a set of personal relations differing in reliability and trustworthiness, ranging from persons with whom there are strong ties to others with whom ties are infrequent or weak.

Collier and Gunning (1999b) and Murphy (2002) apply these ideas to decisions about business expansion in Africa. As they describe the situation, the trusted network members of African entrepreneurs are often others within the same family or ethnic group. The dilemma is that in these trusted circles, new economic information will tend to appear less frequently than in wider networks. But the wider networks include contacts who are not trusted to the same degree, and an entrepreneur hearing of a profit opportunity through such contacts may feel that the risk is simply too great to proceed.

In some settings, an entrepreneur might turn to a third party—say, a firm that conducts creditworthiness checks, audits, and the like—to assess business risks and ensure the reliability of a potential partner. Also, where governments maintain well-functioning and transparent commercial courts, an entrepreneur can expect to recoup some of the losses from a failed partnership and thus limit the downside risks of business expansion. In sub-Saharan Africa, however, the key business service sectors have yet to develop in many cities, and few small-scale entrepreneurs can count on the effectiveness of commercial courts and the impartiality of local officials. In the absence of these institutions, African entrepreneurs must fall back on their trusted network partners and abandon profit opportunities not conveyed through their most trusted local circles. The net effect is a contraction of investment and slower economic growth than might occur in the presence of complementary business services and a coherent legal system.

To sum up our review of spatial concentration and innovation, we find many reasons to believe that localization and urbanization effects can raise productivity and foster economic growth. As our review shows, theories suggesting such effects have well outpaced any supporting empirical research. Hence no strong conclusions can yet be rendered. But we see enough in the combination of compelling theory and (limited) empirical findings to conclude that urban spatial concentration must be one cause of national economic growth.[10] The size of its contribution is not yet known but is surely of considerable significance.

---

[10]One active area of research on spillover effects is the performance of industrial clusters in developing countries (Schmitz and Nadvi, 1999; Bell and Albu, 1999).

Spatial Deconcentration

We have been describing the benefits of the spatial concentration of resources, but these advantages run up against limits imposed by congestion and the rising prices of land and other location-specific nontradeables. Data on urban systems suggest that with economic development comes a tendency toward urban decentralization (Rosen and Resnick, 1980). This tendency is not always evident, and given the structural changes involved, its meaning is debateable. Many factors can influence both development and decentralization, perhaps the most prominent among them being national transportation policies and investments. But monocausal theories of decentralization are seldom seriously advanced in the literature. Most researchers acknowledge the powerful role played by economic forces, but stress that even these forces are not necessarily dominant. Political and historical factors are also given their due, with particular reference to the spatial aspects of political power and access to bureaucrats.

The complexities of decentralization can be seen in two recent empirical analyses using cross-national comparative data. Ades and Glaeser (1995) aim to explain differences in the population size of each country's largest urban agglomeration.[11] Other things being equal, these cities tend to be relatively larger in countries with higher levels of national income per capita and higher ratios of imports and exports to national income. The main city's population is smaller, however, in countries with higher national road densities and greater government expenditures on transport. Taken together, these findings imply that higher levels of income per capita will yield decentralized city systems only if accompanied by deeper investments in transport. Three political factors are found to matter: main cities are larger when they are national capitals, and both political instability and dictatorship forms of government are associated with larger city size. Political effects are also seen in the earlier analysis of Henderson (1982), who shows that decentralized city systems are associated with decentralized political systems.

Gaviria and Stein (2000) revisit some of these issues with panel data on the countries in the Ades–Glaeser sample; they focus on the population growth rate of the largest city rather than its size.[12] Some of the earlier findings survive. For instance, where Ades and Glaeser show that higher levels of GDP per capita are associated with larger main cities, Gaviria and Stein show that faster GDP per capita growth rates are associated with faster city population growth. But Gaviria

---

[11]They include country size as a control variable, which has the effect of expressing all results in relative terms.

[12]Again a control variable—the growth rate of the country's total urban population—is introduced to convert the results to relative terms. See Chapter 4 on the United Nations procedures for estimating city-specific population growth rates and the possibility of measurement errors in these data. Gaviria and Stein find that, with other things held constant, larger cities tend to grow more slowly than smaller ones. This tendency has been well documented by the United Nations (2001) and has long been embedded in its city projection methods.

and Stein fail to confirm the Ades–Glaeser result on dictatorships. They note that the effects of openness to trade depend on geography: the population growth rates of landlocked cities tend to fall with an increase in the ratio of trade to GDP, while no effect of trade can be detected in the growth rates of port cities. It appears that a set of empirically replicable "stylized facts" about urban deconcentration has yet to be established.

As suggested by the analysis of Ades and Glaeser (1995) and by many country case studies, investments in transportation infrastructure can play an important role in decentralization. As improvements are made in transport and communication, firms are freed to seek the locations that offer them the best combination of productivity advantage, rents, and wages. Henderson (1988) describes this process for Korea. In the region surrounding Seoul, manufacturing began to deconcentrate in the 1970s, moving from the inner to the outer rings of the region. Alternative sites in the south of Korea (near Busan) also began to grow more rapidly than Seoul. Firms in the machinery and metal sectors, whose production had become routinized, followed the logic of the product development cycle and sought cheaper land and labor outside the capital. Large firms sometimes maintained head offices in Seoul but decentralized their production plants; other firms relocated all their operations but stayed in contact with Seoul bureaucrats by remaining within a half-hour's drive. In the Korean case, better transport links within and outside the capital region greatly facilitated decentralization; so did the increasing availability of good-quality local public services, which alleviated the concerns of high-skilled workers about relocating. Although the Korean government offered firms a number of targeted incentives for relocation, including tax breaks and preferential access to credit, in Henderson's account these policies had little effect.

As the Korean example makes clear, the process of decentralization combines economic with political elements in a way that limits the explanatory power of narrowly focused economic models. Still, some insights into the process can be gleaned from formal analyses. The most fully articulated of the economic theories is that of Henderson (1982, 1985, 1988), in which the organizing concepts are those of localization and urbanization economies. As discussed above, firms benefiting from localization economies can reap productivity advantages from spatial clustering with other firms in their industries. A system of specialized cities can then emerge, with the smallest cities of the system being dominated by industries whose localization economies are exhausted at low levels of clustering (e.g., in industry employment). The largest cities then house the industries with gains from localization that persist even in large clusters.[13] Specialization of this type establishes the spine of the city system, to which industries drawing benefits from urbanization economies—city size and diversity—then attach themselves.

---

[13] Such localization effects are most powerful when industry prices are held fixed, as in the case of production for export.

In all cities, the effects of clustering on congestion costs, rents, and wages provide counterpressures that keep the agglomerating tendencies in check.

Although Henderson makes only modest claims for the explanatory power of this elegant theory—he offers it as a set of regularities that might be glimpsed beneath the embroidery of other economic relations—the theory has drawn attention because of the ease with which it can be linked to international markets. Cities specializing in goods traded on world markets will be directly affected by changes in world prices. An increase in any given world price will be expressed in a national city system by an increase in the number of cities that specialize in the production of the good in question. Thus, when world prices change for goods in which medium-sized cities specialize, the spatial implications should be evident in this portion of the city hierarchy. National policies that subsidize or tax particular goods will have effects akin to those of international prices. In principle, at least, these are empirically testable propositions, although proper tests would require unusually detailed, city-specific data.

Fujita, Krugman, and Venables (1999) have fashioned an alternative city system theory—one that can also be linked to international markets—from rather different materials. Perhaps the most striking feature of their theory is that it is wholly free of reference to localization and urbanization externalities. Rather, the concepts at the core of the model are those of diversity, increasing returns to scale, and transport costs. As used here, "diversity" refers to the preferences of consumers for a wide range of manufactured goods. When consumers have only weak preferences for diversity, the ensuing pattern of demand encourages firms to produce a narrow range of goods with high levels of output for each, thereby exploiting the available economies of scale. When preferences for diversity are stronger, a greater range of goods is produced but at lower output levels for each.

The cost of conveying finished goods to consumers is a main determinant of the spatial clustering of firms. As firms and their labor forces gather around any one location, the consumer market associated with that location expands, and this, in turn, raises its attractiveness for other firms. Such agglomerating tendencies are countered by the need for firms to exploit profit opportunities in locations that are not so heavily populated by their competitors. After much complex argument—see Krugman (1991) for the seminal paper in this line of research, Fujita, Krugman, and Mori (1999) for some of the detail, and Neary (2001) for a penetrating critique—this approach can be shown to yield an urban hierarchy with a dominant central city and subsidiary cities occupied by industries with high transportation costs. Interestingly, the decentralizing tendencies can be hidden in small populations but are exposed as the national population grows.

In one early expression of these ideas, Livas Elizondo and Krugman (1992) explain how openness to international trade can shape the roles of larger and smaller cities. (The authors have Mexico City and Monterrey, California, in mind, with the United States playing the role of trading partner.) They imagine a scenario in which the population of Monterrey initially equals that of Mexico City. As

protectionism toward the United States increases, the allocation of population between these cities becomes unstable, and a tendency emerges for labor to concentrate in one large city. In this way, market size effects cause closed economies to
produce dominant megacities. When the economy is opened to trade, this lessens
the need for firms seeking large markets to locate in cities and permits a more
dispersed city system.

In these theories, small cities are viewed mainly as small concentrations of
industry. But small and intermediate-sized cities are often linked to the surrounding rural settlements by complex two-way interactions; these include trade;
employment; and the provision of services, such as health care and secondary
education (Hardoy and Satterthwaite, 1986b; Kamete, 1998). One of the most
important linkages is the stimulus that prosperous agriculture can provide for
urban development.

Reviews of urban change often highlight how many of the most rapidly growing urban centers are found in areas where the value of agricultural production
is increasing most rapidly (Manzanal and Vapnarsky, 1986; Hardoy and Satterthwaite, 1988; Blitzer, Davila, Hardoy, and Satterthwaite, 1988; UNCHS, 1996).
Among the most important factors are the value per hectare of the crops (the
higher the value, generally the more local urban development occurs); the potential for local value-added activities (and the scale of forward and backward
multiplier linkages between agricultural production and local urban enterprises);
and the structure of landownership (the greatest stimulus to local urban development generally being the existence of a large number of prosperous, relatively
small farms growing high-value crops) (Hardoy and Satterthwaite, 1988).

Examples of the strong stimuli for urban development provided by agriculture
include fruit production in the Upper Valley of Rio Negro in Argentina (Manzanal and Vapnarsky, 1986) and in Bangalore, India, the multiple interconnections between rural silk cocoon producers and urban enterprises involved in collecting and processing the cocoons, making silk, and making and selling saris
(Bhooshan, 1986; Benjamin, 2000). In some cases, however, prosperous agriculture gives little stimulus to nearby urban development, especially where landownership is highly concentrated and more extensive crops are grown (Hardoy and
Satterthwaite, 1988). Where markets are dominated by large local merchants who
control access to transport and marketplaces and, in many instances, access to capital, credit, and information, much of the value of agricultural production can be
steered out of the region (Tacoli, 1998).

There is little to suggest that governments recognize the potential for prosperous agriculture to support urban development beyond the local level. Many
agricultural towns and cities have been starved of the support they require from
higher levels of government to aid economic expansion and meet the needs of
rapidly growing populations. In some instances, agricultural policies have pre-
vented or discouraged rural producers from diversifying production and trapped
them in low-profit crops with few forward and backward linkages. Examples can

be found in many Asian nations with policies designed to ensure adequate rice production to feed urban populations (Douglass, 1998, 1999). Comprehensive urban/rural development frameworks and regional spatial planning in the 1970s and 1980s generally focused on trying to expand industrial production in smaller urban centers and often failed to identify and support the potential comparative advantages of each locality. However, this failure to support a prosperous agriculture that could in turn underpin urban development also relates to obvious political constraints, such as inequitable landowning structures and pricing and marketing structures that held down rural incomes. While many of these are national-level constraints, the internationalization of trade and production is an increasingly important dimension that affects local economies through the rise of international agro-industry and the resulting marginalization of small farmers (Bryceson, 1999).

Where statistics are available on occupational structures within smaller urban centers, they often show a significant proportion of the labor force working in agriculture, livestock, forestry, or fishing. The panel found no recent studies on occupational structures in smaller urban centers. However, case studies of cities with under 100,000 inhabitants in predominantly rural regions of low-income nations, undertaken during the early 1980s, revealed that it was common for 10–30 percent of the workforce to be employed in agriculture, with many more having occupations that serve demand generated by agricultural production or agricultural incomes (Hardoy and Satterthwaite, 1986b). Agriculture may also provide the livelihoods of a significant proportion of the population in larger cities—although the portion of any city's workforce in agriculture is greatly influenced by how much the urban boundaries extend beyond the built-up areas. The fact that large proportions of the economically active populations in some of the largest cities of China and Bangladesh work in agriculture reflects the setting of urban boundaries that encompass large areas of agricultural land. Statistics on urban occupational structures are also unlikely to include most of those who engage in urban agriculture—for instance, those who do such work on a part-time basis or outside normal hours or who are not registered as working in agriculture (Smit, Ratta, and Nastr, 1996).

Urban Bias Revisited

Few would disagree with the statement that the policies of developing-country governments have often favored large cities and the urban elites (Lipton, 1976). Exchange rate, tariff, and tax policies appear to have penalized rural dwellers more than urban; by distorting economic signals, they have also reduced national output. In recent years, however, such price distortions have been reduced in many developing countries, often through reforms undertaken in programs of structural adjustment (Collier and Gunning, 1999a,b). Many price-related biases no doubt remain, and in rural areas they are compounded by poor transport systems and (in some cases) restrictions on competition among agricultural wholesalers and retailers.

Lipton (1993) argues that price distortions are no longer the main expression of urban bias, and that expenditure biases have become more important. In his view—one that is widely shared—public investments in infrastructure and social spending are often undertaken in cities without sufficient attention to the rates of return that could be secured from alternative rural investments.[14] In many countries in sub-Saharan Africa, public employment appears to have expanded in capital and other cities well beyond what can be justified on efficiency grounds (Becker, Hamer, and Morrison, 1994).

The urban bias argument is in part an argument about missed opportunities to improve economic efficiency through rural investment, but inequities are perhaps its dominant theme.[15] The demographic data presented in earlier chapters of this report—for instance, the data on public service delivery discussed in Chapter 5—document the many disadvantages suffered by rural populations by comparison with their urban counterparts. Although we have also drawn attention to the urban poor, who are themselves disadvantaged, these data serve as a reminder of the gross inequalities between urban and rural residents in many developing countries.

Although no one would dismiss the possibility of an urban bias in expenditures, the element of bias is more difficult to isolate than is commonly recognized. The spatial concentration of urban populations allows economies of scale and scope to be exploited in urban infrastructural investments, and these economies are not readily captured in dispersed rural settings (Becker and Morrison, 1999:1722; Montgomery, 1988). Investing in such rural infrastructure as irrigation, transportation, and agricultural extension can improve rural productivity, reduce food costs, and allow labor to be released for urban occupations. But when capital is scarce and the unit costs of rural investments are high, an argument can be made for an initial focus on urban investments (Williamson, 1965). In principle, one can imagine a fair-minded social planner choosing to schedule investments in urban and then rural phases. But these are speculative arguments. Acknowledging the many difficulties involved in assessing price and expenditure biases, Williamson (1988) points to the curious absence of empirical studies linking such

---

[14]For an analysis of the formidable difficulties involved in assessing rates of return to rural road investments, see van de Walle (2002).

[15]A genre of political–economic models explores these issues, noting that urban interests can sometimes be served by rural investments. In an extreme case (such as the Soviet Union in its industrialization phase), urban elites interested only in industrial development can agree to subsidize rural infrastructure to increase food supplies and keep urban wages low (Dixit, 1969). As Hansen (1979) argues, neither the rural nor urban elites (large landowners and industrialists) can be expected to have much interest in diminishing the pool of subsistence labor in their sectors. While industrialists might see benefits in giving urban workers schooling and other social infrastructure, measures to raise productivity in traditional agriculture may not work to benefit rural landlords and can be disadvantageous for urban industrialists. In this sense, an urban "bias" in public expenditures is to be expected, assuming that government is controlled by wealthy elites.

policy biases even to urbanization. The efforts of Malpezzi (1990) to link urban growth to measures of price distortion yield almost no correlation, and the earlier studies of Montgomery (1987) and Becker and Morrison (1988) are no more successful in isolating an effect. In short, although there is every reason to think that a measure of urban bias continues to plague pricing and expenditure policies in many countries, the magnitude of this bias remains unknown.

ECONOMIC RETURNS TO SCHOOLING

Earlier chapters have described the ways in which economic returns to schooling can affect demographic behavior.[16] That returns to schooling have a spatial dimension is well recognized. As suggested in the preceding section, gaps in schooling returns can be expected to emerge across the national space as economies urbanize and decentralize their city systems. The greater payoff to schooling in urban than rural areas is a main factor—perhaps the dominant one—in higher rates of migration among the educated.

Rates of return to schooling are also potentially important determinants of fertility. When the returns to investing in education are high, this can encourage families to adopt productive and reproductive strategies in which their fertility is reduced and investments in their children's education are increased. The "quantity–quality transition" is a central mechanism in economic development: it ultimately produces slower labor force growth and higher levels of human capital per worker.

The logic of supply and demand prompts doubt, however, about whether high returns to schooling can be sustained (Fallon and Layard, 1975; Montgomery, Arends-Kuenning, and Mete, 2000). In recent years, the supply of educated labor has been increasing rapidly in many developing countries, and although figures specific to urban areas are not widely available, we believe the urban increases have been particularly large. If other things were held constant, such supply shifts would depress the economic returns to schooling and mute the demographic responses described above. Of course, countervailing forces can be at work on the demand side that maintain or even increase high returns to schooling. The accumulation of physical capital can raise the relative demand for better-educated labor if skilled labor is complementary to capital (Fallon and Layard, 1975). Exogenous technological change—perhaps linked to manufactured exports—can also increase demand for better-educated labor. Recent economic theories of endogenous growth and the small empirical literature described above (Rauch, 1993; Moretti, 2000) suggest that urban concentrations of highly educated labor may generate positive spillovers that raise the returns to lower levels of schooling.

---

[16]See Krueger and Lindahl (2001) for a review of the concept and measurement of returns to schooling.

Such demand-side forces could well keep schooling returns high even in the face of rapid shifts in supply.

Psacharopoulos (1985, 1994) summarizes a large number of empirical estimates of the rate of return to primary, secondary, and tertiary schooling. (Many of these estimates are based on urban earnings regression equations.) In the developing world, the private returns to primary education range from 17 to over 40 percent, with the high estimates being found in early studies (some using questionable data) of sub-Saharan Africa. At the secondary-school level, estimates of returns vary from 16 to 27 percent, and at higher levels of schooling they lie in the 19–28 percent range.[17] Although private returns are unreliable guides to the social value of investments in schooling—for that purpose, they would need to be adjusted for educational subsidies, credentialism, and other factors that impart upward bias—they approximate the measures that families themselves consider in making demographic decisions.[18]

Are shifts in the supply of educated labor generally reducing the returns to schooling? There is some evidence to this effect for Korea (Kim and Topel, 1995), where the expansion of university schooling drove down its private rate of return in the 1980s. Elsewhere in Asia there is little evidence of any systematic decline; see Montgomery, Arends-Kuenning, and Mete (2000) for a review. In sub-Saharan Africa, however, unmistakable evidence has emerged of falling rates of return in those countries whose economies have been stagnant or worse. In such settings, the demand-side forces may simply be too weak to maintain the returns to schooling when rapid expansion is underway on the supply side.

The case of Taiwan, a country that has experienced rapid economic growth, is instructive. Lee and Mason (2001) document a substantial increase in the supply of better-educated urban adults. By 1998, about 25 percent of urban men in Taiwan had acquired a junior college or higher degree, and roughly 33 percent had graduated from high school, leaving 42 percent with a junior high school education or less. Urban Taiwanese women had achieved very similar levels of schooling. Yet as the supply of better-educated labor was expanding from 1978

---

[17]Although some high estimates are found in sub-Saharan African, the range is wide even here. For example, Cohen and House (1994) find that in the Sudan, the returns to primary school are lower than those to secondary, which in turn are lower than the tertiary returns—a reversal of the pattern usually assumed to hold—and that the returns are lower at all three levels of schooling than is typically reported in the literature. Bigsten, Collier, Dercon, Fafchamps, Gauthier, Gunning, Isaksson, Oduro, Oostendorp, Pattillo, Soderbom, Teal, and Zeufack (1998), having access to rich longitudinal data on workers in manufacturing firms in five countries (Ghana, Cameroon, Kenya, Zambia, and Zimbabwe), also show that in manufacturing, the returns to schooling are lowest for those with primary education, greater at the secondary level, and still greater for university graduates.

[18]See Knight and Sabot (1990) for an unusually penetrating discussion of the biases in rate-of-return estimates, based on two unusual surveys of wage earners in Nairobi and Dar es Salaam. In addition to years of schooling attained, these data include independent measures of cognitive and reasoning abilities. Earnings were found to be better predicted by cognitive scores—which arguably measure the amount of *learning* that takes place in school—than by years of schooling as such. The findings raise questions about the meaning of conventional rate-of-return calculations using years of schooling.

to 1998, the rates of return to schooling were actually increasing for those with secondary schooling and above, the largest gains being recorded by men with a college or junior college education. Meanwhile, men with less than a junior high school education saw their rates of return to schooling fall. For urban women, rates of return have also been rising among those with a junior college or higher education, although the trends at the low end of the educational distribution are less clear. Evidently, then, over a period of rapid increase in the supply of workers with secondary and tertiary schooling, other forces—perhaps having to do with technological change and capital accumulation—have somehow conspired to enhance the rates of return to that schooling.

The case of Brazil, studied by Lam and Dunn (2001), may exemplify the situation of countries experiencing slower but still positive economic growth. This research focuses on the nine largest Brazilian cities, whose populations together grew by 25 million between 1970 and 2000. The private rate of return to schooling has fallen in these cities, but the decline has been so small as to barely register. For men, the rate of return fell from 13 percent in 1977–1979 to 12 percent in 1997–1999 in the nine cities combined. The largest city, São Paulo, exhibited the lowest rates of return (12.6 and 11.2 percent at the beginning and end of the period, respectively), but the decline here was about the same as elsewhere. There is no evidence that urban rates of return were depressed by labor force growth—the declining rate of return is almost entirely a phenomenon of the 1990s, by which time labor force growth rates were themselves on the decline (Lam and Dunn, 2001: 17). Although the Brazilian data testify to the surprising durability of high private returns to schooling, they do not reveal what demand-side factors could be responsible for that persistence.

In urban Kenya, an expansion in education comparable to that of Taiwan and Brazil has not been accompanied by economic expansion; indeed, urban levels of consumption per capita have fallen steadily, declining by one-quarter from 1978 to 1995 (Appleton, Bigsten, and Manda, 1999). Over this period, the rate of return to secondary schooling deteriorated badly, falling by nearly two-thirds (Appleton, Bigsten, and Manda, 1999: Table 7). For those with primary schooling, the wage gains relative to having no schooling also declined.[19] At the tertiary level, however, it appears that the rates of return to schooling have either been constant or increased with time. Although declines in the quality of secondary schooling may have undermined its rate of return, Appleton, Bigsten, and Manda (1999) are skeptical that school quality can be the main explanation. In their view, the high returns enjoyed by early Kenyan cohorts were probably due to their ability to secure employment in well-protected niches of the urban economy.

The experience of Kenya shows that where macroeconomic growth has halted and deterioration set in, continued expansion of the supply of schooling can drive

---

[19]Nonetheless, the *social* rates of return to primary schooling held steady because there were reductions in the costs of schooling—teacher salaries fell along with the general decline in wages.

down its returns, except perhaps for the relatively small group of students who are able to make their way to university. It is not known whether the Kenyan experience applies to other sub-Saharan countries, although it is surely not atypical of countries in this region and elsewhere suffering from negative economic growth. Knight and Sabot (1990) show that in Tanzania, for example, recent cohorts of primary-school leavers have seen schooling returns of only 12 percent, well short of the 17 percent returns enjoyed by earlier cohorts. In urban Ghana, wage rates for the unskilled in manufacturing firms fell steadily during 1991–1995, as they had been doing for well over a decade, but the wages of skilled workers remained constant over the period, and the returns to skill thus increased (Teal, 2000). Matched worker–firm data assembled by Teal (2000) indicate that in Ghanaian manufacturing, skilled workers are more complementary to capital than are unskilled workers. A modest amount of capital accumulation in Ghanaian manufacturing may well have helped stabilize the wages of the skilled workers.

The lesson to be drawn from this collection of case studies is that educational expansion need not result in declines in urban returns to schooling, although supply shifts can certainly exert downward pressure when not opposed by forces on the demand side. The literature has not yet isolated the most important of the demand-side influences, although there is much speculation about the effects of physical capital accumulation, export orientation, and skill-biased technological change (Montgomery, Arends-Kuenning, and Mete, 2000). This is an area in urgent need of research attention.

MIGRATION AND ECONOMIC MOBILITY

Migration is generally viewed as a behavioral response to spatial differences in standards of living.[20] Much of the literature represents migration in terms of individual decisions involving comparisons of real wages or earnings. But in recent years this literature has substantially broadened, and it now accommodates a variety of assumptions about the relevant set of decision makers and the economic outcomes they may consider. One now sees family models of decision making that stress the distinct opportunities and costs facing women and men (Riley and Gardner, 1993; Yang and Guo, 1999; De Jong, 2000), household production perspectives in which some family members are deployed to urban areas and others to rural so as to maximize expected incomes (Zhao, 1999), and portfolio models in which migration is one tactic in the family's larger strategy for managing risk (Stark, 1991). Although much of the attraction of urban areas for migrants lies in the prospects for upward economic mobility after arrival, very few studies have examined urban income dynamics with the appropriate longitudinal data. Hence,

---

[20]Thorough reviews of the migration literature in economics include Yap (1977), Williamson (1988), Lucas (1997), and Becker and Morrison (1999). We stress the volitional aspects of migration here, recognizing that in some countries and regions, substantial migratory flows result from violence, political repression, and natural disaster.

it is difficult to say whether migrants' expectations generally coincide with the urban realities. This section closes with a review of what little is known about urban economic mobility.

We take the early Todaro (1969) and Harris and Todaro (1970) models of migration as points of departure for a broader discussion. These models are notable for clearly articulating how rural-to-urban migration is linked to the structure of the urban economy, as expressed in its labor market segments and wage rigidities. (The models do not address urban-to-urban migration.) In developing their models, Todaro and Harris placed special emphasis on the urban formal sector, which at the time was conceived to be a segment of the labor market offering relatively high wages and security of tenure. In what follows we review briefly the core elements of these models and describe how the discussion has advanced in the decades since they were formulated.

Revisiting the Todaro and Harris–Todaro Models

Textbook discussions of rural-to-urban migration often depict it as a response to the higher levels of real earnings available in urban areas. If rural and urban earnings are determined by market forces, a gap between them signifies a departure from the textbook ideal of an economy-wide equilibrium in which the value of the marginal product of labor is the same across locations. As rural-to-urban migration takes place, the shift of labor drives down urban real earnings and allows rural earnings to rise, leading the economy toward that equilibrium ideal. Migration thus enhances the efficiency with which the economy's full resources are deployed (Adelman and Robinson, 1978; Morrison and Guo, 1998).

This benign view of labor markets and migration is challenged by Todaro (1969) and Harris and Todaro (1970), who argue that in an important segment of the urban labor market—the so-called "formal sector"—wage rates are institutionally determined and set at levels too high to clear the market. Todaro and Harris further assume that rural residents will migrate or not depending on the prospects for formal-sector employment. Such jobs can be secured, however, only after a period of open unemployment and job search that will commence upon the migrant's arrival. Hence in deciding whether to move, potential migrants will take into account not only the formal-sector urban wage rate w_u, but also the probability p of securing such a job.[21] If the urban expected wage $w_u \cdot p$ exceeds the rural wage w_r, a rural resident will judge migration to be economically rational, provided that moving costs are negligible.[22]

---

[21]The time horizons envisioned in these models differ: Todaro (1969) imagines an infinite horizon with $p(t)$ representing the probability that a migrant has obtained a formal-sector job by t periods of residence in the city; in Harris and Todaro (1970), the migrant's time horizon is the length of a single period, and p is the chance of securing a formal-sector job in that period.

[22]To simplify his presentation, Todaro (1969) assumes that urban informal-sector earnings can be ignored; in effect, these earnings are treated as being fixed at zero. The probability p of securing a formal-sector job is specified by Todaro (1969) as the ratio of the number of new jobs created in a

In this framework, an incentive to migrate persists until $w_u \cdot p = w_r$, that is, until urban expected wages come to equal rural wages. Because urban formal-sector wages are fixed at w_u, additional migration to cities can serve only to increase urban unemployment and reduce p, the probability of employment. Eventually, unemployment will be driven high enough to equate urban expected earnings $w_u \cdot p$ to rural earnings. This is an equilibrium of sorts, but, as Todaro emphasizes, reaching it may require high rates of urban unemployment (Lucas, 1997: 734). The models also imply that attempts to stimulate the demand for labor in urban areas are apt to be counterproductive: with urban wages fixed, such demand-stimulating policies can only induce further rural-to-urban migration, raising the total amount of urban unemployment and possibly increasing the urban unemployment rate.[23] Hence, development effort is better expended on rural areas; if w_r is increased, the spillover benefits will be evident in higher urban employment probabilities.

In the early 1970s, this was seen as a compelling way to frame the issues. The Todaro and Harris–Todaro models drew together several strands of the literature that were just coming into prominence at the time—notably the notion of a dualistic, highly segmented urban labor market and the idea of equilibrium in expectations—and they provided further justification, if any was needed, for development efforts directed to rural populations. Supportive empirical evidence soon emerged in aggregate and some individual-level studies, notably those of Annable (1972), Barnum and Sabot (1977), and Cole and Sanders (1985). But as the Harris–Todaro framework came under increasing scrutiny, several key assumptions that had initially appeared sensible proved difficult to justify (Berry and Sabot, 1978; Kannappan, 1983, 1984, 1985, 1988).

Have urban formal-sector wage rates w_u indeed been rigid and fixed at levels high enough to preclude market clearing? As Watanabe (1976) observes, it must have appeared reasonable to assume so in the immediate postindependence era, when trade union pressures and desires to establish "livable" wage levels resulted in high declared minimum wages in some developing countries. In Watanabe's account, trade unions were particularly vigorous in East Africa, the region that supplied much of the inspiration for the Todaro and Harris–Todaro models. By the late 1970s, however, substantial evidence of wage flexibility had emerged in Kenya (Collier and Bigsten, 1981), and from 1978 to 1995, urban real minimum wage levels fell there by half (Appleton, Bigsten, and Manda, 1999). Even in the

---

period to the number of urban unemployed who would be competing for such jobs; Harris and Todaro (1970) specify p to be a function of the stock of urban employed relative to the full urban labor force. The Todaro approach assumes that once a formal-sector position is assumed, it can be held indefinitely; the Harris–Todaro approach, by contrast, depicts the urban labor market as being a kind of job lottery with wholesale turnover in each period.

[23]Whether the urban unemployment rate would necessarily increase is unclear. In the Harris–Todaro model, rural wages w_r rise with rural outmigration; both w_r and the urban employment probability p can adjust to establish equilibrium. In simple versions of this model, rightward shifts of urban demand reduce the equilibrium urban unemployment rate, although the total numbers unemployed can increase.

late 1960s and early 1970s, according to Watanabe (1976: Table 2), the general tendency across developing countries was to allow the real value of minimum wages to erode with inflation, and there is reason to doubt whether the legal minimums were ever systematically enforced in very many countries (Teal, 2000).

The scope for high, rigid urban wage setting is now believed to be narrow and is perhaps confined mainly to the public sector.[24] To be sure, in some countries government is the dominant formal-sector employer—according to Collier and Gunning (1999a), it accounted for half of formal employment in Kenya as recently as 1990—and wages appear to be set above market-clearing levels in some cases (Knight and Sabot, 1988). There are instances—in Egypt, for example—in which government hiring rules appear to exert a disproportionate influence on urban labor markets.[25] But in many countries, prolonged weak economic performance has created pressures on government budgets, making it increasingly difficult to finance their large public-sector wage bill. Consequently, public workforces have been maintained only by allowing salaries to decline. In the Sudan, for instance, real public-sector wages in the late 1980s had fallen by 30 percent from the levels that prevailed only a decade earlier (Cohen and House, 1996).

Urban open unemployment rates—which also figure prominently in the Todaro and Harris–Todaro models—have likewise proved difficult to interpret. Although exceptions can be found, the evidence has generally failed to show persistently high rates of open unemployment across the spectrum of developing-country cities (Kahnert, 1987; Kannappan, 1988). Open unemployment is simply not a sustainable job-search strategy for many urban job seekers. Fallon (1983), for instance, finds that in urban India, it is mainly secondary school-leavers who are openly unemployed; vigorous demand for university graduates has kept down their unemployment rates, and those who lack secondary schooling have few means to sustain themselves without work of some kind. For Venezuela, Schultz (1982) undertook a careful examination of the role played by unemployment rates in guiding migrants among alternative destinations. Recognizing that

---

[24]We have not discussed "efficiency wage" models that allow firms to set wages for some of their employees above the levels prevailing in the external labor market, either to reduce turnover and training costs or to encourage greater employee effort. These models are fundamentally different from the Harris–Todaro perspective in that the internal wage premium is not rigid, but is determined by the returns to firm-specific human capital, the costs of training and monitoring employees, and external market conditions. See Lucas (1997) and Becker and Morrison (1999) for reviews.

[25]According to Assaad (1997), the Egyptian government has officially guaranteed a public-sector position to all university graduates and graduates of technical secondary schools. The promise of employment has not been honored in recent years—the last cohorts to receive the promised public-sector jobs graduated in the early 1980s—but the guarantee remains on the books and has had a perverse effect on recorded rates of open unemployment. Those who want to maintain a place in the queue for public employment may register themselves as unemployed even as they work (unrecorded) in the private sector. The wage gap between public- and private-sector jobs has fallen in Egypt, according to Assaad, although discrimination against women in the private sector increases the relative attractiveness of public-sector employment for them, as do the nonwage benefits attached to government jobs.

open unemployment might not be a viable job-search strategy for poor potential migrants, he carried out separate analyses of migration by level of education. Schultz uncovered clear evidence that rates of unemployment mattered most for the better-educated potential migrants. Among those with primary schooling or less, unemployment rates exerted no discernible influence on locational decisions. Wage rates, however, mattered for all education groups.

The view that urban labor markets are separable into formal and informal sectors, with the formal sector offering high wages and long tenure and the informal sector low wages and insecure employment, is now recognized as simplistic and in need of substantial reappraisal. We return to the issues later in this chapter. The point to note here is that the distributions of earnings in formal and informal jobs often overlap; many studies have failed to detect any pronounced formal-sector wage advantage for comparable workers. Even where a formal-sector wage advantage once existed, it has tended to erode with time, with the deterioration being especially marked in Africa. As discussed below, a notable development of the past 20 years is the increasing informalization of urban labor and product markets, which has further weakened the case for focusing solely on the formal sector. In short, the assumption that rural migrants are motivated mainly by the prospect of formal-sector employment places more emphasis on this one segment of the urban labor market than is warranted.

Of all the assumptions that motivate the Todaro and Harris–Todaro models, perhaps the most understudied is that migrants must rely on a "move first, then search" strategy with regard to urban employment. Although this assumption cannot be categorically rejected, several case studies suggest that it, too, is open to question. An analysis by Bigsten (1996) of rural-to-urban migration in Kenya shows that many migrants have jobs arranged before they move, with circular migration providing a mechanism for transmitting job information. In a detailed study of migrants to Delhi, Banerjee (1981, 1983, 1986) finds that over half of migrants either had their urban jobs lined up before arrival or had received strong assurances that a position would be available. These Indian migrants tended to take positions similar to those held by their urban relatives and contacts. In Manila (Aratme, 1992) and Bangkok (Phongpaichit, 1993), there is clear evidence of prearranged employment, especially for informal-sector jobs. If these experiences from Kenya, India, the Philippines, and Thailand are indications of what is true more generally, open unemployment upon urban arrival may be less common than envisioned in the early theory.[26]

---

[26]Fields (1975) develops an interesting variant on the Harris–Todaro model in which urban residents can choose either to search full time for a formal-sector position (while being openly unemployed) or to search part time (while holding an informal-sector job) at reduced search efficiency. He retains the assumption of rigid formal-sector wages but allows informal-sector wage rates to be flexible. In the model's equilibrium, the rural wage w_r equals the expected urban wage from full-time search, which in turn equals the expected urban wage derived from informal-sector employment combined with part-time search. Because Fields assumes that informal-sector urban wages are flexible, his model predicts that in equilibrium, urban informal wage rates will lie below the levels of rural wages. A comparison

It is not really surprising that migrants would draw on information from their families, social networks, and other contacts before deciding to relocate. Information chains and social support networks have long been recognized as important to international migration (Palloni, Massey, Ceballos, Espinosa, and Spittel, 2001; Portes, 1995). Social networks have not received the same attention in studies of internal migration, but the literature shows that here, too, the networks of potential migrants can provide information and supportive ties that are helpful in job search. A study of Khartoum (Cohen and House, 1996) finds that urban employers often recruit new workers by asking their current employees to recommend family members or friends; employment information thus tends to circulate along family and ethnic lines. Kannappan (1988) also stresses these informal channels. A number of authors describe how rural-to-urban migran ts take care to maintain their rural connections (Naved, Newby, and Amin, 2001; Townsend and Garey, 1994; Hoops and Whiteford, 1983). In addition to the studies cited above, Hugo (1981), Fuller, Lightfoot, and Kamnuansilpa (1985), Menon (1987, 1988), and Root and DeJong (1991) stress the importance of both family ties and social networks to migration decisions. Moreover, as discussed in Chapter 6, social networks are important in facilitating migrants' adjustment to urban life (Lomnitz, 1997; Pick and Cooper, 1997; Selier, 1997; Srinivasan, 1997).

The Composition of Migrant Streams

Although the point is not much emphasized in economic theories of migration (see Stark, 1991, for an exception), it is obvious that the demographic and economic implications of migration differ depending on whether moves are permanent or temporary in nature. The case of China is of particular interest because in this country, temporary migration was a response to new economic opportunities emerging just as powerful state restrictions on movement were being eased. The Chinese case also illustrates how migration can present men and women with different risks and opportunities.

Yang and Guo (1999) describe temporary migration in China, relying on an unusually detailed study of Hubei province in central China. Here as elsewhere in the country, the household registration system (*hukou*, described in Chapter 4) assigns each citizen either an agricultural or a nonagricultural registration status. In the prereform era, a rural migrant could not gain access to urban employment, education, or social services without first obtaining a nonagricultural registration from the local urban government. When economic reforms began to stimulate new economic activities in Chinese cities, resulting in an increasingly diverse employment structure only a part of which fell under government control, the possibility

---

of wage rates alone would indicate that urban informal workers are poorer than rural residents. Once expectations of securing formal-sector employment are factored in, however, the levels of economic well-being of the two groups are seen to be the same. Expectations of upward mobility just compensate for the low level of current earnings among those currently employed.

emerged for rural migrants to take urban jobs while continuing to be registered as de jure agricultural residents. These migrants—whose urban location differs from their sector of registration—are "temporary migrants" in the sense of the phrase used in China. "Permanent migrants" are those whose registration status has been reconciled with their location, as happens with official job transfers and with better-educated migrants who are more likely to persuade local officials of the need to convert their status.[27]

The consequences of these developments are evident in very large-scale migration flows in China (Yeung, 2001), with credible estimates of the urban "floating population" (*liudong renkou*) of temporary migrants ranging as high as 50 million (Yang and Guo, 1999). The jobs held by temporary migrants offer long hours; poor working conditions; low and unstable pay; and little access to the in-kind benefits available to longer-term urban residents, such as medical insurance, pensions, subsidized transport, child care, and housing (Wang and Zuo, 1999). Construction work is a main source of employment, along with manufacturing, nursemaiding, marketing and services, garment work, and scrap collecting (Yeung, 2001, citing several sources). Temporary migrants are somewhat handicapped in securing better jobs because they lack the social networks that help longer-term residents gain access to information and obtain recommendations.

Temporary migrants in China are predominantly men—about three-quarters of the total, to judge from the Hubei survey used by Yang and Guo—probably because of the risks and stresses of their urban lives and the nature of the available employment. Rural married women are especially unlikely to become temporary migrants, whereas marriage is evidently not a strong disincentive for rural men. Temporary migrants tend to have an intermediate level of educational attainment, roughly equivalent to middle or junior secondary school. Those with less schooling can find it difficult to negotiate the complexities of urban environments, whereas the better-educated are often able to convert to nonagricultural status, thereby becoming permanent migrants. Yeung (2001) notes that permanent migrants are concentrated mainly in the professional and technical occupations and dominate urban-to-urban migration flows, whereas temporary migrants are much more likely to be engaged in rural-to-urban moves.

The sex differences that are so prominent in Chinese temporary migration are not seen across Asia.[28] In Thailand, for instance, the pronounced seasonality of agriculture has given rural women the opportunity for off-season migration to Bangkok, where many take short-term jobs in the service sector. Among

---

[27]Yeung (2001) gives a detailed account of the recent efforts of local governments to establish intermediate statuses, lying between the agricultural and nonagricultural categories of the *hukou* system, that would give rural migrants a degree of legitimacy and access to some urban entitlements, if not the full range.

[28]We do not attempt here a general review of male–female differences in migration, which vary greatly by country, region, and time period. The interested reader might consult Bilsborrow (1993), who provides a wide-ranging survey of female migration in developing countries with particular attention to conceptual and measurement issues, and Singelmann (1993), who offers a statistical portrait.

recent migrants to Bangkok, women outnumber men by the ratio of three to two (Phongpaichit, 1993). Some argue that the export orientation of Thailand, its relatively large urban service and tourist sectors, and employer perceptions that young women will work reliably for low wages have much enhanced the demand for female labor (Lim, 1993).

Phongpaichit (1993: Table 50) shows that social networks of friends and relatives are particularly important sources of employment information for Thai female migrants. Although male migrants also depend on social networks, they are more likely than women to conduct job searches for themselves. Some research suggests a gender-specific pattern in establishing migrant social networks: men are said to migrate first, with their contacts helping to establish networks and reduce risks, thereby facilitating subsequent rounds of migration on the part of women (Guest, 1993).

Urban Economic Mobility

Surprisingly little research has explored urban economic mobility using data with a longitudinal dimension. In part this is because longitudinal data are generally uncommon. Even where such data have been gathered, however, rural income dynamics and rural risks appear to have attracted more interest. The dearth of urban studies also reflects the heterogeneity of urban employment and the difficulties involved in accurately measuring net earnings and household consumption expenditures in any setting.

The few urban studies available tend to divide household consumption levels into quintiles or similar classes and record the transitions made among these classes over time, with a particular focus on transitions out of poverty (usually the lowest consumption quintile). These longitudinal studies challenge the view that upward mobility is more likely in urban than in rural areas. In both sectors, it appears, there can be considerable flux, and the estimates of transition rates for both are probably contaminated by measurement errors.[29]

Grootaert and Kanbur (1995) examine annual panel data on urban and rural households in Côte d'Ivoire from 1985 to 1988, a period in which per capita

---

[29] In addition to the literature reviewed below, see Gibson (2001) for Papua New Guinea. In Gibson's analysis, urban households exhibit less short-term variability in consumption than do rural households. Urban households may be better positioned to smooth consumption, at least over the short term, thanks to easier access to savings and loan accounts and the availability of medical or life insurance. This interpretation is consistent with the literature on savings rates in rural and urban areas reviewed earlier in this chapter, which suggests higher precautionary savings in rural areas. A rather different approach to measuring mobility, focusing on *intergenerational* mobility in the acquisition of schooling, is that of Andersen (2001) for Latin America. This analysis, using 18 surveys fielded in 1995–1998, examines the education attained by young adults as a function of the educational attainment of their parents. The percentage left unexplained by parental schooling is taken to be a measure of intergenerational mobility. Using the full national samples, Andersen finds that more-urbanized countries exhibit greater intergenerational mobility in schooling. However, separate regressions applied to urban and rural samples provide no clear evidence of greater intergenerational mobility in the urban areas.

consumption was falling for the country as a whole. Among the urban households that were initially poor (but not in extreme poverty), the proportion exiting poverty ranged from 15 to 55 percent, depending on the region. Rural households exhibited very similar out-of-poverty transition rates. Carter (1999) investigates economic mobility during 1993–1998 in the South African province of KwaZulu-Natal. He also finds substantial economic mobility in both the urban and rural parts of the province, but uncovers some evidence that upward mobility is more common in the urban areas (Carter, 1999: Table 2, 16).

In a detailed study of Lima, Glewwe and Hall (1998) examine per capita consumption expenditures from 1985 to 1990, this being an era of macroeconomic collapse when average incomes fell by 30 percent across Peru. Their study reveals substantial rates of mobility even for households in the lowest consumption quintile in 1985. Of these initially poor households, 40 percent had risen to the second or higher quintile by 1990. Conversely, among households initially in the second consumption quintile in 1985—those that might be described as near-poor—some 24 percent had descended into the lowest quintile by 1990.

Better-educated Peruvian households exhibited higher initial levels of consumption (in 1985) and were apparently more likely to sustain improvements in consumption even through the ensuing macroeconomic turmoil.[30] Rural migrant households were found to be more vulnerable to consumption declines, as were households with children. Glewwe and Hall show that social network ties among local kin could not provide much protection against consumption declines because all internal transfers dwindled as the Peruvian economy shrank. The small minority of households with international networks of kin and friends tended to be better protected.

Two studies of Malaysia—by Randolph and Trzcinski (1989) and Trzcinski and Randolph (1991)—take a longer-term perspective on mobility, examining individual transitions in relative earnings over the period 1967 to 1976. Using retrospective rather than panel data and restricting their analyses to men, these authors find that rural-to-urban migration combined with occupational change (presumably the common experience among migrants) increased the likelihood of upward mobility in relative terms.[31] Among the urban residents, men with greater education were found to be less likely to experience relative income decline over the period; as in the case of urban Peru, education appears to provide some protection against downward mobility.

---

[30]The latter is a bivariate result, which weakens when multivariate controls are introduced. It is disputed by Schady (2002), who was unable to confirm the result in a reanalysis using additional Peruvian datasets.

[31]The focus of this research is squarely on *relative* mobility. The earnings distribution in 1967 is divided into deciles, as is the 1976 distribution. A man who was in the lowest decline in both years is recorded as having experienced no mobility, even though his absolute income level might have changed considerably. These studies do not analyze urban and rural residents separately, and use retrospective reports of earnings that are of uncertain reliability for the self-employed and farmers.

This smattering of longitudinal studies, in which countries undergoing crises and wholesale structural change are overrepresented, may not be a reliable guide to urban economic mobility in less turbulent times. For the broader picture, it is necessary to consider cross-sectional studies in which migrant earnings can be compared with those of urban natives.[32] Vijverberg and Zeager (1994), who focus on Tanzania in the early 1970s, provide a particularly interesting example of this body of research. They find that rural-to-urban migrants attract lower wage offers than do urban natives in their first decade of city residence, but are able to secure higher earnings thereafter. One explanation for this crossover focuses on the migrants who arrive with the aim of accumulating capital to be used upon their return to the village. Such "target" migrants may well exert greater effort than urban natives in their first few years of city residence, much as international migrants are thought to do in their high-income host countries. Once they pass through an initial period of adjustment to city life, the greater work effort expended by migrants is rewarded by higher earnings.

Something of this pattern is also seen in a study of the Sudan by Cohen and House (1996), which shows increasing earnings for migrants by length of stay in Khartoum, possibly attributable in this case to the accumulation of firm-specific experience.[33] In urban Bolivia, Chiswick, Patrinos, and Hurst (2000) find that rural migrants who have stayed in the city for more than 5 years have significantly higher earnings than migrants who have arrived more recently, although rural migrants evidently never surpass the earnings of urban natives. (By contrast, urban-to-urban migrants in Bolivia achieve higher earnings than city natives.) Female migrants who cannot speak Spanish—mainly older, rural-born women and recent arrivals—face earnings penalties, whereas monolingual Spanish speakers (whether male or female) can command an earnings premium. These earnings paths testify to positive selectivity—on average, migrants must be an unusually energetic and resourceful group—and to the adjustment difficulties faced by many migrants upon arrival.

THE INFORMALIZATION OF URBAN LABOR MARKETS

As we have seen with regard to migration, the proposition that the urban economy can be divided into formal and informal sectors has attracted an enormous amount of research attention over the past 30 years. Doubt has been cast on a number of

---

[32] It has long been recognized that cross-sectional studies of migrant earnings by duration of stay are vulnerable to selectivity bias in that those migrants who have been successful are probably more likely to remain. Although some upward bias is probable, the size of the bias is unknown.

[33] In bivariate analyses, migrants with 6 or more years of residence in Khartoum were found to earn more than native residents in several sectors: public-sector employment, small but protected private employment, and unprotected private employment. Migrants earned somewhat less than urban natives when employed in large private firms and self-employed. These migrant–nonmigrant comparisons were not pursued in detail in multivariate analyses.

assumptions about these sectors, raising the question of whether it is still useful to organize thinking about the urban economy under such broad headings.[34] The categories of formal and informal reflect a general belief that urban markets are separable into segments and that barriers of various kinds hinder movement from one segment to the other. If this is so, then urban economic diversity and inequality can be explained, at least in part, by reference to the barriers that prevent earnings from being equalized.[35] A thorough review of the issues is beyond the scope of this chapter, but in what follows, we touch on some of the arguments that link the formal–informal distinction to urban inequalities and speculate about the implications for urban income growth.

As can well be imagined, urban jobs and economic enterprises are too varied, and the data about them too crude, for two categories of employment to be adequate. In addition, many city dwellers hold multiple jobs, such as when a wage earner in a large firm also operates a small business on the side. To define employment as formal or informal, the International Labour Organization (ILO) has highlighted only three of the many possible dimensions: whether a worker is self-employed; the size of the firm; and coverage by government systems of employment registration, taxation, or regulation. In the ILO definition, the informal sector comprises the self-employed, those who are working in firms with fewer than five employees, workers with no registration, owners of a family business with fewer than five employees, and family members working in a family business without a specified wage.[36] This classification assigns to the formal sector all government employees and both the owners and employees of large firms.

---

[34]Initially inspired by Hart's 1973 work in Ghana, the concept of an informal sector gained popularity in the 1970s, thanks to the efforts of the International Labour Office's World Employment Programme and affiliated researchers (for example, Bromley and Gerry, 1979). Turnham, Salomé, and Schwartz (1990) and Mead and Morrison (1996) provide critical reviews.

[35]Not all conceptions of the informal sector emphasize the barriers to mobility. De Soto (1987) views the informal sector as a response to the excessive power of the state and its overly restrictive regulations. The autonomy enjoyed by small firms and entrepreneurs is risked if by growing larger, they expose themselves to taxation and regulation (Tybout, 2000). Some observers view informal-sector growth as being beneficial because they believe it fosters labor market flexibility and adaptability more generally. An alternative view, held by some neo-Marxist functionalists, is that small-scale production provides a reservoir of labor willing to work at near-subsistence levels (see Déblé and Hugon, 1982), keeping wage levels low (and profits high) in formal-sector enterprises. Informal-sector growth can also reflect efforts by large enterprises to shed costs by outsourcing and subcontracting some of their operations to unprotected workers. For Lautier (1994), the informal economy is not an economic sector in any conventional sense, but rather constitutes a parallel economy in which virtually any activity might be represented, from urban agriculture to transportation and financial services. Even Hart (1995) now proposes to abandon the "informal economy" label.

[36]In 1997, the ILO clarified its 1993 definition (based on size and capitalization of firms), defining the informal sector in terms of characteristics of the production units (enterprises) in which the activity takes place, rather than characteristics of the persons involved or their jobs. Accordingly, the population employed in the informal sector was defined as comprising all persons who are employed in at least one production unit of the informal sector, irrespective of their employment status or whether this employment is their main or a secondary job.

A few examples—using definitions similar if not identical to that of the ILO—may suffice to indicate the extent of the informal sector.[37] Arnaud (1998), reviewing evidence from a number of West African cities, finds it reasonable to classify fully 70 percent of employment as informal. In Kazakhstan, only 27 percent of the country's labor force pays social taxes; even if all of these workers were urban residents, the formal sector thus defined would constitute only 56 percent of the urban labor force (Anderson and Becker, 2001). For Kyrgyzstan, data on social contributions indicate that just 64 percent of the labor force works in the formal sector (Becker and Paltsev, 2001).[38] In urban India, the self-employed accounted for 16 percent of employment in 1987–1988, but by 1993–1994 their share had risen to 34 percent. In Mumbai alone, informal jobs increased from 44 percent of the total in 1971 to 55 percent in 1981 (Deshpande and Deshpande, 1991). In São Paulo, the formal sector's share of employment fell from 54 percent in 1988 to 43 percent in 1998 (Buechler, 2000). Boxes 8.2 and 8.3 provide detailed analysis of the informal sector in Brazil, and São Paulo in particular. To many observers, examples such as these indicate that the informal sector's share of urban employment is large and may be on the rise.

Barriers to Mobility?

It is one thing to say that the informal sector is large and growing, but quite another to assert that those who work there are separated from the formal sector by cross-sectoral barriers. Surprisingly few studies have explored this distinction with data in which individual workers are followed over time. Maloney (1999), who uses longitudinal data from urban Mexico in the early 1990s, uncovers little in his data to support dualistic views. For Mexico, the evidence on employment transitions is more consistent with the operation of "a well-integrated market in which workers search for job opportunities across sectors than with one in which informal workers seek permanent status in the formal sector and stay until they retire" (Maloney, 1999: 291).

The data in question were collected over a 15-month period from 1991 to early 1992, a relatively prosperous period for Mexico characterized by very low (measured) unemployment. Selected transition rates for those working at the beginning and end of this period are shown in Table 8-1. Even over this short time span, high rates of individual mobility are evident, with considerable movement to and from formal-sector salaried employment. (The formal sector comprises all firms with

---

[37]No comprehensive assessment of levels and trends in informal employment can be made here. Sethuraman (1981) provides estimates of the share of the urban labor force working in the informal sector for a number of cities in the late 1970s.

[38]These are upper-bound estimates for Kyrgyzstan because some informal-sector participants maintain nominal formal-sector job status to retain eligibility for benefits, and many outside the official labor force have informal-sector occupations.

BOX 8.2 Rising Informal Employment in São Paulo

Between 1989 and 1999, according to Buechler (2000), public-sector employment in São Paulo shrank from 635,000 to 609,000, and private registered salaried employment also declined, from 3.4 to 2.9 million. The remainder—one measure of São Paulo's informal labor force—grew from 2.4 to 3.7 million, an annual growth rate of over 4 percent. (See Lam and Dunn, 2001, for other measures of informal employment.)

In 1988 industry employed 29 percent of workers in the municipality, but by 1998 this share had fallen to only 18 percent. Schiffer (2000) argues that much of the city's manufacturing activity has relocated to other cities, and that São Paulo has become much more service oriented. There has been a noticeable "casualization" of work, with an increase in small businesses operating at the fringes of the formal economy, engaged in self-employment, part-time work, home work, construction, sweatshop manufacturing, street vending, and other retail trade. Buechler (2000) argues that these sectors have grown as a result of the increasing competition that accompanies economic openness and liberalization—in effect, that globalization has led to informalization.

While manufacturing has declined, there has been considerable growth in high-end, skill-intensive services. With increases in outsourcing, some skilled and professional jobs formerly listed under manufacturing are now classified under services. São Paulo's informal sector has strong links to the formal sector, as is evident in the number of unregistered workers working in large firms and the self-employed who are associated with a single such large firm. As Buechler notes, formal-sector employees may choose to depart for the informal sector in their search for jobs offering greater independence and flexibility (in her qualitative interviews, quits were recorded more often than layoffs). Also, informal-sector growth presumably reflects efforts by employers to evade cost-increasing regulations, taxes, and social payments.

---

six or more workers.) The percentages on the diagonal from upper left to lower right show that formal salaried employment is the most persistent of the statuses, but even these job spells can be short, with some 22 percent of formal job-holders leaving in little more than a year. The likelihood of exiting formal salaried employment declines with education (not shown), suggesting that the better-educated

---

BOX 8.3 Does Urban Population Growth Swell the Informal Sector?

Examining evidence from the nine largest Brazilian cities, Lam and Dunn (2001: Figure 6, Table 2) find no correlation between the percentage of urban workers who are unregistered and the growth rate of either the urban labor force or the urban population. Nor do they find a correlation between unemployment rates and rates of city population or labor force growth. Population and labor force growth rates have been falling since the 1980s, while unemployment rates have been rising.

The rise in urban unemployment in Brazil must have been due primarily to other factors—perhaps macroeconomic shocks and policies. Difficulties in accommodating labor force growth are unlikely to have been a primary cause.

TABLE 8-1 Employment Transitions in Urban Mexico, 1991–1992 (percentages of workers by employment status in 1992, given status in 1991)

1991 Status	1992 Status				
	Unpaid	Self-employed	Informal Salaried	Contract Work	Formal Salaried
Unpaid	27	16	18	6	13
Self-Employed	1	69	9	5	10
Informal Salaried	3	16	41	7	29
Contract Work	0	15	10	45	26
Formal Salaried	0	6	7	5	78

NOTE: The rows do not sum to 100 percent because we have omitted several statuses: out of the labor force, in school, unemployed, and employed in "other" work than listed above.

SOURCE: Maloney (1999: Table 5).

may perceive brighter prospects for advancement within the formal sector than do workers with less education.[39]

Maloney finds that by their own accounts, about two-thirds of those leaving formal salaried positions for self-employment did so voluntarily. Transitions to self-employment are more likely for prime-age workers, probably because some start-up capital is needed to begin a small business. In Mexico, at least, self-employment is not an entry-level sector for the young.[40] These findings echo the views of Gregory (1986), who expresses doubt about dualistic characterizations of urban labor markets in Mexico. Tybout (2000), assembling evidence on rates of formal-sector entry and exit in Chile, Colombia, Morocco, Korea, and Taiwan, also documents high transition rates.

Lacking longitudinal data, other researchers have attempted to glean evidence on formal–informal barriers from data on wage rates or earnings by sector of employment. Unfortunately, evidence of persistent wage differences does not necessarily constitute evidence of barriers to mobility. Any job is associated with a bundle of nonwage characteristics, and the earnings from a particular type of job would be expected to vary systematically with such characteristics.[41] Persistent

---

[39] A study of Côte d'Ivoire also shows that formal education is an important determinant of formal-sector employment, with a suggestion of credentialism on the part of formal-sector employers (Grootaert, 1992).

[40] Similar conclusions were reached by Blau (1986), who studied transitions from employee to self-employed status in Malaysia. He found that among men in their prime working ages, transitions from employee to self-employed are much more likely than transitions from self-employed to employee. Among migrants to urban areas, the likelihood of being self-employed *rises* with time since migration. It appears that in Malaysia, as elsewhere, a significant number of the self-employed are small-scale entrepreneurs whose operations require a base of start-up capital that must be pieced together over time.

[41] Apart from average wages or earnings, the relevant job characteristics include other benefits apart from earnings, such as subsidized health care or social security; the variance of earnings; the future

wage differences (among comparable workers) could be taken as evidence of barriers to mobility, but might instead reflect sorting according to nonwage characteristics. Small-scale entrepreneurs, for instance, could prefer their work to better-paying employment in a large firm because they value the autonomy and independence that comes with being one's own boss. All this renders the interpretation of wage differences problematic.

Interestingly, in the study of Mexico mentioned above, Maloney (1999) finds that transitions from self-employment and contract work to formal salaried employment bring significant declines in earnings, whereas those leaving formal salaried employment for either self-employment or contract work realize significant earnings gains. But it is difficult to be sure that these are real losses and gains, because formal-sector jobs in urban Mexico often provide health benefits as part of the compensation package. Transitions to self-employment from other informal work—which probably do not entail a loss of benefits—also bring substantial increases in earnings.[42] Maloney shows that informal salaried-worker earnings are the lowest among the urban groups he studies, although this finding may be attributable in part to implicit training costs and other unmeasured factors.

Similarly mixed results appear in other research. In a study of urban Brazil, Telles (1993) finds that self-employed men who are protected by labor legislation do as well as or better than their formal-sector counterparts, but unprotected workers fare worse. For urban Peru, Yamada (1996) compares earnings in the informal sector with those in public and private formal-sector jobs. Informal-sector work provides an income premium relative to the private formal sector, perhaps because it gives a greater return to entrepreneurial abilities. In 1985 the Peruvian public sector still offered an earnings premium, but by 1990 this premium had vanished in the wake of repeated macroeconomic shocks and hyper-inflation. In Indonesia, however, Thomas, Beegle, and Frankenberg (2000) show that in 1997, urban public-sector employment provided a substantial wage premium relative to private-sector employees and that this premium increased when the Asian financial crisis reached Indonesia in 1998. The urban self-employed

---

returns to skills and on-the-job training, which may not be fully reflected in current earnings; the risks and stresses of working conditions; the degree of autonomy and independence that can be exercised by the job-holder; and the likelihood of involuntary job loss.

As Maloney (1999) argues, to interpret evidence of earning differentials in terms of market barriers and rigidities, one must have a sense of what these differentials would have been in the absence of such rigidities. In a hypothetical world in which individuals have identical preferences, labor markets are in equilibrium, and earnings are flexible, jobs would provide levels of earnings that would just compensate for their nonwage characteristics (Rosen, 1974). Although they would generally offer different wage rates, in equilibrium all types of jobs would provide the same level of utility. This hypothetical situation can serve as a benchmark against which empirical evidence of earnings differentials can be measured.

[42] Another interpretive difficulty, noted by Lucas (1997: 737), is that data on the earnings of the self-employed may not adequately distinguish *net* earnings from sales, and may overstate the premium associated with self-employment.

had no precrisis earnings advantage over private-sector employees in Indonesia, but made a substantial gain (in relative terms) during the crisis.

In summary, the recent evidence on wage differences by sector is far from uniform, revealing much country-to-country variation and offering few general lessons. Most of the studies reviewed by the panel find that the informal sector contains some groups with decidedly lower earnings than those available in formal-sector jobs. But the informal sector also contains what might be termed an "upper tier" of individuals and enterprises whose net earnings appear to exceed those of formal-sector occupations. The formal sector is itself heterogenous and difficult to characterize, with public-sector employment offering a wage premium in some settings but not in others (Lucas, 1997: 762).

Taken as a group, the studies reviewed here lend little support to the notion that persistent earnings differences are the result of barriers to mobility that separate formal from informal work. We do not see convincing evidence that such barriers are insurmountable or that they cause urban earnings to be more unequal than they might otherwise be. To be sure, the literature on this issue remains thin, but the burden of proof appears to have shifted to those who contend that mobility constraints are significant. Definitive conclusions must await longitudinal data on employment transitions, and for the moment such data remain scarce.

Increasing Heterogeneity

If the developments of the past two decades could be summed up in a sketch, it might read as follows. In the 1980s and 1990s, macroeconomic crises and restructuring had the effect of curtailing wage-earning employment in many public and private enterprises. International assistance was often extended on terms that required reductions in government expenditures, a commitment to privatization, and the imposition of cost containment measures in state-owned enterprises. Where such programs were implemented, parastatal enterprises and many private firms cut employment; in many cases, recruitment to the civil service all but ceased.[43] Some formerly protected, subsidized, traditional industries shrank as governments cut tariff protections and exposed their economies to the world markets. Buenos Aires, for example, lost a third of its industrial jobs from 1974 to 1985, and its unemployment rate rose from 6 percent in 1991 to 18 percent in 1995 (Prévôt-Shapira, 2000). Those who lost wage employment in the formal sector often had little recourse but to take up informal employment.

At the same time, however, informal-sector entrepreneurs moved aggressively into fields that had been largely abandoned by the public sector, such as transportation. Large industrial enterprises developed subcontracting links to informal units that specialized in business services (Sassen, 1994b), such as small maintenance and repair workshops and computer services. In China, the towns and small cities of the Pearl River delta became home to numerous small industrial

---

[43]McCulloch, Baulch, and Cherel-Robson (2000) give a detailed account for the case of Zambia.

units connected by subcontracts to large enterprises in Hong Kong. Where new urban elites emerged, consumer service firms also sprang up to provide them with caterers, couriers, dog walkers, security guards, and home deliverymen, much as in the cities of high-income countries.

In short, while the "lower tier" of the urban informal sector may have been the recipient of substantial inflows from the formal sector and elsewhere, with earnings thereby deteriorating, other segments of the informal sector may well have been revitalized and linked profitably to domestic and even international partners. If in an earlier era the urban economy could be depicted as divided along the lines of formal and informal sectors, today there is an increasing appreciation of the polarization taking place within the informal sector itself (see Crankshaw and Parnell 2003, for the case of Johannesburg). These developments are exceedingly difficult to quantify, and no doubt vary greatly among countries and among cities in any given country; nevertheless, they merit discussion.

In the view of many observers, the changes sketched above have had the effect of making employment more precarious, even for those who hold formal-sector positions. The stratum of supervisors and skilled employees, which might once have appeared reachable by means of steady advancement within a firm, has become unsettled as a result of growing job flexibility and economic reversals. Pressures on government payrolls and formal-sector salaries have presented employees with few options but to seek outside supplements to their incomes.[44] Patterns of work and residence may be becoming increasingly fluid, with many workers alternating between formal and informal activities. Even for skilled workers, fixed-term contracts and the vagaries of international demand have transformed working life from a stable, dependable routine to a ceaseless search for the next contract and connection. In a way, then, even the conditions of employment in the formal economy have become informalized, at least to a degree (Vandemoortele, 1991; Roberts, 1991).

It is an open question whether developments such as these can provide a firm foundation for future urban income growth. Is it really likely that the informal sector, thus roiled and reconstituted, will become sufficiently dynamic to generate economic growth?

Except where migration responds to dramatic growth in demand (as in the case of China described earlier), the opportunities available in the lower tier of the informal sector will probably remain quite limited. Urban agriculture—often practiced by street food vendors who grow their food locally—may have some potential for growth through closer integration with rural areas. The lower tier will probably continue to function as an entry point for some migrants and as a safety net for others, an economic niche where financial considerations are balanced against traditional social obligations (Ellis and Fauré, 1995). The role of crisis

---

[44] In Buenos Aires, the *contratos basuras* are growing in number, and some 20 percent of job seekers are actually currently employed workers looking for a second job because of a drop in their salaries (Prévôt-Shapira, 2000).

regulator and cushion, however, has its limits. It is difficult to imagine that large enterprises are likely to develop or significant skills accumulate within this tier.

One recent study of the informal sector in sub-Saharan Africa reports that the most successful informal firms are neither the smallest nor the largest, but those of intermediate size (Fauré and Labazée, 2000). These enterprises rarely evolve from smaller units, except in the cases of civil engineering and transportation. They are typically formed by the transfer of commercial capital and are created by investors with vocational training, such as skilled workers made redundant in the formal sector. These units often have the capacity to grow in their technical sophistication (auto parts and other small urban metallurgy enterprises are developing in Nigeria, as are manioc and cereal milling firms) and rarely employ recent migrants, perhaps because success requires both skills and urban social connections. Even in this upper tier of the informal sector, however, business profits are not necessarily reinvested in the accumulation of capital. Rather than expand the scale of their operations, many successful small entrepreneurs evidently prefer to diversify their activities and reduce risks by investing in trade, transportation, and construction (Collier and Gunning, 1999a,b).

The continued vitality of the informal sector will depend on access to reliable public services and infrastructure (water, electricity, communications, road networks), on the quality of urban management, and on the development of complementary business services.[45] Infrastructural constraints can be especially frustrating for informal-sector businesses, which typically lack the capital to substitute for poorly delivered public services (for example, by purchasing their own generators to protect against electricity outages). Informal-sector development is also hindered by the absence of complementary business services and by the weaknesses of legal systems and governmental oversight (Collier and Gunning, 1999a,b). It is not surprising, then, that informal-sector profits tend to be used for purposes of diversification rather than capital accumulation.

In summary, our impression is that the informal sector encompasses an increasingly diverse set of activities; one can speak of high tiers and low tiers, of protected and unprotected workers, and yet further distinctions among informal enterprises are doubtless warranted. The formal sector is also more heterogeneous than was recognized in the early theoretical conceptions. In addition, the links between the informal and formal sectors appear to be growing increasingly complex and subtle.

According to our reading of the evidence, no insurmountable barriers appear to divide these two sectors. If this view is correct, then the terms "formal" and "informal" are now useful mainly as evocative labels that suggest general characteristics, rather than being descriptive of deep-seated market rigidities and dualisms. The diversity of both formal and informal sectors, as well as the frequency

---

[45]But for a cautionary view, see Davis, Kang, and Vincent (2001), who find that poor water supplies do not greatly constrain micro enterprises in two Ugandan towns. These small units have water needs not unlike those of households in volume.

of passage between them, means that the root causes of urban inequalities must be sought in the opportunities and constraints that can be found in both sectors.

EARNINGS INEQUALITY: CASE STUDIES

Ideally, the developments described in the three preceding sections—changes in the returns to schooling, the economic mobility experienced by migrants, and the increasing differentiation of both formal and informal urban sectors—could be drawn together to form a comprehensive picture of urban economic inequalities. At the moment, that goal lies beyond reach, but the broad outlines of a portrait of inequality can be glimpsed in selected country case studies. We examine the case of Brazil first, and then consider Taiwan and China.[46]

Brazil

It is plausible to suppose that most countries have rich and poor cities and that much of urban inequality has to do with differences in income across cities. Indeed, earlier chapters of this report have documented substantial socioeconomic differences by city size, as seen in levels of public service provision, children's schooling, and fertility, among other indicators. But the demographic surveys we have relied upon are not of sufficient size to allow within-city inequalities to be clearly exposed.

To examine both inter- and intracity inequality, Lam and Dunn (2001) exploit a 20-year series of large labor force surveys for Brazil, covering the period 1977 to 1999. Restricting attention to the country's nine largest cities, Lam and Dunn (2001: 15) find that earnings inequality is "primarily generated within cities rather than across cities. Although differences in mean earnings between cities are as large as two to one, these differences make a relatively modest contribution to overall inequality, given the much larger earnings differentials observed within every city." Taking the variance of the logarithm of earnings as a measure of inequality, Lam and Dunn show that over 90 percent of earnings variance is attributable to within-city earnings differences.[47]

A large component of earnings variance—about 45 percent—is due, in turn, to variation in the number of years of schooling attained by Brazilians and the

---

[46]Many factors other than those discussed here can affect earnings inequality. For instance, Ashenfelter and Oaxaca (1991) report findings from a set of studies examining labor market discrimination in developing countries. Large earnings differentials between men and women that are attributable to discrimination are found in Tanzania, Brazil, and Nicaragua; similarly large differences are found between Africans (blacks) and non-Africans (Asians) in Tanzania, and between scheduled and non-scheduled castes in Delhi.

[47]Lam and Dunn are unable to adjust nominal earnings for price differences among Brazilian cities, which they acknowledge may be considerable. Such price differences affect the variance of earnings across cities, and leave unclear whether the observed cross-city differentials are nominal or real.

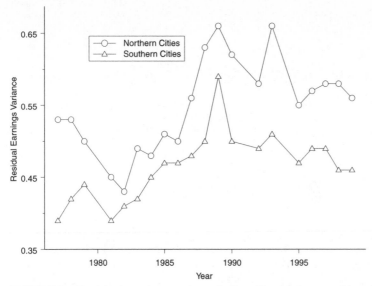

FIGURE 8-1 Residual earnings variance in Brazil's nine largest cities, 1977–1999.
NOTE: The figure shows the s^2 from earnings regressions that include age and educational attainment.
SOURCE: Interpolated from Lam and Dunn (2001).

economic returns to schooling.[48] Schooling in Brazil accounts for an unusually large share of earnings inequality by international standards—taking about three times the share found in the United States. Interestingly, the variance of earnings in São Paulo is the lowest among the nine cities considered by Lam and Dunn, partly because the returns to schooling are slightly lower there.

Although schooling can account for a great deal of earnings variance in Brazil, it leaves a considerable portion of that variance unexplained. Over the 20-year period examined by Lam and Dunn, the unexplained component of earnings variance increased substantially, as can be seen in Figure 8-1. The high inflation of the late 1980s played a role in the rising trend, but that trend must also reflect the increasing heterogeneity of Brazil's urban labor markets discussed earlier (see Box 8.2 for São Paulo).

---

[48]Consider the earnings equation $Y = \beta S + X'\gamma + \epsilon$, where Y is the logarithm of earnings, S is schooling attainment in years, X represents other explanatory factors, and ϵ is a disturbance term uncorrelated with the S and X variables. The variance of Y can be expressed as

$$V_Y = \beta^2 V_S + 2 \cdot \beta C'_{S,X}\gamma + \gamma' V_X \gamma + \sigma_\epsilon^2,$$

where V_Y, V_S, and V_X are variances, and $C_{S,X}$ is a covariance matrix. Lam and Dunn (2001) focus on the two main roles of schooling evident in this expression: the return to schooling coefficient β and the variance of schooling V_S. Their regressions are sex-specific, with age being the only X variable included.

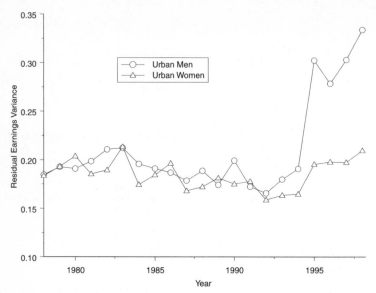

FIGURE 8-2 Residual earnings variance in urban Taiwan, 1978–1998.
NOTE: The figure shows the s^2 from earnings regressions that include age and educational attainment.
SOURCE: Lee and Mason (2001).

Taiwan

Using similar techniques, Lee and Mason (2001) examine changes over time in earnings inequality in Taiwan.[49] Inequality (again measured by the variance in the logarithm of earnings) has been low there by world standards, and from 1978 to 1988 it declined further before rising in the mid-1990s. Within Taiwan's urban sector alone, earnings inequality showed little change from 1978 until the 1990s, when it began to rise. Lee and Mason attribute some of the increase in inequality to the entry of women into the urban labor force, which increases the spread of urban earnings because women generally earn less than men. However, two related factors partly offset this effect: the variance of women's earnings is smaller than that of men, and the male–female earnings gap has begun to close. Higher returns to schooling in urban labor markets have also increased the variance of earnings, but higher schooling attainment has tended to decrease it.

Yet much of the recent increase in urban inequality, at least for Taiwanese men, is due to unmeasured forces that generated markedly higher earnings variances in the 1990s. Figure 8-2 shows the time path of the residual variance in urban earnings for men and women, with these variances estimated net of age and educational attainment for each sex. As can be seen, the residual variances fluctuated with a mild downward drift in the years 1979 to 1994, but then rose sharply.

---

[49]Lee and Mason are not able to include the self-employed in their analyses.

The increase predates the Asian financial crisis years, although the crisis must have had a further unsettling effect. But while earnings variances were rising for men, decidedly less change is evident for women, and nothing akin to the urban increase is apparent in earnings variances in rural areas (not shown). It is tempting to speculate that in Taiwan, increasing urban variances are the product of globalization and informalization, but no direct evidence confirms this notion as yet.

China

Khan, Griffin, and Riskin (1999) find evidence of increasing income inequality within China's cities over the period 1988 to 1995, when many of the work-unit and government subsidies previously enjoyed by urban households all but disappeared. Although the composition of urban incomes changed considerably (cash incomes from employment rose from 44 to 61 percent of household income over this period, while housing and miscellaneous subsidies fell from 39 to 11 percent), inequality also increased within each category of income. The within-category effects were by far the dominant influence on overall urban inequality. Khan, Griffin, and Riskin (1999) also find that measured urban poverty rates increased somewhat over the period, and speculate that greater increases might well have been recorded if proper account could have been taken of urban price changes and the incomes of the enormous "floating population" of migrants, which are not covered in the available data.

Using a sample of large Chinese cities that administer adjacent rural counties, Wei and Wu (2001) show how urban economic growth can spill over to benefit such rural areas, thereby reducing urban/rural inequalities. The main focus of this analysis is on the international trade orientation of Chinese cities in the period 1988–1993. To measure inequality between cities and their rural surroundings, Wei and Wu construct ratios of urban and rural GDP per capita, using city-specific data and including only the rural areas that fall under a city's control. For cities that grew more open with respect to trade—those for which the value of city exports relative to city GDP rose—inequality between the city and its rural counties fell. The results are robust to several changes in empirical specification and are not limited to the coastal cities alone. They hint at the increasing importance of international linkages to the character of internal, national-level economic relationships—a topic explored in the next section.

THE FUTURE OF URBAN LABOR MARKETS: GLOBAL LINKS AND LOCAL OUTCOMES

The increasing speed and depth of international communication and economic exchange will surely have profound consequences for the cities of poor countries. But these countries differ greatly in the extent to which their economies are exposed to such forces: a few are rapidly dismantling barriers to trade and investing heavily in communications infrastructure, others are proceeding at a more cautious pace, and some appear to be decidedly reluctant participants in global networks of exchange. Historical legacies, sunk costs, and policy stances vary so greatly among poor countries that no general pronouncements about globalization and its urban consequences are really possible.

The spatial implications are especially complex. Even a partial list suggests just how many contingencies need to be taken into account in thinking about the local spatial expressions of international linkages. Reductions in trade barriers give local firms access to larger markets and enable them to exploit economies of scale. Yet when firms that were formerly protected make their international debuts, the less efficient among them will likely be driven back to a purely domestic role. When firms in high- and low-income countries are linked in customer–supplier relationships, this link can provide a conduit for the transfer of technology and economic learning, whether about production processes, markets, or commercial strategies. But technology transfer is probably less broadly beneficial when it involves local firms that extract and export raw materials as compared with firms that export manufactured goods. In some countries, manufactured exports are produced in enclaves with easy access to raw materials (or sited across national borders from high-income consumers), whereas the firms that were once sheltered by import substitution policies are found in the large metropolises (Becker and Morrison, 1999: 1719). The returns to having superior transport and communications infrastructure are likely to favor the large cities of most countries, at least until investments can be undertaken in their smaller cities. But if this observation would appear to suggest a measured and orderly spatial progression, consider that in some cases—notably in China's Pearl River delta—massive programs of infrastructural investment as part of the development of the greater Hong Kong metropolitan region have been put in place with surprising speed, enabling smaller cities to exploit specialized niches and linkages in the international economy.

In what follows, then, we attempt no general predictions. Rather, we highlight a few of the developments associated with globalization that appear likely to impinge on urban demography. We first consider how foreign direct investment can shape local economic space. Next, we examine an emerging sector of high-end business services—a notably dynamic element in some large cities with effects that ripple across their populations. Finally, we explore what is known about the risks and economic volatility to which urban populations are exposed as they engage more fully with the international economy.

Foreign Direct Investment

As Douglass (1997) argues, the influence of international linkages on city growth is often overlooked or summarized too glibly in indicators such as ratios of exports to GDP. He writes (p. 12):

> Missing from the analysis have been a wide array of equally powerful
> international relations formed through direct investment in production

---

BOX 8.4 Foreign Direct Investment: Shaping Indonesia's Cities

In Indonesia, the period from the 1970s to the 1990s saw foreign direct investment (FDI) emerge as a powerful force, which encouraged the growth of a network of large cities but generally neglected rural areas and smaller cities (Douglass, 1997).

In the 1970s about three-quarters of total foreign investment went to two sectors: natural resource extraction (mining and forestry) and resource processing (the chemicals, minerals, and metals manufacturing sectors); and textiles, which accounted for about one-quarter of all foreign investment. Investments in manufacturing were concentrated mainly in Jakarta and the surrounding province of West Java. Key port cities along Java's northern coast also attracted investment, as did cities in Sumatra and Kalimantan from which oil, timber, and some cash crops were shipped. FDI was substantially more spatially concentrated, according to Douglass, than were domestic firms. In particular, foreign investment neglected the densely settled rural areas of Java, Bali, and eastern Indonesia, which lacked significant natural resources. By 1985, no less than 76 percent of manufacturing employment was found in Java, and of this, some 86 percent was urban based (Douglass, 1997: 127). The consequences were seen in rapid outmigration from rural Java to Jakarta and the cities on Java's northern coast.

The early 1980s saw steep declines in commodity prices, including oil, accompanied by a dwindling of FDI in the outer islands. Indonesia began to reconfigure its development strategies to emphasize export-oriented manufacturing, an activity in which its newly literate labor force might prove attractive to foreign investors. The country soon became a favored site for Japanese investment. By the latter part of the 1980s, Japan was providing over a third of all foreign investment in Indonesia, and FDI was also flowing in even greater quantities, in total, from Taiwan, Korea, Hong Kong, and Singapore. But the export-oriented manufacturing and foreign investment projects were highly concentrated in spatial terms, being located mainly in Jakarta, Bandung, and Surabaya (Douglass, 1997: 135–6).

More recently, rural dwellers within range of these large cities have been increasingly involved in urban employment, whether as daily and weekly commuters or as short-term residents, thanks to improvements in transport and communication. Such urban connections have clearly improved the incomes of rural families (Douglass, 1997: 137). However, the costs of urban concentration have been high. It is doubtful that the concentration of Indonesian manufacturing in a few large urban centers can be sustained for long, given the stress it places on the urban natural environment and the need for enormous investments in public services to keep pace with expanding populations.

---

and services, licensing agreements, concessionary contracts for the extraction of natural resources, and finance by transnational enterprises, their home governments, and international donor agencies. All of these linkages have, in fact, been expanding much more rapidly than international trade, and when seen together they comprise an increasingly formidable set of parameters. . . .

One important strand in this set of relations—that of foreign direct investment (FDI)—is explored in Box 8.4 for the case of Indonesia. In this instance, a pattern of foreign investment has emerged with clear spatial delineation, unfolding in distinct phases marked by an increase in the urban concentration of investment. We know of no broader treatment than this of the spatial implications of international linkages and capital flows, but as in Indonesia, it is likely that foreign investment often has an urban focus.

As Kaminsky, Lyons, and Schmukler (2001: Figures 1 and 2) show, private capital flows to developing countries have become increasingly important and now account for some 80 percent of the total flows, including official aid. These private flows are a mix of FDI and other financial streams that wend through the capital markets, involving bank and trade-related lending together with portfolio flows, the latter of considerable importance to the economies of Latin America and the East Asia Pacific region. As discussed by the World Bank (2002a), private capital flows are cyclical and sensitive to the macroeconomic and financial conditions of high-income countries, as well as to local risk factors. FDI, although less volatile than portfolio flows, is also subject to pronounced cyclical swings. The peak in FDI to developing countries was reached in 1999, and just 2 years later, investments had fallen by 8 percent from that peak (World Bank, 2002a: 37).

Recent projections indicate that strong FDI growth will probably resume in East Asia and in some countries of other regions. For the foreseeable future, however, only a few developing countries can expect to receive any substantial foreign investment. At present, FDI is highly concentrated in only a handful of very large countries: Brazil, China, and Mexico alone absorb about half of all FDI flows to developing countries (World Bank, 2002a: 39). For the countries that can attract them, such investment flows provide important additional capital, but they also present additional risks of exposure to the economic volatilities transmitted through world financial networks (De Gregorio and Valdés, 2001).

Globally Linked Business Services

Many corporate firms in high-income countries (and some of their counterparts in developing countries) have penetrated multiple regional and international markets, operating directly or through affiliates. International firms operating in local markets often require services that are tailored to these markets and purchased from local suppliers. The globalization of finance; the growth of transnational investment; the spatial dispersal of factories, service outlets, and offices; and the creation of facilitating information technology—all have contributed to a demand for specialized business services (Roberts, 1994; Hampton, 1996; Bagchi-Sen and Sen, 1997; Bowe, 1998; McKee, Garner, and McKee, 2000).

As discussed in Chapter 2, high-end business services can be viewed as complex bundles of inputs. These bundles may involve contributions from several types of specialized professions, and where speed is of the essence in production, only the communications infrastructure and diverse economies of large cities are

---

BOX 8.5 The Internationalization of the Informal Economy

Information technologies, adopted by some migratory networks and diasporas, allow internationalization of the informal economy. A striking example is provided by the networks of Mouride Senegalese migrants, who use Internet connections in Dakar to manage trading in money and goods among New York, Dakar, and Touba (Tall, 2000).

The internationalization of informal sectors is also tied to growth in transnational organized crime. Prostitution, child trafficking, smuggling, and arms dealing are now globalized phenomena. The production and distribution of illegal drugs have important consequences for urban economies through the creation of jobs and the consumer demands of those directly employed. Drug trafficking is probably the principal export of Colombia and Myanmar, where the resources thus generated are invested in real estate and large-scale industrial enterprises. In Colombia, a system of "Mafia-providence" (Le Bonniec and Sauloy, 1992) transforms crime and corruption into factors of economic modernization. In Lagos and Cape Town, trafficking in narcotics provides incomes far in excess of normal formal-sector salaries, and finances enterprises in the trade and transport sectors (Fottorino, 1991).

---

likely to be able to provide the requisite input mix.[50] Once the services have become routinized, however, some elements in their production can be relocated outside the large cities to take advantage of lower rents and congestion costs (Duranton and Puga, 2001). It is the nonroutine, innovative, and customized aspect of business services that tends to keep them concentrated in the larger cities.

In many major cities, then, a new economic core of corporate service activities is being formed, sometimes displacing older manufacturing and administrative activities. In some cases, the scale, power, and profitability of the new corporate core activities are so visible as to suggest the emergence of a new urban economy. To be sure, even in the most dynamic of cities, the corporate services sector is but one part of the larger city economy. Cities with a core of international business functions retain much of their former economic character and still have a great deal in common with cities lacking that core. But as international networks strengthen, the growth paths of internationally linked cities appear likely to diverge from those of other cities. (See Box 8.5.)

Although less clearly apparent in the smaller cities, the emergence of an internationally linked, modern services sector has become evident in those cities as well. Furthermore, regionally focused firms share many of the characteristics of firms with more widely dispersed operations and contacts. Although the regional firms need not negotiate all the complexities of international borders and country regulations, they, too, have regionally dispersed networks of operations that require centralized control and servicing. Hence, regional firms have also fed the demand for business services in their corporate headquarters and regional offices.

---

[50]See Black and Henderson (1999a) for the United States.

The transformation of urban real estate is one vivid indicator of the emerging services sector. Housing is being constructed and remodeled to the tastes of new high-income professionals; firms selling high-profit goods and services are out-bidding lower-profit firms for desirable commercial space. Neighborhood shops tailored to local needs are being replaced by upscale boutiques and restaurants catering to high-income urban elites.

The political economy of these developments is no less important. A growing share of a city's total payroll and tax revenues can be accounted for by the new specialized service core. The high-end business service sector is an increasingly important factor in shaping urban economic diversity and inequality.

Exposure to Risk from World Markets

Because many large cities act as the interface between their national economies and the international markets, their populations are directly exposed to the vari-abilities of these markets. To be sure, rural populations can also be profoundly affected by international developments, such as changes in the world prices of primary products. Rural economies, being less diverse than urban economies, are arguably more vulnerable to certain types of shocks. Cities possess financial and some social welfare institutions that can mitigate risks and help smooth con-sumption (Gibson, 2001). In general, however, the spatial concentration of city populations must enhance the local economic multipliers that transmit economic downturns (and upturns) from one subgroup to another. Urban economies are more monetized than rural economies, and rural strategies for weathering a crisis (e.g., growing food for own consumption) are not available to many of the urban poor. Also, the construction and real estate sectors—notorious for their boom-and-bust cycles and sensitivities to the state of capital markets—are far more im-portant to city than rural economies, as are the inventories held by manufacturing firms. City economies would appear to contain some especially volatile sectors that might raise risks for urban residents overall.

As countries negotiate their way toward liberalization and a deeper engage-ment with world markets, they adopt adjustment policies that mediate the effects of international markets and cause these effects to impinge differently on rural and urban populations. A number of African countries, for instance, have eased marketing restrictions and lifted price ceilings on agricultural goods, thereby re-moving much of the bias against agriculture that was so prominent in the 1970s (Collier and Gunning, 1999b). But even as these reforms work to the benefit of some rural residents, they can hurt urban residents who rely on subsidized food and other goods. In many of the recent economic crises seen across the develop-ing world, international market forces and domestic policies are mingled in a way that makes it very difficult to anticipate the urban consequences.

The complexities are well illustrated in the case of Zambia (McCulloch, Baulch, and Cherel-Robson, 2000), where developments in international markets combined with a host of policy reforms to generate rising rates of urban poverty. The collapse of world copper prices—long that country's largest and most valuable export—in the late 1970s eventually led Zambia to adopt a series of structural adjustment programs beginning in the mid-1980s, which included the removal of ceilings on the prices of maize and other agricultural commodities and major reforms that improved agricultural marketing. These long-overdue reforms clearly benefited rural residents. For urban consumers, however, the removal of subsidies on maize meal sharply increased the cost of living and sparked rioting in Lusaka and other major towns of the Copperbelt. On the international front, Zambia lifted many foreign exchange controls in the early 1990s, removed licensing and quantity restrictions on exporting and importing, and reduced and greatly simplified tariffs on imports. These new policies were intended to lay the foundation for future growth in exports and employment. But in the near term, as McCulloch, Baulch, and Cherel-Robson (2000: 11) write:

> ... the collapse of the manufacturing sector has been dramatic. Companies operating behind high levels of protection have been unable to withstand the simultaneous shocks of trade liberalization and the removal of subsidized credit. Employment in formal manufacturing fell over 40 percent ... the textile industry has almost collapsed.

Urban poverty rates in Zambia (calculated from three surveys with data on household consumption expenditures) rose from 47 percent in 1991 to 63 percent in 1998; meanwhile, rural rates of poverty fell from 88 to 77 percent (McCulloch, Baulch, and Cherel-Robson, 2000: Table 3b).

The experience of Indonesia during the Asian financial crisis also shows how urban and rural populations can be affected differently by international developments. The Indonesian phase of the crisis is usually dated to the collapse of the *rupiah* in January 1998, after which there ensued a period of rapid inflation, tightening credit, and government control over lending that paralyzed banking and nearly brought the construction sector to a halt.

Levinsohn, Berry, and Friedman (1999) studied the price effects associated with this crisis and found that contrary to what is often thought, the very poor do not occupy niches in the urban economy that are somehow sheltered from international economic shocks. Indeed, increases in the cost of living during the crisis were greatest for the urban poor, somewhat smaller for the urban nonpoor, and smaller still for rural households.

The impacts on employment, wages, and earnings are closely examined by Thomas, Beegle, and Frankenberg (2000) and Smith, Thomas, Frankenberg, Beegle, and Teruel (2000). Over the decade leading up to the Asian financial crisis, substantial wage growth benefited Indonesian men and women. As the crisis unfolded through 1998, employment rates that were already high remained so. The impact of the crisis was not seen in employment as such, but rather in wage rates, which fell by some 40 percent in urban and rural areas. This spectacular decline in wages all but erased the gains made by men over the preceding decade and nearly erased the gains for women as well.

The urban declines in wages were slightly larger than the rural declines, and of course in cities, a much higher fraction of workers earn wages (Smith, Thomas, Frankenberg, Beegle, and Teruel, 2000). Wages fell for almost all urban groups, although the percentage declines were evidently larger for low-skilled wage earners, especially among men without government jobs (Thomas, Beegle, and Frankenberg, 2000). For the urban self-employed, hourly earnings fell about as much as wages, on average, although again upper and lower tiers of self-employment can be distinguished, with greater declines occurring in the latter (Thomas, Beegle, and Frankenberg, 2000). In rural Indonesia, the self-employed (mainly farmers) appear to have been left largely unaffected by the Asian financial crisis, and rural family incomes tended to fall less than wage rates, probably because rural households could activate multiple coping strategies. Urban residents could not protect themselves to the same degree, although both Smith, Thomas, Frankenberg, Beegle, and Teruel (2000) and McGee and Firman (2000) detect an increase in urban agricultural work, which might be interpreted in terms of coping strategies.[51]

Frankenberg, Beegle, Thomas, and Suriastini (1999) ask whether Indonesian children were more likely to leave school in the peak year of the crisis (1998) as compared with the previous year. They find marked increases in school dropout rates in both the urban and rural areas of Indonesia, with the increases being relatively small at the primary level of schooling but quite substantial at the secondary level. Urban dropout rates rose more than did rural rates, and although increases were recorded across the economic spectrum, dropout rates rose much more for poor families. Curiously, however, the negative effects of the crisis on children's education were not seen in their health. Frankenberg, Beegle, Thomas, and Suriastini (1999) show that although use of public and preventive health services declined in the crisis, no deterioration in children's health was apparent. Children's height for age and weight for height showed little change from 1997 to 1998, and measures of anemia actually exhibited some improvement.

The possibility of such mixed responses to macroeconomic crisis is emphasized by Schady (2002), who examines changes in urban children's school enrollment in Peru from 1988 to 1992. Peru's crisis was as severe as that faced by Indonesia and might have been expected to produce the same sort of reactions. Yet Schady finds little change in enrollment rates in Lima and other Peruvian cities. Perhaps, as he argues, macroeconomic crises lower the opportunity

---

[51] Sumarto, Wetterberg, and Pritchett (1999) present findings from a large-scale qualitative survey conducted in each of Indonesia's 4025 subdistricts (*kecamatan*). The data—drawn from interviews with local officials in each subdistrict—suggest that households in the middle range of income responded to the crisis by working more, reducing consumption, drawing down savings, and selling assets. In the view of these local officials, the poor households in their districts had far fewer options available to them.

BOX 8.6 Cross-Border Migration Flows Between Kazakhstan and Russia

Employing unusually detailed time-series data from Kazakhstan, Musabek, Becker, Seitenova, and Urzhumova (2001) show how migration is influenced by economic conditions there and in neighboring Russia. Monthly data are available on aggregate flows from 1995 to 1999. The migration flows are substantial: on net, 13 percent of Kazakhstan's urban population (and 9 percent of its rural population) emigrated between 1990 and 1999, with by far the largest outflow going to Russia.

Urban Kazakhstanis have higher propensities to migrate to Russia and are far more sensitive to wages and exchange rate movements than are their rural counterparts. This is especially true for young adults (aged 18–29). Migration responds to changes in relative Kazakhstani/Russian mean wages with a lag of about 7 months and an elasticity estimated to be near unity on average. Migration is also highly responsive to changes in relative capital investments per worker and to movements in exchange rates.

---

costs of schooling by reducing the earnings from children's employment.[52] The marginal benefits of schooling can also be affected if the crisis is expected to be long-lasting. Indeed, when earnings decline more for those with few skills and low education, it is conceivable that a crisis may even raise the perceived returns to schooling.

Few studies have explored the spatial implications of economic crisis in any depth by asking whether certain types or sizes of cities appear more vulnerable. In the formerly socialist countries of West Asia, the prolonged crises associated with economic restructuring appear to have hit the secondary cities harder than the capitals. Bishkek, the capital of Kyrgyzstan, experienced severe difficulties in the first few years of the post-Soviet era, but as its economy steadied, it began to attract migrants from the secondary cities, where local industry had utterly collapsed with dim prospects for recovery. Between 1989 and 2000, Bishkek added about 130,000 people, while the secondary cities of Kyrgyzstan lost 55,000 residents (Government of the Kyrgyz Republic, 2000). Levels of poverty in Bishkek have been low in comparison with rural rates and those of other cities, and its wage rates have been relatively high even when adjusted for differences in human capital (Anderson and Becker, 2001). If anything, the gaps in living standards between Bishkek and the remainder of Kyrgyzstan may well have widened over the 1990s. In many ways, then, the economic crisis and adjustments in Kyrgyzstan appear to have reestablished the favored position of the capital city that was so characteristic of the Soviet era.

In Kazakhstan, both urban and rural areas have lost population, and there are now substantial migratory flows both to and from Russia (see Box 8.6). The total urban population declined from 9.8 million in 1992 to only 8.4 million in 1998

---

[52]This argument requires a narrow definition of opportunity costs: when adult earnings also decline, children's earnings that are lower in money terms can have a large effect in terms of household well-being.

(Government of Kazakhstan 1999, and unpublished data). But the capitals of Almaty and Astana continued to grow, at least during the second half of the 1990s, and again it was the secondary cities that lost population. Health recovery appears to have been stronger in the country's large cities (Becker and Urzhumova, 2001). In both Kyrgyzstan and Kazakhstan, capital-city residents have generally fared better than those in secondary cities during a very difficult period of transition.

CONCLUSIONS AND RECOMMENDATIONS

Conclusions

The urban demographic bonus is both a boon and a challenge for developing-country cities. As population projections make clear, the urban economies of low- and middle-income countries can expect a very large increase in the supply of labor over the next several decades. In addition, as fertility declines, child dependency ratios will decline, and a larger proportion of the population will temporarily move into the working ages (Bongaarts, 2002). In some Asian settings, declining fertility has also been credited as a major contributor to sustained economic growth (Mason, Merrick, and Shaw, 1999; Bloom and Williamson, 1998). Slower growth in the number of school-age children has enabled greater educational investment per child, and lower dependency ratios have produced higher national savings rates and reduced temporarily the need for certain types of public expenditures. In this sense, an extraordinarily large cohort of working-age adults produces a one-time demographic bonus. But for countries to realize their demographic bonus, their economies must be strong enough to absorb the growing workforce without experiencing increased unemployment or depressed wages. Rapid economic and political changes increase the complexity of the challenge.

   Urban labor markets and returns to schooling in developing countries are dependent not only on labor supply, but also on technological change and capital formation. This chapter has examined several key elements in the nature and magnitude of the structure of labor demand and supply in low- and middle-income countries. Urban labor markets determine individual and family incomes, which establish incentives for migration and profoundly influence decisions about investments in children's schooling and family size.

   A popular view is that urban labor markets in developing countries are riddled with imperfections and that unemployment and poverty are the direct result of labor market failure. Yet our review has highlighted the considerable uncertainty that surrounds the functioning of urban labor markets in these settings. Urban economies have changed greatly since the formulation of the highly influential models of Todaro (1969) and Harris and Todaro (1970). Although rapid growth in the supply of labor might appear to threaten the economic returns to schooling, our analysis shows that where macroeconomic growth has been moderate or strong, the urban returns to schooling have generally been maintained, and in some cases returns to university education have increased. On the other hand, where macroeconomic growth has been weak, as in much of sub-Saharan Africa, rapid increases in the supply of better-educated urban labor have resulted in a marked decline in the returns to schooling. Evidently, accumulation of physical capital and technological progress can sustain educational returns even in the face of rapid shifts in labor supply, but if these are lacking, returns to schooling will be threatened.

Although there is substantial fluctuation in individual incomes in urban areas, rural-to-urban migrants are able to attain earnings comparable to those of native urbanites after an adjustment period. Surprisingly little attention has been paid to individual income dynamics within urban areas. The few longitudinal studies available do not clearly reveal higher rates of upward or downward mobility in cities as compared with rural areas; in both there is a great deal of flux. However, studies of migrants—based mainly on cross-sectional surveys that may overrepresent the more successful migrants—generally show that rural migrants undergo a period of adjustment to city life during which their earnings are low, but subsequently achieve earnings levels that rival and sometimes exceed those of urban natives.

Recommendations

Given the partial nature of this review, it is impossible to formulate a list of specific research recommendations on the relationship between population and labor force growth and labor absorption. Space constraints have forced us to ignore many critical issues, such as the role of unions, discrimination, and occupational segregation in the demand for and supply of labor. We have also chosen to overlook issues relating to hours worked, retirement decisions, job attachment, work effort, and the nature of contracts. And finally, we have not discussed the technological advances that might raise the marginal productivity of labor in agriculture. Nevertheless, our review has uncovered two central research themes that will doubtless play a large part of a future research agenda in this area.

Cities and city-regions Our review has underscored the need to place urban demographic issues within an urban economic context. However, we have paid little attention to the economy and demography of the region immediately surrounding cities and metropolitan regions—what we might call the urban-regional economy. Greater attention to this subject in future demographic research is important because these surrounding regions are integrally related to what is happening to cities and metropolitan regions.

Globalization and inequality There has been much recent speculation about whether the globalization of economic relationships heightens urban inequalities. Case studies of Brazil, Taiwan, and China provide some evidence of a growing dispersion of urban incomes in the 1990s. Although

the sources of the trends are not clearly identifiable, such empirical findings are consistent with the view that urban labor markets are increasingly
heterogeneous and volatile, in part because of their exposure to world markets. An examination of the effects on urban populations of international
economic shocks and crises shows that city dwellers can be disproportionately affected; the evidence from Indonesia is especially clear on this point.
The spatial effects are not always focused on cities, however, and urban
residents also draw considerable benefits from exposure to world markets.
Nevertheless, as globalization proceeds, more research will be needed on
both the costs and benefits to urban residents of their increased exposure to
world markets.

9

The Challenge of Urban Governance

The preceding analysis of the demographic, social, and economic aspects of the urban transition has emphasized three important features. First, we have demonstrated the inevitable tendency for the global population to become urbanized. Second, we have illustrated the growth of a system of urban places—at both an international and national level—dominated by very large urban regions that are responsible for generating a significant proportion of national wealth. And third, we have argued that these large urban regions are functional because they have been integrated through improvements in the transactional environment of the flows of people, commodities, capital, and information. One of the least well-understood elements on this list is information.

The information requirements for the management of large cities are important conditioning factors in the cities' institutional elaboration. With the spread of democratization and decentralization now under way almost everywhere, local governments are increasingly being required to operate with the speed and efficiency of private business while facing ever more complex political and regulatory issues. Local governments must digest an immense amount of information to perform their duties in a fair and efficient manner. Yet data are severely lacking in many cities throughout the developing world. The typical 10-year interval between censuses presents a problem for policy analysis and planning for large cities, where the metropolitan population may easily grow by 1 or 2 million inhabitants in 5 years. Moreover, demographic data at the subnational level typically are not processed or made available for several years after a national census has been conducted.

Governments could also benefit greatly from data on population size, growth, and composition; differential fertility and mortality rates; and socioeconomic characteristics for numerous small-area units, which could then be aggregated to analyze trends within various parts of a metropolitan region. Employment data are particularly important here, since population growth has outstripped job growth in urban places in most developing countries. These data are also lacking or at least not readily available to planners and policy makers. Planners often have only rudimentary knowledge of the numbers and characteristics of recent migrants in most large developing-country cities. Moreover, cities' own projections of their future population growth often have been widely off the mark.

Planning is further hampered by limited information about local land markets. Most large cities lack sufficient, accurate, and current data on patterns of land conversion and infrastructure deployment. Frequently, urban maps are 20 to 30 years old and lack any description of entire sections of cities, particularly burgeoning periurban areas.

In most large cities in developing areas, each municipal agency or department typically maintains its own database, often using differing standards and rarely sharing data. Computerization of such data is still relatively uncommon. Many municipal agencies continue to rely on paper files and maps, which are often stored in formats and at scales so diverse that they cannot be compared or collated and are not easily updated (Bernhardsen, 1999). There are almost no examples of integrated databases for the constituent parts of large metropolitan regions. This is hardly surprising given the large number of political entities constituting most metropolitan regions, with their differences in age, socioeconomic needs, and financial and managerial capacity. Typically, there are reasonable data for the central city, with data (often noncomparable) for the outlying municipalities being of varying quality.

This chapter is concerned with the political and institutional implications of the urban transition. For some commentators (Ohmae, 1990; Scott, 1998), the urbanization process is a result of powerful global forces that are, at the same time, leading to a reduction in the political power of the nation state. Whether or to what extent this may be the case, there appears to be ample evidence that the urban transition of the twenty-first century will involve a significant renegotiation of political relationships between national and urban governments. Just as the present system of governance grew out of the replacement of city states by national states (Mumford, 1961), new systems of governance may very well emerge from the current urban revolution.

Underlying these political questions is one fundamental fact. The way in which present patterns of urban growth are being framed territorially differs from that of earlier periods of urbanization. Previously, government was organized on the basis of rural-to-urban responsibilities that were defined both spatially and structurally. Government was organized vertically so that tasks were divided among the national, provincial, and county levels, as well as highly local units of urban administration such as cities and towns. Each of these levels of government was defined in terms of discrete spatial areas, although there were often overlaps in administrative responsibilities.

Today there is general agreement that the rapid urbanization of developing countries should involve some reorganization and even reconceptualization of systems of governance. For example, the increasingly close interaction between central cities and their rural hinterlands (made possible by improvements in transportation and information transmission, among other things) suggests that rural and urban jurisdictions need not always be administered separately. And the fact that very large urban regions (including their hinterlands) are in many countries the source of both major economic initiatives and advances in national productivity suggests that these city-regions should not remain under the restrictive control of other levels of government if they are to reach their full potential for development (see Scott, 2001). Finally, the emerging importance of cities and city-regions in the world economy underlies the generalized shift from power relations based on pyramidal and hierarchical structures to those grounded increasingly in networks and horizontal relationships (Castells, 1997).

This chapter begins with a brief discussion of the concept of urban governance and the issues involved, which are illustrated by the case of the Bangkok Metropolitan Region. We then undertake a detailed review of the major challenges of urban governance in developing countries. Next we examine the question of whether there is, in fact, a single "best" model of urban governance. The final section of the chapter presents conclusions and recommendations.

THE CONCEPT OF URBAN GOVERNANCE

While the concept of governance is widely used today, its common usage in the social sciences is a product of the last decade and a half. In a lengthy discussion of governance as applied to urban examples throughout the developing world, McCarney, Halfani, and Rodriquez (1995) find that an important element in the development process, explicitly lacking in many official and agency-based definitions, is the connection of government, and particularly local government, to emerging structures of civil society. Accordingly, they define governance as "the *relationship* between civil society and the state, between rulers and ruled, the government and the governed" (McCarney, Halfani, and Rodriquez, 1995: 95). Important elements of this definition were adopted by other researchers writing about comparative local government in developing countries (Wilson and Cramer, 1996) and were eventually incorporated into the United Nations Development Program (1997a: 2–3) current definition:

> Governance can be seen as the exercise of economic, political and administrative authority to manage a country's affairs at all levels. *It comprises the mechanisms, processes and institutions through which citizens and groups articulate their interests, exercise their legal rights, meet their obligations and mediate their differences* [emphasis added].

One reason for the emergence of the concept of "governance" or "urban governance" is that the context within which local government operates has become much broader and more complex. In the United States, researchers dealing with metropolitan problems increasingly use the term "metropolitan governance" rather than "metropolitan government" because of the more inclusive connotations of the former (Stephens and Wikstrom, 2000: 47). Similar ideas have begun to take root in Europe. In an important article on France (where a Law of Decentralization was first passed in 1981), Le Galès (1995) argues for a shift in nomenclature from "the government of cities to urban governance." While the term "local government" is associated with a formal description of powers and responsibilities of urban authorities, local politics and the way in which French cities are administered are changing rapidly. According to Le Galès (1995: 60), "the term 'governance' suggests ... functions and actions of government, but without the idea of uniformity, rationality, or standardization. The term 'urban governance' implies a greater diversity in the organization of services, a greater flexibility, a variety of actors, even a transformation of the forms that local democracy might assume, and taking into account citizens and consumers, and the complexity of new forms of citizenship."

The emergence of a discussion of "governance" in a continental European context is of more than purely scholarly interest, since for some time the concept was considered an Anglo-Saxon term, and as such inappropriate outside English-speaking countries. Some Latin American researchers believed the more apt terms to be "governabilidad" and "governabilidade" in Spanish and Portuguese, respectively, which essentially mean "governability." But as Coelho and Diniz (1997) argue, the problem in the case of Brazil after formulation of the 1988 Constitution was not decision-making incapacity (or "ingovernability"), but rather the inability of leadership to achieve sufficient support and legitimacy to implement a whole host of technical measures. As a result, the authors propose retaining the concept of governability (*governabilidad*), but at the same time accepting a new concept, *governance*, to denote the state's command and steering capacity, its capacity to coordinate among politics and interests, and its capacity to implement measures from the level of the center to the local area. The concept of *local governance*, they add, brings to bear the political dimension "and places the interdependence of state and civil society at the center of the debate" (Coelho and Diniz, 1997: 113). The intersection of state and civil society, in this view, takes place at all levels of government—from the most local to the national.

Discussing Africa, the French planning writer Jaglin (1998) first notes how the concept of governance permits the incorporation of a wide variety of actors and groups in both the formal and informal sectors, as well as local, national, and international groups and agencies. The situation in South African cities in the mid-1990s, however, was extreme. In the transition from an apartheid system in which the majority population was totally excluded from power to a (potentially) fully democratic local government system, an elaborate process of dialogue and negotiating forums ensured a relatively smooth movement from exclusion to inclusion. Jaglin argues that the complexity and multisectoral nature of this process can best be described under the rubric of governance. "In imposing a form of representation of the political class, the private sector and local residents (through the 'civics' based in black townships) at the center of the required forums, the law made governance official, since it obliged the different actors to negotiate before local policies could be considered" (Jaglin, 1998: 31).

Beyond the pure concept of governance, which to us denotes the neutral relationship between government and the governed (mediated for some through culture and political practices), many writers and policy makers now speak of "good governance." While one must be careful not to reproduce in such a value-laden concept all the sociocultural and institutional prerequisites of government in developed countries, the notion of good governance carries with it a premise of institutional design that is at once open and accountable to civil society in general, and effective in terms of financial management and policy implementation. Good governance involves an effective balance between the raising of revenue and the proper expenditure of this revenue on services and investments that are based on accountable decisions. This model, in turn, implies that many levels of government and many local stakeholders and social groups will be involved.

The task of analyzing these changes in the patterns of governance in developing countries is complicated by the diverse paths and scenarios of urbanization and socioeconomic development that exist in the developing world. Yet the expansion of the urban built environment is occurring everywhere, and thus the development of systems of urban governance that can cope with urban expansion is a major priority.

The issues associated with urban governance are illustrated by the example of the Bangkok Metropolitan Region (BMR), which consists of the Bangkok Metropolitan Administration (BMA), with a population of 8 million, and the five adjacent provinces. In 2000, the BMR was estimated to contain 11.5 million people. Adding the adjacent industrial heartland of Thailand creates an extended metropolitan region (EMR) of 17.5 million people, making up 28 percent of the total population of Thailand in 2000 (Webster, 2000b: 8).[1] This region has been the focus of much of Thailand's economic development, involving a major change from an agricultural rice-exporting economy to an economy open to foreign direct investment (a high proportion from Japan) in the 1980s and a very rapid increase in export-oriented manufacturing. The result was a period of hypergrowth that made the Bangkok region one of the fastest-growing urban economies in the world, with an annualized growth rate of 17.5 percent in the period 1990 to 1996. With government encouragement, this economic expansion also led to the rapid outward sprawl of the region from the city (Webster, 2000b: 9), resulting in increased traffic congestion; environmental pollution; and serious infrastructure problems, including inadequate provision of water and sewerage and a substantial proportion of the population in the periphery living in substandard housing.

---

[1] Much of the discussion in this section is summarized from Webster (2000b).

As the region grew in size and territory, no adequate system of governance emerged that could solve these problems in a coordinated manner. The city core, the BMA, is under the leadership of an elected governor; 60 elected councilors (one per 100,000 people), making up the Bangkok Metropolitan Council; and a large number of elected councilors in 50 local districts who advise district directors appointed by the governor. While it has a huge staff complement (numbering 82,950, including teachers, in 2001) (Bangkok Metropolitan Administration, 2001), the Metropolitan Administration has limited powers—although much greater than is the case for other local authorities in Thailand. Moreover, many of its key functions, such as water and electricity service, are under the control of national agencies. Outside the BMA, in the BMR, matters are even more complicated as provinces control most of the planning, and there is no overall plan for the EMR. Webster points out there are more than 2,000 local government authorities (many of them serving small villages) in this outer region of urban activity.

The period of hypergrowth in Thailand was abruptly halted by the economic crisis that began in July 1997, which was focused on Bangkok. Between 1997 and 1998, the city product fell by one-half. By 1999 the official unemployment rate had increased from 1.4 percent in 1997 to 5.1 percent, reflecting a decrease in construction employment. But the major effect was a decline in income among the urban informal sector, such as taxi drivers. Inflation caused increases in food and gas prices that also adversely affected the poor. Estimates suggest the slum population of the BMA grew from 1.2 million in 1996 to 1.5 million in 1998, and there appear to have been deteriorating social conditions, including increasing crime, drug use, and suicides (Webster, 2000b). In contrast with the Indonesian case, however, there was no massive social and political disruption, for several reasons. First, households proved very adaptable—adopting strategies of outmigration, sharing of income, and increased participation by women in informal-sector activities. Second, many foreign companies, particularly in the manufacturing sector, did not lay off workers but stopped giving bonuses; this was the case, for example, with a number of Japanese companies. As the *baht* devalued, these firms were able to take advantage of this strategy to export more cheaply. Finally, the government remained stable during this period.

In fact, some writers have argued that the crisis benefited Bangkok, first because the city has been able to rebound more quickly than could either Vietnam or Indonesia, its chief competitors for export-oriented manufacturing in Southeast Asia; and second because the cost of living (including rent) has been substantially reduced, making Bangkok more competitive as a site for foreign investment. In addition to these factors, public works programs designed to provide employment have led to a decrease in pollution and traffic congestion. And the national government has been forced to accelerate its program of administrative decentralization to the local level despite very weak institutional capacity at this level. In this case, important attempts to develop new systems of urban governance are being made during a particularly volatile phase of contemporary globalism.

The urban form of the larger EMR of Bangkok is thus assuming many similarities to other large mega-urban regions in the developing world (see McGee, 1991, and McGee and Robinson, 1995, for a description of mega-urban regions in the Asian region.) Basically, the EMR is divided into three zones—the core, suburbs, and exurbia—on the basis of typical characteristics of each zone. While these three zones function as an economic region, there are sharp differences among them (see Table 9-1).

Is there a preferred governance model that best fits such a mega-urban region? There are essentially four categories of mega-urban governance. These categories reflect attempts in other parts of the world to manage large metropolitan regions, a subject to which we return in the penultimate section of the chapter. The first category, which can be called the *fragmented* model, is characterized by a myriad of autonomous local government units, each with jurisdiction over a particular function and/or territory. There is sporadic and poor coordination among the various units. This model is the most typical of the American approach to metropolitan governance, though some examples exist in developing countries as well. A second category, which can be termed the *mixed* model, encompasses regional governance approaches in which both central and local government play a role in the administration of a region. This approach is typical of most mega-urban regions in developing countries, including the case of Bangkok discussed above. A third form of administration is the *centralized* model. This model, still found in transitional societies such as Vietnam, is dominated by a central government. Finally, we should mention the *comprehensive* metropolitan governance model, although no pure examples of this approach currently exist in developing countries. In this model there is either a single coordinating governance unit for the whole mega-urban region or a two-tier system in which local governments (or municipalities) perform a number of local functions, but cede to a higher metropolitan (subnational) authority the performance of region-wide functions. A version of this model has been operating in Abidjan, Côte d'Ivoire, since 1980, and a "unicity" model has been emerging in South Africa since the local elections of November 2000. Four major Chinese cities that are governed as provinces also fall into this category.

While there is no consensus on the type of mega-urban governance that may emerge in this new era of urbanization, there is general agreement that as the wealth of these regions grows, some new form of governance will be required. As mega-urban regions grow in wealth, however, they will need to develop systems of taxation and governance that operate at both a regional and a highly local level, a process that will involve both decentralization and privatization. The next section reviews some of the major issues involved in both designing and implementing governance structures at the metropolitan level in developing countries.

TABLE 9-1 Extended Metropolitan Region of Bangkok, Characteristics of Main Zones

Population	Economic	Government	Built Form	Main Drivers	Main Threat
Core					
High density	Knowledge	City government elected	Polynuclear	Global and national property developers	Too-rapid decentralization
Longer-term residents	Tourism	National service agencies	Mixed land use		Political and social instability
Generational contrasts	Services		Hotels, convention centers		
Suburbs					
Medium density	Service industry	Provincial Changwad towns	Gated suburbs	Thai property developers	Industry uncompetitive
Outward flow of core households	Specialized agriculture		Shopping malls		Environmental pollution
Some low-income population			Leisure (golf)		
			Market gardens		
Legal and illegal housing			Squatters		
			Expressways		
Exurbia					
Rural migrants	Industry	Provincial Changwad towns	Industrial estates	Foreign direct investment	Overly dependent on exogenous drivers
			In-situ agriculture		
			Squatters		
			Industrial housing		
			Ports		

SOURCE: Adapted from Webster (2000b: 9).

MAJOR CHALLENGES OF URBAN GOVERNANCE IN DEVELOPING COUNTRIES

As the example of Bangkok illustrates, the governance challenges of large metropolitan areas in developing countries are both diverse and complex. It is arguably the case that this diversity and complexity are increasing with population growth and globalization, and that as this process unfolds, new approaches to governance and the management of cities will emerge. To impose some order on a very large subject, we examine these major urban challenges along five major dimensions: *capacity* (with a focus on urban services and service delivery); *financial resources* (with emphasis on generation of local revenues); *diversity* (in particular, issues of inequality and fragmentation, often leading to violence and a failure to regulate social conflicts); *security* (involving crime and violence, and approaches to the preservation of public order and the alleviation of violence); and *authority* (with a focus on decentralization and distribution of powers, local jurisdictional configurations, and political participation).

The literature on these interrelated topics is voluminous, but a certain disciplinary specialization tends to attach itself to each of these dimensions: geographers (with some economists) are more likely to focus on urban services, public finance economists on the financial dimension, sociologists and criminologists on the diversity and security dimensions, and political scientists and public administration specialists on the authority dimension.

Each of these dimensions can be related to demographic dynamics. The sectoral policies adopted to address the challenges associated with each have implications for such demographic variables as urban migration, the differential treatment of gender and age groups in the population, and the quality of life of urban residents.

The Capacity Dimension

During the 1980s, rapid urban growth throughout the developing world began to seriously outstrip the capacity of most cities to provide adequate services for their citizens. Beginning in the 1960s, this incapacity was made visible through the increasing number and extent of slum and squatter settlements in the cities of developing countries. The 1960s and 1970s were a period of extensive contention between municipal (and national) authorities and low-income urban residents. While the authorities sought to limit the use of urban land to the purposes for which it was usually zoned (i.e., high-income residential, commercial, and industrial uses), low-income populations attempted to build individual shelters on some of this land or to organize "invasions" for more concerted attempts to convert the land to their use. Clearly, the supply of cheap, serviced urban land fell far behind the demand for land on the part of a rapidly growing low-income population—a population that, in addition, had to be close to centrally located sources of income and employment to subsist economically.

In many countries, government response to this demand originally took the form of setting up centralized housing banks and construction agencies. For example, the National Housing Bank of Brazil (established in 1964 and closed in 1986) produced around 4 million units; two major agencies in the Ivory Coast produced close to 40,000 units during the 1960s and 1970s; in Egypt, public housing agencies built 456,000 units between 1960 and 1986; and in Singapore, some 460,000 units were built from 1969 to 1985 (UNCHS, 1996: 219).

While this housing made up a substantial proportion of low-income housing in a number of countries by the 1980s, there were major problems: maintenance was poor, public subsidies were high, it was difficult to avoid corrupt practices entirely, and the pace of construction was in any case inadequate to respond to the level of inmigration (Cohen, 1974; Mayo and Gross, 1989; Perlman, 1976; Stren, 1978). Notwithstanding exceptions, such as Hong Kong or Singapore, in which high-quality housing was successfully developed and maintained (Yeung, 1998a: Chapter 4), international agencies turned to more collaborative approaches.

Two policy responses stand out. The first is the *sites and services projects* of the 1970s and 1980s (Cohen, 1983), in which minimally serviced plots in large subdivisions were allocated to low-income applicants, who were expected (with some assistance in the form of training and loans of materials) to build their own homes. The second is *squatter upgrading projects*, which regularized land tenure and improved services and infrastructure in "slum" areas to encourage the orderly improvement of neighborhoods without displacing existing residents. Variants of these approaches are still operative today, but both involve complex, costly planning and administrative organization, as well as the design of an incentive system to encourage investment by the poor and discourage "leakage" to higher-income groups. From the building of housing units, public policy approaches in developing countries have shifted to "enabling" strategies that encourage land and infrastructure development, as well as support for medium-sized and small-scale enterprise (UNCHS, 1996). Prominent among these strategies are reforms in the governance of urban services—from arrangements based entirely within the public sector, to arrangements based on partnerships with private and nongovernmental groups (Fiszbein and Lowden, 1999; Freire and Stren, 2001), to various kinds of arrangements with private service providers (Batley, 1996).

Overall, these enabling and partnership strategies are consistent with what some observers see as a shift toward "neoliberal" economic policies, as applied at the local level. While the typical package of neoliberal policies (such as fiscal discipline, reduction of public expenditures, deregulation, open exchange rates, and trade liberalization) was generally applied at the national level when first introduced, new approaches to reform include social safety nets and decentralization. In the case of the former, many countries began in the late 1980s to develop redistributive programs and agencies targeted at the very poor; these programs were inevitably operated (at least partially) through institutional mechanisms set up locally—though not, in most cases, within existing local government institutions. As for decentralization, while most studies of national reform policies in the 1980s and 1990s relegate it to a minor role, some authors claim it is an essential element of neoliberalism. Vilas (1996), for example, sees the elaboration of what he calls "neoliberal social policy" in the 1990s as having three basic characteristics: privatization, targeting of the poor, and decentralization. Lowi (2000), with special reference to the United States but by implication including developing countries as well, argues that decentralization (which he qualifies as devolution and links to privatization and deregulation) is a fundamental part of strategies to "address the spillover effects of extreme inequalities" caused by neoliberalism. Behind this assertion is the argument that local elites and political institutions in the United States are better able to manage the "fallouts" from continuing and increasing inequalities than are national institutions.

One example of a large city confronting its service and infrastructure challenges in an energetic and innovative fashion is Shanghai. With a population in its metropolitan area of more than 13 million (not including the transitory, unregistered population, which may account for a further 3.3 million) and a total land area of 6,340 square kilometers, Shanghai is the largest city in China and one of the largest in the world. The metropolitan area consists of 14 urban districts in the city proper (2,057 square kilometers) and six suburban counties, all within a single area with the status of a province within the Chinese system of government (Wu, 1999a: 207).

While Shanghai was a major industrial and commercial center from the mid-1850s until the takeover of the Chinese Communist regime, it experienced neglect and disinvestment after 1949. Overall, from 1949 through 1983, some 87 percent of Shanghai's revenue was remitted to Beijing, leaving 13 percent for local allocation. By contrast, Beijing and Tianjin averaged 30 percent during the same period. As a result, Shanghai was known as the "golden milk cow" of the planned economy of China (Yeung, 1996: 9). Limited investment in infrastructure and housing meant that urban amenities suffered, so that "by the 1970s and 1980s, the central city's infrastructure was near collapse. For instance, in the former French Concession, nearly 700,000 dwellings were without flushing toilets. Compared to the national urban average and Beijing (a city of comparable size), Shanghai lagged in several important indices of urban infrastructure, including per capita living space and per capita paved roads" (Wu, 1999a: 208–9).

The central government's neglect of Shanghai began to reverse itself in the early to mid-1980s, culminating in a 1988 agreement between the two to give the city more autonomy in revenue collection and expenditure. In the same year, the city established a foundation to mobilize funds for urban construction; in 1992, this became the Shanghai Urban Construction Investment and Development Company (Wu, 1999b: 2277). This state-owned company allocates funds in many different areas of infrastructure and services and to many different local agencies.

According to Wu (1999b: 2278), the company "has displayed an impressive record of achievement in infrastructure financing since its creation." Wu goes on to say that the company

> ... has employed a wide range of financing mechanisms, particu-
> larly through such non-state channels as international capital, bank
> loans and credits, construction bonds, stock markets and service con-
> cessions. It has entered into concessions with profit-making enter-
> prises to operate the three bridges and a tunnel across the Huangpu
> River. It also has established a number of subordinate entities, mainly
> in charge of water supply, which are listed on the Shanghai Stock
> Market. Available official information shows that in 1995 and 1996,
> funds mobilized by the company accounted for about 76 per cent and
> 90 per cent, respectively, of Shanghai's total urban maintenance and
> construction revenue.

These systematic investments had begun to show results by the mid-1990s in terms of road construction, park expansion, and wastewater treatment. Some massive infrastructure projects were completed, including the beginning of a new subway line, a tunnel, and three large bridges across the Huangpu River.

The most spectacular outcome of the new emphasis on modern infrastructure in Shanghai has been the development of the Pudong New Area, a virtually new district across the river from the old commercial center to the east of the city. Pudong has been designated the country's financial center, "the Wall Street of China" (Saywell, 2000: 58). Major financial institutions, such as the Shanghai Security Exchange, as well as many large international corporations (including Philips, General Motors, Eriksson, and Xerox) have already located their offices in the Lujiazui area of Pudong (Wu, 1999a: 214–15). By the end of 2000, some 70 foreign and joint venture companies had established themselves in Pudong's industrial parks, and some 80 foreign and domestic financial institutions were employing an estimated 150,000 white-collar staff in 20 large office towers (Saywell, 2000: 56).

As impressive as they are, these infrastructure achievements have done lit-tle to improve the living conditions of the large majority of Shanghai's working population, whose per capita living space is no more than 8 square meters on av-erage, with 10 percent of the population living in a space of less than 4 square meters (Wu, 1999a: 208). One of the main problems with housing construction is the cost of urban land. And yet in the future, as land prices increase with ma-jor infrastructure projects and international investments, the cost of housing will rise even higher. The 1996 decision of the Shanghai municipal government to grant residency permits to those from outside the city who purchase an apartment in Pudong worth at least 500,000 renminbi (US$60,200) can only reinforce the polarization of the housing market.

In addition to the rising cost of land, a major factor behind the lag in housing has been a large increase in the city's population, caused partly by migration of rural peasants to urban areas. Most of these migrants (often referred to as the "floating population") do not have official urban status and live in substandard housing. Many live in so-called "villages" named for the provinces from which the migrants originally came. As documented by Solinger (1999), recent rural migrants in major Chinese cities survive under very depressed conditions with respect to access to such major city services as water, electricity, transport, and even cheap food. As one Shanghai citizen complained, "The urban environment is ruined. Wherever there's a large concentration of mobile population, shacks are erected at will, cooking is done outdoors, the streets are used as public toilets, structures are soiled, and public facilities are destroyed" (Solinger, 1999: 119). Box 9.1 describes the extremely marginal conditions under which some migrants subsist in Shanghai. The living conditions of rural-to-urban migrants in some of China's largest cities will be a major public policy issue in the years to come.

Yet in some respects, the Shanghai case is unique and very promising—at least from the point of view of urban services and infrastructure improvement. But on the housing side, with severe backlogs and pressure for improved accommodation for lower-income groups, it is more typical of the situation common in many cities of the developing world. By the end of the 1990s, a huge gap still existed across the developing world between the effective supply of adequately serviced land and minimal standard housing on the one hand and the demand for accommodation as expressed through what poor families are able to pay on the other. Because land and minimal standard housing are, in general, not supplied quickly enough to keep pace with demand on the part of low-income groups, the backlog is expressed in dramatic fashion through the continuing existence of slums, squatter areas, and other forms of informal housing or impermanent structures. These areas, often totally bereft of services and infrastructure (at least in the early stages of their development), are growing in many cities and declining in few.

Estimating the growth in the proportion of the urban population living in "self-help" housing in four major cities of Latin America, Gilbert (1998) shows that the proportion in Mexico City increased from 14 to 60 percent between 1952 and 1990; that in Lima, Peru, increased from 8 to 38 percent from 1956 to 1989; and that in Caracas, Venezuela, increased from 21 to 42 percent from 1961 to 1991. Only Bogota, Colombia, was able to decrease the proportion of the population living in such settlements—in this case, from 40 to 26 percent from 1955 to 1991 (Gilbert, 1998: 82).

The Global Urban Indicators Database of the United Nations Centre for Human Settlements (UNCHS), based on a major survey of 237 cities around the world (some 176 of which were listed as being in "developing" countries) reflects the same trends in housing quality. According to 1993 figures, among cities in Africa, on average only 49 percent of dwellings could be considered in compliance with local building regulations; for the Asia Pacific region (which in the

---

BOX 9.1 Living on the Edge in Shanghai

A stone's throw from the glistening skyscrapers that tower over the eastern Chinese city of Shanghai, three-year-old Wang Kun lives with his parents in a hovel surrounded by festering garbage.

A 15-strong tribe of rubbish collectors live in three rows of jerry-built shacks at the side of a rubbish dump in Shanghai's southeastern Nanhui—one of scores of makeshift villages built on the outskirts of dumps around China's gleaming economic capital.

Wang Kun and his father Wang Jun are from neighboring Jiangsu province while many of their fellow scavengers come from central China's impoverished Sichuan province. Their numbers are growing....

"Rubbish collectors do play an important role in cities and authorities have an ambivalent attitude towards them," said Sophia Woodman, research director of Hong Kong-based Human Rights in China.

Crackdowns on garbage collectors can be triggered for arbitrary reasons ranging from National Day celebrations to a senior leader driving past a cluster of migrant dwellings and "thinking we don't want this in our gleaming modern city," she added.

For 26-year-old Liu Tian, his wife and four-year-old son, who live on a rubbish tip in Sanlitang village in Shanghai's southern suburbs, the insecurity is bearable.

The 800 yuan (97 dollars) Liu can rake in every month operating a smoke-belching machine that turns old plastic bags into rubber is four times more than he would earn in his Jiangsu village.

"It's not a bad life. I earn much more than I would at home and when my son is old enough I want to send him back to school in Jiangsu," Liu said....

The Sanlitang rubbish dump is run by an entrepreneur who hails from Suxian, the same Jiangsu village as Liu Tian and his co-workers. Liu said his boss is doing well for himself but the authorities have asked him to relocate.

"We have to move on in a few weeks, some of the other workers have already moved but we don't know where we're going yet. We have to wait for the boss to tell us," he explained....

However, for Wang Jun, the smell of the refuse and filth as well as the threat of being driven out by police is no deterrent.

"Although work here is dirty and hard, I have more freedom and human dignity than in a factory job," he said.

SOURCE: Agence France-Press (2001)

---

survey does not include Korea, Singapore, or Japan), the figure is 59 percent; and for Latin America, the comparable figure is 74 percent. These figures show that access to adequate housing is still a distant goal for large numbers of people living in these three regions; they also show—all too clearly—that there is a strong relationship between the per capita income of countries (and cities) and the level and quality of housing and urban services supplied to their people (UNCHS, 1999). In general, writes Angel (2000: 320),

> ... while the formal housing sector [has] produced the bulk of housing for high-income groups, and while public housing [has been] of

TABLE 9-2 Percentage of Urban Households Connected to Utility Services, by Region

Region	Water	Sewerage	Electricity	Telephone
Africa	37.6	12.7	42.4	11.6
Asia (Pacific)	63.2	38.5	86.1	26.0
Latin America and the Caribbean	76.8	62.5	91.6	41.2
Industrialized	99.4	97.8	99.4	89.1

SOURCE: United Nations Centre for Human Settlements (1999).

limited scope everywhere—except in Hong Kong and Singapore—most low-income housing in the developing market economies was and is produced by the informal housing sector ... occupying land illegally (squatting) or built in land subdivisions that do not conform to zoning ordinances and planning regulations ... without adequate infrastructure, without any state subsidies, and without any formal housing finance.

This picture of housing supply lagging badly behind demand runs parallel to a variety of other statistical measures of urban service delivery. Based on the same UNCHS database of 237 selected cities, Table 9-2 reveals a major difference between developing and industrialized regions. In terms of water, sewerage, electricity, and telephone connections, the proportion of urban households receiving urban services is much lower in developing regions. By region, however, there is a clear gradation for each of these services from a low in Africa, through Asia and Latin America, to a high in the industrialized world. The poorest countries (in this case those located in Africa) claim the lowest level of urban services, regardless of which service is being measured. A similar gradation of urban service levels—from a low in the poorest cities of Africa to a high in the industrialized world—obtains for virtually all other major urban services not included in this table, including waste disposal, expenditures on roads per person, education, and health services (UNCHS, 1999).

In the specific case of health statistics, the UNCHS database shows that African cities lag considerably behind cities in all other regions. Thus in the 87 cities representing Africa in the database, there is an average of 954 persons per hospital bed, compared with 566 for Asia Pacific (which includes China), 288 for Latin America and the Caribbean, and 132 for the industrialized world. Child mortality (under age 5) is also high in African cities, at a rate of more than twice that in the Asia Pacific region (UNCHS, 1999: socioeconomic development tables), and 30 times greater than that reported for the industrialized world. The low quality of health services in African cities is closely related to poor sanitation. The introduction to a major recent comparative study of waste management in African cities (Onibokun, 1999: 2–3) makes the following observation:

> The rapid rate of uncontrolled and unplanned urbanization in the developing nations of Africa has brought environmental degradation. Indeed, one of the most pressing concerns of urbanization in the developing world, especially in Africa, has been the problem of solid-, liquid-, and toxic-waste management. Recent events in major urban centres in Africa have shown that the problem of waste management has become a monster that has aborted most efforts made by city authorities, state and federal governments, and professionals alike. A visit to any African city today will reveal ... heaps of uncontrolled garbage, roadsides littered with refuse, streams blocked with junk, disposal sites constituting a health hazard to residential areas, and inappropriately disposed toxic wastes.

As many commentators have observed, the poorest cities in the world (which are also among the most rapidly growing) have acute capacity problems when it comes to servicing their populations. Not only is there generally a severe shortage (verging on absence) of trained, professional staff to deal with complex urban management problems, but the overall resource levels of poor municipalities are extremely low. Since water and sewer reticulation systems, to say nothing of electrical and telephone networks, cost no less in developing than in industrialized countries, substantial financial resources must be found to finance major infrastructural investments. But with per capita municipal revenue figures at such levels as US$13.20 in Nairobi, $2.60 in Lagos, $17.10 in Delhi, $27.70 in Dhaka, and $31 in Abidjan, only the most elementary municipal activities and local services can be supported. Latin American revenue figures are somewhat higher—again, depending on the wealth of the country in question—but in rapidly urbanizing countries such as Bolivia (where the revenue per capita in La Paz is US$108) or Guatemala (with Guatemala City having a per capita revenue of $26) (UNCHS, 1999), services and infrastructure cannot even come close to keeping pace with population growth. When services (such as water or electricity) are either partially or fully privatized, the new owners have difficulty raising rates to finance new infrastructural investment.

Cities in the industrialized world (such as Toronto, with municipal revenue per capita of US$2,087; New York, with $5,829; or Amsterdam, with $4,559) have a much larger pool of local resources from which to finance needed infrastructure. While the individual returns may be somewhat unreliable, the UNCHS survey indicates that in 1993, the average per capita revenue received by municipal governments in Africa was US$15.20, in Asia (Pacific) $248.60, in Latin America and the Caribbean $252.20, and in the industrialized world $2,763.30. The ratio between the lowest and highest regions is on the order of 1:182. This ratio is much higher than that between per capita income in sub-Saharan Africa and that in the "high-income" countries (1:51) listed in the *World Development Report* (World Bank, 2000c: 275).

As discussed in the following section, one important means of dealing with local service capacity problems is to devolve more power to local authorities. While there have been problems in many countries with undertaking devolution before the necessary financial resources are available, local governments are often in closer touch than more central authorities with community and other civil society groups that can support service initiatives.

In the Philippines, for example, the Local Government Code of 1991 transferred responsibility for overseeing the implementation of primary health care to local government units. While the Ministry of Health apparently resisted devolution at first, the decentralization of many health services in fact took place on January 1, 1993, at which time 595 hospitals, 12,859 rural and urban health units and health centers, and most health programs were (at least formally) transferred from the national to the local level. Significant financial challenges resulted at the local level since revenues were allocated by the central government on the basis of demographic and poverty measures, not the existing distribution of health facilities and programs (Stover, 1999). Here, civil society helped buffer the shock. Since the central Ministry of Health had expended considerable effort on developing relations with nongovernmental organizations (NGOs), volunteer health workers, and other community organizations at the local level before the advent of mandated decentralization, local governments were able to find partners to carry out their primary health mandate, and according to some, the transition in many areas took place relatively effectively (Bautista, 1998).

The Financial Resources Dimension

While it is impossible to separate the capacity (or incapacity) of cities to deal with the service needs of their population from the financial resources they have at their disposal to do so, it is also the case that the level of resources available is not immutable. While wealthy countries can direct much higher levels of taxes and fees for service to their municipalities and/or private service providers than can poorer countries, the elasticity of supply of municipal revenue in relation to per capita income is clearly greater than zero. One of the reasons for this is that cities and their surrounding regions are often the most dynamic economic units in the country; the more effectively municipalities can build services and infrastructure to facilitate productive economic activity, the more both the country and individual urban citizens will benefit. The logic behind this relationship was at least one of the factors underlying the major decentralization reforms of the 1980s and 1990s throughout the developing world. There is some discussion among researchers as to the fundamental factors behind decentralization in different settings and different countries, as we have seen above, but the balance of opinion on these initiatives appears to be positive. In any case, as a result of these decentralization reforms, local governments (and cities in particular) have been given substantially more power by central governments in many countries around the world. As Manor (1999: 1) points out:

> Decentralization has quietly become a fashion of our time. It is being considered or attempted in an astonishing diversity of developing and transitional countries ... by solvent and insolvent regimes, by democracies (both mature and emergent) and autocracies, by regimes making the transition to democracy and by others seeking to avoid that transition, by regimes with various colonial inheritances and by those with none. It is being attempted where civil society is strong, and where it is weak. It appeals to people of the left, the center and the right, and to groups which disagree with each other on a number of other issues.

The nature of these decentralization policies varies tremendously—from incremental changes in protocols for intergovernmental relations on the one hand to major constitutional amendments or even new constitutional dispensations on the other. Three large countries gave new constitutional powers to municipalities during the period.

In Brazil, a new constitution in 1988 considerably increased the power of municipalities in relation to the states, assigning to them control of intracity transport, preschool and elementary education, land use, preventive health care, and historical and cultural preservation. On the participatory side, municipalities in Brazil were given the right to establish councils of stakeholders (termed in English "municipal boards" or "community councils"). These bodies, established in most of the largest cities in the country, include unelected representatives of community groups and deal with such important matters as urban development, education, the environment, health, and sanitation.

In India, an important constitutional amendment in 1992 provided an illustrative list of functions that were henceforth to be considered appropriate for municipal government; among these functions were planning for economic and social development, alleviation of urban poverty, and even urban forestry. The amendment also limited the degree to which state governments are able to suspend democratic local government (a practice that, until then, had frozen democratic local governments in nearly half of the largest cities in the country), provided for a revision of state–local fiscal relations, and required that no less than 33 percent of all elected local councilors be women.

The new South African constitution of 1996 devotes a whole chapter (containing 14 separate articles) to local government. Among other things, this chapter (Section 152) states that the objectives of local government (including municipal government) are "(a) to provide democratic and accountable government for local communities; (b) to ensure the provision of services to communities in a sustainable manner; (c) to promote social and economic development; (d) to promote a safe and healthy environment; and (e) to encourage the involvement of communities and community organisations in the matters of local government."

There are two clear messages in these reforms. The first is that municipalities (and other local governments) are now expected to undertake *and to finance* a much broader range of services and other economic and social activities. The second is that community and important local stakeholder groups must be engaged in the local governance process.

In spite of this general assignment of greater powers and responsibilities to municipalities in many countries, revenue has not kept pace with expenditure requirements. Not only are most local authorities dependent for up to one-third of their revenue on other levels of government, but their own resources are inadequate. One important reason for this inadequacy of own-source revenue is that it is usually based on fees for service and property taxes, rather than on more lucrative and collectible taxes (such as gasoline and income taxes) (UNCHS, 1996: 178–81). In many countries, even mandated central government transfers are not reliable. In poor countries, collecting fees and property taxes is notoriously difficult. Most municipalities in developing countries cannot borrow, and they cannot run a deficit. In addition, local revenue is highly dependent on both macroeconomic factors (for example, whether national economies are prospering or in distress) and on the level at which municipalities are permitted to borrow through the market. Under recent conditions of crisis in such countries as Argentina, Brazil, and Indonesia, local authorities have been negatively affected even though they have been able to borrow and their potential sources of local revenue have been augmented by improving the tax base.

Comparative data on local government revenues and expenditures are particularly difficult to obtain. Most countries do not supply consistent and reliable revenue and expenditure data. Even the *Government Finance Statistics Yearbook* published by the International Monetary Fund, the primary and most authoritative source of international data on government finance, gives information on local government finance for only 52 of its 114 listed countries in its 1998 edition, with time-series, detailed data being provided for only 12 developing countries (International Monetary Fund, 1998). Revenue and expenditure figures reported in the UNCHS database, referred to above, appear questionable in the case of some developing-country cities. Havana, Cuba, for example, reports revenues of US$1,418 per capita and capital expenditures per capita of $1,318, while Toronto reports, respectively, $2,087 and $253, and New York reports $5,829 and $582 (UNCHS, 1999). For the most part, as argued above, the level of revenues and expenditures for all cities in poor countries is very low.

Given the increase in devolution of powers and responsibilities that has characterized the last decade, figures on municipal expenditures are slowly rising in comparison with national government expenditures, but the levels are still low. Figures published in the 1996 *Global Report on Human Settlements*—covering a sample of 18 wealthy countries; 4 transition countries; and 16 countries in Asia,

Africa, and Latin America—show that on average, local government expenditures are 22 percent of total government expenditures in the first group, 20 percent in the second group, and only 9 percent in the third group (UNCHS, 1996: 174). Unfortunately, many of these figures are over a decade old. Under Bolivia's *Ley de Participación Popular* (the implementation of which began in 1994), municipal governments automatically receive 20 percent of all central government revenues through fiscal transfer. And starting in the early 1990s, Colombia began to transfer an increasing fixed proportion of national recurrent income to municipalities—from 14 percent in 1993 to 22 percent in 2002 (Hoskin, 1998: 105). Looking at municipal spending as a proportion of total public-sector spending between the 1970s and the early 1990s for Colombia, Argentina, Chile, and Peru, one finds increases of, respectively, 10.5 to 15.7 percent, 5.4 to 8.6 percent, 4.7 to 12.7 percent, and 2.2 to 9.2 percent (UNCHS, 1996: 167). There is good reason to believe—as the Colombian example of fiscal transfer already indicates—that these proportions will rise further in the early years of the twenty-first century.

As a result of changes in intergovernmental relations, the financial health of municipalities is slowly improving—at least in some countries. A compilation of data from case studies carried out in the mid-1990s for Brazil, Bolivia, Colombia, Chile, and Peru shows that transfers from other levels of government to the local level are now relatively high, representing 62.7 percent of total local revenue in Brazil, 54.7 percent in Bolivia, 47.8 percent in Colombia, 42.7 percent in Chile, and 58.1 percent in Peru (Aghón and Casas, 1999: 77). At the same time, property tax reforms in some countries have resulted in a much higher level of recovery. In La Paz, for example, after the *Ley de Participación Popular* (1994) devolved property taxes from the central government to municipal jurisdictions, property tax recovery increased considerably—from US$4.6 million in 1993 to $9.3 million in 1996. In Bolivia, the new law also created "vigilance committees" at the central municipal level, composed of local citizens who were to monitor the use of resources by elected mayors and councils, could propose investment projects, and in some cases could censure and dismiss the mayor (Grindle, 2000: 95–7). The creation of these groups contributed to a heightened sense of local "ownership" in municipal government, and probably to the higher rate of tax recovery as well. And in Bogota, Colombia, recovery rose from approximately 9 million pesos in 1993 to 30 million pesos in 1996 once a system of self-evaluation of property tax had been instituted (Aghón and Casas, 1999: 78–9).

That local tax collection and revenue generation may be as much a governance as a technical issue (requiring, for example, changes in tax codes, property attributions, and accounting systems) is illustrated by examples in China and Brazil. In the case of China, market-oriented reforms since the late 1970s have resulted in the devolution of important decision-making powers from the center to localities (Wang, 1994), as well as in changes in the fiscal relations between the two levels of government. While there have been many twists and turns in the redefinition of the fiscal relationship between levels of government, a decentralized market environment has clearly emerged. Local governments now enjoy considerable "off-budget" revenues, generated from such sources as donations by individuals and enterprises to specific public projects, profits from township-owned enterprises, fees for services and fines, and revenue from the leasing of public land to enterprises and developers (Gang, 1999). Indeed, the sale of land use rights has constituted the largest source of income for many cities in the coastal region since the late 1980s (Yeung, 1998b: 177–78, 271–74).

In 1992, the last year in which off-budget revenues were officially counted as fiscal revenue, such revenues had reached 93 percent of total formal budgetary revenues at the local level, and they are presumably still rising, at least in the aggregate. Although observers remark on the difficulty of estimating the contribution of off-budget revenues to large government structures (such as city government), that contribution is undoubtedly considerable. By 1996, such revenues accounted for close to 40 percent of all funding for urban infrastructure (including local public utility and construction charges, transfers from the central government, and regular municipal budgetary allocations) (Wu, 1999b: 2271–72). While there is controversy over the legitimacy of the way these revenues are allocated (see below), local governments use informal revenue generation systems—with the involvement of their citizens—to generate necessary resources for the provision of public goods. Gang (1999: 234–5) remarks on the close connection between local participation and effective mobilization of local tax resources:

> A real challenge ... is to develop a new type of local governance. Case studies in various regions show that in most places where off-budget revenue makes up a large share of local public revenues, some kind of democratic mechanism has emerged spontaneously. For example, people have started to use the local People's Assembly as the mechanism for decision making and monitoring of local public finance. Qingde town of Zhejiang province established three years ago an Assembly subcommittee, a "Financial Committee," as the decision making body for local public finance. Almost 30 percent of the Assembly delegates joined the committee, whose main task is to discuss and decide whether public projects should be initiated, how they should be financed, how the resources should be mobilized and how the revenues (mainly off-budget revenues) should be distributed and used.... In Shahe town of Shantou city in Guangdong province, the local people set up three years ago a special local "Board of Directors for Public Projects." It functions as the decision making (legislative) and administrative body for local public projects, mainly physical projects for infrastructure, including roads, schools and hospitals. The board consists of most of the "elite" of the town, elected by the local people, but includes no current local government officials. It not only makes decisions on projects and fund-raising but

also takes responsibility for project implementation and fund expenditures. In some sense, the board functions like a "parallel government" in charge of special fields of local public affairs. Meanwhile, the local administration plays the role of an outside monitor: it still carries out other government duties and at the same time monitors the work of the board and reinforces the formal government policies which need to be taken into consideration.

In both cases described … we can see the development of democratic mechanisms and a new type of local governance. Such new mechanisms minimise the problems that have arisen with off-budget revenues. As it develops spontaneously, based on solid economic motivations, this local democracy holds promise, with an obviously far-reaching impact on local governance.

While these new participatory mechanisms undoubtedly open some local economic systems to participation from the community, there is another side to this process. On the one hand, as researchers have pointed out, local governments and officials in China have been developing large collective enterprises, whose income (described above as "off-budget") can be used in a constructive fashion for administration, infrastructure improvement, and the establishment of new enterprises that can expand the revenue base of local governments (Oi, 1992, 1995; Walder, 1994). On the other hand, as Sargeson and Zhang (1999) point out in a case study of Xihu, a suburban district of Hangzhou, the provincial capital of Zhejiang, some local officials have taken advantage of these new enterprises to enrich themselves. They have done so by translating their political influence into stock shares, preventing a more balanced distribution of enterprise benefits throughout the local area. The costs and benefits of this decentralized fiscal system in China clearly warrant further evaluation.

Another and much better-known case is the development of "participatory budgeting" in Brazil. While versions of this system have been operating throughout Brazil (see, for example, Singer, 1996), the most well-known example of a city practicing the participatory budget system is Porto Alegre, a city of about 1.3 million in the south of the country. The system—which essentially involves ordinary citizens in planning for the yearly capital budget—is based on the work of 16 forums based on local regions of the city. In addition, there are 5 thematic forums (created in 1994), addressing education, health and social services, transportation, city organization, and economic development. There is also a municipal budget council with representatives from the regional and thematic forums.

The system was originated in 1989 by the Union of Neighborhood Associations. By 1995, some 7,000 people were participating in the regional assemblies and 14,000 more in further meetings to negotiate compromises among regions' conflicting demands. The system is complex and continues virtually throughout the year. The regional forums even micromanage the actual implementation of capital projects (Abers, 2001). According to the municipality, more than 70 cities elsewhere in Brazil and throughout the world (including Buenos Aires, Barcelona, and Saint Denis) have adapted this system to their own needs (Porto Alegre, 1998: 10).

A study of the city management process in Porto Alegre (Pozzobon, 1998) reveals that even from 1992 to 1995, the city increased its total tax receipts by 34 percent. The former mayor of the city claims the popularity of the budgeting system contributed to a tripling of the city's tax revenues during the period 1989–1999 (Pont, 2001). Abers (2001: 140), examining the participatory budget process, emphasizes the widespread democratic learning that was entailed:

> Along the way, [citizen] participants have developed a series of democratic skills. The most elementary are the basic habits of collective decisionmaking—holding coherent meetings, allowing all to speak, and learning how to debate and vote on complex issues where choices are multiple. Participants have also gained critical skills in negotiating with the administration. They pressure agencies to produce information about government actions and to demystify technical rules. They often successfully force administration officials to talk in ordinary people's terms and, in doing so, unmask attempts to veil in technical complexity the real reasons for rejecting or changing the demands prioritized.

Abers also argues that participatory budgeting would not have been possible without the active, time-consuming, and persistent efforts of local government officials to work with neighborhood groups.

Pont (2001), the mayor of the city during the period 1996–2000, implies that the participatory system in Porto Alegre was so popular that it resulted in the mayor's party (the PT or "Worker's Party") winning the state governorship in 1996:

> In the last election [1996] we really guaranteed Olivio Dutra's [the governor's] victory with a huge landslide in Porto Alegre. Rio Grande do Sul has a population of almost 10 million; there are about 7 million voters, and the victory was by 80,000 votes. It was a very tight contest overall, but in the capital we won with a very large margin. So we can say that it was the voters in the capital [Porto Alegre] who guaranteed the victory (Pont, 2001: 146).

While Porto Alegre is the best known of the Brazilian cities practicing participatory budgeting, it is not the only or even the first city to do so. In Piracicaba, a municipality in the state of São Paulo, a Citizens Budgetary Committee—in which popular organizations had seats and votes—was established as early as 1980. The initiative died when a new mayor was elected, but other participatory initiatives were undertaken in such cities as Lages, Fortaleza, and Recife in the 1980s (Souza, 2001). At the time, these cities were not administered by the PT, but by other leftist parties or coalitions. São Paulo had a less-than-successful experience with participatory budgeting under mayor Luisa Erundina during 1989–1992 (Singer, 1996). Since the election in 2000 of another PT administration under Mayor Marta Suplicy, the participatory budgeting process has been revived.

On the more positive side, Belo Horizonte, a relatively affluent city in Minas Gerais State, has organized "priorities caravans" consisting of budget delegates making local bus visits to check directly on the problems identified at subregional meetings. Overall, Belo Horizonte has indicated on its Web site that some 200,000 people have already taken part in participatory budgeting (Souza, 2001: 15). In Recife, a much poorer city in the northeast of Brazil, participatory budgeting began with the election of Mayor Jarbas Vasconcelos in 1985 and has continued to the present, including a recent period when the city was administered under a coalition government. Nevertheless, in Recife as in other cities, a relatively small proportion of the total budget is under discussion in the participatory budgeting process (Melo, Rezende, and Lubambo, 2000). The needs of the poor are a long way from being solved by this process. As a knowledgeable Brazilian writer claims with reference to the process across the country, "although some of the claims and results [of participatory budgeting] deserve more research, the experience does allow low-income segments of neglected areas ... to decide on investment priorities in their communities. Furthermore, it also argues that encouraging participation in highly unequal societies like Brazil should be valued more for heightening citizenship rather than for the material gains it may bring to some areas of the cities" (Souza, 2001: 1).

The Diversity Dimension

As they grow, many cities become increasingly diverse with respect to both the cultural, ethnic, and even religious characteristics of their populations and the nature of their economies. The extraordinary internal diversity of cities has always been a source of stress and conflict, but also of creativity and originality. Hall (1998: 7) suggests that, contrary to gloomy predictions of decline, many of the largest cities of the Western world have also served as platforms for the highest levels of innovation. While "no one kind of city, nor any one size of city, has a monopoly on creativity or the good life ... the biggest and most cosmopolitan cities, for all their evident disadvantages and obvious problems, have throughout history been the places that ignited the sacred flame of the human intelligence and the human imagination." It can be argued that one of the most important measures of a successful city—in both the developed and developing worlds—is the ability to deal effectively with social diversity and to create structures of governance that integrate diverse communities and economic interests into a functioning system (Polèse and Stren, 2000).

Studies of the morphology of cities in developing countries almost always comment on the fragmentation of the population, from both a social and infrastructural point of view. In his classic article on urban planning in developing countries, Balbo (1993: 24–5) points out that, although Western industrial cities are characterized by a certain coherence that is amenable to master planning, almost all cities in developing countries are more complex, both spatially and socially:

> ... the city of the Third World is a city of fragments, where urbanisation takes place in leaps and bounds, creating a continuously discontinuous pattern. In the fragmented city, physical environment, services, income, cultural values and institutional systems can vary markedly from neighbourhood to neighbourhood, often from street to street. An aerial view of the city shows a spatial structure made up of many different pieces drawn together in a rather accidental way. There are more of some kinds than others. Those in the periphery are incomplete and more "fragile," while older areas are well established with clearly defined boundaries.

> Even in Latin America, where most cities date from the sixteenth century, a process of "tribalisation" seems to be under way: the city is splitting into different separated parts, with the apparent formation of many "microstates." Wealthy neighbourhoods provided with all kinds of services, such as exclusive schools, golf courses, tennis courts and private police patrolling the area around the clock intertwine with illegal settlements where water is available only at public fountains, no sanitation system exists, electricity is pirated by a privileged few, the roads become mud streams whenever it rains, and where house-sharing is the norm. Each fragment appears to live and function autonomously, sticking firmly to what it has been able to grab in the daily fight for survival.

This depiction of the situation in the early 1990s has been reinforced by evidence of the further fragmentation of urban and interurban networks in both developed and developing cities. These networks involve such essential urban services as transport, water and sanitation, electrical supply, communications, and even security. As Graham and Marvin (2001:383) argue, the urban world of the last decade has seen a "splintering urbanism" in which "standardized public or private infrastructure monopolies ... laid out to offer broadly similar services at relatively equal user charges over cities and regions, are receding as hegemonic forms of infrastructure management." While a major factor behind these changes in developing-country cities is the inability of service providers to keep pace with demographic growth, more general factors behind these changes include "the widespread retreat of the idea that networked services are 'public' services that should be available to all at standard tariffs" (Graham and Marvin, 2001: 96) and the pervasiveness of the idea that all forms of ownership (public and private) should compete for the supply of local services.

As a result of many of these factors, knowledgeable commentators were still observing social segregation in Latin American cities toward the end of the 1990s. Thus, Gilbert (1996: 91–3) observes that "Latin American cities remain highly segregated.... In Lima, everyone knows that San Isidro and Miraflores are rich while Comas and Villa El Salvador are poor; in Santiago, the extremes are found in affluent Providencia and Vitacure in the north-east and poor La Pintana and La Granja in the south. In Rio de Janeiro, the rich live in Leblon and Ipanema and the poor in the Baixada Fluminense...." While residential segregation is becoming more complex, he argues, there is no sign that it is declining; "indeed, in some respects there is greater polarization." The complex nature of this pattern can be seen in a number of cities, as described below.

Rio de Janeiro

Rio de Janeiro represents a story of "emerging dualization in a historically unequal city" (Ribeiro and Telles, 2000). The Rio metropolitan area, with a population of some 9.7 million spread over 17 municipalities, grew at a rate of only 1.1 percent from 1980 to 1991. As many of the city's population migrated to medium-sized cities in the State of Rio de Janeiro, the outer parts of the city region grew much more quickly than the central portions. The authors' observations, based on census data, show that the poor, the less educated, and nonwhites are concentrated in the periphery and the favelas (spread throughout the metropolitan area), while the white, educated population is concentrated in the city center.

During the period 1980–1991, income concentration increased—the poor became more concentrated in the periphery and the indigent poor in the central parts of the city, while the rich increased their share of total income. At the same time, as salaried employment for the poor was becoming more scarce, and many at the lower end of the income scale were moving to the city center to take advantage of opportunities to work in the personal services sector, large real estate companies "intensified central city polarization, transforming the South Zone into an exclusive citadel, fortified by Rio's steep hills and an ominous public and private police presence. The termination of the housing finance system in the 1970s, the reduced income of workers, and upper middle class desires to live in exclusive zones have made elite housing by far the most viable sector of the real estate market" (Ribeiro and Telles, 2000: 86–7).

As these tendencies toward a duality among the population according to socio-economic status and location evolved, a parallel division emerged in the associations maintained by the two groups. Thus, those who have little education and are poor are much more likely to become involved in neighborhood community and religious associations than in unions, professional associations, and political parties. Those with high income and education, by contrast, join unions, professional associations, and cultural and sports associations and play a more active role in formal political parties. The periphery and the favelas are also characterized by what the authors call "the expansion of criminal and perverse forms of sociability" (Ribeiro and Telles, 2000: 93). These social patterns make coherent governance much more difficult to achieve.

São Paulo

São Paulo is another well-documented example of social fragmentation. The municipality of São Paulo, with some 10 million people, is one of the world's largest cities. Greater São Paulo, which includes an additional 38 municipalities in a continuous urban area of 1,500 square kilometers, contains 17.8 million people (United Nations, 2001: 84) and is the second-largest metropolitan area in Latin America (after Mexico City). As was the case in Rio de Janeiro, the growth rate in the City of São Paulo and the greater São Paulo region slowed during the 1980s, to the benefit of smaller municipalities elsewhere in the State of São Paulo as manufacturing firms relocated from the center to the periphery. Total employment grew more rapidly outside the metropolitan region as well, with the exception of the financial services and communications sectors, which grew more rapidly in the City of São Paulo (Santos, 1996: 229). During the 1980s and 1990s, pockets of poverty and rundown housing developments bedeviled the generally well-equipped central areas of the city; at the same time, more and more of the housing in the peripheral areas of the city was classified as "precarious," with low-quality materials, often on marginal land, with little or no infrastructure, and with few social services. Sposati (1996), a professor of social work and currently an elected municipal councillor, developed a series of maps of social inclusion/exclusion in the mid-1990s. In the introduction to her collection of maps (which depict the presence or absence of various facilities and services throughout the city), she makes the following observation (Sposati, 1996: 5):

> If the city of São Paulo had eyes and could see itself in a large mirror, it would see the broken and shocking view of its inequalities. However, its two eyes would not be similar either. As in the popular song, maybe while one of them was staring, the other one would be floating. Because everything here seems unequal. The largest city in Latin America, with circa 10 million inhabitants, is famous for the presence of the most advanced forms of technological development and the turnover of finance capital. It houses gardened neighborhoods, lavish mansions, dauntless buildings, excellent teaching centers and first class hospitals. A numerous fleet of luxury and imported cars circulates through its avenues or stops in traffic jams. Nevertheless, São Paulo also lives with the most severe forms of deprivation and human suffering. A deprived and unemployed population seeks refuge in slums and shack houses, or is abandoned on the streets. They are

daily victims of violence and do not have access to their rights and justice. They hang on overcrowded buses and trains, and if they get ill, the health service is poor. Their children, when they manage to, attend deteriorated schools, and evasion takes place very soon....

To some writers, this pattern is systemic. Rolnick (1999), a senior planner, argues that the coincidence of precarious housing, low income, and low formal employment that characterizes many peripheral zones of the city actually constitutes a pattern of "territorial exclusion," whereby those groups consigned to live in these areas cannot fully realize the benefits of citizenship and economic growth that are available to people living in other areas of the city. She shows that there is a marked relationship between levels of violence and homicide in the city and levels of basic services available. Using 1991 census statistics showing housing conditions, location, infrastructure availability, and number of rooms per household, she constructs a measure of territorial exclusion for 118 cities within the state, showing an inverse relationship between the ranking on territorial exclusion and homicide rates in both 1991 and 1994. "Territorial exclusion," she explains, "makes daily life insecure and risky. It blocks access to jobs and educational and cultural opportunities, which are concentrated in small and protected enclaves within cities. Since most residences in excluded areas are illegal and mixed use is generally forbidden by municipal land regulations, people are denied the possibility of using assets, such as home ownership, to generate money and create jobs.... [In these excluded areas] living in a permanent condition of denial of basic human environmental needs makes inhabitants feel as if their lives are worthless" (Rolnick, 1999: 17).

In particular, the peripheral areas of the city of São Paulo exhibit many of the preconditions for violence, in that resentment and anger build up when infrastructure and services are not easily available. As Cardia (2000) describes the situation, violence in the metropolitan area is significantly greater in the peripheral areas, where the population growth rate is the highest. Because of inadequate infrastructure, these populations are cut off from services and public authorities in a variety of ways (Cardia, 2000). While residential segregation and unequal infrastructural development do not in themselves produce violence and crime, these writers clearly believe that such conditions raise the likelihood that a culture of violence will be reinforced.

Another approach to describing this pattern of increasing fragmentation of social groups and neighborhoods is offered by Caldeira (1996: 63), who discusses the development of social and spatial segregation in São Paulo from the early twentieth century to the present. During this period, São Paulo went from being a "concentrated city" (from the early part of the century to the 1930s); to a city with "a rich centre and a poor periphery" (from the 1940s to the 1980s); to its present form in the 1990s (and presumably later), which she describes as "proximity and high walls." Her study of a rapidly growing wealthy suburban neighborhood

(Morumbi) shows that fear of violence and crime is a pervasive subject in every-day conversation. However, talk of crime is common throughout all social groups in the city, as "people from all social classes fortify their homes, change their habits, and end up transforming the city and its public areas." The result is a new urban landscape made up essentially of "fortified fragments" from which the poor and marginalized are physically excluded (Caldeira, 1996: 64–5):

> As the spaces for the rich face inwards, the outside space is left for those who cannot afford to go in. In fact, the public is treated as leftover both by the design of the enclaves and by the citizens who create the new private order. The modern public space of the streets is increasingly the area abandoned to the homeless and the street children ... fragmentation enforces separation and expresses not simple differences but irreconcilable inequalities.

Newspaper advertisements appearing between 1985 and 1995 illustrate this trend. These advertisements—aimed at the rich—both reflect and promote an image of security, isolation, racial and class homogeneity, and high levels of services and facilities (Caldeira, 1999: 120).

Manila

A final example of the tendency toward social and institutional fragmentation is the case of Manila, the capital of the Philippines. Metro Manila (or the National Capital Region [NCR]), with a population in 2000 of 10.87 million (United Nations, 2001: 89), is by far the largest city in the country, almost 10 times larger than the next-largest city, Cebu City. Metro Manila incorporates 17 municipalities (or local government units) occupying a territory of 636 square kilometers. According to Laquian (2000: 3), "the urban field of Metro Manila rightfully includes 18 adjacent [local government units] that add another 4 million people resident within a territory of 1,681 square kilometers within the so-called Calabarzon region ... as well as the provinces of Bulacan, Zambales and Pampanga in Central Luzon."

In this mega-urban region, the outlying towns have been growing more quickly than the national capital region since the 1960–1970 intercensal period. Some of these towns registered an annual growth rate of over 6 percent during the period 1980–1990 (Ocampo, 1995: 285). In the process of growth, the net movement of migrants within the region has been outward rather than inward, creating major problems of sprawl and ribbon development. Sprawl has put an extreme strain on public utilities and services, extended travel distances for workers living outside the NCR, and "resulted in social disparities and conflicts of various kinds" (Ocampo, 1995: 287).

One knowledgeable writer has described Metro Manila as a "city of villages" in which "autonomous local units ... have traditionally resisted efforts to centrally control their activities" (Laquian, 2000: 1). Local resistance to higher-level controls is a result of three elements: a relatively entrenched localism that defines neighborhoods as distinct units within the wider metropolitan area; strong local government units, reinforced by the 1991 Local Government Code; and a strong political culture of particularism that makes coalitions difficult to achieve (Laquian, 2000).

Fragmentation at the local level starts with the division of the city into four major types of neighborhoods. First are the *barrios* of the urban poor, often on marginal lands and even huge garbage dumps. Second are the "villages" of the rich, in which the residents lead protected, isolated lives with a full range of public services available for their use. Third are the traditional neighborhoods that house the majority of the population, bound closely by the observance of cultural and religious festivals, and participating in groups such as parent–teacher and neighborhood watch associations. Fourth are the traditional villages on the city's periphery, although these semirural areas are becoming pervaded by pollution and industrial enterprises, and their young are leaving for the city (Laquian, 2000: 1–2).

The fragmentation of neighborhood cultures is reinforced, one author argues, by the control retained by powerful local families in many Manila cities and municipalities. It is further exacerbated by the competitive behavior of certain local units (such as Makati, Quezon City, and Mandaluyong), which vie for large infrastructure investments and buildings that can serve the global economy. One result of this differentiation is that there is a wide disparity in the revenue collection of Metro Manila local governments. In 1997, revenue per capita ranged from 486 pesos in Malabon to 7,656 pesos in Makati, the upscale commercial and financial center (Shatkin, 2000: 2368).

Coordination and planning at the metro level are weak. While there is an upper-tier authority with responsibility for the whole metropolitan area, its powers and even its budget are limited, especially relative to the local government authorities, whose powers were increased under the 1987 Constitution and the 1991 Local Government Code. The power of the metropolitan authority was not enhanced by the fact that Imelda Marcos had been appointed governor at the outset of the authority's life, presiding over the Metro Manila Commission until President Ferdinand Marcos was toppled in 1986. The agency, renamed the Metro Manila Authority in 1990, was assigned a rotating chairman, chosen every 6 months from among the 17 city and municipal mayors of the NCR. In 1995, the Metro Manila Authority became the Metro Manila Development Authority, although it has "remained a weak governance structure" (Laquian, 2000: 8). While NGOs and civil society groups are highly active in Manila as well as throughout the Philippines, these groups have not been able to overcome the innate localism and particularism that obtains at the metropolitan level (Laquian, 2000: 23).

The Security Dimension

Urban security became one of the dominant issues of the 1990s in many developing countries. Since September 11, 2001, an international dimension has been

added to the domestic sources of insecurity generated by some of the urban social conditions considered above. We have chosen to discuss this important subject here since it is closely related to issues of social fragmentation and social
policy, and because we wish to explore the governance implications of different
approaches to dealing with the problem.

There is no question from both macro- and micro-level studies that urban violence has increased in a great many parts of the developing world. At the global
level, crime and violence are generally much higher in Africa and Latin America
than in Asia. A dataset (United Nations Interregional Crime and Justice Research
Institute, 1998) covering 18 developing-country cities[2] shows that Asia consistently ranks the lowest for all types of crime, while Africa and Latin America
share the highest ranking for all types of crime. When the "contact crime" rate
(i.e., incidents involving violence) is analyzed separately, Latin American cities
outstrip African and Asian cities with regard to sexual assault, with a rate of 5
percent of all types of crime (compared with 2.4 percent in the African cities and
1.6 percent in the Asian cities). For assault with force, African cities show a rate
of 3.1 percent, compared with 2.7 percent in Latin America and 0.8 percent in
Asia. For robbery, cities in Latin America have a rate of 8.1 percent, compared
with 4.2 percent in Africa and 1.4 percent in Asia.

Aside from the human and sociological effects of crime and violence, there
is a significant economic cost to the countries in which rates of crime and violence are high. A groundbreaking study by two Colombians (Londoño and Guerrero, 2000) estimates the cost of violence against people and property in terms
of loss of potential urban gross domestic product (GDP). The authors claim
that El Salvador, Colombia, Venezuela, Brazil, Peru, and Mexico lose, respectively, 24.9, 24.7, 11.8, 10.5, 5.1, and 12.3 percent of their urban GDP annually
as a result of violence (Londoño and Guerrero, 2000: 27). Likewise, a study by
the Mexican Health Foundation (Lozano, Hijar, Zurita, Hernández, Avila, Bravo,
de Jesús Ramirez, Carrillo, Ayala, and López, 2000), based on statistics for Mexico City collected in the mid-1990s (when the city's violence rates were increasing), suggests that the annual cost of violence in the city (taking both direct and
indirect costs into consideration) is a staggering $1.897 billion.

Data on homicide in cities are often cited as the most striking indication that
urbanization in the developing world produces a decline in social cohesion and an
increase in conflict and insecurity. Table 9-3 summarizes some data on homicide
rates for different cities in Latin America, indicating major differences among
countries, as well as rather important variations within countries. Rates in Brazil

---

[2]This dataset, collected through the International Crime Victimization Survey, constitutes the most
detailed global dataset on urban violence available. Crime was measured according to five categories:
vehicle-related crime, break-and-enter crime, victimization experienced by the respondent personally
(including robbery, theft of personal property, assault/threat, and sexual incidents), consumer fraud,
and bribery/corruption. Data were collected in the largest city in each of the selected countries. Although not representative of the urban population in each country, this dataset provides a starting point
for regional comparisons of urban crime (bearing in mind such issues as underreporting).

TABLE 9-3 Homicide Rates per 100,000 Inhabitants in
Selected Latin American Cities

City	Country	Year	Homicide Rate
Medellín	Colombia	1995	248.0
Cali	Colombia	1995	112.0
Diadema	Brazil	1997	146.1
Belford Roxo	Brazil	1997	76.5
São Paulo	Brazil	1998	55.8
Rio de Janeiro	Brazil	1998	52.8
Lima	Peru	1995	25.0
Ciudad de México	Mexico	1995	19.6
Santiago	Chile	1995	8.0
Buenos Aires	Argentina	1998	6.4
Caracas	Venezuela	1995	76.0
Guatemala City	Guatemala	1996	101.5
San Salvador	El Salvador	1995	95.4

SOURCE: Carneiro (2000).

and Colombia, for example, are very high by worldwide standards, while rates in cities such as Santiago and Buenos Aires are relatively low.

Trend data from case studies show a general increase in levels of violence in cities of Latin America over the last two decades, although some cities have also experienced a decrease in recent years. Nevertheless, trends may not be consistent even within a country. In Brazil, for example, the critical period for increases in violence was the second half of the 1980s, coinciding with the reestablishment of democracy. More recently, however, Rio de Janeiro has seen a decline in the rate of homicides, while this has not been the case in São Paulo. This finding suggests that urban violence has both local and more systemic explanations.

How to respond to the increasing violence is a major challenge at a number of levels—national, local, and social. Given the broad contours of a model that regards violence as a result of the erosion of physical, human, natural, and social capital, it is possible to identify policy options with the potential to restore these community assets. Of the four types of capital, the most amenable to policy intervention at the local level is social capital. In Chapter 2, we defined social capital as "networks and local associations . . . that might support collective action, enforce norms, generate expectations or reciprocity, or foster feelings of mutual trust." What is the relation between social capital and urban governance?

Among the reasons social capital is important is that both the size and density of social networks and institutions, as well as the nature of interpersonal interactions, significantly affect the efficiency and sustainability of development processes. Violence erodes social capital when it reduces the trust and cooperation within formal and informal social organizations and among their members that are critical for a society to function (Moser, 1998; Moser and Holland, 1997).

Social capital in formal institutions

In contexts characterized by human rights violations and high impunity rates, violence often erodes faith in the relevance and governability of many formal social institutions. When judicial, educational, health, media, and security institutions are no longer able to function appropriately and transparently, democracy itself is challenged. In some contexts, violence-linked industries associated with drugs, diamonds, or other natural resources can erode the state by corrupting institutions and dividing the population. For instance, drug traffickers' systematic threats and attacks against the communications media effectively suppress the effective and peaceful participation of civil society institutions in political decisions at the community and national levels.

Social capital in informal community-level institutions

The capacity for community-level organizations to function depends on levels of cohesion and the ability to meet locally, which in turn hinge on personal safety issues. Sustained violence creates fear and reduces trust among neighbors and communities. Fear of crime is greater where rates of contact crimes are higher (United Nations Interregional Crime and Justice Research Institute, 1998). The response, particularly for women, is frequently to avoid certain places after dark. Such restrictions break down community cohesion.

As noted earlier, fear increases urban fragmentation, resulting in a new urban landscape made up essentially of fortified areas from which the poor and marginalized are excluded. Rodriguez and Winchester (2001) discuss how feelings of insecurity in Santiago, Chile, have led to reduced interaction across social class levels, resulting in neighborhoods more homogeneous in income level and reduced social mobility. Agbola (1997) describes a crime prevention strategy in Lagos, Nigeria, based on environmental design, whereby the physical environment is 'manipulated' to deter crime more effectively through the installment of fences, residential enclaves, and other segregational measures. As discussed earlier, fear of crime in São Paulo has led middle- and upper-income citizens to segregate themselves spatially from the rest of the city (Caldeira, 1996).

In some contexts, violence both contributes to and is the result of the creation of "perverse" social capital.[3] A primary example of perverse social capital is gang involvement, whereby young people bereft of strong family and community support form mutually reinforcing groups. In many poor neighborhoods, gangs form the main nexus of socialization for children, who join as young as age 12 or 13. Often gangs may be at war with rival groups involved in robbery, theft, drug

---

[3] A useful distinction can be made between productive and perverse institutions. While productive institutions aim to provide benefits in order to improve the well-being of the community, perverse institutions benefit their members but are usually detrimental to the community or society at large (Rubio, 1997; Moser and McIlwaine, 2000a: 78).

distribution or consumption, and assaults. In some communities, gangs protect their neighbors, committing crimes elsewhere; in others they prey on their neighbors, creating a climate of fear (Moser and McIlwaine, 2000b; Rodgers, 1999).

In Nicaragua, for example, almost half of all crimes and delinquent acts are attributable to youth gangs. Rodgers (1999) highlights five key factors linked to youth gangs in Latin America: their context is generally that of urban poverty; their behavioral patterns and formation are highly localized; their relationship with the local community may be protective or violent; when involved in drug trafficking, they tend to be more violent; and postwar migration and deportation of illegal immigrants are affecting their formation.

Social capital in household relations

Violence erodes beneficial household relations when it reduces the households' capacity to function effectively as a unit. High levels of stress in conflict zones, for instance, where many men join illegal guerrilla or paramilitary groups, seriously disrupt family life. In poor urban communities, many women identify a direct linkage among male unemployment, alcohol abuse, and increased domestic violence, which may result in increases in female-headed households. In Guayaquil and Budapest, for example, domestic violence was found to be the single most important cause of household restructuring (Moser, 1998; Moser and McIlwaine, 1999).

Family members—both male and female—are put in a vulnerable position when communities are displaced by violence. Women are often more vulnerable than men at the moment of eviction, when they are exposed to the risks of flight and separation from their homes. While men appear better equipped to cope at such times, the reverse is true when displaced households restructure their lives; then the impact is greater for men, who become unemployed and experience a loss of status as breadwinners and a shattering of their sense of masculine identity. Women appear better equipped to develop support networks so they can continue the routines of daily survival and find new ways of earning an income, creating social capital not with other women originating from the same area, but with those sharing the same history of displacement (Meertens and Segura-Escobar, 1996).

There are many initiatives under way to deal with urban violence. Currently in many cities, one of the biggest constraints is not the absence of interventions but the lack of a coordinated approach to reducing violence. The impact of impressive menus of initiatives—implemented by government, private entities, and NGOs—is often limited by fragmented approaches involving narrowly focused, independent programs. If informed policy decisions regarding the relative fiscal returns of different programs are to be made, one of the most important priorities is the development of a cohesive policy that integrates and combines different objectives and instruments for reducing violence, and encompasses monitoring of key indicators as well as rigorous evaluations. This is largely a governance issue.

Ultimately, the debate on preventing urban crime in the developing world cannot be separated from broader issues of improving urban governance and management. This linkage implies closer integration of crime prevention and reduction imperatives within the context of more general city planning and management strategies. In some contexts, coordinated initiatives to respond to the increasing problem of violence have emerged at the city level. The role of local government in reducing violence and crime is increasingly recognized as a practical and effective solution (South Africa, 1998):

> Local government, the level of government which is closest to the citizenry, is uniquely placed to actively participate in social crime prevention initiatives and to redirect the provision of services to facilitate crime prevention.

Local municipal government tends to represent the lowest level at which planning can take into account the needs of local communities and their particular crime problems, and can therefore create effective linkages among locally elected officials, municipal departments, and the national police service (Shaw, 1998). Nevertheless, budget constraints and a lack of capacity often characterize developing-country municipal governments, and the consolidation of local government structures presents an opportunity to integrate crime prevention into the line functions of municipal departments (Shaw, 1998).

Along with government, civil society and local communities have an important role to play. Cohen and Swift (1993), for instance, advocate a public health approach that prioritizes coalition building and the development of networks of service providers. Thus, for example, one local health prevention program encourages family violence services, alcohol abuse agencies, child abuse prevention agencies, rape crisis services, conflict resolution services, drug abuse agencies, and suicide intervention services to form a network of support to coordinate comprehensive prevention services:

> Coalitions can accomplish a broad range of goals that reach far beyond the capacity of any individual member organization. The work of an active coalition can range from information-sharing and co-ordination of services to advocacy for major environmental or regulatory changes. (Cohen and Swift, 1993: 62)

Finally, the community can play an important role in reducing violence by creating its own authorities or groups to tackle the problem. Guha (1998) cites the example of the "peace committees" that are frequently formed in Indian communities after riots. These committees often include members from both conflicting communities, considered to be "respectable citizens" who work to reduce the conflict. The approach was found to be particularly effective in Calcutta for avoiding and containing many incidents that had the potential to escalate into major riots

(Guha, 1998). However, since the causes and manifestations of violence are context specific, the details of integrated intervention frameworks need to be tailored to the requirements of different situations.

The Authority Dimension

The basic parameters of urban governance in many developing countries have undergone a major transformation over the last decade and a half. Contributing to this transformation have been the relentless demographic growth of cities, with associated economic and geographic expansion of the urban base; the worldwide trend toward devolution of both power and financial resources from the national to the local level in most developing and transitional countries (as discussed earlier); the spread of powerful local movements, such as social and environmental movements in Latin America, the "people's power" movement in the Philippines, the anti-apartheid movement in South Africa, and the workers' movement in Poland; and the powerful trend toward democratization and political pluralism, along with the emergence of robust civil society institutions (such as NGOs) at both the local and international levels (UNCHS, 1996: Chapter 5). These driving forces have been reinforced by specific institutional reforms in particular countries, such as the constitutional reforms in Brazil, India, and South Africa discussed above; the *Ley de Participación Popular* in Bolivia; the Local Government Code of 1991 in the Philippines; the extension of communal status to towns and cities, small towns, and all rural settlements in Côte d'Ivoire in 1980, 1985, and 1996, respectively (Crook and Manor, 1998: 141); and a host of other reforms, well documented in the literature on Mexico, Colombia, Uganda, Indonesia, Thailand, and China.

The particular governance structure currently in place in individual countries and cities is a result of the intersection of the decentralization process; the level of democratic reforms expressed through municipal restructuring; and local circumstance, including leadership and the general involvement of civil society groups. Overall, urban governance appears most advanced in Latin America with regard to finding new modalities to manage and relate to growth, followed by Asia and then Africa (at least outside a few selected leaders in urban governance reform, such as South Africa and Côte d'Ivoire). While the focus of this chapter is on large metropolitan regions, the governance structure in these regions is invariably influenced by the overall approach to decentralization and local government in the country as a whole. Some examples follow.

Decentralization—in the sense of genuine devolution of power and financial resources (or the ability to raise finances) from the national to the local level—has had a rather limited trajectory in Africa. One of the reasons for this is certainly the legacy of the centralized, statist bureaucratic regimes of colonial powers that did not cede independence until the 1960s and even later (whereas formal decolonization took place 20 years earlier in South Asia and Indonesia, and a century earlier in Latin America). Another reason is that most postindependence regimes in Africa were ruled initially by powerful leaders and single parties who relinquished little ground to autonomous social formations or localities.

By the 1980s, this picture had begun to change across the continent, and by 1991, only 8 of 54 countries for which reliable data were available could be considered clearly "authoritarian," with 3 more being governed by a system that could best be described as "directed democracy." In addition, 8 countries were "democratic," while 35 were said to be in various stages of "transition" to more democratic forms of government (Africa Demos, 1991).

Through the next decade, the full democratization of South Africa in 1994 and the return to democracy of Nigeria in 1998 were the major events, even though a number of transitional countries became politically unstable. At the end of the decade, the respected NGO Freedom House reported that of 53 countries evaluated, 8 were "free" (i.e., full electoral democracies), 21 were "partly free," and 23 were "not free" (i.e., authoritarian systems) (Karatnycky, 1999). Overall, there was little change over the decade.

Abidjan

A former French colony, Côte d'Ivoire has always had one of the highest levels of urban development and most elaborate urban policy systems of any francophone country (Cohen, 1974). As of 2000, its largest city, Abidjan, had a population estimated at 3.3 million (United Nations, 2001: 86) over a land area of 627 square kilometers (Attahi, 2000: 10). This coastal metropolis, often referred to as "the pearl of the lagoons," represents some 40 percent of the country's total urban population and about 75 percent of its formal employment (Attahi, 2000: 10).

Like other major cities in the West African francophone region, and in spite of its relative affluence in comparison with other cities of the region, Abidjan suffers from insufficient housing and infrastructure (20 percent of its population lives in irregular or "spontaneous" housing in unserviced neighborhoods), struggles to remove ever-increasing amounts of household and industrial refuse, and cannot build enough roads to keep up with the increasing number of motor vehicles. Even though importations of cars and trucks were restricted in 1998 to vehicles no more than 7 years old, the number of these vehicles has been growing at a rate of 9 percent per year (Attahi, 2000: 16)—several times higher than the rate of population growth, estimated at 3.16 percent per annum for the period 2000–2005 (United Nations, 2001: 97). Abidjan's fabled high-quality infrastructure and large formal employment base have been deteriorating since the late 1980s, as population growth has fallen from a high in the 11 percent per annum range up to the late 1970s to a figure closer to 3 percent today, a level lower than that of middle-sized towns in the region (Dubresson, 1997: 266).

Like other ex-colonial states in Africa, Côte d'Ivoire emerged after independence (in 1960) as a relatively centralized country. Then, beginning in 1978, a decentralization process directed by the President saw, in succession, the restoration of "commune" (or municipal) status to the major cities in the country, including 10 communes in Abidjan; the amalgamation of the 10 Abidjan communes into a second-tier government known as the City of Abidjan; and the extension of communal status to 98 smaller towns (in 1985). Finally, 3 years after the death of President Houphouët in 1993, his successor extended municipal status to the remaining rural areas of the country, increasing the total number of local government units from 136 to 196 (Crook and Manor, 1998: 141). In terms of the fastidious details of its planning, as well as the follow-up of support to local councils, the Ivoirian decentralization exercise stands as one of the most thoroughgoing and successful in Africa.

Two aspects of this exercise are worthy of mention here. First, beginning in 1990, the Ivoirian government loosened control over the political system, permitting parties other than the government party to contest both local and national elections. As a result, independents and opposition parties (based on a list system) won 9 of the 135 communes in the 1990 communal elections; in the 1996 elections, the proportion grew to 27 of 196 communes (Crook and Manor, 1998: 149). The real possibility of opposition parties winning local elections and administering local councils clearly enhanced the legitimacy of local government in many parts of the country.

Second, while it decentralized, the government also strengthened its advisory and central administrative systems, so that local councils could receive administrative and technical support as needed. The Department of Local Government (within the Ministry of the Interior) grew impressively, its professional staff reaching 108 in 1995 (Attahi, 1996: 122).

The governance of the Abidjan metropolitan area consists formally of a two-tier structure: at the lower tier are the 10 communes, of differing size and wealth, each having elected councillors and an elected mayor; at the second tier is the City of Abidjan, consisting of the mayors of the 10 constituent communes, plus four more councillors from each commune. The mayor of the City of Abidjan is elected by the mayors of the 10 communes at the first meeting of the collective legislative body, called the "grand council." After his election, he resigns from his communal position, handing the position over to his "assistant mayors" at the local level.

The major functions of the upper-tier government are waste disposal and management; public lighting; sanitation; traffic regulation; maintenance of roads, parks, and cemeteries; and town planning. The communes administer markets, allocate plots for public purposes, deal with the maintenance of primary schools and clinics (but not school or health policy, let alone the supervision and payment of professionals, which are national responsibilities), operate social centers, and share functions with other levels of government with respect to pollution and hygiene. Major services, such as waste removal, electricity, and water, are in the hands of private companies, albeit under some level of surveillance from either the local or national government.

Problems with revenue exist at all levels, even in relatively affluent Abidjan, where the differences among communes are sharp. In the early 1990s, for example, the 3 wealthiest of the 10 communes of the City of Abidjan spent, per resident, an average of 49 times the amount spent by the 3 poorest communes on recurrent expenditures and 6 times the amount for capital expenditures (Dubresson, 1997: 285).

Although the metropolitan system has been functioning for 20 years, observers identify a number of problems. For example, the national government has been less than fully cooperative in permitting the City of Abidjan to exercise some of the functions for which it has a legal mandate. These include the inspection of construction sites, the issuing of drivers' licenses, and the control of firefighting and rescue operations. Since the main source of the City's revenues, the property tax, is collected by the national government and then remitted to the communes (which then pay a fixed proportion to the City), the City has little direct influence over its finances. Major service operations are controlled by private corporations that cannot easily be controlled by the City. Furthermore, since the mayor of the City is not elected at large but chosen by the mayors of the constituent communes, he does not have an independent political base from which to promote metropolitan-wide policies. Already the mayor of the wealthiest commune has resigned from the grand council on the grounds that the obligatory funds (40 percent of revenues) paid to the City could be used more effectively locally. On a more positive note, a number of communes have set up neighborhood management committees and endowed them with an administrative budget. These initiatives have taken place without higher-level support.

In the 1996 local elections, 1 of the 10 municipalities in the Abidjan area—Adjamé—returned a mayor, Marcel Amondji, who was a member of one of the opposition parties. This mayor has since set up 19 neighborhood management councils to involve citizens in local affairs. Each has an annual budget equivalent to US\$4,500 to cover the costs of the local office. According to a *New York Times* observer (French, 1998: 4), Adjamé

> has been all but transformed. Once trash-filled streets are now kept clean by broom-wielding city workers [a program called "extreme hygiene"]. A multistory African-style market is rising to replace a warren of cluttered and dangerous side streets that served as the neighborhood's informal bazaar. And white-smocked inspectors regularly make the rounds of the community's innumerable cafés ensuring that food served to the working class population is not only cheap, but sanitary.

The mayor attributes these changes, at least in part, to the competitive electoral system. "What is being done here," he says, "represents a night and day change from the past, when elections were formalities and the office of mayor was largely an honorific title. We have managed to triple our budget by raising local taxes, and nobody has complained because they see that local government is giving them valuable services for the first time." (Amondji quoted in French, 1998.) In Abidjan, as throughout the country, decentralization has been a relative success, but local resources are still very limited, and the level of activity of civil society is barely perceptible.

Mexico City

Our second example is one of the largest metropolitan areas in the world—Mexico City. For many years, Mexico City's massive, expansive growth was regarded as virtually inexorable. In 1991, for example, the population of the agglomeration was predicted to reach 25–27 million by 2000 (Rowland and Gordon, 1996: 173), although that prediction was scaled down considerably when the 1990 census figures were released. The notion of an urban "leviathan" somehow out of control was reinforced by the city's fabled scarcity of water, its high levels of air pollution and other toxic chemicals, its extreme traffic congestion, and the struggles of its poor citizens to obtain decent and affordable housing and accessible infrastructure.

While the city's service and infrastructure problems remain severe, many well-documented studies cited in earlier chapters show a decrease in its population growth during the 1980s and 1990s, a dispersion of its population from the center to the peripheral areas of the metropolitan region and beyond, and a gradual reduction in the pattern of socioeconomic differentiation among its major areas. Paradoxically, although there appears to have been a decline in social disparities in the city if one takes *delegaciones* as the unit of analysis (Rubalcava and Schteingart, 1987, 2000), at the very local level (Ward, 1999: 30),

> the segmentation, separation, and dividing line (barriers) between rich and working class neighborhoods is probably increasing. Mexico City, like many Latin American cities, has seen a dramatic rise in violence levels in the 1990s. Private security firms are increasingly hired to secure the perimeters of upper and middle income residential neighborhoods, making them effective no-entry zones for working class and outsider populations. Moreover as a growing number of urban services are contracted out to private operators, this serves to segment still further the transactional separation of rich and poor.

Currently, the population of Mexico City—which includes both the Federal District (with 16 *delegaciones*) and 41 municipalities to the north, east, and west in the states of México and Hildago—is estimated at 18.13 million (United Nations, 2001: 88), with an annual growth rate that has been shrinking for many years. Rates of both annual natural increase and inmigration have been declining since the middle of the past century. From a high of 6.7 percent in the 1940s (Ward, 1998: 48), the overall population growth rate for the metropolitan area has declined to an estimated 1.81 percent, and it is projected to fall to as low as 0.35 percent over the next 5 years (United Nations, 2001: 99).

The reasons for this reversal in trends are discussed elsewhere in this volume, but Mexico City remains a relatively poor city with serious problems in both production and distribution of public goods and services. Its current highly limited metropolitan governance system is a product of both the country's history of decentralization and democratization and the unwieldy nature of a jurisdictional division between the Federal Capital district on the one hand and the adjacent municipalities of the State of México on the other.

For decades, governance of the Mexico City metropolitan area was a relatively low-key affair, involving a presidentially appointed *regente* of the Federal District and the mayors and administrations of the adjacent (but much less developed) towns and settlements of the periphery. Because of the importance of the capital city, the *regente* position was a cabinet-level post in the federal government. Given the highly centralized and even personal nature of the Mexican political system until recently, ultimate control of the capital city was in effect vested in the president of the country.

In practice, what planning and coordination existed between the two jurisdictions occurred often through the involvement of federal government ministries in both the State of México and the Federal Republic, reinforced politically by the relationship between the governor of the state and the *regente*, the latter being, until the 1990s, from the same governing party (although the *regente* was a much more senior position in terms of protocol). During the 1970s and 1980s, planning initiatives and institutions tended to operate either at the national level (for the whole country), or in one or the other of the Federal District or the State of México. Metropolitan institutions, such as a Conurbation Commission, a secretariat for planning and budgeting, and a Council for the Metropolitan Area, came and went according to the political inclinations of different *regentes*. But with little or no public participation in planning and a multiplicity of competing and overlapping jurisdictions, the economic and social forces inherent in the growth of the city took their own paths, with little guidance from planners (Ward, 1998: Chapter 5).

Aside from the appointed *regente* and his staff, the city was further subdivided into 16 *delegaciones* (municipalities before 1928), whose administrative directors (*delegados*) were in turn appointed by the *regente*. During the 1970s and 1980s, various local and neighborhood councils were set up to give residents a say in local matters, but these groups had at best a consultative role relative to the senior appointed administrators (Ward, 1998: 118–9). In 1994, an effort was made by the dominant party, the Partido Revolucionario Institucional (PRI), to introduce "citizen advisers" as elected, paid officers at the level of the *delegacion*, mandated to assist with local community service requests. Without explaining its action, however, the government discontinued this reform 3 years after its initiation (Eckstein, 2000: 192). The arbitrary nature of local government in the capital city, at least until nearly the end of the decade, led the author of a textbook on local government in Latin America to state that "few major cities in the world have less local democracy than Mexico City" (Nickson, 1995: 199).

Traditionally, cities had little status in the Mexican system of government and politics. Article 115 of the 1917 Mexican Constitution gave states power over local government but spoke of the *municipio libre* as the cornerstone of territorial administration. It was not until 1983 that a new phase in intergovernmental relations began with a number of amendments and additions to Article 115. In proposing these changes, the president, Miguel de la Madrid (1982–1988), suggested a major "sea change" was in the offing. As one commentator observed of de la Madrid's campaign for the presidency, the candidate made clear in public meetings throughout the country that (as cited in Rodríguez, 1997: 69)

> his purpose is to eliminate, or at least minimize ... excessive central bureaucracy and population concentration, tardiness and inefficiency in some sectors of the federal government, dependency and financial weakness of the municipalities, and so forth. The time has come to "federalize" the "National Life." Each and every aspect of the state's activities which before were forced to centralize, are now obliged to decentralize.

Although de la Madrid went on to establish a system that was increasingly decentralized in administrative terms while remaining highly centralized politically, the changes to Article 115 were the beginning of an altered political environment for the municipalities. The new article approved by Congress in February 1983, to take effect on January 1, 1984, specified the public services for which municipalities had prime responsibility and suggested that the municipalities should be governed according to organic laws passed at the state level. The municipalities were also guaranteed their own sources of revenue, in particular a property tax. For many years thereafter, municipalities still relied largely on transfers from the federal government for the bulk of their revenues, but the potential existed to expand their own-revenue accounts. After the reform was passed, the president set up a National Center for Municipal Studies to serve as an information and research center for reform-related issues.

The most recent constitutional reform relevant to Mexican cities (and to Mexico City) is a revision of Article 115 passed by the Mexican Congress in June 1999. This revision, a result of negotiations among the three major political parties, recognizes local government as an essential level of Mexican government. It not only states that local governments (*municipios*) are to be governed by elected councils consisting of *regidores* and *syndicos*, but also specifies a list of functions and powers that are under their exclusive jurisdiction. Such functions cannot henceforth be limited by the state governments. They include the provision of drinking water and all related services, public lighting, cleaning and waste disposal, markets, police, streets and gardens, planning and land regulation, and other services the municipalities judge to be within their capacity to administer. The municipalities are further empowered to set tax rates and to collect the revenues necessary to carry out the above functions (Guerrero Amparán and López, 2000).

While Mexicans have traditionally elected their mayors and councillors (except in the Federal District), the elections had little meaning for many years as long as the PRI controlled the selection of all candidates. But political pluralism (albeit constrained at first) began to erode this situation as, beginning in 1983, a significant number of municipal elections began to be won by opposition parties. While some of these victories were orchestrated by the PRI itself and some resulted from splits within the dominant party, others (such as those in Durango, Ciudad Juárez, and Chihuahua) reflected genuine support for the Partido Acción Nacional (PAN) (Rodríguez, 1997: 53).

The story of opposition politics at the subnational level in subsequent years is one of conflict between emerging opposition sentiment and (often) PRI tactics to discredit or undermine the local victories of opposition candidates (Rodríguez, 1998: 174–83). By 1996 the PRI controlled 1,551 of the 2,412 municipalities in the country (or 64 percent); the PAN controlled 225 (or 9 percent); the Partido de la Revolución Democrática (PRD) controlled 181 (or 8 percent); and "others" controlled the rest (19 percent), including Oaxaca state, where indigenous groups elected their civic leaders in 413 municipalities (Rodríguez, 1998: 177). At this point, most major cities were under opposition control, with PAN mayors being significant in the more-developed north and the PRD more important in the area around Mexico City and in the south. Rodríguez (1998) argues that the advent of more competitive politics has brought more scrutiny of candidates by voters. This in turn means that more competent individuals are selected and that the quality of governance is enhanced by greater transparency (Rodríguez, 1998: 183). On the other hand, many municipalities—especially smaller, poorer towns and towns in the less industrial and developed areas of the country—are not competitive.

Did the new political pluralism make a difference in urban management? A comparison of three cities with opposition regimes in the 1990s—Tijuana and Córdoba under the PAN and Nezahualcóyotl under the PRD—shows that during the decade, the new regimes were far from fully successful in implementing their campaign promises of administrative rationalization, greater efficiency, and improved citizen participation. Setting aside the case of Nezahualcóyotl, whose municipal council had been elected only a short time before the research commenced, the other two municipalities had been able to improve the delivery of public services to their citizens (in comparison with the previous PRI regimes), and efforts were at least under way to modernize the management of the municipal enterprise. While they did not observe regression, the researchers are far from categorically enthusiastic about the changes that have ensued (Duhau and Schteingart, 1997). And a historical analysis of the politics and policies of various mayors of Mexico City since the 1950s (Davis, 2002) reveals that different mayors have exercised considerable autonomy in developing their own signature policies in spite of the fact that they were not elected until recently, and that this autonomy has been based at least in part on the fact that Mexico City as a political constituency of the national political elite must be heard and responded to (Davis, 2002).

A major reform in Mexico City in particular was the decision by the Mexican government to permit elections in the Federal District, first at the level of the whole district and then at the level of the constituent *delegaciones*. In 1997 for the first time ever, the post of "head of government" of the *Departmento del Distrito Federal* was made an elective one, to be supplemented by elections throughout the city for positions in a new Representative Assembly. Of the 40 elective positions in the assembly, 2 were won by the PAN and the other 38 by the PRD. The new head of government or mayor, who won by an overwhelming margin, was 63-year-old Cuauhtémoc Cárdenas, himself a former candidate for president and the son of a revered former president. At the same time that the PRD won the local government elections, it also captured 28 of the 30 single-member Mexico City congressional district seats in the national elections. A careful interpretation of the vote shows that the main supporters of the PRD were working-class voters who were strongly antagonistic toward the ruling party. Many switched their intended votes during the campaign to align with the party that best expressed their antigovernment sentiments. As in other elections, the Mexico City elections showed that "the prototypical PRI voter was a housewife with limited education; the classic PAN supporter an educated Catholic; and the paradigmatic PRD voter a politically engaged member of the working class" (Lawson, 1999: 151).

Among the watchwords of the new administration were the cleaning up of corruption and crime, efficiency in service delivery, and popular participation. Because the national government did not support, in terms of either resources or policies, the opposition PRD government in the Federal District, the mayor could achieve success in these particular objectives without calling on assistance from the center (Davis, 2002: 251). Nevertheless, Mayor Cárdenas left his position to run (unsuccessfully) for the presidency in 2000. The fact that the mayor had early on demonstrated his interest in national political issues (such as the situation in Chiapas) may have contributed to the widespread feeling among poorer people in Mexico City that, although electoral democratization was important, parties still operated as "clans" and did not represent them. "Residents had learned the hard way to be cynical about political change" (Eckstein, 2000: 194).

Change, however, continued. In 2000, not only did the Federal District mayor stand for general election (won again by the PRD candidate, garnering 1.7 million of a total of 4.3 million votes cast) (Gómez Tagle, 2000: 661), but so, too, did the councillors within individual *delegaciones* (Rodríguez Araujo, 2000: 657). Despite the new, more democratic system in the Federal District, however, no new structures of *metropolitan* governance have been instituted, and the larger metropolitan region is still almost totally bereft of a framework for planning.

Local participation in Chinese cities

Although Western-style pluralist electoral politics is absent in China, major changes in the governance of Chinese cities have been proceeding since the late 1980s. These changes have taken place at the local level of the urban community in Chinese cities and, according to one estimate, affect 200–300 million of its citizens (Choate, 1998: 6). While these changes are complex, they can be discussed from two vantage points: the formal structure of urban government and the operation of the local residents' committees that have become so prominent in the larger cities since the mid-1990s.

During the period of centralized planning and administration in postwar China (roughly 1949–1978), the nation's municipal administrative and political structure was characterized by the penetration of local communist party structures into all levels of urban administration. The secretary of the Communist Party's city committee, representing the party, was the most powerful individual, notwithstanding the fact that he had no position in the city government. The mayor, as the head of the city administrative bureaucracy, was second in importance, but at the same time was usually the party committee's deputy secretary. Decisions were normally initiated by the party and then carried out by the city government. The city government had control over land and construction, but many functions related to urban services (such as health care, housing, and primary education) were under the control of the work unit, or *danwei*, which could be a large government office or an industrial plant.

Beneath the level of the city government, cities were divided into districts (of which the largest cities had up to 14), subdistricts (or street offices), and neighborhood (or residents') committees. In this system of tight vertical control, only individuals who were formally working for a government-approved *danwei* were permitted to live in the city. Rural-to-urban migration was tightly circumscribed, and only those with a resident's permit had access to housing, rationed commodities (including staple grains and oils, meat and fish, cotton cloth, and most consumer durables) and social services. "The government managed not only urban development, but also urban residents' lives" (Zhang, 2001: 187).

With the introduction of market-oriented reforms beginning in 1978, local governments (as discussed above) were given more freedom to raise and distribute financial resources, responsibilities were transferred from the national to the local level, and the government stopped managing every detail of urban citizens' lives. The formal structure of municipal government at the city level (including the relationship between government and party leaders) did not change; around 1985–1986, however, the government began to place much more emphasis on the structure and functioning of submunicipal government, in particular urban residents' committees (Choate, 1998: 10). Behind this decision were a number of important factors: massive movement of rural migrants into the cities, a rapid increase in urban under- and unemployment caused by enterprise restructuring, and a withdrawal of the social safety-net functions formerly provided by large urban work-based units.

From 1989 to 1993, a number of laws reorganizing residents' committees were passed, and a 1992 joint policy paper and a 1994 major government circular laid the groundwork for a more elaborate and stronger role for the local committees. By the late 1990s, these residents' committees (which catered to modal populations of some 2,000 each) were systematically involved in some or all of the following services: information and record keeping; public safety and security; mediation of local civil and family disputes; public health and family planning; environment and sanitation; legal education of the public; provision of "convenience" services, such as fast food restaurants, public transport, and public telephones; social welfare (especially for young children and the elderly); and employment placement (Choate, 1998: 16–25). According to observers, the average age of committee members is declining, and the committees are hiring more educated, experienced, and professional staff; paying more attention to the needs of the people through social surveys and feedback mechanisms; and connecting with newly formed associations, such as volunteer social service groups, proprietor and land development associations, and cultural organizations (Choate, 1998; Read, 2000; Ying, 2000; Zhang, 2001). By the end of the 1990s, there were some 119,000 of these local committees throughout urban China. In Beijing and its suburbs in 1997, for example, there were 10 districts, 118 street offices, and 5,026 neighborhood committtees (Read, 2000: 807–8).

In many of their local initiatives, committees organize to collect fees and develop local projects. Ying (2000: 8–9) gives a good example of the new local management style in Shanghai, a style that often involves city residents actively reporting their complaints to the residents' committee office, which follows up with energetic—and probably financially advantageous—measures:

> The Quxi Road Market for Agricultural and Non-staple Products under the jurisdiction of the Wuliqiao Subdistrict [Street Office] in Shanghai [is a good] example. In 1997 the market was still dirty, chaotic and jammed with traffic. In addition, it was a market without effective management where some small private retailers ran rampant, gave short weight and beat up administrators. The local 2,000 households or more reported all this to the subdistrict office for action. Cadres of the office immediately held a meeting to discuss the matter and took measures. They cut the number of stands in the market from over 300 to 144. They also invested 260,000 yuan in building unified, standard permanent stands. They also organized an all-weather six-member sanitation team which worked on two shifts a day. The law enforcement team also entered the market to exercise supervision and strict management at regular intervals, thus reducing the number of problems. In 1998 the market was elected an advanced

exchange at the city level, and acclaimed by local residents. Finding problems through letters and calls and helping the people allay
their worries and tide over their difficulties have become a distinctive feature of the Wuliqiao Subdistrict Office in its effort to offer
good community service. According to statistics, in 1998 the office
processed 253 letters from the people and received over 4,000 calls.
These changes were not present in or before the early 1990s. They
are also unprecedented in the development history of Chinese cities,
so they are of great historical and practical significance.

While not all local committees may be as effective as this particular example, Choate (1998: 28) reports that, based on his observations and interviews in
14 cities over a 3-year period, "it appears as though the work of residents committees is reasonably well-regarded by the relevant populations themselves." Perhaps as a result, many cities are developing full-service community centers at the
street office and district levels. They are assisted by citizen "boards" or "management committees" consisting of representatives of major mass organizations
and the party (Choate, 1998: 29–31). While these groups are not elected, they
constitute an interesting local solution to the challenge of representing a range of
opinions and professional skills in an increasingly complex social and economic
environment.

IS THERE A "BEST" MODEL OF URBAN GOVERNANCE?

In this chapter we have attempted a limited review of some of the more notable
changes in urban governance in very large cities in the developing regions of Asia,
Africa, and Latin America. This review, while far from comprehensive and systematic (inasmuch as more extensive case studies and comparative data do not yet
exist in the research literature), indicates that new institutional forms are emerging in municipalities across the developing world. Common to most if not all of
these new institutional approaches are three main elements: greater involvement
of NGOs and community groups in local governance, often through a more plural
and democratic electoral system; greater transparency and accountability in both
the planning and implementation of local policy; and the devolution of more legal
and constitutional responsibility for urban affairs from the state or national level
to the local level. From the election of mayors and local councillors across Latin
America, to the increasing pluralism of the political process in Africa, to the incorporation of massive numbers of new actors in the Indian and Philippine municipal
systems, to the involvement of nonstate actors in service and infrastructure provision in China, a massive opening of political space is taking place at the urban
level.

Behind this enhancement of the municipal political role are multiple and complex structural changes: the emergence and more active participation of civil

society at the local level (often together with or as an offshoot of other social movements, such as those involving human rights, environmentalism, and indigenous rights); the connection of municipalities and their activists with networks of other municipalities and elected officials; the decentralization of powers and functions from national to local government units; and the new power and influence that cities—especially large cities—are assuming in a competitive and globalizing world.

Given the diversity of the new institutional arrangements coming into active use, as well as the fact that each country has its own historical and political circumstances that vest local governance with a special logic and legitimacy, can common elements be discerned? This question is particularly pertinent since cities and their surrounding regions increasingly see themselves as being in competition with other cities and regions around the world (Scott, 2001). At stake are potentially large investments on the part of multinational institutions (both private and public) that can make a major contribution to the employment prospects, and thus the economic welfare, of any city. Since the overall quality of governance is regarded as contributing to a city's ability to manage its infrastructure and services and maintain a certain quality of life for its citizens, alternative models of good governance frequently figure in discussions of ways to improve the competitive position of cities.

Reforms in local governance and the technical support needed by developing municipalities to put these reforms into practice effectively in their constrained economic circumstances have been the object of significant program assistance from international agencies. These agencies include the Urban Management Program of UN Habitat (formerly UNCHS); the World Bank; a number of international municipal and local government associations; and various bilateral aid agencies, such as the U.S. Agency for International Development and Germany's Deutsche Gesellschaft für Technische Zusammenarbeit (GTZ). In 1999, Dinesh Mehta, current director of the Urban Management Program, compiled three lists of "good governance" criteria to be incorporated in advice proffered by international agencies: (1) a Habitat II list (including accountability, transparency, participation, the rule of law, and predictability); (2) a United Nations Development Program (UNDP) list (including participation, the rule of law, transparency, responsiveness, consensus orientation, equity, effectiveness and efficiency, accountability, and strategic vision); and (3) a list compiled by Konrad Adenauer Stiftung for the "Better Cities Network of East and South-East Asian Cities" (including accountability, responsiveness, management innovation, public–private partnerships, local government–citizen interaction, decentralized management, networking, and human resource management) (Mehta, 1999).

Of course, each program has developed explanatory text as to how these criteria might be applied, and there are many other lists. Virtually no research of which we are aware has been done on the relative effectiveness of different elements of these lists in either controlled or comparative situations. What is clear from these lists is that an idealized liberal–democratic model of urban governance (in which well-informed citizens protected by legal institutions make periodic democratic choices of teams of politicians and professional bureaucrats to manage and develop their local space) is the suggested institutional format. While improving governance is important in smaller and intermediate-sized cities, the analysis of governance models most commonly involves the largest cities, which have the most at stake in the new economic dispensation.

By common agreement, achieving good governance in the largest metropolitan regions is more difficult than in smaller cities. Populations are larger and more diverse than in smaller cities, the level of resources necessary to institute and maintain services and infrastructure is much higher on an aggregate basis, civil society groups are more organized, and the range of functions for which the city is responsible makes the organization and logistics of urban management much more complex. As an element of his widely discussed argument that much of the world is moving from order toward anarchy, Kaplan (2001: 55) singles out urbanization:

> The 21st century is going to be the first century in world history when more than half of humanity will live in cities. Even sub-Saharan Africa is almost 50 percent urban. Urban societies are much more challenging to govern than rural societies. In rural societies people can grow their own food, so they are less susceptible to price increases for basic commodities. Rural societies don't require the complex infrastructure of sewage, potable water, electricity, and other things that urban societies have. Urbanization widens the scope of error for leaders in the developing world while simultaneously narrowing the scope for success. It is harder to satisfy an urban population than a rural population, especially when that population is growing in such leaps and bounds that governing institutions simply cannot keep pace.

As we have seen, very large cities do indeed present complex problems of urban management, but there is little or no evidence that they are sliding into anarchy. What we can conclude, which is also consistent (but not coterminous) with Kaplan's argument, is that the largest metropolitan areas will be more likely to house a highly diverse range of active civil society groups. Along with this organizational diversity, large cities will harbor important movements of political opposition to the party or regime in power at the center. This tendency is most likely a function of both social and economic diversity and the pervasive presence of global ties among the population. Thus in Kenya, the municipal elections of 1992 and 1997 reflected a largely antiregime sentiment, and both elections in Nairobi (the largest city) produced a majority of councillors representing opposition parties. In Mexico City, as we have seen, the left-wing PDR carried the municipal election in 2000. In Brazil, the most recent municipal elections, in October 2000, produced left-wing majorities (as against the center–left position of the ruling party) in the three largest cities—São Paulo, Belo Horizonte, and Rio de Janeiro. Political opposition may be one reason central governments are notoriously reluctant to agree to municipal reform packages involving greater autonomy for their largest cities.

One major issue arising in the design of governance systems for large metropolitan areas is that of coordination. Aside from the question of scale and size, the physical expansion of large cities in almost all cases extends the population and the rural (or rural/urban) hinterland over which the city holds sway to include a large number of separate and even independent political jurisdictions. Coordinating these jurisdictions is both a political and an organizational challenge, particularly given the tendency of the effectively urbanized area to spread over an ever-larger territory. In one of the classic works on this subject, Jones (1942) argues that growing cities in the United States (including central cities and their suburbs) were increasingly being fragmented into a multiplicity of inadequately coordinated units. "This fragmentation ensured competitive behavior between local governments, an inability to solve regional problems, an uneven distribution of tax resources, a lack of citizen control of local government, and the unequal distribution of services, especially pertaining to mass transit, sewerage and garbage, water supply, public health, law enforcement, and firefighting" (Stephens and Wikstrom, 2000: 40). To solve these problems, Jones argues, new arrangements to ensure metropolitan political integration should be undertaken.

Since the time of Jones's study, a considerable literature has addressed this problem in both Europe and North America. Yet as metropolitan areas grow in both size and number around the world, we are no closer to finding suitable comprehensive solutions. In an overview of four major metropolitan areas in Canada and five in the United States in 1995–1996, Rothblatt (1999) shows that the average metropolitan area in Canada contains 40 municipalities, while that in the United States contains 157 municipalities and counties. This difference in North American cities reflects the American tendency to localized, individualistic solutions as compared with greater acceptance in Canada of a coordinating role for higher levels of government (Goldberg and Mercer, 1986). Nevertheless, there are exceptions to the trend in both countries, and there is today a disturbing tendency toward greater social polarization and fragmentation in both American and Canadian cities. This trend appears on the surface to be positively related to political fragmentation (which permits the separation of groups by income and race), but the relationship cannot be clearly demonstrated. (For the American literature, see National Research Council, 1999: Chapter 3.)

As large cities in developing countries spread outward, the jurisdictional mosaic becomes larger and more complex. As we have seen in the case of Mexico City, the capital region now includes some 41 municipalities in two states, a Federal District, and 16 subunits within that district that are equivalent to municipalities. The metropolitan area of São Paulo consists of 39 separate municipalities, while Greater Santiago is made up of 34 separate communes. Rio de Janeiro has 17 separate municipalities and Buenos Aires 20 local government units. In Africa, Abidjan consists of 10 communes and a second-tier government, but one must also include a number of privatized service agencies and central government ministries that administer important functions in the city region. In South Africa, there is currently a trend toward consolidation, but in the period immediately after democratization (in the early to mid-1990s), Cape Town was made up of 39 local government units and Durban as many as 69. The pattern extends to Asia as well, where, as we have seen, Bangkok consists of a Bangkok Metropolitan Administration (divided into 50 districts) plus 5 adjacent provinces (which themselves include as many as 2,000 small local governments), while the greater Manila area includes 17 municipalities and up to 18 additional local government units in the surrounding mega-urban region.

The governance of large (metropolitan) urban areas is currently a central issue in a number of Latin American countries as they try to reconcile a resurgent local democratic culture with the need to manage complex local functions efficiently so as to safeguard the economic benefits accruing to their city-regions. There are two parallel arguments in the literature on metropolitan governance—a literature that, until recently, was based almost entirely on European and North American evidence. One argument addresses the question of whether there should be a unitary organization of government dealing with the entirety of the built-up metropolitan area. Assuming the answer to this question is positive, a second line of argument has to do with whether there should be a single-tier or two-tier metropolitan government (Sharpe, 1995). In principle, there are three possible organizational models arising from these options: (1) a loosely organized collaborative system involving relatively autonomous local governments that cover the metropolitan area; (2) a relatively unitary form of government incorporating the whole of the built-up area; and (3) a two-tier system of government covering the metropolitan area, with lower-level municipalities undertaking certain defined local functions and a higher-level council or metropolitan government dealing with functions of a regional nature. The first of these models parallels the *fragmented* model discussed earlier in this chapter, while the second and third are variants of what we have called the *comprehensive* model.

While the two-tier model was considered the most desirable system in principle for many years, it has been coming under attack for practical, political, and theoretical reasons (Sharpe, 1995: Chapter 2). Among the practical problems are the difficulty involved in keeping up with the de facto extension of the boundaries of the metropolitan area, the problem of reaching agreement on exactly where the regional government begins and local municipal functions stop, and the distribution of revenue both horizontally and vertically in large areas that are becoming fragmented and differentiated. There are, in addition, two major political problems, one local and one intergovernmental. At the local, metropolitan level, those attempting to coordinate area-wide structures, whatever their democratic credentials (which are, in any case, usually limited) have great difficulty capturing the loyalties and attachments of their citizens. Tasks are too technical, and local-ized political attachments to one's own commune or municipality tend to prevail. Area-wide sentiment, which the metropolitan structure could tap as a political resource, is in short supply; rather, tensions and conflicts among different local structures and communities within the overall metropolitan region appear increas-ingly common. At the intergovernmental level, there is almost always tension between a large and powerful local (metropolitan) government and a higher level of government—such as a state, province, or central government—that must de-centralize functions and allocate revenue to another unit with which it may very well be in political competition.

Some would argue that the fragmented model is theoretically superior to the comprehensive model. An argument can be made, based on public-choice princi-ples, that a number of small local jurisdictions is superior to a single overarching government. Since a variety of small local government units can offer different baskets of services and taxes, the whole local area can operate as a quasi-market, supporting greater efficiency through a kind of competition among jurisdictions based on the choices of citizens about where to live (Tiebout, 1956; Ostrom, Tiebout, and Warren, 1961).[4]

It appears clear that, whatever the challenges to governance in large urban re-gions in the developing world, no single or even dominant model of metropolitan governance is likely to emerge in the foreseeable future. This has not happened in Europe and North America (Lefèvre, 1998) and is unlikely to happen in de-veloping countries, which are even more differentiated in history, geography, and culture. More effective structures for coordination need to be developed, but each solution will have to respond to a myriad of complex political, financial, and tech-nical problems.

What can be said is that more participatory local solutions will be attempted for the myriad of challenges entailed in assessing and collecting taxes; improving transparency and justice in the allocation of capital funding; and involving com-munities in such local services as health care, primary education, and even the construction of basic infrastructure. As these cities grow (albeit more slowly than smaller, intermediate-sized cities), their professional staff will become more pro-ficient and their elected officials more experienced, and the new powers and re-sponsibilities devolved to them will be consolidated. One can only hope that all cities will see the value of democracy, the rule of law, and honest and effi-cient local administration, as well as the importance of supporting strong civil society organizations. However they are eventually constructed, cities must draw on the legitimacy of an emerging localism and commitment to democracy, and they must find nontechnical means to engage the imagination and energies of civil society.

---

[4] Virtually all these arguments came into play in Toronto when, in 1997, the provincial government of Ontario removed the well-known and much-admired upper-tier government and its six second-tier governments and replaced them with a single municipal government covering one-half of the greater Toronto area.

CONCLUSIONS AND RECOMMENDATIONS

Conclusions

The emergence of large urban regions, spread over many jurisdictions, presents acute problems of governance. Partly as a response, important institutional reforms have taken place over the last decade. One way of characterizing these trends is to see them as a movement from "local government" to "local governance." The term "urban governance" implies a greater diversity in the organization of services, a greater variety of actors and stakeholders, and a greater flexibility in the relationship between municipalities and their citizens.

These trends in institutional reform can be illustrated by the example of the Bangkok Metropolitan Region. From this analysis the question may be asked: Is there a preferred governance model that best fits such a mega-urban region? There are four types of mega-urban governance in actual use around the world: the fragmented model, the mixed model, the centralized model, and the comprehensive governance model. The first and last are the most widespread. The comprehensive model exists to some degree in Côte d'Ivoire, is emerging in South Africa with the "unicity," and is in effect practiced (albeit without local structures of democratic political representation) in four of the largest Chinese cities. In discussing some of these variations on an overall theme of mega-urban governance, we looked in this chapter at some of the key challenges faced by all large urban areas: the capacity dimension (involving services), the financial dimension (with a focus on the generation of local revenues), the diversity dimension (where issues of fragmentation and inequality are central), the security dimension, and the authority dimension (looking at the distribution and allocation of power).

As a result of decentralization reforms in many countries, local governments have been given more functions, as well as—after an initial time lag—more power to raise revenues. The range of these reforms is truly vast. Unfortunately, comparative statistics are very incomplete, but what figures we do have show that municipal expenditure levels are slowly rising as a proportion of national government expenditure, although the level is still low.

Local tax collection and revenue generation may be as much a governance issue as a technical finance issue, if we take into account some examples from China and Brazil. In the case of China, reforms since the late 1970s have decentralized decision making from the center to localities and have allowed local governments to enjoy the benefits of substantial "off-budget" revenues. With citizens' involvement, these revenues are a major source of infrastructural investment. In Brazil, many municipalities have adopted various versions of a "participatory budgeting" system, whereby cities are divided into regions or districts, and citizens in those areas participate in a process of determining the shape of the investment budget for each financial year.

Security is an increasingly important dimension of urban governance. During the 1990s and beyond, urban security has become one of the dominant issues. As for policy responses to violence, the emphasis in a myriad of programs throughout the world focuses on strengthening local social capital. Violence erodes social capital when it reduces trust and cooperation within formal and informal social organizations; conversely, when social capital is strong, development processes are supported.

Since the late 1980s, major decentralization initiatives that have strengthened municipal governance have taken place in a large number of countries. Examples such as Abidjan in Côte d'Ivoire, Mexico City, and some of the larger coastal cities in China illustrate a wide variety of institutional reforms that have been taking place at the local level around the developing world. Common to most of these reforms are greater involvement of NGOs and community groups, greater openness and accountability, and the disposition of more legal and financial responsibility for urban affairs at the local rather than at the state or national level.

The issue of coordination of multiple jurisdictions is central to the governance challenge in large city-regions. The literature on metropolitan governance focuses on the fragmented situation typically found in almost all North American metropolitan areas. But developing countries exhibit high levels of jurisdictional incoherence as well. Here there are two competing arguments: one suggesting that a wide variety of jurisdictions and local agencies can be beneficial to citizens since it permits local choice in services and living environments; and another promoting more coherent metropolitan-wide administrative and political solutions. These correspond, respectively, to the "fragmented" model and the "comprehensive" model of governance. As yet, no single model holds sway around the world, but discussions and analyses of competing visions are taking place almost everywhere.

Recommendations

The field of comparative urban governance is relatively new. But to improve our ability to explain and analyze urban governance reforms and policy options, we recommend more comparative studies and better interdisciplinary tools. This will involve, at a minimum:

- Paying more attention comparatively to the local dynamics of policy reform, both among cities within individual countries and across national boundaries. As urban populations increase to staggering dimensions in some cities, and as decentralization devolves substantial powers to municipal governments in the areas of health care, education, social assistance, and urban development, we need to incorporate information on and analysis of local governance into our development and policy discussions in a much more central fashion. Municipal development is real development for a large part of the population and must be treated as such in the research literature. Just as we have good cross-national information on GDP, demographic change, and even income inequality, we need to disaggregate as much of this information as possible to the urban level for comparative purposes.

- Incorporating local governance into our models and analyses of urban change. Until now, research on urbanization has focused primarily on the disciplines (such as sociology and geography) that deal with social and physical change in the urban environment. This was understandable as long as local governments had few powers and little ability to effect changes in the urban situation. But issues of metropolitan reform are on the table in many countries and need to be addressed using analytical approaches that link politics, administrative reform, and the other social sciences in the same discussion.

10

Looking Ahead

It is a rare moment in the world of demographic research when four things coincide: a profound global trend presents itself; the conceptual tools needed to analyze it and rich empirical resources are available; the trend has drawn the attention of closely allied fields and occasioned an outpouring of work by scholars in these fields; and yet the path forward lacks the signposts that would normally have been established by previous research. This is the situation facing demographers as they contemplate the cities of poor countries. The prospects are inviting, but for demographers, at least, this is an urban frontier.

The important urban trends reviewed in this report have been summarized twice: once in the executive summary at the beginning of the volume and again, in more detail, at the end of each of the substantive chapters. Here we touch only on the highlights of this complex picture to draw out the implications for research policy. At the center of the story is the fact that nearly half the world's population and more than three-quarters of the population of high-income countries currently live in cities. Today's world hardly resembles that of the early twentieth century, when only about 14 percent of the world's population was urban, and it is significantly changed even from 1950, when the figure was 30 percent (Grauman, 1976; United Nations, 2002a). By 2030, it is likely that more than 80 percent of the population of North America, Europe, Australia, and Latin America and more than 50 percent of the populations of Asia and Africa will be living in urban areas.

Although demographers have given attention to migration, they have otherwise left unexamined the implications of city life for demographic behavior in poor countries. It is here that the intellectual tools being honed in research on the United States and other rich countries can be applied—the concepts of multilevel analysis, social networks, neighborhood effects, social capital, and diffusion; and the array of measures used to understand the spatial expressions of segregation. When these tools are finally brought to bear on the cities of poor countries, we expect they will unearth many similarities in behavior in rich and poor countries but also many differences, each having the potential to enrich understanding of urban life.

It is not only because more people in the developing world will be living in cities—both large and small—but also because cities are themselves being transformed that a reconsideration of policy and research is necessary. Many of these cities participate in global networks of exchange and circuits of information; international markets, always important to some cities, are taking on greater importance for a wider variety of them; and in many countries, the relations of national and local governments are being reconfigured by decentralization and the transfer of fiscal authority and responsibility for services from national to local units of government. Increasingly, solutions to urban challenges are to be found at the subnational, regional, and local levels.

The management of diversity and inequality is among the fundamental tasks of urban governance. As urbanization brings a greater percentage of the national population into city life, the diversity of experience within cities will become more important to debates on poverty and inequality. All cities contain elite neighborhoods that are well served by good schools, health facilities, and public utilities. All cities contain poor neighborhoods as well, and in many of these the disadvantages of poverty are vividly expressed in demographic indicators. Poor neighborhoods typically suffer from grossly inadequate public infrastructure and services, lower school enrollment rates, less control over fertility, higher risks during pregnancy, lower levels of nutrition, and higher rates of mortality. Spatial segregation and the spatial concentration of poverty are likely to be just as important in the cities of poor countries as in those of the United States.

At present, few local and national statistical systems are engaged in systematic collection of the spatially disaggregated data needed to investigate such issues. National-level surveys, although indispensable for many purposes, generally cannot provide reliable portraits of individual cities and neighborhoods. The great international programs of survey research of the past quarter-century—the World Fertility Surveys and the Demographic and Health Surveys (DHS)—have been all but aspatial in their design. Like most demographic surveys, they allow for little more than the use of crude urban/rural dichotomies. If there were ever value in such simplistic measures, it is being eroded by the blurring of boundaries between cities and their surrounding regions and by the differentiation that increasingly marks rural communities in their connections to urban economies (Coombes and Raybould, 2001; Hugo, Champion, and Lattes, 2001).

For many reasons, then, there is a pressing need to develop the local datasets that can illuminate local realities and inform local policy, planning, and investment decisions. Comparative research on urban neighborhoods is valuable not only as research, but also as a means by which local and national authorities can understand their own situations by reference to similar situations elsewhere. As local governments develop their research and planning capabilities, there will be many opportunities for international technical assistance and funding through both south-to-south and north-to-south transfers. The purpose of this final chapter is to identify several promising directions for future urban demographic research and to suggest ways of improving the basic infrastructure that supports such research.

DIRECTIONS FOR FUTURE RESEARCH

New Conceptualizations of Location

In company with many urban scholars, we have emphasized the need for careful conceptualization and measurement of human settlements. New concepts and measures must recognize the ambiguities of urban boundaries and the many interconnections among rural and urban populations. This is not a new recommendation: in 1952 the United Nations *Demographic Yearbook* urged that settlement systems be considered in terms of a continuum from small clusters to large agglomerations. Many criteria could be used to identify urban areas and their rural linkages. Hugo, Champion, and Lattes (2001) suggest a focus on three key dimensions: settlement size, population density, and accessibility, with the last of these measured in terms of distance to transportation and communication options. Urban researchers have also urged that attention be given to systems for classifying regions so as to clarify the wider roles played by cities. The panel strongly endorses such research efforts.

More Spatially Disaggregated Data

With the spread of democratization and government decentralization now under way in much of the world, local administrations are increasingly being required to operate with the speed and efficiency of private business while facing ever more complex political and regulatory environments. Local governments must digest an immense amount of information to perform their duties in a fair and efficient manner. Effective planning, forecasting, and policy making all require spatially disaggregated data—but at present these data are lacking in many developing countries. Planners often have only the most rudimentary knowledge of the numbers and characteristics of recent migrants and the populations living in the city peripheries. Governments could benefit greatly from small-area unit data on population size, growth, and composition. Differential fertility and mortality rates would be valuable, as would small-area socioeconomic profiles. When such data are lacking, it should come as no surprise that cities' own projections of their population growth often fall wide of the mark. Some of the necessary intraurban data will be gathered by internationally sponsored surveys, but in the main, such data will need to be collected by national statistical services, perhaps with international technical assistance. We urge that such technical assistance be given high priority.

Spatially disaggregated data could bring to light the diversity of health risks to which urban populations are exposed (Chapters 6 and 7), illustrate the distribution of poverty (Chapter 5), and give local governments a means of understanding where service gaps and redundancies lie (Chapter 9). Data on social, economic, and spatial differentiation at the neighborhood level can provide powerful political stimuli. For instance, maps of Accra and São Paulo showing cross-district differentials in health and environmental conditions generated considerable local debate and some policy changes in both of these cities (Stephens, Akerman, Avle, Maia, Campanareio, Doe, and Tetteh, 1997). Such maps can inform neighborhood residents and the politicians who represent them, providing an empirical basis for claims upon national and local resources (as occurred in London, where Charles Booth mapped social and economic differentials in the late nineteenth century).

Considerable capacity building will be required before such visions can become realities. In most of today's large cities, municipal agencies maintain their own databases; computerization and common identifiers that permit data sharing are far more the exception than the rule. There are few examples of integrated databases for the constituent parts of large metropolitan regions. This is an area in which international technical assistance could greatly strengthen local capacities for local analysis.

In each country, a starting point would be to assess what data are available in national censuses. Census data should be among the most valuable sources of information on social and economic differentiation. When complete coverage is achieved, a census allows socioeconomic conditions of city neighborhoods to be described in minute detail. Data at the neighborhood level can be aggregated to depict larger parts of metropolitan regions. Yet census data are not commonly available in such spatially disaggregated small-area units. The lack of recent census data is due in part to the fact that many low-income nations have held no census in the last 15 years. Even where new censuses have been conducted, many countries have lacked the capacity or the willingness to generate the disaggregated figures needed by local governments.

In the view of this panel, additional support may be needed for those international assistance and training programs, such as that of the International Programs Center of the U.S. Bureau of the Census, which support census taking and the analysis of census data in developing countries by national statistical offices.[1] The analysis component of such programs warrants special attention. In the course of training, a focus on developing socioeconomic profiles of small-area units within cities could highlight the importance of spatially disaggregated data.

The Potential of New Technology

Remote sensing technologies are a promising addition to the set of tools used to gauge the spatial extent of cities and monitor change. Data gathered in this

---

[1] See www.census.gov/ipc/www.ta.html for a description of the U.S. Bureau of the Census program.

manner make a useful supplement to socioeconomic data collected by conventional means, especially when the latter are coded in a geographic information system (GIS). Recent research suggests that the combination of remotely sensed and census data may prove valuable in improving estimates of the spatial extent of cities and even their total populations. GIS technology is becoming a powerful tool in long-term strategic planning and management, and it has the potential to assist local governments in performing their diverse functions. The numbers and types of GIS applications are likely to expand rapidly if means can be found to surmount the challenges such technology presents to poor countries and to keep the costs of training and database management affordable.

New Research Themes

Throughout this report we have drawn attention to the distinctive features of urban environments that invite further demographic research. We strongly urge that where possible, such research have a comparative focus. Several dimensions of comparison warrant consideration: the situations of large and small cities; the conditions of the urban poor relative to the nonpoor and rural residents; and among the urban poor, the circumstances of those who are spatially concentrated in slums and those who live in more heterogeneous communities. If progress is to be made in understanding the demographic implications of spatial segregation, urban social networks, social capital, and the like, longitudinal research designs will eventually be needed. Even with richer data, many challenges will confront demographic research and the evaluation of program interventions. Just as in the United States, researchers assessing the impacts of poverty interventions in developing-country cities will need to grapple with the selectivities that arise from migration and program placement (Rosenzweig and Wolpin, 1982, 1988). They will need to make creative use of natural experiments and quasi-experiments. Cross-country comparative research also promises great dividends. As noted in Chapters 6 and 7, the links between urbanization and demographic transitions need to be considered more carefully than was possible in this report. There is still much to be gained, we believe, by further examination of the World Fertility Surveys and the DHS.

IMPROVING THE RESEARCH INFRASTRUCTURE

If urban demographic research is to make a contribution, attention must be paid to the infrastructure that supports such research, as represented by the major international datasets. At present, these data are often inaccessible or coded in such a way as to prevent vital cross-linkages. The data assembled by the United Nations Population Division and summarized in *World Urbanization Prospects*, for example, form the basis for much international research on urban and city growth. Unfortunately, these data have not yet been placed in the public domain. If they were made publicly accessible, the wider research community could then lend assistance in several ways: by uncovering errors in the data series, by helping to resolve inconsistencies, and by developing and testing new methods for estimating and projecting urban and city populations. Below we offer a list of recommendations that, if acted upon, would greatly enhance the value of existing data sources and ongoing data-gathering programs.

Allow comparisons of alternative urban definitions. Many of the controversies in the measurement and definition of urban areas have to do with smaller urban areas—those under 100,000 in population—that are defined to be urban according to country-specific criteria. It is probably futile to ask that uniform criteria be applied in these definitions. Rather, we suggest that whatever a country's urban criteria may be, all areas so designated be listed with their population sizes and other data relevant to the classification. This information should be made available to the United Nations for inclusion in its urban databases. Where possible, we urge that some order be brought to the definitions of urban thresholds, density measures, and measures of megacities.

Computerize the United Nations *Demographic Yearbook*. We encourage the United Nations to release the city population data contained in its *Demographic Yearbook* as a computerized database with identifying codes that would permit the linkage of each city's data across years. Rather than using typographical conventions to indicate urban concepts and isolate cases of doubtful reliability, as is the current practice, such information should be included in standardized fields in the database, with other fields being reserved for comments on country- or city-specific issues. Doing so would facilitate the use of these data for research and allow researchers to make their own decisions about the quality of individual data points. The quality and usefulness of the data in the yearbook could also be improved by close and regular collaboration between United Nations staff and independent researchers.

Expand *World Urbanization Prospects*. We make three recommendations to the United Nations Population Division to strengthen the basis for urban population research.

> **Include smaller cities.** In recent years, the United Nations has not included population estimates or projections for cities of under 750,000 population, with the exception of capital cities. Given the importance of such smaller cities to the urban transition, there is every reason to publish population estimates for all cities with populations of 100,000 and above. Whether projections for smaller cities should also be published is a separate matter calling for the exercise of research judgment.

Make projection inputs public. The task of projecting city sizes is much too large to be relegated to a single division of the United Nations with its limited resources and many commitments. The broader research community could assist in evaluating and refining projection methods if the data used by the United Nations Population Division were made publicly available. Presumably, such data could be included in the *Demographic Yearbook* database mentioned above, so that all available population series for cities could be obtained from a single unified source.

Specify the urban concept. The urban concept used in estimating and projecting city sizes varies considerably across countries, can vary across cities in a given country, and sometimes varies over time even for a single city. It is imperative to specify in the database, by city and by time period, the units used in the reports on city size; to note variations in reporting; and to describe how the projection methods take account of such variability in units.

Refine urban indicators in the Demographic and Health Surveys. We recommend that a thorough review of the DHS be undertaken from the perspective of urban demographic research. The panel has identified a number of areas in which the DHS methods could be improved at low cost. The single most important improvement would be to establish a permission system giving researchers access to spatial identifiers for the survey clusters for surveys fielded before 1999, when the new GIS coding system was put in place. As with the GIS permissions system for recent surveys, a system for the older surveys should be designed so as to protect the privacy and confidentiality of survey respondents (see Appendix F and the discussion in Chapter 4).

In addition, we encourage the DHS program to carefully review the effectiveness of its standard socioeconomic indicators in measuring advantage and disadvantage in urban populations. A set of questions in the areas of water supply, sanitation, and provision of electricity could be designed to better measure service adequacy and reliability. We make further specific recommendations with regard to public service delivery, migration, and reproductive health in Appendix F.

In making these recommendations for the DHS, we are mindful of the many conflicting demands that its survey program must balance. Other things being equal, we might also argue for increases in urban sample sizes and further improvements that could yield more precise and informative measures of urban health and demographic behavior. But there are, no doubt, considerable opportunity costs involved in refashioning the DHS sample designs in such a way, and we remain unsure of the net benefits. Hence, we have not included such recommendations here.

In the very near future, the balance of population in many developing countries will shift from predominantly rural to predominantly urban. For the long run, we believe this to be good news. The challenge over the next 30 years, however, will be to take full advantage of the potential benefits of urbanization. Richer data will be required to illuminate the situations of the urban poor, and new concepts and methods will be needed to understand the changing demography of place—not only between rural and urban areas, but also across the urban spectrum and within large urban agglomerations. Little attention has been paid to these issues to date. It is the panel's hope that the findings of our report will stimulate research into these pressing issues in urban demography.

References

ABER, J. L., M. A. GEPHART, J. BROOKS-GUNN, AND J. P. CONNELL (1997): "Development in Context: Implications for Studying Neighborhood Effects," in *Neighborhood Poverty*, ed. by J. Brooks-Gunn, G. J. Duncan, and J. L. Aber, vol. I: Context and Consequences for Children, pp. 44–61. Russell Sage Foundation, New York.

ABERS, R. (2001): "Learning Democratic Practice: Distributing Government Resources Through Popular Participation in Porto Alegre, Brazil," in *The Challenge of Urban Government: Policies and Practices*, ed. by M. Freire, and R. Stren, pp. 129–143. The World Bank, Washington, DC.

ADAIR, L. S., B. M. POPKIN, AND D. GUILKEY (1993): "The Duration of Breast-Feeding: How Is It Affected by Biological, Sociodemographic, Health Sector, and Food Industry Factors?" *Demography*, 30(1), 63–80.

ADAMS, J. S. (1995): "Classifying Settled Areas of the United States: Conceptual Issues and Proposals for New Approaches," in *Metropolitan and Non-metropolitan Areas: New Approaches to Geographical Definition*, ed. by D. C. Dahmann, and J. Fitzsimmons, no. 12 in *Working Paper* series, pp. 9–83. Population Division, U.S. Bureau of the Census, Washington, DC.

ADELMAN, I., AND S. ROBINSON (1978): *Income Distribution Policy in Developing Countries: A Case Study of Korea*. Stanford University Press, Stanford, CA.

ADES, A. F., AND E. L. GLAESER (1995): "Trade and Circuses: Explaining Urban Giants," *Quarterly Journal of Economics*, 110(1), 195–228.

AFOLABI BAMBGOYE, E., AND O. A. LADIPO (1992): "Oral Contraceptive Marketing in Ibadan, Nigeria," *Social Science and Medicine*, 35(7), 903–906.

AFRICA DEMOS (1991): Newsletter, volume 1, number 4.

AFRICAN POPULATION AND HEALTH RESEARCH CENTER (2002): "Population and Health Dynamics in Nairobi's Informal Settlements: Report of the Nairobi Cross-Sectional Slums Survey (NCSS) 2000," African Population and Health Research Center, Nairobi, Kenya.

AFSAR, R. (1999): "Rural-Urban Dichotomy and Convergence: Emerging Realities in Bangladesh," *Environment and Urbanization*, 11(1).

AGBOLA, T. (1997): *The Architecture of Fear: Urban Design and Construction Response to Urban Violence in Lagos, Nigeria*. IFRA/African Book Builders, Ibadan.

AGENCE FRANCE-PRESS (2001): Excerpt from Hong Kong service, January 5.

AGHA, S. (1998): "Sexual Activity and Condom Use in Lusaka, Zambia," *International Family Planning Perspectives*, 24(1), 32–37.

AGHA, S., A. KARLYN, AND D. MEEKERS (2001): "The Promotion of Condom Use in Non-Regular Sexual Partnerships in Urban Mozambique," *Health Policy and Planning*, 16(2), 144–151.

AGHÓN, G., AND C. CASAS (1999): "Strengthening Municipal Financing: Difficulties and New Challenges for Latin America," in *Fiscal Decentralisation in Emerging Economies. Governance Issues*, ed. by K. Fukusaku, and L. R. de Mello Jr., pp. 75–85. OECD, Paris.

AGRAWAL, R. (1999): *Street Children*. Shipra Publications, Delhi.

AGYEI, W. K., R. B. BIRIRWUM, A. G. ASHITEY, AND R. B. HILL (2000): "Sexual Behaviour and Contraception among Unmarried Adolescents and Young Adults in Greater Accra and Eastern Regions of Ghana," *Journal of Biosocial Science*, 32(4), 495–512.

AGYEI, W. K., J. MUKIZA-GAPERE, AND E. J. EPEMA (1994): "Sexual Behaviour, Reproductive Health and Contraceptive Use among Adolescents and Young Adults in Mbale District, Uganda," *Journal of Tropical Medicine and Hygiene*, 97(4), 219–227.

AGYEI-MENSAH, S. (2002): "Fertility Transition in West Africa," *Journal of African Policy Studies*, 12(2).

AIDOO, M., AND T. HARPHAM (2001): "The Explanatory Models of Mental Health Amongst Low-Income Women and Health Care Practitioners in Lusaka, Zambia," *Health Policy and Planning*, 16(2), 206–213.

AITKEN, I. (1999): "Implementation and Integration of Reproductive Health Services in a Decentralized System," in *Myths and Realities about the Decentralization of Health Systems*, ed. by R.-L. Kolehmainen-Aitken, pp. 111–136. Management Sciences for Health, Boston, MA.

AKIN, J., P. HITCHINSON, AND K. STRUMPF (2001): "Decentralization and Government Provision of Public Goods: The Public Health Sector in Uganda," MEASURE Evaluation Project Working Paper No. WP-01-35 (March). Carolina Population Center, Chapel Hill, NC.

AKIN, J. S., AND P. HUTCHINSON (1999): "Health-Care Facility Choice and the Phenomenon of Bypassing," *Health Policy and Planning*, 14(2), 135–151.

ALAN GUTTMACHER INSTITUTE (1998): *Into a New World: Young Women's Sexual and Reproductive Lives*. Alan Guttmacher Institute, New York.

ALDERMAN, H. (2001): "Multi-Tier Targeting of Social Assistance: The Role of Intergovernmental Transfers," *The World Bank Economic Review*, 15(1), 33–53.

ALESSIE, R., AND A. KAPTEYN (1991): "Habit Formation, Interdependent Preferences and Demographic Effects in the Almost Ideal Demand System," *Economic Journal*, 101, 404–419.

ALLAIN, T. J., A. O. WILSON, Z. A. GOMO, E. MUSHANGI, B. SENZANJE, D. J. ADAMCHAK, AND J. A. MATENGA (1997): "Morbidity and Disability in Elderly Zimbabweans," *Age and Ageing*, 26(2), 115–121.

ALVARADO, R., A. ZEPEDA, S. RIVERO, N. RICO, S. LÓPEZ, AND S. DÍAZ (1999): "Integrated Maternal and Infant Health Care in the Postpartum Period in a Poor Neighborhood in Santiago, Chile," *Studies in Family Planning*, 30(2), 133–141.

ALVES, M. H. M. (2003): "São Paulo: The Political and Socio-Economic Transformations Wrought by the New Labor," in *World Cities in Poor Countries*, ed. by J. Gugler. Cambridge University Press, Cambridge.

ALVI, K., AND R. WONG (1993): "Income Aspirations and Migrant Women's Labour Force Activity in Malaysia," in *Internal Migration of Women in Developing Countries: Proceedings of the United Nations Expert Meeting on the Feminization of Internal Migration*, ed. by United Nations, pp. 290–300. United Nations, New York.

AMIN, S., I. DIAMOND, R. T. HAVED, AND M. NEWBY (1998): "Transition to Adulthood of Female Garment-Factory Workers in Bangladesh," *Studies in Family Planning*, 29(2), 185–200.

AMIS, P. (1995): "Making Sense of Urban Poverty," *Environment and Urbanization*, 7(1), 145–157.

AMIS, P., AND S. KUMAR (2000): "Urban Economic Growth, Infrastructure and Poverty in India: Lessons from Visakhapatnam," *Environment and Urbanization*, 12(1), 185–197.

ANAS, A., R. ARNOTT, AND K. A. SMALL (1998): "Urban Spatial Structure," *Journal of Economic Literature*, 36(September), 1426–1464.

ANDERSEN, L. E. (2001): "Social Mobility in Latin America," Paper prepared for the Inter-American Development Bank Research Network Project on Adolescents and Young Adults: Critical Decisions at a Critical Age.

ANDERSEN, R. M. (1995): "Revisiting the Behavioural Model and Access to Medical Care: Does It Matter?" *Journal of Health and Social Behaviour*, 36, 1–10.

ANDERSON, K., AND C. M. BECKER (2001): "Spatial Patterns of Poverty and Prosperity During Transition: Kyrgyzstan 1993–1997," Paper prepared for the Panel on Urban Population Dynamics, Committee on Population, National Research Council. University of Colorado at Boulder Institute of Behavioral Science, Program in Population Processes.

ANGEL, S. (2000): *Housing Policy Matters: A Global Analysis*. Oxford University Press, New York.

ANNABLE, J. (1972): "Internal Migration and Urban Unemployment in Low-Income Countries: A Problem in Simultaneous Equations," *Oxford Economic Papers*, 24(3), 399–412.

ANTOINE, P., D. OUÉDRAOGO, AND V. PICHÉ (eds.) (1999): *Trois Générations de Citadins au Sahel. Trente Ans d'Histoire Sociale à Dakar, et à Bamako*. L'Harmattan, Paris.

ANTOINE, P., M. RAZAFINDRAKOTO, AND F. ROUBAUD (2001): "Contraints de Rester Jeunes? Evolution de L'Insertion Urbaine Dans Trois Capitales Africaines, Dakar et Yaoundé, Antananarivo," *Les jeunes, hantise de l'espace public dans les sociétés du Sud*, Autre part, 18. IRD/Editions de l'Aube, Paris.

ANZORENA, J., J. BOLNICK, S. BOONYABANCHA, Y. CABANNES, A. HARDOY, A. HASAN, C. LEVY, D. MITLIN, ET AL. (1998): "Reducing Urban Poverty: Some Lessons from Experience," *Environment and Urbanization*, 10(1), 167–186.

APPADURAI, A. (2001): "Deep Democracy: Urban Governmentality and the Horizon of Politics," *Environment and Urbanization*, 13(2), 23–43.

APPLETON, S., A. BIGSTEN, AND D. K. MANDA (1999): "Educational Expansion and Economic Decline: Returns to Education in Kenya, 1978–1995," Working Paper WPS/99-6, Centre for the Study of African Economies, University of Oxford.

APTEKAR, L. (1994): "Street Children in the Developing World: A Review of Their Condition," *Cross-Cultural Research*, 28(4), 195–224.

APTEKAR, L., AND L. M. CIANO-FEDEROFF (1999): "Street Children in Nairobi, Kenya: Gender Differences in Mental Health," in *Homeless and Working Youth Around the World: Exploring Developmental Issues*, ed. by M. Rafaelli, and R. Larson, pp. 35–46. Jossey-Bass, New York.

ARATME, N. (1992): "A Study of the Occupational Mobility of Ilocano Migrants in Metro Manila, the Philippines," University of Chicago, Department of Sociology, paper given at the 1992 Population Association of America meetings.

ARNAUD, M. (ed.) (1998): *Dynamiques de l'Urbanisation de l'Afrique au Sud du Sahara*. ISTED-Ministère des Affaires Etrangères, Paris.

ARROSSI, S. (1996): "Inequality and Health in Metropolitan Buenos Aires," *Environment and Urbanization*, 8(2), 43–70.

ASHENFELTER, O., AND R. OAXACA (1991): "Labor Market Discrimination and Economic Development," in *Unfair Advantage: Labor Market Discrimination in Developing Countries*, ed. by N. Birdsall, and R. Sabot. World Bank, Washington, DC.

ASHURST, H., S. BALKARAN, AND J. B. CASTERLINE (1984): "Socio-Economic Differentials in Recent Fertility," World Fertility Survey *Comparative Studies* No. 42. International Statistical Institute, Voorburg, Netherlands.

ASIAN DEVELOPMENT BANK (1997): *Emerging Asia: Changes and Challenges*. Asian Development Bank, Manila.

ASSAAD, R. (1997): "The Effects of Public Sector Hiring and Compensation Policies on the Egyptian Labor Market," *The World Bank Economic Review*, 11(1), 85–118.

ASTONE, N. M., C. A. NATHANSON, R. SCHOEN, AND Y. J. KIM (1999): "Family Demography, Social Theory, and Investment in Social Capital," *Population and Development Review*, 25(1), 1–31.

ATKINSON, S., J. SONGSORE, AND E. WERNA (1996): *Urban Health Research in Developing Countries: Implications for Policy*. CAB International, Wallingford.

ATKINSON, S. J., AND J. CHEYNE (1994): "Immunization in Urban Areas: Issues and Strategies," *Bulletin of the World Health Organization*, 72(2), 183–194.

ATKINSON, S. J., A. NGWENGWE, M. MACWAN'GI, T. J. NGULUBE, T. HARPHAM, AND A. O'CONNELL (1999): "The Referral Process and Urban Health Care in Sub-Saharan Africa: The Case of Lusaka, Zambia," *Social Science and Medicine*, 49(1), 27–38.

ATTAHI, K. (1996): "Côte d'Ivoire," in *The Changing Nature of Local Government in Developing Countries*, ed. by P. McCarney, pp. 107–126. Centre for Urban and Community Studies and the Federation of Canadian Municipalities, Toronto and Ottawa.

——— (2000): "Gouvernance Metropolitaine en Afrique Occidentale," Unpublished paper prepared for presentation at National Academy of Sciences meeting. Woods Hole, Massachusetts (September).

AUDRETSCH, D. B., AND M. P. FELDMAN (1996): "R&D Spillovers and the Geography of Innovation and Production," *American Economic Review*, 86(3), 630–640.

AXINN, W. G., J. S. BARBER, AND D. J. GHIMIRE (1997): "The Neighborhood History Calendar: A Data Collection Method Designed for Dynamic Multilevel Modeling," *Sociological Methodology*, 27, 355–392.

AXINN, W. G., AND S. T. YABIKU (2001): "Social Change, the Social Organization of Families, and Fertility Limitation," *American Journal of Sociology*, 106(5), 1219–1261.

BAGCHI-SEN, S., AND J. SEN (1997): "The Current State of Knowledge in International Business in Producer Services," *Environment and Planning A*, 29, 1153–1174.

BAH, S. (1993): "Re-Examination of Recent Trends in Under Five Mortality Rates in Zimbabwe: Evidence from the ZDHS, 1988," *Central African Journal of Medicine*, 39(9), 180–183, Published erratum appears in *Central African Journal of Medicine*, August 1995, 41(8):265.

BAHR, J., AND R. WEHRHAHN (1993): "Life Expectancy and Infant Mortality in Latin America," *Social Science and Medicine*, 36(10), 1373–1382.

BAILEY, W., H. H. WYNTER, A. LEE, J. JACKSON, P. OLIVER, J. MUNROE, A. LYEW-AYEE, S. SMITH, AND M. CLYDE (1996): "Disparities in Access to Family Planning Services in Jamaica," *West Indian Medical Journal*, 45, 18–21.

BAIROCH, P. (1988): *Cities and Economic Development: From the Dawn of History to the Present*. University of Chicago Press, Chicago.

BAKER, J. (1995): "Survival and Accumulation Strategies at the Rural-Urban Interface in North-West Tanzania," *Environment and Urbanization*, 7(1), 117–132.

BALBO, M. (1993): "Urban Planning and the Fragmented City of Developing Countries," *Third World Planning Review*, 15(1), 23–35.

BANERJEE, B. (1981): "Rural-Urban Migration and Family Ties: An Analysis of Family Considerations in Migration Behaviour in India," *Oxford Bulletin of Economics and Statistics*, 43, 321–355.

——— (1983): "The Role of the Informal Sector in the Migration Process: A Test of Probabilistic Migration Models and Labour Market Segmentation for India," *Oxford Economic Papers*, 35, 399–422.

——— (1986): *Rural to Urban Migration and the Urban Labour Market*. Himalaya (for the Institute of Economic Growth), Bombay.

BANGKOK METROPOLITAN ADMINISTRATION (2001): *Bangkok Metropolitan Administration*. International Affairs Division, BMA, Bangkok.

BARATA, R. B., M. C. RIBEIRO, M. GUEDES, AND J. D. MORAES (1998): "Intra-Urban Differentials in Death Rates from Homicide in the City of São Paulo, Brazil, 1988–1994," *Social Science and Medicine*, 47(1), 19–23.

BARBOSA, R., Y. CABANNES, AND L. MORAES (1997): "Tenant Today, *Posseiro* Tomorrow," *Environment and Urbanization*, 9(2), 17–41.

BARKER, G., AND F. KNAUL (1991): "Exploited Entrepreneurs: Street and Working Children in Developing Countries," Working Paper No. 1, Childhope-USA, New York.

BARNUM, H., AND R. SABOT (1977): "Education, Employment Probabilities and Rural-Urban Migration in Tanzania," *Oxford Bulletin of Economics and Statistics*.

BARTER, P. A. (1999): "Transport and Urban Poverty in Asia: A Brief Introduction to the Key Issues," *Regional Development Dialogue*, 20(1), 143–163.

BARTLETT, S., R. HART, D. SATTERTHWAITE, X. D. L. BARRA, AND A. MISSAIR (1999): *Cities for Children: Children's Rights, Poverty and Urban Management*. Earthscan, London.

BASSETT, M. T., L. BIJLMAKERS, AND D. M. SANDERS (1997): "Professionalism, Patient Satisfaction and Quality of Health Care: Experience During Zimbabwe's Structural Adjustment Programme," *Social Science and Medicine*, 45(12), 1845–1852.

BATLEY, R. (1996): "Public-Private Relationships and Performance in Service Provision," *Urban Studies*, 33(4/5), 723–751.

BATTEN, D. (1990): "Network Cities Versus Central Place: Building a Cosmo Creative Constellation," in *Cosmo-Creative '90: International Forum on Logistical Development and Its Regional Consequences in Osaka—Towards a Cosmo Creative City, Osaka*, pp. 83–85. Osaka Prefectual Government, Osaka.

BAULCH, B. (1996): "The New Poverty Agenda: A Disputed Consensus," *IDS Bulletin*, 27(1), 1–10.

BAUMANN, T., J. BOLNICK, AND D. MITLIN (2001): "The Age of Cities and Organizations of the Urban Poor: The Work of the South African Homeless People's Federation and the People's Dialogue on Land and Shelter," IIED Working Paper on Poverty Reduction in Urban Areas, IIED, London.

BAUTISTA, V. A. (1998): "Reconstructing the Functions of Government: The Case of Primary Health Care in the Philippines," in *Local Government in the Philippines: A Book of Readings. Volume II. Current Issues in Governance*, ed. by P. D. Tapales, J. C. Cuaresma, and W. L. Cabo, pp. 551–569. Center for Local and Regional Governance and National College of Public Adminsitration and Governance, University of the Philippines, Quezon City.

BEALL, J., AND C. LEVY (1994): "Moving Towards the Gendered City," Overview paper for the Preparatory Committee for Habitat II, Geneva.

BECK, T. (1994): *The Experience of Poverty: Fighting for Respect and Resource in Village India*. Intermediate Technology Publications, London.

BECKER, C. M., AND D. BLOOM (1998): "The Demographic Crisis in the Former Soviet Union: Introduction," *World Development*, 26(11), 1913–1919.

BECKER, C. M., A. M. HAMER, AND A. R. MORRISON (1994): *Beyond Urban Bias in Africa: Urbanization in an Era of Structural Adjustment*. Heinemann, Portsmouth, NH.

BECKER, C. M., AND D. HEMLEY (1998): "Demographic Change in the Former Soviet Union During the Transition Period," *World Development*, 26(11), 1957–1976.

BECKER, C. M., AND A. R. MORRISON (1988): "The Determinants of Urban Population Growth in Sub-Saharan Africa," *Economic Development and Cultural Change*, 36(2), 259–278.

——— (1999): "Urbanization in Transforming Economies," in *Handbook of Regional and Urban Economics*, ed. by P. Cheshire, and E. S. Mills, vol. 3, pp. 1673–1790. Elsevier North-Holland, Amsterdam.

BECKER, C. M., AND S. PALTSEV (2001): "Macro-Experimental Economics in the Kyrgyz Republic: Social Security Sustainability and Pension Reform," *Comparative Economic Studies*, 43(4).

BECKER, C. M., AND D. URZHUMOVA (2001): "Mortality Recovery in Kazakhstan," University of Colorado at Boulder, Institute of Behavioral Science, Program in Population Processes.

BECKER, C. M., J. G. WILLIAMSON, AND E. S. MILLS (1992): *Indian Urbanization and Economic Development Since 1960*. Johns Hopkins University Press, Baltimore, MD.

BEEVERS, D. G., AND J. S. PRINCE (1991): "Some Recent Advances in Non-Communicable Diseases in the Tropics. 1. Hypertension: An Emerging Problem in Tropical Countries," *Transactions of the Royal Society of Tropical Medicine and Hygiene*, 85(3), 324–326.

BEGGS, J. J., V. A. HAINES, AND J. S. HURLBERT (1996): "Revisiting the Rural-Urban Contrast: Personal Networks in Nonmetropolitan and Metropolitan Settings," *Rural Sociology*, 61(2), 306–325.

BEHRMAN, J., H.-P. KOHLER, AND S. WATKINS (2001): "Social Networks, Family Planning, and Worrying About AIDS," Paper presented at the 2001 Annual Meetings of the Population Association of America, Washington, DC.

BELL, M., AND M. ALBU (1999): "Knowledge Systems and Technological Dynamism in Industrial Clusters in Developing Countries," *World Development*, 27(9), 1715–1734.

BELLA, A. F., O. BAIYEWU, A. BAMIGBOYE, J. D. ADEYEMI, B. A. IKUESAN, AND R. O. JEGEDE (1993): "The Pattern of Medical Illness in a Community of Elderly Nigerians," *Central African Journal of Medicine*, 39(6), 112–116.

BENDER, D., T. RIVERA, AND D. MADONNA (1993): "Rural Origin as a Risk Factor for Maternal and Child Health in Periurban Bolivia," *Social Science and Medicine*, 37(11), 1345–1349.

BENJAMIN, S. (2000): "Governance, Economic Settings and Poverty in Bangalore," *Environment and Urbanization*, 12(1), 35–56.

BENNEH, G., J. SONGSORE, J. S. NABILA, A. T. AMUZU, K. A. TUTU, Y. YANGYUORU, AND G. MCGRANAHAN (1993): "Environmental Problems and the Urban Household in the Greater Accra Metropolitan Area (GAMA)—Ghana," Stockholm Environment Institute, Stockholm.

BENNETT, S. (1992): "Promoting the Private Sector: A Review of Developing Country Trends," *Health Policy and Planning*, 7(2), 97–110.

BENZIGER, V. (1996): "Urban Access and Rural Productivity Growth in Post-Mao China," *Economic Development and Cultural Change*, 44(3), 539–570.

BERMAN, P., C. KENDALL, AND K. BHATTACHARYA (1994): "The Household Production of Health: Integrating Social Science Perspectives on Micro Level Health Determinants," *Social Science and Medicine*, 38(2), 205–215.

BERNHARDSEN, T. (1999): *Geographic Information Systems: An Introduction*. 2nd ed., John Wiley & Sons, New York.

BERRY, A., AND R. H. SABOT (1978): "Labor Market Performance in Developing Countries: A Survey," *World Development*, 6(11–12), 1199–1242.

BERRY, B. J. L. (1995): "Capturing Evolving Realities: Statistical Areas for the American Future," in *Metropolitan and Non-Metropolitan Areas: New Approaches to Geographical Definition*, ed. by D. C. Dahmann, and J. D. Fitzsimmons, no. 12 in *Working Paper* series, pp. 85–138. Population Division, U.S. Bureau of the Census, Washington, DC.

BERRY, B. J. L., E. C. CONKLING, AND D. M. RAY (1997): *The Global Economy in Transition*. 2nd ed., Prentice Hall, New Jersey.

BHOOSHAN, B. (1986): "Bangalore, Mandya and Mysore Districts," in *Small and Intermediate Urban Centres: Their Role in Regional and National Developments in the Third World*, ed. by J. E. Hardoy, and D. Satterthwaite, pp. 131–184. John Wiley (UK) and Westview (USA).

BIGSTEN, A. (1996): "The Circular Migration of Small Holders in Kenya," *Journal of African Economies*, 5(1), 1–20.

BIGSTEN, A., P. COLLIER, S. DERCON, M. FAFCHAMPS, B. GAUTHIER, J. W. GUNNING, A. ISAKSSON, A. ODURO, R. OOSTENDORP, C. PATTILLO, M. SODERBOM, F. TEAL, AND A. ZEUFACK (1998): "Rates of Return on Physical and Human Capital in Africa's Manufacturing Sector," Working Paper 98-12, Centre for the Study of African Economics, University of Oxford.

BIGSTEN, A., AND S. K. MUGERWA (1992): "Adoption and Distress in the Urban Economy: A Study of Kampala Households," *World Development*, 20(10), 1423–1441.

BILSBORROW, R. E. (1993): "Internal Female Migration and Development: An Overview," in *Internal Migration of Women in Developing Countries*, ed. by United Nations, pp. 1–17. United Nations, New York.

——— (1998): "The State of the Art and Overview of the Chapters," in *Migration, Urbanization, and Development: New Directions and Issues*, ed. by R. E. Bilsborrow, pp. 1–58. United Nations Population Fund (UNFPA), New York.

BILSBORROW, R. E., AND R. ANKER (1993): *Community-Level Data for the Analysis of Fertility and Other Demographic Behavior: Survey and Questionnaire Design*. International Labour Office, Geneva.

BIRD, R. M., AND M. SMART (2002): "Intergovernmental Fiscal Transfers: International Lessons for Developing Countries," *World Development*, 30(6), 899–912.

BLACK, D., AND V. HENDERSON (1999a): "Spatial Evolution of Population and Industry in the United States," *American Economic Review*, 89(2), 320–327.

——— (1999b): "A Theory of Urban Growth," *Journal of Political Economy*, 107(2), 252–284.

BLAU, D. M. (1986): "Self-Employment, Earnings, and Mobility in Peninsular Malaysia," *World Development*, 14(7), 839–852.

BLITZER, S., J. DAVILA, J. E. HARDOY, AND D. SATTERTHWAITE (1988): *Outside the Larger Cities: Annotated Bibliography and Guide to the Literature on Small and Intermediate Urban Centres in the Third World*. IIED, Human Settlements Programme, London.

BLOOM, D. E., AND J. G. WILLIAMSON (1998): "Demographic Transitions and Economic Miracles in Emerging Asia," *World Bank Economic Review*, 12(3), 419–455.

BLUE, I. (1999): "Intra-Urban Differentials in Mental Health in São Paulo, Brazil," Ph.D. thesis, South Bank University, London.

BLUE, I., AND T. HARPHAM (1998): "Investing in Mental Health Research and Development," *British Journal of Psychiatry*, 172, 294–295.

BOCQUIER, P., AND S. TRAORÉ (1998): "Migration and Urbanization in West Africa: Methodological Issues in Data Collection and Inference," in *Migration, Urbanization, and Development: New Directions and Issues*, ed. by R. E. Bilsborrow, pp. 249–274. United Nations Population Fund (UNFPA), New York.

BOERMA, J. T., A. J. NUNN, AND A. G. WHITWORTH (1999): "Spread of HIV Infection in a Rural Area of Tanzania," *AIDS*, 13, 1233–1240.

BOND, K. C., T. W. VALENTE, AND C. KENDALL (1999): "Social Network Influences on Reproductive Health Behaviors in Urban Northern Thailand," *Social Science and Medicine*, 49, 1599–1614.

BONGAARTS, J. (1990): "The Measurement of Wanted Fertility," *Population and Development Review*, 16(3), 156–162.

——— (2002): "Dependency Burdens in the Developing World," in *Population Matters: Demographic Change, Economic Growth, and Poverty in the Developing World*, ed. by N. Birdsall, A. C. Kelley, and S. Sinding, pp. 55–64. Oxford University Press, New York.

BONGAARTS, J., AND R. G. POTTER (1983): *Fertility, Biology, and Behavior: An Analysis of the Proximate Determinants*. Academic Press, New York.

BONGAARTS, J., AND S. W. WATKINS (1996): "Social Interactions and Contemporary Fertility Transitions," *Population and Development Review*, 22(4), 639–682.

BOONYABANCHA, S. (2001): "Savings and Loans: Drawing Lessons from Some Experiences in Asia," *Environment and Urbanization*, 13(2), 9–21.

BORJAS, G. J. (1995): "Ethnicity, Neighborhoods, and Human-Capital Externalities," *American Economic Review*, 85(3), 365–390.

BOSERUP, E. (1985): "Economic and Demographic Interrelationships in Sub-Saharan Africa," *Population and Development Review*, 11(3), 383–397.

BOWE, M. (ed.) (1998): *Banking and Finance in Islands and Small States*. Pinter, London and Washington, DC.

BRADLEY, J. B., C. STEPHENS, T. HARPHAM, AND S. CAIRNCROSS (1992): *A Review of Environmental Health Impacts in Developing Country Cities*. Urban Management Program, Urban Management and the Environments, The World Bank, Washington, DC.

BRAMBILA PAZ, C. (1998): "A Reassessment of Migration and Urbanization in Mexico in the 20th Century," in *Migration, Urbanization, and Development: New Directions and Issues*, ed. by R. E. Bilsborrow, pp. 59–88. United Nations Population Fund (UNFPA), New York.

BRASS, W., AND C. L. JOLLY (eds.) (1993): *Population Dynamics of Kenya*. Panel on the Population Dynamics of Sub-Saharan Africa, Committee on Population, National Research Council, National Academy Press, Washington, DC.

BROCKERHOFF, M. (1994): "The Impact of Rural-Urban Migration on Child Survival," *Health Transition Review*, 4(2), 127–149.

——— (1995a): "Child Survival in Big Cities: The Disadvantages of Migrants," *Social Science and Medicine*, 40(10), 1371–1383.

——— (1995b): "Fertility and Family Planning in African Cities: The Impact of Female Migration," *Journal of Biosocial Science*, 27, 347–358.

——— (1999): "Urban Growth in Developing Countries: A Review of Projections and Predictions," *Population and Development Review*, 25(4), 757–778.

——— (2000): "An Urbanizing World," *Population Bulletin*, 55(3).

BROCKERHOFF, M., AND E. BRENNAN (1998): "The Poverty of Cities in Developing Regions," *Population and Development Review*, 24(1), 75–114.

BROMLEY, R., AND C. GERRY (eds.) (1979): *Casual Work and Poverty in Third World Cities*. John Wiley and Sons, New York, Brisbane, Toronto.

BROOKS-GUNN, J., G. J. DUNCAN, T. LEVENTHAL, AND J. L. ABER (1997): "Lessons Learned and Future Directions for Research on the Neighborhoods in Which Children Live," in *Neighborhood Poverty*, ed. by J. Brooks-Gunn, G. J. Duncan, and J. L. Aber, vol. I: Context and Consequences for Children, pp. 279–297. Russell Sage Foundation, New York.

BRUGHA, R., D. CHANDRAMOHAN, AND A. B. ZWI (1999): "Viewpoint: Management of Malaria: Working With the Private Sector," *Tropical Medicine and International Health*, 4(5), 402–406.

BRUGHA, R., AND A. B. ZWI (1999): "Sexually Transmitted Disease Control in Developing Countries: The Challenge of Involving the Private Sector [Editorial]," *Sexually Transmitted Infections*, 75(5), 283–285.

BRYCESON, D. (1999): "Sub-Saharan Africa Betwixt and Between: Rural Livelihoods, Practices and Policies," ASC Working Paper no. 43, Africa Studies Centre, Leiden.

BUECHLER, S. (2000): "The Growth of the Informal Sector in São Paulo, Brazil," Paper prepared for the Panel on Urban Population Dynamics, Committee on Population, National Research Council. Columbia University, Department of Urban Planning.

BULATAO, R. A., AND J. A. ROSS (2000): "Rating Maternal and Neonatal Health Programs in Developing Countries," MEASURE Evaluation Paper no. WP-00-26. Carolina Population Center, Chapel Hill, NC.

BURTON, L. M., T. PRICE-SPRATLEN, AND M. B. SPENCER (1997): "On Ways of Thinking about Measuring Neighborhoods: Implications for Studying Context and Developmental Outcomes for Children," in *Neighborhood Poverty*, ed. by J. Brooks-Gunn, G. J. Duncan, and J. L. Aber, vol. II: Policy Implications in Studying Neighborhoods, pp. 132–144. Russell Sage Foundation, New York.

BYARUGABA, J., AND D. KIELKOWSKI (1994): "Reflections on Trauma and Violence-Related Deaths in Soweto, July 1990–June 1991," *South African Medical Journal*, 84(9), 610–614.

BYASS, P., M. D. ADEDEJI, J. G. MONGDEM, A. C. ZWANDOR, S. H. BREW-GRAVES, AND C. J. CLEMENTS (1995): "Assessment and Possible Control of Endemic Measles in Urban Nigeria," *Journal of Public Health and Medicine*, 17(2), 140–145.

CAIRNCROSS, S. (1990): "Water Supply and the Urban Poor," in *The Poor Die Young: Housing and Health in Third World Cities*, ed. by J. E. Hardoy, S. Cairncross, and D. Satterthwaite, pp. 109–126. Earthscan Publications, London.

CALDEIRA, T. P. R. (1996): "Building Up Walls: The New Pattern of Spatial Segregation in São Paulo," *International Social Science Journal*, 147(March), 55–66.

——— (1999): "Fortified Enclaves: The New Urban Segregation," in *Cities and Citizenship*, ed. by J. Holston, pp. 114–138. Duke University Press, Durham and London.

——— (2000): *City of Walls: Crime, Segregation, and Citizenship in São Paulo*. University of California Press, Berkeley.

CALDWELL, J. C. (1976): "Toward a Restatement of Demographic Transition Theory," *Population and Development Review*, 2(3&4), 321–366.

——— (1979): "Education as a Factor in Mortality Decline: An Examination of Nigerian Data," *Population Studies*, 33, 395–413.

——— (1995): "Understanding the AIDS Epidemic and Reacting Sensibly to It," *Social Science and Medicine*, 41, 299–302.

——— (1997): "The Impact of the African AIDS Epidemic," *Health Transition Review*, 7(Supplement 2), 169–188.

——— (2000): "Rethinking the African AIDS Epidemic," *Population and Development Review*, 26(1), 117–135.

CALDWELL, J. C., AND P. CALDWELL (1993): "The Nature and Limits of the Sub-Saharan African AIDS Epidemic: Evidence from Geographic and Other Patterns," *Population and Development Review*, 19(4), 817–848.

——— (2001): "Regional Paths to Fertility Transition," *Journal of Population Research*, 18(2), 91–117.

CAMPOS, R., M. RAFFAELLI, AND W. UDE (1994): "Social Networks and Daily Activities of Street Youth in Belo Horizonte, Brazil," *Child Development*, 65, 319–330.

CARDIA, N. (2000): "Urban Violence in São Paulo," Comparative Urban Studies Occasional Paper no. 33. Woodrow Wilson International Center for Scholars, Washington, DC.

CARE/TANZANIA (1998): "Dar-es-Salaam Urban Livelihood Security Assessment, Summary Report," CARE/Tanzania.

CARME, B., P. KOULENGANA, A. NZAMBE, AND G. D. BODAN (1992): "Current Practises for the Prevention and Treatment of Malaria in Children and in Pregnant Women in the Brazzaville Region (Congo)," *Annals of Tropical Medicine and Parasitology*, 86(4), 319–322.

CARNEIRO, L. P. (2000): *Violent Crime in Latin American Cities: Rio de Janeiro and São Paulo*. World Bank, Washington, DC, World Bank Project on Crime in LAC Countries.

CARPENTIER, L., T. PRAZUCK, F. VINCENT-BALLEREAU, L. T. OUEDRAOGO, AND C. LAFAIX (1995): "Choice of Traditional or Modern Treatment in West Burkina Faso," *World Health Forum*, 16(2), 198–202.

CARTER, M. R. (1999): "Getting Ahead or Falling Behind? The Dynamics of Poverty in Post-Apartheid South Africa," Draft paper, Department of Agricultural and Applied Economics, University of Wisconsin.

CASTELLS, M. (1989): *The Informational City: Information Technology, Economic Restructuring and the Urban-Regional Process*. Blackwell, Oxford, UK.

———— (1997): *The Rise of the Network Society*. Blackwell, Oxford, UK.

CASTERLINE, J. B. (ed.) (1985a): *The Collection and Analysis of Community Data*. International Statistical Institute, Voorburg.

———— (1985b): "Community Effects on Fertility," in *The Collection and Analysis of Community Data*, ed. by J. B. Casterline, pp. 65–75. International Statistical Institute, Voorburg.

———— (1999): "The Onset and Pace of Fertility Transition: National Patterns in the Second Half of the Twentieth Century," Policy Research Division Working Paper No. 128, Population Council, New York.

CASTERLINE, J. B., M. R. MONTGOMERY, D. K. AGYEMAN, P. AGLOBITSE, AND G.-E. KIROS (2001): "Social Networks and Contraceptive Dynamics in Southern Ghana," Paper presented at the 2001 Annual Meetings of the Population Association of America, Washington, DC.

CEESAY, M. M., M. W. MORGAN, M. O. KAMANDA, V. R. WILLOUGHBY, AND D. R. LISK (1996): "Prevalence of Diabetes in Rural and Urban Populations in Southern Sierra Leone: A Preliminary Survey," *Tropical Medicine and International Health*, 2(3), 272–277.

CENTER FOR POPULATION OPTIONS (1992): *Adolescent Fertility in Sub-Saharan Africa*. Center for Population Options, Washington, DC.

CHALKER, J., N. CHUC, T. FALKENBERG, N. DO, AND G. TOMSON (2000): "STD Management by Private Pharmacies in Hanoi: Practice and Knowledge of Drug Sellers," *Sexually Transmitted Infections*, 76, 299–302.

CHAMBERS, R. (1983): *Rural Development: Putting the Last First*. Longman, London.

———— (1989): "Editorial Introduction: Vulnerability, Coping and Policy," *IDS Bulletin*, 20(2), 1–7.

———— (1995): "Poverty and Livelihoods: Whose Reality Counts?" *Environment and Urbanization*, 7(1), 173–204.

CHAMPION, T. (1998): "The Complexity of Urban Systems: Contrasts and Similarities from Different Regions," Australian Development Studies Network, Briefing Paper No. 51, Canberra.

CHANDLER, T. (1987): *Four Thousand Years of Urban Growth: A Historical Census*. St. David's University Press, Lewiston/Queenston, NY.

CHAPPLE, K. (2002): "Out of Touch, Out of Bounds: How Social Networks Shape the Labor Market Radii of Women on Welfare in San Francisco," *Urban Geography*, forthcoming.

CHASKIN, R. J. (1994): "Defining Neighborhood," Background paper prepared for the Neighborhood Mapping Project of the Annie E. Casey Foundation. Chapin Hall Center for Children at the University of Chicago.

CHEN, N., P. VALENTE, AND H. ZLOTNIK (1998): "What Do We Know about Recent Trends in Urbanization?" in *Migration, Urbanization, and Development: New Directions and Issues* ed. by R. E. Bilsborrow, pp. 59–88. United Nations Population Fund (UNFPA), New York.

CHIGUZO, A. (1999): "Factors Associated with the Occurrence of Malaria Epidemics. The Case of Huruma Peri-Urban, Eldoret Municipality, Kenya," Poster presented at the MIM African Malaria Conference, 14–19 March, Durban, South Africa.

CHISWICK, B. R., H. A. PATRINOS, AND M. E. HURST (2000): "Indigenous Language Skills and the Labor Market in a Developing Economy: Bolivia," *Economic Development and Cultural Change*, 48(2), 349–367.

CHOATE, A. C. (1998): "Local Governance in China, Part II. An Assessment of Urban Residents Committees and Municipal Community Development," Working Paper No. 10, Asia Foundation. The Asia Foundation, New York.

CHOE, S.-C. (1996): "The Evolving Urban System in North-East Asia," in *Emerging World Cities in Pacific Asia*, ed. by F.-C. Lo, and Y. M. Yeung, pp. 498–519. United Nations Press, Tokyo.

CHRISTALLER, W. (1933): *Die Zentralen Orte in Süddeutschland*. Fischer, Jena, Germany, (Translated into English as: Baskin, C. W., 1966, *Central Places in Southern Germany*. Prentice-Hall, Englewood Cliffs, NJ).

CITRO, C. F., AND R. T. MICHAEL (eds.) (1995): *Measuring Poverty: A New Approach*. National Academy Press, Washington, DC.

CLELAND, J. (1985): "Marital Fertility Decline in Developing Countries: Theories and the Evidence," in *Reproductive Change in Developing Countries: Insights from the World Fertility Survey*, ed. by J. Cleland, and J. Hobcraft, pp. 223–252. Oxford University Press, Oxford.

CLELAND, J., AND J. HOBCRAFT (eds.) (1985): *Reproductive Change in Developing Countries: Insights from the World Fertility Surveys*. Oxford University Press, Oxford.

CLELAND, J., AND C. WILSON (1987): "Demand Theories of the Fertility Decline: An Iconoclastic View," *Population Studies*, 41, 5–30.

COALE, A. J., AND T. J. TRUSSELL (1974): "Model Fertility Schedules: Variations in the Age Structure of Childbearing in Human Populations," *Population Index*, 40(2), 185–258.

COALE, A. J., AND S. C. WATKINS (eds.) (1986): *The Decline of Fertility in Europe.* Princeton University Press, Princeton, NJ.

COELHO, M. P., AND E. DINIZ (1997): "Governabilidad, Gobierno Local y Pobreza en Brasil," in *Ciudades y Gobernabilidad en América Latina*, ed. by A. Rodriguez, and L. Winchester, pp. 99–152. Editiones Sur, Santiago.

COHEN, B. (1998a): "The Emerging Fertility Transition in Sub-Saharan Africa," *World Development*, 26(8), 1431–1461.

COHEN, B., AND W. J. HOUSE (1994): "Education, Experience, and Earnings in the Labor Market of a Developing Economy: The Case of Urban Khartoum," *World Development*, 22(10), 1549–1565.

——— (1996): "Labor Market Choices, Earnings, and Informal Networks in Khartoum, Sudan," *Economic Development and Cultural Change*, 44(3), 589–618.

COHEN, B., AND J. TRUSSELL (eds.) (1996): *Preventing and Mitigating AIDS in Sub-Saharan Africa: Research and Data Priorities for the Social and Behavioral Sciences*, Panel on Data and Research Priorities for Arresting AIDS in Sub-Saharan Africa, Committee on Population, Commission on Behavioral and Social Sciences and Education, National Research Council. National Academy Press, Washington, DC.

COHEN, L., AND S. SWIFT (1993): "A Public Health Approach to the Violence Epidemic in the United States," *Environment and Urbanization*, 5(2), 50–66.

COHEN, M. (1974): *Urban Policy and Political Conflict in Africa. A Study of the Ivory Coast.* University of Chicago Press, Chicago.

——— (1983): *Learning by Doing. World Bank Lending for Urban Development, 1972–82.* The World Bank, Washington, DC.

——— (2002): "The Five Cities of Buenos Aires: An Essay on Poverty and Inequality in Urban Argentina," in *Encyclopedia of Sustainable Development*, ed. by S. Sassen. United Nations Economic, Social, and Cultural Organization, Paris.

COHEN, R. B. (1981): "The New International Division of Labor, Multinational Corporations and Urban Hierarchy," in *Urbanization and Urban Planning in Capitalist Society*, ed. by M. Dear, and A. J. Scott, pp. 287–315. Methuen, London.

COHEN, S. B. (ed.) (1998b): *The Columbia Gazetteer of the World.* Columbia University Press, New York.

COLE, W. E., AND R. D. SANDERS (1985): "Internal Migration and Urbanization in the Third World," *American Economic Review*, 75(3), 481–494.

COLEMAN, J. S. (1988): "Social Capital in the Creation of Human Capital," *American Journal of Sociology*, 94(Supplement), S95–S120.

——— (1990): *Foundations of Social Theory.* The Belknap Press of Harvard University Press, Cambridge, MA.

COLLIER, P., AND A. BIGSTEN (1981): "A Model of Educational Expansion and Labor Market Adjustment Applied to Kenya," *Oxford Bulletin of Economics and Statistics*, 43(1), 31–49.

COLLIER, P., AND J. W. GUNNING (1999a): "Why Has Africa Grown Slowly?" *Journal of Economic Perspectives*, 13(3), 3–22.

——— (1999b): "Explaining African Economic Performance," *Journal of Economic Literature*, 37(1), 64–111.

COMMITTEE ON IDENTIFYING DATA NEEDS FOR PLACE-BASED DECISION MAKING (2002): *Community and Quality of Life: Data Needs for Informed Decision Making.*

National Academy Press, Washington, DC, Committee on Geography, Board on Earth Sciences and Resources, Division of Earth and Life Studies, National Research Council.

COMMITTEE TO STUDY FEMALE MORBIDITY AND MORTALITY IN SUB-SAHARAN AFRICA (1996): *In Her Lifetime: Female Morbidity and Mortality in Sub-Saharan Africa.* National Academy Press, Washington, DC, C. P. Howson, P. F. Harrison, D. Hotra, and M. Law, eds., Board on International Health, Institute of Medicine.

COOMBES, M., AND S. RAYBOULD (2001): "Public Policy and Population Distribution: Developing Appropriate Indicators of Settlement Patterns," *Environment and Planning C: Government and Policy*, 19(2), 223–248.

CORBETT, J. (1989): "Poverty and Sickness: The High Costs of Ill-Health," *IDS Bulletin*, 20(2), 58–62.

CORNIA, G. A., AND R. PANICCIÀ (1999): "Mortality Changes in Severely Distressed Economies," in *Population and Poverty in Developing Countries*, ed. by M. Livi-Bacci, and G. de Santis, pp. 217–249. Clarendon Press, Oxford.

COUR, J.-M. (1994): *West Africa Long Term Perspective Study.* OECD, ADB, CILSS.

COX, D., B. E. HANSEN, AND E. JIMENEZ (1999): "How Responsive are Private Transfers to Income? Evidence from a Laissez-Faire Economy," Working Paper, Department of Economics, Boston University.

COX, D., AND E. JIMENEZ (1998): "Risk Sharing and Private Transfers: What about Urban Households?" *Economic Development and Cultural Change*, 46(3), 621–637.

CRANE, S. F., AND J. W. CARSWELL (1992): "A Review and Assessment of Non-Governmental Organization-Based STD/AIDS Education and Prevention Projects for Marginalized Groups," *Health Education Research*, 7(2), 175–194.

CRANKSHAW, O., AND S. PARNELL (2003): "Race, Inequality and Urbanisation in the Johannesburg Region, 1946–1996," in *World Cities in Poor Countries*, ed. by J. Gugler. Cambridge University Press, Cambridge.

CREWE, E. (1995): "Indoor Air Pollution, Household Health and Appropriate Technology; Women and the Indoor Environment in Sri Lanka," in *Down to Earth: Community Perspectives on Health, Development and the Environment*, ed. by B. Bradford, and M. A. Gwynne, pp. 92–99. Kumarian Press, West Hartford.

CROOK, R. C., AND J. MANOR (1998): *Democracy and Decentralisation in South Asia and West Africa: Participation, Accountability and Performance.* Cambridge University Press, Cambridge.

DAHMANN, D. C. (1999): "New Approaches to Delineating Metropolitan and Non-metropolitan Settlement: Geographers Drawing the Line," *Urban Geography*, 20(8), 684–694.

DAVIS, D. E. (2002): "Mexico City: The Local-National Dynamics of Decentralization," in *Capital City Politics in Latin America: Democratization and Empowerment*, ed. by D. J. Myers, and H. A. Dietz, pp. 227–263. Lynne Rienner, Boulder, CO.

DAVIS, J., A. KANG, AND J. VINCENT (2001): "How Important Is Improved Water Infrastructure to Microenterprises? Evidence from Uganda," *World Development*, 29(10), 1753–1767.

DAVIS, K. (1955): "The Origin and Growth of Urbanization in the World," *American Journal of Sociology*, 60(5), 429–437.

——— (1958): *The World's Metropolitan Areas*. University of California Press, Berkeley, CA.

——— (1965): "The Urbanization of the Human Population," *Scientific American*, 213(3), 40–53.

——— (1969): *World Urbanization 1950–1970. Vol. I: Basic Data for Cities, Countries, and Regions*. Institute of International Studies, Berkeley, CA.

DE GREGORIO, J., AND R. O. VALDÉS (2001): "Crisis Transmission: Evidence from the Debt, Tequila and Asian Flu Crises," *The World Bank Economic Review*, 15(2), 289–314.

DE JONG, G. F. (2000): "Expectations, Gender, and Norms in Migration Decision-Making," *Population Studies*, 54(3), 307–319.

DE LA PAZ LÓPEZ, M., H. IZAZOLA, AND J. G. DE LEÓN (1993): "Characteristics of Female Migrants According to the 1990 Census of Mexico," in *Internal Migration of Women in Developing Countries: Proceedings of the United Nations Export Meeting on the Feminization of Internal Migration*, ed. by United Nations, pp. 133–153. United Nations, New York.

DE SOTO, H. (1987): *El Otro Sendero: La Revolucion Informal*. Editorial Oveja Negra, Bogota.

DE WIT, J. W. (2002): "Urban Poverty Alleviation in Bangalore," *Economic and Political Weekly*, September 21, 3935–3942.

DEATON, A., AND C. PAXSON (2000): "Growth, Demographic Structure, and National Saving in Taiwan," *Population and Development Review*, 26(Supplement), 141–173.

DEATON, A., AND A. TAROZZI (2000): "Prices and Poverty in India," Unpublished paper, Research Program in Development Studies, Princeton University.

DÉBLÉ, I., AND P. HUGON (eds.) (1982): *Vivre et Survivre dans les Villes Africaines*. PUF, Paris.

DECOSAS, J., F. KANE, J. K. ANARFI, K. D. R. SODJI, AND H. U. WAGNER (1995): "Migration and AIDS," *Lancet*, 346, 826–828.

DEGRAFF, D. S., R. E. BILSBORROW, AND D. K. GUILKEY (1997): "Community-Level Determinants of Contraceptive Use in the Philippines: A Structural Analysis," *Demography*, 34(3), 385–398.

DEL CONTE, A., AND J. KLING (2001): "A Synthesis of MTO Research on Self-Sufficiency, Safety and Health, and Behavior and Delinquency," *Poverty Research News*, 5(1), 3–6.

DELPEUCH, F., AND B. MARIE (1997): "Obesity and Developing Countries of the South," *Medicine Tropicale*, 57(4), 380–388.

DEMOGRAPHIC AND HEALTH SURVEYS (1994): *Description of the Demographic and Health Surveys Individual Recode Data File: DHS II*. Demographic and Health Surveys, Macro International, Version 1.1.

——— (2001): *Description of the Demographic and Health Surveys Individual Recode Data File: DHS III*. Demographic and Health Surveys, Macro International, Version 1.1 (with differences from DHS II).

DESGRÉES DU LOÛ, A., P. MSELLATI, I. VIHO, AND C. WELFFENS-EKRA (2000): "The Use of Induced Abortion in Abidjan: A Possible Cause of the Fertility Decline," *Population*, 12, 197–214.

DESHPANDE, S., AND L. DESHPANDE (1991): "Problems of Urbanization and Growth of Large Cities in Developing Countries: A Case Study of Bombay," Population and Labour Studies Programme, Working Paper no. 17. World Development Program Research.

DEVAS, N., AND D. KORBOE (2000): "City Governance and Poverty: The Case of Kumasi," *Environment and Urbanization*, 12(1), 123–135.

DEVELAY, A., R. SAUERBORN, AND H. J. DIESFELD (1996): "Utilization of Health Care in an African Urban Area: Results from a Household Survey in Ouagadougou, Burkina Faso," *Social Science and Medicine*, 43(11), 1611–1619.

DIETZ, P. (1990): "Youth Reach Their Peers," *Passages*, 10(1), 1–3.

DINYE, R. D. (1995): "A Gender Sensitive Situation Analysis of the Urban Poor, a Case Study in Kumasi, Ghana," *Trialog*, 44, 34–37.

DIXIT, A. (1969): "Marketable Surplus and Dual Development," *Journal of Economic Theory*, 1, 203–219.

DOUGLASS, M. (1989): "The Environmental Sustainability of Development: Coordination, Incentives and Political Will in Land Use Planning for the Jakarta Metropolis," *Third World Planning Review*, 11(2), 211–238.

——— (1997): "Structural Change and Urbanization in Indonesia: From the 'Old' to the 'New' International Division of Labour," in *Urbanization in Large Developing Countries: China, Indonesia, Brazil, and India*, ed. by G. W. Jones, and P. Visaria, pp. 111–141. Clarendon Press, Oxford.

——— (1998): "A Regional Network Strategy for Reciprocal Rural-Urban Linkages: An Agenda for Policy Research with Reference to Indonesia," *Third World Planning Review*, 20(1).

——— (1999): "Rural-Urban Integration and Regional Economic Resilience: Strategies for the Rural-Urban Transition in Northest Thailand," mimeo.

DUBRESSON, A. (1997): "Abidjan: From the Public Making of a Modern City to Urban Management of a Metropolis," in *The Urban Challenge in Africa: Growth and Management of its Large Cities*, ed. by C. Rakodi, pp. 252–291. United Nations University Press, Tokyo.

DUHAU, E., AND M. SCHTEINGART (1997): "Governance and Local Management in Mexico and Colombia," Unpublished paper presented at the GURI Workshop, "Governance in Action" at the Woodrow Wilson International Center for Scholars, Washington, DC (November).

DUNCAN, G. J., J. P. CONNELL, AND P. K. KLEBANOV (1997): "Conceptual and Methodological Issues in Estimating Causal Effects of Neighborhoods and Family Conditions on Individual Development," in *Neighborhood Poverty*, ed. by J. Brooks-Gunn, G. J. Duncan, and J. L. Aber, vol. I: Context and Consequences for Children, pp. 219–250. Russell Sage Foundation, New York.

DURANTON, G., AND D. PUGA (2001): "Nursery Cities: Urban Diversity, Process Innovation, and the Life Cycle of Products," *American Economic Review*, 91(5), 1454–1477.

DURLAUF, S. N. (1999): "The Case 'Against' Social Capital," *Focus*, 20(3), 1–5.

EBERTS, R. W., AND D. P. MCMILLEN (1999): "Agglomeration Economies and Urban Public Infrastructure," in *Handbook of Regional and Urban Economies*, ed. by E. S. Mills, and P. Cheshire, vol. 3, pp. 1455–1495. Elsevier North-Holland, Amsterdam.

ECKSTEIN, S. (2000): "What Significance Hath Reform? The View from the Mexican Barrio," in *Social Development in Latin America: The Politics of Reform*, ed. by J. S. Tulchin, and A. M. Garland, pp. 175–200. Lynne Rienner, Boulder.

EISENSTEIN, E., AND M. T. DE AQUINO (1992): "Project: Street Children and Drugs," Unpublished document for NEPAD and WHO.

EKBLAD, S. (1993): "Stressful Environments and Their Effects on Quality of Life in Third World Cities," *Environment and Urbanization*, 5(2), 125–134.

ELLIS, F. (1998): "Household Strategies and Rural Livelihood Diversification," *Journal of Development Studies*, 35(1), 1–38.

ELLIS, S., AND Y. A. FAURÉ (eds.) (1995): *Entreprises et Entrepreneurs Africains*. Karthala-Orstrom, Paris.

ELLISON, G., AND E. L. GLAESER (1999): "The Geographic Concentration of Industry: Does Natural Advantage Explain Agglomeration?" *American Economic Review*, 89(2), 311–316.

ENTWISLE, B., J. B. CASTERLINE, AND H. A. A. SAYED (1989): "Villages as Contexts for Contraceptive Behavior in Rural Egypt," *American Sociological Review*, 54(6), 1019–1034.

ENTWISLE, B., R. R. RINDFUSS, D. K. GUILKEY, A. CHAMRATRITHIRONG, S. CURRAN, AND Y. SAWANGDEE (1996): "Community and Contraceptive Choice in Rural Thailand: A Case Study of Nang Rong," *Demography*, 33, 1–11.

ESPINOZA, V. (1999): "Social Networks among the Urban Poor: Inequality and Integration in a Latin American City," in *Networks in the Global Village: Life in Contemporary Communities*, ed. by B. Wellman, pp. 147–185. Westview Press, Boulder, CO.

ETEMADI, F. U. (2000): "Civil Society Participation in City Governance in Cebu City," *Environment and Urbanization*, 12(1), 57–72.

EWBANK, D. C., J. G. DE LEÓN, AND M. A. STOTO (1983): "A Reducible Four-Parameter System of Model Life Tables," *Population Studies*, 37(1), 105–127.

EWBANK, D. C., AND S. H. PRESTON (1990): "Personal Health Behavior and the Decline in Infant and Child Mortality: The United States, 1900–1930," in *What We Know About the Health Transition: The Cultural, Social and Behavioral Determinants of Health*, ed. by J. C. Caldwell, S. Findley, P. Caldwell, G. Santow, W. Cosford, J. Braid, and D. Broers-Freeman, vol. I of *Health Transition Series*, pp. 116–149, Canberra. Australian National University.

FALLON, P. R. (1983): "Education and the Duration of Job Search and Unemployment in Urban India," *Journal of Development Economics*, 12, 327–340.

FALLON, P. R., AND P. R. G. LAYARD (1975): "Capital-Skill Complementarity, Income Distribution, and Output Accounting," *Journal of Political Economy*, 83(2), 279–302.

FALLON, P. R., AND R. E. B. LUCAS (2002): "The Impact of Financial Crises on Labor Markets, Household Incomes, and Poverty: A Review of the Evidence," *World Bank Research Observer*, 17(1), 21–45.

FARBER, S. C., AND B. LEE (1984): "Fertility Adaptations of Rural-to-Urban Migrant Women: A Method of Estimation Applied to Korean Women," *Demography*, 21, 339–345.

FAURÉ, Y., AND P. LABAZÉE (2000): *Petits Patrons Africains: Entre Assistance et Marché*. Karthala, Paris.

FAWCUS, S., M. T. MBIZVO, G. LINDMARK, AND L. NYSTROM (1995): "A Community Based Investigation of Causes of Maternal Mortality in Rural and Urban Zimbabwe. Maternal Mortality Study Group," *Central African Journal of Medicine*, 41(4), 105–113.

——— (1996): "A Community-Based Investigation of Avoidable Factors for Maternal Mortality in Zimbabwe," *Studies in Family Planning*, 27(6), 319–327.

FEACHEM, R., R. KJELLSTROM, AND C. MURRAY (eds.) (1990): *The Health of Adults in the Developing World*. World Bank, Washington, DC.

FERRINHO, P., W. VAN LERBERGHE, AND A. D. C. GOMES (1999): "Public and Private Practice: A Balancing Act for Health Staff," *Bulletin of the World Health Organization*, 77(3), 209.

FIELDS, G. S. (1975): "Rural-Urban Migration, Urban Unemployment and Underemployment, and Job-Search Activity in LDCs," *Journal of Development Economics*, 2, 165–187.

FIKREE, F. F., R. H. GRAY, H. W. BERENDES, AND M. S. KARIM (1994): "A Community-Based Nested Case-Control Study of Maternal Mortality," *International Journal of Gynecology & Obstetrics*, 47, 247–255.

FIKREE, F. F., A. KHAN, M. M. KADIR, F. SAJAN, AND M. RAHBAR (2001): "What Influences Contraceptive Use among Young Women in Urban Squatter Settlements of Karachi, Pakistan?" *International Family Planning Perspectives*, 27(3), 130–135.

FIKREE, F. F., F. MIDHET, S. SADRUDDIN, AND H. W. BERENDES (1997): "Maternal Mortality in Different Pakistani Sites: Ratios, Clinical Causes and Determinants," *Acta Obstetricia et Gynecologica Scandinavica*, 76, 637–645.

FILMER, D., AND L. PRITCHETT (2001): "Estimating Wealth Effects Without Expenditure Data—Or Tears: An Application to Educational Enrollments in States of India," *Demography*, 38(1), 115–132.

FINDLEY, S. E., AND A. DIALLO (1993): "Social Appearances and Economic Realities of Female Migration in Rural Mali," in *Migration of Women in Developing Countries*, ed. by United Nations, pp. 244–258. United Nations, New York.

FISCHER, C. S. (1982): *To Dwell among Friends: Personal Networks in Town and City*. University of Chicago Press, Chicago, IL.

FISHMAN, R. (1990): "America's New City: Megalopolis Unbound," *Wilson Quarterly*, 14(1), 24–45.

FISZBEIN, A., AND P. LOWDEN (1999): *Working Together for a Change: Government, Civic, and Business Partnerships for Poverty Reduction in Latin America and the Caribbean*. Economic Development Institute of the World Bank, Washington, DC.

FORSTER, L. M., M. TANNHAUSER, AND H. M. BARROS (1996): "Drug Use among Street Children in Southern Brazil," *Drug and Alcohol Dependence*, 43, 57–62.

FOTTORINO, E. (1991): *La Piste Blanche: L'Afrique sous l'Emprise de la Drogue*. Balland, Paris.

FRANCA, M. C. (2001): "A Cidade Como Palco da Divrsidade Demográphica: O Caso da Cidade do Natal," Paper presented at the 2001 Meetings of the International Union for the Scientific Study of Population (IUSSP), Salvador, Brazil, August. Departamento de Estatistica da UFRN.

FRANKENBERG, E., D. THOMAS, AND K. BEEGLE (1999a): "The Real Costs of Indonesia's Economic Crisis: Preliminary Findings from the Indonesian Family Life Surveys." Labor and Population Working Paper. DRU-2064-NIA-NICHD. University of California at Los Angeles.

FRANKENBERG, E., K. BEEGLE, D. THOMAS, AND W. SURIASTINI (1999b): "Health, Education, and the Economic Crisis in Indonesia," Paper presented at the 1999 annual meetings of the Population Association of America, New York.

FREEDMAN, R. (1979): "Theories of Fertility Decline: A Reappraisal," *Social Forces*, 58(1), 1–17.

FREEDMAN, R., AND J. Y. TAKESHITA (1969): *Family Planning in Taiwan: An Experiment in Social Change*. Princeton University Press, Princeton, NJ.

FREIRE, M., AND R. STREN (eds.) (2001): *The Challenge of Urban Government: Policies and Practices*. The World Bank, Washington, DC.

FRENCH, H. W. (1998): "Breaking the Mold," *Urban Age*, 6(2), 3–5.

FRENK, J., J. L. LONDOÑO, F. KNAUL, AND R. LOZANO (1998): "Latin American Health Systems in Transition: A Vision for the Future," in *21st Century Health Care in Latin America and the Caribbean: Prospects for Achieving Health for All*, ed. by C. Bezold, J. Frenk, and S. McCarthy, pp. 109–142. Institute for Alternative Futures (IAF) and Fundacion Mexicana Para la Salud, Alexandria, VA, and Mexico, DF.

FREY, W., AND Z. ZIMMER (2001): "Defining the City," in *Handbook of Urban Studies*, ed. by R. Paddison, pp. 14–35. SAGE Publications, London.

FREY, W. H., AND A. SPEARE (1995): "Metropolitan Areas as Functional Communities," in *Metropolitan and Non-Metropolitan Areas: New Approaches to Geographical Definition*, ed. by D. Dahmann, and J. Fitzsimmons, no. 12 in *Working Paper* series, pp. 139–190. Population Division, U.S. Bureau of the Census, Washington, DC.

FRIEDMAN, S. R., AND S. ARAL (2001): "Social Networks, Risk-Potential Networks, Health, and Disease," *Journal of Urban Health: Bulletin of the New York Academy of Medicine*, 78(3), 411–418.

FRIEDMANN, J. (1986): "The World City Hypothesis," *Development and Change*, 17(1), 69–83.

——— (1995): "Where We Stand: A Decade of World City Research," in *World Cities in a World-System*, ed. by P. L. Knox, and P. J. Taylor, pp. 21–47. Cambridge University Press, Cambridge.

FRIEDMANN, J., AND J. MILLER (1965): "The Urban Field," *Journal of the American Institute of Planner*, 31, 312–319.

FRIEDMANN, J., AND G. WOLFF (1982): "World City Formation: An Agenda for Research and Action," *International Journal of Urban and Regional Research*, 6(3), 309–344.

FUJITA, M., P. KRUGMAN, AND T. MORI (1999): "On The Evolution of Hierarchical Urban Systems," *European Economic Review*, 43(2), 209–251.

FUJITA, M., P. KRUGMAN, AND A. J. VENABLES (1999): *The Spatial Economy: Cities, Regions, and International Trade*. MIT Press, Cambridge, MA.

FULLER, T. D., J. N. EDWARDS, S. SERMSRI, AND S. VORAKITPHOKATORN (1993): "Housing, Stress, and Physical Well-Being: Evidence from Thailand," *Social Science and Medicine*, 36(11), 1417–1428.

FULLER, T. D., P. LIGHTFOOT, AND P. KAMNUANSILPA (1985): "Rural-Urban Mobility in Thailand: A Decision-Making Approach," *Demography*, 22(4), 565–580.

FURSTENBERG, F. F. (1993): "How Families Manage Risk and Opportunity in Dangerous Neighborhoods," in *Sociology and the Public Agenda*, ed. by W. J. Wilson, pp. 231–258. Sage Publications, Newbury Park, CA.

FURSTENBERG, F. F., AND M. E. HUGHES (1997): "The Influence of Neighborhoods on Children's Development: A Theoretical Perspective and a Research Agenda," in *Neighborhood Poverty*, ed. by J. Brooks-Gunn, G. J. Duncan, and J. L. Aber, vol. II: Policy Implications in Studying Neighborhoods, pp. 23–47. Russell Sage Foundation, New York.

GALLOWAY, P. R., E. A. HAMMEL, AND R. D. LEE (1994): "Fertility Decline in Prussia, 1875–1910: A Pooled Cross-Section, Time Series Analysis," *Population Studies*, 48(1), 135–158.

GANG, F. (1999): "Transition to Fiscal Federalism: Market-Oriented Reform and Redefinition of Central-Local Relations in China," in *Fiscal Decentralization in Emerging Economies. Governance Issues*, ed. by K. Fukusaku, and L. R. de Mello Jr., pp. 223–245. OECD, Paris.

GARNER, C. L., AND S. W. RAUDENBUSH (1991): "Neighborhood Effects on Educational Attainment: A Multilevel Analysis," *Sociology of Education*, 64(4), 251–262.

GARZA, G. (1996): "Social and Economic Imbalances in the Metropolitan Area of Monterrey," *Environment and Urbanization*, 8(2), 31–41.

———— (ed.) (2000): *La Ciudad de México en el Fin del Segunda Milenio*. El Colegio de México, Centro de Estudios Demográficos y Desarrollo Urbanos: Gobierno del Distrito Federal, Mexico City.

———— (2002): "New Forms of Urbanization: Conceptualizing and Measuring Human Settlements in the 21st Century," Paper presented at a conference on "Beyond the Urban-Rural Dichotomy: Towards a New Conceptualization of Human Settlement Systems," Bellagio, Italy, March 11–15, 2002. Mimeographed. El Colegio de México, Mexico City.

GAVIRIA, A., AND E. STEIN (2000): "The Evolution of Urban Concentration Around the World: A Panel Approach," Working Paper no. 414, Research Department, Inter-American Development Bank. Washington, DC.

GEPHART, M. A. (1997): "Neighborhoods and Communities as Contexts for Development," in *Neighborhood Poverty*, ed. by J. Brooks-Gunn, G. J. Duncan, and J. L. Aber, vol. I: Context and Consequences for Children, pp. 1–43. Russell Sage Foundation, New York.

GERSOVITZ, M. (1988): "Saving and Development," in *Handbook of Development Economics, Volume I*, ed. by H. Chenery, and T. Srinivasan, pp. 381–424. Elsevier Science, Amsterdam.

GHOSH, A., S. S. AHMAD, AND S. MAITRA (1994): *Basic Services for Urban Poor: A Study of Baroda, Bhilwara, Sambalpur and Siliguri*, no. 3 in Urban Studies. Institute for Social Sciences and Concept Publishing Company, New Delhi.

GIBBS, J. P., AND K. DAVIS (1958): "Conventional vs. Metropolitan Data in the International Study of Urbanization," *American Sociological Review*, 23, 504–514.

GIBSON, J. (2001): "Measuring Chronic Poverty without a Panel," *Journal of Development Economics*, 65, 243–266.

GILBERT, A. (1994): *The Latin American City*. Latin America Bureau and Monthly Review Press, New York.

——— (ed.) (1996): *The Mega-City in Latin America*. United Nations University Press, Tokyo.

——— (1998): *The Latin American City*. Latin American Bureau, London, revised ed.

GILSON, L. (1997): "The Lessons of User Fee Experience in Africa," *Health Policy and Planning*, 12(4), 273–285.

GILSON, L., AND A. MILLS (1995): "Health Sector Reforms in Sub-Saharan Africa: Lessons of the Last 10 Years," *Health Policy*, 32, 215–243.

GILSON, L., S. RUSSELL, AND K. BUSE (1995): "The Political Economy of User Fees with Targetting: Developing Equitable Health Financing Policy," *Journal of International Development*, 7(3), 369–401.

GINSBURG, N., B. KOPPELL, AND T. G. MCGEE (eds.) (1991): *The Extended Metropolis: Settlement Transition in Asia*. University of Hawaii Press, Honolulu.

GIPOULOU, F. (1998): "Network Cities and the Formation of a Mediterranean Sea in East Asia," Paper presented at the International Conference on Interdependence in Asia Pacific, Stockholm University, Stockholm, Sweden, November 30–December 1.

GIUSTI, D., B. CRIEL, AND X. D. BETHUNE (1997): "Viewpoint: Public Versus Private Health Care Delivery: Beyond the Slogans," *Health Policy and Planning*, 12(3), 193–198.

GLAESER, E. L. (1998): "Are Cities Dying?" *Journal of Economic Perspectives*, 12(2), 139–160.

GLAESER, E. L., H. D. KALLAL, J. A. SCHEINKMAN, AND A. SHLEIFER (1992): "Growth in Cities," *Journal of Political Economy*, 100(6), 1126–1152.

GLEWWE, P., AND G. HALL (1998): "Are Some Groups More Vulnerable to Macroeconomic Shocks Than Others? Hypothesis Tests Based on Panel Data from Peru," *Journal of Development Economics*, 56(1), 181–206.

GLIK, D., W. B. WARD, A. GORDON, AND F. HABA (1989): "Malaria Treatment Practices among Mothers in Guinea," *Journal of Health and Social Behaviour*, 30(December), 421–435.

GOLDBERG, M. A., AND J. MERCER (1986): *The Myth of the North American City: Continentalism Challenged*. University of British Columbia Press, Vancouver.

GOLDSTEIN, S. (1990): "Urbanization in China, 1982–87: Effects of Migration and Reclassification," *Population and Development Review*, 16(4), 673–701.

GOLDSTEIN, S., AND A. GOLDSTEIN (1981): "The Impact of Migration on Fertility: An 'Own Children Analysis' for Thailand," *Population Studies*, 35, 265–284.

——— (1983): "Migration and Fertility in Peninsular Malaysia: An Analysis Using Life History Data," Note N-1860-AID, Rand Corporation, Santa Monica, CA.

——— (1984): "Interrelations Between Migration and Fertility: Their Significance for Urbanization in Malaysia," *Habitat International*, 8, 93–103.

GOLDSTEIN, S., M. WHITE, AND A. GOLDSTEIN (1997): "Migration, Fertility, and State Policy in Hubei Province, China," *Demography*, 34(4), 481–491.

GOLLEDGE, R. G., AND R. J. STIMSON (1997): *Spatial Behavior: A Geographic Perspective*. The Guilford Press, New York and London.

GÓMEZ TAGLE, S. (2000): "Elecciones de Jefe de Gobierno, 1997 y 2000," in *El Atlas de la Ciudad de Mexico*, ed. by G. Garza, pp. 658–666. Departamento del Distrito Federal and El Colegio de México, Mexico D.F.

GOOD, C. (1987): *Ethnomedical Systems in Africa: Patterns of Traditional Medicine in Rural and Urban Kenya*. Guilford Press, New York.

GOTTMAN, J. (1961): *Megalopolis: The Urbanized Northeastern Seaboard of the United States*. The Twentieth Century Fund, Krauss International Publications, New York.

GOULD, W. T. (1998): "African Mortality and the New Urban Penalty," *Health and Place*, 4(2), 171–181.

GOVERNMENT OF INDIA (1993): *Report of the Expert Group on the Estimation of Proportion and Number of Poor*. Planning Commission, Delhi.

——— (2001): "Press Release—Population of Urban and Rural Areas for the Country and States/Union Territories—Census of India 2001," Office of the Registrar General and Census Commissioner, www.censusindia.net.

GOVERNMENT OF KAZAKHSTAN (1999): *Statistical Yearbook 99*. Agency on Statistics of the Republic of Kazakhstan (Goskomstat RK), Almaty.

GOVERNMENT OF THE KYRGYZ REPUBLIC (2000): *Demograficheskii Ezhegodnik Kyrgyzskoi Respubliki 1995–1999 gg*. National Statistical Committee of the Kyrgyz Republic (NSCKR), Bishkek.

GRAHAM, S., AND S. MARVIN (2001): *Splintering Urbanism: Networked Infrastructures, Technological Mobilities and the Urban Condition*. Routledge, London and New York.

GRANOVETTER, M. (1973): "The Strength of Weak Ties," *American Journal of Sociology*, 78(6), 1360–1380.

——— (1985): "Economic Action and Social Structure: The Problem of Embeddedness," *American Journal of Sociology*, 91(3), 481–510.

GRANT, E. (1999): "State of the Art of Urban Health in Latin America," European Commission Funded Concerted Action: 'Health and Human Settlements in Latin America,' South Bank University, London.

GRAUMAN, J. V. (1976): "Orders of Magnitude of the World's Urban Population in History," *Population Bulletin of the United Nations*, 8, 16–33.

GREGORY, D., AND J. URRY (eds.) (1985): *Social Relations and Spatial Structures*. St. Martin's Press, New York.

GREGORY, P. (1986): *The Myth of Market Failure: Employment and the Labor Market in Mexico*. Johns Hopkins University Press, Baltimore, MD.

GRETHER, J.-M. (1999): "Determinants of Technological Diffusion in Mexican Manufacturing: A Plant-Level Analysis," *World Development*, 27(7), 1287–1298.

GREWE, C., AND C. M. BECKER (2001): "Characteristics of Poor Households in Indonesia," Paper prepared for the Panel on Urban Population Dynamics, Committee on Population, National Research Council. University of Colorado at Boulder Institute of Behavioral Science, Program in Population Processes.

GRILICHES, Z. (1957): "Hybrid Corn: An Exploration in the Economics of Technological Change," *Econometrica*, 25, 501–522.

GRIMM, M., C. GUÉNARD, AND S. MESPLEÉ-SOMPS (2002): "What Has Happened to the Urban Population in Côte d'Ivoire Since the 1980s? An Analysis of Monetary Poverty and Deprivation Over 15 Years of Household Data," *World Development*, 30(6), 1073–1095.

GRINDLE, M. S. (2000): *Audacious Reforms: Institutional Invention and Democracy in Latin America*. Johns Hopkins University Press, Baltimore.

GROOTAERT, C. (1992): "The Position of Migrants in the Urban Informal Labour Markets of Côte d'Ivoire," *Journal of African Economies*, 1(3), 416–445.

GROOTAERT, C., AND R. KANBUR (1995): "The Lucky Few Amidst Economic Decline: Distributional Change in Côte d'Ivoire as Seen Through Panel Data Sets, 1985–88," *Journal of Development Studies*, 31(4), 603–619.

GROSS, R., B. LANDRIED, AND S. HERMAN (1996): "Height and Weight as a Reflection of the Nutritional Situation of School-Aged Children Working and Living in the Streets of Jakarta," *Social Science and Medicine*, 43, 453–458.

GUERRERO AMPARÁN, J., AND T. G. LÓPEZ (eds.) (2000): *Reflexiones en Torno a la Reforma Municipal del Articulo 115 Constitucional*. Miguel Angel Porrua, Mexico City.

GUEST, P. (1993): "The Determinants of Female Migration from a Multilevel Perspective," in *Internal Migration of Women in Developing Countries*, ed. by United Nations, pp. 223–242. United Nations, New York.

GUHA, B. (ed.) (1998): *Conflict and Violence in Indian Society*. Kanishka Publishers, New Delhi.

HADDAD, L., M. T. RUEL, AND J. L. GARRETT (1999): "Are Urban Poverty and Undernutrition Growing? Some Newly Assembled Evidence," *World Development*, 27(11), 1891–1904.

HÄGERSTRAND, T. (1952): *The Propagation of Innovation Waves*. Royal University of Lund, London.

——— (1975): "Space-Time and Human Conditions," in *Dynamic Allocation of Urban Space*, ed. by A. Karlqvist, L. Lundqvist, and F. Snickars, pp. 3–12. Saxon House, Teakfield, Farnborough, Hants.

HALL, P. (1966): *The World Cities*. World University Press, London.

——— (1998): *Cities in Civilization*. Weidenfeld and Nicholson, London.

HALL, P., AND U. PFEIFFER (2000): *Urban Future 21: A Global Agenda for Twenty-First Century Cities*. E & FN Spon, London.

HAMID, N. (2001): "Social Exclusion and Women's Health in Lahore, Pakistan," Ph.D. thesis, South Bank University, London.

HAMPSHIRE, K., AND S. RANDALL (2000): "Pastoralists, Agropastoralists and Migrants: Interactions Between Fertility and Mobility in Northern Burkina Faso," *Population Studies*, 54, 247–261.

HAMPTON, M. (1996): *The Offshore Interface: Tax Havens in the Global Economy*. St. Martin's Press, New York.

HANMER, L., AND H. WHITE (1999): *Human Development in Sub-Saharan Africa: The Determinants of Under-Five Mortality*. Institute of Social Studies, The Hague.

HANSEN, B. (1979): "Colonial Economic Development with an Unlimited Supply of Land: A Ricardian Case," *Economic Development and Cultural Change*, 27(4), 611–628.

HANSON, K., AND P. BERMAN (1998): "Private Health Care Provision in Developing Countries: A Preliminary Analysis of Levels and Composition," *Health Policy and Planning*, 13(3), 195–211.

HANSON, S., AND G. PRATT (1991): "Job Search and the Segregation of Women," *Annals of the American Association of Geographers*, 81(2), 229–254.

———— (1995): *Gender, Work and Space: International Studies of Women and Place.* Routledge, London.

HARDEE, K., K. AGARWAL, N. LUKE, E. WILSON, M. PENDZICH, M. FARRELL, AND H. CROSS (1998): "Post-Cairo Reproductive Health Policies and Programs: A Comparative Study of Eight Countries," POLICY Project paper. The Futures Group International, Inc., Washington, DC.

HARDOY, J. E., D. MITLIN, AND D. SATTERTHWAITE (1992): *Environmental Problems in Third World Cities.* Earthscan Publications, London.

———— (2001): *Environmental Problems in an Urbanizing World: Finding Solutions in Africa, Asia and Latin America.* Earthscan Publications, London.

HARDOY, J. E., AND D. SATTERTHWAITE (eds.) (1986a): *Small and Intermediate Urban Centres: Their Role in National and Regional Development in the Third World.* Hodder and Stoughton (UK) and Westview (USA).

———— (1986b): "A Survey of the Empirical Material on the Factors Affecting the Development of Small and Intermediate Urban Centres," in *Small and Intermediate Urban Centres: Their Role in Regional and National Development in the Third World,* ed. by J. E. Hardoy, and D. Satterthwaite, pp. 279–334. Hodder and Stoughton (UK) and Westview (USA).

———— (1988): "Small and Intermediate Urban Centres in the Third World: What Role for Government?" *Third World Planning Review,* 10(1), 5–26.

———— (1989): *Squatter Citizen: Life in the Urban Third World.* Earthscan Publications, London.

HARLOE, M. (1996): "Cities in the Transition," in *Cities After Socialism: Urban and Regional Change and Conflict in Post-Socialist Societies,* ed. by G. Andrusz, M. Harloe, and I. Szelenyi, pp. 1–29. Blackwell, Oxford.

HARPHAM, T. (1994): "Urbanization and Mental Health in Developing Countries: A Research Role for Social Scientists, Public Health Professionals and Social Psychiatrists," *Social Science and Medicine,* 39(2), 233–245.

———— (1997): "Urbanization and Health in Transition," *Lancet,* 349(Suppl. III), 11–13.

HARPHAM, T., AND I. BLUE (eds.) (1995): *Urbanization and Mental Health in Developing Countries.* Aldershot, Avebury.

HARPHAM, T., T. LUSTY, AND P. VAUGHAN (1988): *In the Shadow of the City: Community Health and the Urban Poor.* Oxford University Press, Oxford.

HARPHAM, T., AND C. STEPHENS (1991): "Urban Health in Developing Countries: From the Shadows into the Spotlight," *Tropical Diseases Bulletin,* 88(8), R1–R35.

HARPHAM, T., AND M. TANNER (eds.) (1995): *Urban Health in Developing Countries: Progress and Prospects.* St. Martin's Press, New York.

HARRIS, J. R., AND M. P. TODARO (1970): "Migration, Unemployment, and Development: A Two-Sector Analysis," *American Economic Review,* 60, 126–142.

HART, K. (1973): "Informal Income Opportunities and Urban Employment in Ghana," *Journal of Modern African Studies,* 11(1), 61–89.

———— (1995): "L'Entreprise Africaine et l'Economie Informelle. Reflexions Autobiographiques," in *Entreprises et Entrepreneurs Africians,* ed. by S. Ellis, and Y. A. Fauré, pp. 115–124. Karthala-Orstom, Paris.

HARVEY, D. (1973): *Social Justice and the City.* Johns Hopkins University Press, Baltimore, MD.

HEISE, L. L., A. RAIKES, C. H. WATTS, AND A. B. ZWI (1994): "Violence Against Women: A Neglected Public Health Issue in Less Developed Countries," *Social Science and Medicine*, 39(9), 1165–1179.

HENDERSON, J. V. (1982): "The Impact of Government Policies on Urban Concentration," *Journal of Urban Economics*, 12, 280–303.

——— (1985): *Economic Theory and the Cities*. Academic Press, Orlando, FL.

——— (1988): *Urban Development: Theory, Fact, and Illusion*. Oxford University Press, New York.

——— (2002): "Urbanization in Developing Countries," *The World Bank Research Observer*, 17(1), 89–112.

HENDERSON, J. V., T. LEE, AND J.-Y. LEE (2001): "Scale Externalities in Korea," *Journal of Urban Economics*, 49, 479–504.

HENDERSON, J. V., Z. SHALIZI, AND A. J. VENABLES (2000): "Geography and Development," Unpublished paper, Department of Economics, Brown University.

HENTSCHEL, J., AND P. LANJOUW (1996): "Constructing an Indicator of Consumption for the Analysis of Poverty," LSMS Working Paper No. 124, World Bank, Washington, DC.

HERVITZ, H. M. (1985): "The Effects of Migration on Fertility: The Case of Brazil," *International Migration Review*, 19(2), 293–318.

HEWETT, P. C., AND M. R. MONTGOMERY (2001): "Poverty and Public Services in Developing-Country Cities," Population Council *Working Paper* no. 154. Population Council, New York.

HIGGINS, M. (1997): "Demography, National Savings, and International Capital Flows," Federal Reserve Bank of New York Staff Reports No. 34, New York.

HOFFMAN, M., W. M. PICK, D. COOPER, AND J. E. MYERS (1997): "Women's Health Status and Use of Health Services in a Rapidly Growing Peri-Urban Area of South Africa," *Social Science and Medicine*, 45(1), 149–157.

HOGAN, D. P., AND E. M. KITAGAWA (1985): "The Impact of Social Status, Family Structure, and Neighborhood on the Fertility of Black Adolescents," *American Journal of Sociology*, 90(4), 825–855.

HOLDSWORTH, G., P. A. GARNER, AND T. HARPHAM (1993): "Crowded Outpatient Departments in City Hospitals of Developing Countries: A Case Study from Lesotho," *International Journal of Health Planning and Management*, 8(4), 315–324.

HONDAGNEU-SOTELO, P. (1994): *Gendered Transitions: Mexican Experiences of Immigration*. University of California Press, Berkeley, CA.

HONDURAS MINISTRY OF HEALTH (1999): *Annual Report*. Honduras Ministry of Health, Honduras.

HONG KONG TRADE DEVELOPMENT COUNCIL (1998): *The Rise in Offshore Trade and Offshore Investment*. Trade Development Council, Hong Kong.

HOOPS, T., AND S. WHITEFORD (1983): "Transcending Rural-Urban Boundaries: A Comparative View of Two Labor Reserves and Family Strategies," in *Population Growth and Urbanization in Latin America: The Rural-Urban Interface*, ed. by J. M. Hunter, R. N. Thomas, and S. Whiteford, pp. 261–280. Schenkman, Cambridge, MA.

HOSKIN, G. (1998): "Urban Electoral Behavior in Colombia," in *Urban Elections in Democratic Latin America*, ed. by H. A. Dietz, and G. Shidlo, pp. 91–116. Scholarly Resources Inc., Wilmington, DE.

HOTCHKISS, D. R. (1998): "The Tradeoff Between Price and Quality of Services in the Philippines," *Social Science and Medicine*, 46(2), 227–242.

HOTCHKISS, D. R., AND A. GORDILLO (1999): "Household Health Expenditures in Morocco: Implications for Health Sector Reform," *International Journal of Health Planning Management*, 14, 201–217.

HOWELL, J. (2000): "The Political Economy of Xiamen Special Economic Zone," in *Fujian: A Coastal Province in Transition and Transformation*, ed. by Y. M. Yeung, and D. Chu, pp. 119–142. The Chinese University Press, Hong Kong.

HUGHES, J., AND A. P. MCCAULEY (1998): "Improving the Fit: Adolescents' Needs and Future Programs for Sexual and Reproductive Health in Developing Countries," *Studies in Family Planning*, 29(2), 233–245.

HUGO, G. J. (1981): "Village-Community Ties, Village Norms, and Ethnic and Social Networks: A Review of Evidence from the Third World," in *Migration Decision-Making: Multidisciplinary Approaches to Microlevel Studies in Developed and Developing Countries*, ed. by G. F. DeJong, and R. W. Gardner, pp. 186–224. Pergamon Press, New York.

——— (1993): "Migration as a Survival Strategy: The Family Dimension of Migration," Paper presented at the Expert Group Meeting on Population Distribution and Migration, Santa Cruz, Bolivia. 18–22 January 1993, U.N. Population Division, New York.

HUGO, G. J., A. CHAMPION, AND A. LATTES (2001): "New Conceptualization of Settlement for Demography: Beyond the Rural/Urban Dichotomy," Paper presented at the August 2001 Conference of the International Union for the Scientific Study of Population (IUSSP), Bahia, Brazil.

IGUN, U. A. (1979): "Stages in Health-Seeking: A Descriptive Model," *Social Science and Medicine*, 13, 445–456.

INDÚSTRIA DE EMBALAGENS PLÁSTICAS LTDA (1994): "Plano Metropolitan da Grande São Paulo; 1993/2010," Empresa Metropolitana de Planejamento da Grande São Paulo, SA, São Paulo.

INTERNATIONAL FEDERATION OF RED CROSS AND RED CRESCENT SOCIETIES (1998): *World Disasters Report 1998*. Oxford University Press, Oxford and New York.

INTERNATIONAL MONETARY FUND (1998): *Government Finance Statistics Yearbook 1998*. International Monetary Fund, Washington, DC.

ISLAM, N., N. HUDA, F. B. NARAYAN, AND P. B. RANA (eds.) (1997): *Addressing the Urban Poverty Agenda in Bangladesh, Critical Issues and the 1995 Survey Findings*. The University Press Limited, Dhaka.

JACOBS, J. (1969): *The Economy of Cities*. Vintage, New York.

——— (1984): *Cities and the Wealth of Nations: Principles of Economic Life*. Vintage, New York.

JAFFE, A. B., M. TRAJTENBERG, AND R. HENDERSON (1993): "Geographic Localization of Knowledge Spillovers as Evidenced by Patent Citations," *Quarterly Journal of Economics*, 108(3), 577–598.

JAGLIN, S. (1998): "La Gestion Urbaine en Archipels en Afrique Australe," *Annales de la Recherche Urbaine*, 80–81, 27–34.

JAMES, S. A., A. J. SCHULZ, AND J. VAN OLPHEN (2001): "Social Capital, Poverty, and Community Health: An Exploration of Linkages," in *Social Capital and Poor Communities*, ed. by S. Saegert, J. P. Thompson, and M. R. Warren, pp. 165–188. Russel Sage Foundation, New York.

JAMIL, S., AND F. F. FIKREE (2002a): "Determinants of Unsafe Abortion in Three Squatter Settlements of Karachi," Department of Community Health Sciences, Aga Khan University, Karachi, Pakistan.

———— (2002b): "Incomplete Abortion from Tertiary Hospitals of Karachi, Pakistan: Final Report," Department of Community Health Sciences, Aga Khan University, Karachi, Pakistan.

JARRETT, R. L. (1997): "Bringing Families Back In: Neighborhood Effects on Child Development," in *Neighborhood Poverty*, ed. by J. Brooks-Gunn, G. J. Duncan, and J. L. Aber, vol. II: Policy Implications in Studying Neighborhoods, pp. 48–64. Russell Sage Foundation, New York.

JENCKS, C., AND S. E. MAYER (1990): "The Social Consequences of Growing Up in a Poor Neighborhood," in *Inner-City Poverty in the United States*, ed. by L. E. Lynn, and M. G. H. McGeary, pp. 111–186. National Academy Press, Washington, DC.

JIMENEZ, E. (1995): "Human and Physical Infrastructure: Public Investment and Pricing Policies in Developing Countries," in *Handbook of Development Economics*, ed. by J. Behrman, and T. N. Srinivasan, vol. IIIB, pp. 2773–2843. Elsevier North-Holland, Amsterdam.

JOHANSSON, S. R., AND C. MOSK (1987): "Exposure, Resistance and Life Expectancy: Disease and Death During the Economic Development of Japan, 1900–1960," *Population Studies*, 41(2), 207–235.

JOHNSON, G. (1997): "Changes in Earnings Inequality: The Role of Demand Shifts," *Journal of Economic Perspectives*, 11(2), 41–54.

JONES, G. W. (1984): "Women in the Urban and Industrial Workforce, Southeast and East Asia," Development Studies Centre, Monograph no. 33. The Australian National University, Canberra.

———— (2002): "Southeast Asian Urbanization and the Growth Of Mega-Urban Regions," *Journal of Population Research*, 19(2), 119–136.

JONES, G. W., C. L. TSAY, AND B. BAJRACHARYA (2000): "Demographic and Employment Change in the Mega-Cities of Southeast and East Asia," *Third World Planning Review*, 22(1), 1–28.

JONES, V. (1942): *Metropolitan Government*. University of Chicago Press, Chicago.

JONSSON, A., AND D. SATTERTHWAITE (2000a): "Income-Based Poverty Lines: How Well Do the Levels Set Within Each Country Reflect the Cost of Living in the Larger/More Prosperous Cities and the Cost the Urban Poor Have to Pay for Non-Food Items?" Paper prepared for the Panel on Urban Population Dynamics, Committee on Population, National Research Council.

———— (2000b): "Overstating the Provision of Safe Water and Sanitation to Urban Populations: A Critical Review of the Quality and Reliability of Official Statistics and of the Criteria Used in Defining What Is 'Adequate' or 'Safe'," Unpublished paper prepared for the Panel on Urban Population Dynamics, Committee on Population, National Research Council.

JOVANOVIC, B., AND R. ROBB (1989): "The Growth and Diffusion of Knowledge," *Review of Economic Studies*, 56(4), 569–582.

KAHN, K., AND S. TOLLMAN (2002): "The INDEPTH network: Demographic Surveillance System Site Profiles," Document available from Internet web site http://www.indepthnetwork.net.

KAHNERT, F. (1987): "Improving Urban Employment and Labor Productivity," World Bank Discussion Paper no. 10. The World Bank, Washington, DC.

KAMETE, A. Y. (1998): "Interlocking Livelihoods: Farm and Small Town in Zimbabwe," *Environment and Urbanization*, 10(1), 23–34.

KAMINSKY, G. L., R. K. LYONS, AND S. L. SCHMUKLER (2001): "Mutual Fund Investment in Emerging Markets: An Overview," *The World Bank Economic Review*, 15(2), 315–340.

KANJI, N. (1995): "Gender, Poverty and Structural Adjustment in Harare, Zimbabwe," *Environment and Urbanization*, 7(1), 37–55.

KANNAPPAN, S. (1983): *Employment Problems and the Urban Labor Market in Developing Nations*. University of Michigan, Graduate School of Business Administration, Ann Arbor, MI.

——— (1984): "Tradition and Modernity in Urban Employment in Developing Nations," *Regional Development Dialogue*, 5(2), 55–62.

——— (1985): "Urban Employment and the Labor Market in Developing Nations," *Economic Development and Cultural Change*, 33(4), 419–441.

——— (1988): "Urban Labor Markets and Development," *World Bank Research Observer*, 3(2), 189–206.

KAOTHIEN, U., AND D. WEBSTER (2001): "The Bangkok Region," in *Global City-Regions: Their Emerging Forms*, ed. by R. Simmonds, and G. Hack, pp. 23–37. SPON Press, London and New York.

KAPLAN, R. (2001): "Hope for the Best, Expect the Worst," *Foreign Policy*, 124(May/June), 53–56.

KAPTEYN, A., S. VAN DE GEER, H. VAN DE STADT, AND T. WANSBEEK (1997): "Interdependent Preferences: An Econometric Analysis," *Journal of Applied Econometrics*, 12, 665–686.

KARATNYCKY, A. (1999): "The Comparative Survey of Freedom, 1989–1999. A Good Year for Freedom," Freedom House web page, www.freedomhouse.org/survey99/essays/karat.html, New York.

KAUFMAN, C. E., S. CLARK, N. MANZINI, AND J. MAY (2002): "How Community Structures of Time and Opportunity Shape Adolescent Sexual Behavior in South Africa," Policy Research Division *Working Paper* no. 159. The Population Council, New York.

KAUFMAN, C. E., T. DE WET, AND J. STADLER (2000): "Adolescent Pregnancy and Parenthood in South Africa," Policy Research Division *Working Paper* no. 136. The Population Council, New York.

KAWACHI, I., AND L. F. BERKMAN (2001): "Social Ties and Mental Health," *Journal of Urban Health*, 78(3), 458–467.

KAWACHI, I., B. P. KENNEDY, AND R. GLASS (1999): "Social Capital and Self-Rated Health: A Contextual Analysis," *American Journal of Public Health*, 89(8), 1187–1193.

KAYE, K., AND M. K. NOVELL (1994): "Health Practices and Indices of a Poor Urban Population in Indonesia. Part I: Patterns of Health Service Utilization," *Asia Pacific Journal of Public Health*, 7(3), 178–182.

KAYOMBO, E. J. (1995): "Motor Traffic Accidents in Dar es Salaam," *Tropical Geography and Medicine*, 47(1), 37–39.

KEARNS, G. (1988): "The Urban Penalty and the Population History of England," in *Society, Health and Population During the Demographic Transition*, ed. by A. Brandstrom, and L. Tedebrand, pp. 213–236. Almquist and Wiskell International, Stockholm.

—— (1993): "Le Handicap Urbain et le Déclin de la Mortalité en Angleterre et au Pays de Galles 1851–1900," *Annales de Démographic Historique*, pp. 75–105.

KELLEY, A. C., AND J. G. WILLIAMSON (1984): *What Drives Third World City Growth? A Dynamic General Equilibrium Approach*. Princeton University Press, Princeton, NJ.

KELLY, P. F. (1998): "The Politics of Urban-Rural Relationships: Land Conversion in the Philippines," *Environment and Urbanization*, 10(1), 35–54.

KENNEDY, B. P., I. KAWACHI, AND E. BRAINERD (1998): "The Role of Social Capital in the Russian Mortality Crisis," *World Development*, 26(11), 2029–2043.

KENNEDY, P. (1993): *Preparing for the 21st Century*. Random House, New York.

KHAN, A. R., K. GRIFFIN, AND C. RISKIN (1999): "Income Distribution in Urban China During the Period of Economic Reform and Globalization," *American Economic Review*, 89(2), 296–300.

KILIAN, A. (1995): "Malaria Control in Kaborole and Bundibugyo Districts, Western Uganda," Report on a comprehensive malaria situation analysis and design of a district control programme, Fort Portal, Uganda.

KIM, D.-I., AND R. H. TOPEL (1995): "Labor Markets and Economic Growth: Lessons from Korea's Industrialization, 1970–1990," in *Differences and Changes in Wage Structures*, ed. by R. B. Freeman, and L. F. Katz, pp. 227–264. National Bureau of Economic Research, Chicago.

KIRK, D. (1996): "Demographic Transition Theory," *Population Studies*, 50, 361–387.

KITANGE, H. M., H. MACHIBYA, J. BLACK, D. M. MTASIWA, G. MASUKI, D. WHITING, N. UNWIN, C. MOSHIRO, P. M. KLIMA, M. LEWANGA, K. G. ALBERTI, AND D. G. MCLARTY (1996): "Outlook for Survivors of Childhood in Sub-Saharan Africa: Adult Mortality in Tanzania. Adult Morbidity and Mortality Project," *British Medical Journal*, 312(7025), 216–220, Published erratum appears in *BMJ* 1996 February 24; 312(7029):483.

KLEINMAN, A. (1980): *Patients and Healers in the Context of Culture*. University of California Press, Berkeley.

KNIGHT, J. B., AND R. SABOT (1988): "Lewis Through a Looking Glass: Public Sector Employment, Rent-Seeking and Economic Growth," Research Memorandum RM-108, Williams College Center for Development Economics, Williamstown, MA.

—— (1990): *Education, Productivity and Inequality: The East African Natural Experiment*. Oxford University Press, New York.

KNOBEL, H. H., W. YANG, AND M. HO (1994): "Urban-Rural and Regional Differences in Infant Mortality in Taiwan," *Social Science and Medicine*, 39(6), 815–822.

KNODEL, J., A. CHAMRATRITHIRONG, AND N. DEBAVALYA (1987): *Thailand's Reproductive Revolution: Rapid Fertility Decline in a Third World Setting*. University of Wisconsin Press, Madison, WI.

KNOX, P. L., AND P. J. TAYLOR (1995): *World Cities in a World-System*. Cambridge University Press, Cambridge.

KNUDSEN, A. B., AND R. SLOOFF (1992): "Vector-Borne Disease Problems in Rapid Urbanization: New Approaches to Vector Control," *Bulletin of the World Health Organization*, 70(1), 1–6.

KOSTINSKIY, G. (2001): "Post-Socialist Cities in Flux," in *Handbook of Urban Studies*, ed. by R. Paddison, pp. 451–465. Sage Publications, London.

KRAAY, A. (2000): "Household Saving in China," *The World Bank Economic Review*, 14(3), 545–570.

KRESS, D. H., AND W. WINFREY (1997): "Pakistan Private Sector Population Project: Pakistan Contraceptive Demand and Pricing Study, Final Report (January 31)," The Futures Group International UK.

KRUEGER, A. B., AND M. LINDAHL (2001): "Education for Growth: Why and for Whom?" *Journal of Economic Literature*, 39(4), 1101–1136.

KRÜGER, F. (1998): "Taking Advantage of Rural Assets as a Coping Strategy for the Urban Poor," *Environment and Urbanization*, 10(1), 119–134.

KRUGMAN, P. (1991): "Increasing Returns and Economic Geography," *Journal of Political Economy*, 99(3), 483–499.

KULKARNI, S., AND M. K. CHOE (1998): "Wanted and Unwanted Fertility in Selected States of India," National Family Health Survey Subject Reports no. 6. International Institute for Population Sciences, Mumbai, and East-West Center Program on Population, Hawaii.

LAGA, M., M. ALARY, N. NZILA, A. T. MANOKA, M. TULIZA, F. BEHETS, J. GOEMAN, M. ST. LOUIS, AND P. PIOT (1994): "Condom Promotion, Sexually Transmitted Diseases Treatment, and Declining Incidence of HIV-1 Infection in Female Zairian Sex Workers," *Lancet*, 344(8917), 246–248.

LAM, D., AND C. DUNN (2001): "The Evolution of Urban Labor Markets in Brazil, 1977–1999," Paper prepared for the Panel on Urban Population Dynamics, Committee on Population, National Research Council.

LANGER, A., G. NIGENDA, AND J. CATINO (2000): "Health Sector Reform and Reproductive Health in Latin America and the Caribbean: Strengthening the Links," *Bulletin of the World Health Organization*, 78(5), 667–676.

LAQUIAN, A. (2000): "Metro Manila: People's Participation and Social Inclusion in a City of Villages," Unpublished paper presented at the Urban Governance Workshop, Woodrow Wilson Center, Washington. December 6–7.

LAUTIER (1994): *L'Économie Informelle dans le Tiers Monde*. La Découverte, Paris.

LAWSON, C. (1999): "Why Cárdenas Won: The 1997 Elections in Mexico City," in *Toward Mexico's Democratization: Parties, Campaigns, Elections, and Public Opinion*, ed. by J. I. Dominguez, and A. Poiré, pp. 147–173. Routledge, New York and London.

LE BONNIEC, Y., AND M. SAULOY (1992): *A Qui Profite la Cocaïne?* Calmann-Levy, Paris.

LE GALÈS, P. (1995): "Du Gouvernement des Villes à la Gouvernance Urbaine," *Revue Francaise de Science Politique*, 45(1), 57–95.

LEDENT, J. (1980): "Comparative Dynamics of Three Demographic Models of Urbanization," Research Report RR-80-1, International Institute for Applied Systems Analysis, Laxenburg, Austria.

LEE, B., AND S. C. FARBER (1984): "Fertility Adaptation by Rural-Urban Migrants in Developing Countries: The Case of Korea," *Population Studies*, 38, 141–155.

LEE, B. A., AND K. E. CAMPBELL (1999): "Neighbor Networks of Black and White Americans," in *Networks in the Global Village: Life in Contemporary Communities*, ed. by B. Wellman, pp. 119–146. Westview Press, Boulder, CO.

LEE, R. D. (2000): "Intergenerational Transfers and the Economic Life Cycle: A Cross-Cultural Perspective," in *Sharing the Wealth: Demographic Change and Economic Transfers between Generations*, ed. by A. Mason, and G. Tapinos, pp. 17–56. Oxford University Press, Oxford.

LEE, R. D., A. MASON, AND T. MILLER (2000): "Life Cycle Savings and the Demographic Transition: The Case of Taiwan," *Population and Development Review*, 26(Supplement), 194–222.

LEE, S.-H., AND A. MASON (2001): "Asia's Urban Labor Force, Earnings Growth, and Earnings Inequality," Paper prepared for the Panel on Urban Population Dynamics, Committee on Population, National Research Council. Department of Economics, University of Hawaii.

LEE-SMITH, D., AND C. H. TRUJILLO (1992): "The Struggle to Legitimize Subsistence: Women and Sustainable Development," *Environment and Urbanization*, 4(1), 77–84.

LEFÈVRE, C. (1998): "Metropolitan Government and Governance in Western Countries: A Critical Review," *International Journal of Urban and Regional Research*, 22(1), 9–25.

LERISE, F., A. KIBADU, E. MBUTOLWE, AND N. MUSHI (2001): "Rural-Urban Interactions and Livelihood Strategies: The Case of Lindi and its Region in Southern Tanzania," Rural-Urban Interactions and Livelihood Strategies Working Paper 1, IIED.

LESTHAEGHE, R. (1977): *The Decline of Belgian Fertility, 1800–1970*. Princeton University Press, Princeton, NJ.

——— (1989): "Social Organization, Economic Crisis, and the Future of Fertility Control," in *Reproduction and Social Organization in Sub-Saharan Africa*, ed. by R. Lesthaeghe, pp. 475–505. University of California Press, Berkeley, CA.

LEVIN, C. E., D. G. MAXWELL, M. AMMAR-KLEMESU, ET AL. (1999): "Working Women in an Urban Setting: Traders, Vendors and Food Security in Accra," FCND Discussion Paper No. 66, IFPRI, Washington, DC.

LEVINE, R. A., E. DEXTER, P. VELASCO, S. LEVINE, A. R. JOSHI, K. W. STUEBING, AND F. M. TAPIA-URIBE (1994): "Maternal Literacy and Health Care in Three Countries: A Preliminary Report," *Health Transition Review*, 4(2), 186–191.

LEVINSOHN, J., S. BERRY, AND J. FRIEDMAN (1999): "Impacts of the Indonesia Economic Crisis: Price Changes and the Poor," Working Paper 7194, National Bureau of Economic Research, Cambridge, MA.

LIM, L. L. (1993): "The Structural Determinants of Female Migration," in *Internal Migration of Women in Developing Countries*, ed. by United Nations, pp. 207–222. United Nations, New York.

LIMÃO, N., AND A. J. VENABLES (2001): "Infrastructure, Geographical Disadvantage, Transport Costs, and Trade," *The World Bank Economic Review*, 15(3), 451–479.

LIN, N. (1999): "Building a Network Theory of Social Capital," *Connections*, 22(1), 28–51.

LIN, N., X. YE, AND W. M. ENSEL (1999): "Social Support and Depressed Mood: A Structural Analysis," *Journal of Health and Social Behavior*, 40, 344–359.

LINDEN, E. (1996): "The Exploding Cities of the Developing Regions," *Foreign Affairs*, 75(1), 52–65.

LIPTON, M. (1976): *Why Poor People Stay Poor: Urban Bias in World Development*. Harvard University Press, Cambridge, MA.

——— (1993): "Urban Bias: Of Consequences, Classes and Causality," *Journal of Development Studies*, 29(4), 229–258.

LIU, G., AND S. GOLDSTEIN (1996): "Migrant-Nonmigrant Fertility Differentials in Anhui, China," *Chinese Environment and Development*, 7, 144–169.

LIVAS ELIZONDO, R., AND P. KRUGMAN (1992): "Trade Policy and the Third World Metropolis," Working Paper no. 4238. National Bureau of Economic Research, Cambridge, MA.

LIVI BACCI, M. (1997): *A Concise History of World Population*. 2nd ed., Blackwell, Cambridge, MA.

LLOYD-SHERLOCK, P. (1997): *Old Age and Urban Poverty in the Developing World: The Shanty Towns of Buenos Aires*. St. Martin's Press, New York.

LOAYZA, N., K. SCHMIDT-HEBBEL, AND L. SERVÉN (2000a): "Saving in Developing Countries: An Overview," *The World Bank Economic Review*, 14(3), 393–414.

——— (2000b): "What Drives Private Saving Across the World?" *Review of Economics and Statistics*, 82(2), 165–181.

LOAYZA, N., AND R. SHANKAR (2000): "Private Saving in India," *The World Bank Economic Review*, 14(3), 571–594.

LOMNITZ, L. (1997): "The Social and Economic Organization of a Mexican Shanty-Town," in *Cities in the Developing World: Issues, Theory, and Policy*, ed. by J. Gugler, pp. 204–217. Oxford University Press, Oxford.

LONDOÑO, J. L., AND J. FRENK (1997): "Structured Pluralism: Towards an Innovative Model for Health System Reform in Latin America," *Health Policy*, 41(1), 1–36.

LONDOÑO, J. L., AND R. GUERRERO (2000): "Violencia en América Latina: Epidemiologia y Costos," in *Asalto al Desarrolo, Violencia en América Latina*, ed. by J. L. Londoño, A. Gaviria, and R. Guerrero, pp. 11–57. Interamerican Development Bank, Washington, DC.

LORENZ, N., AND P. GARNER (1995): "Organising and Managing Health Services," in *Urban Health in Developing Countries: Progress and Prospects*, ed. by T. Harpham, and M. Tanner, pp. 48–63. Earthscan, London.

LÖSCH, A. (1954): *The Economics of Location*. Yale University Press, New Haven, CT.

LOWI, T. J. (2000): "Think Globally, Lose Locally," in *Globalization, Governance, and Identity*, ed. by G. Lachapelle, and J. Trent, pp. 17–38. Les Presse de Université de Montréal, Montréal, Canada.

LOZANO, R., M. HIJAR, B. ZURITA, P. HERNÁNDEZ, L. AVILA, M. L. BRAVO, T. DE JESÚS RAMIREZ, C. CARRILLO, C. AYALA, AND B. E. LÓPEZ (2000): "Capital Lesionada: Violencia en Ciudad de México," in *Asalto al Desarrollo: Violencia en América Latina*, ed. by J. L. Londoño, A. Gaviria, and R. Guerrero, pp. 205–232. Interamerican Development Bank, Washington, DC.

LOZANO, R., C. MURRAY, AND J. FRENK (1999): "El Peso de las Enfermedades en Mexico," in *Las Consecuencias de las Transiciones Demografica y Epidemiological en América Latina*, ed. by K. Hill, J. B. Morelos, and R. Wong. El Colegio de México, Mexico City.

LUBIS, F. (1986): "Providing Quality Family Planning and MCH Services in the Urban Areas: The YKB Experience," *JOICFP Review*, 11, 18–22.

LUCAS, R. E. (1988): "On the Mechanics of Economic Development," *Journal of Monetary Economics*, 22, 3–42.

LUCAS, R. E. B. (1997): "Internal Migration in Developing Countries," in *Handbook of Population and Family Economics*, ed. by M. Rosenzweig, and O. Stark, pp. 721–798. Elsevier North-Holland, Amsterdam.

LUKE, N. (2002): "Confronting the Myth of "Sugar Daddies": Linking Age and Economic Asymmetries and Risky Sexual Behavior in Urban Kenya," Paper presented at the Population Association of America Annual Meeting, May 8–11, Atlanta, GA.

LUSK, M. W. (1989): "Street Children Programs in Latin America," *Journal of Sociology and Sociological Welfare*, 16, 55–77.

MACARTHUR, I. W. (1993): "Sheltering Street Youth in Rio de Janeiro, Brazil," Master's thesis, Massachusetts Institute of Technology, Boston.

MACLEOD, S., AND T. MCGEE (1996): "The Singapore-Johore-Riau Growth Triangle: An Emerging Extended Metropolitan Region," in *Emerging World Cities in Pacific Asia*, ed. by F.-C. Lo, and Y. M. Yeung, pp. 417–464. United Nations University Press, Tokyo.

MAGADI, M. A., AND E. ZULU (2002): "Initiation of Sex and Subsequent Sexual Behavior among Female Adolescents in Nairobi Slums," Paper presented at the Population Association of America Annual Meeting, May 8–11, Atlanta, GA.

MAGNANI, R., E. E. SEIBER, E. ZIELINKSKI GUTIERREZ, AND D. VEREAU (2001): "Correlates of Sexual Activity and Condom Use among Secondary-School Students in Urban Peru," *Studies in Family Planning*, 32(1), 53–66.

MAGNANI, R. J., L. GAFFIKIN, E. M. LEÃO DE AQUINO, E. E. SEIBER, M. DE CONCEIÇÃO CHAGAS ALMEIDA, AND V. LIPOVSEK (2001): "Impact of an Integrated Adolescent Reproductive Health Program in Brazil," *Studies in Family Planning*, 32(3), 230–243.

MAHID BIN MOHAMED, D. A. (1998): "Case Study of NSDIs in Countries in Transition: Malaysia," Available on Internet website www.gsdi.org/docs/canberra/malaysia.html. Author is Director General of Survey and Mapping, Malaysia.

MAKANNAH, T. J. (1990): "Policy Measures for Stemming Urban In-Migration," in *Conference on the Role of Migration in African Development: Issues and Policies for the '90s. Vol. 1: Commissioned Papers*, ed. by Union for African Population Studies, pp. 82–95. Union for African Population Studies, Dakar.

MAKINEN, M., H. WATERS, M. RAUCH, N. ALMAGAMBETOVA, R. BITRAN, L. GILSON, D. MCINTYRE, S. PANNARUNOTHAI, A. L. PRIETO, G. UBILLA, AND S. RAM (2000): "Inequalities in Health Care Use and Expenditures: Empirical Data from Eight Developing Countries and Countries in Transition," *Bulletin of the World Health Organization*, 78(1), 55–65.

MALAWI, NATIONAL STATISTICS OFFICE (1994): "Survey of Household Expenditure and Small Scale Economic Activities 1990/91," National Statistics Office, Malawi.

MALONEY, W. F. (1999): "Does Informality Imply Segmentation in Urban Labor Markets? Evidence from Sectoral Transitions in Mexico," *The World Bank Economic Review*, 13(2), 275–302.

MALPEZZI, S. (1990): "Urban Housing and Financial Markets: Some International Comparisons," *Urban Studies*, 27(6), 971–1022.

——— (1999): "Economic Analysis of Housing Markets in Developing and Transition Economies," in *Handbook of Regional and Urban Economies*, ed. by E. S. Mills, and P. Cheshire, vol. 3, pp. 1791–1864. Elsevier North-Holland, Amsterdam.

MAMDANI, M., P. GARNER, ET AL. (1993): "Fertility and Contraceptive Use in Poor Urban Areas of Developing Countries," *Health Policy and Planning*, 8(1), 1–18.

MANOR, J. (1999): *The Political Economy of Democratic Decentralization*. The World Bank, Washington, DC.

MANSKI, C. F. (1993): "Identification of Endogenous Social Effects: The Reflection Problem," *Review of Economic Studies*, 60, 531–542.

MANZANAL, M., AND C. VAPNARSKY (1986): "The Development of the Upper Valley of Rio Niegro and its Periphery Within the Comahue Region, Argentina," in *Small and Intermediate Urban Centres: Their Role in Regional and National Development in the Third World*, ed. by J. E. Hardoy, and D. Satterthwaite, pp. 18–79. Hodder and Stoughton (UK) and Westview (USA), London.

MARSHALL, A. (1890): *Principles of Economics*. 8th ed., Macmillan Press, London (1977 reprint).

MARTINS, S. B., AND G. J. EBRAHIM (1995): "The Female Street Children of Rio De Janeiro: A Qualitative Study of Their Backgrounds," *Journal of Tropical Pediatrics*, 41, 43–46.

MASON, A., T. MERRICK, AND P. SHAW (eds.) (1999): *Population Economics, Demographic Transition, and Development: Research and Policy Implications*. The World Bank, World Bank Institute Working Paper, Washington, DC.

MASON, K. O. (1997): "Explaining Fertility Transitions," *Demography*, 34(4), 443–454.

MASSEY, D. S. (1990): "American Apartheid: Segregation and the Making of the Underclass," *American Journal of Sociology*, 96(2), 329–357.

——— (1996): "The Age of Extremes: Concentrated Affluence and Poverty in the Twenty-First Century," *Demography*, 33(4), 395–412.

MATCHINDA, B. (1999): "The Impact of Home Background on the Decision of Children to Run Away: The Case of Yaoundé City Street Children in Cameroon," *Child Abuse and Neglect*, 23, 245–255.

MAYANK, S., R. BAHL, A. RATTAN, AND N. BHANDARI (2001): "Prevalence and Correlates of Morbidity in Pregnant Women in an Urban Slum of New Delhi," *Asia-Pacific Population Journal*, 16(2), 29–45.

MAYO, S. K., AND D. J. GROSS (1989): "Sites and Services—and Subsidies: The Economics of Low-Cost Housing," in *Government Policy and the Poor in Developing Countries*, ed. by R. M. Bird, and S. Horton, pp. 106–143. University of Toronto Press, Toronto.

MBIZVO, M. T., S. FAWCUS, G. LINDMARK, AND L. NYSTROM (1993): "Maternal Mortality in Rural and Urban Zimbabwe: Social and Reproductive Factors in an Incident Case-Referent Study," *Social Science and Medicine*, 36(9), 1197–1205.

MCCARNEY, P., M. HALFANI, AND A. RODRIQUEZ (1995): "Towards an Understanding of Governance: The Emergence of an Idea and Its Implications for Urban Research in Developing Countries," in *Urban Research in the Developing World. (Vol. 4). Perspectives on the City*, ed. by R. Stren, and J. Bell, pp. 91–141. Centre for Urban and Community Studies, University of Toronto, Toronto.

MCCOMBIE, S. (1995): "Treatment Seeking for Malaria: A Review of Recent Research," *Social Science and Medicine*, 43(6), 933–945.

MCCULLOCH, N., B. BAULCH, AND M. CHEREL-ROBSON (2000): "Poverty, Inequality and Growth in Zambia During the 1990s," Institute of Development Studies Working Paper 114, Institute of Development Studies, Brighton, UK.

MCDADE, T. W., AND L. S. ADAIR (2001): "Defining the 'Urban' in Urbanization and Health: A Factor Analysis Approach," *Social Science and Medicine*, 53, 55–70.

MCDOWELL, L. (1993a): "Space, Place and Gender Relations, Part 1: Feminist Empiricism and the Geography of Social Relations," *Progress in Human Geography*, 17, 157–179.

——— (1993b): "Space, Place and Gender Relations, Part 2: Identity, Difference, Feminist Geometries and Geographies," *Progress in Human Geography*, 17, 305–318.

MCGEE, T. G. (1991): "The Emergence of *Desakota* Regions in Asia: Expanding a Hypothesis," in *The Extended Metropolis: Settlement Transition in Asia*, ed. by N. Ginsburg, B. Koppel, and T. G. McGee, pp. 3–25. University of Hawaii Press, Honolulu.

MCGEE, T. G., AND T. FIRMAN (2000): "Labor Market Adjustment in the Time of 'Krismon': Changes of Employment Structure in Indonesia, 1997–1998," Paper prepared for the Panel on Urban Population Dynamics, Committee on Population, National Research Council.

MCGEE, T. G., AND C. J. GRIFFITHS (1998): "Global Urbanization: Towards the Twenty-First Century," in *Population Distribution and Migration: Proceedings of the United Nations Expert Group Meeting on Population Distribution and Migration, Santa Cruz, Bolivia, 18–22 January 1993*, ed. by United Nations Population Division, pp. 49–65. United Nations, New York, Convened in preparation for the International Conference on Population and Development, Cairo, 5–13 September 1994.

MCGEE, T. G., AND I. M. ROBINSON (eds.) (1995): *The Mega-Urban Regions of Southeast Asia*. University of British Columbia Press, Vancouver.

MCGRANAHAN, G., J. SONGSORE, AND M. KJELLÉN (1999): "Sustainability, Poverty and Urban Environmental Transitions," in *The Earthscan Reader in Sustainable Cities*, ed. by D. Satterthwaite. Earthscan Publications Ltd., pp. 107–130, London.

MCKEE, D., D. GARNER, AND Y. MCKEE (2000): *Offshore Financial Centers, Accounting Services and the Global Economy*. Quorum Books, Westport, CT.

MCPAKE, B. (1993): "User Charges for Health Services in Developing Countries: A Review of the Economic Literature," *Social Science and Medicine*, 36(11), 1397–1405.

MCPAKE, B., D. ASIIMWE, F. MWESIGYE, M. OFUMBI, L. ORTENBLAD, P. STEEFLAND, AND A. TURINDE (1999): "Informal Economic Activities of Public Health Workers in Uganda: Implications for Quality and Accessibility of Care," *Social Science and Medicine*, 49(7), 849–865.

MEAD, D. C., AND C. MORRISON (1996): "The Informal Sector Elephant," *World Development*, 24(10), 1611–1619.

MEEKERS, D. (2001): "The Role of Social Marketing in Sexually Transmitted Diseases/HIV Protection in 4600 Sexual Contacts in Urban Zimbabwe," *AIDS*, 15(2), 285–287.

MEEKERS, D., AND G. AHMED (2000): "Contemporary Patterns of Adolescent Sexuality in Urban Botswana," *Journal of Biosocial Science*, 32, 467–485.

MEEKERS, D., G. AHMED, AND M. MOLATLHEGI (2001): "Understanding Constraints to Adolescent Condom Procurement: The Case of Urban Botswana," *AIDS Care*, 13(3), 297–302.

MEEKERS, D., AND A.-E. CALVES (1997): "'Main' Girlfriends, Girlfriends, Marriage, and Money," *Health Transition Review*, 7(Supplement).

MEERTENS, D., AND N. SEGURA-ESCOBAR (1996): "Gender, Violence and Displacement in Colombia," *Singapore Journal of Tropical Geography*, 17(2), 165–178.

MEHTA, D. (1999): "Urban Governance: Lessons from Best Practices in Asia," Unpublished paper, New Delhi.

MEJIA-SOTO, G. (1998): "Morbilidad de 'los Ninos de la Calle'," *Adolescencia latinoamericana*, 1(3), 175–182.

MELO, M., F. REZENDE, AND C. LUBAMBO (2000): "Urban Governance, Accountability and Poverty: The Politics of Participatory Budgeting in Recife, Brazil," Project on Urban Governance, Partnerships and Poverty, University of Birmingham.

MENON, R. (1987): "Job Transfers: A Neglected Aspect of Migration in Malysia," *International Migration Review*, 21(1), 86–95.

———— (1988): "How Malaysian Migrants Pre-Arrange Employment," *Sociology and Social Research*, 72(4), 257–259.

MENSCH, B. S., M. ARENDS-KUENNING, A. JAIN, AND M. R. GARATE (1997): "Avoiding Unintended Pregnancy in Peru: Does the Quality of Family Planning Services Matter?" *International Family Planning Perspectives*, 23, 21–27.

MENSCH, B. S., J. BRUCE, AND M. E. GREENE (1998): *The Uncharted Passage: Girls' Adolescence in the Developing World*. Population Council, New York.

MENSCH, B. S., P. C. HEWETT, AND A. ERULKAR (2001): "The Reporting of Sensitive Behavior among Adolescents: A Methodological Experiment in Kenya," Policy Research Division *Working Paper* no. 151, Population Council, New York.

MENSCH, B. S., B. L. IBRAHIM, S. M. LEE, AND O. EL-GIBALY (2000): "Socialization to Gender Roles and Marriage among Egyptian Adolescents," Policy Research Division *Working Paper* no. 140, Population Council, New York.

MEYER, D. R. (1998): "World Cities as Financial Centres," in *Globalization and the World of Large Cities*, ed. by F.-C. Lo, and Y. M. Yeung, pp. 410–432. United Nations University Press, Tokyo.

MIGUEL, E., P. GERTLER, AND D. I. LEVINE (2001): "Did Industrialization Destroy Social Capital in Indonesia?" Department of Economics, University of California at Berkeley.

MILNE, D. (2001): "The Advantages to a City of Spatial Information to Enable Service Delivery," Unpublished paper prepared by the interim GIS coordinator for the City of Cape Town, South Africa.

MINSA (1996): *Annual Report of Nicaraguan Ministry of Health*. Nicaraguan Ministry of Health, Managua.

MITCHELL, J. C. (ed.) (1969): *Social Networks in Urban Situations: Analyses of Personal Relationships in Central African Towns*. Manchester University Press, Manchester, UK.

MITLIN, D., AND D. SATTERTHWAITE (2001): "Urban Poverty: Some Thoughts about its Scale and Nature and about Responses to It," in *Facets of Globalization: International and Local Dimensions of Development*, ed. by S. Yusuf, W. Wu, and S. Evenett, pp. 193–215. World Bank, Washington, DC.

MITLIN, D., D. SATTERTHWAITE, AND C. STEPHENS (1996): "City Inequality," *Environment and Urbanization*, 8(2), 3–7.

MITRA, A. (1999): "Agglomeration Economies as Manifested in Technical Efficiency at the Firm Level," *Journal of Urban Economics*, 45, 490–500.

———— (2000): "Total Factor Productivity Growth and Urbanization Economies: A Case of Indian Industries," *Review of Urban and Regional Development Studies*, 12(2), 98–108.

MOCK, C. N., F. ABANTANGA, P. CUMMINGS, AND T. D. KOEPSELL (1999): "Incidence and Outcome of Inquiry in Ghana: A Community-Based Survey," *Bulletin of the World Health Organization*, 77(12), 955–964.

MOCK, N. B., T. A. SELLERS, A. A. ABDOH, AND R. R. FRANKLIN (1993): "Socioeconomic, Environmental, Demographic and Behavioral Factors Associated with Occurrence of Diarrhoea in Young Children in the Republic of Congo," *Social Science and Medicine*, 36(6), 807–816.

MOLBAK, K., P. AABY, L. INGHOLT, N. HOJLYNG, A. GOTTSCHAU, H. ANDERSON, L. BRINK, U. GANSTED, A. PERMIN, AND A. VOLLMER (1992): "Persistent and Acute Diarrhoea as the Leading Causes of Child Mortality in Urban Guinea Bissau," *Transactions of the Royal Society of Tropical Medicine and Hygiene*, 86(2), 216–220.

MOLINA, R., C. PEREDA, F. CUMSILLE, L. M. OLIVA, E. MIRANDA, AND T. MOLINA (1999): "Prevention of Pregnancy in High-Risk Women: Community Intervention in Chile," in *Abortion in the Developing World*, ed. by A. I. Mundigo, and C. Indriso, pp. 57–77. Zed Books Ltd., London.

MOLYNEUX, C. S., V. MUNG'ALA-ODERA, T. HARPHAM, AND R. W. SNOW (1999): "Maternal Responses to Childhood Fevers: A Comparison of Rural and Urban Residents in Coastal Kenya," *Tropical Medicine and International Health*, 4(12), 836–845.

MONTEIRO, C. A., D. A. BENICIO, W. L. CONDE, AND B. M. POPKIN (2000): "Shifting Obesity Trends in Brazil," *European Journal of Clinical Nutrition*, 54(4), 342–346.

MONTGOMERY, J. D. (1992): "Job Search and Network Composition: Implications of the Strength-of-Weak-Ties Hypothesis," *American Sociological Review*, 57(5), 586–596.

MONTGOMERY, M. R. (1987): "The Impacts of Urban Population Growth on Urban Labor Markets and the Costs of Urban Service Delivery," in *Population Growth and Economic Development: Issues and Evidence*, ed. by D. G. Johnson, and R. D. Lee, pp. 149–188. University of Wisconsin Press, Madison, WI.

——— (1988): "How Large Is Too Large? Implications of the City Size Literature for Population Policy and Research," *Economic Development and Cultural Change*, 36(4), 691–720.

——— (2000): "Perceiving Mortality Decline," *Population and Development Review*, 26(4), 795–819.

MONTGOMERY, M. R., M. ARENDS-KUENNING, AND C. METE (2000): "The Quantity-Quality Transition in Asia," *Population and Development Review*, 26(Supplement), 223–256, in C.Y. Cyrus Chu and Ronald D. Lee, eds., *Population and Economic Change in East Asia*.

MONTGOMERY, M. R., AND J. B. CASTERLINE (1993): "The Diffusion of Fertility Control in Taiwan: Estimates from Pooled Cross-Section, Time-Series Models," *Population Studies*, 47(3), 457–479.

——— (1996): "Social Learning, Social Influence, and New Models of Fertility," *Population and Development Review*, 22(Supplement), 151–175, In John B. Casterline and Ronald D. Lee and Karen A. Foote, eds., *Fertility in the United States: New Patterns, New Theories*.

MONTGOMERY, M. R., M. GRAGNOLATI, K. A. BURKE, AND E. PAREDES (2000): "Measuring Living Standards with Proxy Variables," *Demography*, 37(2), 155–174.

MOOMAW, R., AND A. M. SHATTER (1996): "Urbanization and Economic Development: A Bias Toward Large Cities," *Journal of Urban Economics*, 40 (July), 13–37.

MOORE, G. (1990): "Structural Determinants of Men's and Women's Personal Networks," *American Sociological Review*, 55(5), 726–735.

MORETTI, E. (2000): "Estimating the Social Returns to Education: Evidence from Longitudinal and Repeated Cross-Section Data," Working paper, Department of Economics, University of California at Los Angeles.

MORICONI-EBRARD, F. (1994): *GEOPOLIS: Pour Comparer les Villes du Monde*. Economica, Anthropos, Collection "Villes," Paris.

MORRILL, R. (1995): "Metropolitan Concepts and Statistics Report," in *Metropolitan and Non-Metropolitan Areas: New Approaches to Geographical Definition*, ed. by D. C. Dahmann, and J. D. Fitzsimmons, no. 12 in *Working Paper* series, pp. 191–250. Population Division, U.S. Bureau of the Census, Washington, DC.

MORRISON, A. R., AND X. GUO (1998): "Measuring the Macroeconomic Impact of Internal Migration: A Production Function Approach with Evidence from Peru," in *Migration, Urbanization, and Development: New Directions and Issues*, ed. by R. E. Bilsborrow, pp. 221–246. United Nations Population Fund (UNFPA), New York.

MOSER, C. O. N. (1987): "Mobilization as Womens' Work: Struggles for Infrastructure in Guayaquil, Ecuador," in *Women, Housing and Human Settlements*, ed. by C. O. N. Moser, and L. Peake, pp. 166–194. Tavistock Publications, London and New York.

——— (1993): "Urban Social Policy and Poverty Reduction," Working Paper, Urban Development Division, TWURD WP 10, October.

——— (1996): "Confronting Crisis: A Summary of Household Responses to Poverty and Vulnerability in Four Poor Urban Communities," Environmentally Sustainable Development Studies and Monographs Series 7, The World Bank, Washington, DC.

——— (1998): "The Asset Vulnerability Framework: Reassessing Urban Poverty Reduction Strategies," *World Development*, 26(1), 1–19.

MOSER, C. O. N., A. J. HERBERT, AND R. E. MAKONNEN (1993): "Urban Poverty in the Context of Structural Adjustment: Recent Evidence and Policy Responses," TWU Discussion Paper DP no. 4, Urban Development Division, The World Bank, Washington, DC.

MOSER, C. O. N., AND J. HOLLAND (1997): *Urban Poverty and Violence in Jamaica*. World Bank, Washington, DC.

MOSER, C. O. N., AND C. MCILWAINE (1999): "Participatory Urban Appraisal and Its Application for Research on Violence," *Environment and Urbanization*, 11(2), 203–226.

——— (2000a): *Urban Poor Perceptions of Violence and Exclusion in Colombia*. The World Bank, Washington, DC.

——— (2000b): *Violence in a Post-Conflict Context: Urban Poor Perceptions from Guatemala*. The World Bank, Washington, DC.

MOZAMBIQUE MINISTRY OF PLANNING AND FINANCE, EDUARDO MONDLANE UNIVERSITY, AND INTERNATIONAL FOOD POLICY RESEARCH INSTITUTE (1998): "Understanding Poverty and Well-Being in Mozambique: The First National Assessment (1996–97)," IFPRI, Washington, DC.

MROZ, T. A., K. A. BOLLEN, I. S. SPEIZER, AND D. J. MANCINI (1999): "Quality, Accessibility, and Contraceptive Use in Rural Tanzania," *Demography*, 36(1), 23–40.

MUHURI, P. K., AND S. O. RUTSTEIN (1994): "Socioeconomic, Demographic, and Health Indicators for Subnational Areas," DHS Comparative Studies no. 9. Macro International, Calverton, MD.

MULGAONKAR, V. B., I. G. PARIKH, V. R. TASKAR, N. D. DHARAP, AND V. P. PRADHAN (1994): "Perceptions of Bombay Slum Women Regarding Refusal to Particpate in a Gynaecological Health Programme," in *Listening to Women Talk about Their Health: Issues and Evidence from India*, ed. by J. Gittelsohn, M. E. Bentley, P. J. Pelto, M. Nag, S. Pachauri, A. D. Harrison, and L. T. Landman, pp. 145–167. Har-Anand Publications, The Ford Foundation, New York.

MUMFORD, L. (1961): *The City in History. Its Origins, Its Transformations, and Its Prospects.* Harcourt, Brace, San Diego.

MUNA, W. F. (1993): "Cardiovascular Disorders in Africa," *World Health Statistical Quarterly*, 46(2), 125–133.

MURPHY, J. T. (2002): "Networks, Trust, and Innovation in Tanzania's Manufacturing Sector," *World Development*, 30(4), 591–619.

MUSABEK, E. N., C. M. BECKER, A.-G. S. SEITENOVA, AND D. S. URZHUMOVA (2001): "The Migration Response to Economic Shock: Lessons from Kazakhstan," Paper prepared for the Panel on Urban Population Dynamics, Committee on Population, National Research Council. Institute of Behavioral Science, Program in Population Processes, Boulder, CO.

MUTATKAR, R. K. (1995): "Public Health Problems of Urbanization," *Social Science and Medicine*, 41(7), 977–981.

MWENESI, H. (1993): "Mothers' Definition and Treatment of Childhood Malaria on the Kenyan Coast," Faculty of Medicine, University of London.

NARAYAN, D., AND L. PRITCHETT (1999): "Cents and Sociability: Household Income and Social Capital in Rural Tanzania," *Economic Development and Cultural Change*, 47(4), 871–897.

NATIONAL RESEARCH COUNCIL (1997): *The New Americans: Economic, Demographic, and Fiscal Effects of Immigration.* National Academy Press, Washington, DC.

——— (1999): *Governance and Opportunity in Metropolitan America.* National Academy Press, Washington, DC.

——— (2000): *Beyond Six Billion: Forecasting the World's Population.* National Academy Press, Washington, DC, Panel on Population Projections. J. Bongaarts and R. A. Bulatao, eds. Committee on Population.

——— (2001): *Diffusion Processes and Fertility Transition: Selected Perspectives.* National Academy Press, Washington, DC, J. B. Casterline, ed.

NAVARRO, L. (2001): "Exploring the Environmental and Political Dimension of Poverty: The cases of Mar del Plata and Necochea-Quequen Cities," *Environment and Urbanization*, 13(1), 185–199.

NAVED, R. T., M. NEWBY, AND S. AMIN (2001): "The Effects of Migration and Work on Marriage of Female Garment Workers in Bangladesh," *International Journal of Population Geography*, 7(2), 91–104.

NEARY, J. P. (2001): "Of Hype and Hyperbolas: Introducing the New Economic Geography," *Journal of Economic Literature*, 39(2), 536–561.

NELSON, K., R. MAGNANI, AND K. BOND (2000): *The "Youth Friendliness" of Health Services and Service Utilization by Adolescents and Young Adults in Lusaka,*

Zambia. FOCUS on Young Adults Program/Pathfinder International, Washington, DC.

NGALANDE-BANDA, E., AND G. WALT (1995): "The Private Health Sector in Malawi: Opening Pandora's Box?" *Journal of International Development,* 7(3), 403–421.

NICHTER, M. (1996): "Self-Medication and STD Prevention [Editorial; Comment]," *Sexually Transmitted Diseases,* 23(5), 353–356.

NICKSON, R. A. (1995): *Local Government in Latin America.* Lynne Rienner, Boulder, CO.

NOTESTEIN, F. (1953): "Economic Problems of Population Change," in *Proceedings of the Eighth International Conference of Agricultural Economists,* pp. 13–31. Oxford University Press, London.

OCAMPO, R. B. (1995): "The Metro Manila Mega-Region," in *The Mega-Urban Regions of Southeast Asia,* ed. by T. G. McGee, and I. M. Robinson, pp. 282–295. University of British Columbia Press, Vancouver.

ODERO, W. (1995): "Road Traffic Accidents in Kenya: An Epidemiological Appraisal," *East African Medical Journal,* 72(5), 299–305.

ODERO, W., P. GARNER, AND A. ZWI (1997): "Road Traffic Injuries in Developing Countries: A Comprehensive Review of Epidemiological Studies," *Tropical Medicine and International Health,* 2(5), 445–460.

OGUNBEKUN, I., A. OGUNBEKUN, AND N. OROBATON (1999): "Private Health Care in Nigeria: Walking the Tightrope," *Health Policy and Planning,* 14(2), 174–181.

OHMAE, K. (1990): *The Borderless World: Power and Strategy in the Interlinked Economy.* Harper, New York.

OI, J. (1992): "Fiscal Reform and the Economic Foundations of Local State Corporatism in China," *World Politics,* 45(1), 99–126.

——— (1995): "The Role of the Local State in China's Transitional Economy," *The China Quarterly,* 144, 1132–1149.

OKELLO, D. O., R. LUBANGA, D. GUWATUDDE, AND A. SEBINA-ZZIWA (1998): "The Challenge to Restoring Basic Health Care in Uganda," *Social Science and Medicine,* 46(1), 13–21.

OKONOFUA, F. E., C. ODIMEGWU, B. AINA, P. DARU, AND A. JOHNSON (1996): "Women's Experiences of Unwanted Pregnancy and Induced Abortion in Nigeria: Summary Report," New York: Population Council.

OLDS, K., AND H. W. YEUNG (1999): "(Re)shaping 'Chinese' Business Networks in a Globalising Era," *Environment and Planning,* 17, 535–555.

O'LOONEY, J. (2000): *Beyond Maps: GIS and Decision Making in Local Government.* Environmental Systems Research Institute Press, California.

ONIBOKUN, A. G. (ed.) (1999): *Managing the Monster: Urban Waste and Governance in Africa.* International Development Research Centre, Ottawa.

OSTROM, V., C. M. TIEBOUT, AND R. WARREN (1961): "The Organization of Governments in Metropolitan Areas," *American Political Science Review,* 55(4).

OUCHO, J. O., AND W. T. S. GOULD (1993): "Internal Migration, Urbanization, and Population Distribution," in *Demographic Change in Sub-Saharan Africa,* ed. by K. A. Foote, K. H. Hill, and L. G. Martin, pp. 256–296. National Academy Press, Washington, DC.

PACK, H., AND J. PAGE (1994): "Accumulation, Exports and Growth in the High-Performing Asian Economies," *Carnegie-Rochester Conference Series on Public Policy*, 40, 199–236.

PAIEWONSKY, D. (1999): "Social Determinants of Induced Abortion in the Dominican Republic," in *Abortion in the Developing World*, ed. by A. I. Mundigo, and C. Indriso, pp. 131–150. Zed Books Ltd., London.

PALLONI, A., D. S. MASSEY, M. CEBALLOS, K. ESPINOSA, AND M. SPITTEL (2001): "Social Capital and International Migration: A Test Using Information on Family Networks," *American Journal of Sociology*, 106(5), 1262–1298.

PALMORE, J., AND R. FREEDMAN (1969): "Perceptions of Contraceptive Practice by Others: Effects on Acceptance," in *Family Planning in Taiwan: An Experiment in Social Change*, ed. by R. Freedman, and J. Takeshita, pp. 224–240. Princeton University Press, Princeton.

PAN AMERICAN HEALTH ORGANIZATION (PAHO) (1998): *Health in the Americas*. PAHO, Washington, DC.

PANTER-BRICK, C., A. TODD, AND R. BAKER (1996): "Growth Status of Homeless Nepali Boys: Do they Differ from Rural and Urban Controls?" *Social Science and Medicine*, 43, 441–451.

PARISH, W. L., AND R. J. WILLIS (1993): "Daughters, Education, and Family Budgets: Taiwan Experiences," *Journal of Human Resources*, 28(4), 863–898.

PARRY, C. (1995): "Quantitative Measurement of Mental Health Problems in Urban Areas: Opportunities and Constraints," in *Urbanisation and Mental Health in Developing Countries*, ed. by T. Harpham, and I. Blue, pp. 193–224. Aldershot, Avebury.

PASHA, O., F. F. FIKREE, AND S. VERMUND (2001): "Determinants of Unmet Need for Family Planning in Squatter Settlements in Karachi, Pakistan," *Asian-Pacific Population Journal*, 16(2), 93–108.

PATEL, S., AND D. MITLIN (2001): "The Work of SPARC and Its Partners Mahila Milan and the National Slum Dwellers Federation in India," IIED Working Paper Series on Urban Poverty Reduction, IIED, London.

PEARLMAN, E., H. JONES, M. GOROSH, C. G. VOGEL, AND M. OJERMARK (1998): "Urban and Rural Family Planning Services: Does Service Quality Really Matter?" in *Clinical-Based Family Planning and Reproductice Health Services in Africa: Findings from Situation Analysis Studies* ed. by K. Miller, R. Miller, I. . Askew, M. C. Horn, and L. Ndhlovu, pp. 143–156. Population Council, New York.

PEBLEY, A. R., N. GOLDMAN, AND G. RODRÍGUEZ (1996): "Prenatal and Delivery Care and Childhood Immunization in Guatemala: Do Family and Community Matter?" *Demography*, 33(2), 231–247.

PERLMAN, J. (1976): *The Myth of Marginality: Urban Politics and Poverty in Rio de Janeiro*. University of California Press, Berkeley.

PHILLIPS, D. (1990): *Health and Health Care in the Third World*. Routledge, London.

PHONGPAICHIT, P. (1993): "The Labour Market Aspects of Female Migration to Bangkok," in *Internal Migration of Women in Developing Countries*, ed. by United Nations, pp. 178–191. United Nations, New York.

PICK, W. M., AND D. COOPER (1997): "Urbanisation and Women's Health in South Africa," *African Journal of Reproductive Health*, 1(1), 45–55.

PICK, W. M., AND C. M. OBERMEYER (1996): "Urbanisation, Household Composition and the Reproductive Health of Women in a South African City," *Social Science and Medicine*, 43(10), 1431–1441.

PICKERING, H., M. OKONGO, A. OJWIYA, D. YIRRELL, AND J. WHITWORTH (1997): "Sexual Networks in Uganda: Mixing Patterns Between a Trading Town, Its Rural Hinterland and a Nearby Fishing Village," *International Journal of STDs and AIDS*, 8(8), 495–500.

PIETERSE, E. (2000): "Metropolitan Governance Under Construction: Notes on the Unicity Experiment in Cape Town," Unpublished paper, Isandla Institute.

POLÈSE, M., AND R. STREN (eds.) (2000): *The Social Sustainability of Cities: Diversity and the Management of Change.* University of Toronto Press, Toronto.

POLICY PROJECT (2000): "Health Reform, Decentralization, and Participation in Latin America: Protecting Sexual and Reproductive Health," The Futures Group International, Inc., Washington, DC.

PONT, R. (2001): "A Conversation with Raul Pont, Mayor of Porto Alegre," in *The Challenge of Urban Government: Policies and Practices*, ed. by M. Freire, and R. Stren, pp. 145–150. The World Bank, Washington, DC.

POPKIN, B. M. (1999): "Urbanization, Lifestyle Changes and the Nutrition Transition," *World Development*, 27(11), 1905–1916.

POPULATION REFERENCE BUREAU (2001): *Youth in Sub-Saharan Africa: A Chartbook on Sexual Experience and Reproductive Health.* Population Reference Bureau, Washington, DC.

POPULATION SERVICES INTERNATIONAL AND POPULATION REFERENCE BUREAU (2000): *Social Marketing for Adolescent Sexual Health: Results of Operations Research Projects in Botswana, Cameroon, Guinea, and South Africa.* Population Reference Bureau, Washington, DC.

PORTES, A. (1995): *The Economic Sociology of Immigration: Essays on Networks, Ethnicity, and Entrepreneurship.* Russell Sage Foundation, New York.

PORTO ALEGRE (1998): *Porto Alegre: Socioeconomics.* Porto Alegre City Hall, Porto Alegre.

POTGIETER, F., D. VENTER, E. P. THOMAS, J. R. SEAGER, G. MCGRANAHAN, AND M. KJELLÉN (1999): *Port Elizabeth 1000 Household Environment and Health Survey*, no. 6.1 in Port Elizabeth Household Environment and Health Series Report 1, Urban Environment Series. Stockholm Environment Institute and South African Medical Research Council, Cape Town.

POTTER, R. G., AND F. E. KOBRIN (1982): "Some Effects of Spouse Separation on Fertility," *Demography*, 19(1), 79–96.

POZZOBON, R. M. (1998): *Os Desafios da Gestão Municipal Democrática, Porto Alegre.* Instituto Polis, São Paulo.

PRESTON, S. H. (1979): "Urban Growth in Developing Countries: A Demographic Reappraisal," *Population and Development Review*, 5(2), 195–215.

PRESTON, S. H., AND M. R. HAINES (1991): *Fatal Years: Child Mortality in Late Nineteenth-Century America.* Princeton University Press, Princeton, NJ.

PRESTON, S. H., AND E. VAN DE WALLE (1978): "Urban French Mortality in the Nineteenth Century," *Population Studies*, 32(2), 275–297.

PRÉVÔT-SHAPIRA, M.-F. (2000): "Segregacão, Fragmentacão, Secessão: A Nova Geografia Social de Buenos Aires," *Novos Estudos*, 56, 169–183.

PRYER, J. (1989): "When Breadwinners Fall Ill: Preliminary Findings from a Case Study in Bangladesh," *IDS Bulletin*, 20(2), 49–57.

PSACHAROPOULOS, G. (1985): "Returns to Education: A Further International Update and Implications," *The Journal of Human Resources*, 20(4), 583–611.

——— (1994): "Returns to Investment in Education: A Global Update," *World Development*, 22(9), 1325–1343.

PUTNAM, R. D. (2000): *Bowling Alone: The Collapse and Revival of American Community*. Simon and Schuster, New York.

QUIGLEY, J. M. (1998): "Urban Diversity and Economic Growth," *Journal of Economic Perspectives*, 12(2), 127–138.

QUINN, T. C. (1995): "Population Migration and the Spread of Types 1 and 2 Human Immunodeficiency Viruses," in *Infectious Diseases in an Age of Change: The Impact of Human Ecology and Behavior on Disease Transmission*, ed. by B. Roizman, pp. 77–97. National Academy Press, Washington, DC.

——— (1996): "Global Burden of the HIV Pandemic," *Lancet*, 348, 99–106.

RAKODI, C. (1995): "Poverty Lines or Household Strategies? A Review of Conceptual Issues in the Study of Urban Poverty," *Habitat International*, 19(4), 407–426.

——— (1998): "Review of the Poverty Relevance of the Peri-Urban Interface Production System Research," Report for the DFID Natural Resources Systems Research Programme.

RAKODI, C., R. GATABAKI-KAMAU, AND N. DEVAS (2000): "Poverty and Political Conflict in Mombasa," *Environment and Urbanization*, 12(1), 153–170.

RAKOWSKI, C. A., AND G. KASTNER (1985): "Difficulties Involved in Taking Health Services to the People: The Example of a Public Health Care Center in a Caracas Barrio," *Social Science and Medicine*, 21(1), 67–75.

RANDALL, S., AND T. LEGRAND (2001): "Is Child Mortality Important? Reproductive Strategies, Decisions and Outcomes in Senegal," Paper presented at the Workshop on Mortality and Reproductive Decision-Making in Sub-Saharan Africa, International Union for the Scientific Study of Population, Salvador de Bahia, Brazil, August.

RANDOLPH, S., AND E. TRZCINSKI (1989): "Relative Earnings Mobility in a Third World Country," *World Development*, 17(4), 513–524.

RAUCH, J. E. (1993): "Productivity Gains from Geographic Concentration of Human Capital: Evidence from the Cities," *Journal of Urban Economics*, 34(3), 380–400.

——— (2001): "Business and Social Networks in International Trade," *Journal of Economic Literature*, 39(4), 1177–1203.

READ, B. L. (2000): "Revitalizing the State's Urban 'Nerve Tips'," *The China Quarterly*, 163(September), 806–820.

RECCHINI DE LATTES, Z., AND S. M. MYCHASZULA (1993): "Female Migration and Labour Force Participation in a Medium-Sized City of a Highly Urbanized Country," in *Internal Migration of Women in Developing Countries: Proceedings of the United Nations Expert Meeting on the Feminization of Internal Migration*, ed. by United Nations, pp. 154–177. United Nations, New York.

REDDY, N. (1992): *Street Children of Bangalore: A Situational Analysis*. National Labour Institute, Ghaziabad, India.

RIBE, H., AND T. P. SCHULTZ (1980): "Migrant and Native Fertility in Colombia in 1973: Are Migrants Selected According to their Reproductive Preferences?" Discussion Paper no. 355, Economic Growth Center, Yale University.

RIBEIRO, L. C. D. Q., AND E. E. TELLES (2000): "Rio de Janeiro: Emerging Dualization in a Historically Unequal City" in *Globalizing Cities: A New Spatial Order?* ed. by P. Marcuse, and R. van Kempen, pp. 78–94. Blackwell Publishers, Oxford, UK.

RICHMOND, P. (1997): "From Tenants to Owners: Experiences with a Revolving Fund for Social Housing," *Environment and Urbanization*, 9(2), 119–39.

RILEY, N. E., AND R. W. GARDNER (1993): "Migration Decisions: The Role of Gender," in *Internal Migration of Women in Developing Countries*, ed. by United Nations, pp. 195–206. United Nations, New York.

RIP, M. R., C. S. KEEN, D. L. WOODS, AND H. A. VAN COEVERDEN DE GROOT (1988): "Perinatal Health in the Peri-Urban Township of Khayelitsha, Cape Town," *South African Medical Journal*, 74, 629–632.

RIZZINI, I. (1998): "Poor Children in Latin America: A Case Example of Social Inequality," *Children's Legal Rights Journal*, 18, 50–70.

ROBERTS, B. (1991): "The Changing Nature of Informal Employment: The Case of Mexico," in *Towards Social Adjustment: Labour Market Issues in Structural Adjustment*, ed. by G. Standing, and V. Tokman, pp. 115–140. International Labour Office, Geneva.

ROBERTS, S. (1994): "Fictitious Capital, Fictitious Spaces: The Geography of Offshore Financial Flows," in *Money, Power and Space*, ed. by R. Martin, and N. Thrift. Blackwell, Oxford.

RODENBURG, J. (1993): "Emancipation or Subordination? Consequences of Female Migration for Migrants and Their Families," in *Internal Migration of Women in Developing Countries: Proceedings of the United Nations Expert Meeting on the Feminization of Internal Migration*, ed. by United Nations, pp. 273–289. United Nations, New York.

RODGERS, D. (1999): "Youth Gangs and Violence in Latin America and the Caribbean: A Literature Survey," Urban Peace Program Series, Latin America and Caribbean Region Sustainable Development Working Paper no. 7. The World Bank, Washington, DC.

RODRIGUEZ, A., AND L. WINCHESTER (2001): "Santiago de Chile: Metropolización, Globabizatió, Desigualdad," *Eure*, 27(80), 121–139.

RODRÍGUEZ, V. E. (1997): *Decentralization in Mexico: From Reforma Municipal to Solidaridad to Nuevo Federalismo*. Westview, Boulder, CO.

——— (1998): "Opening the Electoral Space in Mexico: The Rise of the Opposition at the State and Local Levels," in *Urban Elections in Democratic Latin America*, ed. by H. A. Dietz, and G. Shidlo, pp. 163–197. Scholarly Resources Inc., Wilmington, DE.

RODRÍGUEZ ARAUJO, O. (2000): "Govierno, Reformas Politicas y Democratizacion del Distrito Federal, 1940–2000," in *El Atlas de la Ciudad de Mexico*, ed. by G. Garza, pp. 653–657. Departamento del Distrito Federal and El Colegio de México, Mexico D.F.

RODRIK, D. (1997): "TFPG Controversies, Institutions and Economic Performance in East Asia," NBER Working Paper 5914, National Bureau of Economic Research, Cambridge, MA.

ROGERS, A. (1982): "Sources of Urban Population Growth and Urbanization, 1950–2000: A Demographic Accounting," *Economic Development and Cultural Change*, 30(3), 483–506.

——— (1986): "Parameterized Multistate Population Dynamics and Projections," *Journal of the American Statistical Society*, 81(393), 48–61.

———— (1995): *Multiregional Demography: Principles, Methods and Extensions*. John Wiley and Sons, Chichester, UK.

ROGERS, A., AND L. J. CASTRO (1981): "Model Migration Schedules," Research Reports no. RR-81-30, International Institute for Applied Systems Analysis, Laxenburg, Austria.

ROLNICK, R. (1999): "Territorial Exclusion and Violence: The Case of São Paulo, Brazil," Comparative Urban Studies Occasional Papers Series, No. 26, Woodrow Wilson International Center for Scholars.

ROMIEU, I., AND M. HERNANDEZ (1999): "Air Pollution and Health in Developing Countries: Review of Epidemiological Evidence," in *Health and Air Pollution in Rapidly Developing Countries*, ed. by G. McGranahan, and F. Murray, pp. 43–56. Stockholm Environment Institute, Stockholm.

ROOT, B. D., AND G. F. DEJONG (1991): "Family Migration in a Developing Country," *Population Studies*, 45, 221–233.

ROOT, G. (1997): "Population Density and Spatial Differentials in Child Mortality in Zimbabwe," *Social Science and Medicine*, 44(3), 413–421.

ROSEN, K. T., AND M. RESNICK (1980): "The Size Distribution of Cities: An Examination of the Pareto Law and Primacy," *Journal of Urban Economics*, 8, 165–186.

ROSEN, S. (1974): "Hedonic Prices and Implicit Markets: Product Differentiation in Pure Competition," *Journal of Political Economy*, 82(1), 34–55.

ROSENZWEIG, M. R., AND T. P. SCHULTZ (1982): "Child Mortality in Colombia: Individual and Community Effects," *Health Policy and Education*, 2, 305–348.

ROSENZWEIG, M. R., AND K. L. WOLPIN (1982): "Government Interventions and Household Behavior in a Developing Country," *Journal of Development Economics*, 10, 209–225.

———— (1988): "Migration Selectivity and the Effects of Public Programs," *Journal of Public Economics*, 37(3), 265–289.

ROSERO-BIXBY, L., AND J. B. CASTERLINE (1993): "Modelling Diffusion Effects in Fertility Transition," *Population Studies*, 47, 147–167.

ROSS, J., J. STOVER, AND A. WILLARD (1999): "Profiles for Family Planning and Reproductive Health Programs," The Futures Group International, Glastonbury, CT.

ROSSI, E. (2000): "Meeting the Growing Demand for Quality Reproductive Health Services in Urban Africa: Partnerships with Municipal Governments," Lessons Learned from SEATS' Urban Initiative. Family Planning Service Expansion and Technical Supprt (SEATS) Project, John Snow, Inc., Arlington, VA.

ROTHBLATT, D. N. (1999): "Summary and Conclusions," in *Metropolitan Governance Revisited: American/Canadian Intergovernmental Perspectives*, ed. by D. N. Rothblatt, and A. Sancton, pp. 475–525. Institute of Governmental Studies Press, University of California at Berkeley, Berkeley.

ROUTH, S., A. A. THWIN, T. T. KANE, AND A. H. BAQUI (2000): "User-Fees for Family-Planning Methods: An Analysis of Payment Behavior among Urban Contraceptors in Bangladesh," *Journal of Health, Population, and Nutrition*, 18(2), 69–78.

ROWLAND, A., AND P. GORDON (1996): "Mexico City: No Longer a Leviathan?" in *The Mega-City in Latin America* ed. by A. Gilbert, pp. 173–202. United Nations University Press, Tokyo.

RUBALCAVA, R. M., AND M. SCHTEINGART (1987): "Estructura Urbana y Diferenciación Sociospacial en la Zona Metropolitana de la Ciudad de México," in *El Atlas de la Ciudad de Mexico*, ed. by G. Garza, pp. 108–115. Departamento del Distrito Federal and El Colegio de México, Mexico D.F.

—— (2000): "Segregación Socioespacial," in *La Ciudad de México en el Fin del Segundo Milenio*, ed. by G. Garza, pp. 287–296. Gobierno del Distrito Federal y El Colegio de México, Mexico City.

RUBIO, M. (1997): "Perverse Social Capital: Some Evidence from Columbia," *Journal of Economic Issues*, 31(3), 805–816.

RUEL, M. T., AND J. L. GARRETT (1999): "Overview," *World Development*, 27(11), 1885–1890.

RUEL, M. T., L. HADDAD, AND J. L. GARRETT (1999): "Some Urban Facts of Life: Implications for Research and Policy," *World Development*, 27(11), 1917–1938.

RUSSELL, S. (1996): "Ability to Pay for Health Care: Concepts and Evidence," *Health Policy and Planning*, 11(3), 219–237.

SABATINI, F., AND F. ARENAS (2000): "Entre el Estado y el Mercado: Resonacias Geográficas y Sustentabilidad Social en Santiago de Chile," *EURE*, 26(79), 95–113.

SALAFF, J. W. (1981): *Working Daughters of Hong Kong: Filial Piety or Power in the Family?* Asa Rose Monograph. Cambridge University Press, Cambridge.

SAMPSON, R. J. (2002): "Crime and Public Safety: Insights from Community-Level Perspectives on Social Capital," in *Social Capital and Poor Communities*, ed. by S. Saegert, J. P. Thompson, and M. R. Warren, pp. 89–114. Russel Sage Foundation, New York.

SAMPSON, R. J., AND J. D. MORENOFF (1997): "Ecological Perspectives on the Neighborhood Context of Urban Poverty: Past and Present," in *Neighborhood Poverty*, ed. by J. Brooks-Gunn, G. J. Duncan, and J. L. Aber, vol. II: Policy Implications in Studying Neighborhoods, pp. 1–22. Russell Sage Foundation, New York.

—— (2000): "Public Health and Safety in Context: Lessons from Community-Level Theory on Social Capital," in *Promoting Health: Intervention Strategies from Social and Behavioral Research*, ed. by B. D. Smedley, and S. L. Syme, pp. 366–390. National Academy Press, Washington, DC.

SAMPSON, R. J., J. D. MORENOFF, AND T. GANNON-ROWLEY (2002): "Assessing 'Neighborhood Effects': Social Processes and New Directions in Research," *Annual Review of Sociology*, 28, 443–478.

SAMPSON, R. J., AND S. W. RAUDENBUSH (1999): "Systematic Social Observation of Public Spaces: A New Look at Disorder in Urban Neighborhoods," *American Journal of Sociology*, 105(3), 603–651.

SANDERS, D., J. KRAVITZ, S. LEWIN, AND M. MCKEE (1998): "Zimbabwe's Hospital Referral System: Does It Work?" *Health Policy and Planning*, 13(4), 359–370.

SANDERSON, D. (2000): "Cities, Disasters and Livelihoods," *Environment and Urbanization*, 12(2), 93–102.

SANTOS, M. (1996): "São Paulo: A Growth Process Full of Contradictions," in *The Mega-City in Latin America*, ed. by A. Gilbert, pp. 224–240. United Nations University Press, Tokyo.

SAPIR, D. (1990): "Infectious Disease Epidemics and Urbanization: A Critical Review of the Issues," Paper prepared for the WHO Commission on Health and Environment, Division of Environmental Health, WHO, Geneva.

SARGESON, S., AND J. ZHANG (1999): "Re-Assessing the Role of the Local State: A Case Study of Local Government Interventions in Property Rights Reform in a Hangzhou District," *The China Journal*, 42(July), 77–99.

SASSEN, S. (1991): *The Global City: New York, London, Tokyo*. Princeton University Press, Princeton, NJ.

―――― (1994a): *Cities in a World Economy*. Pine Forge Press, Thousand Oaks, CA.

―――― (1994b): "The Informal Economy: Between New Developments and Old Regulations," *The Yale Law Journal*, 103(8).

―――― (2000): *Cities in a World Economy*. 2nd ed., Pine Forge Press, Thousand Oaks, CA.

―――― (2001a): "Cities in the Global Economy," in *Handbook of Urban Studies*, ed. by R. Paddison, pp. 256–272. Sage Publications, London.

―――― (2001b): *The Global City: New York, London, Tokyo*. 2nd ed., Princeton University Press, Princeton, NJ.

―――― (ed.) (2002): *Global Networks, Linked Cities*. Routledge for the United Nations University/Institute of Advanced Studies, New York.

SASTRY, N. (1996): "Community Characteristics, Individual and Household Attributes, and Child Survival in Brazil," *Demography*, 33(2), 211–229.

SASTRY, N., A. PEBLEY, AND M. ZONTA (2002): "Neighborhood Definitions and the Spatial Dimension of Daily Life in Los Angeles," Paper presented at the 2002 Annual Meetings of the Population Association of America, Atlanta, GA.

SATTERTHWAITE, D. (1993): "The Impact on Health of Urban Environments," *Environment and Urbanization*, 5(2), 87–111.

―――― (1995): "The Under-Estimation and Misrepresentation of Urban Poverty," *Environment and Urbanization*, 7(1), 3–10.

―――― (1996a): "The Scale and Nature of Urban Change in the South," International Institute for Environment and Development (IIED) Working Paper, London.

―――― (1996b): "Urban Poverty: Reconsidering Its Scale and Nature," IIED Paper Series on Poverty Reduction in Urban Areas, IIED, London.

SAVITCH, H. V. (1996): "Cities in a Global Era: A New Paradigm for the Next Millennium," in *Preparing for the Urban Future: Global Pressure and Local Forces*, ed. by M. A. Cohen, B. A. Ruble, J. S. Tulchin, and A. M. Garland, pp. 39–65. Woodrow Wilson Center Press, Washington, DC.

SAYWELL, T. (2000): "Pudong Rises to the Task," *Far Eastern Economic Review*, pp. 56–58.

SCHADY, N. R. (2002): "The (Positive) Effect of Macroeconomic Crises on the Schooling and Employment Decisions of Children in a Middle-Income Country," Working paper, The World Bank, Washington, DC.

SCHEJTMAN, A. (1999): "Urban Dimensions in Rural Development," *Cepal Review*, (67), 15–33.

SCHIFFER, S. R. (2000): "Recent Trends in the São Paulo Labor Market," Paper prepared for the Panel on Urban Population Dynamics, Committee on Population, National Research Council.

SCHMITZ, H., AND K. NADVI (1999): "Clustering and Industrialization: Introduction," *World Development*, 27(9), 1503–1514.

SCHOEN, R., AND Y. J. KIM (1993): "Two-State Spatial Dynamics in the Absence of Age," *Theoretical Population Biology*, 44, 67–79.

SCHULTZ, T. P. (1982): "Lifetime Migration within Educational Strata in Venezuela," *Economic Development and Cultural Change*, 30(3).

SCHWARTZ, J. B., D. K. GUILKEY, AND R. RACELIS (2002): "Decentralization, Allocative Efficiency and Health Service Outcomes in the Philippines," Working Paper no. WP-01-36, MEASURE Evaluation Project. University of North Carolina, Chapel Hill, NC.

SCHWARTZ, J. B., R. RACELIS, AND D. K. GUILKEY (2000): "Decentralization and Local Government Health Expenditures in the Philippines," Working Paper no. WP-01-36, MEASURE Evaluation Project. University of North Carolina, Chapel Hill, NC.

SCOTT, A. J. (1998): *Regions and the World Economy: The Coming Shape of Global Production, Competition, and Political Order*. Oxford University Press, Oxford, UK.

——— (ed.) (2001): *Global City-Regions: Trends, Theory, Policy*. Oxford University Press, New York.

SELIER, F. (1997): "Expanded Family and Extended Community: Migrants in Karachi," in *Family and Gender in Pakistan: Domestic Organization in a Muslim Society*, ed. by H. Donnan, and F. Selier, pp. 156–170. Hindustan Publishing Corporation, New Delhi.

SENANAYAKE, M. P., A. RANASINGHE, AND C. BALASURIYA (1998): "Street Children: A Preliminary Study," *Ceylon Medical Journal*, 43, 191–193.

SENDEROWITZ, J. (1995): "Adolescent Health: Reassessing the Passage to Adulthood," World Bank Discussion Paper 272. International Bank for Reconstruction and Development, Washington, DC.

SENDEROWITZ, J., AND C. STEVENS (2001): "Leveraging the For-Profit Sector in Support of Adolescent and Young Adult Reproductive Health Programming." (June) The Futures Group International, Inc.

SETHURAMAN, S. V. (1981): *The Urban Informal Sector in Developing Countries: Employment, Poverty and Environment*. International Labour Organization, Geneva.

SHAPIRO, D., AND B. O. TAMBASHE (2001): "Fertility Transition in Urban and Rural Sub-Saharan Africa: Preliminary Evidence of a Three-Stage Process," *Journal of African Policy Studies*, 7(2–3), 111–136.

SHARLIN, A. (1986): "Urban-Rural Differences in Fertility in Europe During the Demographic Transition," in *The Decline of Fertility in Europe*, ed. by A. J. Coale, and S. C. Watkins, pp. 234–260. Princeton University Press, Princeton, NJ.

SHARPE, L. J. (ed.) (1995): *The Government of World Cities. The Future of the Metro Model*. John Wiley, Chichester.

SHATKIN, G. (2000): "Obstacles to Empowerment: Local Politics and Civil Society in Metropolitan Manila, the Philippines," *Urban Studies*, 37(12), 2357–2375.

SHAW, M. (1998): "The Role of Local Government in Crime Prevention in South Africa," Occasional Paper No. 33 (August). Pretoria: Institute for Security Studies. Web document: http://www.iss.co.za/Pubs/PAPERS/33/Paper33.html.

SHI-XUN, G. (1999): "Factors Affecting Induced Abortion Behavior among Married Women in Shanghai, China," in *Abortion in the Developing World*, ed. by A. I. Mundigo, and C. Indriso, pp. 78–97. Zed Books Ltd., London.

SHORT, K. (2001): "Where We Live: Geographic Differences in Poverty Thresholds," Paper presented at the Annual Meeting of the Society of Government Economists, New Orleans, LA.

SHORT, K., T. GARNER, D. JOHNSON, AND P. DOYLE (1999): "Experimental Poverty Measures: 1990 to 1997," U.S. Census Bureau, Current Population Reports, Consumer Income, P60-205, U.S. Government Printing Office, Washington, DC.

SHOWERS, K. B. (2002): "Water Scarcity and Urban Africa: An Overview of Urban-Rural Water Linkages," *World Development*, 30(4), 621–648.

SHRESTHA, A., T. T. KANE, AND H. HAMAL (1990): "Contraceptive Social Marketing in Nepal: Consumer and Retailer Knowledge, Needs and Experience," *Journal of Biosocial Science*, 22, 305–322.

SHUKLA, V. (1996): *Urbanization and Economic Growth*. Oxford University Press, Delhi.

SIMMONDS, R., AND G. HACK (eds.) (2000): *Global City Regions: Their Emerging Forms*. SPON Press, London and New York.

SIMON, C. P., AND L. BLUME (1994): *Mathematics for Economists*. Norton, New York.

SINGELMANN, J. (1993): "Levels and Trends of Female Internal Migration in Developing Countries, 1960–1980," in *Internal Migration of Women in Developing Countries*, ed. by United Nations, pp. 77–93. United Nations, New York.

SINGER, P. (1996): "Budgeting and Democracy," in *International Workshop on Local Governance*, ed. by R. H. Wilson, and R. Cramer, pp. 101–122. Lyndon B. Johnson School of Public Affairs, University of Texas, Austin, TX.

SINGH, S., AND G. SEDGH (1997): "The Relationship of Abortion to Trends in Contraception and Fertility in Brazil, Colombia and Mexico," *International Family Planning Perspectives*, 23(1), 4–14.

SIVARAMAKRISHANAN, K. (1996): "Urban Governance: Changing Realities," in *Preparing for the Urban Future: Global Pressure and Local Forces*, ed. by M. A. Cohen, B. A. Ruble, J. S. Tulchin, and A. M. Garland, pp. 225–241. The Woodrow Wilson Center Press, Washington, DC.

SMIT, J., A. RATTA, AND J. NASTR (1996): *Urban Agriculture: Food, Jobs and Sustainable Cities*, Publication Series for Habitat II. UNDP, New York.

SMIT, W. (1998): "The Rural Linkages of Urban Households in Durban, South Africa," *Environment and Urbanization*, 10(1), 77–87.

SMITH, J. P., D. THOMAS, E. FRANKENBERG, K. BEEGLE, AND G. TERUEL (2000): "Wages, Employment and Economic Shocks: Evidence from Indonesia," Working Paper 00-07, Labor and Population Program, RAND. The RAND Corporation, Santa Monica, CA.

SNOW, J. (1855): *On the Mode of Communication of Cholera*. John Churchill, London.

SOBRINO, L. J. (2002): "Urbanización y Competitvidad Local en México," Working paper, El Colegio de México.

SODERMANN, M., M. S. JAKOBSEN, K. MOLBAK, I. C. A., AND P. AABY (1997): "High Mortality Despite Good Care-Seeking Behavior: A Community Study of Childhood Deaths in Guinea-Bissau," *Bulletin of the World Health Organization*, 75(3), 205–212.

SOLINGER, D. (1999): *Contesting Citizenship in Urban China: Peasant Migrants, the State and the Logic of the Market*. University of California Press, Berkeley and Los Angeles.

SONGSORE, J. (1992): "Review of Household Environmental Problems in the Accra Metropolitan Area, Ghana," Working Paper, Stockholm Environment Institute.

SONGSORE, J., AND G. MCGRANAHAN (1998): "The Political Economy of Household Environmental Management: Gender, Environment and Epidemiology in the Greater Accra Metropolitan Area," *World Development*, 26(3), 395–412.

SOUTH AFRICA (1998): "Draft White Paper on Safety and Security," Government of South Africa, Pretoria.

SOUTH AFRICAN DEPARTMENT OF HEALTH (1998): *South African Demographic and Health Survey 1998*. South African Department of Health, Pretoria.

SOUZA, C. (2001): "Participatory Budgeting in Brazilian Cities: Limits and Possibilities in Building Democratic Institutions," Working Paper No. 28, University of Birmingham project in Urban Governances, Partnership and Poverty.

SPEIZER, I., S. MULLEN, AND K. AMEGEE (2001): "Gender Differences in Adult Perspectives on Adolescent Reproductive Behaviors: Evidence from Lomé, Togo," *International Family Perspectives*, 27(4), 178–185.

SPOSATI, A. (1996): "Social Exclusion/Inclusion Map of the City of São Paulo," Unpublished document, São Paulo.

SRINIVASAN, S. (1997): "Breaking Rural Bonds Through Migration: The Failure of Development for Women in India," *Journal of Comparative Family Studies*, 28(1), 89–102.

STARK, O. (1991): *The Migration of Labor*. Basil Blackwell, Cambridge, MA.

STECKLOV, G. (1997): "Intergenerational Resource Flows in Côte d'Ivoire: Empirical Analysis of Aggregate Flows," *Population and Development Review*, 23(3), 525–553.

STEPHENS, C. (1996): "Healthy Cities or Unhealthy Islands? The Health and Social Implications of Urban Inequality," *Environment and Urbanization*, 8(2), 9–30.

STEPHENS, C., M. AKERMAN, S. AVLE, P. B. MAIA, P. CAMPANAREIO, B. DOE, AND D. TETTEH (1997): "Urban Equity and Urban Health: Using Existing Data to Understand Inequalities in Health and Environment in Accra, Ghana and São Paulo," *Environment and Urbanization*, 9(1), 181–202.

STEPHENS, C., I. M. TIMAEUS, M. AKERMAN, S. AVLVE, P. B. MAIA, P. CAMPANARIO, B. DOE, L. LUSH, D. TETTEH, AND T. HARPHAM (1994a): "Collaborative Studies in Accra, Ghana and São Paulo, Brazil, and Analysis of Urban Data of Four Demographic and Health Surveys," London School of Hygiene and Tropical Medicine, London.

——— (1994b): "Environment and Health in Developing Countries: An Analysis of Intra-Urban Differentials Using Existing Data," Monograph, London School of Hygiene and Tropical Medicine, London.

STEPHENS, G. R., AND N. WIKSTROM (2000): *Metropolitan Government and Governance. Theoretical Perspectives, Empirical Analysis, and the Future*. Oxford University Press, New York.

STEYN, K., J. FOURIE, C. LOMBARD, J. KATZENELLENBOGEN, L. BOURNE, AND P. JOOSTE (1996): "Hypertension in the Black Community of the Cape Peninsula, South Africa," *East African Medical Journal*, 73(11), 758–763.

STIERLE, F., M. KADDAR, A. TCHICAYA, AND B. SCHMIDT-EHRY (1999): "Indigence and Access to Health Care in Sub-Saharan Africa," *International Journal of Health Planning Management*, 14(2), 81–105.

STOLOFF, J. A., J. L. GLANVILLE, AND E. J. BIENENSTOCK (1999): "Women's Participation in the Labor Force: The Role of Social Networks," *Social Networks*, 21(1), 91–108.

STOVER, C. C. (1999): "Financing, Service Delivery, and Decentralization in the Philippines and Kenya," in *Myths and Realities about the Decentralization of Health Sys-*

tems, ed. by R.-L. Kolehmainen-Aitken, pp. 27–37. Management Sciences for Health, Boston, MA.

STREN, R. (1978): *Housing the Urban Poor in Africa. Politics, Policy and Bureaucracy in Mombasa, Kenya*. Center for International Studies, University of California, Berkeley.

────── (2002): "The Newest Decentralization: Can We Sustain It?" Unpublished paper, University of Toronto.

STREN, R., AND M. HALFANI (2001): "The Cities of Sub-Saharan Africa: From Dependency to Marginality," in *Handbook of Urban Studies*, ed. by R. Paddison, pp. 466–485. Sage Publications, London.

STUEBING, K. W. (1997): "Maternal Schooling and Comprehension of Child Health Information in Urban Zambia: Is Literacy a Missing Link in the Maternal Schooling–Child Health Relationship?" *Health Transition Review*, 7, 151–171.

SUMARTO, S., A. WETTERBERG, AND L. PRITCHETT (1999): "The Social Impact of the Crisis in Indonesia." The World Bank, Washington, DC, and Jakarta.

SURJADI, C. (1993): "Respiratory Diseases of Mothers and Children and Environmental Factors among Households in Jakarta," *Environment and Urbanization*, 5(2), 78–86.

SUTTON, P. C. (2000): "An Overview of Efforts at Estimating Urban Populations Using Nighttime Satellite Imagery and Geo-Location," Paper presented at the Workshop on Gridding Population Data, CIESIN, 2–3 May.

SWART-KRUGER, J., AND L. M. RICHTER (1997): "AIDS-Related Knowledge, Attitudes and Behaviour among South African Street Youth: Reflections on Power, Sexuality, and the Autonomous Self," *Social Science and Medicine*, 45, 957–966.

SWYNGEDOUW, E. A. (1995): "The Contradictions of Urban Water Provision: A Study of Guayaquil, Ecuador," *Third World Planning Review*, 17(4).

SZRETER, S. (1997): "Economic Growth, Disruption, Deprivation, Disease and Death: On the Importance of the Politics of Public Health for Development," *Population and Development Review*, 23(4), 693–728.

SZWARCWALD, C. L., C. L. T. DE ANDRADE, AND F. I. BASTOS (2002): "Income Inequality, Residential Poverty Clustering and Infant Mortality: A Study in Rio de Janeiro, Brazil," *Social Science and Medicine*, 55(12), 2083–2092.

TABATABAI, H., AND M. FOUAD (1993): *The Incidence of Poverty in Developing Countries: An ILO Compendium of Data*. A World Employment Programme Study, International Labour Office, Geneva.

TABIBZADEH, I., A. ROSSI-ESPAGNET, AND R. MAXWELL (1989): *Spotlight on the Cities: Improving Urban Health in Developing Countries*. World Health Organization, Geneva.

TACOLI, C. (1998): "Bridging the Divide: Rural-Urban Interactions and Livelihood Strategies," Sustainable Agriculture and Rural Livelihoods Programme, Gatekeeper Series 77, IIED, London.

TAI-WHAN, K., J. HEE, AND C. SUNG-NAM (1999): "Sexuality, Contraception, and Abortion among Unmarried Adolescents and Young Adults: The Case of Korea," in *Abortion in the Developing World*, ed. by A. I. Mundigo, and C. Indriso, pp. 346–367. Zed Books Ltd., London.

TALL, M. (2000): "Les Investissements Immobiliers à Dakar des Émigrés Sénégalais," Ph.D. thesis, Université Louis Pasteur, Strasbourg.

TAMANG, A., N. SHRESTHA, AND K. SHARMA (1999): "Determinants of Induced Abortion and Subsequent Reproductive Behavior among Women in Three Urban Districts of Nepal," in *Abortion in the Developing World*, ed. by A. I. Mundigo, and C. Indriso, pp. 167–190. Zed Books Ltd., London.

TANNER, M., AND T. HARPHAM (1995): "Action and Research in Urban Health Development: Progress and Prospects," in *Urban Health in Developing Countries*, ed. by T. Harpham, and M. Tanner, pp. 216–220. Earthscan, London.

TANTCHOU, J., AND E. WILSON (2000): "Post-Cairo Reproductive Health Policies and Programs: A Study of Five Francophone African Countries. (August)," POLICY Project paper. The Futures Group International, Inc., Washington, DC.

TASCHNER, S. P., AND L. M. M. BÓGUS (2001): "São Paulo, Uma Metrópole Desigual," *EURE*, 27(80).

TAYLOR, C. E. (1993): "Learning from Health Care Experiences in Developing Countries," *American Journal of Public Health*, 83(11), 1531–1532.

TAYLOR, P. J. (2000): "World Cities and Territorial States Under Conditions of Contemporary Globalization," *Political Geography*, 19, 5–32.

TAYLOR, P. J., AND D. R. F. WALKER (2001): "World Cities: A First Multivariate Analysis of Their Service Complexes," *Urban Studies*, 38(1), 23–47.

TEAL, F. (2000): "Real Wages and the Demand for Skilled and Unskilled Male Labour in Ghana's Manufacturing Sector: 1991–1995," *Journal of Development Economics*, 61(2), 447–461.

TELLES, E. (1993): "Urban Labor Market Segmentation and Income in Brazil," *Economic Development and Cultural Change*, 41(2), 231–249.

THAVER, I. H., T. HARPHAM, B. MCPAKE, AND P. GARNER (1998): "Private Practitioners in the Slums of Karachi: What Quality of Care Do They Offer?" *Social Science and Medicine*, 46(11), 1441–1449.

THOITS, P. A. (1995): "Stress, Coping, and Social Support Processes: Where Are We? What Next?" *Journal of Health and Social Behaviour*, Extra Issue, 53–79.

THOMAS, D., K. BEEGLE, AND E. FRANKENBERG (2000): "Labor Market Transitions of Men and Women During an Economic Crisis: Evidence from Indonesia," Working Paper 00-11, Labor and Population Program, RAND. Santa Monica, CA: RAND.

THOMAS, D., J. STRAUSS, AND M. H. HENRIQUES (1991): "How Does Mother's Education Affect Child Height?" *Journal of Human Resources*, 26, 183–211.

THOMAS, E. P., J. R. SEAGER, E. VILJOEN, F. POTGIETER, A. ROSSOUW, B. TOKOTA, G. MCGRANAHAN, AND M. KJELLÉN (1999): "Household Environment and Health in Port Elizabeth, South Africa," Urban Environment Series Report 6, Stockholm Environment Institute and South African Medical Research Council.

THOMPSON, J., I. T. PORRAS, E. WOOD, J. K. TUMWINE, M. R. MUJWAHUZI, M. KATUI-KATUA, AND N. JOHNSTONE (2000): "Waiting at the Tap: Changes in Urban Water Use in East Africa over Three Decades," *Environment and Urbanization*, 12(2), 37–52.

TIEBOUT, C. M. (1956): "A Pure Theory of Local Expenditures," *Journal of Political Economy*, 64, 416–424.

TIMAEUS, I. M. (1998): "Impact of the HIV Epidemic on Mortality in Sub-Saharan Africa: Evidence from National Surveys and Censuses," *AIDS*, 12(Suppl. 1), S15–S27.

TIMAEUS, I. M., AND A. LOPEZ (1996): "Introduction," in *Adult Mortality in Latin America*, ed. by I. M. Timaeus, J. Chackiel, and L. Ruzieka, pp. 5–13. Clarendon Press, Oxford.

TIMAEUS, I. M., AND L. LUSH (1995): "Intra-Urban Differentials in Child Health," *Health Transition Review*, 5(2), 163–190.

TODARO, M. P. (1969): "A Model of Labor Migration and Urban Unemployment in Less Developed Countries," *American Economic Review*, 59(1), 139–148.

TODD, A. (1996): "Health Inequalities in Urban Areas: A Guide to the Literature," *Environment and Urbanization*, 8(2), 141–152.

TOMES, N. (1998): *The Gospel of Germs: Men, Women, and the Microbe in American Life*. Harvard University Press, Cambridge, MA.

TORRES, H. A. (2001): "Cambios Socioterritoriales en Buenos Aires Duratne la Decada de 1990," *EURE*, 27(80), 33–56.

TOSTA, N. (1997): "National Spatial Data Infrastructures and the Roles of National Mapping Organisations," in *Framework for the World*, ed. by D. Rhind, pp. 173–186. John Wiley & Sons, New York.

TOSTENSEN, A., I. TVEDTEN, AND M. VAA (eds.) (2001): *Associational Life in African Cities: Popular Responses to the Urban Crisis*. Nordiska Afrikainstitutet, Uppsala, Sweden.

TOWNSEND, N., AND A. I. GAREY (1994): "Men, Households, and Children in Botswana: An Exploration of Connections Over Time and Space," Paper presented at the 1994 Annual Meetings of the Population Association of America, Miami.

TOWNSEND, R. M. (1994): "Risk and Insurance in Village India," *Econometrica*, 62(4), 539–591.

TRZCINSKI, E., AND S. RANDOLPH (1991): "Human Capital Investments and Relative Earnings Mobility: The Role of Education, Training, Migration, and Job Search," *Economic Development and Cultural Change*, 40(1), 153–168.

TSAI, I.-J., C. C. CHU, AND C.-F. CHUNG (2000): "Demographic Transition and Household Saving in Taiwan," *Population and Development Review*, 26(Supplement), 174–193, in C.Y. Cyrus Chu and Ronald D. Lee, eds., *Population and Economic Change in East Asia*.

TSUI, A. O. (1985): "Community Effects on Contraceptive Use," in *The Collection and Analysis of Community Data*, ed. by J. B. Casterline, pp. 77–99. International Statistical Institute, Voorburg.

TSUI, A. O., J. N. WASSERHEIT, AND J. G. HAAGA (eds.) (1997): *Reproductive Health in Developing Countries: Expanding Dimensions, Building Solutions*. National Academy Press, Washington, DC.

TULCHIN, J. S. (1998): "Global Forces and the Future of the Latin American City," Comparative Urban Studies Program Occasional Paper Number 4. Woodrow Wilson International Center for Scholars, Washington, DC.

TURNHAM, D., B. SALOMÉ, AND A. SCHWARTZ (1990): *The Informal Sector Revisited*. OEDC, Paris.

TYBOUT, J. R. (2000): "Manufacturing Firms in Developing Countries: How Well Do They Do, and Why?" *Journal of Economic Literature*, 38(1), 11–44.

UNAIDS (2000): Reports on the Global HIV/AIDS Epidemic. UNAIDS/00.13E. World Health Organization, Geneva.

UNITED NATIONS (1949): *Demographic Yearbook*. United Nations, New York.

———— (1953): *Demographic Yearbook*. United Nations, New York.

———— (1969): *Growth of the World's Urban and Rural Population, 1920–2000*. United Nations, New York.

———— (1974): *Manual VIII: Methods for Projections of Urban and Rural Population*, no. 55 in Population Studies. United Nations, Department of Economic and Social Affairs, New York.

———— (1980): *Patterns of Urban and Rural Population Growth*, no. 68 in Population Studies. United Nations, Department of International Economic and Social Affairs, New York.

———— (1987): *1985 Demographic Yearbook*. United Nations, Department of International Economic and Social Affairs, Statistical Office, New York.

———— (1991): *World Urbanization Prospects 1990*. United Nations, Department of International Economic and Social Affairs, New York.

———— (1992): *1991 Demographic Yearbook*. United Nations, Department of Economic and Social Development, Statistical Office, New York.

———— (1994): "Programme of Action of the 1994 International Conference on Population and Development," (A/CONF.171/13). Reprinted in *Population and Development Review* 21(1):187–213 and 21(2):437–461.

———— (1998a): *1996 Demographic Yearbook*. United Nations, Department of Economic and Social Affairs, New York.

———— (1998b): *World Urbanization Prospects: The 1996 Revision*. United Nations, Department of Economic and Social Affairs, Population Division, New York.

———— (2000): *1998 Demographic Yearbook*. United Nations, Department of Economic and Social Affairs, New York.

———— (2001): *World Urbanization Prospects: The 1999 Revision*. United Nations, Department of Economic and Social Affairs, Population Division, New York.

———— (2002a): *World Urbanization Prospects: The 2001 Revision. Data Tables and Highlights*. United Nations, Department of Economic and Social Affairs, Population Division, New York.

———— (2002b): *World Urbanization Prospects: The 2001 Revision. Special Tabulations*. United Nations, Department of Economic and Social Affairs, Population Division, New York.

UNITED NATIONS CENTRE FOR HUMAN SETTLEMENTS (1993): *Support Measures to Promote Rental Housing for Low Income Groups*. United Nations Centre for Human Settlements (Habitat), HS/294/93E, Nairobi.

———— (1996): *An Urbanizing World: Global Report on Human Settlements 1996*. Oxford University Press for the United Nations Centre on Human Settlements (Habitat), Oxford and New York.

———— (1999): "Global Urban Indicators Database," United Nations Centre on Human Settlements (Habitat) website www.urbanobservatory.org/indicators/database.

———— (2001): *Cities in a Globalizing World: Global Report on Human Settlements 2001*. Earthscan Publications, London.

UNITED NATIONS DEVELOPMENT PROGRAM (1997a): *Governance for Sustainable Human Development*. United Nations, United Nations Development Program (UNDP), New York.

———— (1997b): *Human Development Report 1997.* Oxford University Press for the United Nations Development Program, Oxford.

———— (1998): *Combating Poverty: The Korean Experience.* United Nations Development Programme (UNDP), Seoul.

UNITED NATIONS INTERREGIONAL CRIME AND JUSTICE RESEARCH INSTITUTE (1998): *Victims of Crime in the Developing World,* no. 57. United Nations, United Nations Interregional Crime and Justice Research Institute, Rome.

UNITED STATES GOVERNMENT (1999): "HIV/AIDS in the Developing World," U.S. Bureau of the Census, Report WP/98-2. U.S. Government Printing Office, Washington, DC.

———— (2001): "IDB Summary Demographic Data," www.census.gov.

UPCHURCH, D. M., C. S. ANESHENSEL, C. A. SUCOFF, AND L. LEVY-STORMS (1999): "Neighborhood and Family Contexts of Adolescent Sexual Activity," *Journal of Marriage and the Family,* 61(4), 920–933.

URBAN RESOURCE CENTRE—KARACHI (2001): "Urban Poverty and Transport: A Case Study from Karachi," *Environment and Urbanization,* 13(1), 223–233.

URZHUMOVA, D., AND C. M. BECKER (1999): "Demographic Trends in Kazakhstan and their Economic Significance," Almaty: USAID Central Asian Republics regional office, Pension Reform Project, presentation at the Republican Seminar for Akims of Oblasts, Cities, and Regions (Astana, December 1999).

U.S. BUREAU OF THE CENSUS (2001): *An Aging World 2001.* International Programs Center, Washington, DC.

VAN DE KAA, D. J. (1996): "Anchored Narratives: The Story and Findings of Half a Century of Research into the Determinants of Fertility," *Population Studies,* 50, 389–432.

VAN DE WALLE, D. (2002): "Choosing Rural Road Investments to Help Reduce Poverty," *World Development,* 30(4), 575–589.

VAN DEN EEDEN, P., AND H. J. M. HÜTTNER (1982): "Multi-level Research," *Current Sociology,* 30(3), 1–182.

VAN POPPEL, F., AND C. VAN DER HEIJDEN (1997): "The Effects of Water Supply on Infant and Child Mortality: A Review of Historical Evidence," *Health Transition Review,* 7, 113–148.

VAN RIE, A., N. BEYERS, R. P. GIE, M. KUNNEKE, L. ZIETSMAN, AND P. R. DONALD (1999): "Childhood Tuberculosis in an Urban Population in South Africa: Burden and Risk Factor," *Archives of Disability in Children,* 80(5), 433–437.

VAN ROSSEM, R., AND D. MEEKERS (2000): "An Evaluation of the Effectiveness of Targeted Social Marketing to Promote Adolescent and Young Adult Reproductive Health in Cameroon," *AIDS Education and Prevention,* 12(5), 383–404.

VANDEMOORTELE, J. (1991): "Labour Market Informalisation in Sub-Saharan Africa," in *Towards Social Adjustment: Labour Market Issues in Structural Adjustment,* ed. by G. Standing, and V. Tokman, pp. 81–113. International Labour Office, Geneva.

VANLANDINGHAM, M. J., S. SUPRASERT, W. SITTITRAI, C. VADDHANAPHUTI, AND N. GRANDJEAN (1993): "Sexual Activity among Never-Married Men in Northern Thailand," *Demography,* 30(3), 297–313.

VASQUEZ, L. A., C. T. GARCIA, S. CATASUS, M. E. BENITEZ, AND M. T. MARTINEZ (1999): "Abortion Practice in a Municipality of Havana, Cuba," in *Abortion in the*

Developing World, ed. by A. I. Mundigo, and C. Indriso, pp. 117–130. Zed Books Ltd., London.

VERMA, S. (1999): "Socialization for Survival: Developmental Issues among Working Street Children in India," in *Homeless and Working Youth Around the World: Exploring Developmental Issues,* ed. by M. Raffaelli, and R. Larson, no. 85 in New Directions for Child and Adolescent Development. Jossey-Bass, San Francisco, CA.

VIJVERBERG, W. P., AND L. A. ZEAGER (1994): "Comparing Earnings Profiles in Urban Areas of an LDC: Rural-to-Urban Migrants vs. Native Workers," *Journal of Development Economics,* 45, 177–199.

VILAS, C. (1996): "Neoliberal Social Policy: Managing Poverty (Somehow)," in *North American Congress on Latin America (NACLA) Report on the Americas,* 29(6), (May/June), 16–21.

VILLA, M., AND J. RODRIGUEZ (1996): "Demographic Trends in Latin America's Metropolises, 1950–1990," in *The Mega-City in Latin America,* ed. by A. Gilbert, pp. 25–52. United Nations University Press, Tokyo.

VISARIA, P. (1997): "Urbanization in India: An Overview," in *Urbanization in Large Developing Countries: China, Indonesia, Brazil, and India,* ed. by G. W. Jones, and P. Visaria, pp. 266–288. Clarendon Press, Oxford.

VÖGELE, J. (2000): "Urbanization and the Urban Mortality Change in Imperial Germany," *Health and Place,* 6(1), 41–55.

WALDER, A. G. (1994): "Corporate Organization and Local Government Property Rights in China," in *Changing Political Economies: Privatization in Post-Communist and Reforming Communist States,* ed. by V. Milor, pp. 53–66. Lynne Rienner, Boulder, CO.

WALKER, A. R. (1995): "Cancer Outlook: An African Perspective," *Journal of the Royal Society of Medicine,* 88(1), 5–13.

WALKER, A. R., AND P. SARELI (1997): "Coronary Heart Disease: Outlook for Africa," *Journal of the Royal Society of Medicine,* 90(1), 23–27.

WALKER, A. R., AND I. SEGAL (1997): "Health/Ill-Health Transition in Less Privileged Populations: What Does the Future Hold?" *Journal of the Royal College of Physicians, London,* 31(4), 392–395.

WANG, F., AND X. ZUO (1999): "Inside China's Cities: Institutional Barriers and Opportunities for Urban Migrants," *American Economic Review,* 89(2), 276–280.

WANG, Y. (1994): "China: Urban Development and Research Towards the Year 2000," in *Urban Research in the Developing World. Vol. 1. Asia,* ed. by R. Stren, pp. 253–321. Centre for Urban and Community Studies, University of Toronto, Toronto.

WANG'OMBE, J. K. (1995): "Public Health Crises of Cities in Developing Countries," *Social Science and Medicine,* 41(6), 857–862.

WARD, P. (1998): *Mexico City.* 2nd ed., revised. John Wiley, Chichester.

――― (1999): "Mexico City's Future in an Era of Globalization: Dealing with the Demographic Downturn," Paper presented at National Academy of Sciences workshop on "World Cities in Poor Countries," (October), Washington, DC.

WATANABE, S. (1976): "Minimum Wages in Developing Countries: Myth and Reality," *International Labour Review,* 113(3), 345–358.

WAWER, M. H., K. J. LASSNER, AND B. B. C. HANFF (1986): "Contraceptive Prevalence in the Slums of Rio de Janeiro," *Studies in Family Planning,* 17(1), 44–52.

WEBBER, M. (1963): "Order in Diversity: Community Without Propinquity," in *Neighborhood, City and Metropolis*, ed. by R. Gutman, and D. Popenoe, pp. 792–781. Random House, New York.

WEBER, A. (1909): *Über den Standort der Industrien.* Tübingen, Germany, (Translated into English as: Friedrich, C. F., 1929, *Alfred Weber's Theory of Location of Industries.* University of Chicago Press, Chicago).

WEBSTER, D. (2000a): "Financing City-Building: The Bangkok Case Discussion Paper," Asia Pacific Research Center, Institute for International Studies, Stanford University.

——— (2000b): "Bangkok: Evolution and Adaptation under Stress," Paper delivered at Conference on World Cities in Poor Countries, National Academy of Sciences, Washington, DC.

WEEKS, J. R. (2002): "Using Remote Sensing and Geographic Information Systems to Identify the Underlying Properties of Urban Environments," Paper prepared for the conference "New Forms of Urbanization: Conceptualizing and Measuring Human Settlement in the Twenty-First Century," organized by the IUSSP Working Group on Urbanization, Bellagio, Italy, March 11–15.

WEEKS, J. R., A. GETIS, X. YANG, T. RASHED, AND M. S. GADALLA (2002): "Spatial Patterns as Predictors of Fertility in Cairo, Egypt," Paper presented at the Annual Meeting of the Population Association of America, May 8–11, Atlanta, GA.

WEI, S.-J., AND Y. WU (2001): "Evidence from Within China," Working Paper 8611, National Bureau of Economic Research, Cambridge, MA.

WELLINGTON, M., F. NDOWA, AND L. MBENGERANWA (1997): "Risk Factors for Sexually Transmitted Disease in Harare: A Case-Control Study," *Sexually Transmitted Diseases*, 24(9), 528–532.

WELLMAN, B., AND B. LEIGHTON (1979): "Networks, Neighborhoods, and Communities: Approaches to the Study of the Community Question," *Urban Affairs Quarterly*, 14(3), 363–390.

WHITE, M. J. (1987): *American Neighborhoods and Residential Differentiation.* Russell Sage, New York.

——— (2000): "Migration, Urbanization, and Social Adjustment," in *Urbanization, Population, Environment, and Security: A Report of the Comparative Urban Studies Project*, ed. by C. Rosan, B. A. Ruble, and J. S. Tulchin, pp. 19–23. Woodrow Wilson International Center for Scholars, Washington, DC.

——— (2001): "Demographic Effects of Segregation," in *Encyclopedia of the Social and Behavioral Sciences*, vol. 19, pp. 13250–13254. Elsevier Science.

WHITE, M. J., Y. K. DJAMBA, AND N. A. DANG (2001): "Implications of Economic Reform and Spatial Mobility on Fertility in Vietnam," Working paper, Population Studies and Training Center, Brown University.

WHITE, M. J., L. MORENO, AND S. GUO (1995): "The Interrelationship of Fertility and Migration in Peru: A Hazards Model Analysis," *International Migration Review*, 29, 492–514.

WILKINSON, R. G. (1996): *Unhealthy Societies: The Afflictions of Inequality.* Routledge, London.

WILLIAMSON, J. (1965): "Regional Inequality and the Process of National Development," *Economic Development and Cultural Change*, 13, 3–45.

—— (1988): "Migration and Urbanization," in *Handbook of Development Economics, Volume 1*, ed. by H. Chenery, and T. N. Srinivasan, pp. 425–465. Elsevier North-Holland, Amsterdam.

WILLIS, R. J. (1973): "A New Approach to the Economic Theory of Fertility Behavior," *Journal of Political Economy*, 81(2, part 2), S14–S64.

WILSON, R. H., AND R. CRAMER (eds.) (1996): *International Workshop on Local Governance, Second Annual Proceedings*. Lyndon B. Johnson School of Public Affairs, University of Texas, Austin, TX.

WILSON, W. J. (1987): *The Truly Disadvantaged: The Inner City, the Underclass and Public Policy*. University of Chicago Press, Chicago.

WING, S., G. GRANT, M. GREEN, AND C. STEWART (1996): "Community Based Collaboration for Environmental Justice: South-East Halifax County Environmental Re-Awakening," *Environment and Urbanization*, 8(2), 129–140.

WINSTON, C. M., AND V. PATEL (1995): "Use of Traditional and Orthodox Health Services in Urban Zimbabwe," *International Journal of Epidemiology*, 24(5), 1006–1012.

WIRTH, L. (1938): "Urbanism as a Way of Life," *American Journal of Sociology*, 44(1), 1–24.

WITTIG, M. C., J. D. WRIGHT, AND D. C. KAMINSKY (1997): "Substance Abuse among Street Children in Honduras," *Substance Use and Misuse*, 32, 805–827.

WOLCH, J., AND M. DEAR (eds.) (1989): *The Power of Geography: How Territory Shapes Social Life*. Unwin Hyman, Boston.

WONG, K.-Y., R.-Q. CAI, AND H.-X. CHEN (1992): "Shenzhen: Special Experience in Development and Innovation," in *China's Coastal Cities: Catalysts for Modernization*, ed. by Y. M. Yeung, and X.-W. Hu, pp. 264–290. University of Hawaii Press, Honolulu.

WORKING GROUP ON DEMOGRAPHIC EFFECTS OF ECONOMIC AND SOCIAL REVERSALS (1993): *Demographic Effects of Economic Reversals in Sub-Saharan Africa*. National Academy Press, Washington, DC, Panel on the Population Dynamics of Sub-Saharan Africa, Committee on Population, Commission on Behavioral and Social Sciences and Education, National Research Council.

WORKING GROUP ON FACTORS AFFECTING CONTRACEPTIVE USE (1993): *Factors Affecting Contraceptive Use in Sub-Saharan Africa*. National Academy Press, Washington, DC, Panel on the Population Dynamics of Sub-Saharan Africa, Committee on Population, Commission on Behavioral and Social Sciences and Education, National Research Council.

WORLD BANK (1994): *World Development Report 1994: Infrastructure for Development*. Oxford University Press, New York.

—— (2000a): *Entering the 21st Century: World Development Report 1999/2000*. Oxford University Press, Oxford and New York.

—— (2000b): "Interhousehold Transfers: Using Research to Inform Policy," *PREM Notes*, 36.

—— (2000c): *World Development Indicators, 2000*. The World Bank, Washington, DC.

—— (2001): *World Development Report 2000/2001: Attacking Poverty*. Oxford University Press, Oxford and New York.

—— (2002a): *Global Development Finance: Financing the Poorest Countries*. The World Bank, Washington, DC.

———— (2002b): *World Development Report 2002: Building Institutions for Markets.* Oxford University Press for the World Bank, New York.

WORLD FERTILITY SURVEY (1984): *World Fertility Survey: Major Findings and Implications.* Alden Press, Oxford.

WORLD HEALTH ORGANIZATION (1992): *Our Planet, Our Health.* Report of the WHO Commission on Health and Environment, World Health Organization, Geneva.

———— (1993): *The Urban Health Crisis: Strategies for Health for All in the Face of Rapid Urbanization.* World Health Organization, Geneva.

———— (1996): *Investing in Health Research and Development: Report of the Ad Hoc Committee on Health Research Relating to Future Intervention Options.* World Health Organization, Geneva.

———— (1997): "Substance Abuse among Street Children and Other Children and Youth in Especially Difficult Circumstances," WHO Fact Sheet, www.who.int/inffs/en/fact151. html, World Health Organization, Geneva.

———— (1998): *Unsafe Abortion: Global and Regional Estimates of Incidence of and Mortality Due to Abortion, with a Listing of Available Country Data.* 3rd ed., Division of Reproductive Health, World Health Organization, Geneva.

WRATTEN, E. (1995): "Conceptualizing Urban Poverty," *Environment and Urbanization,* 7(1), 11–36.

WRIGHT, J. D., D. C. KAMINSKY, AND M. WITTIG (1993): "Health and Social Conditions of Street Children in Honduras," *American Journal of Diseases of Children,* 147, 279–283.

WU, F. (2000): "The Global and Local Dimensions of Place-Making: Remaking Shanghai as a World City," *Urban Studies,* 37(8), 1359–1377.

WU, W. (1999a): "City Profile—Shanghai," *Cities,* 16(3), 207–216.

———— (1999b): "Reforming China's Institutional Environment for Urban Infrastructure Provision," *Urban Studies,* 36(13), 2263–2282.

WU, W., AND S. YUSUF (2003): "Shanghai: Rising in a Globalizing World," in *World Cities in Poor Countries,* ed. by J. Gugler. Cambridge University Press, Cambridge.

WYSS, K., D. WHITING, P. KILIMA, D. G. MCLARTY, D. MTASIWA, M. TANNER, AND N. LORENZ (1996): "Utilisation of Government and Private Health Services in Dar es Salaam," *East African Medical Journal,* 73(6), 357–363.

YAMADA, G. (1996): "Urban Informal Employment and Self-Employment in Developing Countries," *Economic Development and Cultural Change,* 44(2), 289–314.

YANG, X., AND F. GUO (1999): "Gender Differences in Determinants of Temporary Labor Migration in China: A Multilevel Analysis," *International Migration Review,* 33(4), 929–953.

YAP, L. Y. (1977): "The Attraction of Cities: A Review of the Migration Literature," *Journal of Development Economics,* 4, 239–264.

YESUDIAN, C. (1994): "Behaviour of the Private Sector in the Health Market of Bombay," *Health Policy and Planning,* 9(1), 72–80.

YEUNG, Y. M. (1995): "Globalization and World Cities in Developing Countries," in *Perspectives on the City,* ed. by R. Stren with J. K. Bell, vol. 4, Urban Research in the Developing World, pp. 189–226. University of Toronto Press, Toronto.

———— (1996): "Introduction," in *Shanghai: Transformation and Modernization under China's Open Policy,* ed. by Y. M. Yeung, and Y. W. Sung, pp. 1–23. The Chinese University Press, Hong Kong.

—— (1998a): "The Urban Poor and Urban Basic Infrastructure Services in Asia: A Substantive Review of Past Approaches," in *Urban Development in Asia: Retrospect and Prospect*, ed. by Y. M. Yeung, pp. 95–141. Hong Kong Institute of Asia-Pacific Studies, The Chinese University of Hong Kong.

—— (ed.) (1998b): *Urban Development in Asia: Retrospect and Prospect.* Hong Kong Institute of Asia-Pacific Studies, The Chinese University of Hong Kong.

—— (1999): "The Emergence of Pearl River Delta's Mega Urban-Region in a Globalizing Environment," Occasional Paper No. 90, Hong Kong Institute of Asia-Pacific Studies, The Chinese University of Hong Kong (in Chinese).

—— (2000): *Globalization and Networked Societies: Urban-Regional Change in Pacific Asia.* University of Hawaii Press, Honolulu.

—— (2001): "Migration in China under Openness and a Marketizing Economy," Background paper prepared for the Panel on Urban Population Dynamics, Committee on Population, National Research Council.

YEUNG, Y. M., AND D. CHU (eds.) (1998): *Guangdong: Survey of a Province Undergoing Rapid Change.* 2nd ed., The Chinese Univesity Press, Hong Kong.

—— (eds.) (2000): *Fujian: A Coastal Province in Transition and Transformation.* The Chinese University Press, Hong Kong.

YEUNG, Y. M., AND X.W. HU (eds.) (1992): *China's Coastal Cities: Catalysts for Modernization.* University of Hawaii Press, Honolulu.

YEUNG, Y. M., AND Y. W. SUNG (eds.) (1996): *Shanghai: Transformation and Modernization under China's Open Policy.* The Chinese University Press, Hong Kong.

YING, W. (2000): "Self-Governance for City Residents and Changes in Community Management Styles," Website, IDS Civil Society and Governance Project, Sussex.

YIRRELL, D. L., H. PICKERING, G. PALMARINI, L. HAMILTON, A. RUTEMBERWA, B. BIRYAHWAHO, J. WHITWORTH, AND A. J. BROWN (1998): "Molecular Epidemiological Analysis of HIV in Sexual Networks in Uganda," *AIDS*, 12(3), 285–290.

YITNA, A. (2002): "Levels, Trends, and Determinants of Fertility in Addis Ababa, Ethiopia," *Journal of African Policy Studies*, 12(2).

YOUNG, A. (1995): "The Tyranny of Numbers: Confronting the Statistical Realities of the East Asian Growth Experience," *Quarterly Journal of Economics*, 110(3), 641–680.

ZHANG, L., AND S. X. ZHAO (1998): "Re-Examining China's 'Urban Concept and the Level of Urbanization'," *The China Quarterly*, 154, 330–381.

ZHANG, T. (2001): "Public Participation in China's Urban Development," in *Handbook of Global Social Policy*, ed. by S. S. Nagel, and A. Robb, pp. 183–207. Marcel Dekker, New York.

ZHAO, Y. (1999): "Leaving the Countryside: Rural-to-Urban Migration Decisions in China," *American Economic Review*, 89(2), 281–286.

ZWI, A. B., S. FORJUOH, S. MURUGUSAMPILLAY, W. ODERO, AND C. WATTS (1996): "Injuries in Developing Countries: Policy Response Needed Now," *Transactions of the Royal Society of Tropical Medicine and Hygiene*, 90(6), 593–595.

Appendices

Appendices

A

Concepts and Definitions of Metropolitan Regions

For many years, urban geographers have struggled to find conceptual categories in which to place those settlements that spread beyond the political or administrative bounds of the "city" itself. In high-income countries, much effort has gone into devising new categories appropriate to the evolving nature of cities, beginning with the recognition of suburbanization in Europe and North America (Champion, 1998). The metropolitan concept that evolved over much of the twentieth century emerged from industrial urban forms: concentrated, core-oriented production that, by agglomerating industry and employment in a single center and packing the population around the center and along radiating transport networks, provided a spatial solution to the problem of slow and expensive transport (Adams, 1995; Berry, 1995). The production and distribution of goods and an emphasis on radial movement to and from the urban core gave way to the rise of the service economy, with communications increasingly substituting for movement and movement occurring in all directions at all times of the day and week, in this way generating what has been termed an "urban field" (Adams, 1995; Friedmann and Miller, 1965).

Recent literature has drawn attention to conceptual analogies in the cities of poor countries, particularly in terms of the growth and outward spread of metropolitan areas and the tendency for initially separate urban centers to be merged in wider metropolitan regions. There is a suggestion that the megacities of low- and high-income countries may have more in common with each other, irrespective of their locations on the globe, than they have with other parts of their own urban systems (Champion, 1998). McGee and Griffiths (1998), for example, note the convergence of Bangkok and Los Angeles, both being territorially vast, amorphous, multicentered regions with populations residing up to 100 kilometers from the city core.

481

In recent years, many researchers have argued that the simple classifications of "central city" and "suburb" have become obsolete. In the United States and elsewhere, these researchers see an emerging pattern of settlement taking the form of increasingly dispersed and decentralized centers of activity and residential zones (Berry, 1995; Castells, 1989; Fishman, 1990). To try to incorporate this new and evolving reality into a definition of settlement forms for use in the dissemination of statistical data is clearly a daunting task.

In the decade leading up to the 2000 Census, the U.S. Bureau of the Census oversaw a large-scale review of alternative approaches to delineating metropolitan and nonmetropolitan settlements as part of an examination of metropolitan area (MA) statistical standards. This review was unusually thorough and is perhaps as interesting for its participatory process as for its conclusions. The overriding concern was that metropolitan standards had become needlessly complex, both conceptually and operationally.

Greatest attention was paid to the definition of building blocks—the smallest territorial units from which cities and metropolitan regions are formed—the methods of aggregating these blocks, and territorial coverage. Four papers were commissioned for the review, and these papers outlined four rather different approaches (Adams, 1995; Berry, 1995; Frey and Speare, 1995; Morrill, 1995). Some of the researchers advocated the use of census tracts as the basic geospatial unit, with journey-to-work data being used to define clusters. The authors of two papers favored the use of counties, however, with one of these papers suggesting that commuting time be used as a clustering criterion and the other suggesting the use of population density.

The analytic task was complicated by external constraints and pressures, including political pressure from local interests. Many smaller cities expressed an interest in being designated as standard metropolitan areas (SMAs) for prestige and business reasons, and many developed public relations campaigns and applied political pressure on their congressional delegations (Dahmann, 1999).

In the end, the review resulted in a recommendation that a core-based statistical area (CBSA) classification replace the MA classification. The cores (i.e., the densely settled concentrations of population) would be Census Bureau–defined urbanized areas and smaller densely settled "settlement clusters" identified in Census 2000. The CBSA classification identified three types of areas on the basis of total population of all cores in the CBSA: (1) *megapolitan areas*, defined around cores of at least 1 million population; (2) *macropolitan areas*, defined around cores of 50,000 to 999,999 population; and (3) *micropolitan areas*, defined around cores of 10,000 to 49,000 population. The identification of micropolitan areas extended the concepts of core-based approaches to smaller population centers, which had previously been relegated to a nonmetropolitan residual category. This new approach addressed the problem that the area outside metropolitan settlements, which includes more than 10,000 smaller cities and towns, huge expanses of open country, and over four-fifths of U.S.land, had been consigned to an uncategorized and undifferentiated status.

Because data on counties and their equivalents are both available and familiar, the review recommended continued use of these entities as the building blocks for statistical areas, although it did not preclude the adoption of subcountry entities, such as tracts or mail (ZIP) code areas, for the future. It was further decided that commuting (journey-to-work) data from the Census Bureau (which will soon be available on an annual basis from the Census Bureau's American Community Survey) should continue to be regarded as the most reliable measure of functional integration between areas. The utility of other data measuring functional ties—including telephone traffic patterns, cellular telephone service, media market penetration, Internet use, and purchasing patterns—was evaluated. The review generated the recommendation that a commuting threshold of 25 percent be adopted to establish qualifying linkages between outlying counties and counties containing CBSA cores. It was noted that the percentage of a county's employed residents who commuted to the central county or counties (or who commuted from outlying to central counties) was an unambiguous, clear measure of whether a potential outlying county should qualify for inclusion.

In a striking departure from the previous MA standard, a recommendation of the review was not to use measures of "settlement structure." In the previous standard, the level of population density, the percentage urban, and population growth rates were all used, together with measures of commuting, to establish whether outlying counties should be included in an MA. The review led to the conclusion that with the changes in the nature of settlement, commuting patterns, and communications technologies, settlement structure had lost much of its former connection to industrial, occupational, and family structure and could no longer serve as a reliable indicator of metropolitan character.

B

Mathematical Derivations

This appendix explains the basis for the mathematical results presented in Chapter 4. The form in which the equations are presented follows that of Rogers and colleagues (e.g., Rogers, 1995), who have put emphasis on their links to stable population theory. Alternative approaches can also be found in the literature; for example, some authors develop their equations in terms of net rather than gross migration rates, and others define rates of migration in terms of destination rather than origin populations.

The fixed-rates model described in the first section of Chapter 4 can be written in matrix form as follows:

$$\begin{bmatrix} U_t - U_{t-1} \\ R_t - R_{t-1} \end{bmatrix} = \begin{bmatrix} n_u - m_{u,r} & m_{r,u} \\ m_{u,r} & n_r - m_{r,u} \end{bmatrix} \begin{bmatrix} U_{t-1} \\ R_{t-1} \end{bmatrix}, \qquad (B.1)$$

with all terms defined as in the text. This is the most convenient form for present purposes. If analytic solutions are desired, the equations can be re-expressed as

$$\begin{bmatrix} U_t \\ R_t \end{bmatrix} = \begin{bmatrix} 1 + n_u - m_{u,r} & m_{r,u} \\ m_{u,r} & 1 + n_r - m_{r,u} \end{bmatrix} \begin{bmatrix} U_{t-1} \\ R_{t-1} \end{bmatrix},$$

and the stable solution is one in which the urban and rural populations grow at the same rate r, such that in equilibrium,

$$\begin{bmatrix} U_t \\ R_t \end{bmatrix} = (1 + r) \cdot \begin{bmatrix} U_{t-1} \\ R_{t-1} \end{bmatrix}.$$

As in conventional stable population models, r can be derived from the eigenvalues of the projection matrix. Rogers (1995: 15–16) outlines the method for the general case; a survey of solution techniques can be found in Simon and Blume (1994). These techniques are needed in models with age structure, but in the simple model at hand, r is easily found (Ledent, 1980).

Returning to the form of the model shown in equation (B.1), we obtain expressions for urban and rural growth rates and the share of total urban growth attributable to migration from the rural sector. These are, respectively,

$$\frac{U_t - U_{t-1}}{U_{t-1}} = n_u - m_{u,r} + \frac{R_{t-1}}{U_{t-1}} \cdot m_{r,u}, \tag{B.2}$$

$$\frac{R_t - R_{t-1}}{R_{t-1}} = n_r - m_{r,u} + \frac{U_{t-1}}{R_{t-1}} \cdot m_{u,r}, \tag{B.3}$$

and

$$\begin{aligned} MS_t &= \frac{m_{r,u} \cdot R_{t-1}}{(n_u - m_{u,r}) \cdot U_{t-1} + m_{r,u} \cdot R_{t-1}} \\ &= \left(1 + \frac{U_{t-1}}{R_{t-1}} \cdot \frac{n_u - m_{u,r}}{m_{r,u}}\right)^{-1}. \end{aligned} \tag{B.4}$$

Equations (B.2) and (B.3) can be solved for the equilibrium urban/rural population balance,

$$b \equiv \lim_{t \to \infty} \frac{U_t}{R_t},$$

provided that this limit exists and is greater than zero (see Schoen and Kim, 1993). If such a limit exists, then asymptotically the urban and rural growth rates both equal r, the stable population growth rate. To find b, one equates the right-hand sides of equations (B.2) and (B.3), and the value of b is obtained as one of the roots of a quadratic equation. With the solution for b determined, equation (B.2) establishes the long-term rate of urban growth. The long-term share of migration is similarly found by inserting b into equation (B.4).

The other measures we discuss can be derived from these equations. The *level of urbanization*, denoted by $P_{u,t}$ in the main text, is expressed as

$$P_{u,t} = \frac{U_t}{P_t}$$

in the terms employed here. The rate of *national population growth* is

$$\frac{P_t - P_{t-1}}{P_{t-1}} = \frac{U_{t-1}}{P_{t-1}} \cdot n_u + \frac{R_{t-1}}{P_{t-1}} \cdot n_r, \tag{B.5}$$

which is a weighted average of the urban and rural rates of natural increase. The *rate of urbanization*, which can be expressed as the difference between the urban growth rate and that of the national population, is given by

$$\frac{U_t - U_{t-1}}{U_{t-1}} - \frac{P_t - P_{t-1}}{P_{t-1}} = -m_{u,r} + \frac{R_{t-1}}{P_{t-1}} \cdot (n_u - n_r) + \frac{R_{t-1}}{U_{t-1}} \cdot m_{r,u}. \tag{B.6}$$

The difference between the urban and rural growth rate is

$$URGD_{t-1} = (n_u - m_{u,r}) - (n_r - m_{r,u}) + \frac{R_{t-1}}{U_{t-1}} \cdot m_{r,u} - \frac{U_{t-1}}{R_{t-1}} \cdot m_{u,r}. \quad \text{(B.7)}$$

This relationship plays an important role in United Nations projections.

C

Linking DHS Surveys to
United Nations City Data

Until 2000, the city population data published in the United Nations *Demographic Yearbook* were not computerized in any publicly accessible form. Thanks to the efforts of Alice Clague of the United Nations, the panel was able to secure a new database (United Nations, 2000) containing a prepublication version of the city population data that appear in the *1998 Demographic Yearbook*. Although our computer file lacked some of the detail of the published table, it supplied the framework we needed to construct the merged city population dataset used throughout this report. To lengthen the time span of these data, we supplemented the computer file by keying in city population data from three earlier years of the *Demographic Yearbook* (United Nations, 1987, 1992, 1998a).

Drawing on these data and another computer file (United Nations, 2001) containing the statistical annexes to a recent volume of *World Urbanization Prospects*, we assembled a composite city database that includes the following:

- Raw population counts and estimates for capital cities and agglomerations of 100,000 population and above, taken from four recent volumes of the United Nations *Demographic Yearbook*

- Extrapolated data series from *World Urbanization Prospects* (United Nations, 2001) for cities of 750,000 population and above, covering the period 1950 to 2000 at 5-year intervals

- Recent population estimates for capital city urban agglomerations, also taken from United Nations (2001) and earlier years of this publication

For cities of under 750,000 population (other than capital cities), only the *Demographic Yearbook* population counts are available.

487

The panel then faced a problem in linking the United Nations city-level data to survey data on individuals and households from the Demographic and Health Surveys (DHS). Until recently the DHS program did not release information on the geographic locations of its sampling clusters, evidently to protect the confidentiality of the survey respondents. In the surveys available to the panel, not even the city name is provided for urban residents. This restriction means that if the DHS data are to be linked to data on cities, the only option is to forge the link using whatever geographic indicators *are* reported in the surveys.[1]

Most DHS surveys provide information on the region of the country in which a sampling cluster is located, although the surveys vary greatly in the extent of regional detail, with some countries specifying regions very broadly in geographical terms. All DHS surveys contain information on whether the sampling cluster is urban or rural in character, presumably following the definitions used by the country's national statistics office. Unfortunately, the population size of the urban area in which a cluster is located is not given; rather, its size is loosely characterized in broad, almost qualitative terms. In Round 1 of the DHS program, urban areas were characterized as being either large or small cities. Since Round 2, three categories have been used: capitals and large cities, small cities, and towns. Large cities are defined as those with populations of 1 million or more; the small city category contains all cities in the wide range from 50,000 to 1 million population; and towns are the residual category for urban areas below 50,000 in size (Demographic and Health Surveys, 1994, 2001).

THE MATCHING PROCEDURE

Faced with these difficulties, the panel undertook to match the DHS data on region and city size, as broadly and qualitatively defined, to the United Nations estimates of the population sizes of specific individual cities.[2] Using the available DHS data and reports, together with geographic atlases (e.g., Cohen, 1998b), we found that we could link the data in two ways. Often enough information was available for us to match a sampling cluster to a specific city. Sometimes, however, we lacked sufficiently detailed geographic variables from the DHS to identify a specific city of residence, but were able to winnow the possibilities to a set of cities. The latter type of linkage occurred more often in the Round 1 DHS surveys (whose urban characterizations were cruder than those in Rounds 2 and 3) and in more populous countries and those with higher levels of urbanization (which usually have more cities in any given geographic region).

---

[1] We are indebted to Narayan Sastry of RAND Corporation for providing us with sampling cluster identifiers for the 1986 Brazilian DHS, a survey undertaken in an era in which the DHS program supplied such identifiers. Of the 90 DHS surveys used in our analyses, this is the only one allowing a precise match between sampling clusters and residence in particular cities.

[2] Edward Hui (Brown University) made a major contribution to this effort.

In the case of the unique matches, the panel assigned a city size value taken from the merged United Nations database described above. Our aim was to use a city population estimate for 1990—a year roughly midway in the course of the DHS program—or the nearest available year. In deciding among the different United Nations population estimates, we gave first preference to the *World Urbanization Prospects* estimate, but if this was unavailable turned to the *Demographic Yearbook* estimate for the urban agglomerations or, if necessary, to the *Yearbook* estimate for the city proper.

For the cases in which a DHS sampling cluster could be linked only to a set of cities, we constructed the weighted average of the 1990 populations for the cities in the set, using the city populations themselves as weights, and assigned this weighted average to the DHS sampling cluster. The idea was to assign the city population value that would be expected if a person were to be drawn at random from the set of cities.

THE RESULT: CITY SIZE RANGES

Clearly there is much room for subjective errors and imprecision in the final results of this matching procedure. It is unfortunate that until recently the DHS program has had no mechanism in place to allow its survey clusters to be linked directly to city identifiers; having such a mechanism would have eliminated one source of error (see Appendix F for the panel's recommendation for meeting this need). As we have discussed, the United Nations population estimates are themselves subject to errors and substantial differences in definitions. In view of the many uncertainties involved, all city sizes are classified in ranges of population size in the panel's analyses using DHS data, rather than being expressed as point estimates. We chose ranges that appeared to be narrow enough to be informative, yet broad enough to mitigate the effects of matching and other errors. In our analyses of DHS data, we do not make use of population growth rates for cities and sets of cities, although that possibility deserves further research attention.

DHS SURVEYS USED IN THIS REPORT

The following tables provide information on the DHS surveys examined in this report, which are limited to those datasets that had been released and were available to the panel as of the beginning of 2000. (Many more DHS surveys have been made available since then, but they could not be included.) Table C-1 lists the countries whose surveys were examined by the panel, with the year of the survey indicated. Table C-2 gives each country's urban definition precisely as it is recorded by the United Nations. Table C-3 lists the cities of these countries whose populations fell into the 1–5 million range in 1990 or the closest year to it for which a calculation was possible, and also lists the cities with more than 5 million population.

TABLE C-1 Countries with a Demographic and Health Survey Included in the Panel's Dataset, by Region (survey year in parentheses)

Region	Countries Surveyed
North Africa	Egypt (1988, 1992, 1995), Morocco (1987, 1992), Tunisia (1988)
Sub-Saharan Africa	Benin (1996), Botswana (1988), Burkina Faso (1993), Burundi (1987), Cameroon (1991, 1998), Central African Republic (1994–95), Chad (1996–97), Comoros (1996), Côte d'Ivoire (1994), Ghana (1988, 1993, 1998–99), Kenya (1989, 1993, 1998), Liberia (1986), Madagascar (1992, 1997), Malawi (1992, Mali (1987, 1995–96), Mozambique (1997), Namibia (1992), Niger (1992, 1998), Nigeria (1990), Rwanda (1992), Senegal (1986, 1992–93, 1997), Sudan (1989–90), Tanzania (1991–2, 1996), Togo (1988, 1998), Uganda (1988–89, 1995), Zambia (1992, 1996), Zimbabwe (1988, 1994)
South-East Asia	Indonesia (1987, 1991, 1994, 1997), Philippines (1993, 1998), Thailand (1987)
South and West Asia	Bangladesh (1993–94, 1996–97), India (1992), Kazakhstan (1995), Republic of Kyrgyzstan (1997), Nepal (1996), Pakistan (1990–91), Sri Lanka (1987), Turkey (1993), Uzbekistan (1996), Yemen (1991)
Latin America	Bolivia (1989, 1994, 1998), Brazil (1986, 1996), Colombia (1986, 1990, 1995), Dominican Republic (1986, 1991, 1996), Ecuador (1987), El Salvador (1985), Guatemala (1987, 1995, 1999), Haiti (1994–95), Mexico (1987), Nicaragua (1998), Paraguay (1990), Peru (1986, 1991–92, 1996), Trinidad and Tobago (1987)

TABLE C-2 Urban Definitions in the Countries with a DHS Survey in the Panel's Dataset, as Recorded by the United Nations

Country	Definition
Bangladesh	Places having a municipality (*pourashava*), a town committee (*shahar* committee), or a cantonment board.
Benin	Localities with 10,000 or more inhabitants.
Bolivia	Localities with 2,000 or more inhabitants.
Botswana	Agglomerations of 5,000 or more inhabitants where 75 percent of economic activity is nonagricultural.
Brazil	Area internal to the urban perimeter of towns and cities as defined by municipal law.
Burkina Faso	The sum of 14 towns.
Burundi	Commune of Bujumbura.

TABLE C-2 *continued*

Country	Definition
Cameroon	Urban centers.
Central African Republic	Twenty principal centers with a population of over 3,000.
Chad	Administrative centres of *préfectures*, *sous-préfectures* and administrative posts.
Colombia	Population living in a nucleus of 1,500 or more inhabitants.
Comoros	Administrative centers of *préfectures* and localities with 5,000 or more inhabitants.
Côte d'Ivoire	Urban agglomerations containing more than 10,000 inhabitants; agglomerations of from 4,000 to 10,000 persons with more than 50 percent of households engaged in nonagricultural activities; and the administrative centers of Grand Lahoun and Dabakala. Excludes the *milieux urbain* of Bouna, which has a population of 11,000.
Dominican Republic	Administrative centers of *comunas* and municipal districts.
Ecuador	Capitals of provinces and cantons.
Egypt	Governorates of Cairo, Alexandria, Port Said, Ismailia, and Suez; frontier governorates; and capitals of other governorates and district capitals (*markaz*).
El Salvador	Administrative centers of *municipios*.
Ghana	Localities with a population of 5,000 or more.
Guatemala	*Municipio* of Guatemala Department; officially recognized centers of other departments and municipalities. Urban population for 1981 is officially adjusted to include the urbanized suburbs bordering the *municipio* of Guatemala, consistent with the previous census.
Haiti	Administrative centers of communes.
India	Towns (places with municipal corporation, municipal area committee, town committee, notified area committee, or cantonment board); and all places having 5,000 or more inhabitants, a density of not fewer than 1,000 persons per square mile or 390 per square kilometer, pronounced urban characteristics, and at least three-fourths of the adult male population employed in pursuits other than agriculture.
Indonesia	Municipalities (*kotamadya*), regency (*kabupaten*) capitals and other places with urban characteristics.
Kazakhstan	Cities and urban-type localities, officially designated as such, usually according to the criteria of number of inhabitants and predominance of agricultural or nonagricultural workers and their families.
Kenya	Towns with 2,000 or more inhabitants.
Kyrgyzstan	Cities and urban-type localities, officially designated as such, usually according to the criteria of number of inhabitants and predominance of agricultural or nonagricultural workers and their families.

(continued)

TABLE C-2 *continued*

Country	Definition
Liberia	Localities with 2,000 or more inhabitants.
Madagascar	Centers with more than 5,000 inhabitants.
Malawi	All townships, town planning areas, and district centers.
Mali	Localities with 5,000 or more inhabitants and district centers.
Mexico	Localities with 2,500 or more inhabitants.
Morocco	Urban centers.
Mozambique	*Conselho* of Maputo and Beira.
Namibia	The censuses are thought to be underenumerated, but the underenumeration is almost solely in the rural areas. Hence, the census population counts for urban areas (1951 and 1960) and for Windhoek (1951, 1960, 1981) are accepted, but the 1992 Revision for the total population is used to estimate the "true" census count for all three dates. The 1951 and 1960 percentage urban is estimated by dividing the census count of urban population by the above-estimated "true" census counts. To obtain the urban population at the time of the 1981 census, it was noted that in 1951 and 1960, 30 percent of the urban population lived in Windhoek. Therefore for 1981, the census-counted Windhoek population was accepted and was divided by 0.30 to obtain an estimated urban population.
Nepal	Localities with 9,000 or more inhabitants (*panchayats*).
Nicaragua	Administrative centers of departments and *municipios*.
Niger	Urban centers (27 towns).
Nigeria	Towns with 20,000 or more inhabitants whose occupations are not mainly agrarian.
Pakistan	Places with municipal corporation, town committee, or cantonment.
Paraguay	Administrative centers of the official districts of the Republic.
Peru	Populated centers with 100 or more dwellings grouped contiguously and administrative centers of districts.
Philippines	All cities and municipalities with a density of at least 1,000 persons per square kilometer; administrative centers, barrios of at least 2,000 inhabitants, and those barrios of at least 1,000 inhabitants which are contiguous to the administrative center, in all cities and municipalities with a density of at least 500 persons per square kilometer; and all other administrative centers with at least 2,500 inhabitants.
Rwanda	Kigali; administrative centers of *préfectures* and important agglomerations and their surroundings.
Senegal	Agglomerations of 10,000 or more inhabitants.
Sri Lanka	Municipalities, urban councils, and towns.

TABLE C-2 *continued*

Country	Definition
Sudan	Localities of administrative or commercial importance or with a population of 5,000 or more inhabitants.
Thailand	Municipalities.
Togo	Seven urban communes.
Trinidad and Tobago	Port-of-Spain, Arima borough, and San Fernando town.
Tunisia	Population living in communes.
Turkey	Population of the localities within the municipality limits of administrative centers of provinces and districts.
Uganda	Population of all settlements as small as trading centers with as few as 100 inhabitants.
United Republic of Tanzania	Gazetted townships.
Uzbekistan	Cities and urban-type localities, officially designated as such, usually according to the criteria of number of inhabitants and predominance of agricultural or nonagricultural workers and their families.
Yemen	The entire former colony of Aden, excluding the oil refinery and villages of Al Burayqah and Bi'r Fuqum for the former Democratic Yemen, and six main towns for the former Yemen.

SOURCE: United Nations (1998b: 37–55).

TABLE C-3 Large Cities in the Countries Covered by DHS Surveys in the Panel's Dataset, by Region

	Population *circa* 1990	
Region	1 to 5 Million	Over 5 Million
North Africa	*Egypt*: Giza, Alexandria; *Morocco*: Rabat, Casablanca; *Tunisia*: Tunis	*Egypt*: Cairo
Sub-Saharan Africa	*Cameroon*: Douala; Côte d'Ivoire: Abidjan; *Ghana*: Accra; *Kenya*: Nairobi; *Mozambique*: Maputo; *Nigeria*: Ibadan; *Senegal*: Dakar; *Sudan*: Omdurman, Khartoum; *Tanzania*: Dar es Salaam; *Zimbabwe*: Harare	*Nigeria*: Lagos
Southeast Asia	*Indonesia*: Palembang, Tangerang, Medan, Surabaya, Bandung; *Philippines*: Quezon City	*Indonesia*: Jakarta; *Philippines*: Manila; *Thailand*: Bangkok
South, Central, West Asia	*Bangladesh*: Chittagong; *India*: Ludhiana, Varanasi, Kalyan, Visakhapatnam, Bhopal, Ulhasnagar, Madurai, Patna, Coimbatore, Indore, Vadodara, Kochi, Surat, Jaipur, Lucknow, Nagercoil, Napur, Kanpur, Pune, Ahmedabad, Bangalore, Hyderabad; *Kazakhstan*: Almaty; *Pakistan*: Multan, Rawalpindi, Peshawar, Gujranwala, Faisalabad, Lahore; *Turkey*: Konya, Izmir, Ankara; *Uzbekistan*: Tashkent	*Bangladesh*: Dhaka; *India*: Madras, Delhi, Calcutta, Mumbai; *Pakistan*: Karachi; *Turkey*: Istanbul
Latin America	*Bolivia*: La Paz; *Brazil*: Santos, Belém, Campinas, Nova Iguaçu, Brasilia, Curitiba, Fortaleza, Salvador, Recife, Porto Alegre, Belo Horizonte; *Colombia*: Barranquilla, Cali, Medellín, Santa Fe de Bogota; *Dominican Republic*: Santo Domingo; *Ecuador*: Quito, Guayaquil; *El Salvador*: San Salvador; *Guatemala*: Guatemala City; *Haiti*: Port-au-Prince; *Mexico*: Ecatepec, Netzahualcoyotl, Puebla de Zaragoza, Monterrey, Guadalajara,	*Brazil*: Rio de Janeiro, São Paulo; *Mexico*: Mexico City; *Peru*: Lima

D

United Nations
Estimates and Projections

The urban/rural growth rate difference, or $URGD$, is the centerpiece of the method developed by the United Nations Population Division to estimate and project urban populations. In its initial formulation, however, the United Nations method did not exploit the full implications of equation (B.7) in Appendix B. Here we first discuss the extrapolation method as it was presented by the United Nations (1974: 29), and then show how the refinements later introduced by the United Nations (1980: 10–11) exploited the equation.

With data at two points in time, say, $t-1$ and t, the urban/rural growth rate difference can be approximated by

$$URGD_{t-1} = \ln \frac{U_t}{R_t} - \ln \frac{U_{t-1}}{R_{t-1}}.$$

Taking the growth rate difference to be constant at $URGD = d$ and expressing the urban/rural balance in t as a function of a base year balance, we may write

$$\frac{U_t}{R_t} = \frac{U_0}{R_0} e^{dt}.$$

To convert the urban/rural balance at time t into an expression for the level of urbanization, we make use of the relation

$$P_{u,t} = \frac{U_t/R_t}{1 + U_t/R_t},$$

and obtain, after substitution,

$$P_{u,t} = \frac{(U_0/R_0)e^{dt}}{1 + (U_0/R_0)e^{dt}}.$$

495

With $\alpha_0 \equiv \ln (U_0/R_0)$, the level of urbanization can be written in a standard logit form,

$$P_{u,t} = \frac{e^{\alpha_0+d\cdot t}}{1 + e^{\alpha_0+d\cdot t}}. \tag{D.1}$$

This is the essence of the so-called "United Nations method" for estimating the level of urbanization from data on a country's urban and rural populations at two points in time.[1]

In the format of *World Urbanization Prospects*, estimates (and projections) are published for 5-year intervals beginning in 1950. To produce these estimates, the United Nations uses equation (D.1) to interpolate between censuses and to provide reasonable guesses of urban proportions between 1950 and the first national census available after that date (United Nations, 1998b: 33).

The weak point of the United Nations method emerges when it is employed to generate forward projections of urbanization levels. The method assumes constancy in the $URGD$, and this is an untenable assumption in medium- and long-term projections. The simple analytic model of Appendix B shows that, with other things held constant, the $URGD$ should decline with urbanization. Referring to equation (B.7), we see that as the urban/rural balance U_{t-1}/R_{t-1} rises, a reduction in the growth rate difference must result, except in the unlikely case in which both $m_{r,u}$ and $m_{u,r}$ are zero. Noting this, the United Nations (1980: 10–11) sought and found in the empirical record supporting evidence for $URGD$ decline.

Since 1980, therefore, the United Nations has incorporated in its projections a function that ensures a progressive decline in growth rate differences over the course of each country's projection. The United Nations (1998b: 33–4) gives a concise summary of the function, which is based on a simple regression model estimated on data from all countries, whether developing or developed, with more than 2 million inhabitants in 1995 (a total of 113 countries). The function has the effect of slowing the projected rate at which countries with high levels of urbanization approach the upper limit of unity, but it also induces somewhat faster projected urbanization for countries with low levels of urbanization (United Nations, 1980: 11). Note also that whereas the United Nations *estimates* of urban population are based only on country-specific census data, the *projections* of urban population use both country-specific and cross-country data, with the latter including developed as well as developing countries.

The United Nations method for estimating and projecting the population of individual cities is, in broad outline, little more than an application of the $URGD$ method to different data. Rather than working with the urban/rural balance U_t/R_t, however, the method considers a city's population in relation to the national total less the population of the city in question.[2] Let i denote the city whose population

---

[1] Note that the maximum urbanization level implied by the equation is unity.

[2] The approach is a revised version of a method set forth earlier by the United Nations (1974), in which each city's population was examined in relation to the total *urban* population of the country,

is being estimated and projected, and let $U_{i,t}$ be its population in year t. The estimation exercise for city i begins with

$$\frac{U_{i,t}}{P_t - U_{i,t}},\tag{D.2}$$

and the population of city i is then estimated from the differences in growth rates of numerator and denominator found in the most recently available intercensal period. The method is applied independently, city by city within a country, to all those cities whose populations are to be estimated (United Nations 1980: 44–47, 1998b: 35).

As is the case when urban totals are projected, the projections of city population must rely upon additional research judgments. The United Nations (1980) introduced a method for keeping the projected growth rates of large cities within reasonable bounds. In this study, the United Nations noted a U-shaped relationship between city size and city growth rates, with the highest growth rates evident in small (under 500,000 population) and very large (over 4 million population) cities. At the time of the study, however, there were relatively few very large cities in developing countries, and the United Nations concluded that the relationship between city size and growth rates was predominantly negative. City size was found to be only a weak predictor of city growth, however, with the raw correlation between city growth rates and the log of city size being only -0.083. The United Nations (1998b: 36) revisited the issue, again using both developed and developing countries, and confirmed what had been seen earlier: a weakly negative relationship between city size and growth.[3]

Although mindful of the thin empirical justification, the United Nations has judged it sensible to embed a negative relationship between city size and growth in its city population projections. As explained by the United Nations (1998b), the method relies upon the results of a cross-country regression, estimated using the sample of 113 developed and developing countries described above (which contains some 1,982 cities). The dependent variable of the regression is the difference in growth rates between the city and the country's total *urban* population (rather than the total population used in the denominator of equation (D.2)); the explanatory variable is the log of initial city size. This regression produces a predicted value for the city–urban growth rate difference given the size of the city.

---

rather than the national total. The growth rate of city i is of course linked to the growth rate of the country's urban population—the linkage is obvious in countries where the urban sector is dominated by a few large cities. Hence in the approach favored by the United Nations (1974: 46–47), the city projections were to be made iteratively, beginning with the country's largest city and the projected urban total, and at each subsequent step removing from the denominator of the equation (an expression analogous to equation (D.2)) those cities whose populations had already been projected.

[3] In view of this low bivariate correlation, it is surprising that in the multivariate regressions reported by Preston (1979: Table 2) and Brockerhoff (1999: Table 4), where one might have expected a weak city size effect to disappear altogether, city size remains negatively and significantly associated with the rate of city growth.

Consider a projection of the population of city i in year t, which relies on the size projected for that city in year $t - 1$. The projection for t relies in large part on the $URGD$ for city i in the most recent intercensal period, but the projected value is modified to reflect the regression equation described above, which is multiplied by a year-specific weight. The sequence of weights is chosen so as to force the projected city–urban growth difference toward the relationship implied by the regression equation. The United Nations (1980: 45–47) gives a lucid account of this procedure.

We would not want to leave the impression that these city estimates and projections are little more than a mechanical extrapolation of assumptions. United Nations researchers have long recognized the possibility of errors and have attempted to take them into account. The United Nations (1974: 45, 48) warned of the possibility of considerable error if the city projection method were to be applied mechanically and urged that the results of the exercise be carefully scrutinized. Recently, the United Nations (1998b: 36) conceded that, even with a dampening function in place, when the city population projections are aggregated to the country level, they can show a tendency to grow more rapidly than the country's total projected urban population. This is not, in itself, evidence of an inconsistency between the two types of projections—recall that small urban areas do not usually have their populations estimated and projected. But care must obviously be taken to ensure that the total of the projected city populations does not exceed the total projected for all urban areas.

When the aggregate of the city-specific projections happens to grow more rapidly than the projected urban total (the United Nations, 1998b: 36, suggests that this situation is common), yet another adjustment is applied to bring the projected rates of city growth more in line with that of the urban total. Each city's growth rate is reduced by the same amount in such a way that, over the full course of a projection, the projected city total can never exceed the projected urban total. Finally, additional adjustments are made in cases of negative estimated or projected city growth rates; in the final adjusted estimates and projections, such negative growth rates are generally replaced by zero growth rates (or so it appears, to judge from the United Nations, 1998b: 36).

The result of all this is a complicated algorithm whose success in estimating and projecting city populations is far from being assured. Although the United Nations has been careful to describe the main features of the methods it applies, it has not fully developed the demographic justification for its projection adjustments, nor has it presented a clear rationale for commingling developed- and developing-country population data in these projections. The consequence is that the United Nations' city population projections are linked across countries and over time in ways that are difficult to defend. Criticisms of this nature can also be leveled at the projections of total urban populations, although where these projections are concerned, the adjustments are fewer and somewhat better justified.

E

Measuring Relative Poverty with DHS Data

This appendix briefly describes how the panel defined urban poverty for the purposes of its DHS analyses, leaving a more complete account to Hewett and Montgomery (2001). Recall that in the DHS program, no information is collected on incomes or consumption expenditures, the two variables commonly used to measure household standards of living. However, a few other items are collected that can serve as crude proxy measures of living standards. We can distinguish three categories of such items: the ownership of various consumer durables; descriptors of the quality of housing; and measures of access to services, such as water supply and electricity. Of the three, we limit attention to the consumer durables and housing measures. This is because we want to explore whether poverty is associated with a lack of access to public services, and with that goal in mind, poverty cannot be defined in terms of these same services. The items used in the panel's index are ownership of a refrigerator, television, radio, bicycle, motorcycle, or car; the number of sleeping rooms in the dwelling; and whether its floor is of a finished material. Montgomery, Gragnolati, Burke, and Paredes (2000) and Filmer and Pritchett (2001) discuss the performance of such proxies as measures of living standards.

Using these durables and housing quality items, we proceeded to define poverty in *relative* terms. We carried out a principal components analysis—a method not unlike factor analysis—to extract from the DHS indicators a single score that could be interpreted as an index of the household's standard of living. (Hewett and Montgomery, 2001, compare results from confirmatory factor analysis with those from principal components analysis and find little empirical difference between them.) For each DHS survey, we classified as "relatively poor" those urban households whose index scores fell into the lowest quartile of the urban scores for that survey. The same approach was used to characterize rural households.

This emphasis on the relative aspect of poverty was all but forced upon us by the nature of the data collected in the DHS surveys. The proxy measures form a heterogenous group and are not directly comparable to measures of income or consumption. These data do not provide the necessary raw materials for a defensible measure of absolute poverty. Furthermore, ownership of consumer durables differs so greatly between urban and rural settings that to form one index common to both settings might well be misleading. Having decided to estimate separate indices for urban and rural households, we were left with little alternative but to rank households within their sectors of residence. One advantage of such sector-specific relative poverty measures is that they retain their meaning when we make comparisons across countries at different levels of income per capita, whereas absolute poverty measures would be too closely associated with national income per capita to allow for meaningful comparisons.

Unfortunately, the durables and housing measures are not always available and consistently defined in all DHS surveys. In Round 1 of the DHS program, questions on these measures were asked only of households that happened to have in residence a woman of reproductive age. Hence for the 27 DHS surveys in this round, the data gathered are not representative of the general population of households. The situation changed in Rounds 2 and 3 of the DHS program, when such information began to be collected for all households. Even in these rounds, however, the availability of any particular item in a survey is not guaranteed. The problem is compounded by differences in the coding schemes across surveys and by the lack of variation of some items in particular countries or sectors. The durables and housing measures that can be used to construct an index will therefore vary from one country to another, and within countries from urban to rural areas.

Although the panel's intention had been to explore rural differences in relative living standards as well as urban, we found that the DHS-based indices could not always identify a lowest quartile of rural households. This is especially so in very poor countries, where many households lack most or all of the consumer durables items. Further research on this front is needed, but to pursue the issue of rural diversity in any greater depth would have led the panel away from its main priorities.

Tables E-1 and E-2 (mentioned in Chapter 5) shed light on the likelihood of (relative) poverty and access to services for households containing a woman who is a recent migrant, by comparison with other households.

TABLE E-1 Urban Migrant–Nonmigrant Differences in Poverty and Access to Services, All Recent Migrants, by Region

DHS Surveys in Region	Relatively Poor	Access to		
		Piped or In-home Water	Flush Toilet	Electricity
	Migrant Proportion Less Nonmigrant Proportion			
North Africa	0.015	0.037	0.011	−0.016
Sub-Saharan Africa	0.009	0.029	0.042	0.025
Southeast Asia	0.035	0.036	0.056	0.042
South, Central, West Asia	0.014	0.035	0.042	0.062
Latin America	0.054	−0.018	0.001	−0.015
TOTAL	0.022	0.021	0.031	0.023
	Number of Surveys and Significance			
North Africa				
Surveys	6	3	2	1
Significant	1	1	0	0
Significant migrant disadvantage	1	0	0	0
Sub-Saharan Africa				
Surveys	39	36	33	35
Significant	8	13	16	6
Significant migrant disadvantage	5	2	1	1
Southeast Asia				
Surveys	4	4	3	3
Significant	1	0	2	1
Significant migrant disadvantage	1	0	0	0
South, Central, West Asia				
Surveys	11	9	10	6
Significant	5	4	4	4
Significant migrant disadvantage	2	0	1	0
Latin America				
Surveys	18	14	16	9
Significant	10	3	3	3
Significant migrant disadvantage	10	3	1	3
TOTALS				
Surveys	78	66	64	54
Significant	25	21	25	14
Significant migrant disadvantage	19	5	3	4

NOTE: Estimates and tests from probit models, adjusted for city size and woman's age.

TABLE E-2 Urban Migrant–Nonmigrant Differences in Poverty and Access to Services, by Type of Origin Area and Region

DHS Surveys in Region	Relatively Poor	Access to Piped or In-home Water	Flush Toilet	Electricity
North Africa				
Surveys	6	3	2	1
Disadvantage, city origin	0	0	0	0
Disadvantage, town origin	0	0	0	0
Disadvantage, rural origin	5	0	0	0
Sub-Saharan Africa				
Surveys	33	32	29	31
Disadvantage, city origin	1	1	0	0
Disadvantage, town origin	2	0	0	1
Disadvantage, rural origin	11	9	11	11
Southeast Asia				
Surveys	4	4	3	3
Disadvantage, city origin	1	0	0	0
Disadvantage, town origin	2	0	0	0
Disadvantage, rural origin	2	0	0	0
South, Central, West Asia				
Surveys	7	5	7	3
Disadvantage, city origin	1	0	0	0
Disadvantage, town origin	0	0	0	0
Disadvantage, rural origin	4	0	2	0
Latin America				
Surveys	15	12	13	7
Disadvantage, city origin	2	1	0	0
Disadvantage, town origin	6	0	1	1
Disadvantage, rural origin	11	5	7	4
TOTALS				
Surveys	65	56	54	45
Disadvantage, city origin	5	2	0	0
Disadvantage, town origin	10	0	1	2
Disadvantage, rural origin	33	14	20	15

NOTE: Estimates and tests from probit models, adjusted for city size and woman's age.

F

Recommendations for the Demographic and Health Surveys

Definition of urban The First Country Report that accompanies the release of each DHS survey should clearly state what the term "urban" means in the context of the survey. This would be particularly helpful for researchers concerned about the definition of towns. Even if the defining criteria are the same as those used by the national statistical office—as the panel suspects they usually are—the definition should be prominently displayed in the report. It would also be helpful to know how the answers given by respondents—say, to a question on place of previous residence—are converted into the urban classifications used in the published data. Remarkably little of this basic information can be found in the DHS reports.

City size categories Current DHS practice in reporting city size categories must be revised. The current practice is to define "large and capital cities" as those cities of 1 million population and above, leaving a broad residual category of "small cities," which includes every city of between 50,000 and 1 million population. The smallest urban units, "towns," are those whose population is below 50,000 but that meet country-specific criteria for defining a locality as urban. This coding yields too little information on the range and variety of urban locations. At a minimum, the number of city size classes used in the standard DHS location variables should be increased. If it is feasible to do so, these city size codings should be applied throughout each survey in, for example, questions referring to childhood and other previous residences.

City population sizes The population sizes of all cities of 100,000 and above should be listed, city by city, in the First Country Report, organized according to the most disaggregated regional classification given in the dataset.

503

Ideally, the population counts would be the most recent available to the national statistics office; a second-best solution would be to report the city populations given in Table 8 of the United Nations *Demographic Yearbook* or the appropriate table of *World Urbanization Prospects*.

Confidentiality: Two levels of access Until recently, the DHS program did not release detailed geographic identifiers, evidently out of a desire to protect the confidentiality of the survey respondents. An authorization mechanism should be developed that would allow researchers to apply for permission to use geographically detailed identifiers for earlier DHS surveys, which are not covered in the new system. This mechanism might take the form of a two-level permission system whereby:

- Some authorized researchers would have access to a data file linking sampling cluster codes to city names, thus permitting use of complementary city-level data in their analyses.

- Other authorized researchers would have access to a more detailed data file linking sampling cluster codes to geographic information system (GIS) codes, thus permitting use of both city-level and neighborhood-level data.

Migration status for all women If possible, the household questionnaire should elicit the migration status of *all* women in the household, not just those of reproductive age who are selected for individual interviews.

Migration status for men If possible, the household questionnaire should elicit the migration status of *all men* as well.

Duration in current residence For women who participate in individual interviews, duration of residence in the current location should be categorized more clearly. For migrants, duration of residence is required to properly allocate conceptions and births between current and former residences and likewise to apportion risks of child death. Ideally, information would be provided on the month of the most recent move in the 5 years before the survey. Presumably this information could be gathered even in cases in which it is not feasible to collect a full migration calendar.

Water supply For urban residents, data on access to drinking water need to be supplemented with information on the variability of water supply. Weekly or biweekly recall periods would probably be feasible. Questions should also be included on the time (i.e., waiting to use a well) and money costs of water supply.

Private access to sanitation Some countries include questions on private access to pit toilets and latrines, but this is definitely not the norm. Every effort should be made to include such questions in the standard survey and to supplement them with questions on the time (i.e., waiting) and money costs of access to public or private latrines.

Electricity For urban residents, data on access to electricity need to be supplemented with information on the variability and money costs of supply. Weekly and biweekly recall periods would appear to be feasible.

Reproductive health services As discussed in Chapter 6, urban populations make far greater use of private-sector sources of reproductive health services than do rural populations. The DHS program should consider how to expand its measures of knowledge and access to include more information on private-sector sources of family planning and other reproductive health services. The time and money costs of access should also be included. It may prove useful as well to inquire into the location of services vis-à-vis place of work.

Urban community modules At present, DHS community surveys and inventories of public services and clinics are fielded mainly in rural communities. Urban communities and neighborhoods are more difficult to define than rural, and some believe that urban communities are so much better supplied with reproductive health (and other) services that there is little to be gained from fielding urban community surveys. Yet situation analyses—as shown in Chapter 6—indicate that neither access to services nor service quality should be assumed to be superior in urban as compared with rural areas. Hence the panel urges the DHS program to begin to field urban community modules, working on an experimental basis in selected cities or countries, to gain experience in the construction of meaningful assessments for these communities.

Biographical Sketches of
Panel Members and Staff

Mark R. Montgomery (*Cochair*) is professor of economics at the State University of New York, Stony Brook, and senior associate at the Population Council. He has also served as senior fellow in the Department of Geography and Planning at the University of Lagos, Nigeria, and as assistant professor at the Office of Population Research, Princeton University. He was a member of the National Research Council's (NRC) Committee on Population and has served on numerous other NRC committees. He participated in a Committee on Population study on reproductive health in developing countries and an Institute of Medicine study on unintended pregnancies. His research includes analyses of social networks and diffusion processes in Africa and Asia; research on social learning, mortality, and children's schooling; and research on the link between urban growth and economic growth (for the 1986 National Academy of Sciences report, *Population Growth and Economic Development: Policy Questions*). He earned a B.A. degree from the University of North Carolina and a Ph.D. in economics from the University of Michigan.

Richard Stren (*Cochair*) is professor of political science at the University of Toronto and former director of the Centre for Urban and Community Studies. Over the past 35 years he has carried out extensive research on African cities, having done fieldwork in Nairobi, Mombasa, Dar es Salaam, Abidjan, and Makurdi. During the 1990s he traveled extensively within Latin America. His main research areas are urban politics in the developing world and comparative public administration. His major publications include *Housing the Urban Poor in Africa, African Cities in Crisis, Sustainable Cities, An Urban Problematique, Socially Sustainable Cities,* and *The Challenge of Urban Government: Policies and Practices.* A forthcoming book (written with Patricia McCarney) is entitled *Urban Governance in the Developing World: Innovations and Discontinuities* (to be published by the Woodrow Wilson Center and the Johns Hopkins University Press). For 8 years he coordinated the Global Urban Research Initiative undertaken at the University of Toronto with support from the Ford Foundation. He received his B.A. in economics at the University of Toronto and his M.A. and Ph.D. in political science from the University of California at Berkeley.

Charles Becker is research professor of economics and director of the American Economic Association's Summer Minority Program at the University of Colorado (Denver), and a research associate with the Population Program in the Institute of Behavioral Science at the University of Colorado (Boulder). Dr. Becker also serves as a senior advisor to the Kazakhtstan Actuarial Center. For 7 years he served as president of the Economics Institute in Boulder, Colorado. He has published widely on issues in economic development, urbanization, income distribution, and demographic and economic change in the former Soviet Union. Dr. Becker is the author of several books on urban development including *Studies in Indian Urban Development* (with Edwin Mills, published by Oxford University Press in 1986), *Indian Urbanization and Economic Growth Since 1960* (with Edwin Mills and Jeffrey Williamson, published by the Johns Hopkins University Press in 1992), and *Beyond Urban Bias: African Cities in an Age of Structural Adjustment* (with Andrew Hamer and Andrew Morrison, published by Heinemann and James Currey Ltd. in 1994). He is currently working on demoeconomic modeling, forecasting of pension systems, and forecasting of interregional migration in Central Asia.

Ellen M. Brennan-Galvin is a visiting fellow at Yale University and a consultant for the RAND Corporation. During 2001–2002 she was a Fellow at the Woodrow Wilson International Center for Scholars in Washington, D.C. She previously was chief of the Population Policy Section of the United Nations Population Division. For more than 25 years, Dr. Brennan-Galvin has conducted research on urbanization and urban environmental issues. She is the author of more than a dozen case studies on megacities, published by the United Nations. In addition, she has been in charge of numerous research projects in such areas as reproductive health and rights, abortion law and policies, HIV/AIDS, and international migration policies. For the National Academy of Sciences, she is currently a member of the Committee on Population and served as a member of the Committee on the Geographic Foundation for Agenda 21. She also served as a member of the substantive secretariat at the International Conference on Population and Development (Cairo, 1994), participating in the drafting of the Programme of Action. Dr. Brennan-Galvin is a Phi Beta Kappa graduate of Smith College; holds an M.A. and a Ph.D. from Columbia University; and was a Population Council Fellow, studying demography at the Office of Population Research, Princeton University.

Martin Brockerhoff was an associate in the Policy Research Division of the Population Council in New York at the time he served on the panel. Previously he served as a population and health program officer at the U.S. Agency for International Development. Dr. Brockerhoff has worked on a broad array of demographic issues, mainly in sub-Saharan Africa. His research has focused on urban health and urban poverty and has included fieldwork in Kenya. His research has also dealt with the consequences of urban growth, migration, child health in Africa, and the effectiveness of urban family planning programs. His publications include *Child Survival in Big Cities: Are the Poor Disadvantaged?* (published by the Population Council, Policy Research Division, in 1993); *Fertility and Family Planning in African Cities: The Impact of Female Migration* (published by the Population Council, Policy Research Division in 1994); *The Impact of Rural–Urban Migration on Child Survival* (published in *Health Transition Review* 4:127–149, 1994); *The Poverty of Cities in the Developing World* (written with Ellen Brennan, published by the Population Council, Policy Research Division in 1996); *Migration, Sexual Behavior and HIV Diffusion in Kenya* (written with Ann E. Biddlecom, Population Council, Policy Research Division in 1998), *Urban Growth in Developing Countries: A Review of Projections and Predictions* (published by the Population Council, Policy Research Division in 1999); *An Urbanizing World* (*Population Bulletin* 55:3, published in 2000); and *The Urban Demographic Revolution* (published in *Population Today* Aug./Sept. 2000). He holds a B.A. in political science and an M.A. in economics from Columbia University and a Ph.D. in sociology from Brown University. Dr. Brockerhoff resigned from the panel in August 2001.

Barney Cohen is study director for the Panel on Urban Population Dynamics and director of the National Academies' Committee on Population. Since 1992 he has worked on a wide variety of projects at the National Academies. His published volumes include *From Death to Birth: Mortality Decline and Reproductive Change* (edited with Mark R. Montgomery, published by National Academy Press in 1998), *Adolescent Reproductive Behavior in the Developing World* (edited with John Bongaarts, published in a special issue of *Studies in Family Planning* 29(2) in 1998), *Changing Numbers, Changing Needs: American Indian Demography and Public Health* (edited with Gary D. Sandefur and Ronald R. Rindfuss, published by National Academy Press in 1996), *Preventing and Mitigating AIDS in Sub-Saharan Africa: Research and Data Priorities for the Social and Behavioral Sciences* (edited with J. Trussell, published by National Academy Press in 1996), *Population Dynamics in Senegal* (edited with Gilles Pison, Kenneth Hill, and Karen Foote, published by National Academy Press in 1995), and *Social Dynamics of Adolescent Fertility in Sub-Saharan Africa* (edited with Caroline H. Bledsoe, published by National Academy Press in 1993). Dr. Cohen holds a Ph.D. in demography from the University of California, Berkeley, an M.A. in economics from the University of Delaware at Newark and a B.A. in pure mathematics and statistics from the University College of Wales, Aberystwyth, Dyfed.

Michael Cohen is Director of the Graduate Program in International Affairs at the New School University in New York. He was previously senior advisor in environmentally sustainable development in the Latin America and Caribbean Regional Office of the World Bank and on the Faculty of Architecture and Urban Design at the University of Buenos Aires. In September 1999, he joined the International Center for Advanced Studies at New York University for 2 years. Previously Dr. Cohen served as senior advisor and chief of staff in the Office of the Vice-President for Environmentally Sustainable Development at the World Bank's Washington Office. Prior to that he served as chief of the Urban Development Division at the World Bank. He is the author or co-author of many books and articles on urban development. Recent publications include *Preparing for the Urban Future: Global Pressures and Local Forces* (written with B. Ruble, J. Tulchin, and A. Garland; published by Johns Hopkins University Press in 1996); *The Human Face of the Urban Environment* (written with I. Serageldin, published by the World Bank in 1995), *Enabling Sustainable Community Development* (written with I. Serageldin and J. Leitman; published by the World Bank in 1995), and *Argentina in Collapse? The Americas Debate*, (edited with Margarita Gutman, published by The New School in 2003).

Alain Dubresson is professor at the University of Paris-X at Nanterre and director of the postgraduate school "Milieux, cultures et sociétés" since 2001. He also serves on the scientific council for ORSTOM, now IRD (French Research Institute for Development). Between 1990 and 1997 he served as director of the Center for Geographic Studies on Sub-Saharan Africa. Dr. Dubresson is the author of 10 books on the geography and demography of sub-Saharan Africa, including *Villes et industries en Côte d'Ivoire* (published by Karthala in 1990), *Pouvoirs et cités d'Afrique noire* (written with S. Jaglin, published by Karthala in 1993), *Petites et moyennes villes d'Afrique noire* (written with M. Bertrand, published by Karthala in 1997), and *L'Afrique subsaharienne: Une géographie du changement* (written with J-P. Raison, published by Masson in 1998).

Gustavo Garza is a research professor at the Center for Demographic and Urban Development Studies at El Colegio de Mexico. He was director of the center during 1986–1988. He has also served as scientific advisor to the Urban Development Programme of the Federal District Department (1985–1988); associate member of the Centro de Estudios Prospectivos, A.C., Mexico City (1987–present); member of the Board of Editors of the Institute of Geography of the National University (1988–present); member of the Scholarship Selection Committee in the field of urban studies at the National Council for Science and Technology (1980–present); and general director of the Institute for Urban Studies of Nuevo Leon (1994–1995). He has published approximately 190 articles in specialized journals and 18 books on various aspects of urban economics and planning issues in Mexico. Notable works include *The Urban Development of Mexico* (1976), *Industrialization Process of Mexico City* (1985), *Macroeconomic Dynamics of Mexican Cities* (1994), *Local Management in the Metropolitan Area of Monterrey* (1998), *Mexico City at the end of the Second Millennium* (2000), and *Urban Planning in Great Metropolis: Detroit, Monterrey and Toronto* (2003).

Trudy Harpham is professor of urban development and policy at South Bank University, London. She has been one of the main researchers on urbanization and health in developing countries for the last 15 years. Her books on urbanization include *In the Shadow of the City: Health and the Urban Poor in Developing Countries* (written with T. Lusty and P. Vaughan, published by Oxford University

Press in 1988); *Urbanization and Mental Health in Developing Countries* (written with I. Blue, published by Avebury in 1995*); Urban Health in Developing Countries: Progress and Prospects* (written with M. Tanner, published by Earthscan in 1995); and *Healthy Cities in Developing Countries* (written with E. Werna, I. Blue, and G. Goldstein, published by Earthscan in 1998). She is international advisor to the World Health Organization's only Collaborating Centre for Urban Health (in South Africa). An urban geographer by training, her current interest is in urbanization and mental health, particularly with regard to the role of social support and social networks.

Terry McGee is professor emeritus of Asian research. He was formerly director of the Institute of Asian Research, as well as professor of geography at the University of British Columbia, Canada. He has held previous appointments in the University of Malaya, Victoria University (New Zealand), Hong Kong University, and the Research School of Pacific Studies in the Institute of Advanced Studies at Australia National University. He is a fellow of the Australian Academy of Social Sciences and has been president of the Canadian Geographical Association and the Canadian Council of Southeast Asian Studies. During the past 30 years, Dr. McGee has concentrated his research on development studies in the Asia Pacific region with particular attention to the processes of urbanization. He is the author and editor of more than 10 books and 150 articles dealing with these subjects. Among his books are *The Southeast Asian City* (1967*), The Urbanization Process in the Third World* (1971), *Hawkers in Southeast Asian City Planning* (1977), *Theatres of Accumulation* (1985), and *The Mega-Urban Regions of Southeast Asia* (1996).

Caroline Moser is currently senior research associate, Overseas Development Institute, and adjunct professor, New School, New York. From 1990 to 2000 she worked at The World Bank, first in the Urban Development Division, and later as lead specialist for social development in the Latin American Department. Previously she was a lecturer at the London School of Economics, and before that at the Development Planning Unit, University College, London. Her recent research includes participatory urban appraisals of urban violence and exclusion in Colombia, Guatemala, and Jamaica, and research on urban poverty in the context of adjustment in Ecuador, Zambia, Philippines, and Hungary. Dr. Moser received a Ph.D. in social anthropology from Sussex University, a postgraduate diploma from Manchester University, and a B.A. from Durham University. Among the numerous publications for which she has been author, co-author, or editor are *Gender Planning and Development: Theory, Practice and Training* (1993); *Confronting Crisis: A Comparative Study of Household Responses to Poverty and Vulnerability in Four Poor Urban Communities* (1996); *Violence in a Post-Conflict Context: Urban Poor Perceptions from Guatemala* (2000); *Urban Poor Perceptions of Violence and Exclusion in Colombia* (2001); *Gender, Armed Conflict and Political Violence* (2001); *Women, Human Settlement and Housing* (1987).

Holly E. Reed is program officer for the Committee on Population of the National Academies. She also serves as study director for the Roundtable on the Demography of Forced Migration and has written and edited several publications on the demography of displaced persons, including *Forced Migration and Mortality*. Ms. Reed is currently a member of the International Union for the Scientific Study of Population's Working Group on the Demography of Conflict and Violence. She has a B.S. in foreign service and an M.A. in demography from Georgetown University.

Saskia Sassen is Ralph Lewis Professor of Sociology at the University of Chicago and Centennial Visiting Professor at the London School of Economics. She is currently completing her forthcoming book *Denationalization: Territory, Authority and Rights in a Global Digital Age* (to be published by Princeton University Press in 2003), based on her 5-year project on governance and accountability in a global economy. She has also just completed for UNESCO a 5-year project on sustainable human settlement for which she set up a network of researchers and activists in more than 50 countries. Her most recent books are *Guests and Aliens* and the edited *Global Networks, Linked* (published by Routledge in 2002). A new, fully updated edition of *The Global City* was published in 2001. Her books have been translated into 14 languages. She serves on several editorial boards and is an advisor to several international bodies. She is a member of the Council on Foreign Relations and chair of the new Information Technology, International Cooperation and Global Security Committee of the Social Science Research Council.

David Satterthwaite is a senior fellow at the International Institute for Environment and Development and on the teaching staff of the Development Planning Unit, University College, London and the London School of Economics. He has been editor of the journal *Environment and Urbanization* since its foundation in 1989. Most of Dr. Satterthwaite's work since 1979 has been on issues of housing, health, environment, urban development, and rural–urban linkages. He has served as an advisor on urban issues to many international agencies including UNICEF, UN-Habitat, Department of International Development, the World Health Organization, the Swedish International Development Cooperation Agency, the Development Directorate of the European Commission, the United Nations Population Division, United Nations Research Institute for Social Development, ActionAid, WaterAid, and the Brundtland Commission. He is the author or editor of 15 books on various aspects of urban development, including *An Urbanizing World: Global Report on Human Settlements 1996* (published by Oxford University Press), *The Environment for Children* (published by Earthscan Publications in 1996), *Environmental Problems in an Urbanizing World* (written with J. Hardoy and D. Mitlin, published by Earthscan in 2001), *The Poor Die Young: Housing and Health in Third World Cities* (co-edited with J. Hardoy and S. Cairncross, published by Earthscan in 1990), *Squatter Citizen: Life in the Urban Third World* (written with J. Hardoy, published by Earthscan in 1989); and *Urbanization and Its Implications for Child Health* (published by the World Health Organization in 1988).

Pravin Visaria was director of the Institute for Economic Growth in Delhi, India. He worked closely with the Indian government's Planning Commission, Department of Statistics, Office of the Registrar General, and Ministry of Health and Family Welfare. Previously he was professor and director of the Gujarat Institute of Development Research, Ahmedabad. He held positions with the University of Bombay and The World Bank. He published numerous articles and books on mortality, fertility, migration, urbanization, labor force and employment, population projections, censuses and surveys, poverty, and population policy, especially in the Indian context. He also held leadership positions with many important academic and policy organizations, including the Indian Association for the Study of Population, the National Sample Survey Organization of India, and the Gujarat Economic Association. His publications include *The Sex Ratio of the Population of India* (published by the Office of the Registrar General, New Delhi in 1971), *Infant Mortality in India: Differentials and Determinants* (published by Sage in 1988), *Non-Agricultural Employment in India: Trends and Prospects* (published by Sage in 1993), *Contraceptive Use and Fertility in India: A Case Study of Gujarat* (published by Sage in 1995), and *Urbanization in Large Developing Countries* (co-edited) (published by Clarendon Press in 1997). Most recently, he co-edited a volume titled *Urbanization in Large Developing Countries* with Gavin Jones (published by Oxford University Press in 1997). Dr. Visaria passed away in February 2001, and this volume is dedicated to his memory and his many contributions to the field of urban studies.

Michael J. White is professor and chair of the Department of Sociology and a faculty associate for the Population Studies and Training Center at Brown University. He has also served as senior research associate at the Urban Institute and on the faculty of Princeton University. Dr. White works broadly in the field of social demography, with a concentration in population distribution. His current research agenda includes studies of migration and environmental change, urbanization in Ghana, and immigrant adaptation in the United States. Dr. White has been involved in data collection efforts of the Population Studies and Training Center in developing countries, including the Coastal Ghana Population and Environment Survey, the Ethiopian Southern Region Study, and the United Nations Population Fund Migration and Health Study. His publications include *American Neighborhoods and Residential Differentiation* (published by the Russell Sage Foundation in 1987), *Techniques for Estimating Net Migration* (written with D. Bogue and K. Hinze, published by the Chicago Community and Family Study Center in 1982), and *Urban Renewal and the Changing Residential Structure of the City* (published by the Chicago Community and Family Study Center in 1981). Dr. White is a member of the Demographic and Behavioral Sciences review panel, National Institutes of Health. He holds a B.A. in urban studies from Harvard University and a Ph.D. in sociology from the University of Chicago.

Yue-man Yeung is professor of geography, director of the Hong Kong Institute of Asia-Pacific Studies, and head of Shaw College of the Chinese University of Hong Kong. His rich and varied career has spanned teaching, research, international development, and university administration, being divided among Singapore, Canada, and Hong Kong. His wide-ranging research interests have recently focused on China's coastal cities and development, South China, globalization, and Asian cities. He has published 28 books and more than 100 articles and book chapters. Recent books include *Globalization and the World of Large Cities* (written with Fu-chen Lo, published by UNU Press in 1998), *Urban Development in Asia* (published by CUHK in 1998), *Guangdong* (written with David Chu, published by Chinese University Press in 1998), *Fujian* (written with David Chu, published by Chinese University Press in 2000), *Globalization and Networked Societies* (published by University of Hawaii Press in 2000), and *New Challenges for Development and Modernization* (published by Chinese University Press in 2002).

Index

A

Abidjan, 225, 391–394
Abortion rates, 219–220
Absolute poverty, 180–184
  numbers of urban residents living in, 2
  research focused on, 287–288
Access to services, 2, 167–180, 196, 251–255
  decentralization of reproductive health
    services, 251–253
  differences by city size, 172–174
  examples of intracity differentials in water
    supply, 178
  factors blocking, 253–254
  improving the quality and accessibility of
    care, 253–254
  measures of in the demographic and health
    surveys, 170
  need to improve data systems on, 4
  poverty among the underserved migrants,
    176–177
  services and the poor, 174–176
Accidents, higher urban rates of, 263
Accra, Ghana, 178, 180, 213, 220, 260, 286–287
Adaptation hypothesis, regarding migrants,
  243
Addis Ababa, 231
Adult educational attainment, rural and urban
  areas, 162
Africa
  cities of more than 750,000 population
    in, 100
  colonial background of, 100–101
  marginalized in new global economy,
    101–102
  population doubling in, 12
  population growth in cities and towns of, 3
  urban population change in, 99–102

  urbanization decoupled from
    industrialization, 82
Agency for International Development, 402
Agglomeration economies, 307–312
Aggregate census-based method, 121
AIDS awareness, variation within urban settings
  in, 5
Albania, 66
American Community Survey, 483
Argentina, 95
Arms dealing, 347
Asia
  cities of more than 750,000 population in,
    103
  HIV levels in, 224
  population doubling in, 12
  population growth in cities and towns of, 3
  population trends in, 91
  urban population change in, 102–106
  See also Pacific Asia
Asian Development Bank's *Cities Data Book*,
  168
Asian "triangles," 79
Aspatial analysis of poverty, 232–238, 302
Assets, 4, 62, 165
Authority dimension of urban governance,
  390–401

B

Bangalore, 49, 150
Bangalore Urban Poverty Alleviation
  Programme (BUPP), 49
Bangkok, 19, 357–362, 481
  characterization of main zones in the
    extended metropolitan region of,
    362

515

growth rate in, 64
HIV levels in, 224–225
migrants to, 329
Bangladesh
    cities abandoned by public sector services
        in, 254
    intraurban differences in infant mortality
        rates in, 285
    urban boundaries in, 317
Barriers to mobility, 333–337
Basic services, 165
    in which urban environments differ from
        rural, 70
Beijing, 84
Beijing-Seoul-Tokyo (BESETO), 78
Belo Horizonte, Brazil, 378
"Better Cities Network of East and South-East
    Asian Cities," 402
Bhilwara, India, 179
Birth attendance, variation within urban settings
    in, 5
Botswana, 213
    HIV in, 222
Boundaries
    city, 136–137
    jurisdictional conflicts, 2
Brasília, 140
Brazil, 340–341
    declining growth rates experienced by
        largest cities in, 120
    foreign direct investment in, 78
    impact of better education in, 321
    Northeastern, child mortality rates in, 39
    "participatory budgeting" in, 376–378
    population pyramid for urban, 129
    residual earnings variance in Brazil's largest
        cities, 341
    rising inequalities in urban incomes, 7
    urban relative to rural age composition of
        men and women in, 129
Breastfeeding, 212n
"Bridging," role of social networks, 48
Broken windows theory, 40
Buenos Aires, 96, 158, 285, 337
    gated communities, 159
Bulawayo, Zimbabwe, 240, 242
BUPP. *See* Bangalore Urban Poverty Alleviation
    Programme

C

Cairo, 14, 68, 69, 99, 136–138, 203
Calcutta, 105, 224
Cambodia, 48
Cameroon, 251
Cancers, higher urban rates of, 263
Capacity dimension in urban governance, 7–8,
    363–371
Cape Town, South Africa, 17, 245
Capital formation, 352
Cardiovascular disease, 263
Caribbean
    cities of more than 750,000 population in, 97
    HIV levels in, 224
Cartagena, Colombia, 185
CBOs. *See* Community-based organizations
CBSA. *See* Core-based statistical area
    classification
Census-based method
    aggregate, 121
    problem of intervals, 355
Centralized model, of urban governance, 361,
    407
Chandigarh, India, 194
Chiang Mai, Thailand, 246
"Chicago School," 30
Child mortality, 127, 278–282, 295–297
"Child quality," 34–35
Child trafficking, 347
Children's health, 272–278, 296
Children's lives, 188–195
China, 337–338, 343–344
    changing urban definitions in, 134
    Cultural Revolution in, 145, 307
    family planning needs in, 245
    foreign direct investment in, 78
    household registration system in, 327
    impact of national economic restructuring
        on rural populations near cities, 63
    a predominantly rural country, 104
    rising inequalities in urban incomes, 7,
        183–184
    urban boundaries in, 317
Chronic "lifestyle" diseases, 268–269
Circular migration, 225
Cities
    amid global forces, 76–81
    characteristics of, 10

concentration of social and economic
resources in, 2
emerging regional networks, 78–79
financial services and foreign direct
investment, 77–78
forced to redefine their comparative
advantages, 1
growth rates in large versus small, 15
markets and volatility, 78, 80
mortality and morbidity in, 5–6, 22–23,
259–299
networks in, 75
optimal size, 56n
with over a million residents, 84
problems of poorest, 370
reinventing themselves, 77
their regions, and the international
economy, 23–25
world cities, 80–81
See also individual cities and countries
Cities Data Book project, 167–168
City boundaries, 136–137
City growth from migration and natural increase,
112–114
City-level population data, 135–141
Brasília, 140
city boundaries, 136–137
Kitwe, Zambia, 141
Niamey, Niger, 140
São Paulo, 139
Shubra-El-Khema, 138
United Nations population estimates,
138–141
City size categories, 489
City systems and city-regions, 58–64
Clustering, 36–37
advantages of, 309
Cobb-Douglas production function, 311n
Cochabamba, Bolivia, 245
Collective socialization, 37
Colombia, 252
Commercial sex work, 225
Common resources, 36–37
Communicable diseases, 73
greater vulnerability of city dwellers to, 259
impact on children's health, 264
new and reemergent, 269–270
Community-based organizations (CBOs), 49

Community dynamics, social capital and, 41–42
Completed schooling for adults, in rural and
urban areas, 161, 163
Comprehensive model, of urban governance,
361, 405–407
"Compression," of social relationships, 45
"Computable general equilibrium" model, 304
Congestion, 2
Contraceptive use, 5, 214–216, 219
Core-based statistical area (CBSA)
classification, 482–483
Coronary heart disease, 263
Côte d'Ivoire, 160
Countries covered by DHS surveys, 490
Crime rates, 56
"Crisis-led" fertility, 226, 230
Cultural conflict, 38
Cultural Revolution, 145
Cumulative measures, 112
Currencies, world markets in, 80

D

Dakar, 205
Dakshinpuri, India, 240, 242
DALY. *See* Disability-adjusted life year
predictions
Dar es Salaam, Tanzania, 178, 186, 269
Data systems
need to computerize, 147, 356
need to improve, 4
Decentralization, 64–66, 95, 390, 408, 411
Deconcentration, 313–317
Definition and measurement issues, 128–141
Delhi, 105
Demand for manufactured goods and services,
income elasticity of, 302
Democratization, 95
Demographic and Health Surveys (DHS), 27, 94,
108, 120, 122–128, 152, 154, 156, 163,
177–179, 200, 227, 229, 488–494, 505
on children's health needs, 261, 272,
277–279, 282
limitations of, 109, 411, 503
linking to United Nations city data, 487–494
measuring relative urban poverty with data
from, 499–502
need for spatial identifiers for all surveys, 4

recommendations for, 503–505
refining urban indicators in, 416–417
showing declines in both urban and rural
    mortality, 6
Demographic behavior theory, 34–40
social learning via social networks, 35–36
Demographic features of the urban transition,
    81–95
Demographic transformation, 11–17
Demographic transition theory, 21
Demographic Yearbooks, 26–27, 109, 131,
    135–139, 412, 415, 487, 504
Depression, 267
Desakota zones, 61–62, 67
Deutsche Gesellschaft für Technische
    Zusammenarbeit (GTZ), 402
Dhaka, Bangladesh, 5, 22, 105, 206, 254, 285
DHS. *See* Demographic and Health Surveys
Diffusion, 5
Disability-adjusted life year (DALY)
    predictions, 264–266, 269
Disease spectrum, 262–272, 297
chronic "lifestyle" diseases, 268–269
injuries, 265–267
mental health, 267–268
new and reemergent communicable diseases,
    269–270
the urban penalty, 270–272
See also Communicable diseases
Diseconomies of proximity, 56
Disruption hypothesis, regarding migrants, 243
Diversity, 204, 315
ability of local governments to cope with, 8
dimension in urban governance, 378–384
in economic interactions, 51–57
effects of, 54
in Manila, 383–384
in Rio de Janeiro, 380–381
in São Paulo, 381–383
spatial theories of, 20, 52–56
See also Socioeconomic diversity and
    inequality
Doi Moi program, 244
Drinking water, measures of access to, 170
Drug trafficking, 347

E

Earnings inequality case studies, 340–343
Brazil, 340–341

China, 343
Taiwan, 342–343
East Asia, 88, 94n
Economic crises, 66, 230, 282–283
in cities of Kazakhstan, 283
fertility transitions and, 226–231
Economic resources, concentrated in cities, 2
"Ecumenopolis." *See* Beijing-Seoul-Tokyo
Education, 4, 196–197, 248–249
dropout rates, 350
"Efficiency wage" models, 325n
Electricity, 4, 63, 170, 505
Elite neighborhoods, 19
Employment
    See Urban labor markets
EMRs. *See* Extended metropolitan regions
Engel's law, 302–304
Environmental hazards, 4, 7, 262
Epidemics, 282–283
Export Group Report, 183
Extended metropolitan regions (EMRs),
    19
External economies, of proximity, 54–56

F

Faisalabad, Pakistan, 254
Families
    embedded in social contexts, 29
    reproductive strategies of, 256
Family planning programs
    private sector in, 254–255
    urban, 107
Family Planning Service Expansion and
    Technical Support (SEATS) project,
    253
FDI. *See* Foreign direct investment
Fertility and reproductive health, 4–5, 20–22,
    199–258
access to services, 257–258
contraception, 214–216
fertility behavior and trends, 256
fertility transitions and economic crises,
    226–231
HIV/AIDS, 222–226
maternal care, 221–222
migrants, 242–246
sexual unions and first marriage, 212–214
social and economic contexts, 201–206

total fertility rates in rural and urban areas, 210

unmet need for contraception and unintended fertility, 216–221

urban adolescents, 247–251

the urban dimension, 200–209

the urban poor, 231–242

urban service delivery, 251–255

Fertility declines

mortality decline following, 94–95

urbanization as a precondition for, 21

Financial resources, 371–378

Financial services, 8, 77–78

Fixed-rates model, 484

"Floating" population, 134, 177

Floods, 187

Foreign direct investment (FDI), 77–78, 305n, 344–346

Formal institutions, social capital in, 387

Formal sector

versus informal sector, 289

jobs in, 301

wages in, 324

For-profit services, versus not-for-profit, 289

Fragmented model, of urban governance, 361, 405–407

G

Geocoded data, 8

Geographic information systems (GIS), 109–110, 147–151, 414, 504

GEOPOLIS database, 134

Ghana, 36, 130, 322

GIS. *See* Geographic information systems

Global Burden of Disease, 269

Global circuits, 1, 24

Global economy, 101–102

Global Report on Human Settlements, 373

Global Urban Indicators Database, 368–369

Globalization, 75–76, 95, 106

Governance. *See* Urban governance

Government Finance Statistics Yearbook, 373

Governments

dimension in which urban environments differ from rural, 70

moving to "governance," 64–67

operating on a territorial basis, 20

pervasive influence of, 74

spatial organization of activities of, 34

Growth

contribution of migration to urban growth, 89–90

natural increase and migration, 89–92

rate of, 485

rural-to-urban migration rates, 90–92

Growth "triangles," 79

GTZ. *See* Deutsche Gesellschaft für Technische Zusammenarbeit (GTZ)

Guayaquil, Ecuador, 178

H

Habitat II, 402

Hanoi, Vietnam, 255

Havana, 220, 373

Hazards. *See* Environmental hazards

Health, 1–2, 22–23, 40–41, 70, 297, 299

See also Communicable diseases; Reproductive health services

Health service provision, 289–295

HIV/AIDS epidemic, 222–226, 282–283

Homicides, 266, 386

Hong Kong, 77, 81n, 94, 102, 338

Household age composition, in rural and urban areas, 131

Household registration system, 327

Household relations, social capital in, 388–390

Household structure, factors disrupting, 194

Housing, 50, 73, 364

HPI. *See* Human Poverty Index

Human capital, 70, 72, 160–163, 196–197

Human Development Report, 164n

Human Poverty Index (HPI), 164n

Hyderabad, 150

I

Ile-Ife, Nigeria, 220

ILO. *See* International Labour Organization

Income, 4, 6, 165

Income elasticity, 302

India, 48, 149–150, 309

Indian Remote Sensing (IRS) satellites, 149

Indonesia, 7, 94, 102, 306, 345, 350

Inequality. *See* Socioeconomic diversity and inequality

Infant mortality rates, 127, 271, 278–282, 295–296
Infectious diseases, 5
Informal economy
    earnings in, 323n
    versus formal sector, 289
    internationalization of, 347
    tiers within, 339
    urban population growth swelling, 334
Informalization of urban labor markets, 331–340
Injuries, 265–267
Inter- and intraurban differentials, 2, 6
"Intergenerational closure," of individual social networks, 41
Intergovernmental transfers, and targeted social assistance, 66
Internal economies, of scale and proximity, 53–54
International Crime Victimization Survey, 385n
International Labour Organization (ILO), 332
International Monetary Fund, 373
International Programs Center, 413
IRS. *See* Indian Remote Sensing satellites

J

Jakarta, Indonesia, 19, 145, 235n
Jordan, 150–151
Jos, Nigeria, 220
Jurisdictional conflicts, 404–405, 408

K

Kaplan-Meier estimator, 278
Karachi, Pakistan, 105, 145, 220, 238, 240, 257
Kazakhstan, 283, 333, 351–352
Kelley-Williamson, 304
Kenya, 36, 321–322
Kinshasa, Zaire, 237
Kitwe, Zambia, 139, 141
Korea, 59, 314
Kuala Lumpur, 77
Kumasi, Ghana, 179
Kuwait, 150
KwaZulu-Natal province, South Africa, 246, 330
Kyrgyzstan, 188, 333, 351

L

Labor force, urban economy and, 6–7, 23–25, 57, 300–354

Lagos, 14, 99, 142
Lahore, Pakistan, 240
"Land invasions," 74
Landslides, 187
Large cities, 84–89
    in the countries covered by DHS surveys, 494
    unique needs of, 16
Larkana, Pakistan, 255
Latin America
    cities of more than 750,000 population in, 97
    HIV levels in, 224
    homicide levels in, 266, 386
    migration rates in, 91
    population doubling in, 12
    population growth in cities and towns of, 3
    social and environmental movements in, 390
    urban growth slowing in, 98
    urban population change in, 96–99
    urbanization in, 12, 87, 95
Lesotho, 292
Ley de Participación Popular, 374, 390
Local participation, in Chinese cities, 399–401
Localization economies, 308–311
"Localization effects," 53n, 54
Location, 29–74
    city systems and city-regions, 58–64
    dimensions in which urban environments differ from rural, 70
    from government to governance, 64–67
    intergovernmental transfers and targeted social assistance, 66
    neighborhoods and demographic behavior theory, 34–40
    neighborhoods and larger structures, 46–49
    new conceptualizations needed, 412
    social capital, 40–42
    spatial segregation, 42–46
    spatial theories of, 52–56
    sustaining diversity in, 51–57
    the urban/rural divide, 67–74
    using multiple data sources to define urbanness in Cairo, 69
Locational price differences and nonfood needs, 180–183
    adjusting poverty rates for geographic differences in prices in the United States, 181

London, 77, 80, 85
Los Angeles, 33, 481

M

Macroeconomic stability, 66
Macropolitan areas, 482
Madras, 150
Mahila Milan, 48, 71, 167
Malaria, 263
Malawi, 224
Malaysia, 94, 102, 149–150
Malnutrition, 263
Manila, 19, 383–384
Manufacturing, advanced economies shifting
    away from, 1
Marriage, 256
Marshall, Alfred, 310
Maternal care, 221–222
    percentage of women with recent births
        attended by physicians or
        nurse/midwives in rural and urban areas,
        221
    percentages of women delivering recent
        births at home, in a public sector
        institution, or in a private-sector in rural
        and urban areas, 222
Maternal mortality rates (MMRs), 241, 263
Megacities, 1, 14–17, 88–89
"Megalopolis," 60
Megapolitan areas, 482
Mental health, 267–268
Metropolitan regions, concepts and definitions
    of, 481–483
Mexico
    calculating production benefits in, 310
    disability-adjusted years of life lost in,
        265
    employment transitions in urban, 335
    foreign direct investment in, 78
    migration in, 122n
    urban share of national economy in, 303
    urban transformation in, 60
    worker mobility in, 333–336
Mexico City, 68, 85, 87, 96, 143, 394–398
    openness of international trade in, 315
    political parties in, 397–398, 403–404
    socioeconomic levels by geostatistical
        areas, 44

    urban subsystem of, 18
    varying levels of income across, 43
Micropolitan areas, 482
Midwives, 290
Migrant shares of urban growth, 111, 114,
    120–121
Migrants, 122–125, 242–246
    permanent versus temporary, 328
    poverty among underserved, 176–177
    pre-arranged employment among, 326–327
    urban migrant-nonmigrant differences in
        poverty and access to services of,
        501–502
Migration, 2
    changes in rural and urban crude birth rates
        and age structure with, 119
    contribution to urban growth, 89–90
    and nature of previous residence, 278–279
    rural-to-urban, contribution to urban growth,
        3, 152, 243
    selectivity hypothesis, disruption hypothesis,
        and adaptation hypothesis, 243
    in the spread of AIDS, 225
    studies of, 7
    and urban age structure, 117–120
    urban-to-rural, in West Africa, 91n
Migration and economic mobility, 322–331
    composition of migrant streams, 327–329
    revisiting the Todaro and Harris-Todaro
        models, 323–327
    urban economic mobility, 329–331
Mixed model, of urban governance, 407
MMRs. *See* Maternal mortality rates
Mongolia, 232
Monterrey, Mexico, 178
Mortality and morbidity in cities, 5–6, 22–23,
    259–299
    boosting the contribution of natural increase
        to urban growth, 3
    child survival and child health, 295–297
    crisis in Russia, social capital and, 41
    crude death rates by neighborhood in
        Accra, 260
    the disease spectrum, 262–272, 297
    distinctive aspects of urban health,
        262
    health service provision and treatment
        seeking, 289–295
    a penalty for the urban poor, 284–289

recent evidence on children's health and
    survival, 272–283
trends over time, 299
the urban health penalty, 297
"Moving to Opportunity" experiment, 50
Mumbai, 85, 238
    federation of low-income groups in, 48
    GIS initiatives in greater, 150
    HIV levels in, 224
    informal jobs in, 333
    urban growth fueled by rural poverty, 105

N

Nairobi Cross-Sectional Slums Survey,
    238–239, 249, 286
Nashville, Tennessee, 45n
Natal, Brazil, 201
National population growth, 116–117, 485
National Slum Dwellers Federation (NSDF), 48,
    71, 167
National statistical systems, 303
Natural disasters, 74
Natural increase, contributing to urban growth, 3
"Natural neighborhoods," 31–32
Neighborhoods, 31–51
    clustering, common resources, and
        contagion, 36–37
    and demographic behavior theory, 34–40
    elite, 19
    federation of low-income groups in Mumbai,
        48
    influence on fertility decisions, 5
    and larger structures, 46–49
    need for data on, 8
    participatory urban poverty programs in
        Bangalore, 49
    services and the physical environment,
        39–40
    social comparisons and subculture conflict,
        38–39
    social learning via social networks, 35–36
Neoliberalism, 365
Neo-Malthusians, 23
Neo-Marxist functionalists, 332n
Nepal, 255
Network effects, 56
    See also Periurban networks; Rural
        networks; Social networks

New York City, 77, 80, 85, 87
Newly industrializing economies (NIEs), 102
NGOs. *See* Nongovernmental organizations
Niamey, Niger, 139–140
NIES. *See* Newly industrializing economies
Nonagricultural occupations, 73
Nonagricultural population of cities and towns
    (NPCT), 134
Nongovernmental organizations (NGOs), 47, 49,
    255
    operating on a territorial basis, 20
    paying attention to street children, 194
    spatial organization of activities of, 34
NPCT. *See* Nonagricultural population of cities
    and towns
NSDF. *See* National Slum Dwellers Federation
Nurse/midwives, proportion of women with
    recent births attended by, 236

O

Obesity, 268–269
Occupational health and safety risks, in urban
    and rural areas, 73
OECD. *See* Organisation for Economic
    Cooperation and Development
Organisation for Economic Cooperation and
    Development (OECD), 145

P

Pacific Asia
    dramatic economic growth in, 102
    formation of "urban corridors" in, 78
    rapid emergence of international orientations
        in, 24
    urbanization accelerating in, 2
Pakistan, 241
"Participatory budgeting," in Brazil, 376–378
"Peace communities," 389
Pecuniary externalities, 51, 308
"People's power" movement, 390
Periurban networks, 36
Permanent migrants, versus temporary, 328
Philippines, 48, 252–253, 372, 390
Phnom Penh, Cambodia, 224
Piped water, advantage enjoyed by large urban
    areas versus small, 4
Planning, barriers to, 355–356
Poisson models, 219n

Poland, workers' movement in, 390
Policy reform, local dynamics of, 408–409
Poorest cities, problems of, 370
Population data, need for adequate and
    comparable, 3–4
Population Division, 4, 82, 109, 132, 153, 172
    World Urbanization Prospects, 26, 109,
        135–139, 142, 152, 414–416, 487, 489,
        496, 504
Population growth, 3
    declining rate of, 11, 89
    estimated and projected, 12, 14
    urban and rural, by region, 83
Port Elizabeth, South Africa, 179
Porto Alegre, Brazil, 377
Poverty, 4, 262
    among underserved migrants, 176–177
    aspatial analysis of, 232–238
    and children's health, 275–277
    comparisons of urban and rural, 183–184
    dealing with, 166–167
    factors intensifying, 194
    spatially concentrated, 232, 238–242
    and well-being, 197
    See also Absolute poverty; Relative urban
        poverty; Urban poverty
Prices, 70, 81
Princeton European Fertility Project, 21
Private access to sanitation, recommendations
    regarding, 504–505
Private medical sources of contraception,
    234
Private providers, 290–291
Private sector, 5, 254–255, 291, 294
Productivity benefits, 309, 310
Projections of urban populations, 141–146
Prostitution, 347
Proximity, 32, 46, 53–54, 71
    diseconomies of, 56
    external economies of, 54–56
    "and high walls," 157
    internal economies of, 53–54
    spatial, 204
Prussian *Kreise*, 21
Public infrastructure, 165
Public services. *See* Access to services;
    Services
Purdah, 206
Pure externalities, 308

Q

Qatar, 148
Quality of care issues, 293–294
"Quantity-quality trade-offs," 51, 204–205, 230
Quxi Road Market for Agricultural and
    Non-staple Products, 400–401

R

Rate of urbanization, 112
Recent evidence on children's health and
    survival, 272–283
    epidemics and economic crises, 282–283
    infant and child survival, 278–282
Reclassification, 89
Reference groups, influence on fertility
    decisions, 5
Referral system issues, 291–292
Regional differences in urban population
    change, 95–106
    Africa, 99–102
    Asia, 102–106
    Latin America, 96–99
Regional networks, 78–79
Regional urban linkages, the Asian "triangles,"
    79
Relative mobility, 330n
Relative urban poverty, 174, 499–500
    measuring with DHS data, 499–502
    predicted enrollment for children by, 190
    urban migrant-nonmigrant differences in
        poverty and access to services of recent
        migrants, 501–502
Remotely sensed data, 8
Reproductive health services
    access to, 257–258
    decentralization of, 5
    defining, 199
    recommendations regarding, 505
Reproductive tract infections (RTIs), 242n
Residual earnings variance
    in Brazil's largest cities, 341
    in Taiwan, 342
"Residual" method, 120–121
Respiratory disease, higher rural rates of,
    263
"Reverse polarization," 98
Rio de Janeiro, 17, 85, 96, 285, 380–381
    HIV levels in, 225

Risk and vulnerability, 184–188
RTIs. *See* Reproductive tract infections
Rural areas
    access to services, 168–172
    AIDS awareness, 237
    children's height for age and weight for
        height at 2 years in, 273–274, 296
    contraceptive use, 216, 217
    infant and child mortality for rural and urban
        areas, 127
    levels of fertility and mortality, 125–128
Rural fertility, 233
Rural growth, rate of, 486
Rural networks, 36
Rural populations, infant mortality estimates for,
    281
Rural-to-urban migration
    contributing to urban growth, 3, 108, 118
    and earnings, 353
    rates of, 90–92
Rural total fertility rates less urban rates by
    region, in economic crises, 229
Rural/urban dichotomies. *See* Urban/rural
    dichotomies
Russia, mortality crisis in, 41
Rwanda, 224

S

Safety nets, 165
San Pedro Sula, Honduras, 264
Sanitary movement, 271
Santiago, Chile, 33–34, 220
    spatial concentration of the elites of, 158
Santo Domingo, 220
São Paulo, 9–10, 14, 17, 24, 60, 61, 87, 96, 139,
    284–285, 333, 334, 381–383
Savings rates, 305–306
Scale
    a defining feature of life in cities, 16
    internal economies of, 53–54
    of urban economy and labor force, 6
School enrollments in urban areas, 188–191
Schooling, 160–163
    advantage enjoyed by large urban areas
        versus small, 4
    economic returns of, 301, 319–322
    impact on contraceptive use, 4
SDI. *See* Shack/Slum Dwellers International

SEATS. *See* Family Planning Service Expansion
    and Technical Support (SEATS) project
Sectoral influences, 304–307
    industrialization and social capital in
        Indonesia, 306
    versus spatial, 302
Security dimension in urban governance,
    384–390
Selectivity hypothesis, regarding migrants,
    243
Self-medication, 290
Seoul, 102
Services
    blocks to delivery of, 252–253
    and the physical environment, 39–40
    provision of better in cities than rural areas,
        196
    public versus private, 289
    recommendations regarding delivery of, 198
    See also Access to services
Sex workers, HIV prevalence among, 224
Sexual networks, urban, 207, 261
Sexual unions, and first marriage, 212–214
Sexually transmitted diseases (STDs), 200–202,
    212, 246, 255, 261, 270
    pharmacists treating, 255
    See also HIV/AIDS epidemic
SEZs. *See* Special Economic Zones
Shack/Slum Dwellers International (SDI), 48
Shanghai, 220, 365–368
Shantou, a Special Economic Zone, 104
Shanty towns, 2
Shelter, 165
Shenzhen, a Special Economic Zone, 77, 104
Shubra-El-Khema, 137–138
Silk industry, 316
Singapore, 94, 102
Size distributions, and primacy, 58–60
Slum Development Teams, 49
Small cities
    combined impact of, 15
    disadvantages of, 257–258
    health care needs in, 298
    including in *World Urbanization Prospects*,
        415
"Smart interpolation" programs, 147
SMAs. *See* Standard metropolitan areas
Smuggling, globalization of, 347
Snow, John, 35

Social accounting matrix techniques, applying to trade in West Africa, 303

Social capital, 40–42, 71
    and community dynamics, 41–42
    in formal institutions, 387
    health and, 40–41
    in household relations, 388–390
    in informal community-level institutions, 387–388
    and the mortality crisis in Russia, 41

Social cohesion, 2, 288

Social comparison theory, 38–39

Social comparisons, and subculture conflict, 38–39

Social contagion, 36

Social contexts of fertility and reproductive health, 201–206
    the program and services environment, 206–209
    spatial differences in fertility rates in greater Cairo, 203

Social dimension, in which urban environments differ from rural, 70

Social embeddedness, 68

Social externalities, 51

Social infrastructure, investments in greater in cities, 5

Social learning
    influence on fertility decisions, 5
    via social networks, 35–36

Social marketing programs, 237, 250, 255

Social networks
    "bridging" role of, 48, 311
    social learning via, 35–36
    strong and weak ties in, 43n, 204

Social relationships, "compression" of, 45

Socialization, institutional, 37–38

Society for the Promotion of Area Resource Centres (SPARC), 48, 71, 167

Socioeconomic diversity and inequality, 4, 19–20, 155–198
    access to public services, 167–180, 196
    childrens lives, 188–195
    within cities, 19–20
    human capital, 196–197
    measuring absolute poverty in cities, 180–184
    multiple dimensions of urban poverty, 165

    need to attend to the spatial aspects of, 20
    poverty and well-being, 197
    recommendations, 197–198
    risk and vulnerability, 184–188
    a spatial perspective, 157–160
    urban well-being: concepts and measures, 164–167

South Africa
    anti-apartheid movement in, 390
    groups of the poor in, 48
    and the imprint of inertia, 57n
    likelihood of recent sex among adolescents in, 248
    new constitution in, 372–373

South Asia, 78

South Korea, 94

Southeast Asia
    changes in rural economies and lifestyles in, 23
    fertility decline preceding mortality decline in, 94n
    selected city growth rates in, 88

Soviet republics, 105–106

Space and measurement, 17–19

SPARC. *See* Society for the Promotion of Area Resource Centres

Spatial aspects of diversity and inequality, need to attend to, 20

Spatial deconcentration, 313–317

Spatial influences, 157–160, 203, 307–312
    versus sectoral, 302

Spatial proximity, 204

Spatial segregation, 42–46

Spatial theories, 52–56
    producer services and high-skill labor markets, 55

Spatially concentrated poverty, 232, 238–242
    urban/rural differences in maternal mortality in Pakistan, 241

Spatially disaggregated data, 412–413

Special Economic Zones (SEZs), 77, 104

"Splintering urbanism," 379

Squatter settlements
    expanded by migrants into cities, 2
    projects to upgrade, 364

Standard metropolitan areas (SMAs), 482

Statistical systems
    African initiatives, 148–149
    decomposition of national, 303

for disaggregated data, 146–151
and GIS, 148–151
STDs. *See* Sexually transmitted diseases
Stocks, 80, 112
Street children, 191–195, 192–195
alcohol and drug use by, 193
demographic profile, 192–193
interventions, 194–195
life on the street and its consequences,
193–194
origins and causes, 194
sex of, 193
"Stunted" children, 272
Sub-Saharan Africa
contraceptive use in, 36
deteriorating health conditions in, 6
fertility rates in, 228
GEOPOLIS database for, 134
having highest infant and child mortality
rates worldwide, 295–296
HIV seroprevalence rates, 222
infant and child mortality rates increasing in,
296
lack of foreign direct investment in, 78
urban children fostered into care of rural
relatives, 62
weak macroeconomic growth in, 6
Suburbanization, 481
Sudan, 331
Sugar daddies, 249

T

Taichung, Taiwan, 30, 36, 202
Taipei, 19, 102
Taiwan, 342–343
growing rates of per capita income in, 94
impact of better education in, 320–321
residual earnings variance in, 342
rising inequalities in urban incomes, 7
Tanzania, 322, 331
TBAs. *See* Traditional birth attendants
Technological change, 2
Kelley-Williamson simulations of, 304
skill-bias in, 305
urban labor force dependent on, 352
Technological externalities, 51
Tegucigalpa, 224–225
Temporary migrants, versus permanent, 328

TFRs. *See* Total fertility rates
Thailand
groups of the poor in, 48
growing rates of per capita income in, 94
newly industrializing economies in, 102
Time costs, 165
Todaro and Harris-Todaro models, 323–327
Tokyo, 77, 80, 85, 87
Total fertility rates (TFRs), 201, 210–211,
226–229
estimates of, 126
in rural and urban areas, 127, 210
Total population of cities and towns (TPCT), 134
Total urban population
growth by national income level, 13
and number of urban areas by size, 85
TPCT. *See* Total population of cities and towns
Traditional birth attendants (TBAs), 241
Traditional healers, 290
Traditional providers, versus modern, 289
Traffic accidents, 266–267
Transformation of cities, 17–25
demographic, 11–17
fertility and reproductive health, 20–22
governance, 25
health, 22–23
and the international economy, 23–25
socioeconomic diversity within cities, 19–20
space and measurement, 17–19
Transient populations, in the spread of AIDS,
225
Treatment seeking, 289–291
health service provision and, 289–295
patterns of, 290
private providers, 290–291
self-medication, 290
traditional healers, 290
Tuberculosis, 270

U

UNCHS. *See* United Nations Centre for Human
Settlements
Undernutrition, 269
UNDP. *See* United Nations Development
Programme
Unemployment, 325
UNICEF, 192
Unintended fertility, 216–221

Unipolar depression, 267
United Nations
  Demographic Yearbooks, 26–27, 109, 131,
    135–139, 152, 415, 487, 504
  estimates and projections from, 11–16, 84,
    88–90, 96, 106–107, 486, 489, 495–498
  estimates of the contributions of migration
    and reclassification to urban growth in
    developing countries, 90
  linking DHS data to city data from, 487–494
  need for critical review of data and
    methodology of, 4, 82
  Population Division, 4, 82, 109, 132, 153,
    172
  Statistical Office, 132, 135
  underestimating city populations, 19, 99,
    143, 498
United Nations Centre for Human Settlements
  (UNCHS), 27, 97, 100, 103, 155,
  367–369
United Nations *Demographic Yearbook*,
  computerizing, 415
United Nations Development Programme
  (UNDP), 164n, 357
United Nations Habitat, Urban Management
  Program, 402
"United Nations method." *See* Urban/rural
  growth difference method
Unmet need for contraception, and unintended
  fertility, 216–221
Upward mobility, expectations of, 327n
Urban adolescents, 247–251
Urban advantage, 5–6
  calling into question, 5
  demographic bonus, 352
  little significant erosion in for children,
    296–297
  in reproductive health, 238, 257
Urban age structure, 128
Urban agglomerations, 52, 86, 136
Urban areas
  access to services, 168–172
  children's height and weight in, 272–274,
    296
  current use of modern contraceptives in,
    216
  environmental problems in, 262
  infant and child mortality for rural and urban
    areas, 127

  infant and child mortality in, 280
  levels of fertility and mortality, 125–128
  measures of access to basic public services,
    170
  poverty-related problems in, 262
  school enrollments in, 188–191
Urban bias, 317–319
Urban concepts, specifying in *World
  Urbanization Prospects*, 416
"Urban corridors," formation of in Pacific Asia,
  78
Urban definitions
  allowing comparisons of alternative, 415
  in the countries with a DHS survey, 490–493
  inconsistent, 132–135
Urban diseconomies, 98
Urban economy and labor force, 6–7, 23–25, 57,
  300–354
  earnings inequality case studies, 340–343
  economic returns to schooling, 319–322
  global links and local outcomes, 343–352
  informalization, 331–340
  migration and economic mobility, 322–331
  sectoral influences, 304–307
  spatial deconcentration, 313–317
  spatial influences, 307–312
Urban family planning programs, 107
Urban future, 11–14
Urban governance, 7–8, 25, 355–409
  the authority dimension, 390–401
  a "best" model of urban metropolitan
    governance, 401–406
  the capacity dimension, 363–371
  the concept of urban governance, 357–362
  the diversity dimension, 378–384
  the financial resources dimension, 371–378
  major challenges of urban governance in
    developing countries, 363–401
  the security dimension, 384–390
Urban growth, 3, 93, 111, 114–117, 486
Urban health, distinctive features of, 259
Urban labor force
  consequences of rapid growth in, 6
  dependent on technological change and
    capital formation, 352
Urban labor markets, 331–340, 343–352
Urban Management Program, 402
Urban migrants, 123–124, 126
Urban penalty, 259–260, 270–272, 284–289

Urban poor, 231–242
    infant mortality estimates for, 281
    inferior access to basic amenities, 4
    inferior access to reproductive health
        services, 257–258
    mortality risks facing, 6, 297–298
    spatially concentrated poverty in, 238–242
    vulnerability to crises and disasters, 4, 267
Urban population dynamics, 3–4, 17–19,
        108–154
    city growth from migration and natural
        increase, 112–114
    definition and measurement, 128–141
    fertility, mortality, migration, and urban age
        structure, 120–128
    key concepts and notation, 110–112
    migrant shares as calculated from censuses,
        120–121
    migrants as recorded in the demographic and
        health surveys, 122–125
    migration and urban age structure, 117–120
    projecting urban populations, 141–146
    statistical systems for disaggregated data,
        146–151
    urban age structure, 128
    urban and national population growth,
        116–117
    urban and rural levels of fertility and
        mortality, 125–128
    urban growth and the rate of urbanization,
        114–116
Urban population growth, 75–107, 111
    cities amid global forces, 76–81
    key demographic features of the urban
        transition, 81–95
    major regional differences, 95–106
    swelling the informal sector, 334
Urban poverty, 165, 174, 197, 499–500
Urban/rural dichotomies, 2, 4, 6, 70, 152, 256
Urban/rural growth difference (URGD) method,
        132, 135, 141, 495–498
Urban/rural interface
    linkage issues, 294–295
    population growth rates within metropolitan
        São Paulo, 61
    spaces and networks at, 60–64
Urban service delivery, 251–255
    decentralization of reproductive health
        services, 251–253

improving the quality and accessibility of
    care, 253–254
the private sector in family planning,
    254–255
Urban sexual networks, 207
Urban sociological research, 31
Urban-to-rural migration flows, in West Africa,
    91n
Urban total fertility rates by region, in economic
    crises, 227
Urban treatment seeking, 289–291
    private providers, 290–291
    self-medication, 290
    traditional healers, 290
"Urban villages," 31
Urban well-being, concepts and measures,
    164–167
Urbanization
    accelerating in Pacific Asia, 2
    benefits derived from, 2, 8
    decoupled from industrialization in Africa,
        82
    effects of, 53n
    inevitable tendency toward, 355
    level of, 485
    as a precondition for fertility decline, 21
    rate of, 92–93, 485
    "splintering," 379
    URGD declining with, 496
    without development, 93
Urbanization economies, 308–309
"Urbanness," 172
    in Cairo, using multiple data sources to
        define, 69
URGD. *See* Urban/rural growth difference
    method
U.S. Bureau of the Census, 95, 482
    American Community Survey, 483
    HIV/AIDS Surveillance Data Base,
        224
    International Programs Center, 413
User fee issue, 292–293

                                V

Vietnam, migration in, 244
"Vigilance committees," 374
Violent crime, 266

W

Waste disposal, 4, 170–171
"Wasted" children, 272
Water supply, 63, 178, 504
  See also Drinking water; Piped water
Weak ties, in social networks, 204
Weibull estimator, 278
West Africa, 91n, 303
WFS. *See* World Fertility Survey
Women, 123–124, 221, 222, 225, 234, 236,
    238, 266, 300, 504
World Bank, 183–184, 185n, 310, 346, 402
World cities, 80–81
World Development Report, 371
World Fertility Survey (WFS), 211, 226–227,
    229, 261, 282, 299, 411
World Health Organization, 186n, 267, 292

World population growth, 1, 3–4, 108–154
    concentrated in urban areas, 82–84,
      106
    distribution by urban/rural and national
      income level, 13
World Urbanization Prospects, 26, 109,
    135–139, 142, 152, 414–416, 487, 489,
    496, 504

X

Xiamen, 104

Z

Zambia, 224, 283, 348–349
Zhuhai, 104
Zimbabwe, 237, 293

OTHER TITLES FROM EARTHSCAN

ENVIRONMENTAL PROBLEMS IN AN URBANIZING WORLD
Jorge E Hardoy, Diana Mitlin and David Satterthwaite

'It's rare to encounter a work as authoritative and accessible as this. It is a mine of useful information from cities in every corner of the Third World, which does not shy away from the immensity of the problems, but says as much about the solutions to them as about the problems themselves' JONATHON PORRITT

'One of the finest guides available is this book that addresses the problems and potential solutions squarely, honestly and pragmatically... There are good examples of how well things can be done and models of good practice. The book provides basic science and information to understand the problems and thorough discussion of the obstacles to be overcome... This book challenges and informs. It stimulates and questions. It should be required reading in all courses dealing with urban issues. It already is for my students' URBAN STUDIES

This updated and much expanded edition of the classic *Environmental Problems in Third World Cities* describes environmental problems and their effect on human health, local ecosystems and global cycles. It points to the political causes that underpin many of these problems.

Pb 1-85383-719-9

THE EARTHSCAN READER IN SUSTAINABLE CITIES
Edited by David Satterthwaite

'David Satterthwaite has compiled an impressive volume of high quality papers with the intention to create an internationally relevant, comprehensive basis of the very complex issue: sustainable cities... The Reader is an impressive collection of papers on a potential, sustainable urban future. It attempts to cover all currently relevant issues and does so successfully... It is recommendable as an informative source of reference for professionals and researchers wanting to widen or supplement their knowledge on sustainable cities' HOUSING STUDIES

The last five years have brought an enormous growth in the literature on how urban development can meet human needs and ensure ecological sustainability. This collection brings together the most outstanding contributions from leading experts on the issues surrounding sustainable cities and urban development.

Pb 1-85383-601-X • Hb 1-85383-602-8

CITIES FOR CHILDREN
Children's Rights, Poverty and Urban Management
Sheridan Bartlett, Roger Hart, David Satterthwaite, Ximena de la Barra and Alfredo Missair

'This extremely well researched and well referenced book will make a valuable resource for a very wide range of readers... The final section detailing the resources the authors used to research the work is worth the cost of the book alone... Without doubt, this is a very valuable and well-written work that will support students, academics, practitioners and policy-makers in many countries' Planning Theory & Practice

Urban authorities and organizations are responsible for providing the basic services that affect the lives of urban children. *Cities for Children* will help them understand and respond to the rights and requirements of children and adolescents. It looks at the responsibilities that authorities face, and discusses practical measures for meeting their obligations in the context of limited resources and multiple demands. The book emphasizes the challenges faced by local government, and contains information that would be useful to any groups working to make urban areas better places for children.

Pb 1-85383-470-X • Hb 1-85383-471-8

THE CHALLENGE OF SLUMS
Global Report on Human Settlements 2003
United Nations Human Settlement Programme (UN-HABITAT)

'Slums represent the worst of urban poverty and inequality. Yet the world has the resources, knowhow and power to reach the target established in the Millennium Declaration. It is my hope that this report, and the best practices it identifies, will enable all actors involved to overcome the apathy and lack of political will that have been a barrier to progress, and move ahead with greater determination and knowledge in our common effort to help the world's slum dwellers to attain lives of dignity, prosperity and peace' From the Foreword by KOFI A ANNAN, Secretary-General, United Nations

Almost 1 billion people live in slums, the majority in the developing world where over 40 per cent of the urban population are slum dwellers. *The Challenge of Slums* presents the first global assessment of slums, emphasizing their problems and prospects. Using a newly formulated operational definition of slums, it presents estimates of the numbers of urban slum dwellers and examines the factors at all levels, from local to global, that underlie the formation of slums as well as their social, spatial and economic characteristics and dynamics. It goes on to evaluate the principal policy responses to the slum challenge of the last few decades.

Pb 1-84407-037-9 • Hb 1-84407-036-0

WATER AND SANITATION IN THE WORLD'S CITIES
Local Action for Global Goals
United Nations Human Settlement Programme (UN-HABITAT)

'In a rapidly urbanizing world, the battle for water and sanitation will have to be fought in human settlements, particularly in slums and shanties of the growing urban areas of developing countries. Achieving these avowed goals will remain a distant dream if we do not focus on the slums of Nairobi, the bustees of Calcutta and the favelas of Rio. The analytical work in this report and its key finding – that local solutions are key to achieving global goals – should provide a valuable input to the work of the Millennium Task Force' ANNA KAJUMULO TIBAIJUKA, Under-Secretary-General, United Nations, and Executive Director, UN-HABITAT

'This is surely the most impressive and important publication to come out of the UN system for many years. It brings together 20 years of evidence from attempts to build the foundations of public health in the developing world – hygiene, sanitation and water supply – and shapes that evidence into the lessons and insights that show the way forward' PETER ADAMSON, founder, *New Internationalist*, and author and researcher of UNICEF's *The State of the World's Children* from 1980 to 1995

The world's governments agreed at the Millennium Summit to halve the number of people who lack access to safe water, mainly in the world's cities, by 2015. This influential publication sets out in detail the scale of inadequate provision of water and sanitation. It describes the impacts on health and economic performance, showing the potential gains of remedial action; it analyses the proximate and underlying causes of poor provision and identifies information gaps affecting resource allocation; it outlines the consequences of further deterioration; and it explains how resources and institutional capacities – public, private and community – can be used to deliver proper services through integrated water resource management.

Pb 1-84407-004-2 • Hb 1-84407-003-4

THE VULNERABILITY OF CITIES
Natural Disasters and Social Resilience
Mark Pelling

'An ambitious book which tackles subjects of fundamental importance to the future of the planet' open house international

When disaster strikes in cities the effects can be catastrophic compared to other environments. But what factors actually determine the vulnerability or resilience of cities? *The Vulnerability of Cities* examines the too-often overlooked impact of disasters on cities, the conditions leading to high losses from urban disasters and why some households and communities withstand disaster more effectively than others.

Three detailed studies of cities in the global South are drawn from countries with contrasting political and developmental contexts: Bridgetown, Barbados – a liberal democracy; Georgetown, Guyana – a post socialist-state; and Santo Domingo, Dominican Republic – an authoritarian state in democratic transition.

Pb 1-85383-830-6 • Hb 1-85383-829-2

EMPOWERING SQUATTER CITIZEN
Local Government, Civil Society and Urban Poverty Reduction
Edited by Diana Mitlin and David Satterthwaite

Produced by the highly respected Human Settlements Programme at the International Institute for Environment and Development (IIED), this book offers a fresh look at the complex causes of urban poverty. It goes beyond conventional, official definitions based only on income or consumption levels to include considerations of housing conditions, tenure, infrastructure and service provision, the rule of law, and civil and political rights, including 'voice' and the right to influence policy and practice on the ground. It makes the case for redirecting support to local organizations and processes.

Worldwide case studies of innovative government organizations and community-driven processes form the core of the book, showing new ways to address urban poverty shows that poverty reduction in urban areas is as much about building and supporting competent, accountable local organizations as about attempting to improve incomes.

Pb 1-84407-101-4 • Hb 1-84407-100-6 • May 2004